Russian politics and society

'It should be on the shelf of anyone seeking to make heads or tails of the . . . problems of Yeltsin's Russia.'

Guardian

'The most comprehensive and detailed analysis and assessment of post-Soviet Russian politics to be found in a single volume . . . No student can afford to miss it.'

Peter Shearman, *Journal of Area Studies*

Richard Sakwa's *Russian Politics and Society* is the most comprehensive study of Russia's post-communist political development. It has, since its first publication in 1993, become an indispensable guide for all those who need to know about the current political scene in Russia, about the country's political stability and about the future of democracy under its post-communist leadership.

This is the ideal introductory textbook: it covers all the key issues; it is clearly written; and it includes the most up-to-date material currently available. For this second edition, Richard Sakwa has updated the text throughout and restructured its presentation so as to emphasize the ongoing struggle for stability in Russia over the last five years. This edition includes:

– the full text of the constitution of 1993
– new material on recent elections, the new parliament (State Duma and Federation Council), the development of the presidency and an evaluation of the country's political evolution during the 1990s
– up-to-date details on the development of a federal system and on local government
– a thoroughly updated bibliography

This new and revised edition consolidates the reputation of *Russian Politics and Society* as the single most comprehensive standard textbook on post-Soviet Russia.

Richard Sakwa is Professor of Russian and European Politics at the University of Kent at Canterbury. He is the author of *Soviet Politics: An Introduction* and of *Gorbachev and His Reforms, 1985–1900*; in addition, he has edited Ruslan Khasbulatov's *The Struggle for Russia*.

Russian politics and society

Second edition

Richard Sakwa

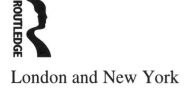

London and New York

First published 1993
by Routledge
11 New Fetter Lane, London EC4P 4EE
29 West 35th Street, New York, NY 10001

Second enlarged and revised edition published 1996
by Routledge
11 New Fetter Lane, London EC4P 4EE

Simultaneously published in the USA and Canada
by Routledge
29 West 35th Street, New York, NY 10001

© 1993, 1996 Richard Sakwa

Typeset in Times by
Ponting–Green Publishing Services, Chesham, Buckinghamshire

Printed and bound in Great Britain by
T. J. Press (Padstow) Ltd.

British Library Cataloguing in Publication Data
A catalogue record for this book is available from the
British Library.

Library of Congress Cataloging in Publication Data
A catalogue record for this book has been requested.

ISBN 0–415–15483–9 (hbk)
ISBN 0–415–12160–4 (pbk)

Contents

Appendix 3 The Russian Constitution   395

Figures

Tables

Preface to the second edition

The rebirth of Russia! How quickly these words have become worn and stale. Not so very long ago they reflected the aspirations of a people apparently toiling under the burden of an alien ideology, which suppressed democratic aspirations and separated the country from international life. Today these early hopes are easily mocked as democracy itself appears to be a cover for self-serving politicians, the decay of public morals, and, from the Russian perspective, the repugnant self-interest of the international order that the country was once so keen to join.

Some three years have passed since the publication of the first edition and much indeed has changed. The speeding up of history noted in the earlier edition still shows no sign of abating. Russian politics retain their capacity to surprise; crisis appears to be the normal condition of Russian affairs. Whereas earlier there appeared to be some discernible reason and direction to Russia's hurtling troika, we are now a little less sure. Having never shared the much-maligned 'euphoria' attending the fall of communism, I nevertheless felt that Russia enjoyed a unique and perfectly realistic opportunity not simply to join the international community but also to establish a political order which respected human dignity and international norms of associational life, including the rudiments of democracy, while making its own unique contribution to the resolution of problems of social and international organisation. I still believe this to be the case, but the context and time-scale have had to be modified.

Russian history is characterised by relatively clearly defined phases, and today a seventh Russia is emerging whose features we are just beginning to perceive and which will take its place alongside the previous six. The first was Kievan Rus', lasting until the Mongol invasions destroyed the achievements of this period and isolated the country from the rest of the world, a separation whose consequences are still felt. The Mongol occupation from roughly 1240 to 1480 gradually gave way to the reconstitution of the state, this time based on Moscow; and to this day the degree of rupture between Muscovite Russia and the older Kievan civilisation is a matter of considerable historical (and political) controversy. The Muscovite period established Russia as a society with profound spiritual and cultural depths whose relationship with the rest of European civilisation remains ambivalent. The era was marked also by territorial expansion, symbolised by the fall of the Kazan Khanate in 1552 and the occupation of territories further to the East.

The fourth period was inaugurated by Peter the Great's construction of St Petersburg as a 'window to the West', the transfer of the capital to that city in 1712, and the declaration of Russia as an empire in 1721. The St Petersburg phase of Russian history was marked by a confusion between ideas of nation and empire, and simultaneously (and some would argue consequently) by a failure effectively to separate the state from the monarchy, a dereliction that led ultimately to the overthrow of the autocracy in February 1917. In the subsequent brief liberal interlude Russia grappled simultaneously to establish democracy, fight a war, control a social revolution in the countryside, contain class war in the cities, and to come to terms with the aspirations for national self-determination of numerous peoples within the Russian empire. Marked by an enormous political creativity and despite solid achievements (often overlooked by its critics) the democratic polity (consisting of the Provisional Government, the soviets, various dumas, and many other social organisations) was overwhelmed by failure to institutionalise its rule or to impose legal forms of political contestation.

The Bolsheviks from October 1917 were the beneficiaries, a period marked by a single-minded ruthlessness in the seizure and maintenance of power, and despite the warnings by some of the senior figures (Kamenev, Zinoviev and others) that one-party communist rule would entail civil war and oceans of blood, Lenin was undeterred and launched Russia into its sixth phase, Soviet power. We shall have more to say about the Soviet legacy later in this book; and at the same time the failure of democracy in Russia in 1917 stands as a stark warning to the present, seventh, period. At the level of personal freedoms and human dignity life today is immeasurably better than it was under the Soviet regime, but Russia's democracy is flawed, its society fragmented, social relations distorted by enormous inequality and poverty, and its market institutions rudimentary.

This edition has been largely rewritten and reordered. Some of the extremely long chapters of the earlier version have been broken down into smaller units, and topics have been grouped into associated parts. There is some thematic continuity between the parts which can be described as follows.

The first focuses on the age-old problem of what is Russia, and who are the Russians. This is, for want of a better term, the civilisational question, raising issues of national identity, purpose and interests. Russia is being reborn as a state, a polity, an economy, a society, but perhaps above all as a nation. But what does nation mean in this context? – not just ethnic Russians (*Russkie*) but all who live within the reconstituted Russian Federation (*Rossiyani*); and nation in the modern context also has political attributes, suggesting citizenship and political representation. Russian history is marked by ambiguous relationships between state, nation, empire, society and polity, and this legacy has left a firm imprint on contemporary changes.

The second theme examines the attempt to structure the political space that has emerged with the fall of communism. Politics was reborn under Gorbachev, but the institutionalisation of the new freedoms remains deficient. The first attempt at democratisation was overthrown in 1917 (leaving aside contingent factors) because of the failure to integrate the vibrant civil and political society into an effective polity; and today a distinctive hybrid political system is emerging that is torn between conflicting imperatives: democracy, state unity, transformative goals, and the simple desire of elites to stay in power. Thus the second theme focuses on the tension between democracy as a goal and the process of 'democratisation'.

The third theme is the tension between globalisation and nativisation. In the late twentieth century a country can try policies of economic autarchy and political isolation, but the penalties are enormously high. On the other side, globalisation is not necessarily at variance with nativisation, the attempt to find some indigenous path of development and global integration on national terms. Japan has managed effectively to combine the two, and China may well be on its way to finding a unique balance reflecting its traditions and geopolitical realities.

Globalisation does not take place in a vacuum but requires an effective national context and a social subject that can act as the carrier of international economic and political processes. If this social subject is excessively narrow the whole globalisation project is liable to be rejected, as it was in Iran in 1979. Thus adaptation to the international system has certain limits and is not necessarily incompatible, as Japanese experience since the 1850s suggests, with nativisation. The problem, however, is to find the optimum balance between the two, a median point that Russia does not appear yet to have found.

The fourth theme is the whole question of modernisation. While the notion of 'modernisation' in its 1950s sense has been somewhat discredited, because of its suggestion of universal developmental processes leading to the emulation of Western societies by the rest of the world, the problem has not gone away. While the tension between globalisation and nativisation is part of the question, the larger issue is the nature of contemporary modernity, and the degree to which the logic of modernity imposes its own structures on individual societies. In the Russian context we have the specific problem of the Soviet experience, which sought a separate sort of modernity, rejecting the Western capitalist model, that gave rise to a distinctive type of polity with pre-modern features and an economy that combined huge achievements with aspects that we label 'mismodernisation'. The social consequences, for example, of an economy skewed towards military production and huge plants where workers and managers find a common interest against the centre and dominate local politics clearly have no parallel in Western societies. The introduction of market relations in this context can have wholly unpredictable consequences.

Overshadowing all the above, however, is the larger theme of the reconstitution of a viable social order. Without this, all the rest is placed in jeopardy. More specifically, the question focuses on the nature of politics in a post-communist society, and the quality of the social relations accompanying the 'building of democracy' and economic reform. The late Soviet experience demonstrated that stability on its own is not a sufficient indicator of a viable social order. Viability entails the incorporation of social and intellectual traditions and new ideas into the operation of a polity, with interaction and mutual enrichment between civil society and government. By this standard, of course, some Western societies can be found wanting, and we should beware of imposing on others standards that we ourselves do not meet – the defining feature of contemporary imperialism.

The emerging polity and society in Russia will take their own distinctive forms, drawing on native traditions and civilisational experiences while responding to the challenges of globalisation, modernity and modernisation. Russia is indeed a society in transition, engaged in multiple processes of social transformation, but the result of these endeavours will no doubt amaze us yet.

Canterbury
January 1996

Acknowledgements

My thanks go to the following who at various times have shared their time and knowledge: Roy Allison, Vladimir Amelin, Gleb Anishchenko, Pavel Baev, Sergei Chugrov, Elena Danilova, Vladimir Gelman, Leonid Gordon, Agnes Horvath, Yurii Igritskii, Anatolii Kulik, Krishan Kumar, Peter Lentini, David McLellan, Sergei Mitrokhin, Oleg Mramornov, Sergei Peregudov, Valentin Peshchanskii, Nikolai Petrov, Peter Rutland, Alexei Salmin, Victor Sheinis, Svetlana Sidorenko, Alexander Sobyanin, Victor Sumskii, Sergei Veselovskii, Michael Urban and Stephen White. I am particularly grateful to Jeff Gleisner, Arpad Szakolczai and Andrei Zagorskii who have read part or all of the text, and their comments were much appreciated. The faults, of course, remain my own. Caroline Wintersgill and Patrick Proctor at Routledge, like Gordon Smith earlier, displayed truly heroic patience and understanding of the problems of trying to bring order out of chaos. I am most grateful for the secretarial assistance of Nicola Cooper and Marilyn Spice. It is my pleasure to thank the Nuffield Foundation for their generous assistance in the preparation of this edition.

Note on style, spelling and transliteration

Words like Party are capitalised to indicate that the proper noun referred to is a concrete entity that existed or exists in the Soviet Union or Russia. The word 'democrat' is usually used without inverted commas, although the attempt by a particular group to appropriate the term for themselves is clearly problematical; similarly, for stylistic reasons, the use of 'self-styled democrat' or 'so-called democrat' is kept to a minimum.

The spelling of geographical areas tries to follow the changes, but in most cases has resisted the conversion back to Sovietised forms. Moldavia has thus become Moldova, and its capital Kishinev has become Chisinau, and there they stay despite the reversion to the earlier usage in the Russian media. The same goes for Belorussia's conversion to Belarus; Kirghizia's to Kyrgyzstan; Tataria's to Tatarstan; and Alma Ata's change to Almaty.

The transliteration system is the standard British one (a modified version of the Library of Congress system), used in most cases except when convention has decreed otherwise. Thus, El'tsin becomes Yeltsin, Ekaterinburg is Yekaterinburg, Iaroslavl' is Yaroslavl'. The 'iu' letter becomes 'yu', 'ia' becomes 'ya', and at the beginning of names 'e' become 'ye' (Yevgenii rather than Evgenii). The diacritical (representing the soft sign) is also omitted from the end of frequently used words like *oblast'* (region) and Belarus', and from the end of words or names, thus Lebed rather than the more strictly accurate Lebed' and Rossel rather than Rossel', although when the soft sign is in the middle of a name (e.g. Luk'yanov, Zor'kin) it is retained.

Glossary of terms, acronyms and acrostics

ABM	Anti-ballistic missile (installation)
Afghantsy	Those who fought in the Afghan war, 1979–89
Apparatchik	Worker in the Communist Party's Central Committee apparatus
Apparatchiki	Full-time Communist Party Officials
ASSR	Autonomous Soviet Socialist Republic
CC	Central Committee (of the CPSU)
CMEA	Council for Mutual Economic Assistance, Comecon
CEE	Central and Eastern Europe
Chinovnik	(Tsarist) civil servant
CFDP	Council for Foreign and Defence Policy
CPD	Congress of People's Deputies
CPSU	Communist Party of the Soviet Union
CSCE	Conference on Security and Cooperation in Europe (see also OSCE)
EU	European Union
FIS	Foreign Intelligence Service (see SVR)
FSB	*Federal'noi sluzhby bezopasnosti*, Federal Security Service
FSK	*Federal'noi sluzhby kontrrazvedki*, Federal Counter-Intelligence Service
Guberniya	Province, unit of Tsarist administration
IMF	International Monetary Fund
Ispolkom	*Ispolnitel'nyi komitet*, Executive committee (of the soviets)
KGB	*Komitet gosudarstvennogo bezopastnosti*, Committee of State Security
Komsomol	*Kommunisticheskii soyuz molodezhi*, Young Communist League
Krai	Territory
MB	*Ministerstvo bezopastnosti*, Ministry of Security
MID	*Ministerstvo inostrannykh del*, Ministry of Foreign Affairs
MVD	*Ministerstvo vnutrennykh del*, Ministry of Internal Affairs
NACC	North Atlantic Cooperation Council
Nato	North Atlantic Treaty Organisation
Nomenklatura	The Communist system of political appointments, came to designate the class of office-holders
Obkom	*Oblastnoi komitet, oblast* committee (of the CPSU)
Oblast	Region
OECD	Organisation for Economic Co-operation and Development
Okrug	District, region

OSCE	Organisation for Security and Cooperation in Europe (the name for the CSCE from Decembér 1994)
PfP	Partnership for Peace
Raion	District, borough
RF	Russian Federation
RSFSR	Russian Soviet Federated Socialist Republic
SALT	Strategic Arms Limitation (Talks) Treaty
SCSE	State Committee for the State of Emergency, established during the attempted coup of August 1991
SSR	Soviet Socialist Republic
START	Strategic Arms Reduction (Talks) Treaty
SVR	*Sluzhba vneshnoi rezvedky*, Foreign Intelligence Service
USSR	Union of Soviet Socialist Republics
WTO	Warsaw Treaty Organisation, Warsaw Pact
Zemlya (pl zemli)	Territory, comparable to the German *Länder*
Zemstvo	Unit of Tsarist local administration

Part I

The fall of communism and the rebirth of Russia

1 The fall of communism

But what I believe to be certain is this: if you were to give all these grand, contemporary teachers full scope to destroy the old society and build it anew, the result would be such obscurity, such chaos, something so crude, blind, and inhuman that the whole structure would collapse to the sound of humanity's curses before it could ever be completed.

Fyodor Dostoyevsky[1]

In March 1985 Mikhail Gorbachev came to power committed to revitalising the Soviet Union. Within months he launched a programme called *perestroika* (restructuring), which in the space of 6 years moved from hesitant attempts to rationalise the system, through a phase of liberalisation to a democratisation phase that began to transform the society and polity but which culminated in a final stage of disintegration. The changes could not be constrained by a regime-led reform, and by 1991 pressure for a radical change of system became overwhelming. The attempt in August 1991 by a group to hold back the tide of change precipitated the result that they had sought to avert: the dissolution of the communist system of government and, by the end of the year, the disintegration of the Union of Soviet Socialist Republics (USSR). The dissolution of the communist regime and the disintegration of the USSR are two linked but analytically separate processes.

Thus ended one of the most ambitious attempts at utopian social engineering in human history, launched after the Bolsheviks came to power in Russia in October 1917 and lasting, with significant modifications, 74 years until swept away in the aftermath of the failed coup of August 1991. Gorbachev's attempts to find a more humane, efficient and democratic form of socialism gave way in Russia to a leadership committed to the restoration of capitalism in the shortest possible time and to the establishment of a democratic form of government. As in 1917, the country was at a crossroads, and instead of reform, a profound transformation was taking place. Russia faced the challenge not only of building a new economic and political system but also of making a new state.

THE FAILURE OF PERESTROIKA

Perestroika, launched by Gorbachev soon after becoming General Secretary of the Communist Party of the Soviet Union (CPSU) in March 1985, was the last great attempt at communist reform. During the long rule of Leonid Brezhnev (October 1964–November 1982) the country entered into a period of what later became known as stagnation (*zastoi*). Even before coming to power Gorbachev had realised that the old system had sunk into corruption, with the economic system beset by rot, scientific and cultural life stultified by crippling secrecy, and politics dominated by a corrupt elite. Visiting Canada in May 1983 Gorbachev shared his concerns with the Soviet ambassador there, Alexander Yakovlev, who would later become one of the architects of perestroika. Yakovlev reports that they spent hours discussing the disasters awaiting the Soviet Union if nothing was done: 'The most important common understanding . . . was the idea that we could not live this way anymore'.[2] By starting a 'revolution within the revolution' Gorbachev hoped to save the essentials of the system, above all the leading role of the Party and the planned economy, through greater responsiveness introduced by *glasnost* (openness) and elements of competition through democratisation and limited marketisation.

Gorbachev believed that the old system remained viable, that it was still a powerful motor that required only some fine tuning: perestroika, he insisted, has 'been prompted by an awareness that the potential of socialism has been underutilized'.[3] Despite the revolutionary language, his was essentially a reformist programme. His tragic fate was to act as the destroyer rather than the builder; the more that he tinkered with the system, the deeper the crisis. His reform communism only exacerbated the problems of what was already a system in crisis, and worsened the legacy facing the post-communist governments. It fell to his successors in Russia and the other republics to rebuild economies and to nourish the fragile shoots of democracy that perestroika had encouraged. We shall examine below the three main phases of the old regime in its death agonies.

1 Rationalisation, 1985–86

In this phase some of the themes of Yurii Andropov's authoritarian reform programme were revived. Andropov had been head of the Committee of State Security (KGB) from 1967 until shortly before becoming General Secretary of the CPSU following Brezhnev's death in November 1982, and thus he, better than anyone, knew the real state of affairs in the country. In the few months remaining to him (he died in February 1984) he launched a campaign against corruption and attempted to tighten up on labour and social discipline. Konstantin Chernenko's brief rule (February 1984–March 1985) sought to turn the clock back to the comfortable corruption of the last Brezhnev years.

To Andropov's programme Gorbachev added the notion of *uskorenie* (acceleration), trying to rejuvenate the existing economic system by the vigorous application of old remedies. The government led by Nikolai Ryzhkov devoted yet more resources to investment and re-investment (the improvement of old plant and facilities), imports were cut back and once again the needs of the long-suffering Soviet consumer were neglected. During this period grand programmes were announced, such as the promise that by the year 2000 every Soviet citizen would have an apartment of their own, although how this was to be achieved remained unclear. The programme of acceleration sought both to reform the economy and increase output at the same time, contradictory demands that failed to achieve either.[4] The misconceived anti-alcohol campaign launched at this time, inspired by the 'conservative reformer' Yegor Ligachev, led to the increased production of bootleg liquor (*samogon*) and devastating losses to the budget revenues of central and local authorities.

Rationalisation, according to László Póti, entails 'a series of superficial, partial and non-conceptual measures that, however, indicate a certain degree of unintentional discontent with the system'.[5] The period of rationalisation entailed a recognition of the problem accompanied by the belief that the solution lay within the framework of the existing system. Gorbachev, however, soon came to understand that more radical measures were required.

2 Reform, January 1987–March 1990

The second phase of perestroika can itself be divided into two sub-periods: a discussion phase from January 1987 to the Nineteenth Party Conference (28 June–1 July 1988) marked by debates over *demokratizatsiya* (democratisation) and the revelations of glasnost (openness), a period which proved to be the high point of perestroika; and an implementation phase from summer 1988 to March 1990 which proved far more difficult than the reform communists anticipated. This reform phase corresponds to the stage of liberalisation discussed in the literature on transitions.[6]

In the discussion period increasingly bold strategies for the political regeneration of the political system were considered to tap the alleged hidden potential of the Soviet model of development. The January 1987 plenum of the Central Committee (CC) of the CPSU marked a watershed in the move away from authoritarian towards democratic reform. The plenum called for the extension of competitive elections in the workplace, the soviets and in the Party itself. In June 1987 a further plenum of the CC adopted a plan for the economic transformation of the country which focused on greater autonomy for enterprises and increased rights for workers to elect their own managers. However, rather than strengthening the system, the revelations made possible by glasnost about the crimes of the past and the inadequacies of the present only undermined the legitimacy of the regime as a whole.

The Nineteenth Party Conference marked the transition to attempts to implement programmes of reform. Attempts were made to formulate a grand strategy of political reform to modernise the entire system within the framework of one-party democracy and one-party parliamentarianism. Gorbachev's strategy was based on the CPSU retaining a predominant role,[7] but the Party was now to guide rather than to lead. The overall principle was to be the creation of a 'socialist legal state', the separation of powers and a revived legislature. In December 1988 legislation was adopted by the USSR Supreme Soviet for the creation of a three-chamber Congress of People's Deputies (CPD), two chambers of which (the Soviet of the Union and the Soviet of Nationalities) were to be chosen in multi-candidate elections, while the third (what can be called the Soviet of Representatives) was to be made up of delegates from social organisations, including 100 guaranteed seats for the Communist Party. The CPD was to meet twice a year while current parliamentary business was to be conducted by a smaller Supreme Soviet drawn from the CPD.

The semi-free elections of March 1989 for the new assembly saw the defeat of many communist officials and the return of some democrats, though they numbered no more than 400 out of a total of 2,250 CPD deputies. At the first convocation of the CPD in May 1989 Gorbachev was elected chairman of its new 542-member Supreme Soviet, a post he had achieved without facing the electorate at any stage. The Congress was the scene of vigorous debates, and appeared to mark the onset of effective parliamentary politics. The CPD and its Supreme Soviet passed a significant body of reformist legislation, with new laws on freedom of conscience and religious belief and freedom of the press. The first steps were taken towards the creation of a law-governed state (*Rechtsstaat*), if not a democracy, something that distinguished perestroika from the rest of Soviet history. The structure of the new parliament, however, was deeply flawed – perhaps intentionally so. The Congress itself was unwieldy and, lacking the necessary committee structures, could not focus on key issues or set a coherent legislative agenda, while the Supreme Soviet itself became a permanent forum for wide-ranging debates but failed to establish the necessary routines for effective legislative activity (adoption *and* implementation) or oversight of the executive.

The attempt to reconcile representative democracy with a leading role for the CPSU proved impossible. One-party democracy was a contradiction in terms, and the attempt to achieve the 'socialist pluralism of opinions' was challenged by the growth of genuine political pluralism in society. The very existence of the Soviet state within its old borders was challenged by the Baltic republics and others. The period was marked by accumulating failures, above all in the economic sphere. Reform plan followed reform plan, but none were consistently implemented. The country became increasingly ungovernable as Ryzhkov's government blocked radical reforms while failing to come up with effective policies of its own. The emergence of an active workers' movement in the form of miners' strikes from June 1989 marked the point at which Gorbachev's strategy of reform from above was transformed into a revolutionary challenge from below.

Thus reform can be defined as 'the substantial extension of the rationalisation measures in depth and rate with increased awareness of the tensions of the system, but still within that framework'.[8] Gorbachev's attempt to implement reforms within the framework of the one-party system proved unfeasible; the strategy of reform communism known as perestroika was not implemented because it was unimplementable. The period was characterised by a mass of contradictions, and it soon became obvious that one-party parliamentarianism was self-defeating. A 'socialist' legal state appeared to be an obstacle to the development of a straightforward legal state in which the rights of citizens could be defended by law and in which powers were separated and defined. The reform consensus that existed in 1985 was undermined; by implementing reforms, Gorbachev undermined the very concept of reform itself.

3 Transformation, March 1990–August 1991

The third phase was characterised by the dissolution of Gorbachev's definition of perestroika as a Party-led programme of reform and culminated in the coup of August 1991. From mid-1989 the miners' strikes had demonstrated that new independent forces were entering the stage of Soviet politics. The 'vodka' riots of the New Year of 1990 were followed by a wave of demonstrations and the dismissal of unpopular regional Party leaders in Volgograd, Murmansk, Sverdlovsk, Tyumen and elsewhere under the pressure of mass protest. The politics of resentment against elite privileges was as strong as the hunger for democratic ideals.[9] This wave of protest culminated with a demonstration of perhaps half a million people in Moscow on 4 February 1990 calling for multiparty democracy.

The revolutions in Eastern Europe in the last months of 1989 swept away the communist regimes in East Germany, Czechoslovakia, Bulgaria and Romania, and, afraid that this might happen to them too, the Central Committee plenum of 5–7 February 1990 agreed to modify Article 6 of the 1977 Soviet constitution to remove the constitutional monopoly of the CPSU on political power. This was confirmed by the third (emergency) meeting of the CPD on 14 March, which the next day strengthened Gorbachev's presidential powers. Thus an era of one-party rule which had in effect begun in October 1917 came to an end: free elections were introduced, the half-truths of glasnost gave way to genuine freedom of speech, and Party perestroika gave way to Presidential perestroika. The transformation of the political system at last allowed liberalisation to give way to genuine democratisation.

This phase of perestroika could not be anything but a transitional period. It was characterised by intensified conflicts over economic policy, national issues and political strategies. Gorbachev had been able to consolidate his power faster than any previous Soviet leader, yet he still faced formidable opposition. Above all, the very forces he hoped to use to implement his reforms, the Party and the ministerial bureaucracy, resisted his policies. In the early years of perestroika Gorbachev had been able to mobilise a reform coalition of groups (including the military and the KGB) who, if not welcoming change, realised that some reform of the economy and the political system was essential if the Soviet Union was to meet the challenge of technological and social modernisation. However, by 1990 it was clear that the reform coalition was disintegrating and Gorbachev's own brand of communist reformism was losing support.

A group of diehard reactionaries emerged, warning that Gorbachev's policies would lead to the betrayal of socialism and the destruction of the country. The letter by a Leningrad chemistry teacher, Nina Andreeva, expressed the anger of the old generation and urged a 'balanced' assessment of Stalinism and condemned the classless 'humanism' espoused by perestroika.[10] Conservatives like Ligachev were willing to accept some change but were intent on trying to salvage the Soviet past. The growing democratic movement also now diverged from perestroika's reformism and was united if only on one thing, namely the need to transform the old structures of Soviet power and to introduce the basic features of a modern democratic system. Looming over all of these, however, was the growing nationalist unrest in the republics.

The democratic and national currents critical of Gorbachev's policies at last found an individual upon whom opposition could focus, Boris Yeltsin. Already at the Twenty-seventh Party Congress between February and March 1986 Yeltsin, at the time Party leader in Sverdlovsk *oblast* (region) and soon to be transferred to head the Moscow Party Organisation, had been the first top Party leader openly to condemn the privileges of the Party elite, and his stress on social justice earned him the probably undeserved soubriquet of a populist. Yeltsin's attack on the leading conservative, Ligachev, at the CC plenum of 21 October 1987 signalled the end of the monolithic rule of the CPSU and resulted in his dismissal as head of the Party in Moscow; and his open confrontation with Ligachev, broadcast to millions on television, at the Nineteenth Party Conference on 1 July 1988 revealed the deep splits in the Party.[11] In the elections of March 1989 a tired and angry people gave him overwhelming support in Moscow, 89 per cent of the vote, against the candidate of the old Party system, Yevgenii Brakov. In the CPD he was one of the leaders of the 400-strong Interregional Deputy's Group advocating the radicalisation of the reforms.

Perestroika-style institutions were duplicated in each of the USSR's fifteen republics. The elections to the Russian CPD of 4 March 1990 were relatively more democratic (although by no means free) than the Soviet elections of 1989, with nomination through social organisations dropped and the district registration meeting, used by officials in the earlier elections to screen out undesirable candidates, abolished (see chapter 5). Democratic groups achieved significant victories, assisted by the Democratic Russia electoral bloc established in January 1990 with branches in all the major Russian towns. Some 20 per cent of the seats in the Russian CPD were taken by democrats,[12] taking 63 out of 65 seats assigned to Moscow in the Russian parliament, and 25 out of 34 in Leningrad.[13] The economist Gavriil Popov came to head the

Moscow Soviet, in Leningrad the law professor Anatolii Sobchak came to power, and in Sverdlovsk (Yeltsin's home town), the democrats took control. There was a marked regional dynamic to the elections, with half of the establishment candidates north of Moscow's latitude suffering defeat, whereas south of that line hardly any.

As long as the struggle was between a decaying old regime and a rising new order, the democrats could muster a majority against the communist old guard. Even before August 1991 the second and third echelons of the ruling elite began to throw in their lot with the rising alternative as the rule of the *nomenklatura* (the class of people appointed by or deriving their power from the Communist Party), ebbed away. 'Workers and intelligentsia, collective farmers and military officers, militiamen and former dissidents, Party secretaries in enterprises and non-party informals', were all moving over to the other side of the barricades against the higher officials of state and Party who, because of the distorted electoral process of 1990, were elected in almost equal numbers to the Congress.[14] The 'new class' of which Milovan Djilas had spoken was finally coming into its own; born under Stalin, freed from the terror under Nikita Khrushchev, given job security under Brezhnev, harangued by Gorbachev in the cause of a restructured humane socialism, this class now cast aside the final shreds of communist ideology and claimed the role of the universal (middle) class of modernity.

At the first convocation of the Russian CPD, after three ballots and by a margin of only four votes, on 29 May 1990 Yeltsin was elected its chairman.[15] Henceforth the search for All-Union solutions to the country's problems would give way to each republic trying to find its own way forward. It was clear that Gorbachev's attempts to revive the Soviet system ideologically through reform communism had failed and now some of the fifteen republics of the USSR began to take on responsibility for themselves. The blockage on democratic breakthrough at the All-Union centre encouraged the insurgency against the communist regime to take on national forms.

Already, a year earlier at the first meeting of the Soviet CPD, the idea that Russia itself could leave the Union had been first mooted. In an impassioned speech the writer Valentin Rasputin spoke of environmental and moral issues and warned of the growing anti-Russian sentiments in some of the other republics:

> Russophobia is spreading in the Baltic and Georgia, and it has penetrated other republics as well ... Anti-Soviet slogans are combined with anti-Russian ones, and emissaries from Lithuania and Estonia travel about with such slogans, seeking to create a united front.

In such circumstances, he warned the non-Russian republics:

> Perhaps it is Russia which should leave the Union, since you hold her responsible for all your misfortunes ... Without fear of being called nationalists, we [Russians] could then pronounce the word *Russian* and speak openly about our national self-awareness; we could end the mass corruption of the soul of our youth, and we could finally create our own Academy of Sciences.[16]

Sentiment like this prompted the Russian CPD on 12 June 1990 to adopt by an overwhelming majority a Declaration of State Sovereignty of the RSFSR (Russian Soviet Federated Socialist Republic), whose principles were to lie at the basis of post-communist government in Russia. The Declaration stated that Russia was 'a sovereign state, created by historically united nations'; that 'RSFSR sovereignty is the unique and necessary condition for the existence of Russian statehood'; that 'the RSFSR retains for itself the right of free departure from the

USSR'; and much more that stressed the priority of the Russian constitution and laws over Soviet legislation.[17] To paraphrase Stalin, Russia's insurgency was national in form but democratic in content.

An accompanying Decree on Power represented a revolutionary programme for the liquidation of the power of the *apparatchiki* (full-time Communist Party officials), insisting that 'Any anti-legal interference by political parties, party-political organs and other social organisations in the work of state power and administration, the economic and socio-cultural activity of state enterprises, institutions and organisations must cease immediately and absolutely decisively.'[18] The Decree sought to separate the CPSU from state management, and in particular tried to end the practice whereby local Party leaders were simultaneously chairmen of local soviets (councils). Although challenged in the courts by Gorbachev, several local soviet chairmen resigned their Party posts.[19] Nevertheless, the great majority of local soviet leaders right up to the coup of August 1991 were members of the local Party committee, and in numerous cases local Party leader as well.

A view prevalent today is that the Declaration laid the foundations for the collapse of the USSR. This interpretation is categorically rejected by Ruslan Khasbulatov (at the time Yeltsin's deputy chairman of the Russian Supreme Soviet), who insisted 'The Declaration [did] not, in essence, deal with sovereignty at all, but only with decentralisation of the excessively centralised Union state.' He noted how much remained under Soviet control: 'the combined armed forces, common rail network, airlines, defence' and much more, 'practically all the basic functions which make a state a state'.[20] This may well be true, but the Declaration acted as a spur to the other republics, and from Autumn 1990 provoked a 'war of the laws' between the Union authorities and components of the USSR that ultimately undermined the integrity of the state. The assertion, moreover, that in his struggle with Gorbachev Yeltsin destroyed the Union does not bear close historical examination: while personality conflicts certainly played their part, the titanic shift of geopolitical relations in Eurasia was part of a much deeper process.

Other republics followed Russia's lead, and on 16 July Ukraine adopted an extremely radical declaration of sovereignty, passed unanimously by its parliament, calling for respect for human rights, multiparty democracy, and a separate national army. The precise meaning and juridical status of these declarations remained unclear, but they demonstrated that Gorbachev's attempts to negotiate a new 'Union Treaty' for the USSR would have to take into account the aspirations of the republics for autonomy. Declarations of sovereignty were not restricted to Union Republics but began to be adopted by regions and even by boroughs in Moscow and other cities. The 'war of the laws' focused above all on the contested jurisdictions of Union and republican power. As the Soviet administrative system came apart at the seams, both the republics and the centre claimed priority for their laws, leading in most cases to the implementation of neither.

The emergent Russian state became the main opposition to the decaying Soviet regime, and as Khasbulatov noted, 'we find ourselves in an unprecedented situation in world history: a legitimate government in opposition'.[21] Gorbachev had planned a gradual deconcentration of power to society, yet his hesitancy in relinquishing the concept of Party rule, or indeed his failure to split the CPSU at the Twenty-eighth Party Congress in July 1990 and place an avowedly Social Democratic party at the head of the democratic transformation of the USSR, meant that as power leaked away from the old administrative-command system it was absorbed by the republics. The media, the black economy and corrupt networks also became residual legatees of the declining system, but it was not so much civil society that gained in strength as its most degenerate features. The increased power of the republics indicated not the triumph of civil society but the establishment of the borders within which civil society might later develop.

Despite a host of difficulties, such as complex registration laws and harassment, numerous parties were established in this period of insurgency. Gorbachev's 'socialist pluralism of opinions' was now superseded by structured political conflict and the veritable rebirth of politics. The problem soon became one not of the lack of alternatives but the sheer abundance of new parties that failed to coalesce into a coherent force that could challenge the CPSU or provide the basis for viable government. The decline of the Interregional Group of Deputies prefigured the decline of the USSR CPD itself. The democratic deputies, led by Yeltsin and Andrei Sakharov, were greatly outnumbered by the remainder of the 2,250 deputies, whom the radical democrat Yurii Afanas'ev dubbed the 'aggressively obedient majority'.[22] The group was weakened by splits over national issues, with the Baltic group barely participating at all, and over tactics, the degree to which reform should remain within the one-party system; by late 1990 they had lost direction and coherence, especially with the death of Sakharov in December 1989.

Gorbachev's inability to convert the CPSU into a genuine instrument of reform was one of the main reasons for the failure of perestroika;[23] the end of its monopoly on power did not denote a sudden conversion to democracy by the Party's leading structures. The old regime at this time tried to coopt the resurgent Russian nationalism for its own purposes, but succeeded only in stimulating reactionary Russian nationalism and awakening the aspirations to statehood of some of the minorities within Russia, threatening the unity of the country. The CPSU sponsored various 'front' organisations, like the United Front of Workers (OFT), which tried to appeal to the loyalist instincts of blue-collar workers, and sought to influence the policies of the new parties established after March 1990. As late as March 1991 the CPSU was still giving orders to government ministries, a year after having given up its constitutional 'leading role'. The USSR had moved from one-party rule to a limbo of non-party governance as the CPSU refused to move out of the way to allow new forces to take over. The Communist Party still claimed to be the only force that could fill the political vacuum.

One of the cardinal principles that had kept the Party together was democratic centralism, an institutional theory that suggested participation of lower bodies in the decisions of higher ones but which in practice imposed a rigid hierarchical subordination.[24] Lenin's 1921 'ban on factions', moreover, prohibited horizontal contacts between Party cells. Gorbachev now weakened this element of democratic centralism, allowing an upsurge in factional activity. The Democratic Platform called for the radical democratisation of the CPSU, while the Marxist Platform called for a return to a purer form of Marxian socialism.[25] The Party also began to split into its constituent national parts. In December 1989 the Lithuanian Communist Party under Algirdas Brazauskas broke away from the national CPSU in the belief that only by allying with nationalist forces could it hope to have a voice in Lithuanian politics. The creation in June 1990 of the hardline Communist Party of the RSFSR (CP RSFSR) headed by Ivan Polozkov finally gave separate representation for the 58 per cent of CPSU membership who were in Russia, but it was also an attempt by the conservatives to build a separate power base to thwart Gorbachev's more radical reforms. This they achieved at the Twenty-eighth Party Congress where Gorbachev had to fight hard to have his draft democratic programme of the

Party adopted. The Party seemed constitutionally unable to reform itself, and thus far from being in the vanguard of reform it lagged behind and indeed obstructed change.

The Central Committee of the CPSU, though much changed at the Congress, remained resistant to radical reform. At the same Congress the Politburo, a body that had in effect been the supreme government of the country, was radically transformed. Membership shifted from professional-territorial to largely territorial representation, with the heads of the republican and some regional Party organisations, and certain key officials. At a stroke the Politburo was reduced in power, and the Party was crippled as a functioning political machine. As the linchpin of the Soviet political system, the CPSU had always been more than a political party. But 'the Party' as such was a fiction; it was the Party's full-time apparatus staffed by the half million apparatchiki that was the effective core both of the Party and the state, while a million more were on the Party's teaching staff in the dense network of Party schools and departments of 'social science' in colleges. The ability of the rest of the membership to influence policy was severely limited by the practices of democratic centralism. During perestroika Gorbachev had tried to broaden the influence of the rank-and-file by democratising the Party through the use of elections, and at the same time sought to weaken the grip of the Party bureaucracy by strengthening state bodies and the legislature.[26]

The CPSU's popularity fell sharply from its peak at the height of perestroika, and by May 1990 only 18.8 per cent of the electorate would have voted for it if there had been elections.[27] The Party began for the first time to suffer a financial crisis.[28] Party members themselves were disillusioned, and only 27 per cent stated that if given a choice they would join a second time.[29] Party membership peaked in October 1988 when it stood at 18.9 million members and 416,000 candidates, a total of 19.3 million.[30] In 1989 for the first time since the purges membership actually fell;[31] in the last quarter of 1989 alone 279,000 communists failed to renew their membership, and another 670,000 failed to do so by 1 April 1990.[32] Communists in Armenia and Azerbaijan left *en masse*, and few in the rest of the country felt moved to join what was increasingly perceived as a discredited organisation. This was a period marked therefore by mass defections, with membership falling from the peak of 19.3 million to some 15 million in August 1991.

By the time of the coup the CPSU had lost its ideological and organisational integrity and had failed in its attempts to convert itself from a state structure to a campaigning political organisation.[33] The CPSU was marginalised, its membership was falling and it was splitting into various factions. Communist dominance was challenged by various informal groups and movements, accompanied by the emergence of genuine pluralism in intellectual and political life. The Communist Party was by definition an expansive and monopolistic body that had left civil society, the proper sphere for political parties, after October 1917 and had occupied the state; it was now faced with the prospect of being ousted from its strongholds in the factories, the army and the KGB to become a normal parliamentary party subject to the vagaries of electoral politics. Gorbachev on this crucial issue could not follow his usual centrist position, because the centre had disappeared and he had to come off the fence: either Party rule or genuine multiparty politics. His failure to choose only protracted the crisis, preventing either side from taking the initiative, and weakening his own position.

By 1990 Gorbachev had broadly decided in favour of establishing a market economy, but like most of the population he was unwilling to face the hardships – or the political price – that would inevitably accompany the transition. Gorbachev's failure in September 1990 to support the plan proposed by Stanislav Shatalin and devised by Grigorii Yavlinskii, envisaging a rapid transition to the market in '500 days' and which would have devolved Great Powers to the republics while maintaining a single economic space and currency, was in retrospect probably the moment when the USSR passed the point of no return and could no longer be held together. It appeared that no single economic reform plan could work for all of the USSR, and hence each republic had to devise its own. Yeltsin had supported the Shatalin plan, and its failure led him to launch Russia's own economic reforms in November 1990. If every republic had to devise its own reform plan, then what was the point of Gorbachev's 'renewed union'?

Gorbachev's repudiation of the 500-days plan represented a capitulation to the conservatives who now launched the so-called 'winter offensive' of 1990–91. For reasons that remain unclear, Gorbachev appeared to become hostage to the conservatives, and this was reflected in personnel policy. The liberal Vadim Bakatin was replaced as minister of the interior (MVD) by the pugnacious Boris Pugo, and on 27 December 1990 Gorbachev imposed as his vice-president Gennadii Yanaev. Even the usually compliant USSR CPD, now chaired by Gorbachev's old friend from his Moscow University days Anatolii Luk'yanov, baulked at ratifying the appointment of a tired second rate official who epitomised the faults of the Soviet bureaucratic system. On 20 December 1990 Eduard Shevardnadze, who had been foreign minister since July 1985, resigned, warning darkly of the threat of a conservative coup.

The conservative offensive was not limited to displacing liberal officials in Moscow but attempted to crush the nationalists in the republics. The low point of this period came with the storming of the Lithuanian TV building in January 1991, in which fifteen people were killed. Gorbachev's role in these events is still not clear, publicly defending the ministers responsible for the bloodshed but denying any responsibility. He might well have gone along with what turned out to be a dress rehearsal for the events of August, and then at the last minute repudiated the attempt by the conservatives to seize power in Lithuania. In economic policy this period was if anything even more catastrophic than anything that had come before. In December 1990 Ryzhkov was replaced as prime minister by Valentin Pavlov, a man who had earlier been minister of finance and had almost single-handedly destroyed the rouble by printing money as fast as the budget deficit grew. He now set about destroying the whole economy by his refusal to countenance a rapid advance to the market and by his poorly planned currency reform and price rises.

At the time of the crisis of January 1991 Yeltsin had not hesitated to rush to the Baltic states to declare his support for their independence. While often seen as no more than a ploy in his struggle with Gorbachev, Yeltsin's action nevertheless represented a remarkable repudiation of Moscow's traditional empire-building role and created the conditions for a remarkably peaceful dissolution of what now came to be known as the Soviet 'empire'. Gorbachev's attempt to relegitimise the authority of the Soviet Union in the following months by renegotiating the federation was always a fragile affair, having been delayed too long while he had been distracted by the excitement of foreign affairs and the struggle with his Party opponents. The referendum on 17 March 1991 on a renewed Union gave a notably ambiguous response. While 71.3 per cent of the RSFSR's 79.4 million turnout (75.1 per cent of the total electorate) voted 'yes' to the proposition 'Do you consider necessary the preservation of the Union of Soviet Socialist Republics as a renewed federation of equal sovereign republics, in which the rights and freedom of the individual of any nationality will be fully guaranteed?', almost exactly the same number (69.6 per cent) voted in favour of a second question added to the ballot in Russia – the creation of a Russian presidency – which implicitly challenged the postulates of the first (see Appendix 2.2).

The counter-attack of the conservatives was halted by a renewed wave of labour unrest. On 1 March 1991 a national strike of miners began with economic and political demands, including calls for the resignation of Gorbachev and Pavlov, and the dissolution of the USSR Supreme Soviet. Many miners continued to strike until early May 1991, and they were joined by workers in other industries in Belarus in April. All of this warned Gorbachev that alliance with the conservatives eroded his position. At the opening of the Third Russian (Emergency) Congress of People's Deputies, called by the conservatives in an attempt to oust Yeltsin, Gorbachev ordered 50,000 MVD troops into Moscow to prevent a demonstration in support of Yeltsin, yet perhaps a quarter of a million people defied his ban.

Gorbachev at this point turned once again to the democratic forces, and in the 'nine-plus-one' agreement of 23 April at his dacha at Novo-Ogarevo conceded greater power to the leaders of the nine republics involved and an accelerated transition to the market economy. Yeltsin went on to pacify the miners, and announced that the mines were to be transferred to Russia. The new Union Treaty between the republics of what had been the Soviet Union would be one built from the bottom up, founded on the sovereignty of the republics. The treaty was to have been signed on 20 August.

Yeltsin's position was consolidated on 12 June 1991 when for the first time in history Russia chose its president in a popular vote (see appendix 2.3), with Alexander Rutskoi (the leader of the Communists for Democracy faction that had emerged at the Third CPD) selected as his vice-president. On the same day Popov was elected mayor of Moscow with 65 per cent of the vote; in Leningrad Sobchak was elected mayor with 69 per cent, and at the same time 54 per cent voted to rename the city St Petersburg. At his inauguration on 10 July 1991 Yeltsin proclaimed his readiness to embark on a far-reaching democratic transformation and the fundamental renewal of the Russian Federation. He supported the plan for a restructured Union and promised cooperation with the other republics, but at the same time he stressed the sovereignty of the RSFSR and its role in the world, not simply as part of the USSR but as a sovereign state in its own right. He painted a vision of a rejuvenated Russia 'rising from her knees' and drawing on its cultural and spiritual heritage and its great past, re-entering the world community freed of imperialist ambitions and embracing the principles of freedom, property, the rule of law and openness to the world.[34] Yeltsin appealed to Russian patriotism against the communist regime, but at the same time offered a new synthesis of the national and democratic revolutions.

He continued the assault on the privileges of the CPSU and on 20 July issued a decree banning party structures in government offices and enterprises, and he also proposed legislation that would ban the Party from the armed forces.[35] 'Departification' meant that communist officials would have to choose between their party and jobs. The depoliticisation decree came into effect on 4 August, and the CPSU was still considering its response when the coup intervened. Even Gorbachev appeared to lose patience with the dogged un-reformability of the Party, vividly in evidence at the last plenum of the CPSU's Central Committee on 25–26 July 1991, and announced that an emergency Party congress would be held in December 1991 to adopt a radical new programme that would return the Party to its social democratic roots.[36] Gorbachev at last appeared to accept the necessity of splitting the Party and placing himself at the head of the radical reforming faction.

Conservatives realised that the treaty would make the old structures of power redundant. In

July 1991 twelve leading politicians, writers and generals signed a 'Word to the People', written by Alexander Prokhanov (a journalist with close links to the military), that served as the manifesto of the coup. In emotional language, the address warned of the

enormous, unprecedented misfortune that has befallen us . . . Why is it that sly and pompous rulers, intelligent and clever apostates and greedy and rich moneygrubbers, mocking us, scoffing at our beliefs and taking advantage of our naivete, have seized power and are pilfering our wealth, taking homes, factories and land away from the people, carving the country up into separate parts . . . excommunicating us from the past and debarring us from the future . . . our differences are nothing in the face of the general calamity and distress, in the face of the general love for the homeland, which we see as a single, indivisible entity that has united fraternal peoples in a mighty state, without which we would have no existence.

The Address urged the creation of a nationwide movement of resistance to enemies like 'thoughtless and inept parliamentarians', but was vague on what form this should take.[37]

THE AUGUST COUP

The attempted coup of August 1991 sought to resolve the crisis of power and end the struggle of conflicting ideologies. The leading conspirators were Pavlov (prime minister), Vladimir Kryuchkov (head of the KGB), Dmitrii Yazov (minister of defence), and Yanaev (vice-president). On Saturday 17 August they met and discussed the new Union Treaty to be signed on 20 August. They were joined by Luk'yanov, who realised that the devolution of power to the republics would in effect mean the end of the old centralised structures, including probably the national parliament and with it his own job. On learning that Gorbachev was unaware of their plans, he refused formally to join them but agreed to write against the treaty and at the same time assisted the putschists by delaying the convocation of the Soviet parliament for a week.[38]

On Sunday 18 August the plotters sent a delegation to Gorbachev in his holiday home in Foros in the Crimea. The group included Valerii Boldin, on Gorbachev's personal staff since 1981 and accepted almost as one of the family; Oleg Shenin, a member of the CC Secretariat; Oleg Baklanov, first vice-chairman of the Defence Council, and General Valentin Varennikov, commander-in-chief of ground forces. They sought a presidential decree establishing a state of emergency or agreement to hand over power to the vice-president. Gorbachev condemned their actions and refused to have anything to do with the plot, warning that 'You and the people who sent you are irresponsible. You will destroy yourselves, but that's your business and to hell with you. But you will also destroy the country and everything we have already done.'[39] Gorbachev's communications with the outside world were cut off, but there remains a suggestion that Gorbachev might have done more to try to prevent the coup.

On Monday 19 August the country woke up to announcements by the mass media about the imposition of a state of emergency. A declaration by the State Committee for the State of Emergency (SCSE) was read out, signed by the original four plotters now joined by another four: Pugo, the hardline minister of the interior; Baklanov; Alexander Tizyakov, president of the Association of State Enterprises; and Vasilii Starodubtsev, chair of the government-sponsored Peasant's Union. Yanaev announced that Gorbachev was ill and unable to fulfil his duties, and thus was taking over in the interim. Troops entered Moscow, and for three days the Russian White House, the seat of parliament and the presidency, was defended by citizens.

The plotters had stumbled into launching the coup with very little real preparation, and they had sent the troops into Moscow with no detailed instructions about what they were supposed to do once they got there. As Yazov admitted during later interrogations, 'We had no real plan.'[40] Russians remarked at the time that the coup had been organised with the same level of competence as the country had been run for the last few years.

The Russian leadership acted far more resolutely. On 19 August Yeltsin, Khasbulatov and Ivan Silaev (the Russian prime minister) drafted an 'Appeal to the Citizens of Russia', condemning the coup in no uncertain terms as 'a right-wing, reactionary, unconstitutional coup' and branding the SCSE an illegal body.[41] Within three days it was all over, defeated by the opposition of the Russian leadership, the heroism of the people who took to the streets unarmed against tanks, the resistance in the army, the media and the factories, and by the lack of resolution of the plotters themselves.

However paradoxical it might appear, this was in a sense a 'constitutional coup'. The plotters tried to present their actions as being in conformity with the constitution and thus sought to draw legitimacy from their formal legality. They hoped that Luk'yanov's delay in convening the USSR Supreme Soviet would allow the country to settle down and accept the coup as a *fait accompli*. There was only one problem for the plotters, and that was that Gorbachev refused to step down, even temporarily, and thus they were in fact subverting the constitution. The 'manifesto' of the putschists played down the ideological appeal to communist values; instead, they sought to ground their venture on Soviet nationalism, the attempt to maintain the Soviet Union as a centralised state, and Soviet populism, to gain popular support by denouncing the unpopular cooperatives and other new forms of business activity which the Address quoted above had termed 'bloodsuckers'.

The plotters were not reactionaries, realising that the clock could not be turned back to before 1985 and thus were willing to accept some of Gorbachev's reforms, but insisted that the time had come to stop the retreat. They represented a return to Andropov's authoritarian reform and a rejection of Gorbachev's democratising reforms. The attempted coup was therefore a conservative one, trying to preserve the USSR and its political system but ready to accept some necessary changes. The plotters sought to find a path midway between the out-and-out reactionaries, who would not have objected to Stalin's return, and the reform communists of Gorbachev's ilk who were allegedly betraying the achievements of Soviet socialism.

The coup was statist in two senses: in favour of the preservation of the *territorial* integrity of the Soviet state; and the preservation of the *institutions* of the Soviet state, with or without the Communist Party. Not only the democrats but the conservatives as well realised that the CPSU had had its day, and for the first time since Stalin a major initiative had been launched by-passing the Party leadership. While the Central Committee was not slow in drumming up support for the coup, and neither the Politburo nor the CC Secretariat defended their own General Secretary imprisoned in the Crimea, the coup was as much a defeat for the Communist Party as it was for Gorbachev personally.

Yeltsin's counter-coup destroyed not only the putschists but also the whole system of Soviet power. On 22 August anti-communist demonstrations took place around the country, and the headquarters of the CPSU in Old Square in Moscow was in danger of being stormed. The statue of Felix Dzerzhinskii, the founder of the KGB's forerunner, the Cheka, in front of the Lubyanka was removed with the assistance of the Moscow city authorities. The demonstrations on that day looked as if they might turn into pogroms against Party officials and institutions.

In Moldova and the Baltic republics statues of Lenin were taken down, and one after another the republics announced their independence.

Yeltsin transformed the coup into a revolution. At a session of the Russian parliament the next day the CPSU was suspended in Russia by a stroke of Yeltsin's pen. The CC and Moscow City Communist Party offices in Old Square were sealed to stop documents being destroyed, and Yeltsin ordered a number of communist newspapers to stop publication, including *Pravda* and *Sovetskaya Rossiya*. The retreat of the Party turned into a rout. On 24 August Gorbachev resigned as General Secretary of the CPSU and called for the dissolution of the Central Commitee. On 29 August the USSR Supreme Soviet suspended the CPSU, and on 6 November 1991 Yeltsin banned the Party in Russia.[42] Party organisations were forbiden in military units and state institutions, and the property and bank accounts of the CPSU were placed under the control of the Russian authorities. Amid revelations of the abuse of state and Party funds, on 26 August N. Kruchina, a key worker in the CC's International Department which had been illicitly funding foreign communist parties, committed suicide. Details emerged of a Party-funded shadow economy, a secret financial empire organised by a Business Directorate in the Central Committee to maintain its financial position even if the Party lost political power.[43] Some Party administrators involved in this activity committed suicide, and other highly placed officials also did away with themselves. The Party's links with other communist parties and its subversive activities became known.[44]

There were major changes in the Soviet leadership too. Kryuchkov was replaced as head of the KGB by Bakatin; Pugo (who had committed suicide as the coup unravelled), was replaced as head of the MVD by V. Barannikov; and the minister of defence, Yazov, was replaced by Yevgenii Shaposhnikov. On 24 August Silaev was appointed the head of the State Economic Committee, and on 28 August Boris Pankin was appointed minister of foreign affairs to replace Alexander Bessmertnykh, who had equivocated during the coup. Some of the old guard in state posts also committed suicide, notably Marshal S. F. Akhromeev on 24 August, in despair at seeing the destruction of his life's work in building the USSR.[45]

The failure of the attempt by conservatives to halt the tide of disintegration by staging a coup in August 1991 only accelerated the demise of the old system and the state. While the nature of the August events remains controversial, their effect is clear; the collapse of the once all-powerful Communist Party and the disintegration of the Soviet Union itself. The coup was the final act of 'one of the cruelest regimes in human history'.[46] The Soviet system had destroyed the old Russian middle class and the cultural intelligentsia; it had destroyed the self-sufficient peasantry and Russia's agriculture; the system had squandered the vast natural resouces of the country and the wealth accumulated from the past; and in its final act the cannibalistic regime devoured itself.

THE DISINTEGRATION OF THE USSR

The defeat of the putschists in the August revolution served the insurgent forces well, relegitimising the democratic project and instilling a new pride in Russian statehood, symbolised by the ubiquitous presence of the pre-revolutionary Russian tricolour (white, blue and red), which became the official Russian flag. At the funeral of the three young men who had died in the defence of the White House Yeltsin stressed that 'this conspiracy, this coup, was directed above all at Russia, the federation, the parliament, the president. But the whole of Russia stood up in its defence'.[47] The coup was followed by what can be considered the fourth and final phase of perestroika: disintegration.

The coup accelerated the revolutionary process in the Soviet Union and justified a whole series of formally anti-constitutional measures adopted by the Russian and other republican governments. All the major institutions of the Soviet state were discredited, with the partial exception of the military. The system was no longer in crisis but in a condition of catastrophic breakdown; few of its institutions were capable of reform or regeneration and after the coup were destroyed in their entirety.[48] Whatever the ultimate outcome there was an immediate sense of popular relief that at last some of the problems besetting the country could be faced. A poll conducted by the All-Union Institute of Public Opinion (VTsIOM) on 7 September 1991 found that 46 per cent of Muscovites were more optimistic than in early August, 32 per cent were as before, and only 15 per cent less optimistic.[49]

For the new anti-revolutionary system to be considered secure it had to base itself not only on the negative legitimation of having withstood the coup, but also on a positive programme of convincing, if not always popular, policies. With the destruction of the common enemy, the communist regime, the democratic and national coalition in Russia disintegrated. How was the country to be governed, and indeed, what country, Russia or the Soviet Union?

On his return from the Crimea early on 22 August 1991 Gorbachev remarked that he felt as if he was returning to 'a different country'.[50] In political terms, the world had indeed changed radically, and the next few months revealed that Gorbachev himself was increasingly marginalised by the accelerating disintegration of the USSR. The centre had in effect destroyed itself, and the coup prompted the transformation of the declarations of sovereignty of the republics into declarations of independence. Lithuania had declared its independence on 11 March 1990 and Georgia on 9 April 1991, and even as the coup progressed other republics joined them: Estonia on 20 August; Latvia on the 21st; Ukraine on the 24th; Belarus on the 25th; Moldova on the 27th; Azerbaijan on the 30th; Kyrgyzstan and Uzbekistan on the 31st; Tajikistan on 9 September; Armenia on 23 September and Turkmenistan on 27 October. This formally left only Russia and Kazakhstan in the Soviet Union. Kazakhstan in particular favoured a union because of its own delicate ethnic balance, split almost equally between Russians and Kazakhs, and because of its high degree of economic integration with the rest of the country.

Following the suspension of the CPSU its property was sequestered, and the democratic forces indulged in a rather undignified scramble for the pickings. The magnificent headquarters of the Central Committee on Old Square was taken over by the Russian government, and sessions of the Russian Council of Ministers would henceforth be held in the former offices of the Politburo. Up and down the country former Party headquarters were taken over by local administrations and organisations, and the Party's offices in factories and offices were turned over to new purposes. Very soon the ubiquitous presence of the Communist Party, once feared but more recently reviled, was but a fading memory.

The coup was followed by institutional changes and the creation of transitional structures. The next casualty after the CPSU was the semi-democratic USSR Congress of People's Deputies. As a democratic paper noted at the time, 'Far from being in opposition to the apparatus of totalitarian authority, [the Congress] served as a legal shelter for that authority.'[51] An Emergency Congress from 2–5 September put an end to itself and thus also to one of the major elements of perestroika-style politics. Its last act was a Declaration of Human Rights and Freedoms which committed the country to international standards of legal, citizenship,

Figure 1 The USSR in 1991

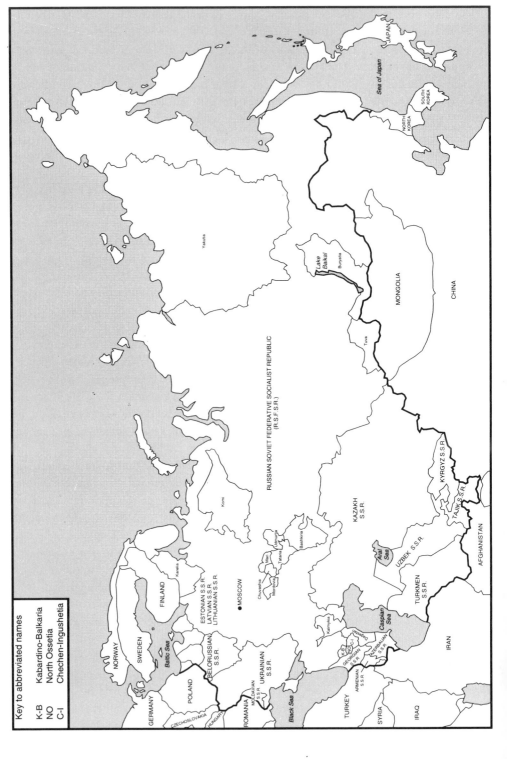

Key to abbreviated names

K-B	Kabardino-Balkaria
NO	North Ossetia
C-I	Chechen-Ingushetia

Table 1 Population of the USSR in 1989

Republic	Population	Percentage of USSR population	Titular nationality					
			living in USSR (thousands)	percentage of USSR population	living in their own titular republic (thousands)	(%)	living outside their own titular republic (thousands)	(%)
Russia	147,386,000	51.4	145,155	50.6	119,866	82.6	25,289	17.4
Estonia	1,573,000	0.5	1,029	0.4	963	93.8	64	6.2
Latvia	2,681,000	0.9	1,459	0.5	1,388	95.1	71	4.9
Lithuania	3,690,000	1.3	3,067	1.1	2,924	95.3	143	4.7
Moldova	4,341,000	1.5	3,352	1.2	2,795	83.4	557	16.6
Belarus	10,200,000	3.6	10,036	3.5	7,905	78.8	2,131	21.2
Ukraine	51,704,000	18.0	44,186	15.4	37,417	82.6	6,767	15.3
Armenia	3,283,000	1.1	4,623	1.6	3,084	66.7	1,539	33.3
Azerbaijan	7,029,000	2.5	6,770	2.4	5,805	85.7	965	14.3
Georgia	5,449,000	1.9	3,981	1.4	3,787	95.1	194	4.9
Kazakhstan	16,538,000	5.8	8,136	2.8	6,535	80.3	1,601	19.7
Kyrgyzstan	4,291,000	1.5	2,529	0.9	2,230	88.2	299	11.8
Tajikistan	5,112,000	1.8	4,215	1.5	3,172	75.3	1,043	24.7
Turkmenistan	3,534,000	1.2	2,729	0.9	2,537	93.0	64	6.2
Uzbekistan	19,906,000	6.9	16,698	5.8	14,142	84.7	2,556	15.3
TOTAL	286,717,000							

Source: *SSSR v tsifrakh v 1989 godu* (Moscow, Finansy i statistika, 1990, pp. 36, 38; *USSR: Facts and Figures Annual*, edited by Alan P. Pollard, vol. 15, (Gulf Breeze, FL, Academic International Press, 1991), p. 504.

property, and social rights, including the right to work, and religious freedom and the right to use one's own language.[52] In the context, however, it was meaningless since there were no institutions that could guarantee these rights, and how could the rights of citizenship be defended in a country that existed only in name? Hopes for a democratic USSR were disappointed, and in the opinion of the self-styled democrats were probably unrealisable since empires and democracy are by definition incompatible. But the question that was to haunt post-communist state building immediately arose: what if the USSR was not an empire but the core of a multinational community that could have survived as a democratic confederal state?

Disintegration was facilitated by the bankruptcy of existing Union institutions, so vividly exposed by the coup, and by the absence of 'democratic' institutions covering the whole country. The very logic of the struggle against the communist 'centre' had undermined all attempts to create alternative *national* institutions and had focused attention on establishing the state institutions of individual republics. In these circumstances only a strong centre could have managed the transition from Soviet unitarism to a genuine confederation, but in this matter (as in so many others), Gorbachev had equivocated for too long and lost the opportunity that might have existed in the period 1988–89.

The absence of a clear demarcation between Union and Russian institutions now gave rise to a dangerous vacuum of authority. Russia in effect suffered from a form of dual power, with two presidents and two parliaments, which gave rise to a type of 'dual powerlessness' and a paralysis of government.[53] This hesitancy was illustrated by Yeltsin's own behaviour. Instead of taking advantage of the enormous boost to his own popularity given by victory over the coup by launching decisive measures (including possibly pre-term elections to Russia's parliament and local soviets) to consolidate the democratic revolution, he went on vacation to Sochi to ponder the future and thus missed the opportunity. Khasbulatov notes that 'The extraordinary passivity of the state during this period [from August to late October] remains a mystery to me', and he argued that only the preparations for the Fifth Congress of People's Deputies 'saved us from the final collapse. . . . The executive was roused from its hibernation and somehow we began to act'.[54]

It is precisely Yeltsin's failure to dissolve the Russian parliament, ironically, for which he is most condemned. In his second volume of memoirs, however, Yeltsin questions whether elections at that time would really have brought forward 'good' deputies, and notes that his resistance to the sort of acts suggested by the democrats, like the abolition of the state security system and vigorous 'decommunisation' measures, was based on the fear of provoking popular violence against the old regime, an approach that might have 'turned August into another October 1917', with all of the attendant violence and bloodshed.[55] The spectre of October and the fear of popular mobilisation inhibited the deepening of the democratic revolution, and thus instead of harnessing the enthusiasm of August to effect radical change, events now shifted gear into intra-elite intrigues and institutional wrangling – giving rise, not surprisingly, to popular disillusionment. The Russian authorities now stumbled into a war of manoeuvre with Gorbachev and the other republics, and as much by necessity as by desire they engaged in a form of 'salami tactics' as slice by slice Russia took over the powers of the Union.

Four main provisional structures operated to fill the vacuum resulting from the collapse of the old regime. First the Congress was replaced by a new USSR Supreme Soviet made up of representatives from the republics to coordinate policy. If nothing else, the new parliament was intended to act as a counterweight to the Russian parliament.[56] The modified Supreme

Soviet had the right to call a full Congress but never did so. Many of the republics failed to send delegates to the new USSR legislature, and few regretted its abolition.

The second and most important body was the twelve member State Council made up of the leaders of the republics with Gorbachev in the chair as president of what remained of the USSR (the three Baltic republics and Georgia did not participate). Gorbachev's acceptance of the new system ranks amongst his highest achievements, but his position would have been stronger if he had unequivocally accepted the confederalisation of the Union before the coup rather than after. During the coup all the structures on which he had relied betrayed him (the CPSU, the army, the KGB and the MVD), but even earlier Gorbachev's instincts led him to try to find a new power base, the collective authority of the presidents of the republics in the Novo-Ogarevo process that had given rise to the Union Treaty, and this was now formalised by the creation of the State Council. Leaders of the democratic opposition had long called for a 'round table' conference of the Eastern Europe sort, but the coup made it clear that the only round table that would have any meaning in the USSR would be one involving not political movements but the leaders of the republics. The State Council took the key strategic decisions in the interim, recognising the independence of the three Baltic republics, but delayed the recognition of the independence of Armenia, Georgia and Moldova or that of Ukraine.

The third transitional structure was the USSR presidency itself. Gorbachev in the immediate post-coup period looked out of touch with current realities, reiterating his commitment to the renewal of the Communist Party and to notions of a renewed socialism. He had expected to carry on as before, but he was soon disabused of this illusion. He was harried and bullied by Yeltsin in the Russian parliament on 23 August, and popular opinion held him partly responsible for the coup because of his appointment of discredited figures and his failure to stand up to the conservatives. The need to keep certain Union structures to manage the transition meant, however, that he was able to stage one of his more remarkable political resurrections and recover some lost ground. Gorbachev's mastery of compromise now worked to his advantage as he tried to achieve some sort of centrist democratic consensus in the post-communist era, as reflected in his appointments to the new Political Consultative Council under the presidency. Moreover, it now seemed to be in the interests of the non-Russian republics to keep an independent centre alive, if only to act as a counterweight to the power of Russia.

The fourth transitional body was the State Council's Inter-Republican Economic Committee, headed from 16 September by the former prime minister of Russia, Silaev. The committee acted as the government of the USSR to provide central direction in the transition to the market. Silaev's appointment reflected tensions within Yeltsin's camp, especially since he was, together with the reform economist Yavlinskii, convinced of the need to maintain a single economic space in the old Union. To this end an economic accord between ten of the former Soviet republics (excluding the three newly independent Baltic states, and Armenia and Georgia) was signed in Almaty in October 1991.

By the end of 1991 it was clear that the old centre could play only a very limited role in post-communist politics. Gorbachev's power was increasingly limited, and very much overshadowed by the Russian government and by Yeltsin personally. The republics were unwilling to delegate functions to the centre and they could now decide the terms and intensity of the relationships with each other. In the early post-coup days the republics had reached agreements on cooperation in economic, scientific, ecological and human rights matters, and above all agreed on the principles of collective security and defence; but these commitments, like the economic accords, remained vague and soon gave way to the complete republicanisation of politics.

There had been a creeping Russification of All-Union institutions even before the coup and now Russian normative acts increasingly replaced Union laws. Already in April 1991 the coal industry had been transferred to the control of the Russian government in exchange for ending the miners' strikes, and now the coup accelerated the process of Russia 'gathering in' economic responsibilities. In mid-November Yeltsin took over Soviet oil exports and the gold and diamond industries, most of which are on Russian territory. The transitional institutions established in September 1991 had little authority to take firm decisions and implement them; in effect, the Union presidency headed by Gorbachev and the old institutions continued as if by sufferance from Yeltsin, and enjoyed only as much authority as he was willing to grant them. To the alarm of the other republics, Russia began to take on the mantle of the old Union centre.

Since Russia had led the democratic struggle against the coup and against the communist regime as a whole, it came as a surprise to the leadership to find in the months after the coup that the hostility of the other republics was now directed against itself, and instead of reaping gratitude for defeating the communist regime, Russia found itself isolated. The process that Russia had started was then completed by Ukraine in its steadfast refusal to have anything to do with the new Union. Russia discovered that the distrust had been directed not so much towards the old regime but against any strong power in Moscow, be it in a Soviet authoritarian guise or a Russian democratic one. The failure to realise this led to several ill-considered acts, such as the announcement by Yeltsin's press secretary Pavel Voshchanov soon after the coup that the borders of republics that declared their independence would be questioned. This only seemed to confirm the suspicions of the republics that Russia was now the imperial hegemon replacing the Soviet regime, and put paid to Russia's hopes of establishing a genuine confederation to replace the USSR. Moreover, the republican leaderships that had wavered during the coup sought to bolster their positions by appealing to anti-Russian and nationalist sentiments, a ploy that was remarkably successful in allowing renamed neo-communist regimes to stay in power in many republics.

Gorbachev's position was increasingly untenable and ultimately he failed to find a role either for himself or for the Union bureaucracy. He tried to coopt the leaders of the republics into a reconstituted centre by offering them seats on the State Council, but the leaders themselves had to respond to pressure in their own republics. Beneath the veneer of republic power the old bankrupt Union bureaucracy remained virtually intact, funded now by making the money-printing presses work even harder. Silaev was given the impossible task of initiating reform from within the existing structures in a way that would suit both the republics and the centre. Russia's adoption of a separate economic reform plan at this time also contributed to splitting the Union.

These contradictions came to a head over attempts to negotiate a new Union Treaty of twelve sovereign states in a reconstituted entity that would be a subject of international law. Gorbachev insisted on the continuation of what he called 'the Novo-Ogarevo process', the search for a new Union of Sovereign States (USS), and this in November 1991 resulted in the fifth draft of the Union Treaty which conceded yet more powers to the Union Republics.[57] The strongest support for confederation came from the president of Kazakhstan, Nursultan Nazarbaev, and Yeltsin, who considered the maintenance of some sort of Union to be in Russia's interests. However, several republics quite simply refused to have anything to do with a renewed centre.

Hopes for a new Union Treaty foundered on the rocks of Ukrainian aspirations and ultimately the whole Union was broken by the attempt to keep Ukraine part of it. While Gorbachev, and indeed Yeltsin, insisted that a Union without Ukraine was meaningless, Ukraine nevertheless abstained from all active participation in negotiations until the presidential elections and referendum of 1 December 1991. The Ukrainian prime minister Vitold Fokin prepared to issue a separate Ukrainian currency, which would effectively end its direct links with the old Soviet economic space. The overwhelming vote in Ukraine on 1 December 1991 to confirm the provisional declaration of independence of 24 August, and the election of Leonid Kravchuk as president at the same time, demonstrated that henceforth it would be the republics that would determine policy and would relate to each other directly without going through Union structures.

If Ukraine and other republics refused to have anything to do with a new Union Treaty, then what was Russia to do? If Ukraine became independent and began to issue its own currency, then there was a danger that Russia would be flooded by the surplus roubles of 52 million Ukrainians. Yeltsin adopted the strategy long advocated by his close adviser, Gennadii Burbulis, namely the development of specifically Russian, as opposed to Soviet, policies. A number of consequences followed from this, including the appointment of a new radical government headed by Yeltsin personally in early November 1991, with Yegor Gaidar responsible for economic reform (see p. 149). Another was the pronunciation of the death sentence on the Soviet Union, all of which was tantamount to a Russian declaration of independence and, as we shall see, the attributes of full Russian statehood soon followed.

On 7–8 December 1991 the leaders of the three Slavic republics (Russia, Ukraine and Belarus), met in a hunting lodge in the Belovezha Pushcha nature reserve in western Belarus, to discuss the future of the Union. Since the three countries were the original signatories of the Union Treaty of December 1922 that had created the USSR, they claimed the right to dissolve what they had once formed. The Belovezha Accords declared that 'The USSR as a subject of international law and as a geopolitical entity has ceased to exist' and announced the formation of a Commonwealth of Independent States (CIS).[58] While coming as a shock to the rest of the world, the Ukrainians had long been considering the option: their ideas for a confederation had been dismissed by Gorbachev, and they plainly considered that attempts to renegotiate the Union Treaty were futile.[59] No records of the meeting survive, but two factors clearly precipitated the decision: the need to accommodate Ukraine's drive for independence; and the perception of Russia's 'government of reforms' that they stood a much better chance on their own to launch a radical transformation of the economy. For Yeltsin, moreover, the act of dissolution had two advantages: it put a summary end to the Gorbachev era; and he apparently believed that the CIS would become a new union with a new president, himself.[60]

The signatories reaffirmed their commitment to 'the goals and principles of the UN Charter, of the Helsinki Final Act and of other CSCE [Conference on Security and Cooperation in Europe] documents' (Preamble). Despite the resounding commitment to 'universally recognised norms concerning human rights', no method of implementing these goals was indicated. Article 3 expressed the commitment to the 'preservation and progress of the ethnic, cultural, linguistic and religious identity of national minorities', but stopped short of recognising their right to political self-determination. The agreement attempted to maintain the territorial *status quo*, and Article 5 forcefully committed the member states to 'recognise and respect the territorial integrity of each other and the inviolability of the existing borders within the Commonwealth', although there was to be free movement of people and information within the Commonwealth. Above all, Article 6 committed the member states to 'maintain a common military-strategic space under joint command, including unified control over nuclear weapons'.[61]

The Central Asian leaders, and in particular Nazarbaev, were deeply offended by the creation of what appeared to be an exclusively Slavic union. They met on 12 December in Ashgabat, the capital of Turkmenistan, and resolved to join the new body. On 21 December all eleven republics that would make up the new Commonwealth met in the Kazakh capital, Almaty. The eight that had not met in Minsk (Armenia, Azerbaijan, Kazakhstan, Kyrgyzstan, Moldova, Tajikistan, Turkmenistan and Uzbekistan) signed a Protocol making them equal High Contracting Parties with the original signatories. The Protocol committed them to the Belovezha Accords and made them founder members of the Commonwealth. On that day Nazarbaev announced that the USSR was no more, though it formally came to an end on 31 December 1991. The presidents signed six documents addressing some of the key problems facing the post-USSR world. They established a single economic space, unified control of nuclear arms and strategic forces, pledged that the international treaties of the USSR would be upheld, and that the existing borders would be respected. The documents, however, were declarations of intent rather than binding treaties. Above all, the Almaty Accords declared that the new Commonwealth 'is neither a state nor a supra-state entity'.[62] It lacked serious central coordinating institutions and in effect abolished 'the centre' altogether, something that facilitated the ratification of the accords by the respective republican parliaments. It appeared that the CIS was to be a transitional phenomenon to manage the change and secure the orderly disaggregation of military and economic structures. This at least was the view of Ukraine and some other republics, but as we shall see (chapter 16), Russia, Kazakhstan and some others hoped for rather more.

The disappearance of the USSR meant the abolition of the post of president, and thus Gorbachev's rule was over. It would be an exaggeration to suggest that Yeltsin agreed to the abolition of the USSR in order to remove his rival Gorbachev, yet the personal factor is important.[63] As time passes the depth of Gorbachev's domestic unpopularity at the time is easily forgotten; a poll in late November found that he was the seventeenth most popular politician, barely squeaking in above the populist Vladimir Zhirinovskii, and way behind the most popular figure, Yeltsin.[64] Gorbachev resigned on 25 December 1991 and declared his critical support for the reforms: 'There can be no justification whatsoever for my going into opposition either from a political point of view or when it comes to the interests of the country. . . . As long as Russia follows the path of democratic change, I will not only support her I will defend her, particularly at this difficult stage'.[65] Gorbachev and Yeltsin came to an agreement whereby the former president would enjoy certain privileges as long as he kept out of active politics. He established an International Foundation for Socio-Economic and Political Studies, known as the Gorbachev Foundation, and invited many of his former colleagues to work in it, including Yakovlev and many others of the perestroika generation.

The foundation of the CIS and the overthrow of the Soviet president, bypassing the constitution and the law, was the last act of the counter-coup launched in August 1991 and marked Yeltsin's conclusive triumph over his rival. It was at least legitimated by the fact that the majority of the eleven presidents who disposed of the USSR had been directly elected in their republics, whereas Gorbachev owed his position to bureaucratic manoeuvring. The USSR Supreme Soviet was not convened as requested by Gorbachev, to give at least some legal form to what was after all not only the dissolution of the USSR but of a geopolitical area that had taken some 500 years to be 'gathered together'. Political expediency and national principles combined to put an end to the USSR, but somewhere along the line democracy was the casualty.

THE END OF SOVIET POLITICS

The Soviet regime had been born in a revolution and it died in one. If a revolution is defined as a significant shift in power and property relations, accompanied by the use of extra-constitutional measures and involving a degree of mass mobilisation, then the events of August 1991 represented a no less profound revolution than the one that had brought the Bolsheviks to power.[66] The revolution of 1991 was accompanied by elements of spontaneity, as in the defence of the White House, but the coup by the communist conservatives was matched by a counter-coup of the democrats, who took advantage of the opportunity to destroy the old power system. But if a revolution is defined as a major shift in elite structure, then this was very much an incomplete revolution with important consequences that shall be explored later in this book.

The second Russian revolution of 1991 was a very special type of revolution: not a revolution within the revolution (despite Gorbachev's assertions to this effect),[67] but a revolution to put an end to revolution, repudiating the revolutionary socialist path of development and returning Russia to the mainstream of European development. In contrast to most revolutions, the anti-revolution was almost bloodless. To borrow Joseph de Maistre's distinction, the restoration of the democratic project overthrown in 1917 was not 'a *contrary revolution*, but the *contrary of revolution*'.[68] In other words, this rejection of revolutionary socialism was not what the Bolsheviks and other revolutionaries called 'counter-revolution', but instead was opposed to the revolutionary process in its entirety. This is one of the reasons why the destruction of the old political order and the attempt to create a new one was achieved with so little physical violence.

Gorbachev's attempts to revive socialism appeared increasingly irrelevant and thinking moved beyond reform communism towards civil society, from liberalisation to liberalism, and from democratisation to democracy. Gorbachev himself only slowly moved beyond destalinisation to a recognition that the Leninist legacy itself might be flawed. The reform communists quite simply, it appeared, had lost the philosophical debate – already much weakened by the invasion of Czechoslovakia 20 years earlier that had snuffed out Alexander Dubcek's 'socialism with a human face', reforms that were remarkably similar to Gorbachev's. Thereafter popular movements in Eastern Europe sought to transcend socialism rather than to reform it. During perestroika Gorbachev created new institutions which could give voice to some of the long-suppressed aspirations of society; these new institutions, however, lacked the legitimacy or ability to resolve any of the key problems facing the country. Gorbachev hoped to find a third path between the essentially repressive rule of the CPSU and full-blooded popular sovereignty expressed through democratic elections and representative government. Perestroika also sought some new form of economic system that could reduce the absurdities of the command economy but without fully embracing the capitalist alternative. No such 'third path' was found.

Solutions to Russia's problems were no longer sought within the Soviet or socialist experience but from Western and pre-revolutionary Russian traditions. Early excitement about the rehabilitation of Nikolai Bukharin and discussion of Khrushchev's reforms from the early 1950s to 1964 gave way to a new interest in the classics of Western liberalism like John Stuart

Mill and James Madison, Montesquieu and de Tocqueville. There was a revived fascination in the Russian religious philosophy of the turn of the century, above all the works of Nikolai Berdyaev and Vladimir Solovy'v, and the social philosophy of Semyon Frank, Sergei Bulgakov and Peter Struve, some of whom had begun as Marxists but who had soon realised its spiritual limitations and the philosophical poverty of revolutionism, a problem analysed in the collection of essays called *Landmarks* (*Vekhi*) of 1909 which marked an epochal shift in the Russian intelligentsia's understanding of processes of social change and political order.[69]

Communism in the Soviet Union fell in 1991 with minimal resistance. Gorbachev's reforms during perestroika had undermined the system from within, and by 1991 formerly mighty institutions were no more than hollow shells.[70] The CPSU was riddled with factions and had lost not only its much-prized ideological unity but also its ability to rule. While Gorbachev's achievements in ending the Cold War and returning consciousness to the people by lifting the burden of fear ensure him his place among the greats in the pantheon of history, his legacy was profoundly flawed. In contrast to his predecessors at the head of the Soviet state, his political flexibility allowed the decoupling of ideology and power and his responsiveness to popular aspirations allowed the Soviet system to be transformed in a relatively peaceful manner. His earlier insistence that the Communist Party should remain at the head of the reform process gradually gave way to a more pluralistic understanding of the process of political change.

Gorbachev's style, however, tended to achieve the maximum confusion for the minimum advantage. His approach to policy-making perpetuated the arbitrariness that had always characterised the Soviet system. While he had a broad strategic vision of overcoming world divisions, he lacked the ability to formulate a convincing middle level range of policy options that could command popular support or address the immediate needs of a society in turmoil. By 1991 he had even lost the support of the Party's liberal wing while not regaining the trust of the conservatives. Later he admitted that 'I should have taken advantage of the stability and popular consensus that existed in the first stage of perestroika, and moved more swiftly towards a market economy'.[71] As politics took on a public and parliamentary form, Gorbachev's mastery of bureaucratic intrigue became irrelevant. Gorbachev's tragedy was that he was unable to make the transition from Party functionary to national leader, and the longer he delayed making the choice, the less he was able to fulfil either.[72]

The failure of perestroika, however, was more than a question of Gorbachev's personality. Gorbachev was only the last of a line of reformers who had tried to make the Leninist system work. Perestroika was the third major attempt at reform of the Soviet system, following the New Economic Policy (NEP) of the 1920s and Khrushchev's reforms in the 1950s.[73] The economist Abel Aganbegyan and other reform communists argued that perestroika was a 'continuation of the October Revolution'[74] in the belief that there were hidden reserves in the system and in the ideology. Gorbachev was the last idealistic Bolshevik, but by returning to Lenin the reform communists were returning to the system that had given birth to Stalinism and the problems that they were trying to overcome. Leninism, in other words, was part of the problem rather than part of the solution. Not only did Gorbachev's reforms fail, but the whole history of Soviet reformism failed too. All tried to find the optimum balance between one-party socialist government and economic dynamism and political participation in the absence of markets and representative government. None could find this balance, and the accumulation of botched and half-hearted reforms only made things worse for their successors.

Perestroika had died even while Gorbachev clung to the remnants of power. Solzhenitsyn's evaluation of Gorbachev's reforms was scathing:

> And what have five or six years of the much-heralded 'perestroika' been used for? For some pathetic reshuffling within the Central Committee. For the slapping together of an ugly and artificial electoral system designed to allow the Party to continue clinging to power. For the promulgation of flawed, confusing and indecisive laws.[75]

The basic framework and premisses on which it was based were acceptable neither to the conservatives nor to the democrats. From March 1990 it was clear that Gorbachev's attempts to devise a viable form of late communism, characterised by a high degree of democratic mass participation within a predominantly state-managed economy loyal to Leninist principles of single party dominance, was doomed. From that time the system itself became increasingly de-ideologised and stopped looking for an overarching theoretical principle and simply became a system trying to stay in power. The concept of a Party-guided process of socialist reform known as perestroika was dead, and the USSR could not survive without the communist system that had given it birth.

In 1991 the communist experiment in Russia, one of the most sustained attempts in social engineering ever undertaken by humanity, came to an end. The revelations of glasnost encouraged the view that the whole Bolshevik period had been one gigantic 'mistake', reflected in the popular slogan of the time 'seventy years on the road to nowhere'. In principle, there cannot be 'mistakes' in history; what happened, happened, and the historian's task is to understand why. Few would argue that Hitlerism was a mistake; regrettable certainly, but not a mistake as such: it arose out of specific social and political circumstances. Similarly, Bolshevik power in Russia did not emerge like a bolt out the blue but was prepared by such factors as the autocracy's resistance to political modernisation; the immiseration of large sections of the peasantry and the nascent working class; the horrors of the war on the Eastern Front; the irreconcilable oppositionism of the Russian intelligentsia (the mental world of Russia's revolutionaries is brilliantly detailed in Dostoevsky's *The Devils*); the obstacles preventing the emergence of an interactive political sphere; and bitter social conflicts.

However, the conscious nature of the Soviet regime, its attempt to plan the future, do provide grounds for calling it a mistaken attempt to apply an extreme version of Enlightenment rationality to the organisation of human affairs. The theory quite clearly did not work as expected by Marx, and instead of the replacement of private property by collective ownership and planning releasing huge reserves of hidden productive and creative potential, it increasingly led to the immiseration of the entire society. Apart from parts of Central Asia, this was not an absolute immiseration but relative, both in contrast with the dynamic development of Russian culture and society before the revolution and in comparison with the seemingly irrepressible energy of post-war Western capitalist societies. By 1989 comparisons of this sort were no longer restricted to radicals but had entered the mainstream Soviet press: *Komsomolskaya pravda* (the official paper of the youth organisation), for example, pointed out that before the 1917 revolution Russia ranked seventh in the world in per capita consumption but had now slipped to seventy-seventh – 'just after South Africa but ahead of Romania'.[76]

The debate over the Soviet past was to cast a long shadow over the post-communist future. Much had been achieved since the revolution in terms of economic and social development, but achieved at great cost and often in wasteful and superfluous forms. For all its distortions the Soviet regime nevertheless represented a recognisably 'Western' pattern of development.

Communism claimed to be an improved and more effective version of the modernity prevalent in Western countries, and measured by such features as childcare, employment and leisure, Soviet society was attractive to many – one of the reasons for the nostalgia for the Soviet epoch in post-communist Russia. In terms of urbanisation, industrialisation, education and all the other attributes of modern life, the Soviet Union simulated universal modernisation processes. However, while in Central Asia this was largely perceived as being progressive, in the Baltic, parts of the Ukraine and elsewhere, the Soviet framework of modernisation appeared to be regressive, separating economies and societies from effective participation in the global economy and international society. Thus the Soviet pattern of modernisation was thoroughly ambivalent, modern and traditional at the same time, giving rise to a distinctive alternative modernity. The search for this parallel modernity, to overcome the alleged crisis tendencies of the capitalist system by abolishing the private ownership of the means of production, gave rise to *mismodernisation*. This is a society that emulates the characteristic features of developed industrial societies, with major advances in urbanisation, education and research, but which lacks the critical dynamism that can make the system self-reproducing – in short, modernisation without modernity.

In the USSR these 'ontological' or intrinsic characteristics of a marketless and 'politics-less' system were joined by a number of conjunctural features that precipitated the dissolution of the regime. Communist rule rested on a dynamic link between ideology and organisation: although the ideology was subject to permanent modification (from Lenin's internationalism to Stalin's Soviet nationalism through to Brezhnev's complacent 'developed socialism'), and organisational forms evolved (from Lenin's party-centredness to Stalin's cult of personality through to Khrushchev's revival of the Party as a functioning institution), the important element was the link itself; power justified by the appeal to an overriding ideological imperative. When that link was broken by Gorbachev, the whole edifice of communist rule collapsed. This in turn precipitated the disintegration of the national territory. Russia was the central actor in the destruction of the USSR, although the Declaration of State Sovereignty of 12 June 1990 was not intended to signal the end of the USSR. Underlying the Declaration and those that followed in other republics was a desire to see the federal Union with a strong centre give way to a confederation of sovereign and equal states. The Declaration, however, unleashed a destructive dynamic that ended with the disintegration of the country. Lacking roots in any national community, the USSR proved susceptible to nationalist mobilisation once the political grip of the CPSU weakened. Above all, the search for security by the USSR ultimately became self-defeating – literally so, and the country collapsed under the weight of direct and indirect military expenditure. The USSR was not defeated in war but by an ideology that perpetuated the need to prepare for war beyond what the economy could sustain.

Mismodernisation gave rise to a society deprived of international contacts and meeting places, of self-sustaining and self-regenerating cultural and economic systems, and above all of a public sphere where responsible individuals could become citizens. The darkened streets of late communism, the empty shops and frustrated careers, the potholes and tawdry buildings, the general coarseness of social life, and the pervasive dishonesty of the ubiquitous bureaucracy degraded all that it came into contact with. The impoverishment of daily life reflected an exhausted ideology and an exhausted society. It was against this background that the new society and polity struggled to be born, rejecting the view that history is destiny, but stamped by its provenance in the administrative-command system.

The Soviet Union did not just fall, it collapsed. The failure of perestroika turned into a catastrophic breakdown of society and economy. All the institutions that maintained Soviet statehood were shattered simultaneously: the Communist Party, the secret police, the economic apparatus and the state mechanism. All of this was in terrible fulfilment of George Kennan's prediction soon after the Second World War that 'Soviet power, like the capitalist world of its conception, bears within it the seeds of its own decay'. He warned that if 'anything were ever to disrupt the unity and the efficacy of the party as a political instrument, Soviet Russia might be changed overnight from one of the strongest to one of the weakest and most pitiable of national societies'.[77] This indeed came to pass, and in the space of a few years Soviet Russia was transformed from one of two superpowers to a supplicant at the gates of the West. The psychological and political consequences of such a dramatic fall have yet to work themselves out.

2   The rebirth of Russia

Nothing destroyeth authority so much as the unequal and untimely interchange of power pressed too far, and relaxed too much.

Francis Bacon[1]

In his speech to the Fifth Russian Congress of People's Deputies on 28 October 1991 Yeltsin noted the weakness of Russian statehood and the need to establish the legal basis for the new Russia.[2] A new state entered the concourse of humanity that was at the same time one of the oldest, Russia, subsumed in the USSR for decades, now returned to claim its place in the community of nations.

THE RUSSIAN STATE

Basic ambiguities surround the emergence of the contemporary Russian state. We speak of an independent Russia, but at what point did it actually become independent? The other Soviet successor states in 1990–91 declared their independence, whereas Russia, while declaring its sovereignty on 12 June 1990, was the only state simply to emerge as the residual legatee of the Soviet state following the latter's dissolution in December 1991. The reborn Russian state, moreover, has no precedents; its borders correspond to no previous historical entity and the polity is based on entirely new principles.

While 1991 represented a fundamental moment of rupture in both geopolitical and governmental terms, elements of continuity, of course, remain. The primordial drive for territorial consolidation is accompanied once again by attempts to strengthen the state at the centre. State building takes four practical forms, leaving aside for the moment questions of national and cultural identity: ability to defend the national territory; effective integration of the centre and periphery; ordered relations between the institutions of governance; and elements of reciprocity between the state and society. The Tsarist system was found wanting on all four counts, having suffered repeated defeats in the Great War; while the Soviet system was certainly able to defend itself, probably against the rest of the world combined, it was less successful in the other three aspects. The reborn Russian state now faces these challenges, once again in the context of balancing influence abroad and political reconstruction at home.

Of the successor states, only Russia has the capacity to become a global power. Russia comprised 76.2 per cent of the entire territory, having half the population of the former USSR, just under 150 million people, and the country is richly endowed with natural resources and a skilled workforce. Russia has the world's fifth largest population (after China, India, the

United States and Indonesia), with 128 recognised nations and ethnic groups. Stretching 9,000 km from East to West, Russia covers one-eighth of the earth's land surface (17.1 million sq km, of which 1.3 million sq km is arable); its borders range a total of 58,562 km (with 14,253 km bordering sixteen foreign states and 44,309 km coasting two oceans and eleven seas). Russia has 90 per cent of the oil, 80 per cent of the natural gas, 70 per cent of the gold production and 62 per cent of the electricity output of the former Soviet Union. The great majority of the research institutes and educational establishments are also to be found here. It is this fundamental geographical and material imbalance that later made it so difficult to find a political balance in relations between Russia and the other successor states.

On the political level Russia had been far more subsumed into the Soviet identity than the other republics, leading them (and many outsiders) to confuse Russia with the Soviet Union. The Russian language was the official state language, and Russians predominated at all levels of government and administration: Russians traditionally were the second secretaries of the republican Party organisations and usually headed the local KGB. Native cultures were Sovietised and the use of their languages, especially in higher educational establishments and in political life, was stymied by the use of the imperial *lingua franca*. Russians represented Soviet power and thus Sovietisation was often perceived as synonymous with Russianisation (the cultural domination of Russia), and in places Russification (the conscious attempt to suppress other cultures in favour of Russia's) as well.

In Russia itself the problem of national identity was more complex. Here Sovietisation was no less intense than in the non-Russian republics, but the largely Russian face to the Soviet regime masked the devastation that Russian culture and society also suffered. While political representation was denied Russia, the opportunities for social advancement in the Soviet regime were enhanced and the cultural prestige of Russia was augmented. It is for this reason that Russian nationalism was to stand in a far more complex relationship to the communist regime and democratic revolution than elsewhere.

Russian predominance did not necessarily mean that the Soviet state governed in the interests of Russia – a point made with great force by 'dissidents' like Solzhenitsyn and then taken up by the democratic insurgency in the late 1980s with Yeltsin at their head. In institutional terms as well, the RSFSR was dissolved into the amorphous USSR. The other fourteen republics had been endowed with the attributes of statehood in the form of republican governments, parliaments and Communist Party organisations, and had developed distinct national identities even within the centralised framework, whereas Russia lacked its own Academy of Sciences, its KGB, its MVD, its trade union or Komsomol organisations, its own national television and radio stations, and its Council of Ministers was firmly subordinated to the Soviet government.

Above all, until 1990 the RSFSR had no Party organisation of its own even though it made up 58 per cent (10.6 million) of CPSU membership. The Russian Party organisation had been abolished with the adoption of the Union Treaty of December 1922 setting up the USSR, when Lenin had argued that the threat of 'great Russian chauvinism' would thus be diminished, but he showed little concern for the political representation of Russians themselves. The interests of RSFSR communists under Khrushchev were represented by a Bureau established in 1956, but this also was abolished in 1966 and thereafter Russian communists lacked direct representation and were managed by All-Union Party bodies.[3] As Khasbulatov notes, 'The lack of rights and the grievous condition of Russia itself was a result of the deliberate policy of the central administration, which "dissolved" the republic in All-Union Party, economic

Table 2 National composition of the Russian Federation in 1989

Ethnic group	Total number	Percentage of RF population	Living on the territory of their own ethno-federal unit	
			number	percentage of the national group
Total population	147,021,869	100		
of whom:				
Russians:	119,865,946	81.53		
living outside				
ethno-federal areas	108,063,409	73.50		
living in others'				
ethno-federal areas	11,802,537	8.03		
Tatars	5,521,096	3.75	1,765,404	31.97
Ukrainians	4,362,872	2.96		
Chuvash	1,773,645	1.21	906,922	51.10
Bashkirs	1,345,273	0.91	863,808	64.21
Belarusians	1,206,222	0.82		
Mordvinians	1,072,939	0.72	313,420	29.21
Chechens	898,999	0.61	734,501	81.71
Germans	842,000	0.57		
Udmurts	714,833	0.49	496,522	69.46
Maris	643,698	0.44	324,349	50.39
Kazakhs	635,865	0.43		
Avars	544,016	0.37	496,077	91.19
Jews	536,846	0.36	8,887	1.65
Armenians	532,390	0.36		
Buryats	417,425	0.28	341,185	81.74
Ossets	402,275	0.27	334,876	83.24
Kabards	386,055	0.26	363,492	94.15
Yakuts	380,242	0.26	365,236	96.05
Dargins	353,348	0.24	280,431	79.36
Azerbaijanis	335,889	0.23		
Komis	336,309	0.23	291,542	86.69
Kumyks	277,163	0.19	231,805	83.63
Lezgins	257,270	0.17	204,370	79.43
Ingush	215,068	0.15	163,762	76.14
Tuvans	206,160	0.14	198,448	96.26
Peoples of the North	182,000	0.12		
Moldovans	172,671	0.12		
Kalmyks	165,821	0.11	146,316	88.28
Gypsies	153,000	0.10		
Karachais	150,332	0.10	129,449	86.11
Komi-Permyaks	147,269	0.09	95,215	64.65
Georgians	130,688	0.09		
Uzbeks	126,899	0.09		
Karelians	124,921	0.08	78,928	63.18
Adygeis	122,908	0.08	95,439	77.65
Koreans	107,000	0.07		
Laks	106,245	0.07	91,682	86.29
Poles	95,000	0.06		
Tabasarans	93,587	0.06	78,196	83.55
Greeks	92,000			
Balkars	78,341	0.05	70,793	90.36
Khakas	78,500	0.05	62,859	80.07
Nogais	73,703	0.05	28,294	38.39
Lithuanians	70,000	0.05		

Table 2 continued

Ethnic group	Total number	Percentage of RF population	Living on the territory of their own ethno-federal unit	
			number	percentage of the national group
Altaians	69,409	0.05	59,130	85.19
Cherkess	50,764	0.03	40,241	79.27
Nenets	34,190	0.02	29,786	87.12
Evenks	29,901	0.02	3,480	11.64
Khants	22,283	0.01	11,892	53.37
Rutuls	19,503	0.01	14,955	76.68
Aguls	17,728	0.01	13,791	77.79
Chukchis	15,107	0.01	11,914	78.86
Koryaks	8,942	–	6,572	73.49
Mansis	8,279	–	6,562	79.26
Dolgans	6,584	–	4,939	75.01
Tsakhurs	6,492	–	5,194	80.00

Source: *RSFSR v tsifrakh v 1989g.* (Moscow, Financy i statistika, 1990), pp. 23–25, modified.

and administrative structures.'[4] The history and traditions of Russia and its peoples were distorted and Russia itself overlain by the Soviet system.

Towards the end of perestroika, in response to stirrings of national consciousness, and indeed to pre-empt the national movement and at the same time to relegitimate Soviet rule in a national garb, attempts were made to give shape to the aspirations for Russian statehood. On 27 July 1989 Russia's last communist prime minister, Alexander Vlasov, informed the Russian Supreme Soviet of plans to give greater economic autonomy to Russia, reminding deputies that Russia accounted for 60 per cent of Soviet GNP yet retained less than half of its national income, whereas other Union Republics retained virtually all the national income they produced. He informed deputies of plans to increase Russia's sovereignty by the creation of new institutions which existed at the All-Union level but not yet at the republican level. These included a separate Russian Academy of Sciences, various social institutions, ministries, as well as a new television channel to cater to Russian needs.[5] The Leningrad Party organisation on 26 August called for the creation of a separate Russian republican Party organisation, but warned against any attempts to convert the CPSU into a confederation of republican parties.[6] In response to these demands in December 1989 a 'Russian Bureau' of the CPSU was created, headed by Gorbachev himself.

This desultory measure satisfied few and the structural asymmetries between Russia and the other republics were maintained. Despite Gorbachev's opposition, as we have seen, in June 1990 a separate CP RSFSR was established by fundamentalists who hoped to use the new party as a bulwark against democratising reforms. This clumsy manoeuvre achieved little except to encourage Yeltsin and the Russian parliament to redouble their efforts to strengthen the Russian state as an instrument in the struggle against the Soviet communist regime. In 1990 Russia also gained its own Academy of Sciences, trade union and Komsomol organisations.

The centre of political life gradually shifted to Russia and the other republics as politics became 'renationalised'. The struggle against the communist monopoly was now focused on

Table 3 The republics of Russia

Name of republic	Capital	Population	Titular nationality (percentage)	Russians percentage	number
Adygeya	Maikop	446,800	22.0	68.0	303,824
Altai	Gorno-Altaisk	196,700	31.0	60.4	118,807
Bashktostan	Ufa	4,042,000	22.0	40.0	1,616,800
Buryatia	Ulan-Ude	1,056,600	24.0	69.0	729,054
Chechen-Ingush	Grozny	1,235,000	70.7(1)	23.1	306,075
Chuvashia	Cheboksary	1,359,000	67.8	26.7	362,853
Dagestan	Makhachkala	1,925,000	80.2(2)	12.0	231,000
Kabardino-Balkaria	Nal'chik	785,900	58.6(3)	32.0	251,488
Kalmykia	Elista	321,700	45.4	37.7	121,281
Karachai-Cherkessia	Cherkessk	434,000	41.0(4)	42.0	182,280
Karelia	Petrozavodsk	799,600	11.0	72.0	575,712
Khakassia	Abakan	583,000	11.5	80.0	466,400
Komi	Syktyvkar	1,246,000	23.3	57.5	716,450
Marii-El	Ioshkar-Ola	764,000	43.0	48.0	366,720
Mordovia	Saransk	963,800	32.5	60.8	585,990
North Ossetia	Vladikavkaz	651,000	53.0	29.9	194,649
Sakha (Yakutia)	Yakutsk	1,074,000	33.4	50.3	537,000
Tatarstan	Kazan	3,723,000	48.5	43.3	1,612,059
Tyva	Kyzyl	306,000	64.3	32.0	97,920
Udmurtia	Izhevsk	1,642,800	30.9	58.9	967,609
	TOTAL	21,161,000	48.7	51.3	10,864,073

(1) Chechens comprised 57.8 per cent and Ingush 12.9 per cent of the total population.
(2) This percentage represents the sum for all the indigenous peoples of Dagestan made up of the following peoples: Agul 0.8 per cent; Avar 27.5; Dargin 15.6; Kumyk 12.9; Lak 5.1; Lezgin 11.3; Nogai 1.6; Rutul 0.8; Tabasaran 4.3; Tsakhur 0.3.
(3) Kabards 49 per cent and Balkars 9.6 per cent of the population.
(4) Karachai 31 per cent and Cherkess 10 per cent of the population.

Note: Population figures are for 1 January 1993; no separate figures are available for the Chechen and Ingush republics.

Source: *Novaya Rossiya: Informatsionno-statisticheskii al'manakh* (Moscow, Mezhdunarodnaya akademiya informatizatsii, 1994), pp. 137–45, modified.

'democracy in one republic' rather than on Gorbachev's apparently futile attempts to democratise the Union and its institutions. The Declaration of State Sovereignty on 12 June 1990, as noted, marked the turning point in relations between the republics and the Union as Russian statehood was formally reborn and Russian laws were to take precedence over Union legislation. The Decree on Power that followed achieved what the democrats had earlier hoped that the Soviet Congress would do, namely assume the full powers of the state. The decree stipulated the separation of the Communist Party from the government in Russia and outlawed the 'party-political system of leadership' in the state, in enterprises, the KGB and the army. A resolution adopted at the same time forbade leading state officials to hold other posts, including those in political or social organisations.[7]

The Soviet state had been federal-unitary; federal in form, it was in effect unitary. The heart of the old state system, the CPSU, had never pretended to be federal and instead had been a unitary body governed by its Central Committee and Politburo in Moscow. The fourteen republican Party organisations were subordinated to the Central Committee of the national Party in Moscow and constrained by democratic centralism. Within Russia only certain autonomous areas populated by national minorities were the subjects of ethno-federalism,

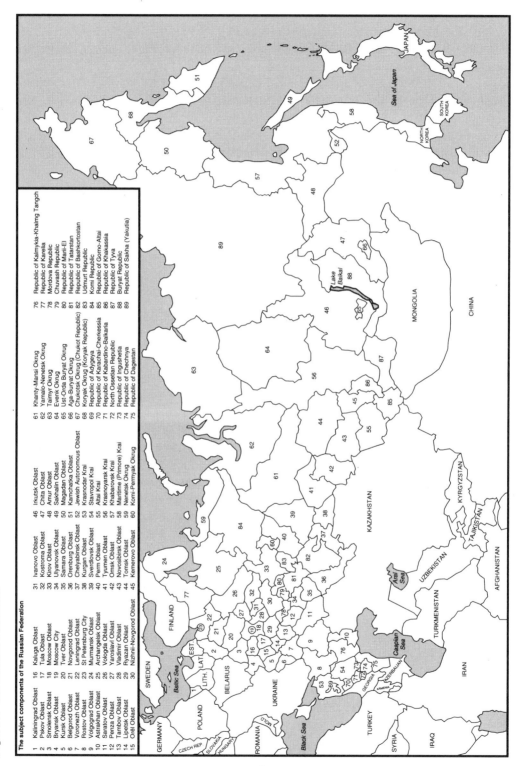

Figure 2 The Russian Federation

The subject components of the Russian Federation

1 Kaliningrad Oblast	16 Kaluga Oblast	31 Ivanovo Oblast
2 Pskov Oblast	17 Tula Oblast	32 Kostroma Oblast
3 Smolensk Oblast	18 Moscow Oblast	33 Kirov Oblast
4 Bryansk Oblast	19 Moscow City	34 Ulyanovsk Oblast
5 Kursk Oblast	20 Tver Oblast	35 Samara Oblast
6 Belgorod Oblast	21 Novgorod Oblast	36 Orenburg Oblast
7 Voronezh Oblast	22 Leningrad Oblast	37 Chelyabinsk Oblast
8 Volgograd Oblast	23 St Petersburg City	38 Kurgan Oblast
9 Volgograd Oblast	24 Murmansk Oblast	39 Sverdlovsk Oblast
10 Astrakhan Oblast	25 Archangelsk Oblast	40 Perm Oblast
11 Saratov Oblast	26 Vologda Oblast	41 Tyumen Oblast
12 Penza Oblast	27 Yaroslavl Oblast	42 Omsk Oblast
13 Tambov Oblast	28 Vladimir Oblast	43 Novosibirsk Oblast
14 Lipetsk Oblast	29 Ryazan Oblast	44 Tomsk Oblast
15 Orël Oblast	30 Nizhnii-Novgorod Oblast	45 Kemerovo Oblast

46 Irkutsk Oblast	61 Khanty-Mansi Okrug	76 Republic of Kalmykia-Khalmg Tangch
47 Chita Oblast	62 Yamalo-Nenetsk Okrug	77 Republic of Karelia
48 Amur Oblast	63 Taimyr Okrug	78 Mordova Republic
49 Sakhalin Oblast	64 Evenk Okrug	79 Chuvash Republic
50 Magadan Oblast	65 Ust-Orda Buryat Okrug	80 Republic of Mari-El
51 Kamchatka Oblast	66 Aga-Buryat Okrug	81 Republic of Tatarstan
52 Jewish Autonomous Oblast	67 Chukotsk Okrug (Chukot Republic)	82 Republic of Bashkortostan
53 Krasnodar Krai	68 Koryak Okrug (Koryak Republic)	83 Udmurt Republic
54 Stavropol Krai	69 Republic of Adygeya	84 Komi Republic
55 Altai Krai	70 Republic of Gorno-Altai	85 Republic of Gorno-Altai
56 Krasnoyarsk Krai	71 Republic of Karachai-Cherkessia	86 Republic of Khakassia
57 Khabarovsk Krai	72 Republic of Kabardino-Balkaria	87 Republic of Tyva
58 Maritime (Primore) Krai	73 North Ossetian Republic	88 Buryat Republic
59 Nenetsk Okrug	74 Republic of Ingushetia	89 Republic of Sakha (Yakutia)
60 Komi-Permyak Okrug	75 Republic of Chechnya	
	76 Republic of Dagestan	

whereas regions populated by the titular nationality (Russians) were part of the unitary and centralised state.

Russia replicated the federal-unitary structure of the USSR (for population of ethnic groups see Table 2). Up to 1990 the RSFSR was made up of 88 administrative units, 73 of which were primary and 15 were secondary (i.e. subordinated to one of the former). The primary units consisted of 16 Autonomous Soviet Socialist Republics (ASSR), 6 krais (territories), 49 oblasts (regions) and the cities of Moscow and St Petersburg, which ranked as oblasts. The 15 secondary units reflected the hierarchical matryeshka doll-like construction of Soviet government, with 5 autonomous oblasts within the krais, and 10 autonomous okrugs (districts), two of which were part of krais and the rest part of oblasts (see Figure 2 and Tables 3 and 4). There are also 1,834 rural *raions* (districts) and 1,067 cities, 13 with a population of over a million.

The end of communism was accompanied by the 'republicanisation' of Russia, with the sixteen ASSR dropping the word 'autonomous' (and most the words 'soviet' and 'socialist' as well). One of the republics (Chechen-Ingushetia) split in two in 1992, four of the five autonomous oblasts declared themselves republics, and most of the autonomous okrugs declared themselves sovereign, freeing themselves from the control of the corresponding oblast or krai and becoming subjects of federation in their own right. Thus by 1993 the Russian Federation consisted of 21 republics, 1 autonomous oblast (Birobijan), 10 autonomous okrugs, 49 administrative oblasts, 6 krais and the cities of Moscow and St Petersburg, a total of 89 administrative areas (for the full list, see article 65.1 of the constitution). As we shall see (Part III), opinion divided between those who sought to make all the components of Russia equal subjects of federation, and those who tried to maintain a hierarchy in the relationship between the republics and the rest.

The natural corollary of the question 'what is Russia?' is the question 'who are the Russians?'. The population of Russia at the time of the 1989 census was 147.02 million, 51.4 per cent of the USSR's population of 286.72 million. The proportion of ethnic Russians in the Soviet population was 50.78 per cent, and in Russia itself 81.5 per cent (119.86 million).[8] Thus 18.5 per cent of the population of the Russian Federation (some 27 million people) are ethnically non-Russian (*Rossiyane* rather than *Russkie*); and slightly less, some 25 million, ethnic Russians live beyond its borders. The fundamental ambiguity over the definition and status of Russians abroad (described by terms like 'compatriots' or 'Russian speakers') reflects ambiguity over the identity of Russia itself.

Nation building in Russia faced some of the problems that had brought down the USSR. Russians comprised 10.4 million (45.1 per cent) out of a total population of 23.1 million people living in the republics, and in nine of the twenty (Chechen–Ingushetia counted as one) were in a majority (see Table 3). The aspirations of some of Russia's republics (Chechnya and Tatarstan in particular) replicated those of the Baltic and Transcaucasian republics earlier, threatening to tear the federation apart. There are major differences, however, and these will be examined below and in later chapters.

In the non-Russian republics the awakening of political consciousness during perestroika quickly took on national forms: the struggle against Sovietisation was accompanied by the attempt to separate from the 'centre' in Moscow, thus implicitly taking on an anti-Russian hue. The rebirth of Russia, however, was a struggle not only against the communist centre but also against elements of Russia's own history. Here it was not only the story of the imposition of a foreign ideology borne by an alien culture, but of destroying a system that in a degenerate form had made Russia great. While nationalism and anti-communism marched hand in hand

Table 4 Non-republic ethno-federal components of the Russian Federation

Names of component	Titular nationality (percentage)	Russians (percentage)
Jewish Autonomous Oblast (Birobidjan)	4.2	83.2
Aga Buryat Autonomous Okrug	54.9	40.8
Chukchi Autonomous Okrug	7.3	66.1
Evenk Autonomous Okrug	14.0	67.5
Khanty-Mansi Autonomous Okrug	1.4	66.3
Komi-Permyak Autonomous Okrug	60.2	36.1
Koryak Autonomous Okrug	16.5	62.0
Nenets Autonomous Okrug	11.9	65.8
Taimyr (Dolgan-Nenets) Autonomous Okrug	13.7	67.1
Ust-Orda Buryat Autonomous Okrug	36.3	56.5
Yamalo-Nenets Autonomous Okrug	4.2	59.2

Source: *Argumenty i fakty*, no. 13 (March 1991), p. 1, where the administrative divisions are those of 1989, but the figures are updated 1989 census returns reflecting the situation of early 1991.

in the non-Russian republics, in Russia the old regime encouraged the aspirations of Russia's own nationalities to counter the growing challenge from the democrats, a development that placed anti-communist Russian patriots in a very awkward position.

The democratic insurgency in Russia tended to avoid identification with the symbols of nationalism, considering them tainted by Russian and Soviet imperialism. During perestroika groups like *Memorial* focused on the crimes committed by Stalin rather than taking up the themes of the Russian nationalist dissidents, many of whom had long argued that rather than being privileged, Russia itself was exploited by the other nationalities, and in particular the absence of a Russian Communist Party weakened Russia's position.[9] Thus issues of national rediscovery at this stage took second place to the recovery of historical memory. Russia thus differed from the other republics and Eastern Europe, where communism was seen as something alien and imposed and where national and democratic aspirations appeared to coincide. In Russia the democratic movement took shape before the emergence of a significant national movement; but the very ambivalence of Russian democracy towards nationalism, while at the same time encouraging the rebirth of the Russian state, would expose it to the charge of betraying Russian national interests later. The attempt artificially to separate the recreation of Russian statehood from national rebirth could not be sustained for long, and the ground was prepared for the later rapprochement between statism and nationalism.

The insurgency against the communist regime took the form of a struggle for the restoration of Russian statehood (*gosudarstvennost*). The Russian concept of 'statehood' is alien to the Anglo-Saxon mind, suggesting both a strong state in domestic politics and a vigorous presence in foreign policy. Statehood was being returned to Russia in two senses: as a political state at last freeing itself from the suffocating tutelage of the Communist Party; and as a republic with the attributes of statehood separate from the USSR. Russia's rebirth as a political state entailed the development of the institutions of political sovereignty, such as an independent parliament, government and presidency. Russia's rebirth as a republic, however, was to be a complex process, involving the development of a new national identity distinct from the Tsarist or Soviet imperial past. The very name of the state changed, with the Sixth CPD in April 1992 adopting a constitutional amendment that abolished the name 'RSFSR' and introduced 'Russia' and 'Russian Federation' as names with equal legal validity.

The crisis of Russian national identity was reflected in very different views on the organisation of the state. For patriots, nationality as such was not an adequate principle for state building and rather the state itself and its principles were tautologically sufficient to build the new order. At the extreme, they favoured the abolition of the ethno-federal system in its entirety and the re-establishment of the Tsarist unitary system based on the purely administrative region called the *guberniya* (province). But the principles of nationality and statehood remained fundamentally ambiguous, and it was not clear what would be the nation, defined both in terms of territory and people, on which the new Russian 'nation-state' would be based. The new republic was a truncated form of the larger Russia for which the White armies had fought during the Civil War of 1918–20, and which ultimately the Bolsheviks rebuilt after their victory and formalised by the Union Treaty of December 1922 establishing the USSR. The rebirth of Russian statehood was accompanied by the tension between internal state-building and external withdrawal. However arbitrary the borders that Russia inherited, the recreation of a larger Russian state was impossible by democratic means, and probably even more unfeasible by military means. Thus a fractured Russian statehood emerged in which the national-patriots could argue that the problems associated with building the institutions of an independent Russia internally were provoked by Russia's separation from some of its historical territories and peoples externally. It was along the line of this fracture that much of post-communist Russian politics flowed.

THE POLITICS OF TRANSITION

The August coup of 1991 in Russia might be taken as a symbolic moment of rupture between the old and the new, year zero of the new order; but at the same, while history might have accelerated, it did not move in leaps. Enormous continuities remained across the symbolic divide: Russia was not a *tabula rasa* on which the new authorities could write at will.

One of the main themes of post-communist politics must necessarily be the interaction between continuity and change, between the existing conditions in society, the economy and politics, and the process of change itself reacting with these historically determined conditions. Matters are complicated, however, by the fact that post-communist Russia had two 'old regimes' against which to measure itself and to draw on, the Tsarist and the Soviet. While it was by no means certain that the factors that had given rise to Bolshevism in the first place had been overcome, it was clear that the 74 years of Soviet power would profoundly influence the post-communist period: there could be no direct return to pre-revolutionary Russia. In 1991 the self-declared 'democrats' came to power, but this did not necessarily entail the triumph of democracy, and it soon became clear that post-communism was a distinctive syndrome of its own and not entirely synonymous with democracy. The fall of the communist regime was a necessary but not a sufficient condition for the triumph of democracy in Russia.

The nature of the changes and ways of measuring them are clearly open to differing interpretations – a theme we shall return to in Part VI. Would it be possible to move from totalitarianism, however decayed, to democracy without an intervening stage of authoritarianism, anarchy, or even the national disintegration that had marked the Revolution and Civil War from 1917 to 1921? Is 'democratisation' an adequate term to describe the transition, or is some broader term like 'modernisation' or 'creating a new political order' more appropriate? The whole notion of 'transition', indeed, has a deterministic air, suggesting that the destination is known and that the transition from communism to democracy is inevitable. That some of the actors insist that the goal is democracy is no reason why we should accept the assertion at face value, although it may be part of the truth.

The second Russian revolution destroyed the unity of the Soviet power system but its elements remained embedded in the Russian body politic. The nomenklatura class, for example, did not disappear with the fall of the old regime; it only lost its role in the Party-led system of power, but generated its own interests (however fragmented). The thousands of informers of the secret police, the corrupt judges, the dedicated communists building socialism on the bones of the peasantry, all these people are the 'citizens' of the new Russia.

Russian democracy is characterised by traditional elements combined with radical innovation. The August regime (the term we shall use to describe the system emerging in the immediate post-communist years), was unable simply to formalise the existing structure of power and property but sought to utilise elements of the old while creating a new socio-economic and political order. The August regime was a distinctive hybrid system: appealing to universal norms of democracy and liberal rights, while at the same time engaged in a radical reconstitution of the social order that goes under the name of 'democratisation'. The tension between democratisation and democracy itself became a potent source of conflict.

The relationship between economic and social structures and political authority and rulers, a subject that preoccupied Max Weber, is still not clear. Modernisation theorists would suggest that the Soviet system had been its own gravedigger, modernising society to the extent that it could no longer be constrained by the authoritarian carapace of the Soviet regime.[10] The maturation of Soviet society now led on to the democratic revolution, but the nature of Soviet modernisation was highly ambivalent and so too was its relationship to democracy. Whereas in nineteenth-century Britain democracy was grafted onto a liberal system of property and law, in Russia political democracy is in search of a social base. In his speech of 28 October 1991 Yeltsin observed that the economic basis for statehood had to be sought through land reform, privatisation and the market: 'We have defended political freedom; now we have to give economic freedom.'[11] The democratic revolution came before the bourgeois revolution; political changes preceded the economic and social basis on which they could be rooted. The state itself not only had to maintain order but to take upon itself 'the organisation of enrichment'.[12]

De Tocqueville argued that the political institutions of America reflected the spirit and ethos of the people.[13] Democracy is both a system of government and a way of life; and it is not clear how democratic institutions can be grafted on to a society whose spirit and ethos are apparently antithetical to democratic norms. The mere presence of numerous political parties and a democratic constitution are no guarantee of democratic practices. Democracy can only with difficulty be 'built from the roof down' (to use the common Russian phrase), but requires the elements of a civic culture like toleration and restraint in society to allow the growth of democracy from below.

There is a considerable literature on the prerequisites for democratic development and the process of transition from authoritarian to democratic regimes. Pluralist writers like Robert Dahl suggest that power in America is exercised not by any particular elite or social class but by competing groups whose influence depends on their strategic location and resources in regard to any particular issue.[14] In what Dahl calls polyarchy – the rule of the many – he describes a system of competing elites in which the state is limited to providing an environment in which various interests compete over policy. A polyarchical system presupposes a basic consensus over the aims and purpose of policy, something which is lacking in Russia today.

The decline of totalitarianism and the end of the elite rule of the Communist Party has been replaced by a society marked by the presence of many interest and pressure groups, but the organised representation of these groups is only in its infancy, and the structural aggregation of interests at the level of the state is embryonic.

The study of post-communist development in Russia and elsewhere draws on the literature of an earlier age, in particular for the comparative study of 'developing countries'. Talcott Parsons argued that all societies make up a social system, operating through a number of subsystems, which tend to be self-regulating to achieve a state of equilibrium.[15] Other scholars – predominantly American – of this school tried to apply the formulae of structural functionalism, with its inputs and outputs and feedback loops, to examine the prerequisites for democratic development in developing countries.[16] Apart from being excessively ethnocentric, these studies proved of little use in forecasting the actual course of development in these countries. Much contemporary writing of the same ilk on democratisation will probably be of similar use in predicting the future of post-communist states. These writers shared a minimalist definition of democracy. Seymour Lipset announced the arrival of a democratic utopia,[17] yet he, too, followed Joseph Schumpeter in arguing that democracy was not a form of society but a method to choose and change governing officials.[18] Dahl adopted an equally diluted definition of democracy, seeing it as a system of decision-making with only formal reference to the non-leaders.

The hybrid character of the August regime has generated a specific type of revulsion against democracy in Russia today; a phenomenon reinforced by the communist regime's use of the term to describe itself, although its language of total democracy (for the working class) led to total dictatorship. While democracy was the universal language of the anti-communist revolution, its practical interpretation took many forms. While upholding democratic principles, liberals prioritised the economic transformation and warned darkly of the dangers of the propertyless *lumpen*. Patriots, while usually nodding in the direction of democracy, fell back on the language of national elitism to guard against what they perceived as the destructiveness of international capitalism. Nationalists made no bones about the redundancy of democracy in the primordial struggle for the development of the Russian state. Paradoxically, former communists united in reconstituted neo-communist parties often made the best democrats – at least when in opposition.

The retreat of government has been accompanied by the retreat of politics. The minimalist definition of democracy suggests a limited role for politics itself; implying indeed that democracy is a form of government rather than a way of life. The pastoral concept of Soviet power has been rejected in favour of a return to the Greek concept of citizenship and laws. In the transition from communist community (*Gemeinschaft*) to capitalist civil society (*Gesellschaft*) individuals are no longer comrades but citizens, and their citizenship is at best partial as they retreat into private life and the pursuit of wealth, if not happiness. The Marxist language of power has given way to Weberian notions of domination (*Herrschaft*), qualified by notions of legitimacy. Weber analysed three ideal type bases for legitimacy, the traditional, the charismatic and the legal-rational, and post-communism is very much identified with the latter. In Russia Yeltsin bestrode the post-communist scene as a charismatic figure, yet sought to legitimise his rule in normative forms of legal–rational rule.

The question of whether Russia enjoys the prerequisites (or indeed, the nature of the prerequisites themselves) for democracy remains open. One of the more popular approaches of the earlier age was the notion of political culture, and in particular the question of the civic culture, the ideas and attitudes that sustain a political system.[19] At a time of rupture, the attitudes and values engendered by the political socialisation of the earlier era, both official and unofficial, cast a long shadow over the new politics. While a type of democratic politics is formalised at the level of the state it is not integrated into the patterns of daily life.

POST-COMMUNIST POLITICS

Four phases can be identified in recent Russian politics.

1. The first encompasses the *insurgency* against the communist system and lasted up to August 1991. This period saw the dissolution of communist rule accompanied by the emergence of movements united on little other than their opposition to the old regime. The insurgency was conducted under the banner of democracy, but once in power democracy was found to be expendable. The first post-communist generation of democrats were themselves former communists used to governing by orders and decrees. The chaotic, negative and personalised pattern of politics associated with the insurgency phase lives on to this day.

2. The second phase from August 1991 to October 1993 was characterised by *polarisation* along a number of axes. The stark contrast between the communist regime and the 'democratic' insurgency now gave way to a number of new conflicts: the centre against the periphery; the republics against the regions; and, above all, the presidency against parliament which came to a head in the bloodshed of October 1993 (see chapter 6). The polarisation phase was marked by bitter controversies over whether Russia should have remained part of some larger union, and was accompanied by claims that the August regime, in launching radical economic reforms, was turning Russia into a primary raw materials supplier for the West. Economic reform saw living standards drop sharply and industrial output collapse. An apparently deindustrialised Russia was becoming no more than a foreign policy lapdog of the West: this, at least, was the claim of the opposition.

It was in this phase that a number of political currents emerged that in broad outline remain to this day. The collapse of the Union polarised opinion between *divisionists* and *rejectionists*.[20] The divisionists accepted the disintegration of the USSR, and some were even prepared to see Russia divide as well, on the grounds that Russia's traditional centralism threatened democracy. They were suspicious of the 'centre', and indeed of anything that looked like recreating the old unitary system and the empire. Notable representatives of this tendency include the historian Yurii Afanas'ev and Sakharov's widow, Elena Bonner. The rejectionists condemned the August regime but were not always agreed on precisely what was to be rejected; most condemned the fall of the Union and opposed the secession of territories from Russia, but were split over the market and democracy. What can be called 'right democrats' hoped to salvage something of the territory and values of pre-revolutionary Russia, accepted some form of market system and broadly acknowledged elements of democracy, while bitterly condemning the Belovezha Accord. Typical of this trend were the 'enlightened patriots' in the Popular Accord bloc who, fearing the 'destructive' tendencies in the 'democratic' camp, staged a dramatic walkout during Democratic Russia's Second Congress on 10 November 1991.[21] The rejectionist front stretched through various neo-communist and communist organisations to nationalist movements. The struggle between divisionists and restorationists partly coincided with contrasting views over such issues as economic reform, decentralisation within Russia, relations with the CIS, and attitude towards the West.

The characteristic feature of the post-communist Russian liberal democratic movement is its fragmentation. There are, moreover, differences in nuance between *liberals* and *democrats*, with the former prioritising economic reform and macroeconomic stabilisation, while democrats espouse a rather more active approach to the universal struggle for human rights, standards of civil liberty and are more consistent in their support for the principle of national self-determination in the former USSR.[22] Both favoured the rapid move to the market economy, and on most issues were united until about mid-1992 when the democrats hoped to deepen the anti-communist revolution. The liberals were most concerned with the establishment of the economic basis for civil society, whereas the democrats were concerned to ensure the functioning of democratic processes and changes in the elite structure to disposses the old nomenklatura. Confident in their ability to forge a new post-communist identity without rummaging too much in the apple box of history, the liberals, prominent in the 'government of reforms' established in November 1991, appeared to be running out of steam by early 1993.

The liberal programme was thus in tension with the democratic one and suffered from its own inadequacies. To many it appeared that the liberal reforms from late 1991 gave birth, not to a genuinely entrepreneurial system, but to various financial combines and economic interest clans (above all in the oil and gas industries) who fought for influence not in the market but in the corridors of power. It appeared that privatisation and associated reforms would not on their own stimulate the creation of a market but allowed the old elites to seize state property for themselves.

One of the important strands in liberal-democratic thinking has been dubbed *Atlanticism*. The term reflects a commitment to close relations with the West, the 'return to civilisation', integration into the world economy, while at the same time maintaining Russia as a post-imperial power. The notion reflects something unique in Russian history, a commitment to integration in international affairs *in the Western way*, the abandonment of claims to uniqueness and to a distinctive path, and thus reflects a new concept of Russia itself. For the first time the form and content of international integration coincided. There are problems with the notion of Atlanticism, however, beyond the obvious ones about the loss of national identity in an amorphous 'Atlantic' civilisation which itself is resisted by many of its participants. The notion of Atlanticism suggests a homogeneity in world affairs which simply does not exist, and it neglects the very real differences between American and European (let alone Japanese or Chinese) perspectives.

Atlanticism was countered by *Eurasianism*, an idea that became one of the main elements in the views of the so-called *centrists* and *democratic statists*. Eurasianism proposed that Russia was not really part of Western civilisation but a civilisation distinct and sufficient unto itself. The debate was at the same time one over developmental paths. Many prominent centrists represented the old state or newly-privatised enterprises, espousing above all a form of national capitalism that would ensure the survival of an indigenous industrial base. This implied generous state subsidies, certain forms of corporatism and the privileging of domestic industry at the expense of global integration and the international division of labour. These were the policies defended by various industrial lobbies.

While the democrats were mostly concerned with transforming the masses into a citizenry, the task as seen from the centre was to make a state, and indeed to reforge the Russian nation. Centrists were often dubbed 'statists' (*gosudarstvenniki*), espousing strong state power and resisting centrifugal tendencies within Russia itself, and asserting vigorous policies in relation to the former Soviet republics and the rest of the world. They insisted that Russian industry should be supported by the state, and that a strong military establishment and the associated defence industries should be protected from the ravages of neo-liberal policies. Centrists favoured technocratic solutions for the maintenance of Russian industry, exemplified by the 'Civic Union' of centrist parties created in mid-1992.

This was the position of vice-president Rutskoi until he moved further into the national-patriotic camp, and as memories of the coup faded he was joined by Sergei Stankevich and many other former democrats. Khasbulatov, formerly Yeltsin's ally and his replacement as chairman of the Russian Supreme Soviet, became the standard bearer of the conservative opposition to the neo-liberal policies of the first post-communist Russian government. The prime minister from December 1992, Viktor Chernomyrdin, reflected much of their thinking but was ultimately forced to pursue economic policies that were only marginally distinguishable from the alleged 'shock therapy' policies of the Gaidar-type liberals. The centre of gravity of Russian politics shifted from the liberal-democratics to the managerial centrists and the national-democratic wing; condemning the divisionists, but not entirely comfortable with the rejectionists.

National-patriots stressed the Great Power interests of the Russian state and were therefore also called *gosudarstvenniki*, but in addition they insisted that Russia should be a Great Power and were thus also dubbed *derzhavniki* (pursuers of Great Power status). They stressed the need to maintain Russia's military potential, and with it the defence industries, and at the same time urged that the retreat of Russian power should not become a rout. For national-patriots the destruction of the communist system was not the same thing as destroying the USSR that covered much the same territory as the historical Russian empire, and they insisted that the borders of post-communist Russia inherited from the Soviet regime did not correspond to the historical borders of Russia.

One of the great tragedies of post-communist Russian politics was the inability of the patriots to sustain an anti-imperialist democratic programme of Russian national rebirth. The weakness of the *patriots* in comparison with nationalist views means that for convenience we can talk of a single national-patriotic bloc, although the distinction between the nationalists and the patriots should be stressed. Nationalists were more willing to make compromises with the former communists, whereas the patriots were more anti-communist and defined Russian identity less in national than in cultural terms (their views are discussed in chapter 10). Communists were only too willing to relegitimise themselves in nationalist garb, while many national-patriots appeared ready to replace the democratic regime, with its many faults, with an outright authoritarian regime to defend Russia's alleged interests more robustly and to save the military-industrial complex.

Russian *nationalists* believed that the West was responsible for the disintegration of the USSR, holding an eclectic mix of Jews, masons, imperialists, Western intelligence services and others responsible for the disasters that had befallen Russia in the twentieth century. The West's plan now, they asserted, was to deindustrialise Russia and turn it into a Third World exporter of cheap raw materials to fuel capitalist prosperity. The most effective proponent of a form of populist nationalism was Vladimir Zhirinovskii, the leader of the so-called Liberal Democratic Party of Russia (LDPR), which was neither liberal nor democratic, and not much of a party either. In the Russian presidential elections of June 1991 Zhirinovskii came in third place with 8 per cent of the ballot, and in the December 1993 elections gained nearly 23 per cent of the popular vote. His solution to Russia's problem was simple: 'I will gain power and I'll give the people everything they need. And it will be very simple: I'll send troops to the former GDR and do a bit of sabre-rattling, including the nuclear threat, and we'll get everything we need.'[23] Faced with such rhetoric, it was clearly in the West's interests to keep Yeltsin in power.

During perestroika the terms 'left' and 'right' were inverted: the 'left' came to denote the free market democrats and liberals, and the 'right' the devotees of socialism and the communist system; but within a short period left and right were back in their usual places, and that is how we shall use the terms. The *neo-communists* were strong in the Russian parliament and supported continued state intervention in industry, were hostile towards Russia's new alliance with the West, and sought to salvage something from the old Soviet system. Exponents of Marxist revivalism, including the revived Communist Party of the Russian Federation (CPRF) (re-established in February 1993), insisted that Stalinism rather than Leninism or Bolshevism had collapsed in the period 1989–91. They argued that a reinvigorated form of Marxism–Leninism offered a third choice between the discredited bureaucratic authoritarianism of the state capitalist systems that had collapsed and the corrupt liberal capitalism offered as the only alternative by the West.[24] While the neo-communists condemned the August regime they were willing to fight within the framework of the August settlement, a paradox that led to their condemnation by the more irreconcilable rejectionists. The *communist rejectionists* sought to revive the traditions of revolutionary socialism and with it to restore the greatness of the Soviet Union.

Populism is defined as a direct appeal to the people, avoiding institutions and claiming some unique insight into the sources of the woes of the nation. Its central prescription is the fairer distribution of economic or political resources. After August 1991 the claim that Yeltsin was a populist was clearly ill-founded since he based himself firmly on the new institutions of the state, and indeed as president personified them, and his economic policies were far from populist. Some of his erstwhile supporters, however, took up his earlier denunciations of inequalities and now condemned the privileges of the new elite. The slogan of 'social justice' retained a residual appeal to the egalitarianism that was deeply ingrained in Soviet society.

Many different versions of populism emerged in post-communist Russia. Conservative populism was based on a dangerous alliance of disaffected and often anti-marketising workers and old-style bureaucrats. Yeltsin in an earlier period had been accused of radical populism, the onslaught against the privileges and inequalities of the old nomenklatura system. Reactionary populism appealed to discipline, order, abundance, the end of corruption and the simplicities of the earlier age of Soviet power. There remained a deep undercurrent of nostalgia for the days of Stalinist 'order' (*poryadok*) when the shops seen through the rose-tinted spectacles of memory were full and accessible.

3. The third phase can be characterised by *democratic adaptation*: the various parties and movements that had emerged during the insurgency phase and contested the very idea of Russia as a separate democratic state during the polarisation phase now (after October 1993) began to adapt to the rules of parliamentary politics and to accept the smaller Russia that had emerged out of the USSR. The rejectionist front was fragmented and marginalised, and while strong opposition remained to the whole post-1991 order much of the opposition now sought to change the system by constitutional means.

4. The fourth phase was marked by *political differentiation*. The big constitutional questions had largely been settled and now political differentiation took place within the broad parameters of the August settlement. More will be said about these phases in later chapters.

THE NEW POLITICAL ORDER

What has emerged out of these phases of post-communist political development? Democrat-isation is part of the current process of change, but that is only part of the story: there is no perfect democracy and no perfect market, and to suggest otherwise would be to fall into the trap of the Utopian thinking that has caused so much misery in Russia already this century. Liberal democracy takes very diferent forms in different countries, ranging from monopolistic liberal democracy in Japan to the multiparty British parliamentary model to the American presidential system, each being a distinctive blend of history, social structure and traditions; and so too Russia's new political order, while formally democratic, operates in ways unique to Russian conditions. Thus continuity and change should not be contrasted too sharply, since the changes themselves are part of an ongoing continuity adapting to new conditions.

The nature of the new order, with its social structure, political institutions and behavioural patterns will be at the centre of attention in this book. According to Michel Foucault, sanctioned forms of rational discourse are governed in societies by systems of order, appropriation and exclusion, which he termed the archeology of power, a concept which in his view was associated with knowledge.[25] Francis Bacon observed that 'Knowledge is power', but for Foucault the relationship was a more subtle one that evolved with the historical contours of a society, and in particular during the crucial formative stage of transition from early modern to modern Europe at the end of the eighteenth century when new 'technologies' of governance emerged. The central question then and now was power, but not in the brutally simplified Leninist version of 'who whom' (*kto kogo*) – who controls the state and its 'bodies of armed men'?, but power as a social and psychological principle governing daily life. Thus power cannot be 'abolished' by vesting it in working class organisations like soviets, as suggested by Lenin, and neither is social knowledge (or ideology) a mask to cover the oppression of the working class, as argued by Marx. Power is a set of relationships formalised in daily life and expressed in forms of habitual rationality rather than a substantive asset that can be appropriated by any particular group in society.

The 'democratic revolution', therefore, is a far more complex phenomenon than a group of self-declared 'democrats' coming to 'power'. The central question of who or what came to power in post-communist Russia can be examined within the framework of a series of dominant discourses, like democracy, liberalism, human rights, and patriotism, that interrelate with society, and different parts of society, in different ways. Seldom has the discourse of democracy been posed as explicitly as in the post-communist countries of Eurasia today, but, just as in the newly independent countries of the Third World in the 1950s and 1960s (when the idea was equally explicit), the brute reality of the societies and their place in the international system gives rise to a series of unintended consequences. Democratisation is therefore a multi-dimensional process rather than a project to be implemented instrumentally. There are various 'strategies of power', once again to use a Foucauldian term, that intervene to desubstantialise 'the tyranny of globalising discourses'.[26] The economic approach to power is only one way of analysing the interrelationship of material forces and ideas.

Between the collapse of the old order and the birth of the new there lay a period of disorientation and disorder, a new Time of Troubles like that in the first decade of the seventeenth century. The dissolution of communist power was accompanied by a crisis of governance threatening chaos and social disorder. The optimum balance between stability and transformation proved elusive as the Soviet crisis of governance re-appeared in an accentuated form. The weakness of post-communist state institutions was not compensated by the growth of other mechanisms to achieve the 'reign of peace' in civil society, giving rise to an almost primeval pre-liberal struggle of all against all, as Hobbes would have put it. The distinctive feature of post-communist Russia was the almost palpable retreat of government: the high tide of state power under the Soviet regime ebbed and society was left exposed and vulnerable to its own morbid elements; venality, criminality and corruption. Once again it appeared that decrees were issued and laws passed only to be ignored by a society apparently living according to a different set of rules. The economic collapse and the threat of social disorder accompanying the transition from communism raised fears that once again, as in 1917, the democratic experiment would be still-born.

This in turn encouraged the reconstitution of state power. According to the constitution 'The repository of sovereignty and the sole source of authority in the Russian Federation is its multinational people' (Article 3.1), yet in practice popular sovereignty gave way to what can be described as *authoritarian democracy* organised in what we shall call a 'regime system' of governance. The notion of regime here draws on two ideas: that a new but unstable bloc came to power after August 1991 that we have called the August regime; and as a partial and imperfect democratic system, imperfect in the sense of incomplete democratisation, giving rise to a hybrid system combining both democracy and authoritarianism. The August regime was based on a distinctive and unstable alliance: dominated by a section of the Russian bureaucracy that had matured for reform, its ideological programme came from liberal Westernisers, while fragmented democratic movements acted largely as auxiliaries.[27] A revolution represents a change in power, property and of the ruling class. Russia has undergone an incomplete revolution: the structure of power has changed; property relations are being transformed; but the ruling class by and large remains in place deprived only of the top echelon of the old political system.

The concept of 'authoritarian democracy' is deliberately paradoxical, reflecting the hybrid and contradictory features of the emerging power system. Democracy is never without its coercive features: the necessary condition for the functioning of a democratic state is a strong and authoritative government, able not only to act as the umpire between various interests but also with the authority to impose its policies on social groups and economic interests; responsive to but not dominated by society. The response to governmental inadequacy and the weakness of the social base of democracy in Russia was intensified authoritarianism, not acting directly against democracy but as its accompaniment. The subtle and complicated systems of democratic governance could only slowly take root, and in the meantime more robust methods of government appeared necessary in this form of soft authoritarianism.

The inversion of the usual pattern of liberalism preceding democracy left its mark on the democratic process. The state was to act as the creator of the social basis on which democracy was to stand, and thus a new type of substitutionism took place where the 'democratic' state acted as the *locum tenens* for liberal social forces; and once again law and legality were subordinated to political expediency. In the name of the defence of the constitution and the legally constituted powers Yeltsin had called for the defence of the Russian White House; but as soon as the 1991 coup was defeated the democratic forces ran roughshod over the constitution and legal powers and once again, as under the Bolsheviks, there was a conflict between ends and means. In the name of democracy Yeltsin issued decrees (for example, confiscating the property of the CPSU without legal sanction) and ignored the wishes of elected bodies. The development of a presidential form of government without the adoption of a new constitution limiting and defining presidential powers threatened the tenuous achievements of democracy. The crisis of constitutional legitimacy that was so marked under perestroika continued until the dramatic confrontation between parliament and president in October 1993, and even then was not entirely resolved.

The transition from communism to liberal democracy, in the absence of a liberal class, appeared to have to pass through a stage of renewed authoritarianism. The intellectual tradition in favour of the 'strong hand' (*silnaya ruka*) from above imposing reform on society has deep roots in Russian political thinking. In the specific conditions of the exit from communism the idea was borrowed from the Chinese where the concept of the 'new authoritarianism' was proposed by policy intellectuals around the former secretary of the Chinese Communist Party, Zhao Ziyang and above all by Bao Tong. In the USSR during perestroika it was advocated by reformers like Igor Klyamkin and Andranik Migranyan,[28] and had to a degree been implemented by Gorbachev in his creeping presidential coup from late 1988. The key argument of the new authoritarians was that it was impossible to move directly from totalitarianism to democracy without an intervening stage of authoritarianism. The strong state would substitute for popular democracy to allow economic reform and the stabilisation of new social relations. Only after a liberal or market economy had been established and the institutions and cultural habits of civil society matured could the institutions of a developed democracy be established. In other words, full democracy had to be suspended for a time in order to save it from being swept away by more reactionary forms of authoritarianism.

Authoritarianism in the post-communist states came in many different forms. In Georgia president Zviad Gamsakhurdia provoked nationalist tensions in South Ossetia and elsewhere in a form of nationalist authoritarianism. In some other republics a type of 'liberal communism' was strongly marked. In Kazakhstan Nazarbaev expressed his admiration for Lee Kuan Yew's *authoritarian modernisation* in Singapore and developed a distinctive brand of radical market reform within an authoritarian political framework. Nazarbaev's rule was more of a techno-cratic authoritarianism open to marketising reforms designed precisely to avoid provoking nationalist tensions. He advocated the 'Chinese option', an authoritarian political approach combined with liberal economic policies.[29] Democracy, it appeared, would have to be sacrificed on the alter of the market, a hybrid which Boris Kagarlitsky dubbed 'market Stalinism'.

Thus the question of the relationship of political power to economic reform was posed with redoubled force. Is democracy a necessity of economic reform, or is it dispensable? Popov indeed argued that democracy and excessive public involvement in politics impedes economic reform.[30] The argument assumes that a strong regime can impose tough economic policies and reform administration more easily than a fully democratic one. Popov, like Sergei Stankevich and other insurgency democrats, had now become what can be called 'democratic statists'; Stankevich in particular was an admirer of Peter Stolypin, prime minister between 1906 and 1911, who advocated an authoritarian political framework to pursue liberal economic reforms. The problem, however, is how to control the modernising authority and how to ensure that it really is reforming and does not degenerate into corruption and begin to rule for its own sake. The experience of Pinochet's dictatorship in Chile suggested that military rule is compatible with economic modernisation, but military government by the 'black colonels' in Greece from 1967 is a strong counter-example. The authoritarian modernising regimes in South Korea, Taiwan and elsewhere all faced this problem, and ultimately moved towards classical democratic representative government.

In a country like Russia, with few institutionalised democratic traditions, the appeal to the strong hand was inevitably tempting and perhaps an inevitable part of the transition process. It did not, however, command universal support, with only 35 per cent supporting the idea of a 'strong hand' in a poll in October 1991, while 51 per cent supported 'democracy'.[31] The regime system of authoritarian democracy relied on simplified democratic procedures and operated through increased presidential powers, though it still ultimately governed through the parliamentary system and legality. As a Moscow entrepreneur put it soon after the coup, 'The "democrats" are exercising the powers they gained after last month's failed putsch in the same way as their predecessors.'[32] The problem, however, was more than a question of personalities: in the absence of a developed social base the only force capable of imposing democracy and the market appeared to be a strong state. The logic of the liberal revolution came into conflict with the logic of the democratic revolution.

The appointment of commissar-like presidential envoys to the regions following the coup smacked of the old authoritarianism and illustrates the dilemmas of the democratic transition in post-communist Russia. In a speech of 2 September 1991 Yeltsin jokingly referred to the envoys as 'the eyes and ears of the Tsar' as if to emphasise traditional Russian practices. In Tambov the head of the oblast soviet executive committee, like thirteen others, had supported the putschists. After the coup Yeltsin dismissed him, but he was promptly reinstated by the Soviet. The latter, formally, was the more democratic, but Yeltsin was trying to impose another order of democracy from outside. The tension between democracy and reform gave rise to the 'Morton's fork' of democracy in Russia: if the democrats operated according to the strict letter of the old constitution and the law, then the entrenched Soviet structures would soon undermine the attempt to establish a new economic and political order; but if the democrats tried to impose the new order they would have to apply authoritarian measures, which undermined the democratic principles which they proclaimed. The dilemma appeared insoluble and led to a prolonged political crisis.

The authoritarian democracy of the regime system emerged out of these dilemmas and then assumed a life of its own as Yeltsin and the associated power system and elites fought to survive. After August 1991 democracy at last found a national vessel, despite the opposition of the rejectionists, in the shape of a slimmed down Russian state, but this state was the heir not only of grand traditions but also of the generalised breakdown of the institutions of a modern state. The convergence between former democrats, centrists and parts of the national-patriotic opposition from 1993 was based on a shared belief in a strong state at home and Russia's role as a Great Power abroad. In the economic sphere the Chinese option of authoritarian modernisation was clearly ill-suited to Russia. The Soviet regime, for all its faults, had endowed Russia with a relatively developed economy and an educated and literate society. Overall Russia ranks as a medium developed country and it requires not so much modernisation, the development of the infrastructure of a modern society, but remodernisation, the development of the spirit of enquiry, entrepreneurship and independence characteristic of modernity.

Similarly, the combination of authoritarianism and democracy is inherently unstable. We now see an accelerated process of state building, but not necessarily the building of a 'republic' with the rule of the people by the people. Popular sovereignty requires a constitution, the rule of law and the whole juridical apparatus that can regulate the relationship between the people and the trustees of power, the government and the state in general. But in the unsettled conditions of post-communist Russia these norms have little meaning, and instead there is a complicated equation involving class factions, new and old elites, and state power itself acting as a relatively autonomous force. A new 'economy' of power[33] with its own 'regime of truth' is beginning to restore the shattered governmentality as it inscribes its authority in social institutions and popular consciousness. The consolidation of Russia into a distinctive form of liberal democracy cannot be discounted; but neither can the emergence of authoritarian patterns of rule. The tension between these two principles will be analysed below.

Part II

Political institutions and processes

3 Constitutionalism and the law

The stability of any constitution depends not so much on its form as on the social and economic forces that stand behind and support it; and if the form of the constitution corresponds to the balance of those forces, their support maintains it unchanged.

James Bryce[1]

The re-emergence of a separate Russia out of the Soviet shell ranks as one of the great state-building endeavours of the twentieth century. Born in crisis and the confusion attending the collapse of one of the greatest geopolitical units the world has ever known, the Russian state emerged with few immediate advantages. Its legal system enshrined a punitive and vindictive ethos, its system of government had to be built from scratch, and there appeared no way in which to devise a new constitution that could act as the rallying point of a new national consensus. Gogol's careering troika dragging Russia no-one knew whither had not yet been tamed, and the three key pillars of the state, the presidency, parliament and the judiciary, still did not pull in harness. While the wild convulsions of earlier years had passed and a sense of direction had been established, the journey proved a stormy one.

THE NEW CONSTITUTIONAL ORDER

The Soviet regime adopted constitutions in 1918 (for what was then the RSFSR), 1924, 1936 and 1977 (the RSFSR adopted a similar version on 12 April 1978), but the concept of 'sham constitutionalism', a term used by Max Weber to describe the constitution (Basic Law) adopted for imperial Russia on 23 April 1906 because the Tsar's power allegedly was not reduced, might be more appropriate for the Soviet rather than the earlier period.[2] In fact, the constitution of 1906 was not a sham but introduced a constitutional monarchy, albeit a monarchy with considerable legislative privileges.[3] The attempt by the monarch to retain the earlier concept of 'unlimited' (*neogranichennyi*) power failed; the fact that Nicholas II refused to be bound by its provisions is another matter. As the collective Tsar, the Communist Party also placed itself above constitutional constraints, and its Statutes were in effect more important than the constitutions themselves. The Soviet system can be labelled pre-constitutional because its constitutions did not do what constitutions are supposed to do, namely regulate the division of labour within the branches of the state and allocate functions between the centre and the localities.

The Soviet regime was pseudo-constitutional since it ignored the real balance of power in society, and in particular the leading role of the Communist Party. The 1918 constitution and its successors might well have proclaimed 'all power to the soviets', but the actual mechanism whereby soviets were to exercise power and the role of the CPSU was left vague. Article 6 of the 1977 constitution defined the Communist Party as the 'leading and guiding force in Soviet society', but did not specify, and thereby limit, its functions. The Soviet polity actually operated according to the conventions of an 'unwritten constitution' of normative acts and administrative practices that left the formal constitution no more than declaratory window-dressing for the regime. The Soviet system had constitutions without the necessary framework of law that could achieve genuine constitutional government. Quite why the Soviet regime felt obliged to proclaim its adherence to constitutionalism remains a mystery, but part of the answer lies in the fact that the Soviet system, despite its repudiation of liberalism, felt constrained by its appeal to a democratic legitimation.[4]

In the last years of the Soviet regime Gorbachev sought through *perestroika* to achieve the renewal of the soviet representative system, the reorganisation of the higher bodies of state power, the reform of the electoral system, and to change the judicial-legal process in its entirety. In short, Gorbachev's programme represented a profound constitutional reform but one that was to be constrained by the concept of the 'socialist legal state'.[5] This programme was given legal form in the constitutional amendments of 1 December 1988, including the creation of the partially elected USSR Congress of People's Deputies, and on 9 June 1989 the CPD established a Constitutional Commission headed by Gorbachev.[6] In the event, the fall of the regime in late 1991 led to the unceremonial abandonment of the Soviet constitution and the gradual reform process as a whole. Thus a precedent was set for constitutional transformation to take place in unconstitutional, indeed revolutionary, ways.

The task now was to write Russia's first ever democratic constitution to consolidate the transformatory process. Russia drew on the experience of the West but ultimately the constitution and the legal system had to be tailored to Russian conditions. The drafting procedure was very different from that followed for the old Soviet consititutions in which a bureaucratic committee, with advice from experts and select groups, would propose a draft which was then publicised in a brief nationwide 'discussion' followed by a unanimous vote in the Supreme Soviet. The drafting of the new Russian constitution reflected the real divisions of society, and even in the best of times the designing of laws and institutions *ab initio* is an exhilarating but dangerous venture. Numerous choices have to be made: between a unitary, federal or confederal system; a parliamentary or a presidential republic or something in between; the balance to be drawn between limited government and effective governance; the equation to be drawn between individual and group rights, between majorities and minorities. If rights are assigned to minority groups, then is there not a danger that members will identify with that community rather than as citizens of the larger state?

The genesis of the Russian constitution

The birth of the new constitution was a long and painful process.[7] Four days after the revolutionary Declaration of Sovereignty of the RSFSR on 12 June 1990, the First Russian CPD on 16 June established a Constitutional Commission to prepare a document that would reflect Russia's new juridical and political status. The commission, made up of 102 deputies, was nominally chaired by Yeltsin with Khasbulatov its vice-chairman, but the main work was carried out by a smaller working group of some fifteen deputies chaired by the commission's secretary, Oleg Rumyantsev.

The first version, rejecting the whole notion of socialism and communism, was ready by November 1990.[8] The draft declared that 'the Russian Federation is a sovereign, democratic, social and legal state of historically united peoples' (article 1.1) and broke decisively with Bolshevik traditions by defending the inviolable rights of the individual (article 1.3). Russia, however, was defined as a 'social state' guaranteeing extensive collective and welfare rights based 'on the principles of social democracy and justice' (article 1.8). Not surprisingly, the draft was attacked as being 'anti-Soviet' and the Supreme Soviet refused to place it on the agenda for adoption by the Second CPD in December 1990.

Against the background of the 'winter offensive' by the so-called conservatives, from late 1990, the Communists of the Russia faction in the legislature prepared an alternative and more traditional draft constitution.[9] Another draft was prepared by a group of legal experts from Saratov University's Faculty of Law. After much discussion the Constitutional Commission came out with a compromise draft in time for discussion by the Third CPD (28 March–4 April 1991); but by then the context had dramatically changed: the 17 March referendum established the post of a Russian president and the Communists of Russia split and a reformist faction (Communists for Democracy) emerged led by Rutskoi. In June 1991 the Fifth CPD (first convocation) rejected the compromise draft, insisting that it failed to formulate Russia's rights against the centre and that it was full of contradictions, and instructed the commission to prepare another version.

The August 1991 coup and the subsequent dissolution of the Soviet system added a new urgency to the constitutional question, and the commission rapidly produced a second version,[10] which was presented by Rumyantsev to the Supreme Soviet on 10 October 1991.[11] With the fall of Soviet power ideological issues, such as individual rights, civil society and judicial reform, were no longer so contentious, but new points of disagreement had emerged. These focused above all on the separation of powers on the horizontal level (between executive and legislative power), and on the vertical level (between the central authorities and components of the federation). The territorial organisation of the state proved particularly divisive since the draft sought to move away from Bolshevik ethno-federal principles towards a classic territorial federalism (see chapter 9). As a result, the Supreme Soviet failed to muster the required 50 per cent of deputies to place the constitution on the reconvened Fifth CPD's agenda for approval.[12]

In response, the Constitutional Commission met on 23 October and authorised Yeltsin to place a slightly revised draft before the CPD 'for discussion' (*k svedeniyu*), rather than adoption.[13] This he did on 2 November,[14] and Congress then instructed the commission to prepare yet another version in time for the Sixth CPD scheduled for spring 1992.

Work on the document was now torn between what appeared to be irreconcilable forces: on the one hand, most of the former autonomous republics rejected the Constitutional Commission's draft for failing to recognise their sovereign status; while, on the other, many of Russia's regions condemned it on the grounds that it gave excessive privileges to the republics. The working group sought to find a compromise, and on 2 March 1992 completed a third version which, after slight modifications, was published on 24 March.[15] This draft proposed a parliamentary republic but with broad powers for the president within the framework of parliamentary oversight and with the clear separation of powers between the executive, legislative and judiciary. As far as supporters of the legislature were concerned, 'In the absence of a civil society in our country, parliament and the Congress of People's Deputies are today virtually the only guarantors that can stop our country from plunging into a dictatorship of individuals'[16]. The signing of the three-tiered Federation Treaty on 31 March (chapter 9) appeared to resolve some of the sharpest conflicts over the federation.[17]

On the eve of the Sixth CPD of April 1992 alternative draft constitutions emerged, and at least two revised communist drafts. Sergei Shakhrai, Yeltsin's legal adviser, put forward his own version which sought to subordinate parliament to presidential structures.[18] A second was concocted by Sobchak, the mayor of St Petersburg and a former professor of economic law, together with Sergei Alekseev, both having been members of the commission drafting the new USSR constitution from the summer of 1989. Their version, presented on 30 March, gave strengthened powers to the executive.[19] Their work drew freely from Andrei Sakharov's proposed new constitution for the USSR.[20]

Sobchak subjected parliament's draft to scathing criticism, asserting that the parliamentary commission had worked in total secrecy and without the help of legal advice, resulting in a document that was 'the former Soviet constitution with democratic phrases'.[21] Their failure to understand the principle of the separation of powers allowed the emergence of dual power rather than cooperation between the various branches of power. Sobchak criticised the alleged extension of constitutional jurisdiction in the draft Basic Law, insisting that in spirit it remained close to Soviet concepts in claiming to regulate not only the state but also society, whereas for Sobchak 'society has lived, is living and will continue to live according to its own laws, which are not really laws but are only statements expressed in a legal form'.[22] Sobchak thus defended a particularly impoverished version of the liberal ideal, one closer to Anglo-American neo-liberalism than to the social liberalism espoused by Vladimir Solovyov, Boris Chicherin and other pre-revolutionary thinkers. Ironically, the section on civil society (chapter 3), of which Rumyantsev and his associates were particularly proud because it provided a theoretical basis for the rejection of the country's totalitarian past, was now condemned as 'socialist' by Sobchak, a criticism that Yeltsin came to share despite his earlier defence of the draft.[23]

The Supreme Soviet this time placed the constitution on the agenda, recommending that it be adopted at its first reading to avoid exhaustive debate over individual clauses. However, the Sixth CPD, while rejecting the Sobchak and communist drafts, merely approved the general outline (*za osnovu*) of the commission's version, calling for yet more revisions.[24] Against the background of a sharp deterioration in relations between the president and parliament, including fears that Yeltsin might dissolve the legislature and put his (Shakhrai's) draft to a national referendum, the Congress somewhat moderated its assault against the president's economic policies and political prerogatives, extending his right to rule by decree to the end of 1992 but forcing him to step down as prime minister. The Congress went on to make numerous amendments to the existing 'Brezhnev' constitution, including the bodily in-corporation of the Federation Treaty.[25]

The constitutional process had now reached an impasse. Only the CPD had the right to amend or adopt the constitution, and Yeltsin's attempts to raise the million signatures necessary to hold a referendum did not offer a way out since adopting the constitution through a referendum was unconstitutional, and in any case required the approval of the Congress. The opposition in the Congress, on the other hand, used the right to make constitutional amendments with increasing boldness and for short-term political advantage. Of the 340 amendments made to the old constitution by early 1993, an astonishing 258 were adopted in 1992 alone.[26] The work of the commission continued, however, and issued a fourth version on 11 November 1992.[27] Work on the new constitution continued in parallel with amendments to the old, allowing, according to Rumyantsev, a gradual convergence of the two. He claimed that this enabled a 'balanced and consistent modernisation of the legal space of the Federation' rather than a constitutional revolution,[28] an assessment that was too sanguine by far.

Fearing the loss of a powerful weapon in their struggle with the president, and hesitant to commit themselves to elections, the Seventh CPD in December 1992 once again failed to adopt the prepared draft constitution. According to Rumyantsev, this was a major mistake and allowed the president to seize the initiative and encourage other drafts which, according to Rumyantsev, were inferior to the parliamentary version in that they introduced numerous 'conjunctural' elements. However long and convoluted the parliamentary version, Rumyantsev insisted, it was nevertheless permeated by a democratic spirit that was in sharp contrast to the Soviet-era constitutions.[29] Agreement had been reached at the Congress on putting the basic principles of the new constitution before the people in a referendum, but Khasbulatov's call in February 1993 for pre-term presidential and parliamentary elections ruptured the fragile compromise and once again opened up the question.

The president now released details of his own, much more presidentialist, constitutional draft devised by Alekseev, Shakhrai and Sobchak on the eve of the referendum of 25 April 1993.[30] This envisaged the abolition of the old Congress and Supreme Soviet and their replacement by a bicameral legislature to be known as the Federal Assembly. The lower chamber (the State Duma) was to be elected on a proportional basis, while the upper (the Federation Council) was to be made up of the elected presidents of Russia's republics and the heads of regional administrations. Only the president's nomination for the post of prime minister was to be ratified by parliament, while all other ministerial appointments were to be approved 'in consultation' with the upper chamber. The president had the power to dissolve parliament and call new elections, while only the Federation Council had the right to impeach the president. The post of vice-president was to be abolished, and it was now made more difficult to amend the constitution. These ideas lay at the basis of the constitution adopted in December 1993.

An extended process of consultation followed in which the views of members of the federation were sought.[31] The results of the April 1993 referendum were interpreted as supporting the president's accelerated programme of constitutional change; and indeed, following the referendum the struggle between the executive and the legislature now focused on the constitution.[32] By the same token, as both sides courted the regions and republics, the Russian constitutional process was ever more frequently likened to the Novo-Ogarevo process whereby Gorbachev sought to adopt a new Union Treaty to maintain the unity of the state – but in the event precipitated its disintegration.[33] The presidential draft was presented to the Constitutional Commission on 6 May 1993, and on the next day was rejected.[34] It remained unclear how his draft, or any other, could be adopted without the support of the existing Congress and Supreme Soviet.[35]

At the same time, the communists published a new version of their own constitution.[36] The patriotic movement also sought not to be left out, and at a conference on 29 June 1993 presented the result of its labours. Patriots insisted that the source of authority for the new constitution should be the national traditions of the country. Victor Aksyuchits, the leader of the Russian Christian Democratic Movement (RCDM), insisted that the spiritual rebirth of Russia was linked with such traditional values as a constitutional monarchy and local self-government.[37] Attempts to revive the fortunes of the patriotic alternative by devising a joint constitution once again came to nought.

Work had continued on the Constitutional Commission's draft, and on 7 May 1993 the Commission approved the fifth 'Khasbulatovite' parliamentary version.[38] The equality of members of the federation was stressed 'apart from those allowed by the constitution'. Republics were recognised as states, enjoying the full panopoly of state powers on their territory, apart from those that remained the prerogative of the Russian Federation. Other members were labelled simply as state-territorial formations. The upper house was to be called the Federation Council, while the lower house, the State Duma, was to be elected by a simple first-past-the-post system. The president was to become merely the ceremonial head of state and not head of the executive branch.[39] The draft was to be discussed by parliamentary committees and a final version was to be published by 15 October and discussed by a special convocation of the CPD to meet on 17 November.[40]

Yeltsin could not ignore this direct challenge to his constitutional status, and on 20 May he decided to finesse the constitutional question by taking up the option long advocated by the Russian Democratic Reform Movement led by Sobchak and Popov,[41] namely the convocation of a special Constitutional Assembly to accelerate the constitutional process.[42] However, whereas Popov had insisted that the Assembly should meet for only one purpose, the adoption of a new consitution, Yeltsin's Constitutional Assembly was intended to shape a draft that could then be sent round to members of the federation for their approval. The Constitutional Assembly opened on 5 June 1993 and was composed of some 750 representatives of the federation as well as from social organisations.

In his opening speech Yeltsin likened the period with 1917 and insisted that the new Assembly was continuing the work of the Provisional Government in devising a democratic constitution for Russia, work brought to a violent end by the Bolshevik seizure of power and the dispersal of the Constituent Assembly in January 1918.[43] Yeltsin's attempt to base the rebirth of the Russian constitutional order on this tradition (the brief attempt to establish democracy in Russia in 1917), rather than the Tsarist, let alone the Soviet, was significant and symbolised the attempt to portray the Soviet period not just as an aberration but as fundamentally illegitimate; an interregnum in Russia's search for democracy. Indeed, his insistence that soviets and democracy were fundamentally incompatible was one of the factors that led to the final rift between himself and the parliamentary speaker, Khasbulatov.[44] Yeltsin branded the attempt by the Supreme Soviet to manage a smooth transition by maintaining continuity and observance of the existing constitution as being no more than 'a weapon in the hands of an illegitimate new ruling class, with whose assistance they try to retain their illegal power'.[45]

Despite the president's fighting talk the work of the Assembly proceeded in a conciliatory atmosphere, and in its committees many of the ideas put forward by parliamentary representatives were adopted, giving rise to a 'mixed' form of government.[46] The Assembly came up with a new version on 12 July drawing on both the presidential draft of April 1993 and parliament's.[47] There was much on which they agreed, such as the rights and obligations of the citizen and the right to all forms of property, but they differed radically over the role of the president and parliament. The Assembly's version represented Yeltsin's last attempt to achieve some agreement with the old legislature over the constitution: the problem still remained of how to adopt it.[48] In an attempt to win over the regions a Federation Council was established at a meeting in Petrozavodsk on 13 August of the Council of the Heads of the Republics, when Yeltsin called for the creation of a type of mini-parliament to resolve the constitutional crisis. The new Council was to consist of a representative apiece from the executive and legislative powers in each region and republic, making a total of 176 from the 88 subjects of the federation willing to participate (Chechnya refused).[49] At its first meeting on 18 September, however, Yeltsin failed to get them to sign a founding document.

The Supreme Soviet was still working to its own timetable of constitutional reform, ignoring the Constitutional Assembly, and in the event this attempt to give substance to a parallel constitutional process that threatened to strip the president of his powers proved a grave miscalculation. Yeltsin struck first, and on 21 September 1993 dissolved the legislature and suspended the constitution.[50] His action raises grave moral issues: to what extent are unconstitutional acts valid in the attempt to establish the rule of law? The new constitutionalism was based on the view that the Soviet system was unreformable, and hence in a revolutionary process law is subordinate to political expediency. In other words, the constitution became a tool in the struggle for reform, an instrumental view that absolved the 'reformers' of the need to subordinate themselves to the rule of law. From this perspective, current events were no more than the final triumph of the 'counter-revolution' against the Bolshevik usurpation of power in October 1917. This was in sharp contrast to the Gorbachevite view favouring continuity in the evolution from Soviet constitutional practices into the new democratic era. These two approaches reflected divergent views over the nature of the transition.

Following the dissolution of the Supreme Soviet the Constitutional Assembly was reorganised to include a 'public chamber'[51] and shortly afterwards a 'state chamber' (the work of both was regularised on 11 October), to complete work on the constitution under the aegis of a committee chaired by Sergei Filatov, the president's chief of staff. The committee drew on the Constitutional Assembly's synthesis but also borrowed directly on earlier presidential and parliamentary drafts. Alekseev noted that earlier versions, above all the Assembly's draft, had in the spirit of compromise incorporated 'pro-soviet elements' that undermined democratic principles.[52] The draft constitution was published on 10 November and, as expected, proposed a strongly presidential system and modified some of the privileges accorded the republics and regions when they had been able to take advantage of the struggle between the president and parliament.[53] A final section of the new version made a number of provisions for the transitional situation, stipulating that the president must serve his full term until June 1996 and thus ended speculation about pre-term presidential elections. It was this version that was placed before the people for approval on 12 December 1993 (see chapter 5) and became Russia's first democratic constitution.

Basic principles of Russian constitutionalism

The Russian constitution of 1993 is liberal in its overall conception but some of its democratic procedures might be flawed. The document reflects the tendency that has been paramount in Russia's post-communist transition, namely that liberalism takes precedence over democracy. Nevertheless, the constitution upholds certain basic principles of democratic state building such as the separation of powers, defining the rights and duties of various levels of government. According to its critics, however, while the principle might have been upheld, the lack of balance in the separation of powers undermined the principles which it claimed to enshrine.

The new constitution is a liberal document, meeting world standards in its provisions for human and civic rights (outlined in its second chapter, see appendix 3). It enshrines the civil rights of citizens, outlawing the incarceration of dissidents and restricting the monitoring of correspondence and bugging of telephone calls. The constitution forbids censorship and guarantees freedom of the press. It allows Russians to travel abroad as a right, forbids the government from sending citizens into foreign exile or stripping Russians of their citizenship. It also promises freedom of movement within Russia, and in an important advance over Rumyantsev's draft, enshrined 'the right to travel freely and choose one's place of stay and residence' (article 27), thus making the dreaded *propiska* residence permits unconstitutional (although Moscow city continued to apply the system). It also guarantees the right to private property, and thus seals this core aspect of the liberal revolution, including the right for citizens to buy and sell land (articles 35, 36). Provision was made for an ombudsman for human rights, whose duties would be specified by a special law: thus the new document sought to overcome the legacy of legal arbitrariness of the Soviet years.

In addition, Russia was defined as a 'social state' (article 7) and numerous rights and entitlements were guaranteed to its citizens. The emphasis on social as well as political rights draws on the social-democratic element in Bolshevik thinking and on the 'social liberal' tendency in pre-revolutionary Russian thought, but fundamentalist liberals insist that 'social' is no more than a tame word for 'socialist'.[54] Whatever the inspiration, a question remains over the degree to which these social rights can be fulfilled since entitlements to positive rights are even more difficult to enforce in a court of law than the negative rights concerning the inviolability of the individual. The listing of entitlements is alien to the Anglo-Saxon tradition but reflects the tendency in Continental social philosophy to assume that what is unregulated in society does not exist.

There is a more fundamental problem, however, than simply the abstract enumeration of polical and social rights. Some of these rights are accompanied by qualifications that could be used to stifle political opposition. In particular, article 29.2 forbids the incitement of social, racial, national or religious hatred and has been cited as an unwarranted limitation on political and expressional rights. More seriously, the defence of state security or the legitimate rights of others (article 55.3) could be used for repressive purposes. Article 80 grants the president certain reserve powers as 'guarantor of the constitution', powers that could in certain circumstances be used to subvert the constitution. The constitution failed to state that voting (except for the president, article 81.1) takes place on the basis of free and *equal* representation, thus making it impossible to appeal to the constitution to prevent, for example, constituencies varying greatly in the number of electors. Moreover, the proclamation of unfulfillable promises of social justice, such as the right to free health care (article 41.1) and a 'decent environment' (article 42) might well be seen as undermining the very basis of trust on which the constitution rests. In this category come the guarantees for trial by jury (article 47.2) when there is as yet no such system in general operation, and the prohibition on 'the use of evidence obtained by violating federal law' (article 50.2), both alien concepts to Russia's immediate past. If these are not fulfilled, then what price all the other promises?

However, these criticisms perhaps overstate the case. This constitution is very much a normative document, establishing the principles on which an ethically desirable state could be established rather than suggesting that it can be achieved immediately. If we accept Bogdan Kistiakovskii's argument that law and the state originally existed independently and that independent courts could be introduced under conditions of absolutism, so too today we can appreciate the new constitution in terms of asynchronicity in the introduction of the rudiments of liberalism, democracy and, indeed, social democracy. While Western democracies have spent the better part of the twentieth century introducing a social corrective to classical liberalism – until the rise of neo-liberalism in the 1980s – post-communist Russia faces the problem of enormously extended social, and indeed political, demands in conditions in which it lacks the ability to meet these demands, resulting in a gulf between aspiration and achievement. As in pre-revolutionary Russia, however, the tendency to subordinate law to the political struggle only creates more obstacles in the way of achieving the goal of a *pravovoe gosudarstvo* (a state ruled by law), let alone a rule of law state.

In a sharp break with the past the constitution makes no reference to any state ideology or religion and instead guarantees freedom of conscience, religion, thought and speech (articles 28 and 29) based on political pluralism and a multiparty system. However, this does not mean that the constitution is not an ideological document: it represents a clear commitment to certain values, including the notion of a 'social' and 'secular' state based on private property, the rule of law and popular sovereignty. However, the enunciation of the rationale behind these views is no longer as explicit as in earlier drafts. The section explicitly devoted to civil society was dropped, ostensibly for the sake of brevity but also reflecting sensitivity over the criticisms made by Sobchak earlier. What was lost, however, was a clear repudiation of Russia's statist traditions and the commitment to the development of the sphere of freedom and autonomy associated with the notion of civil society.

State and government

The constitution established the foundations of the new polity, but the structure remained to be built. A constitutional system is a much broader concept than the constitution itself and reflects the ethical bases of society.[55] It is quite possible to have a constitution but no constitutional order (as under the Soviet regime); or to have a constitutional order but no constitution (as in Britain): the aim in Russia today is to combine the two. The legal functions of a constitution are only one among many, and this is particularly the case with this constitution which sought to repudiate the communist political and philosophical legacy and to establish the basis of a new constitutional order.

Russia is only at the beginning of a constitutional process requiring the development of a whole system of laws and conventions. The adoption of the constitution was only the first act of a titanic process of legislative renewal based on a division between federal constitutional laws (those defining constitutional principles and processes) and routine federal laws.[56] A vast programme of legislative activity awaited the new parliament, with the constitution itself alluding to 10 constitutional laws (requiring a two-thirds majority), 44 federal laws, 5 existing laws needing substantial changes to bring them into line with the new constitution, together with 6 acts governing the activity of the Federal Assembly itself and 4 dealing with the work of the president, a total of 70 acts that would give legislative form to its general principles. Some of these acts were prepared by the presidential Commission for Legislative Suggestions, headed by M. Mityukov, that had by 17 December drawn up a list of the required legislation.[57] The most urgent new laws were those governing states of emergency and martial law, on the prerogatives of the Constitutional and Supreme Courts, labour and tax laws, on social movements, on elections to the State Duma and on the composition of the Federation Council. Laws to be changed included those governing the status of the capital and on the procuracy.

For the first time in Russian history a constitution made a serious attempt to define and limit state power. The final vestiges of the communist legacy were swept away as the new document promised economic liberalism and the democratic separation of powers. Yeltsin argued that the constitution was designed to lay down a 'firm, legal order' for a democratic state, marking an end to the 'dual power' between the presidency and the legislature.[58] The constitution sought to create a 'democratic, federal, rule-of-law state with a republican form of government' (article 1.1). The new version incorporated elements from the previous drafts, above all the section on human and civil rights, but significantly augmented presidential authority and limited the powers of parliament and the republics. The model of governance that emerges from the document is both pseudo-parliamentary and super-presidential, while the government itself has the potential to become a relatively autonomous third centre of power. (The constitution's provisions concerning the institutions of the state and federalism are discussed in the appropriate parts of this book.)

The constitution debated

According to Yurii Stroev, the editor of *Konstitutsionnnyi vestnik*, 'the constitution of 12 December 1993 did not resolve the crisis but forced it deeper'.[59] While this may be an overly negative assessment, the document is nevertheless marked by certain problems: particularly the inadequate legal defence of the civic and human rights of individuals; the lack of balance in the relationship between the executive and the legislative; the tension between federal and unitary principles in the relationship between the centre and localities; the large area of rules and procedures (for example, governing elections) that are not written into the constitution but regulated by acts and decrees; and the lack of a realistic procedure for adopting constitutional amendments.[60]

The constitution is much more difficult to change than Soviet-era constitutions, a feature that might well transform political conflict into a constitutional crisis. The constitution's ninth chapter discusses amendments and revisions, in effect making it easier to abolish the constitution than to amend it. Amendments to chapters 3–8 require a two-thirds majority of the State Duma, the support of three-quarters of the members of the Federation Council, and then ratification by the legislatures of no less than two-thirds of the subjects of the federation (articles 108 and 136). Special rules apply to the 'fundamental' articles of the constitution, chapters 1 and 2, dealing with general rights, and chapter 9 itself, where changes require a three-fifths vote of both houses and a Constitutional Assembly, convened in accordance with federal constitutional law (article 135). This would, in principle, make it easier to change the 'inviolable' chapters than the others, not requiring the ratification of the subjects of the federation. According to some commentators, the difficulties attending constitutional revisions could lead to attempts to kill off the constitution as a whole.[61]

Other criticisms of the constitution include the charge that it is too long, infringing Talleyrand's dictum that 'A constitution should be short and unclear' (*sic*). The authors of America's constitution adhered to this principle, but the post-war framers of the West German constitution did not. The West German constitution (Basic Law) came into force on 23 May 1949 and in great detail established the country as a federal, social, legal state based on a parliamentary system of rule in which the president is the non-executive head of state.[62] The constitution sought to avoid the mistakes of the Weimar republic and enshrined the principle that 'democracy must be able to defend itself', including a ban on parties that challenge the existing constitutional order. There was no place for referenda and other forms of plebiscitary democracy. In terms of length the new Russian constitution veers to the long side, but was much shorter than the unadopted Rumyantsev version.

The constitution as politics

Ralf Dahrendorf has distinguished between constitutional and normal politics; in the former, 'the hour of the lawyers' strikes as they attempt to root modern political society in a constitutional order, whereas in the latter legislative activity concentrates on managing the established system.[63] While useful, the distinction is too abstract since the new constitution had to be prepared at a time of profound political and economic changes: the work of the lawyers was overseen by politicians. Valerii Zor'kin, chairman of the Constitutional Court, indeed argued that the crisis of power was 'a natural result of the policy of "shock therapy"'.[64] Constitution-making became part of the political struggle, and indeed in a peculiar way itself became the prize in the struggle between the executive and the legislature. Moreover, while 'the hour of the lawyer' might have struck, with numerous Western legal experts invited to Moscow to advise on the new constitution, the role of political scientists in 'crafting democracies' has been neglected.[65]

Post-communist Russian politics is characterised by the tension between questions of 'polity' – the nature of the state – and 'policy', specific problems of public policy.[66] While policy or 'normal' politics was strengthened after December 1993, the struggle over the nature of the constitutional order (the polity problem) is by no means over. Indeed, much of normal politics in Russia has consisted of the appeal to constitutional and ethical absolutes, while constitutional debates have often served immediate political interests. Once again, Russian exceptionalism has taken the form of appealing to utopian abstractions and Russia's special path, too often no more than a cover for anti-Western and sectional interests.

The process of constitution drafting had revealed the tendency in Russian political life for individuals or groups to carve out a niche for themselves. Rumyantsev's opponents alleged that he had tried to take the whole constitutional process under his wing as part of the chronic tendency towards the feudalisation of Russian politics (derived from the Soviet era) where groups carve out fiefdoms for themselves. Indeed, it might be noted that the 'territorialisation' of politics affected all aspects, with some using foreign policy issues to advance their careers and others the national question. In this case, Rumyantsev was accused of desperately wanting to be known as the 'father' of the 'Rumyantsev Constitution' and thus ensuring his place in the history books.[67]

Rumyantsev has frequently talked about the foundations of the constitutional order in Russia, the concept of *stroi* (system) in the broadest sense,[68] and he is right to do so. As V. Leontovich argued for pre-revolutionary Russia, it was the absence of a developed civil structure, 'something that is essential for any liberal constitution', that led to the disappearance of political freedom and the destruction of the constitutional system in Russia in 1917.[69] The constitutional process in Russia reflected contradictory processes of social development; a constitution can hardly be more effective than the society which it seeks to regulate. At the same time, this constitution is an act of deliberate political intervention in the evolution of the polity. The constitution is designed not to reflect an existing social order but to mould a new one, a task very different from that confronting the Founding Fathers in Philadelphia in 1787. The instrumental and normative elements in the document, the attempt to design a new social order, have given rise to a number of tensions: was the constitution drafted in terms of expediency rather than right; and does the idea of order rather than freedom lie at its heart?

The constitution represented the culmination of the democratic revolution against communism but at the same time became a casualty of this struggle as it became subsumed into self-sustaining (and self-serving) politics. The constitution, moreover, represented a conscious revolt against the alleged lack of a democratic political culture in Russia, but at the same time reflected the very cultural problematic that it sought to undermine. In other words, the constitution remained ideologised (in the traditional sense) insofar as it acted as an instrument of reform in the hands of 'the Bolsheviks of the marketplace'.

There remains a long way to go before Russia's political life is fully constitutionalised. As Sheinis noted, 'It is, of course, not enough to adopt a constitution in order to create a stable democratic society, but this is a necessary and, at present, urgent prerequisite.'[70] As long as the institutions of civil society and the associated 'habits of the heart', as de Tocqueville put it, of a democratic and free people remain weak, the naturally predatory instincts of the state will find little resistance. The precise nature of societal self-defence mechanisms that can resist the encroachment of the state remain disputed, but liberals would no doubt suggest that they include secure property rights and effective participatory mechanisms in the local and national community. The adoption of a constitution is the core constitutive act of state building and defines the ethical essence of a new state. Russian statehood has now achieved a stable juridical form and the new political order has achieved a degree of constitutional stabilisation.

THE CONSTITUTIONAL COURT

Even the most splendid constitution on paper is valueless if there are no effective mechanisms to ensure compliance. The Law on the Constitutional Court of 12 July 1991 established a Court of fifteen independent judges, appointed for their personal qualities, to deal with all the main questions of constitutionality, but who were prohibited from examining political cases.[71] Under its chairman, Zor'kin, the Court sought to mark out the centre ground that could establish civic peace and maintain the unity of the country. The court was thus accused of placing political considerations above the defence of the laws and constitution of Russia, though with such a malleable constitution the position of the court was unenviable.

The Court asserted its authority against the executive authorities when on 14 January 1992 it overturned a presidential decree establishing a joint ministry of security and internal affairs. The court's attempt to modify the referendum held on 21 March 1992 in Tatarstan failed, though Zor'kin was vigorous in condemning the perceived threat to the unity of the country. Its ruling in November 1992 on the constitutionality of Yeltsin's ban on the Communist Party after the coup found a compromise solution that ruled that the ban on the Party apparatus had been constitutional, but not that on the rank-and-file organisations.

In December 1992, during Russia's first genuine *constitutional* crisis, when executive and legislative power were locked in conflict, the Court acted as a mediator and once again found a compromise solution (see chapter 6). The prestige of the Court, however, was undermined when in January 1993 Zor'kin changed his mind and condemned the idea of a referendum as destabilising, and confidence in his judgement was further diminished when he rushed to condemn Yeltsin's announcement on 20 March 1993 of 'special rule' even before he had seen the document in question.[72] An even greater challenge to the Court's authority was posed by Yeltsin's decree of 21 September 1993 suspending the constitution. The decree urged the Court not to meet until the Federal Assembly began its work, but in the event ten out of the fourteen judges condemned the presidential decree,[73] and in October Yeltsin decreed the suspension of the Court. The Court had tried to assert its authority as a worthy representative of judicial authority to achieve the separation of powers, but the titanic struggle between executive and legislative authority marginalised the judiciary and trampled on the rule of law in its entirety. The Constitutional Court was placed in the invidious position of defending a discredited constitution. Its procedures, moreover, encouraged acts of political adventurism.

The dissolution of the old legislature and the fate of the Court appeared to illustrate the old Russian principle that law is subordinate to politics.[74] The 1993 constitution established a new Constitutional Court of nineteen judges (article 125) with the judges appointed by the Federation Council but nominated by the president. The reorganised Court had a more restricted brief than its highly politicised predecessor, depriving it of the right to initiate cases itself. Designed to ensure that federal laws and decrees comply with the constitution, the Court lost some of its prerogatives concerning relations between the central authorities and components of the federation. Much-needed gate-keeping mechanisms were established to make appeals to the court more difficult as part of the attempt to transform it into a more professional and less politicised body.[75] The Court now has a stable constitution to work with rather than the earlier constantly changing text.

The new law concerning the Constitutional Court adopted in mid-1994 considerably reduced its scope for independent political activity. The judges were no longer allowed to accept matters for consideration on their own initiative, and the range of 'official entities' that could put matters to them was severely restricted. Whereas earlier any deputy (and there were over a thousand of them) could send questions, now this could only be done with the approval of one-fifth of the deputies of any one chamber or by a majority vote of the Federal Assembly as a whole. In certain respects, however, its authority was increased. A ruling by the court, for example, on the constitutionality of a presidential decree, a government resolution or a parliamentary law, is final and cannot be appealed, any legal act that is ruled as un-constitutional loses its force. The Court was to examine cases in the strict chronological order in which they were presented, although similar cases could be considered together.

Some of the judges remained from the old Court, but the confirmation of the new took over a year to complete because the president's nominations were repeatedly rejected. Finally, on 7 February 1995 the Federation Council approved the nomination of the nineteenth judge and the court could commence its work.[76] Vladimir Tumanov was selected chairman of the Constitutional Court, insisting that 'in the transitional period constitutional stability is the highest value', but he feared that lack of respect for the law was the gravest challenge facing the court.[77]

LAW AND THE STATE

The late Tsarist period was marked by an important debate by legal scholars and others over the concept of *pravovoe gosudarstvo* (a 'law-based state'). The Russian notion of this is derived from the German concept of a Rechtsstaat and thus differs from the Anglo-American concept of the 'rule of law'. As Donald D. Barry has noted, 'The concept of Rechtsstaat is based on the positivist assumption that the state itself is the highest source of law'.[78] Thus a *pravovoe gosudarstvo*, as Harold J. Berman put it, 'is rule *by* law, but not rule *of* law'; the latter is sustained by the theory of natural law suggesting that there is a law higher than statutory law governing the normative acts of society.

Many of the more notable Russian moral philosophers and legal scholars condemned the positivist tradition, so strong in Germany. Solovyov, indeed, developed the notion of a type of social liberalism based on the idea of the 'right to a dignified existence' within the context of a society and state formally ordered by law, a view that sharply distinguished him from the revolutionary socialist challenge to Western liberalism but that brought him closer to Bismarck Germany's Rechtsstaat liberals.[79] Strong echoes of Solovyov's thinking can be found in Russia's new constitution. At the turn of the century the name of Boris Chicherin is most strongly identified with the idea of a constitutional legal order and restraints on monarchical power, condemning the positivist tradition while calling for a type of defensive liberalism which he came to call 'liberal conservatism'. His views, also, are particularly resonant in the new constitution, as in his notion of 'liberal measures and strong government',[80] a formula adopted enthusiastically by Yeltsin's 'government of reforms'. Above all, his defence of the ethical attributes of the juridical sphere encompassed by civil society and the notion of freedom that it represents went far beyond Hegel's rather grudging acceptance of this sphere of conflicting private interests, and firmly rejected Marx's critique, views that in effect make Chicherin the intellectual 'godfather', albeit unacknowledged, of Russia's new constitution.

The legal revolution has a dual character. The achievement of a Rechtsstaat in Russia today reflects the attempt in nineteenth-century Germany to limit the arbitrariness of the absolutist *Polizeistaat* (policy state). The term Rechtsstaat was used to describe Germany in the second part of the nineteenth century where a legalism devoid of principle (positive law) pre-dominated. If correct bureaucratic procedures were followed, then an act was legal, and thus in these terms Hitler's regime was legal since he used the provisions of the Weimar constitution to establish his rule. The Soviet police state in its way was governed by law but public power remained arbitrary.[81] Russia now sought to combine the principles of a Rechtsstaat with natural law, which suggests that there is a law higher than the state to which the state itself should be subordinate.

The establishment of a Rechtsstaat, is *limiting*, but the establishment of the rule of law is *expansive*. The 'rule of law' is a concept associated with the Anglo-Saxon common law tradition, whereas Russia is part of the Continental Roman law tradition: according to common law individual rights are defended by the courts, whereas in the continental tradition they are enshrined in a constitution. Thus, to the Anglo-Saxon mind the registration of political parties and religious organisations might seem superfluous, since they are protected by common law and the courts on the principle that 'everything that is not forbidden is permitted'. The Continental system, however, relies on regulation to avoid conflict and to manage social affairs. The constitutional process in Russia today can therefore be seen as a dual revolution: to achieve both a *pravovoe gosudarstvo* (a state governing by law, based on the classical positivist conception of law); and to create a society governed by the rule of law to which the state itself is subordinated. It is this latter concept, based on the theory of natural law which has never taken root in Russia but that was acknowledged in the 1993 constitution.

For Russia the achievement of rule by law (if not yet the rule of law) would be no mean achievement. The gulf between aspiration and achievement remains large, but certain tangible advances towards the goal have been achieved, notably the adoption of the constitution itself. The system moved beyond the nebulous concept of 'socialist legality' towards a law-based state. The concept of law of the revived Russian constitutionalism is indebted to the debates of the late Soviet period. The aim here was above all to separate the Party from the state and to remake the state as an autonomous political and ordered entity. At the same time, the overweening powers of the state were to be limited by the establishment of legal safeguards for individual rights. Associated with the second project was the discourse of civil society, a concept that figured prominently in the draft version of the CPSU's final Programme and in early drafts of the new Russian constitution. There remained, however, a tension between the attempt to reconstitute the state and at the same time to limit it.

A legal (positivist) state is not necessarily a democratic one, but a democratic state is by definition governed by the rule of law. The task facing the Russian legal system was nothing short of revolutionary. The old Bolshevik system of jurisprudence, and the principles on which it was based, were clearly inadequate for a democratic market-based society, and thus a new system in its entirety had to be created. The old system, in common with so much inherited from the old regime, could not be reformed – it had to be rebuilt from scratch. There was, nevertheless, a large degree of continuity in the first period, and judicial reform moved slowly.

From the 1860s urban Russia had seen the development of a relatively free judiciary and the development of the jury system, but these achievements had been swept away by the Bolshevik regime. Only under Gorbachev did the judiciary begin to achieve a measure of political autonomy, but this had been precarious and it fell to the democratic regime to consolidate judicial independence. Under the Soviet regime each republic had its own legal code (as well as their own constitutions), but they varied very little from All-Union standards. The struggle for statehood from 1990 had, naturally, been accompanied by legal conflicts between republican and union legislation. During the 'war of the laws' of late 1990 the Russian Supreme Soviet insisted that Russian laws took precedence over All-Union laws.[82] Only after the August coup did Russia seriously embark upon building a new legal system.

The establishment of a Rechtsstaat in itself comprises a revolution. It means judicial review of legislation and executive acts, a system of citizen's rights, structures for the pluralistic interaction of groups, and in the post-communist context of Russia, the development of a market economy. Communists had always understood that the law is a special kind of normative system, and the truth of this judgement was now reflected in the comprehensive reorientation of the legal system based on a new set of values. Legal reform took place in the special conditions of the transition from a one-party system to a multiparty parliamentary democracy, accompanied by the transition from the command economy to the market. The social function of law played a prominent part in all the post-communist societies. Not only is law a method of exercising and controlling state power, establishing the rules for the conduct of power politics, but it bears a system of values enshrined in such principles as legal security, the freedom to own property, and the protection of rights.

Democratic Russia, however, was born out of a revolution, defined here as the abrogation of law in order to achieve what is perceived as necessary. Following the coup the CPSU and its property was expropriated by executive order, without ceremony and without legal sanction. The death of the USSR was once again accompanied by a minimum of legal niceties, and Russia unceremoniously took over much All-Union property. Faced by what he perceived to be a conservative majority in parliament the Russian president tended to rule by *ukaz* (decree) rather than governing by law. However, accusations of neo-Bolshevism were misleading in the sense that the cumulative impact of the decrees would make rule by decree in future more difficult. Nevertheless, the delay in adopting the new constitution only exacerbated the tension between the form and content of the new political order. Even with the new constitution Russia's legal culture remained primitive, with arbitrariness and inconsistency reigning supreme. Endless administrative regulations modified and often subverted laws; executive officials often issued secret decrees; the laws themselves were often poorly drafted and subject to endless modification that undermined respect for the law; some regional and even more republican leaders claimed that their laws were superior to those of the legislature in Moscow;

and everywhere there was a defiance of the law if they were found to be inconvenient, an attitude to be found at the very top of Russia's administrative system as much as in the semi-criminal lower ranks.

LEGAL REFORM AND THE JUDICIAL SYSTEM

The Soviet system eliminated the independence of the judiciary; irrespective of the personal probity or otherwise of individual judges, the legal system was subservient to the Party-state. Now the institutional context of the legal system changed dramatically, and at the same time legal reform was accompanied by the internationalisation of Russia's political and economic systems. Russia became a full member of the Council of Europe, and its attempts to enter into contractual relations with international economic organisations such as the European Union (EU) and the International Monetary Fund (IMF) meant that Russian standards had to adapt to international ones.

The legislative activity of the Russian parliament operated within these constraints. There were seven key areas of legislation: the jurisdiction of state administrative bodies and the legal status of administrative bodies and political officials; constitutional reform and the establishment of a Constitutional Court; judicial reform, the rebuilding of the Russian legal system; laws regulating public life, the registration of political parties, laws on assembly and association, electoral regulations; laws on local government; laws concerned with the transformation of the economy, foreign trade and association laws, regulating the market economy, trading standards, accounting, tax, privatisation and land laws; and laws concerning the social sphere and welfare politics, social security, unemployment, benefits, labour laws.

The sheer volume of new legislation threatened to overwhelm the legislators and society alike, yet gradually the above agenda resulted in a mass of new legislation, although it must be admitted that many of the new laws were flawed. Social legislation lagged far behind economic laws, and acts were often drafted in an ambiguous manner leaving loopholes for the bureaucracy to exploit. The economic sphere was still overbureaucratised, with a mass of regulations governing the operation of enterprises. Thus instead of deregulation, too often there was yet more regulation. The principles of the new ownership structure were only haphazardly applied. There was as much an economic as a political need for a clear and consistent legal system, so that the economic community did not need to worry too much about political considerations and could instead concentrate on business. Above all, the organised input of social influence on the drafting of laws was still very weak. Social consultative mechanisms were embryonic and there was the danger that the only popular input would be demonstrations and other forms of protest. To balance the above, the committees and commissions of the Supreme Soviet and the subsequent State Duma did examine legislation and draw on expert opinion. The major result of this work was the adoption by the Duma of a new Criminal Code in 1995, to replace the RSFSR one adopted in 1960, with new sections defending individual rights and freedoms regulating economic activity.[83] The second half of the Civil Code, governing economic activity, was passed by the Duma on 22 December 1995.

The Supreme Court of the Russian Federation is the highest body in civil, criminal and administrative law. It oversees the work of all lower courts, and its judges are granted personal inviolability and can only be arrested with the permission of the Constitutional Court. The civil courts are subordinate to the Ministry of Justice and have traditionally acted as branches of the state. According to the constitution, judges of the Constitutional Court, the Supreme

Court and the Supreme Arbitration Court (dealing with economic conflicts) are nominated by the president and endorsed by the Federation Council and are meant to be irremovable. The Procurator-General is nominated by the president, but formally his or her appointment and dismissal is the responsibility of the Federation Council.

The constitution sought to regularise the judicial process and to preclude the possibility of the emergence once again of 'emergency courts' and the like (article 118). Assertions that the president controls the judicial process are exaggerated, at least according to the letter of the constitution, but the fate of successive Procurators-General suggests that the independence of the judiciary remains tenuous. Valentin Stepankov was less than enthusiastic about the president's dissolution of the legislature in September 1993, and was dismissed in the wake of the October events. Yeltsin bitterly opposed the Duma's 'amnesty' of 26 February 1994 for the putschists of August 1991 and October 1993, yet the new Procurator-General (Alexei Kazannik) felt it his duty to release the prisoners, but then resigned. The incident suggests scope for independence of the judiciary (and, incidentally, for parliament), but also illustrates the political pressures on the legal system. The main danger perhaps lies elsewhere, and the new constitution has enshrined the rights of local elites over the judicial process (article 129.3). Local procurators are appointed by regional and republican authorities, hence facilitating corruption and undermining the independence of the judiciary. The separation of powers between the regions and the centre is flawed.

The constitution sought to guarantee judicial independence (articles 10, 120 and 124) but this might appear to lack substance in the absence of life tenure for judges or of provisions for financial autonomy. Above all, the tension in Russia between legal and political thinking was particularly sharp. In 1878, after all, the jury had acquitted Vera Zasulich despite the fact that she had shot General F. Trepov, the Tsarist police commandant in St Petersburg. This can be interpreted as a contradiction between liberalism and democracy, with liberals appealing to the individual and law, whereas the democrats to the people (*narod*): morality (defined as the good of the people) for Russia's populistic democrats has always been regarded as something higher than law – another factor in the contemporary revulsion against democracy and the support by patriots for an authority over and above popular sovereignty. The continuing process of revolutionary upheaval in Russia may once again prevent the combination of the two. In this context, however, it should be stressed that the 1993 constitution is direct-acting, requiring no further legal enactments for its provisions to take effect, and thus the document remains the central reference point for legal and political processes in the country.

The first ever congress of the Russian judiciary in October 1991 adopted a series of proposals for judicial reform, including the return to the jury system abolished by the Bolsheviks in October 1917.[84] Caught between 'the masses', allegedly rendered degenerate by the Bolsheviks' 74-year experiment, and the authorities, some leading reformist jurists later turned against the jury system.[85] Popular attitudes played their part in framing the new legal system, but law-making as such is not a democratic but an elitist pursuit since legal reform can sometimes be inhibited by vengeful popular prejudices. This applies particularly to the question of capital punishment, with public opinion surveys showing support for the death penalty running consistently between 62–67 per cent.[86] The number of offences liable to capital punishment had traditionally been high, with some sixty capital offences in the RSFSR Criminal Code, and the USSR led the international league for the use of the death penalty. Between 1962 and 1989 21,025 people (750 a year) were executed in the USSR, though during perestroika the number declined to 195 in 1990.[87] Some 95 per cent of those condemned were executed for first-degree murder, but doubts were cast on the competence of the courts to categorise the offence as such, and little account was taken of the mental state of the defendants. In addition, many wrongful verdicts were passed in the absence of juries and there were no courts of appeal in the USSR. The Soviet judicial system was imbued with a harsh and repressive ethos, and the system was heavily biased towards guilt, with few acquittals and with a high proportion of judicial errors.[88]

According to Tumanov, too much effort had been spent in the judicial reforms on establishing trial by jury, an aspect of criminal law covering only one per cent of the cases. The main emphasis, he argued, should have been placed on defending the rights of citizens, a much broader question. He insisted that judicial districts should not coincide with territorial areas (regions and republics), in order to preserve the independence of judicial authorities from local administrations. In pre-revolutionary Russia judicial districts encompassed several *gubernii*, and in America the fifty states are covered by only thirteen federal appellate court districts. This would be difficult to do since many of the legislators in the Federation Council, responsible for framing the judicial reforms, were at the same time regional bosses and were not in the least inclined to give up their powers.[89] Russia's criminal justice system still fails to protect the civil rights of the accused, and although much has been achieved in judicial reform a legal order has not yet been achieved.[90]

CRIME AND THE MAFIA

The Russian legal system had to be rebuilt against the background of a society edging towards ungovernability. The power vacuum left by the demise of the communist regime was exploited by criminal syndicates in which power, money and crime, according to Stephen Handelman, forged a 'seamless connection'. In his view, 'The Russian mafiya's (*sic*) connection with government, born of its symbiotic relationship with the former communist establishment, makes organised crime a dagger pointed at the heart of Russian democracy.'[91] The state had already been criminalised by the old elites, and now the arbitrariness of the Soviet system was converted into widespread societal lawlessness. The criminal gangs that had emerged under Stalin, the thieves' world (*vorovskoi mir*) with a code of honour enshrined in popular song, now turned their attention to the emerging entrepreneurs. New and even more ruthless gangs, estimated to number at least 5,000,[92] drew freely on ex-servicemen, the KGB, the army and the militia to deal in pornography, narcotics, money laundering and protection rackets. At the same time, senior officials of the old regime even before the coup of August 1991 had prepared themselves 'for the struggle for the control of Russia's financial and industrial base', and the semi-corporatist post-communist economy provided rich pickings for them.[93]

Already, under Gorbachev crime figures had shown an alarming increase, and by 1991 this had reached awesome proportions accompanied by a sharp increase in motiveless crimes. A record 2.76 million crimes were recorded in 1992, a 27 per cent increase over the previous year, and the clear-up rate fell also.[94] In 1993 the rise appeared to slow down, with the 2.79 million recorded crimes representing an increase of only 1.4 per cent over the previous year.[95] It appeared that the marked long-term rise in recorded crime, since at least the mid-1970s, was beginning to slow down, and at the same time by 1993 the detection rate had improved significantly as Russia's state agencies began to work rather more effectively. Nevertheless, the fear of crime etched itself deeply on the consciousness of the post-totalitarian society.

In 1994 some 32,300 premeditated murders were recorded in Russia, double the 15,600 in

1990 and a rate considerably higher than that typical in Western Europe.[96] Contract killings in particular rose from 102 in 1992[97] to at least 2,500 in 1995, with some 6,500 others probably falling into this category.[98] These killings were marked by a chilling cold-bloodedness as former soldiers, accustomed to death in Russia's many 'little wars', profited from their 'professionalism'. Prominent victims included bankers and MPs, as well as the journalist Dmitrii Kholodov, blown up by an exploding briefcase in October 1994, and the television star Vladislav List'ev, shot in the entrance hall to his appartment block in March 1995. The so-called mafia itself adapted to new circumstances, with criminal gangs gaining a legal foothold by registering as private detective agencies. Their international links also appear to have improved, helped by the enormous increase in the number of Russians travelling abroad, with Britain alone issuing 88,158 visas in 1994 compared to 11,500 in 1987. Nevertheless, fears of a 'tidal wave' of organised crime engulfing Britain and the West appear to have been exaggerated.[99]

Rising crime had prompted Yeltsin in 1992 to relax the controls on the bearing of arms, thus weakening the state's monopoly on firepower that had been imposed by the Bolsheviks soon after they came to power. Citizens now had the right to bear arms to protect themselves and their property. Businesses threatened by criminal gangs were forced to pay protection money, but this in turn stimulated the proliferation of some 8,000 private security companies employing around 1.3 million people by 1995.[100] Official anti-crime organisations lost some of their best agents as an estimated one-third of the state's policemen, security officials and professional soldiers were attracted by promises of better wages and more prestige. The work of the courts was further impeded by the threats of criminals against witnesses and their families.

Budgetary constraints and problems of low morale inhibit the work of law enforcement agencies. The Ministry of the Interior, responsible for the militia, suffered a haemorrhage of experienced officers and was itself mired in criminality. The Democratic Russia leader, Arkadii Murashev, was appointed Moscow's police chief in autumn 1991 and argued that 'The ultimate objective is to transform the militia into a well-equipped police force of the Western type'.[101] His resignation in late 1992 represented a blow to the development of an independent and uncorrupt police force. The renewed anti-corruption campaign waged by the new minister of the interior, Anatolii Kulikov, from mid-1995 revealed awesome depths of venality in the MVD.

While the old regime lacked freedom, it did at least ensure a degree of security. The new freedoms after the fall of communism were accompanied by such a degree of job and physical insecurity that many yearned for the old days. The interpenetration of organised crime and politics led some to argue that Russia's second revolution had been 'stolen' by an unholy alliance of communists-turned-speculators and the criminal underworld. According to Handelman, whole regions and cities had fallen into the hands of criminal networks, senior officers happily traded weapons for cars, while the clandestine trade in nuclear materials threatened the rest of the world. He suggested that Russia had become a 'criminal state' run by and for criminals, while the honest lost out.[102] The close connection between political and criminal elites originated in Soviet times but had grown in depth and scale after 1991. It would be an exaggeration, however, to argue that Russia had become a 'criminal state' since far too much remained beyond the control of criminal-political elites. It would be more accurate to say that Russia was a state marked by widespread criminality reaching into the upper echelons of central and local power; but this does not make Russia – any more than it makes Italy – a mafia state.

THE SECURITY APPARATUS

From the very first days of Soviet power the security apparatus played a major role in the life of the state. Barely a few weeks after coming to power, Lenin, on 20 December 1917 established the Cheka, the forerunner of the KGB. Despite some attempts to curb its powers, the security apparatus, through several changes of name, became the bedrock of Stalin's power and the guarantor of communist rule after his death. The KGB, reorganised in the early 1950s with more limited powers, penetrated society at all levels. In the final stages of perestroika the KGB under Kryuchkov worked with the Party elite to save the old system, trying to discredit the Russian leadership and isolating Gorbachev behind a wall of disinformation.[103]

The Russian authorities after the coup were faced with the challenge of how to put down this monster.[104] The republican branches of the KGB were transferred to the new states, and on 11 October 1991 the State Council abolished the central KGB and its functions were divided between some seven agencies. The main successor organisation, headed briefly by Vadim Bakatin, was the Inter-republican Security Service (ISS), which after the disintegration of the USSR in December 1991 was swallowed up by the Russian Ministry of the Interior (MVD) to form a huge security apparatus called the Ministry of Security and Internal Affairs (MBVD – *Ministerstvo bezopastnosti i vnutrenykh del*), reminiscent of Stalin's monstrous People's Commissariat of Internal Affairs (NKVD). The merger was rejected by the Supreme Soviet and reversed by the Constitutional Court on 14 January 1992, and a separate MVD re-emerged, headed by Victor Yerin, and a new Ministry of Security (MB – *Ministerstvo bezopastnosti*) was created, headed by Yeltsin's ally, Victor Barannikov.

The Soviet Central Intelligence Service assumed the KGB's spying and counter-espionage functions, becoming after the fall of the USSR the Russian Foreign Intelligence Service (SVR – *Sluzhba vneshnoi rezvedky*). The SVR took over the KGB First Directorate's enormous network of foreign agents, electronic monitoring and communications networks, Space Intelligence Centre and much more. Academician Yevgenii Primakov, its first director, stressed that the SVR would not be under political, individual or corporate control, and its sole purpose would be to protect the state.[105] Its main functions were ensuring the non-proliferation of nuclear weapons, monitoring technology vital for the country, preventing regional conflicts, fighting international crime, and checking business partners of the Russian government. Following Primakov's elevation to the foreign ministry in January 1996, his replacement, Vyacheslav Trubnikov, was a career intelligence officer with a strong record of service to the Soviet regime. The other CIS states lacked sophisticated foreign intelligence operations and were forced to rely on the Russians. The Law on Foreign Intelligence of 8 July 1992 subordinated the SVR to the president, with oversight by parliament and the Prosecutor's Office,[106] while the new law on foreign intelligence of December 1995 unequivocally subordinated the SVR to the president while stressing the importance of human rights.[107]

The Ministry of Security assumed the KGB's internal role and often appeared to be little different from its predecessor, taking over much of its structures and personnel. The ministry had 135,000 employees, 50,000 of them employed in counter-espionage, and the rest, now that its services against dissidents and democrats were no longer required, turned their attention to crime.[108] The pervasive corruption within the MVD accentuated the role of the security apparatus.[109] As the conflict between parliament and the president intensified, the MB's position became increasingly difficult, and while the MVD's Yerin pledged his loyalty to Yeltsin, Barannikov's attempts to maintain an independent role, together with corruption charges and the inadequacies of the Border Troops under his jurisdiction in fighting on the Tajik-Afghan border, led to his dismissal in July 1993. His replacement, Nikolai Golushko, was a career KGB officer, but his failure to warn the Kremlin of the gathering insurgency by parliamentary forces led to his own dismissal after the October 1993 events. He was replaced by Sergei Stepashin and, following the unexpected success of Zhirinovskii's nationalists in the 1993 elections, the MB on 21 December 1993 was reorganised to become the Federal Counter-Intelligence Service (FSK). The decree abolishing the MB argued that it had proved impossible to reform the agency, yet Yeltsin had done little to advance the cause of liberalisation, having used the agency to secure his own power base and foiling attempts by parliament to ensure oversight over state security and intelligence bodies.[110] The president, parliament and the Prosecutor-General now share responsibility for oversight over security agencies.

The security agency soon recovered its confidence and often acted in a manner reminiscent of the KGB, in particular condemning foreign organisations in Russia as front organisations for the CIA. A leaked FSK document suggested that its attitudes had barely changed, condemning the activities of foreign academic research centres in Russia as part of America's attempts to undermine Russia as a Great Power.[111] Yeltsin stressed the FSK's role in protecting Russia's economic interests to ensure that the country did not end up 'on the sidelines of the world economy'.[112] The FSK was responsible for the covert war against Dudaev in Chechnya from the summer of 1994, and it was Stepashin who on 7 December 1994 authorised aircraft to bomb Grozny in direct contravention of a ceasefire brokered by the defence minister, Andrei Grachev. The creation of the Federal Security Service (FSB) in the aftermath of the Chechen war[113] and the appointment on 24 July 1995 of the former *Kommendant* of the Kremlin, Mikhail Barsukov, to replace Stepashin as its head signalled a new prominence for the agency. The FSB absorbed several other security agencies, with a staff not to exceed 77,640 (both officers and civilian personnel), and although in principle subordinated to the government and president, the body remained dangerously independent and on 20 June 1996 its head was once again sacked.

The FSB appeared to recreate a monstrous multi-functional agency. Former KGB personnel permeated into many aspects of Russia's post-communist life and the new agencies inexorably extended their influence over Russian life. The Law on Security of March 1992, for example, endowed the MVD, the customs and revenue services, and even the transport sector among others with security functions.[114] The July 1992 Law on the Federal Organs of State Security stated explicitly that the MB was 'a body of executive power', and endowed it with broad prerogatives to combat subversive activity against Russia by foreign agencies and domestic threats to constitutional order, territorial integrity and defence capability.[115] Former KGB censors and Party officials influenced the media, quite apart from using their old contacts to line their pockets. Above all, the security agencies sustained huge parallel armies separate from the official military establishment. The MVD had some 70,000 Interior Troops (VV), with about half deployed in the defence of government establishments, while the other half, the *Opnaz*, became a highly professional mobile strike force.

Following the October 1993 events a separate Presidential Security Service (PSB) was carved out of the Main Guard Directorate (GUO) to provide a military force loyal to the president; it was headed by Yeltsin's long-time personal security guard, Alexander Korzhakov.

In December 1994 PSB troops marched across Moscow to raid the offices of MOST-bank, which among other things sponsored the independent television station NTV. Korzhakov at this time sought to intervene in crucial policy areas such as arms exports and high technology transfers, and, stepping far beyond his official duties, wrote an intemperate letter to the prime minister warning against the removal of quotas on energy exports. Korzhakov apparently encouraged military intervention in Chechnya, no doubt hoping that a short victorious war would restore his master's fortunes in the presidential elections, while failure would only serve to confirm the need for the PSB and the security services to combat terrorism in Moscow. Korzhakov's prominence cruelly exposed the factional nature of Yeltsinite politics until he, too, was fired following the first round of the presidential elections in June 1996.

The influence of a multiplicity of secret services suggested the emergence of a 'security state'. One commentator notes that Russia (and the CIS) is prey to a 'self-perpetuating Chekist culture'[116] that permeates the new social, political, economic and, indeed, criminal structures. Old habits die hard and, despite constitutional guarantees to the contrary, the last years of the Yeltsin presidency were marked by a revival of an autonomous role for the security services. The former head of the government apparatus, Vladimir Kvasov, argued that all telephones and offices in the White House (now the seat of the government) were bugged, and even Sergei Filatov, the head of the Presidential Adminstration, made the astonishing admission that he too might be under surveillance.[117]

The Chechen war provided further evidence of the consolidation of a traditional security state and revealed the awesome implications of the reconstitution of a reborn security complex. The emergence of what came to be called 'the party of war' suggested that Russian politics were becoming increasingly militarised as the executive came under the influence of a security complex beyond parliamentary control. This militant group included the head of the PSB, Korzhakov, the head of the FSK, Stepashin, and the head of the MVD, Yerin. They were joined by the militant nationalities minister, Nikolai Yegorov, who had urged a forceful resolution of the Chechnya crisis but who became one of the first political casualties of the intervention, being sacked in late January 1995. The unity of the so-called 'power ministries', however, should not be exaggerated. Inter-service rivalries were pronounced and the inadequacies of the war effort brought home to Yeltsin the limits of the security apparatus and the awesome costs in domestic popularity and international isolation that their dominance would entail.

DECOMMUNISATION

The 'Nuremberg question' has haunted all post-communist states. To what degree were the perpetrators of the mass murders and other crimes of the communist regime to be brought to account, as some of the Nazis were in the Nuremberg trials during 1945–6? To what extent was the plea 'only obeying orders' to be admissible? How deep should the purging of the past go? For Solzhenitsyn 'A public admission by the Party of its guilt, its crimes, and its helplessness would at least be the first step towards alleviating the oppressiveness of our moral atmosphere.'[118] Shortly after the coup A. Yakovlev argued that 'Democracy is not thirsty for revenge',[119] and Gorbachev also insisted that there should be no witchhunt.[120] The democrats, however, insisted that there should be a public trial of the leading bodies of the CPSU, which 'had for decades imposed a terroristic regime on the country', and called for lustration ('ceremonial washing') laws against top Party and KGB officials to prevent them occupying responsible posts.[121] Rather than the issue dying away, in early 1993 Democratic Russia

(Demrossiya), a party political umbrella organisation, put forward its own version of a lustration law based on Japanese experience to ban former *apparatchiks* from jobs in certain sensitive occupations to stimulate the creation of a new state administrative class.[122]

Any serious decommunisation process, accompanied by dismissals and in certain cases trials, would involve unimaginable numbers and was liable to tear society, and indeed family and friends, apart, and sow misery and discord. Prosecutions for war crimes are always of the defeated by the victors, thus rendering judicial equity questionable.[123] In Poland the first post-communist government drew a 'thick line' under the past, but the line did not hold and in May 1992 legislation allowed the exposure of the names of politicians and state officials who had collaborated with the communist regime.[124] The lustration law of October 1991 in Czecho-slovakia affected more than 250,000 top officials and allowed the pasts of journalists and others to be exposed in a merciless process that judged people guilty until proven innocent, and in the court of public opinion innocence is almost impossible to prove. Instead of 'drawing a line under the past' in the former East Germany, the new authorities pursued collaboraters of the Stasi (secret police) with unparalleled vigour. A law that went into effect on 1 January 1992 gave all citizens access to their Stasi dossiers, some six million of which were in the archives covering half the adult population. Many former dissidents and respected individuals (including the writer Christa Wolf) were accused of collaboration and many lost their jobs despite protestations of innocence. Legal and administrative mechanisms to enable people to defend themselves were inadequate.[125]

Lithuania went the furthest of the former Soviet republics in desovietising state adminis-tration. The independence movement Sajudis established a special commission, composed of intellectuals and MPs, to consider staging a Nuremberg-style 'trial of Bolshevism'. Several deputies in 1992 were discovered to have collaborated with the KGB, including Virgilijus Cepaitis, a close associate of president Vytautas Landsbergis and a former leader of Sajudis, and even the former prime minister, Kazimiera Prunskiene, was accused of collaboration.[126]

The long shadow of the secret police poisoned post-communist politics. As the Poles discovered, Party officials and state functionaries who did not need to be pressed into its service would not have secret police records, and neither would the millions who kept silent and thus acquiesced in the lie. Only those who tried to resist were the subject of police pressure; and now their sufferings were to be prolonged by the moral crusade of the new leaders, most of whom had not fought against the regime when it had been dangerous to do so. During the 'épuration' (purification) following the liberation of France in 1944 some 11,000 people accused of collaboration were executed, usually without trial. If popular vengeance were to be unleashed against the perpetrators of the Bolshevik crimes a new bloodbath would sweep Russia. Demands by the democrats for lustration laws were resisted by the Russian authorities, perhaps fearful of their own pasts. Yeltsin took the view that former communists had to be employed (unless they had committed a specific crime) since they represented the largest pool of professionalism.

In Russia the problem of identifying who was guilty for the years of suffering inflicted on the population was even more acute than in Germany. With the disintegration of the USSR the moral question arose, as it did in Germany: if the state and system on whose behalf the crimes were committed no longer exists, to what extent is the guilt transferred to the successor state which has repudiated the principles in whose name the crimes were committed? The guilt, shame and responsibility of a society which on the whole had condoned the crimes, if only by silence, etched themselves in to the post-communist national consciousness.

Perhaps less morally correct, but probably the only practical option, was to behave as the Germans did once the Cold War came into full swing in the late 1940s, neglecting the prosecution of Nazis and avoiding a full-scale 'épuration'. This approach was based not only on pragmatic considerations, but also on the moral revulsion against Bolshevik absolutism. Sergei Kovalev, the head of parliament's human rights committee, opposed all attempts to divide society into the 'clean' and 'unclean', arguing 'There are no judges among us, not a single one. Everyone is to blame.'[128] The ethical rejection of the Bolshevik cause was no longer accompanied by the denial of the humanity of Bolshevism's servants. In his film *The Inner Circle* Andrei Konchalovsky raised the issue of the degree to which the sources of Stalinism were to be found in the people themselves. Did not the ordinary people play a part in creating the conditions that made their victimisation possible?

4   Party development

In the Russian Federation ideological diversity is recognized. No ideology may be established as the state ideology or as a compulsory ideology. In the Russian Federation political diversity and a multiparty system are recognized. Social associations are equal before the law.

Russian constitution[1]

Political parties have a fundamental role to play in the development of modern representative democracy.[2] They connect civil and political society, advance the perceived interests of individuals, groups and social strata while aiming consciously to develop these constituencies, and provide a link between civil society and the state, espousing the claims of the one and enforcing the rules of the other.[3] In post-communist Russia the emerging parties and party system only marginally fulfilled these functions. This chapter will examine the tortuous process of party formation in Russia, noting that a multiplicity of parties does not of itself demonstrate the existence of a functioning party *system*.

PHASES OF PARTY FORMATION

Party development in Russia evolved through four main phases, corresponding to the periodisation established in chapter 2.

1. Insurgency

The dissolution of communist power was accompanied by the emergence of movements covering social, environmental, gender and other issues, as well as the formation of the first political popular fronts and proto-parties.[4] The tumultuous proliferation of *neformal'nye* (informal, known colloquially as *neformaly*) organisations and an independent press revealed the strong currents of civic endeavour flowing beneath the stagnant surface of Soviet life.[5] While the politics spawned by the insurgency phase might have been untidy and anarchic, they were nevertheless stamped by a profound commitment not only to democratic goals but also to the democratic method, and demonstrably repudiated political cultural theories stressing Russian passivity and innate authoritarianism.[6] The integration of this upsurge of civic activism into a new polity, however, remained problematical.

The Leninist-Stalinist terror and decades of stifling one-party rule ruptured continuity with the past. Pre-revolutionary Russia was characterised by hundreds of societies and clubs, and this rich associational life continued into the early Soviet period but thereafter dried up to the degree that only three social organisations were created in the Brezhnev years.[7] Early studies of the neformaly blurred the distinction between political and social activities; the key point at this stage was autonomy from administrative structures and interest-orientation was a secondary consideration. This autonomy, however, was at first considered part of the shift from 'administrative-command' to hegemonic strategies of rule within the framework of perestroika.[8]

The establishment of the Democratic Union (DS – *Demokraticheskii soyuz*) on 9 May 1988 can be taken as the beginning of the renewed era of multiparty politics in Russia. Rejecting Gorbachev's attempts to expand the base of the Party regime by incorporating new social forces, the party declared its outright opposition to Soviet power and its allegiance to a 'peaceful democratic revolution'.[9] The party adopted a strongly anti-communist line, favouring the introduction of Western-style liberal democracy and market economy. Many of the DS's campaigns at first appeared blasphemous but soon entered the vocabulary of the public and then became official policy. It was the DS which first raised the Russian tricolour at the Kazan Cathedral in St Petersburg and Pushkin Square in Moscow, and indeed which first launched the campaign to rename Leningrad. After the coup the DS insisted that the revolution was still to come, that a change of symbols had taken place but not the revolution of democracy itself. They insisted that popular consciousness was permeated by a totalitarian mentality and had simply transfered its loyalty from the Bolsheviks to the 'good Tsar' Yeltsin and had still not attained a sense of civic responsibility.[10] The problems attending the development of the party, like poor organisation, leadership splits and low membership, were to be mirrored by countless other parties later.

At this stage, however, party formation was the exception rather than the rule. In the other republics the informal movement took the form of popular fronts, with Sajudis in Lithuania one of the largest representing aspirations for national autonomy and, later, independence. These popular fronts were catch-all single-issue movements and acted as the substitute for political parties. Most towns and regions at some time had popular front organisations 'in support of perestroika', but, like Solidarity in Poland, they inhibited the development of a firm multiparty system.

In Russia the absence of an all-encompassing national issue meant that popular fronts were weak and no single movement for the whole nation emerged. Democracy took the place of nationality politics as a mobilising force, and as mass electoral politics emerged, Democratic Russia (Demrossiya) came the closest to covering all of Russia. Democratic Russia was formally established in January 1990 as an umbrella organisation to fight the March local and republican elections, and at its formal inaugural congress on 20–21 October some eighteen social movements and nine political parties came together. It played a leading part in maintaining the pressure on Gorbachev in the year before the coup and its candidate, Yeltsin, emerged triumphant in the presidential elections of June 1991. After the coup, however, Burbulis was the only major figure from Democratic Russia offered an important political post, and the rest had to be satisfied with jobs in the localities or in administration.

The insurgency phase in Russia was both shorter in time and more anarchic than in Poland, while in Hungary the opposition played a lesser role in the transformation of the system, and here a more traditional form of party politics was the first to emerge.[11] The ending of the CPSU's guaranteed monopoly on power in March 1990 was followed by a wave of new parties, formalised by the Soviet Law on Public Associations passed on 9 October 1990 which placed political parties and independent trade unions on a legal footing. By late 1990 there were at least 457 political or politicised organisations in Russia, confronting analysts with major problems of classification.[12] Many of the new parties were barely distinguishable from the burgeoning mass of neformaly, but by early 1991 Russia had some 100 organisations that could be recognised as political parties, of which only about twenty recruited in other republics.[13] The problem soon became one not of the lack of parties but one of 'over-partification', hundreds of small groups covering every known, and some newly-discovered, nook and cranny of the political and social spectrum, and some several times over. Broadly speaking, up to August 1991 Russian politics were characterised by a bipolar struggle between communist and 'democratic' movements, with the embryonic national and patriotic movements torn between the two.

The end of the CPSU's monopoly allowed informal movements to take on more structured forms but they remained stamped by the politics of insurgency. Elections before August 1991, and in particular those in March 1990, were not fought between different social and political groups on the basis of alternative platforms and social groups defending their interests, but rather as voting alliances against a discredited regime (see chapter 5).[14] The onset of electoral politics *preceded* the emergence of a multiparty system, something that distorted the whole process of party formation. Elections were dominated by the anti-politics of opposition to the communist regime, and movements were largely unable to make the transition from mobilisational to representational politics.[15] Practically all respondents in a survey of middle level Demrossiya activists stressed that the movement prospered because of its commitment to the removal of the CPSU from power and the transition to a new social order.[16] Thus unity in the insurgency phase was forged by the negative programme of opposition to the communist regime, in favour of greater civic freedom and a looser form of federation, but failed to define positive political and social programmes.

While it was difficult for traditional electoral parties to take root in Russia, the struggle against the CPSU made it extremely easy for numerous pseudo-parties to emerge. While the term proto-parties suggest a natural evolution to full-blooded partyhood, pseudo-parties were caricatures of the conditions in which multiparty politics came to Russia. Dozens of parties emerged and scored easy victories with the minimum of organisational or intellectual resources against the debilitated CPSU and the decaying partocratic system in its entirety. Who needed a defined programme when the old system provided such a vulnerable target? Thus the new parties were marked by 'numerical weakness, weak and amorphous organisational structures (particularly at the local level), regionalism, ideological vagueness and a negativism bordering on populism, and low-calibre leaders who, for the sake of self-affirmation, actively set themselves up against other parties, even ones that were ideologically close to them'.[17] The emerging multiparty system was highly fragmented: if the process within the CPSU can be described as from party to faction, then the larger process can be described as from faction to party, a transformation that very few groups actually achieved.

2. Polarisation, August 1991–October 1993

The second phase accompanied the triumph of the August regime, the period of relatively liberal economic policies and, in the absence of elections, of a peculiar sort of 'phoney democracy' as the regime born of the August coup consolidated itself. By 20 February 1992 thirty-eight political organisations had been registered with the Russian Ministry of Justice,[18] and by April of that year, according to Stankevich, there were 820 registered public associations, including twenty-five political parties, encompassing over 300,000 people.[19] By May 1993 the number of organisations registered with the Ministry of Justice had risen to 1,800.[20] The new parties, however, palpably failed to become the basis of the new political system, and Russia moved from being a one-party state to a non-party state, albeit accompanied by numerous pseudo-parties. The onset of pluralism in Russia was not the same thing as the establishment of a multiparty system, and instead politics focused on the struggle between institutions rather than between parties in parliament.

The elimination of the CPSU following the coup and the ensuing vacuum opened up new political spaces but failed to trigger political mobilisation. Highly fragmented political parties divided over political, economic and nationality policy. Against the background of the kaleidoscopic formation, division and reformation of *groupuscules* calling themselves parties, a broadly bipolar system emerged in which 'democrats' stood against various nationalist, patriotic and communist splinter organisations, with the whole flank dubbed 'red-browns', the alliance of communist rejectionists and nationalist reactionaries.

Maurice Duverger stresses the electoral and parliamentary origins of modern political parties,[21] and in the absence of either in the polarisation phase party formation inevitably stagnated. If the *leitmotiv* of the alternative society in the insurgency phase had been unity across the political spectrum and between republics, the spirit of the August period was disintegration. Politics polarised over the fall of the USSR, the course of radical economic reform and the new constitutional order. The development of the party system was inhibited by the emergence of a distinctive type of dual power in which a presidential apparatus was superimposed on the nascent parliamentary system with little coordination between the two. While the government gained a degree of institutional autonomy, parties were left hanging in the air with little constructive purpose.

The second period was marked by the decline of the movements associated with the politics of insurgency. Expectations that environmental politics would be one of the major cleavage lines of post-communist party development proved false and environmental movements were marginalised under the impact of severe economic recession; while housing and other movements failed to respond to the new challenges. The official trade union movement was reformed and de-étatised, while the new trade unions were subject to the factionalism and splits typical of the pseudo-parties.[22] The ideological homogeneity of the insurgency phase now gave way to programmatic divergence over such issues as the powers of the presidency, relations with the 'near abroad' and, above all, economic reform. Programmes began to reflect the realities of contemporary Russian politics rather than idealised versions of abstract transitional processes to 'the market' or of 'rejoining world civilisation'.[23] Anti-communist unity now gave way to polarisation not only in the content of programmes, as the umbrella 'democratic' movement ceded ground to patriotic and nationalist organisations, but also in the 'irreconcilable' style of politics that came to predominate at this time.

The coup was followed by the decline not only of movements but also by many of the parties spawned by the struggle against communism. Pseudo-parties had been sustained by a variety of extraneous circumstances that did not reflect either their popular appeal or organisational resources. According to Popov, mayor of Moscow between June 1991 and June 1992, the democratic movement could not have been expected to achieve much since its social base was so heterogeneous, from intellectuals, security officials to pensioners, united only by their 'hatred for the bankrupt CPSU regime'.[24] The dominance of Demrossiya on the reformist flank inhibited the development of more sectional party politics. The failure of social movements to 'particise' themselves, notably in the case of Demrossiya and also the Civic Union later, is one of the distinctive features of the transition in Russia.[25]

After December 1991 'national' politics was defined on a smaller scale, but numerous parties were unable to adapt to narrower horizons and continued to support some larger political entity covering the former Soviet Union. The disappearance of the CPSU removed the incentive for the 'opposition' to unite, while much of the old CPSU elite made a smooth transition and became part of the new establishment. Groups like Demrossiya were disoriented and responded by calling for lustration laws and a continued mobilisational effort against manifestations of the old regime, something that now threatened Yeltsin's own position. A gulf remained between the parties emerging from below and official representation in the legislature, with parliamentary and popular organisations operating on separate levels, inhibiting the development of distinct party identities and organisations.

The polarisation phase was characterised by the emergence of a type of bloc politics whereby various movements sought to subsume, and indeed replace, parties in broader forms of coalition politics. Khasbulatov noted that 'The basic political unit is not the party and not even the party bloc but mass movements, that is, a type of political organisation which is unsuited to demands of stability under conditions of parliamentarianism'.[26] Four major tendencies can be identified in this stage of party formation: liberals and democrats; centrist parties, above all representatives of state industry; national-patriotic movements; and neo-communist and revolutionary socialist organisations.[27]

Liberal and democratic movements fell prey to fragmentation. Demrossiya tried to remain a united organisation but, deprived of the fruits of victory, in the wake of the coup began to break up. In November 1991 the split came over the issue of whether to preserve the Union in some form or to support its dissolution. The majority favoured Sakharov's idea of a loose commonwealth with the right of secession, whereas the three parties in Popular Accord called for a 'united and indivisible Russia' and insisted on 'protection of the rights of Russians in former Union Republics'. They accused the 'radical democrats' of continuing to use communist methods, ignoring moral and formal laws in favour once again of 'telephone law', and of trying as before to control economic and political processes. They insisted that a market economy could not be built with a 'strong hand' and that any attempt to reach the market through authoritarianism would lead not to economic renaissance but to a super-corrupt version of Latin American corporatism. Victor Aksyuchits, the leader of the Russian Christian Democratic Movement (RCDM), attacked Demrossiya for being a leader-dominated body seeking to become some sort of 'super-party'.[28]

The organisational weakness of the Russian democratic spectrum was remarkable, and attempts to create a political bloc in support of Yeltsin and his reforms repeatedly failed. A number of parties were established in 1993 in anticipation of general elections: notably Gaidar's Russia's Choice, representing the 'party of power'; Sergei Shakhrai's Party of Russian Unity and Concord (PRES), which adopted a moderately critical stance even though some of its leaders were in government; and a bloc bringing together 'oppositional democrats' headed by Yavlinskii, Yurii Boldyrev and Vladimir Lukin, the Russian ambassador to America, to form a group based on their initials, Yabloko (Apple).

Various centrist organisations represented the second major tendency. In June 1992 the All-Russian Union for Renewal (*Obnovlenie*) was formed by Arkadii Vol'skii, the chairman of the Russian Union of Industrialists and Entrepreneurs (RUIE, formerly the Scientific Industrial

Union), and was soon dubbed the 'party of managers'. Renewal sought to act as a coalition of three key groups of decision-makers: the managers of state enterprises, the new private entrepreneurs, and the chief executives of local government, many of whom were appointed by Yeltsin himself. On 21 June 1992 Vol'skii's Renewal joined with Alexander Rutskoi's People's Party of Free Russia (PPFR), formerly the Communists for Democracy faction formed in March 1991, and Nikolai Travkin's Democratic Party of Russia (DPR) to establish the Civic Union, a 'constructive' and 'loyal opposition' bloc against not Yeltsin but Gaidar's economics team whose policies, they insisted, could provoke a social explosion.[29]

The Civic Union favoured a slower and more socially oriented approach to economic reform, and sought to prevent the 'Kuwaitisation' of Russia by defending its native industries and technologies by selective import controls and state subsidies.[30] The group was wary of the West, favoured greater integration within the CIS and adopted what they called a broadly Eurasianist perspective.[31] Thus a political organisation was established to represent one of the most solid social bases in Russia and offered a potential alternative government to Gaidar's – if it could remain together. There was no love lost between Travkin's and Rutskoi's parties, divided in terms of personalities and policies; the DPR supported the rapid liberalisation and marketisation of the economy,[32] whereas Rutskoi came out in opposition to radical economic reform as he migrated into the national-patriotic camp.

The Civic Union was not an ideological alliance but a pragmatic attempt to rally the opposition of the centre. Vol'skii hoped to convert the RUIE into a fully-fledged Industrial Party, but hesitated out of fear of creating 'yet another flash-in-the-pan party formed "from the top"'.[33] In the event, following a disappointing performance at the Seventh Congress of People's Deputies in December 1992, the Civic Union withered away. Travkin's DPR also faced considerable difficulties in maintaining its earlier momentum, and his attempts to build a genuine organisation by establishing a strictly hierarchical structure contrasted with Civic Union's greater flexibility.[34] Neither approach was effective, and by late 1994 the DPR was severely weakened by the desertion of its regional membership, Travkin was deposed as leader and replaced by the economist Sergei Glaz'ev, and in 1995 the party split.

The third main tendency was the national-patriot movement, itself covering a wide spectrum from national-socialists at one extreme to democratically minded Russian 'statists' at the other, (the difference between patriots and nationalists will be discussed in chapter 10). The journalist K. Medvedev argued, 'We should not fool ourselves: this movement will inevitably come to power, if only because it is the only political force which played no part in the crimes, mistakes and oversights of recent years.' Just as Yeltsin had overcome Gorbachev because of his intuitive understanding of the mood of Russia, so the national-patriotic forces would triumph because of their understanding that Russia was tired of humiliation and of experiments, whether of the communist sort or those copied from Western models.[35] This analysis was powerful but over-stated the case.

The national-patriots weakened their own position by emphasising one strand of Russian statism at the expense of the other. Their stress on a greater Russia, encompassing other Slavic areas, appeared not only futile but dangerous as well, carrying within it the potential for war with Ukraine, Kazakhstan and others: the slaughter that accompanied Serbia's claims to defend the rights of Serbs in Croatia and Bosnia by incorporating them stood as an awful warning of what could happen in the former USSR. From December 1991 Yeltsin began to talk of a 'red-brown' coalition between rejectionist communists and revanchist Russian nationalists. Such an anti-Yeltsin coalition did indeed begin to take shape and presented a radical challenge to the August settlement. They had a cause, the rights of Russians 'abroad', the bowing to the West, the alleged economic incompetence of Gaidar's government and the catastrophic fall in standards of living and levels of production.

Quite apart from the lack of a coherent economic programme, the national-patriotic movement suffered from a fatal tendency to drift towards irreconcilable extremism. This also characterised the Slavic Assembly (*Slavyanskii sobor*), reflecting the alliance of Soviet and Russian nationalists; the *Nashi* (Ours) movement which brought together Alexander Nevzorov, the presenter of the investigative Leningrad televison programme '600 Seconds', Victor Alksnis of the Soyuz group, and Sergei Kurginyan, one of the leading conservative intellectuals and leader of the 'Postperestroika' group; the Russian Popular Union (*Russkii obshchenarodnii soyuz*, ROS), led by Sergei Baburin and Nikolai Pavlov; the Russian National Assembly (*Russkii obshchenatsionalnyi sobor*, RONS) led by former KGB general A. Sterligov, and many more. Sterligov noted that the 7 years of perestroika had completed the 70-year process of the 'total destruction of the life of the Russian people and its statehood', and sought 'by constitutional means to overthrow the present government of national betrayal'.[36] A lawyer by training, Baburin emerged as an effective and convincing publicist and organiser; he and his allies insisted that Russia *was* the former USSR and supported a strong state, collective property and mystical notions of Russian community.

The political centre moved towards more assertive statist, if not nationalist, positions, and even the so-called democrats began to rediscover the value of patriotism and tried to reclaim the idea from the right. The nationalists and some patriots, however, adopted ever more extreme positions, calling not only for the overthrow of the government but by mid-1992 challenged the president himself. The creation of the National Salvation Front (NSF), reminiscent of similar bodies established in the Baltic republics at the height of the 'winter offensive' against democracy during 1990–91, signalled a deepening of political polarisation. Established at a founding congress of some 3,000 communists and nationalists on 24 October 1992, the NSF brought together some of the more irreconcilable nationalists including the writers Rasputin, V. Belov, A. Prokhanov, academician I. Shafarevich, the well-known figures from the old Soviet Congress, Alksnis and A. Makashov, as well as Baburin and Mikhail Astaf'ev (leader of the Constitutional Democratic Party). The core of the NSF was the oppositional parliamentary bloc 'Russian Unity'. Shafarevich argued that the plan for the destruction of Germany and its pastoralisation at the end of the Second World War was now being imposed on Russia,[37] while the chairman of the organising committee, the MP Il'ya Konstantinov, explained that the movement sought to overthrow Yeltsin, create a coalition government, restore state control over prices, halt the conversion of the defence industry and stop the withdrawal of troops from Eastern Europe.[38] The NSF was declared unconstitutional by Yeltsin on 28 October 1992, the first political movement to be banned in Russia since the coup. Konstantinov questioned whether Yeltsin had the constitutional power to disband public organisations, and insisted that only a court could do so, and indeed on 12 February 1993 the Constitutional Court lifted the ban. The NSF went on to lead the military resistance to the dissolution of the Supreme Soviet in October 1993.

A distinctive mix of great Soviet patriotism, populism and Russian nationalism was propounded by Vladimir Zhirinovskii, leader of the clearly misnamed Liberal Democratic Party of Russia (LDPR). At its founding congress on 31 March 1990 Zhirinovskii, a 44-year-old lawyer working in a publishing house, had been elected leader. He had been born in Alma Ata (then called Verny), the capital of Kazakhstan, and like many from the periphery was more of a nationalist than those living in the metropolis. Zhirinovskii made much of the fact that he was one of the few Russian leaders who had never been a member of the Communist Party, though he apparently worked closely with the security establishment. His programme in the presidential elections of June 1991 was a simple one: to cut the price of vodka, to restore Russia's greatness by renaming the USSR (including the Baltic republics) Russia, and to keep Soviet troops in Eastern Europe until 'Russia' was ready for their return. This programme attracted six million voters, some 7.8 per cent of the electorate.

In early 1991 he called for the imposition of a state of emergency and the banning of all political parties, and naturally he supported the August 1991 coup, though he called the whole episode a 'show'.[39] He went on to urge a second coup to establish order, though this time, he insisted, the coup would be successful and bring him to power. He bitterly attacked Yeltsin for pursuing an 'anti-national, anti-Russian policy', and proclaimed: 'I deliberately say today that we must not give free rein to political democracy. We have to suspend the activities of all parties for now, and we must put all our efforts in the economy.'[40] He averred that the majority of Russians were in favour of dictatorship and called for the restoration of the Russian empire, firstly within the borders of the former USSR and later to encompass the former Tsarist empire, including Poland, Finland and Alaska.[41] Zhirinovskii directed his appeal to disaffected sections of society threatened by marketisation, and part of the business community who valued stability above democracy. The LDPR kept its distance from the maelstrom of nationalist movements and was able to take advantage of the political vacuum created by the destruction of many militant nationalist movements in October 1993 to score his apparent triumph in the elections of December 1993.

Communists represented the fourth main tendency. The fall of communist power was followed by a debate over whether the CPSU had been a party at all or a 'quasi-state organisation that concentrated all the basic functions of power in its hands'?[42] A group of thirty-six Russian MPs appealed to the Constitutional Court to adjudicate the legality of Yeltsin's three decrees issued between 23 August and 6 November 1991, banning the CPSU in Russia and confiscating its property.[43] A counter-petition by a group of Russian MPs led by Rumyantsev claimed that the Party's activities had been subversive and illegal, 'usurping state power and undermining state sovereignty that belongs exclusively to the people', and thus that the ban had been constitutional.[44] The Court on 26 May 1992 ruled that the two petitions would be considered together, and the hearings on the legality of the three decrees opened on 7 July 1992 and soon turned into a trial of the Party's activities since October 1917. The presidential team argued that the CPSU had not been a party but a state organisation, and therefore not the courts but the president had the right to decide its fate.[45] On 30 November 1992 the Court ruled that Yeltsin had acted lawfully in banning the CPSU's ruling bodies, but not its local branches. In effect, the Party was divided into two: the local membership and the governing bodies dominated by apparatchiki. The latter, as Yeltsin asserted, had become entwined with the state and were illegal; but the mass of the rank-and-file membership had been perfectly legitimate members of a political organisation and were entitled to renew their activities.[46]

Following the Court's ambivalent ruling Valerii Kuptsov, the last leader of the CP RSFSR, insisted that the Party would start reorganising and called for Yeltsin's impeachment. His associate, Ivan Rybkin, organiser of the Communists of Russia parliamentary fraction, announced that an extraordinary congress of the Russian Party would be convened and insisted that 93 per cent of the former Party's property belonged to the four main successor organisations, and only 7 per cent to the state.[47] The Communist Party of the Russian Federation (CPRF) came back to life on 13–14 February 1993 at a conference not far from Moscow. Four of the successor parties attended, including Roy Medvedev's Socialist Party of Working People (SPWP) and Alexei Prigarin's Union of Communists, and the whole session was presided over by Rybkin. Old-style Stalinists and pensioners were well represented, but the words 'of the Russian Federation' in the party's name signalled its recognition of existing borders. Gennadii Zyuganov, long associated with the Russian nationalist wing of the movement and formerly leader of the so-called 'Committee of the National-Patriotic Forces of Russia' and author of 'A Word to the People' (the manifesto of the coup), was elected leader. Viktor Anpilov's militant Russian Communist Workers' Party (RCWP) refused to join, and Nina Andreeva's Stalinist All-Union Communist Party of Bolsheviks (VKPB) also kept its distance, but even without them the CPRF soon eclipsed all other parties, drawing on the support of the revived local committees and incorporating a large part of the militant RCWP (including its Kemerovo organisation) which defected to the CPRF.

The CPRF was one of the few political movements that transcended the politics of insurgency and drew on reserves of organisational and political experience matched by no other. The CPRF became Russia's largest party, with a membership of over half a million. It claimed to be the official successor to the CPSU, and thus hoped to have some of its property restored by the courts. Rejecting the calls of some of the irreconcilable oppositionists to boycott the December 1993 elections, Zyuganov led the party to a respectable third place (after Russia's Choice and the LDPR) gaining 12.4 per cent of the national vote giving them thirty-two of the party-list seats in the Duma and another ten constituency seats.

In the polarisation phase the proto-parties of the insurgency stage gave way to a system marked by numerous pseudo-parties, all seeking a niche in the ideological spectrum and organisational life of the post-communist polity. Overpartification stimulated the tendency to move from party to bloc politics, while the absence of disciplined party blocs endowed parliamentary politics with a fractious fluidity. Parties neither guided the president nor formed the government, and parliament and the parties in it were marginalised. Parties fulfilled the communicative and link functions between the political elite and the people only fitfully. The failure to integrate parties into the operation of the political system undermined the stability of the new democratic institutions and forced ever greater reliance on a technocratic ideology of democratic and marketising reforms from above (the regime system). The absence of a multiparty system impeded the development of serious parties, but at the same time the absence of serious parties inhibited the development of a multiparty system.

3. Towards democratic adaptation, late 1993–1995

The third phase was inaugurated by the dissolution of the CPD and its Supreme Soviet on 21 September 1993 and the events of 3–4 October, when the White House was stormed and Yeltsin's opponents crushed. This adaptation stage was marked by the adoption of a new constitution and the first genuine national multiparty elections of 12 December 1993. The elections ended the era of sharply polarised politics, clarified the pattern of party affiliation and effectively 'parliamentarised' Russia's nascent party political system. Electoral politics fragmented the so-called democratic movement and the 'red-brown' flank, and instead a complex pattern of multipolar politics emerged. The consolidation of the party system as an integral part of Russian government proved problematical but the characteristic feature of this period was the adaptation of political parties to the conventions of democratic electoral and parliamentary politics. The extremes of left and right were marginalised.

Following world practice,[48] the electoral system was manipulated by reformers to promote specific goals, above all to encourage the development of a multiparty system (see pp. 104–6). The electoral law provided for a mixed system in which half the seats to the new 450-member State Duma would be elected from single-member constituencies, but the other half would be elected from party-lists. The mixed proportional and constituency system, according to Victor Sheinis, one of its main architects, would not only foster a party system but also avoid 'an atomised parliament with factions like those we have today, representing no more than interest clubs'.[49] According to Nikolai Ryabov, the head of the Central Electoral Commission (CEC), the proportional elections played a positive role 'in the development of the parties and movements themselves, assisting the development of multipartyism in Russia'.[50] Others, however, have argued that the electoral system worked more to strengthen parliamentary factions than parties.[51]

The adoption of the hybrid electoral system only revealed more starkly the fault lines in Russian society. The pseudo-parties of the August system were at last faced with the hard school of an election, in which their inflated claims of support could finally be put to the test; few withstood the challenge, and most faded into the obscurity whence they had come. Thirteen parties and electoral blocs negotiated the hurdles to stand in the election, and of these only eight cleared the 5 per cent threshold (see appendix 2.5). The aim set by Popov earlier, to 'parliamentarianise' the opposition by offering them a forum away from their accustomed street politics, was only partially fulfilled.[52] A new generation of parties emerged, some of whom drew their provenance from earlier stages and adapted to the new conditions, but most were newly created. The elections contributed to the development of parties by forcing the development of organisations and alliances, but it was the adoption of the constitution that provided the institutional framework in which parties could operate.

The establishment of a viable parliamentary system finally created a forum in which party politics could flourish. Hopes that the elections would kick-start the party system, however, were only partially fulfilled, and the presence of nearly a dozen relatively small factions and groups in the Fifth Duma prevented the establishment of a stable majority, inhibited the development of parliamentary government and perpetuated the supraparty system of regime politics. Party factions were once again relatively fluid and deputies were marked by a lack of discipline. Many deputies elected on the party lists, moreover, were not even members of the parties they officially represented, notably in Zhirinovskii's LDPR, whose caucus in the Duma fell prey to endless splits. The lack of correspondence between the composition of parliament and the formation of the government, moreover, accentuated the fragmentation of the Russian party system. Viktor Chernomyrdin had been appointed prime minister in December 1992, and although his government was modified as a result of the elections it remained largely technocratic and 'above politics'. The major centres of power were based on personalities, many of whom were outside the parliamentary and party system altogether, and within parties links between the leadership and membership were tenuous. Parties are trapped between strong executive authority and an amorphous civil society.

To heal the wounds inflicted by the October events and to stabilise the political situation, Yeltsin sponsored a Charter for Civic Accord, signed by 148 political, trade union, religious and public figures on 28 April 1994.[53] The president promised not to launch early parliamentary elections, while the signatories in return promised not to demand early presidential elections, and a ban on strikes was to be observed. Zhirinovskii signed up, but the opposition was notable by its absence, with the CPRF and its close ally, the Agrarian Party of Russia (APR) refusing to sign, while Yavlinskii did not even attend the ceremony, regarding the whole exercise as pointless, imposing no obligations on anyone.[54] The opposition, meanwhile, had organised its own Accord for Russia, including the CPRF, the APR, Rutskoi, and the former head of the Constitutional Court, Zor'kin. Both the oppositional Accord for Russia and Civic Accord reflected the traditional pattern of 'supraparty' bloc politics and harked back to the inclusive 'popular front' politics of the insurgency phase.

The 1993 elections were followed by a new wave of party fragmentation and creation, in which some of the electoral blocs sought to turn themselves into fully fledged parties in anticipation of the parliamentary elections of December 1995. The relative failure of the democrats in the December 1993 elections led many to distance themselves from the policy of radical reform. At the congress of the Russian Democratic Reform Movement (RDRM) on 29 January 1994 its leader, Popov, claimed that the 'Westernising' model of Russian reforms had failed and called for the creation of a 'Democratic Alternative for Russia' (DAR) bloc as a 'constructive opposition' not only to the policy of 'shock therapy' but also to 'the reform model based on Western prescriptions'.[55] With their roots in the insurgency phase when success had fallen into their hands, reformist parties failed to broaden their appeal from the capital's intelligentsia to address the needs of the provinces and ordinary wage earners.

Gaidar's attempts to convert Russia's Choice into a party uniting all the democrats failed miserably. A plenary meeting of Demrossiya's Council of Representatives on 19–20 February 1994 revealed the bitterness of the movement's regional organisations, condemning the dominance of the 'communo-democratic *nomenklatura*' in the regions and criticised the leaders of Russia's Choice for their incompetence in the elections. One of Demrossiya's leaders, Lev Ponomarev, noted that support for the democrats continued to decline throughout Russia, and the meeting voted not to join Gaidar's party.[56] Activists condemned Demrossiya's 'degeneration' from a movement expressing the aspirations of the people into the 'bourgeois' Russia's Choice.[57] Demrossiya was a classic case of the failure to move from the mobilisational politics of insurgency to representational politics typical of a revolution's consolidation phase, and only at moments of crisis against a clearly defined enemy was it able to find a role for itself.

Gaidar went on to establish a new 'liberal conservative' party, Russia's Democratic Choice (DVR), in June 1994, although the Democratic Choice movement continued to exist in parallel alongside the new party, causing considerable confusion.[58] Russia's Choice was the single largest party in the Duma, with seventy-five deputies in its faction, and had branches in sixty-eight of Russia's federal components. Many of Demrossiya's activists joined the new party, but in the regions the choice between remaining in Demrossiya or joining Gaidar's party was a difficult one.[59] In the event, DVR failed to cross the 5 per cent threshold in December 1995.

The Chechen war from late 1994 saw a realignment within the ranks of the 'democrats' themselves. Strong support for the war came from deputy prime minister Shakhrai's PRES, dubbed in the regions the Party of the Indivisible Empire (PIE). Shakhrai had formerly been nationalities minister and in the Security Council had voted for intervention. A Cossack from the North Caucasus, he had long advocated a forceful resolution of the crisis, a fact that did not enhance the electoral prospects of his party and its party-list failed to enter parliament in December 1995. Former finance minister Boris Fedorov's December 12 Liberal Democratic Alliance, now sharply critical of Russia's Choice even though Fedorov had until December

1993 been a member of Gaidar's cabinet, sought to place a confidence motion before parliament and called for a new government and pre-term elections. Fedorov's initial support for the war was later tempered by disgust at the incompetence and brutality of its conduct, and he sought the government's dismissal on grounds of incompetence. Fedorov's 'Forward Russia!' (established in February 1995) staked out a position combining democracy and patriotism, and was not afraid in calling for a strong state or for 'the restoration of order', and indeed he took up Peter Stolypin's favourite maxim, 'reform and order'.[60]

The CPRF itself had gained in political weight in the 1993 elections, ending up with 12.4 per cent of the popular vote giving it thirty-two seats, with another ten deputies elected in single-member constituencies, and would no doubt have done better if Zhirinovskii's LDPR had not diverted votes. The CPRF adapted remarkably well to parliamentary life, but certain identity problems remained. While pledging to support 'workers' collectives' the latter were divided by industry and profession, and the CPRF's relationship with enterprise managers was ambivalent. Over 80 per cent of directors implemented with a greater or lesser degree of enthusiasm Gaidar-type policies.[61] By the time of its Third Congress in January 1995 the CPRF claimed some 550,000 members and 20,000 primary organisations, making it by far the largest party, but the absence of a clear-cut ideology (torn between Marxist revivalism, socialist reformism and communist nationalism) and the aged profile of its membership, inhibited the mobilisation of these resources. The party placed itself firmly in the camp of the constitutional opposition, but its economic programme was populistic, its calls for the reunion of the former Soviet republics smacked of imperialism, its Russian nationalism sat uneasily with its socialist internationalism, while its Eurocommunist-style political programme was as contradictory as that of the original Eurocommunists in the 1970s.[62] Questioning the viability of the smaller Russia to survive, doubts remain over the degree to which the party has embraced pluralistic market-oriented policies. Its nationalist aspirations, socialist loyalties and democratic commitments are not yet convincingly integrated.

The CPRF only tentatively shuffled along the path towards transforming itself from a revolutionary socialist party to adopting the positions of its erstwhile social-democratic enemies. While much attention has been devoted to regime transition, the question of political party transition – the transformation of communist parties into reformist parliamentary parties, in the context of the return to power of many of these parties – is no less important.[63] The CPRF became 'parliamentarianised', although a vociferous section in the party hesitated to embrace evolutionary social democratic positions. The programme adopted at its Third Congress in January 1995 dropped the concept of class struggle altogether and instead talked in terms of a three-stage struggle: the removal from power of Yeltsin's 'anti-people regime' either by gaining an absolute majority in the elections or by popular pressure; the 'restoration of the power of the soviets' from top to bottom; and only then 'socialist development in a renewed form' marked by equality, fairness and the predominance of socialised forms of ownership. The theoretical part of the programme insisted that capitalism was a dead end, but the alternative of 'stable development' was vague in the extreme and reflected the hesitancy with which neo-communists use the word 'communism'.[64] The programme was laced with Zyuganov's heady mix of statism and Slavophilism, reflected in such notions as *obshchinnost* (communality), *derzhavnost* (great powerness), *sobornost* (collegiality) and 'the Russian idea', a notion inaccessible to the Western mind but which in his view was profoundly socialist.[65] The programme was marked by a lack of constructive economic ideas and by a confrontational style that was considered essential for a party in opposition struggling for power.[66] The CPRF found itself in a difficult position over the Chechen war, in general supporting the 'restoration of order', but not by Yeltsin and his generals.[67] Zyuganov supported the principle of Russia's territorial integrity, insisting that 'We face a thousand times more bloodshed in the future unless Russia's territorial fragmentation is stopped now.'[68]

The CPRF under Zyuganov became one of the few genuine mass parties, with a large membership, a strong if contradictory programme and a serious national organisation. The continuing economic crisis and the corruption associated with the August regime once again made the CPRF a credible force. With reformed and renamed communist parties having returned to power in Lithuania, Poland, Hungary and Bulgaria, its prospects looked bright. This was reflected in its notable success in the December 1995 elections, coming top in the proportional part of the elections with 22.3 per cent of the vote, giving it ninety-nine seats in the Duma plus another fifty-eight single-member seats (see appendix 2.6). It is not clear whether the return of communists to influence in Russia is an indication of the failure of the democratic transition or evidence of its success.

It is against the background of a fragmented party scene and with presidential elections due in June 1996 that an attempt was made to impose an ordered two-party system from above. The idea had already been mooted by Burbulis in 1992, and it was now taken up by the presidential apparatus, and in particular by Shakhrai. The plan was to unite the centre-right parties around a political bloc to be led by Chernomyrdin, while the centre-left would be anchored around a movement led by Rybkin, the speaker of the Duma. It soon became clear that Rybkin's bloc would not be much more than a loose alliance of parties, losing even the support of his own APR, and it failed to enter the Sixth Duma.

Chernomyrdin's bloc fared rather better. At its founding congress on 11 May 1995 the new party adopted the grand name of 'Russia Our Home' (*Nash dom Rossii*, NDR), dedicated to 'progress without shocks' and promising to lead Russia into an era of stability and strength. Chernomyrdin declared that the era of 'emotional democracy' was over, and called for a new politics of 'dignity and stability'. The aim was to create a centre-right party that could overcome the fragmentation of the centre and ensure that the CPRF or nationalist forces did not win the elections. The new party was launched with Yeltsin's support and included many ministers. The hardline deputy prime minister Oleg Soskovets and Konstantin Titov, governor of Samara, became deputy chairs under Chernomyrdin, while the majority of the 126 men (no women) on the bloc's standing committee represented the regions. The 300 delegates were largely drawn from the old Soviet bureaucracy and regional elites, including Leonid Polezhaev, governor of Omsk and chair of the powerful Siberian Accord group of regions, and Anatolii Tyazhlov, governor of Moscow oblast and chair of the Union of Governors of Russia. Apart from PRES, New Regional Policy and the 'Russia' factions, few of the established political parties joined the new grouping, and PRES itself left in August 1995. There were allegations that the energy lobby, and in particular Chernomyrdin's old fiefdom Gazprom, were improperly funding the new venture. Its key slogan was 'pragmatism', but the way the party was conceived and built suggested a new attempt at 'nomenklatura democracy', a top-down attempt to secure the existing order.

In the run-up to the parliamentary elections of December 1995 Russia's already fragmented party system atomised even further. By May 1995 seventy-nine parties had been registered by the Ministry of Justice to fight the elections, and by the time the process was complete in late November forty-three groups were registered to stand, making the ballot paper an extraordinarily thick document. All the familiar features of post-communist party building were taken to new extremes: the emphasis on personalities, amorphous and poorly drafted programmes, the deinstitutionalising influence of regional politics, the constant splitting and sub-dividing of parties and factions, and the absence of party discipline. Although the major players came from above, there was an enormous ferment of primary activity in the wards and the degree of grass-roots democracy should not be minimised. The campaign was marked by a novel professionalism, with numerous image-making agencies at work and vigorous fund-raising activities.

The results of the 1995 election came as a surprise to many, above all the strength of the combined rejectionist vote (CPRF and LDPR). The 'centre' was anchored in the relatively disappointing vote for Russia Our Home, while Yabloko was the only 'democratic' party to enter the Sixth Duma. Although the centre of Russian politics, rooted in marketising reforms, international integration and representative democracy, lacked convincing political representation, the adaptation phase had to a large degree universalised these policies, albeit without some of the liberal rhetoric of the earlier era.

4. Political differentiation

Against this broad characterisation of the contemporary Russian party scene, fragmented and amorphous though it was, there were discernible tendencies transforming it into something approaching the emergence of a party system with viable and effective parties. Differentiation took place in three ways: frenetic party formation and reformation continued, but the December 1995 elections distinguished a small group with representation in the Duma from the mass of pseudo-parties; the programmes and policies of this small group were now far more clearly differentiated along the classical political spectrum – the CPRF on the left, Russia Our Home in the centre, Yabloko on the centre right, and the LDPR on the nationalist right, although cross-cutting issues allowed alliances across the spectrum; and, thirdly, Russian society itself began to develop a contoured political structure.

Differentiation in the Russian population was reflected in more stable party alignment between demographic and economic groups. At the time of the December 1995 elections Women of Russia, Russia's Democratic Choice and the LDPR attracted younger people, while the Communists and Agrarians appealed to the older generation. People with little education preferred the Agrarians, LDPR, and Communists, while Russia's Choice and Yabloko attracted the more highly educated. Reformist parties were best represented in the capitals of Moscow and St Petersburg, while the APR dominated the villages, although the Communists had growing support, while the democrats were rarely supported here. The Communists, APR and LDPR found support among poorer segments of society.[69] Many of the new generation of parties were now better funded and began to sink local roots, drawing on a well of consistent support with name and programme recognition. Parties began to mobilise their resources more effectively and to devise programmes that reflected Russia's genuine problems.

The draft 'Law on Political Parties', finally adopted by the Duma on 8 December 1995 to supersede the 1990 Soviet law on public associations, regulates the types of parties that can be formed, procedures for creating and registering them, their rights and responsiblities, and ways of monitoring their activity. Three types of political parties may be established: national, with regional organisations in at least forty-five components of the Russian Federation; interregional, with membership from at least two components; and regional. The law stipulated that a party could only be formed by a group numbering at least ten people. The law prohibits parties that seek forcibly to change the constitutional system, violate the integrity of the Russian Federation, undermine state security, create armed formations, or to foment social, racial, ethnic discord and enmity. Party groups were prohibited from forming in executive agencies or local government, the armed forces, law enforcement agencies, or in the staffs of state or local legislative authorities. No mention was made of Yeltsin's decree of 1 August 1991 prohibiting party organisations from enterprises. Funding for the election campaigns of national parties was to come from federal funds, although they can engage in economic activity of their own and accept donations.[70]

The bureaucratic politics of the August regime began to break down and made space for a new stage in Russia's political evolution. Yavlinskii considered the victory of only four parties in the party-list contest in the December 1995 elections a sign that Russia had outgrown the 'infantile stage of multi-partyism'.[71] Popov noted that the general-democratic stage of the transformation was complete, the fundamentals of democracy had been introduced, and the first phase of privatisation was complete. More importantly, Russia's political configuration changed. We have argued that the transition was based on an alliance between reformist sections of the Soviet bureaucracy and a programme drawn from liberal Westernisers, marginalising the democratic movements born during the insurgency against communism. Now a new model began to emerge in which political regeneration from below and the regions, the emergence of a structured political space, and the fragmentation of the old elite allowed competition between genuinely competing political programmes.

FEATURES OF PARTY DEVELOPMENT

The political and social environment attending the emergence of a party system in Russia was in certain respects reminiscent of the early American experience. The American constitution from the beginning was explicitly biased against parties, termed factions by James Madison. To the present day the two major US parties act as loose coalitions rather than the relatively disciplined and structured parliamentary parties of the West European sort. Emerging from the suffocating tutelage of the Communist Party, anti-party views fell on fertile ground in Russia. Anatolii Khimenko noted that the many years of communist dominance had 'discredited the very concept of "party"'.[72] In his book *Rebuilding Russia* Solzhenitsyn argued against party politics to allow the organic fabric of community to develop.[73] He noted that:

> Party rivalry distorts the national will. The principle of party-mindedness necessarily involves the suppression of individuality, and every party reduces and coarsens the personal element. An individual will have views, while a party offers an ideology.[74]

Presidential systems in the best of circumstances tend to inhibit the emergence of party government, while Yeltsin's insistence on the non-party essence of presidential rule further reduced their potential. Yeltsin's first act on being elected chairman of the Russian Congress on 29 May 1990 was to suspend his membership of Demrossiya, insisting that he would defend 'the interests not of separate groups or parties or organisations but the interests of the peoples of the Russian Federation'.[75] On resigning his CPSU membership on the last day of the Twenty-eighth Congress in July 1990 Yeltsin declared that he would join no party and declared himself to be above party politics. Demrossiya had provided crucial support for Yeltsin's presidential victory in June 1991, yet his victory did not lead to its consolidation as the 'party of power', or indeed, to its consolidation as a party at all. Yeltsin clearly felt more at ease working through his own 'team' free of political or social control, and his claim to be president of all Russians only strengthened the tendency towards charismatic above-party leadership implicit in the regime system in post-communist Russia. In the presidential elections of 1996 he ran as an independent. The new president after June 1996 was required to renounce party membership, something that Zyuganov promised to do. In the event, Yeltin's re-election meant the maintenance of the *status quo*.

The state did little to assist the development of parties or a party system, and little came of Yeltsin's promise to provide assistance at a meeting with the leaders of fifteen of the largest parties on 12 December 1991.[76] The institutional framework of post-communist politics, moreover, inhibited the development of a functioning party system, with the government chosen, as we have seen, on a non-party basis. The character of the state formation following communism was crucial in establishing the context for party development. As M. Steven Fish notes of the perestroika period, the nature of political groups was determined largely by 'the character of state power'. The role of ideas and the convictions of individual politicians is minimised, while the critical legacy of a society thoroughly permeated by an activist state is given prominence.[77] Post-communist Russian state building proved inimical to the conversion of the insurgent political formations into genuine political parties.

The fate of parties and the structure of party politics depended on timing and the type of electoral system adopted. The electoral process is itself a major stimulus for the development of parties and a party system, and the absence of a general election up to December 1993 inhibited further democratisation. Parties in this period, quite simply, had nothing to do. In the absence of elections most political associations before December 1993 barely qualified to be termed parties, failing to meet Sartori's basic definition of a political party as 'any political group that presents at elections, and is capable of placing through elections, candidates for public office'.[78] The elections of December 1993, however, did little to consolidate the party system and indeed it could be argued that the hasty formation of *impromptu* electoral associations, eight of which entered the Duma, disrupted the process of party organisation and consolidation. The LDPR registered notable success in gaining fifty-nine of the 225 party list seats, yet the organisation was less a party, with 40 per cent of its deputies not even members of the party) than a vehicle for Zhirinovskii's charismatic leadership.

The attempt to manipulate the electoral system to encourage the consolidation of effective electoral parties proved only partially successful. The version of the electoral law presented to the Constitutional Assembly in June 1993 by a group of experts led by the deputy Victor Sheinis proposed a mixed system on the German model of direct constituency elections and party lists, intended precisely to encourage the development of a party system.[79] The establishment of the party-list system for the election of half the deputies to the State Duma in December 1993, and the retention of this system for the December 1995 elections, although designed to stimulate the creation of solid political parties, in practice accelerated the fragmentation of the party system. The 1995 electoral rules, for example, allowed only twelve Moscow politicians on the party list, encouraging those lower down the list to form their own electoral blocs.

If the presidency and the electoral system did little to encourage the development of a functioning party system, the old Supreme Soviet did even less. While Khasbulatov stressed the importance of the development of multiparty politics,[80] in practice representation of parliament as a single entity, as a 'party' in and of itself acting as the 'opposition' to presidential government, undermined the development of party politics in the first period.

Gatherings of deputies were fragmented and failed to vote along party lines. Instead, parliamentary factions took on a central significance, with the gradual emergence in parliament of blocs reflecting the various political tendencies in the country.[81] Though elected by the people, deputies came to parliament representing ultimately no one but themselves and were thus responsible to no one. The absence of constituency structures meant that there was no collective party responsibility for the conduct of deputies. This, incidentally, allowed many to become unashamed lobbyists for various interests; bloc politics was no substitute for party politics.

The 1993 elections played a significant role in parliamentarianising the nascent party system; but this was not the same as the partification of parliament. Elections make parties, but party affiliation made little difference to the vote in the constituencies. Over a hundred State Duma deputies were elected as independents, and this was then reflected in the fluidity of factions in the Duma. The formation of parliamentary committees on the party principle was an attempt to kick-start the party system into operation, as was the rule that a party group required a minimum of thirty-five deputies to be registered. According to Mikhail Mityukov, the chair of the presidential commission on legislative proposals and the main author of the regulations governing the work of the new assembly, the rules prevented the emergence of a new Khasbulatov and by focusing on party factions promoted the development of a party system. The chair of the Duma and the vice-chairs were to belong to different factions, and instead of a Presidium there was a Conference consisting of the chairs and delegates from factions and groups with voting power in proportion to their size. The Conference's role was to be purely organisational. The rules, moreover, allowed a faction or bloc to recall a deputy and replace him or her with one further down the party list.[82]

While groups of deputies with defined positions did emerge, they were in constant flux. The experience of the Fifth Duma suggested that 'a proportional system in a country with an undeveloped civil society only impedes the growth of genuine multipartyness'.[83] The establishment of electoral blocs allowed numerous small parties, which independently would not have been able to cross the 5 per cent threshold, to gain seats in the new Duma. Travkin noted that electoral pacts undermined the development of a normal parliamentary party system,[84] and his warnings were justified. With the exception of the CPRF and the APR, few Duma factions retained their original identity: Russia's Choice reformed, the DPR split, PRES barely survived, Yabloko survived only thanks to Yavlinskii, the LDPR (where, as noted, 40 per cent of the deputies elected under its banner were not members of the party), barely remained together as a faction, and so on. The formation of associations to fight elections was governed by one logic – the attraction of star leaders, the search for campaign sponsors and the like – which does not correspond to the logic of genuine party formation, the patient consolidation of regional organisations, the honing of a programme and the establishment of a permanent central staff. The four factions in the Sixth Duma, however, were in a better position to consolidate themselves as stable party caucuses.

In contrast to the 'golden age' of parties from the late nineteenth century to the 1970s, the contemporary era is marked by a plurality of competing forms of political representation (in particular, single issue pressure groups), and the space in which parties operate has changed dramatically. Above all, the electronic media acts as the functional equivalent of political parties, able to mobilise an electorate and substitute for a network of party committees. Much of Zhirinovskii's electoral success has been attributed to his masterly performance on television. The traditional baggage of political organisation and nationally organised political parties appears dispensable when an effective performance and advertisements on the silver screen count for so much – as American politicians long ago realised.

The predominance of individuals inhibited the transformation of movements into structured political organisations, and parties were often little more than vehicles to project the personalities of the leader. This afflicted 'Travkin's' DPR, and was markedly the case with the Russian Democratic Reform Movement (RDRM), a movement made up of generals and few soldiers. The historical tradition of Russian *krugovshchina*, the tendency for political movements to fracture around dominant personalities, appeared to have reasserted itself. Few parties remained unaffected by splits, with Demrossiya in a constant state of disintegration and reformation. There were, by definition, few professional politicians in the anti-communist movement, and their amateurish enthusiasm, polarised world view and inability to compromise marked the first phase of post-communist politics. In this respect the CPRF differed significantly, and organisation compensated for Zyuganov's rather dour personality.

The drain of the most active and able people into the new administrative structures hampered the emergence of a party system. The most talented of the 'democrats' entered the new post-communist bureaucracy in executive or legislative structures, and had little time to devote to their parties. Indeed, Popov cited this as one of the reasons for his resignation as mayor in June 1992, and he pledged to devote himself to the RDRM.[85] At the same time, most parties were marked by limited recruitment. The post-communist model of parties as electoral organisations focused on parliamentary life and party-list elections undermined the need for large constituency organisations. The large numbers involved in the demonstrations, marches and so on during the insurgent 'movement' phase of party formation was not translated into party membership in the second phase of 'pseudo-partification', even more so as political mobilisation declined dramatically once the old system fell.

There were plenty of 'divan' parties, whose membership would fit on to one sofa, and the first wave of what we call pseudo-parties withered away. Only the CPRF became a mass party, with its half million members in 1995 probably double the membership of all other parties taken together. By 1994 only 3 per cent of adults were members of any of the parties, movements and associations.[86] Party affiliation was remarkably low, with only 31 per cent in June 1991 identifying with a party, a percentage that fell sharply once the CPSU was disbanded.[87] Disillusioned by cross-ideological alliances, reflecting too often opportunism rather than principle, society was depoliticised. However, the surpisingly high 64.5 per cent turnout for the referendum of 25 April 1993, and the equally surprisingly high support for Yeltsin and his policies,[88] would suggest that this withdrawal was from party politics, narrowly defined, rather than from politics in general. This was broadly confirmed by the 1993 election, with an official turnout of 54.8 per cent exceeding expectations, and once again in December 1995 the turnout of 64 per cent and in June 1996 69 per cent suggested an active engagement in the political process by a significant proportion of the population.

An open political 'market' emerged in Russia, not monopolised by any single party or category of parties, but the potential market finds very strong 'consumer' resistance to joining parties and political activism. Two sets of reasons can be postulated to explain this resistance. The first looks to the emerging parties, which have been fractious and incompetent in achieving mass appeal; while the second suggests that however effective parties might be, in existing post-communist conditions there are few takers, explained by such factors as alienation because of the Bolshevik experience, the struggle to survive, and the charismatic type of politics that have emerged, focused on presidential politics. Social cleavages characteristic of the early part of the century, based on class, religious and regional politics, have largely been superseded. The traditional class structure had been overturned, organisations and associations destroyed, and quasi-political forms of mobilisation instituted that tend to weaken political participation.

The absence of a recognisable social base to the new political parties was perhaps the single most important factor inhibiting the development of party politics. New parties in Russia suffered a two-fold estrangement: from the social and political interests that they claimed to represent; and from the coherent formulation of a forward-looking policy taking into account actually existing realities rather than an ideologised version of what should be. This double disassociation inhibited the consolidation of a coherent governing coalition or an effective opposition. The disjuncture between marrying an ideology to an organisation and a social group was stark; the absence of real social subjects, who could express their interests imbued politics with vacuous personality teasing. The ruptured fabric of society provided a thin skein on which to develop art, literature and culture in general, and the institutions of political society in particular. Ludmilla Alekseeva, for example, notes that 'The role of political parties among workers is extremely small.'[89] In an ironic version of 'catching up and overtaking', and indeed of 'combined and uneven development', post-communist Russia displayed the symptoms of an advanced 'post-modern' social structure while stamped by the homogenising legacy of totalitarianism. The whole notion of the 'social interest' is diffuse, while sectarian versions of the 'national interest' have, to date, gained little support.

Against the background of a homogenised social landscape, the actual structure of the Russian social terrain is extraordinarily complex. Post-communist political life is even more fractured than the 'post-modern' and 'post-industrial' societies of the West. The extreme pluralism that might be expected to emerge in these conditions is likely to give rise to a permanently fractured party system and unstable democratic politics.[90] While numerous groups existed, it is probably premature to talk of interest group politics: few generated a homogeneous 'interest' and politics was not as yet 'subsystem dominant'. The weakness of the state did not necessarily mean the strength of society but indicated a general crisis of political institutions and civil associations in post-communist Russia.

The increasingly regional character of Russian politics suggested that conditions were lacking for the development of a mass national political party. Mndoyants and Salmin note that 'Russian parties are not complete formations. Sections in Moscow and organisations in the provinces can differ substantially over ideological and other matters.' One and the same party labels could mean very different things to people in various parts of the country.[91] No single party could hope to encompass the regional, national, ethnic, class, group, elite and other cleavages in society, and nor could a single party mediate the multiple social forces, processes and ideologies that buffeted intellectual life. The sheer size of the country made it difficult to constitute a genuinely national party covering not only the major cities but also provincial towns, rural areas and the national republics.

While the centre–periphery cleavage in Russia has lost none of its force, the language of 'national self-determination' has become compromised while regional political organisations have been weak. The establishment of the Urals Transformation of the Fatherland bloc by Eduard Rossel, the governor of Sverdlovsk oblast, in 1995 was the first serious regional organisation. By contrast, Catalan aspirations after Franco found a strong and self-sufficient party ready to express them. Parties based on ethnic politics are wholly delegitimated, while those in favour of new state identities are as yet weak. In Tatarstan, for example, in the forefront of the struggle for autonomy if not yet independence, the leading role is taken not by a party but by a social movement, the Tatarstan Social Centre (TOTs) based, like most nineteenth century national movements, overwhelmingly on the intelligentsia. The case of Chechnya is a maverick one in all respects and can hardly be fitted in to our perspective of party-building.

The distinction between parties in government and those in opposition was unclear, and instead a syncretic political process predominated. Russia's Choice was established as the party of government, yet ministers in that very same government were members of oppositional parties. In the 1995 elections Russia Our Home managed the remarkable feat of presenting itself as the party of government while at the same time criticising the shortcomings of that very same government. Yeltsin's attempts to achieve political consensus by administrative means, as in his Charter for Civic Accord of April 1994, reaffirmed his commitment to a vision of social harmony in which contestatory parties were to be subordinated to the national interest. The Accord reflected Yeltsin's traditional incomprehension about the operation of a multiparty system and his attempts to incorporate active political forces into a dynamic and mobile form of consensus politics run from the top. Yeltsin's apparent attempt to bring in the CPRF by offering them places in a coalition government was in keeping with the inclusionary tendencies of the regime system.[92]

PARTIES AND THE MULTIPARTY SYSTEM

Russia is undergoing a state and nation-building endeavour that matches any in history, yet the language and processes defining this transition remain indistinct. New cleavages have emerged, based above all between those able and willing to take advantage of the new more risk-oriented society and those committed or dependent on security-oriented policies, but these cleavages are only beginning to take party political forms. The social basis of the August regime is strong where people can take advantage of the new opportunities, like the industrial north, Moscow, St Petersburg and Nijhnii Novgorod.

The current fever of party formation has much in common with Russia's first attempt to establish a multiparty system between 1905 and 1917. The dominance of individuals, the relative lack of influence on government, shifting leadership alliances, poor ties with the mass membership, wild sloganeering and the tendency for abstract ideological demands to take the place of immediate political programmes, are all reminiscent of the earlier period.[93] In addition, the upsurge of party formation and hopes for a fundamental constitutionalisation of Russian politics during the period 1904–7 was ultimately inhibited by the reconstitution of imperial power;[94] and likewise the insurgency phase of party formation up to 1991 was eventually constrained by the emergence of the regime system. The question why the Bolsheviks, being only one among many political parties, were able to come to power and establish a one-party system, has been faced directly as a warning of what might come of Russia's contemporary bacchanalia of party formation and mutation.[95] According to a survey ranging from 1917 to 1990, the central feature of Russian party formation has been the absence of a broad social basis and the presence of archaic monolithicity in both Tsarist and Bolshevik forms combined with statist forms of industrial development.[96]

The formative phase of a social formation is indeed crucial, and, as in so many other spheres, insurgency, polarisation, adaptation and differentiation politics each left their mark on Russian party formation. The manner in which the old regime dissolved gave rise to a distinctive establishment phase. The legacy of the unprecedented concentration of political power and claims to ideological predominance by the CPSU provided an inauspicious terrain for parties to claim a share in power. Post-communist Russian politics does not operate on a *tabula rasa* but in a context where traditional social institutions and groups try to preserve their position while challenged by new social actors. The deceptive ease with which the old regime finally fell masked the resilience of the former structures, both formal (e.g. the nomenklatura elite) and informal (mafia-type structures). Kulik noted the emergence of a vicious circle in which parties developed but were weak because of the 'post-totalitarian condition of Russia', while society could not be democratically integrated into the state without powerful parties.[97]

In the insurgency phase mobilisation took place largely on ideological grounds, whereas during the polarisation and adaptation phases this shifted to a variety of forms but was marked by the weakness of organised social groups in civil society coming together to seek political representation. The fluid politics associated with the insurgency phase continued into later years. The negative connotations of the concept of 'party' led many groups to call themselves 'unions', 'movements' or 'associations'. The general revulsion against Bolshevik organisational practices converted democratic centralism into democratic disorganisation: most parties avoided rigorous membership criteria, and allowed both group and individual membership. This led to many peculiar situations in which, for example, an individual in the regions could maintain simultaneously their membership of Demrossiya and the DPR, even though the latter at the national level had left the movement in November 1991. Another feature of insurgency and polarisation politics was the weakness of the link between parties and political representation in legislative bodies. A great mass of deputies had been swept into the soviets as part of the democratic tide of 1990, yet as individuals they lacked a structured political identity and as a mass reflected the amorphousness of the party system in its entirety. Above all, the politics of insurgency were marked by the ability of groups and leaders to achieve victories and fame with relatively small organisational, membership and, indeed, financial, resources. Parties were stamped by the formative stage and largely remained elitist organisations with a fairly small mass base and fluid organisational structures.

The polarisation phase marked the transition from an expanding political community to the restriction of political activism to a relatively small but bitterly divided elite in which regional and other forms of cleavage in effect failed to gain autonomous party representation. The adaptation phase at last allowed political conflict to be conducted within political institutions, while relations between institutions were formalised by the new constitution. The differentiation phase began to bring ideology, social interests and party structures into alignment. The inescapable conclusion, however, is that Russia remained distant from a real multiparty system, and that as the dust settled on frenetic party formation and reformation the country was left with only one genuine party – the Communist Party, inherited from the previous age.

The party-political system remains the weakest link in the new state. The relationship between voter preferences and the formation of the government remains unclear. There are no more than a handful of serious parties; apart from the CPRF doubts remain over the viability of Yabloko, Russia our Home and the LDPR, while most of the others are pseudo-parties. One cannot, however, adopt a too rigid definition of parties in the Russian context for the simple reason that 'parties' as such are only one among a multiplicity of forms of political mobilisation. In elections all sorts of movements, including trade unions and women's organisations, participate (usually as part of a larger electoral bloc), together with ideologically-motivated voter's clubs, associated umbrella movements like Demrossiya, and numerous *ad-hoc* groupings of individuals. The veteran human rights activist Kronid Lyubarskii goes so far as to argue that 'the attempt to conduct "party" elections in an atomised and essentially "non-party" country failed'. Instead of allowing parties to represent the interests of specific social groups, the elections only contributed to the political chaos and allowed full rein to the ambitions of individual leaders, and the resulting parliament in his view did not reflect the real balance of forces in society.[98]

Party development in Russia reflects in an exaggerated form processes common to most post-communist countries.[99] How can we explain the amorphousness of Russian party development? Is there something specifically post-totalitarian inhibiting the development of an effective party system, or is the problem broader, reflecting a general crisis of party systems in mature industrial democracies? Classical analyses, notably that of Stein Rokkan, attribute the features of emerging party systems to the cleavage lines generated by the great processes of nation and state building: workers and capitalists, church and state, centre and periphery, giving rise to certain categories of parties (socialist, Christian, conservative, liberal and so on), although the correspondence between the cleavage and a particular party may be based on any number of independent variables.[100] In addition, according to Rokkan, there is an extraordinary continuity in the political alignments and party systems in Europe between those of the 1920s and the 1960s, suggesting that parties first in the game capture most of the resources available to support a party (voter loyalty, programmes and so on) leaving the system 'frozen' and making it very difficult for new parties to break in, irrespective of the changes that may have transformed society.[101] Rokkan suggested differing processes of political mobilisation between the establishment phase of party alignment and the continuity phase, with changes later tending to be channelled through existing parties rather than through the establishment of new ones. Russia is still far from this, and rather than being 'frozen', Russia's party scene remains excessively fluid.

It is often asserted that Russian political culture is hostile to the emergence of political parties because of a popular commitment to collective values and a predilection for a single authoritative source of political authority.[102] Our argument is that it is not Russia's political culture but the specific conditions under which the multiparty system emerged that provided its essential characteristics. The general debilitation of all social forces was compensated by the emergence of regime governance. The latter could have been institutionalised in the form of one-party predominance if, instead of taking the presidential path, Yeltsin's insurgency had transformed itself into a single governing party, possibly something akin to Mexico's Party of the Institutionalised Revolution (PRI). This outcome was improbable, however, given Russia's inchoate and loosely structured insurgency.

The travails of party development in Russia are perhaps part of the apparent general crisis, or at least the 'unfreezing', of parties in European politics.[103] The shift from materialist to post-materialist preferences in the value system of voters and the eclipsing of parties by new forms of participation such as social movements and alternative forms of political communication (such as television), have given rise to a new volatility in established party systems. The fluidity, and possibly indeed exhaustion, of existing party political systems has been exacerbated by the demise of the bloc politics associated with the Cold War that provided an artificial environment sustaining continuities that might otherwise have given way to new forms of voter alignment and political participation. In particular, the old cleavage between left and right lost its force in the confused modern political terrain, and the idea of the left as a party has certainly come to an end.[104] The age of mass parties appears to be over, and parties in general appear to be obsolete as vehicles of popular mobilisation, regional and national identity, individual development, and, in the Russian context, even as instruments of power.

The secular–religious divide also appears in a new light in post-communist conditions, although it should be stressed that in the West, too, the party alignments derived from this cleavage are waning. In Russia the Orthodox Church had acquiesced in its own subservience to the regime, and this ambiguity tended to undermine its political and moral authority in the post-communist period. Even in Poland where the Catholic Church had been unambiguous in its call for political openness, the advanced secularisation of society prevented the emergence of a serious religiously based party in the aftermath of Solidarity. It might well appear that socialist movements, too, have had their day; a phenomenon of the late nineteenth to the late twentieth century inappropriate for the challenges facing the world entering the twenty-first century. As a response to modernisation, industrialisation and the onset of mass society, a reflection of resistance to the market economy and the secularisation and individualisation of social life, the apparent triumph of liberalism has left the distinctive features of alternative politics without an anchor. Both Christian and Social Democracy were responses to the traumas accompanying the rise of market capitalism but have found it difficult to sustain alternative policies in mature industrial societies.

In Russia, of course, the capitalist social formation is only now emerging and their critiques are acutely relevant. Their weakness, therefore, is all the more mystifying. Part of the answer lies in the perceived problem of lack of choice, of which regime politics was both a cause and consequence. In the early stages of party formation the monolithicity of the CPSU was reproduced in an inverted form by the emerging oppositional movements, united only in their desire to destroy the communist monopoly. This negative unity was perpetuated after the fall of the regime by a commitment to the broad principle of creating a market system in Russia, even those movements which evinced a growing suspicion of capitalism being unable to sustain an effective alternative programme. In this limited sense we can argue that post-communist party formation was inhibited by the post-historical period in which it was born, using history in the sense argued by Fukuyama, namely the absence of a universal alternative to liberal capitalist modernity.[105]

The general crisis of parties, however, also has deeper causes. While post-modernism might well be an over-used and abused term, it does nevertheless signal problems characteristic of our times. In particular, the fusion of microprocessing technology and communications has accelerated the creation of an information society in which politics has become ever more spectral, reduced to the level of images and attractions that have little relation to the irreducible realities of public life. As Jacques Derrida has noted, the media has rendered the professional politician 'structurally incompetent' by generating a set of demands associated with performance-on-air and image-projection, and at the same time a political space has been formed that displaces parties and parliaments.[106] Parties are an expression of the attempt to institutionalise the diverse interests of civil society but, given the fracturing of social activism today, there might be reasons to suspect that parties are no longer the predominant political vehicle for this process. The consolidation of democracy appears to be a far broader process than the formation of a multiparty system; parties are only one aspect of the representative structure of complex democratic societies.[107] Thus the formation of a structured party system in Russia is inhibited by the intrinsic weakness of civil society, the rise of new forms of representing social interests, the fragmentation of 'interests' themselves, and the dissolution of the art of representative politics. The 'American exception' – the absence of ideologically defined mass parties of the socialist sort – has now become the norm.

5 Electoral politics

For forms of government let fools contest,
That which is best administered is best.

Alexander Pope[1]

Elections play a crucial part in the development of a democratic society, but in and of themselves they do not denote the achievement of democracy, defined here as popular control over the executive through effective representation in a legislature. There remains a question over the degree to which popular sovereignty has been achieved and, indeed, over the very definition of popular sovereignty in the context of regime politics. The relationship between election results and the formation of governments is by no means clear-cut.

THE EXPERIENCE OF ELECTIONS

Despite flaws in their conception and implementation, elections have nevertheless played an important part in the development of Russian democracy. Unlike most other post-communist countries, relatively free elections were held in Russia some two years *before* the fall of communism. This gave rise to a peculiar amalgamation of the structures and elites of the old regime with a novel legitimacy derived from their partial adaptation to democratic electoral politics. This hybrid system, in which change was led largely from within the system itself, marginalised the democratic insurgency and helped insulate the regime from the usual effects of electoral politics. Below we shall briefly review the experience of elections in Russia, and then analyse some of their key features.

The emergence of electoral politics

Competitive, if not yet multiparty, elections were the centrepiece of Gorbachev's liberalisation programme. Rather than relegitimising the Soviet system, however, they acted as a powerful vector contributing to its dissolution. The first attempt at competitive elections was in the local soviet elections of 1987, where some 5 per cent of seats were fought in multi-candidate contests.[2] The elections in spring 1989 to the new USSR Congress of People's Deputies (CPD) marked an important new stage in competitive elections, but the choices were limited. We have noted (chapter 1) the role that the spring 1989 elections played in revealing popular hostility to the old regime. The actual operation of the Soviet 'parliament', moreover, revealed the limitations of 'perestroika democracy', a legacy that also impeded the development of genuine parliamentarianism in Russia later.

Russian republican elections, 1990

The Russian parliamentary elections of 4 March 1990 (with the second round on 18 March) marked an important stage in the development of the democratic insurgency and, of greater long-term importance, the shaping of a distinctively Russian political identity. The vessel of democratic politics was no longer the USSR but 'Russia', or as the democrats tended to put it at the time, 'the country'. Only Russia retained the two-tier legislature, and the elections were to a 1,068-member CPD, which in turn selected a smaller Supreme Soviet responsible for current parliamentary matters. Constitutional and other high policy matters were the prerogative of the Congress.

Following widespread criticism of the 1989 elections, the electoral system was modified to remove some of the filters on the nomination of candidates, abolishing the pre-electoral district meetings and the bloc of seats reserved for 'social organisations'.[3] This allowed a wave of independent candidates to be nominated, supported by numerous voters' associations established in the wake of the disappointments of the previous year. This did not prevent numerous violations, with nominated independent candidates arbitrarily being refused registration, preventing their names being placed on the ballots, and with fraudulent counting in areas beyond the supervision of independent observers. The democrats' strength lay in industrial regions and cities, whereas in the countryside the apparatus was able to push its candidates through.[4] There is little evidence, however, of widespread fraud, especially since the electorate had become more politicised since the previous year, partly by the spectacle of the televised Soviet CPD debates. The adaptation of communist elites to democratic procedures (and indeed, the adaptation of democratic proceduralism to the constraints of regime politics) is a characteristic feature of the transition in Russia.

The Communist Party was still the only party represented in the Russian legislative elections of March 1990, but by then it was so divided, with leaders of the opposition still officially members, that it would be fair to characterise the elections as non-party. The elections of March 1990 were contested by four broad groupings: Russian nationalists and neo-Stalinists, who made relatively little impact but began to forge an alliance that would take them to the coup; communist traditionalists supporting Leninist politics, above all the maintenance of the one-party state and the command economy, who would in June 1990 act as the driving force behind the creation of the fundamentalist RSFSR Communist Party; reform communists, supporting Gorbachev's perestroika; and self-styled 'democrats', made up of neformaly and some prominent public figures (above all Yeltsin himself), organised under the broad umbrella of Democratic Russia (Demrossiya).

The elections were semi-free, in the sense that the media was still largely dominated by the old regime and traditional structures of Party influence were still firmly in place, but the common image that the deputies were no more than communist stooges, with a sprinkling of democrats, is not altogether accurate. Deputies were elected if they received more than 50 per cent of the votes cast, and for the vote to be valid there had to be at least a 50 per cent turn out. Candidates stood unopposed in only thirty-three constituencies (3 per cent, compared to 10 per cent – 147 out of 1,500 – the previous year), and in 906 there were more than three candidates. Almost 80 per cent of candidates had to go through to a second round.[5] Although

86.3 per cent of the deputies elected were communists, the CPSU did not stand as a united party and communists in the majority of constituencies competed against each other. Only 1,061 deputies were elected, seven having failed to attract 50 per cent of the electorate.[6] Deputies from the national territories were not necessarily members of the titular ethnic group, and indeed the nomenklatura in 1990 found them a safe haven from the democratic storm.[7]

The 'democrats' could count on about 350 seats in the new assembly. Democratic candidates in Moscow took 57 out of 64 seats, and 28 out of 44 in St Petersburg. In elections to local soviets held at the same time democrats won 240 out of the 400 seats available in the Leningrad Soviet, and in the Moscow Soviet Democratic Russia bloc took 280 out of the 500 seats in the first round.

The electoral gap and referendum, August 1991–December 1993

Schmitter has noted that 'what definitely is most peculiar about Russia's transition is the role that elections have (not) played in it'.[8] This is not quite accurate, since the elections to the Soviet Congress in March 1989, to the Russian Congress a year later, and the presidential elections of June 1991, were defining moments in the dissolution of the old order and the emergence of the new. Nevertheless, the absence of general elections for some two years following the coup, at a time of accelerated political development, is remarkable. The absence of elections reflected the logic of the Russian transition, above all attempts to maintain its consensual and evolutionary nature. In the by-elections that were held at this time attempts to fill vacancies failed because of the inability to reach the 50 per cent threshold against the background of popular apathy and disillusionment with the unseemly struggle between president and parliament.

The question remains, however, of why no elections were held after the coup in autumn 1991, when Yeltsin's popularity was at its peak and the 'democrats' could have been expected to cruise home. Fresh elections would no doubt have promoted the development of a genuine multiparty system, relegitimised the Russian state and assisted the development of state institutions. Numerous factors inhibited this strategy. First, the Russian Supreme Soviet had played an enthusiastic part in the defeat of the coup, and it would have been a poor reward for it to be dissolved at the first opportunity. The CPD, moreover, appeared willing to go along with Yeltsin's plans, above all with his priorities for radical economic reform and a new constitution, and at its meeting from late October 1991 granted him yet more powers to impose economic reforms by decree. Second, before elections could be held it was clear that there would have to be a drastic reorganisation of Russian representative institutions, above all the abolition of the unwieldy Congress.

Third and most importantly, the relegitimation of Russia's representative institutions would have placed the development of the presidency at risk. Russia at this time was still a parliamentary republic and Yeltsin's powers were enjoyed only insofar as they were delegated by the legislature: and what was delegated could be revoked. Finally, elections at this time would have reinforced Yeltsin's dependency on Democratic Russia and the 'democratic' movement as a whole; and as a corollary, the deepening of the democratic revolution would have entailed an assault against the nomenklatura class, something Yeltsin was loathe to do since he soon came to rely on precisely these managerial and administrative elites. Yeltsin tactically marginalised Democratic Russia and the democratic movement as a whole, and they exercised little influence on appointments:[9] at times of crisis, however, he was not above calling on them as his footsoldiers in the struggle against the current enemy.

As the tension between the president and parliament intensified, Democratic Russia prepared to collect the one million signatures required to hold a referendum that could prepare the way for pre-term parliamentary elections. In the event, despite numerous threats, Yeltsin procrastinated. Only when relations had thoroughly deteriorated did Yeltsin seek to renew his popular mandate. The referendum of 25 April 1993 gave people four choices: support for president Yeltsin; support for his economic policies; and whether they favoured early presidential and parliamentary elections. The Ninth CPD stipulated that the vote required 50 per cent of the registered voters (not just a simple majority of those taking part) to be binding, but following an appeal the Constitutional Court ruled that only the last two questions required the higher threshold since they involved constitutional issues. In the event the turnout (64.5 per cent) and support for Yeltsin was higher than expected (see appendix 2.4). Yeltsin received a ringing personal endorsement, with some 59 per cent of the turnout expressing confidence in him, and even his policies, despite the hardship they had caused, were supported by 53 per cent of the vote. The 49 per cent vote for pre-term presidential elections and the thumping 67 per cent (43 per cent of the electorate) for early parliamentary elections, however, were not binding since they failed to reach the required 50 per cent of registered voters.

Elections and referendum of 12 December 1993

Only after the October 1993 events did Russia embark on its first genuine multiparty electoral campaign, but the circumstances were hardly propitious for a fair and honest election.[10] The referendum, however, provided Russia with a constitution which, despite its many flaws, established the ground rules for a democratic political process and the development of genuine parliamentarianism while at the same time defending liberal principles of human rights and the separation of powers (see chapter 3). The principle of popular sovereignty, at the heart of the democratic insurgency against the communist regime, was reaffirmed. The results, however, revealed the profound divisions in Russian society and the absence of consensus over many key issues. The absence of a clear majority in parliament, paradoxically, promoted the parliamentarianisation of Russian politics by forcing the development of consensual forms of government.

Yeltsin's decree of 21 September 1993 'On Gradual Constitutional Reform in the Russian Federation' dissolved the Russian CPD and the Supreme Soviet and transferred their powers to a new bicameral Federal Assembly, and simultaneously suspended the operation of the old constitution.[11] The existing Federation Council was vested with the functions of the upper chamber of the Assembly, while elections to the new lower chamber, the State Duma, were to take place on 12 December 1993. Accompanying the decree were acts establishing the electoral system.[12] The new legislature and the rules regulating its election were thus born in a process that was both unconstitutional and anti-constitutional. This irregular procedure, while breaking the impasse in the struggle between the Supreme Soviet and the presidency, undermined the development of a legal basis to Russian government. During the course of the campaign, moreover, the rules governing the election and the referendum were modified by the president, further undermining their legitimacy.[13] The duration of the new legislature, moreover, was reduced from four to two years.

By a decree of 15 October voters were asked to participate in a plebiscite on the constitution.[14] The support of the majority of the registered electorate, as stipulated by the 16

October 1990 referendum law, was no longer required for adoption but simply 50 per cent of those who voted,[15] although the minimum 50 per cent turnout was retained. The draft constitution was published on 10 November, and the question placed on the ballot paper on 12 December was a simple one: 'Do you support the adoption of the new Russian constitution?'. This method of adopting the constitution is clearly open to criticism.[16] The use of the plebiscite is the favoured technique of dictators, and the judgement of a simple 'yes' or 'no' to a complex question is hardly the most democratic way of adopting such a crucial document; this was the method employed, however, by De Gaulle in 1958 to adopt the constitution establishing the Fifth Republic in France.

Some 106.2 million citizens were eligible to vote and the official turnout figure of 54.8 per cent was rather lower than anticipated, but exceeded the 50 per cent threshold (see appendix 2.5).[17] Official figures show that the constitution was supported by 58.43 per cent of the vote; while 41.6 voted against it.[18] Only 30.7 per cent of the total electorate voted in favour, and in seventeen republics and regions the constitution was rejected.[19] While the majority of the republics supported its adoption, even though their claims to sovereignty were excluded, the closeness of the vote weakens the constitution's legitimacy. The constitution came into force on 12 December 1993, although it was only officially published in the Russian media on 25 December;[20] 12 December is now a national holiday, Constitution Day.

According to the new constitution (article 95.2), the Federation Council consists of one representative each from executive and legislative authorities in the federal components. This laid up a whole minefield of potential problems since the relationship between *ex officio* membership and changes in local administration was not clear. Was the membership of the Council to be changed each time a local leader was changed? After the October events Yeltsin decided that the Federation Council's first convocation would be elected.[21] Two seats were available in each of Russia's 89 republics, regions, federal cities and other federal areas; a total of 494 candidates fought directly for seats in the 178-seat upper house. Some 40 per cent of candidates to the Federation Council were leaders of executive authorities and 16 per cent were heads of legislatures.[22] The elections to the Federation Council, were conducted almost entirely on an individual rather than a party basis.

The electoral system for the State Duma first tried out in December 1993 differed from Soviet practices in three main ways. First, instead of a simple first-past-the-post system, a mixed proportional and majoritarian system was adopted, with half the seats to the 450-member State Duma to be elected from single-member constituencies and the rest to be chosen on a proportional basis from federal party-lists. This drew on German experience but was adapted to Russian conditions. The old majority electoral system used in Russia up to that time was unusual, with most other other post-communist countries having reverted to the proportional systems prevalent before communism, and indeed the elections in November 1917 to the Constituent Assembly had been proportional. Second, the method of nominating candidates was changed from the Soviet emphasis on labour collectives and gatherings of electors to a uniform system of gathering signatures. Candidates simply had to gather enough signed support to be registered. Third, the subject of the electoral process changed from amorphous labour collectives to electoral associations and blocs. All three changes were intended to promote the development of a party-political system in Russia.[23] The abolition of the second round in single-member districts was particularly criticised, but according to a study by Alexander Sobyanin it is unlikely that its retention would have made much difference to the results in December 1993.[24]

Michael Urban calls the new system 'democracy by design', whereby 'those in control of the state machinery attempt to shape the institutions and procedures of a competitive election in ways that ensure an outcome favorable to the designers themselves'.[25] The whole history of the evolution of British (and much of European) democracy is, of course, based on this principle, but in the Russian case the attempt to shape the rules to the advantage of the ruling elite had an effect opposite to that intended. The increase in the proportion of Duma deputies elected from party-lists from the earlier proposed one-third, to a half, for example, was condemned by independent democrats as liable to exaggerate the support of certain blocs:[26] a warning borne out by events – Zhirinovskii's LDPR topped the party-list vote but won only five seats in single-member constituencies. To stand, a party or bloc required at least 100,000 nominations, with no more than 15,000 signatures drawn from any one of Russia's 89 regions and republics, so that the bloc or party had to have demonstrable support in at least seven.[27] This provision was designed to stimulate the creation of a national party system and to avoid the dominance of Moscow, and at the same time to force the creation of larger blocs to overcome the fragmentation of Russian political life. According to Victor Sheinis, one of the main architects of the new electoral law,[28] the aim was to ensure that local leaders did not exercise an undue influence on the elections.[29]

A representation threshold was incorporated into the party-list system to prevent the proliferation of small parties. To enter parliament a party had to take at least 5 per cent of the national vote, with the whole country considered one giant constituency. It was assumed that this would give reformist candidates an advantage since their natural strength in the big cities, above all in Moscow and St Petersburg, would counteract the conservatism of rural areas. In contrast to earlier practice the elections were to be held in one round, thus abolishing run-off contests, and the old minimum turnout requirement of 50 per cent was reduced to 25 per cent. To be elected a candidate had to poll not, as before, the majority of votes (50 per cent plus one) but simply gain more votes than rivals as long as the minimum turnout requirement was met. The Central Electoral Commission (CEC) headed by Ryabov monitored the whole process. The CEC itself became a permanent agency and was later dubbed 'the ministry of elections'.[30]

Candidates required a minimum of 1 per cent nominations to enter the contest in single-member districts unless they had been nominated officially by one of the party blocs, in which case the necessity of obtaining what on average was 4–5,000 signatures was waived. Coming soon after the October events, the requirement that the passport number had to be included alarmed many potential signatories and made canvassing by opposition groups difficult. In the event, 1,586 candidates contested the elections in Russia's 225 single-member constituencies.[31]

The other 225 seats in the State Duma were distributed to the parties on a proportional basis as long as they cleared the 5 per cent threshold. By September 1993 thirty-seven political parties and over 2,000 public organisations had been officially registered in Russia,[32] although the CEC issued a list with only ninety-one all-Russian political and social organisations with the right to nominate candidates.[33] Electoral associations had to register with the CEC at least six weeks before the election, by midnight 6 November, having provided the minimum 100,000 signatures. Groups allied to the National Salvation Front, which had played a central role in the insurgency of October 1993, were banned from participating in the election, as was Victor Anpilov's militant Russian Communist Workers' Party (RCWP); but so too initially were two more mainstream parties, the CPRF and Rutskoi's People's Party of Free Russia.[34] Subsequently the Ministry of Justice allowed the CPRF and individuals from the other banned groups to stand.

Thirty-one associations scrambled to form electoral blocs in time for the deadline, and twenty-one sought to find the required list of nominations. There are many suggestions that the authorities hindered the signature campaign, amid allegations that the police detained oppositional activists and confiscated the signatures that they had managed to collect.[35] The Russian All-People's Union (ROS), headed by Yeltsin's bitter opponents Sergei Baburin and Nikolai Pavlov, claimed that the police had raided its offices and stolen some 20,000 signatures and impeded their campaign in other ways.[36] They failed to qualify, although Baburin fought the election as an individual candidate in his native Omsk, and won. In sum, eight out of the twenty-one blocs were turned down by the CEC after the documents were checked. Thirteen 'electoral associations' (the official name given them by the CEC) were allowed to proceed, fielding a total of 1,717 candidates, giving a grand total of 3,797 candidates in all categories.[37]

If, during the April 1993 referendum some 60 per cent of voters supported Yeltsin and some 40 per cent the opposition, by December 1993 the picture had changed (see appendix 2.5). The two explicitly pro-government parties, Russia's Democratic Choice and PRES, jointly polled 22.2 per cent of the vote, less than the LDPR alone. The total opposition vote now reached 43.2 per cent (22.9% LDPR, 12.4%, CPRF, and 7.9% APR); whereas the proportion voting for the 'democrats' (both in power and in opposition) had fallen to 33.2 per cent (15.5% Russia's Choice, 7% Yabloko, 6.7% PRES and 4% Sobchak); while the Women of Russia bloc (8%) inclined towards the communists, and Travkin's DPR (5.5%) and the Civic Union (1.9%) sought to occupy what appeared to be a disappearing centre. Another interpretation, of course, for the weak performance of the openly centrist parties is that all the others now moved to occupy 'centrist' positions – all, that is, with the exception of Zhirinovskii's LDPR.

The failure to collect 100,000 signatures eliminated a number of important groupings from the election itself, while the establishment of a 5 per cent threshold excluded from parliament parties which together won 8.7 per cent of the total vote. There were, moreover, persistent claims that the vote was marked by widespread fraud. The main accusation is that regional administrations, which in these elections organised the local electoral commissions, exaggerated voter turnout in order to ensure that the 50 per cent threshold for the adoption of the constitution was exceeded.[38] Sobyanin argues that the results to the Federation Council were the most distorted, while those to the State Duma in the single-member constituencies the least, with some 9.2 million ballot papers allegedly falsified in one way or another. Local heads of administration sought to ensure victory to the Federation Council by raising their vote but were then forced to alter the tallies in the other three votes to ensure a correspondence between the turnout and votes cast, and thus they added votes to what they thought would be the less noticeable variants, above all the LDPR.[39] Changes in the number of registered electors remain unexplained.[40] The CEC finally came up with a figure of 106.17 million in its results published on 15 February, yet the figure of registered voters given earlier was 105.28 million.[41] Even the new figure fell short of the 107.31 million registered for the referendum of 25 April 1993.[42] What had happened to over a million voters? There had been no demographic dip in the birthrate a generation earlier, and if anything, since April 1993 the Russian population had increased as refugees and migrants came in from the former Soviet republics.

Any judgement on the political situation in Russia based on these elections must be tempered by the relative arbitrariness of the results. If the elections had been held only on a proportional system, the LDPR would have been the single largest group; but if the old two-stage single-member system had been retained, the LDPR would hardly have figured. While support for reformist candidates remained strong in Moscow, St Petersburg and some other places, in the provinces their support fell sharply: by 15 per cent in Vologda oblast, in Vladimir oblast by ten per cent, and so on. Lyubarskii argues that the riddle is easily resolved: widespread fraud by the old Soviet apparatus. He insists that support for reformist forces had not declined but had probably increased.[43]

The results suggest a highly discerning and sophisticated pattern of voter behaviour, able to take advantage of the multiple voting choices offered by the interweaving of the various campaigns. The case of Nizhnii Novgorod illustrates some of the processes at work. In casting their ballots for the Federation Council and single-member candidates, voters supported local reformist candidates, but in voting for the LDPR in the party-list section the electorate was clearly signalling dissatisfaction with the overall course of government policy. Support for Zhirinovskii can also be interpreted as a sign of dissatisfaction with the Moscow elite that had come to power following the August coup.[44] The absence of a second round, moreover, reduced further the possibility of achieving a popular mandate in single-member constituencies. In many cases (as in Novosibirsk), if the total vote cast for reformist candidates is combined this exceeds the number of votes cast for oppositionists on the party lists. Thus the party-list vote was used as a classic instance of the 'protest' vote (dissatisfaction with national policies and so on); whereas in the single-member constituencies they voted *for* rather than *against* particular candidates and programmes.[45]

In this context, only tentative conclusions can be drawn from these elections: the confused results reflected genuine confusion in the Russian political scene. A large number were seduced by the promises of easy solutions and the restoration of Russia's Great Power status; but a solid bloc at the same time voted for the continuation of reforms. The populace had sent two mutually exclusive signals: in apparently accepting the constitution they were voting for stability; but in voting for the opposition they were rejecting the existing basis for order. The results can be interpreted as not only a protest vote against the 'monetarist' policies pursued by the liberals since late 1991, but perhaps above all against the political establishment that had come to power in Russia in the wake of the August 1991 coup. Political and social structures were separated from the realities of Russian life; the political order represented by the August regime did not reflect the inherent order of society. Aware of this, the August democrats had launched a revolution to establish their social base through rapid privatisation but they had been inhibited in carrying the revolution to its logical conclusion because the nature of their revolution was, by definition, anti-revolutionary and democratic. However, before the rejectionists could consolidate their victory they had to do more than reflect the desperation of society but also to lead it, and here their intellectual poverty forced them to accommodate to the 'centre'.

State Duma elections of 17 December 1995

Granted only a 2-year term, there were attempts to prolong the Fifth Duma's mandate. Ryabov, however, insisted that any delay would infringe the constitution,[46] and the view that the constitution would become meaningless if its provisions were altered at will by the political bureaucracy triumphed.[47] According to the constitution (article 84.a) the president sets the date for elections, an announcement that must be made at least four months before an election falls due; if the president fails to do this, then the electoral law gives the CEC the right. The elections were duly announced, although wrangling over the new electoral law continued up to the last minute, in particular over attempts to reduce the 5 per cent threshold.

The president's draft electoral law of November 1994 exempted groups already represented in the Duma from having to collect signatures to support their candidacy, a provision that was dropped later, as was the prohibition on candidates standing simultaneously in party-list and single-member elections. The presidential draft proposed reducing the proportion of those elected from party-lists from half to a third (returning to the original proposal in 1993), and while Vladimir Isakov (head of the Duma's legislative committee) admitted that there were solid grounds for this 'since the weight of parties in society is still not very high', he accepted that political realities prevented any change.[48]

The electoral law adopted in June 1995 forced party leaders to prune the number of Moscow-based politicians on the party-list to twelve, with the rest to be chosen from the regions. The law stipulated that only parties or movements registered six months before parliamentary elections could enter the campaign, thus drawing a clear cut-off point beyond which party formation would be pointless. The number of parties nevertheless proliferated to reach some 300 and engaged in frenetic bloc-making to collect signatures. The number of signatures now required for the registration of electoral associations doubled to 200,000, with no more than 7 per cent from any one of Russia's eighty-nine component units. To stand in a single-member district a candidate had to collect signatures from 1 per cent of the voters (which could count towards the 200,000 if the candidate was officially part of a bloc), and the candidate who gained a simple plurality of votes won.

The retention of the 225:225 split in the election and the unchanged minimum voter turnout threshold at 25 per cent signalled not only the strength of vested interests of the factions already in parliament but a continued commitment to the belief that a proportional system stimulates the development of parties. The retention of the 5 per cent threshold for party-list candidates to enter parliament, however, was bitterly contested on the grounds that a significant proportion of the vote might end up unrepresented in the Duma; instead, a 'representation threshold' was suggested by presidential aide Georgii Satarov whereby the threshold percentage would be gradually lowered until 75 per cent of votes cast were represented.[49] Sheinis defended the law on the grounds that tiny parties 'do not have the right to exist' and that it should encourage the creation of strong parties. He admitted that the lack of a second round in single-member districts was the electoral law's greatest flaw.[50]

Despite rhetorical allegiance to unity, splits continued among the party elites. The rule restricting central party lists to a maximum of twelve from Moscow limited the scope for coalitions, while large electoral blocs were inhibited by the rule that blocs had to re-register if one party left.[51] By the deadline of midnight 22 October, 43 out of the 69 electoral associations that had earlier signalled their intention to stand turned in their signatures.[52] This was still not the end of their travails, and the registration of some blocs was refused by the CEC on technical grounds. For obvious reasons Ryabov was keen to reduce the number of parties standing, but despite accusations that bans on groups like Yabloko and Derzhava were politically motivated it was more likely a case of bureaucratic pedantry.[53] The role of the courts in these elections was notable, with the Supreme Court ruling that groups, including Democratic Russia, were to be reinstated.

Each of the forty-three party-lists was headed by three names which appeared on the ballot paper, with a total of 5,670 candidates registered on the party-lists. The CEC registered 2,751 candidates in the single-member districts, an average of twelve for each of the 225 constituencies, one-third of whom were independents. The candidates on both systems included a pleiad of stars from the arts and entertainments. Some 370 military figures were registered as candidates, some 150 of whom were serving officers, with the majority aligning themselves with the opposition, although some well-known names appeared on the Russia Our Home (NDR) list and on Boris Gromov's 'My Fatherland' list.[54] Whereas General Alexander Lebed was forced to leave the army because of his political activites, General Rokhlin on the NDR list remained on active duty. The Ministry of Defence even went so far as to create a separate unit to support military candidates – in the event to little avail.

Why did the number of groups seeking to enter parliament proliferate? This extreme fragmentation was not simply a result of the leaders' ambitions, ideological differences, or the increased activity of special interest groups entering politics; it was, rather, a sign of a profound crisis in Russia's multiparty system. With the decline of the democratic insurgency and waning public interest in politics, parties came to represent only a few professional politicians, concerned mainly about their own status and position on the party-list. Focused entirely on elections, parties did not require a large number of activists or regional organisations: it was enough to have a few qualified organisers and resources to collect signatures and put up posters. The Communists were precisely distinguished from the others because they did not limit themselves to electoral work.[55]

The two-party system envisaged by Yeltsin in April 1995 had not materialised. Even more than in 1993, the 'democratic' part of the political spectrum fragmented into small groups. Party leaders calculated that by gaining access to free air time by heading a party-list group their chances in single-member districts would be enhanced; they thus placed their individual interests above those of the movement, something not restricted to the democratic camp.[56] The tactic worked for Irina Khakamada of Common Cause, returning to the Duma from a single-member district although her party failed to cross the threshold, as it did for Boris Fedorov from Forward Russia! (which sought to attract the patriotic as well as the democratic vote); for Vladimir Lysenko from the Pamfilova-Gurov-Lysenko Bloc (established in summer 1995 on the basis of the Republican Party of Russia which had earlier been part of Yabloko); and for Konstantin Borovoi from the Party of Economic Freedom. Gaidar's Russia's Democratic Choice – United Democrats failed to reach agreement with Yabloko, although they tried to avoid candidates in single-member districts standing against each other. The Democratic Russia movement headed by Lev Ponomarev at the last moment called for its supporters to vote for Yabloko.

The centre right was dominated by Chernomyrdin's NDR, while the centre left was much more crowded. Rybkin's Electoral Bloc went through several permutations and was challenged by a number of social democratic, trade union, and manufacturers' associations, as well as the Women of Russia bloc running with a federal list of eighty women.[57]

The left was dominated by the CPRF, the Agrarian Party of Russia headed by Mikhail Lapshin, and a number of extreme rejectionist parties, above all Victor Tyulkin's and Victor Anpilov's bloc Communists-Working Russia-For the Soviet Union. Zyuganov's CPRF came into the elections the beneficiary of the widespread discontent with the course of reforms and the victor in numerous regional elections. Gaidar, however, argued that the result of the elections would depend on the turnout and whether young people participated in the elections, insisting that communists lacked a political base among those under 30 years of age and were very weak among those aged between 30 and 40.[58] He noted that 'If our Communist Party were a good, charming reformist party of a social-democratic nature I would not attach any importance to the elections. But it requires enormous ignorance to confuse our Communist

Party with the reformist parties of Eastern Europe.'[59] Zyuganov rejected claims that his party appealed to the aged population, but agreed that his programme would be incompatible with the existing constitutional order: he proposed 'a constitution of soviet popular power' (*narodovlastie*), which he thought could be achieved by the 'popular-patriotic' victory in the polls.[60] The CPRF's electoral manifesto was more a blend of patriotic populism than communism, avoiding a commitment to specific Soviet policies while stressing the re-integration of the USSR. Zyuganov sought to reassure Western business that the CPRF would not destroy the private sector if it came to power.

The nationalist wing was once again dominated by Zhirinovskii's LDPR. It had won almost a quarter of the vote in 1993 but was now forced to share the national-patriotic vote with numerous other groups. Patriotic centrists were represented by the Congress of Russian Communities (*Kongress Russkikh obshchin*, KRO), whose leader was the former secretary of the Security Council, Yurii Skokov. Second on the list was General Lebed (retd), formerly commander of the Twelfth Army in Moldova, who made clear his presidential ambitions. The KRO had been established by Dmitrii Rogozin in 1993 but he had ceded first place later to Skokov. Lebed announced his entrance into active politics in April 1995, when he joined forces with Skokov, and he resigned his commission in May. There were tensions within the KRO, and in particular between Lebed and Skokov, who also nurtured presidential ambitions and allegedly noted that Lebed's 'education is inadequate. He is not ready yet to be president'.[61] Lebed's major advantage was that he was not tainted by association with the existing powers; his policies were more than a pale reflection of Zhirinovskii's: like the majority of candidates in these elections he promised to extirpate corruption and to resist Nato expansion; but unlike Zhirinovskii he unequivocally condemned chauvinism and refused to label himself a nation-alist, calling for Russia to be a state for all its peoples without a hierarchy of 'elder' or 'younger' brothers. He rejected the *velikoderzhavnost* (Great Power ambitions) of Russians and supported KRO's calls for a Union of Peoples.[62] His calls to restore order, with an 'iron fist' if necessary, appealed to the 80 per cent of Russians identified by Levada as placing order above democracy,[63] but at the same time insisted that 'it is impossible to build a state according to military principles'.[64] In late October 1995 he established his own movement 'Honour and Motherland' (*Chest' i Rodina*) whose aim was to reform the army and to 'restore a strong, peaceful and dynamically developing Russia'.[65]

One does not have to be a political scientist to note the 'farcical' elements in the December 1995 elections, hence the calls for postponement until a more sensible electoral law was adopted.[66] The law 'On the Status of Deputies' provided, extensive immunity, making Duma membership extremely attractive to criminals. The large number of parties running for seats in the Duma, according to Gaidar, demonstrated the immaturity of the Russian political system.[67] With the major exception of the CPRF, the campaign focused not so much on programmes but on personalities; with so many associations on the ballot, voters could only distinguish between them by identifying certain key individuals. Far too many associations stood and far too few entered the Sixth Duma (see appendix 2.6). Fears about the steepness of the 5 per cent threshold proved amply justified as only 50.5 per cent of the party-list votes were actually represented, indicating to some that the Sixth Duma was unrepresentative and illegitimate. As in 1993, the electoral system amplified the representation of the four parties making it over the threshold, and voters supporting the other thirty-nine blocs were in effect disenfranchised. With some 34 million votes in 1995 'wasted', the political tendencies that had formed in society were only partially reflected in the Duma. All of this once again raised the question of changing the electoral system: lowering the 5 per cent threshold; reducing the proportion of MPs elected from party-lists or abolishing the proportional part of the election entirely; and reintroducing a second round in single-member districts.

Gaidar had moved into opposition to the government, but his vote fell dramatically and Russia's Democratic Choice failed to cross the threshold. As for the 'democratic' opposition, Yabloko became the main standard-bearer of reformist policies in the Sixth Duma. As a newly established party, Russia Our Home did well to enter parliament at its first outing, but its weak showing in single-member constituencies revealed its inability to capitalise on its ruling status in the regions; indeed, its status as the 'party of power' was bitterly resented. In standing as the ruling party, Russia Our Home repeated the mistake of Russia's Choice in 1993, drawing upon itself the protest vote against the war in Chechnya and the social injustice arising from the reforms. Although the vote for 1995's party of power, Russia Our Home, had declined from the 15 per cent registered for Russia's Choice in 1993, this now appeared to be a more stable vote and a more stable faction in the Sixth Duma.

While the vote in 1993 for the LDPR represented the 'soft' backlash against the government's policies,[68] the vote for the CPRF in 1995 was the 'hard' backlash. The strong showing for the CPRF not only reflected anger at the suffering imposed on the population by the reforms but also a broader disenchantment with the post-August 1991 political order. It should be noted, however, that the CPRF's 22 per cent represented only 15.2 million votes: the total oppositional vote of some 37 per cent was less than in 1993, while the pro-reform parties' vote fell to 22 per cent. The LDPR's vote halved from that in 1993, yet, contrary to many predictions, successfully crossed the party-list threshold but won only one single-member seat. The failure of patriotic organisations like KRO to enter parliament was the greatest surprise of the elections. Ethnic Russian voters in the republics had been alienated by Skokov's attempt to create a Union of Peoples uniting moderate Russian nationalists with separatists from the non-Russian regions. In contrast to 1993, the 1995 electoral law set specific limits on campaign spending for parties and candidates, although these were clearly exceeded by some of the blocs.

Did the results mean the rejection of the whole polity established since 1991, or only protest against its policies? Despite the fluidity of the party scene the elections were accompanied by an upsurge in popular political interest, with voter turnout rising to 64 per cent, although most consider that voting is unlikely to change anything very much.[69] Institutionalised politics began to make an impact on public consciousness, although this politicisation tended to be more negative than positive in nature. The 1993 elections were characterised by competition between those in power and oppositional groups, the so-called 'party of power' against the 'party of society', which took on an intensely ideological form in the wake of the October events. The programmes of leading contestants by 1995 had become more focused, seeking to defend the interests of specific groups and with more defined programmes. The Russian electorate had matured, with voters increasingly choosing candidates on the basis of party affiliation rather than on personality. The closer alignment between votes cast for party-lists and single-member candidates (with the exception of the LDPR) suggests greater commitment to programmes, increased differentiation among the electorate and the emergence of a more stable value system. In short, divisions between policies had now come to the fore, suggesting that the post-1991 polity had begun to stabilise.

The Sixth Duma was less fragmented than its predecessor, and the presence of only four factions dramatically altered its voting dynamics, with fewer smaller factions to mediate and moderate policy-making. The more radical deputies elected from the party lists were diluted by members elected from the constituencies, often without any clear political affiliation, but the cost was a lack of clear political orientation in the Duma itself.[70]

Presidential elections of June–July 1996

For the first time elections were to be held for the head of state of a sovereign and independent Russia. Candidates registered with the CEC by 15 April 1996, enclosing their tax returns for the previous two years and submitting one million signatures (with no more than 70,000 from any one region), a way of eliminating outside candidates.[71] No candidate obtained more than 50 per cent of the vote in the first ballot (held on 16 June 1996) so the two front-runners entered a run-off poll a fortnight later on 3 July (see appendix 2.7).

Yeltsin's own chances of re-election were reduced by the horrors of the Chechen war and his own ill-health. His popularity had fallen dramatically, from 37 per cent in December 1992 to 6 per cent in June 1995.[72] Neither the 'democratic' camp nor the opposition, however, could agree on a single candidate, repectively, to oppose Yeltsin and thus his chances, in a straight run-off against a communist or a nationalist, remained high. The December 1995 Duma election acted as a primary for the presedential election, identifying the strongest candidates and eliminating the weakest. Several contenders announced their candidacy, including Yeltsin, Zyuganov, Lebed, Yavlinskii, Gorbachev and, of course, Zhirinovskii, without whom no election would be complete in Russia.[73] Those outside power structures sought to build up a popular base, while those who could draw on the administrative resources of an executive position were less concerned with organisational questions.[74]

The first round largely confirmed Russia's traditional electoral geography, with Zyuganov gaining strong support on the southern fringe and the 'red-belt' to the south-west of Moscow, although Yeltsin unexpectedly defeated the opposition in the Far East. Yeltsin fought a surprisingly effective campaign, looking fitter than before and focusing on the threat posed by the communists. The media fell in behind his candidacy, fearing the consequences of a communist victory, as did a large proportion of the electorate. Lebed's strong showing owed something to the covert support of Yeltsin's team, but much more to his own charisma: if in December 1995 he had been an 'iron-fisted populist', by June 1996 he appeared to have become an iron-fisted democrat. Between rounds Yeltsin sacked some of his more unpopular officials (including defence minister Pavel Grachev and presidential security head Korzhakov) and appointed Lebed secretary of the Security Council and presidential national security adviser with the brief to root out corruption and crime. Yavlinskii fought a poor campaign, failing to become the candidate of a united 'third force', while Zhirinovskii was pushed into fifth place. Yeltsin secured a convincing victory in the second round from an electorate afraid that a change of president would entail a change of regime. The 30 million votes cast for Zyuganov represented a large constituency of dissatisfied citizens but he failed to broaden his support beyond the communist and national-patriotic opposition. Despite continuing fears over his health, Yeltsin successfully exploited the slogans of continuity, stability and reform.

ELECTIONS AND THE RUSSIAN POLITICAL SYSTEM

The notion of a founding election figures prominently in the literature on transition,[75] but in Russia the issue is by no means clear cut. The elections of 1989 to the Soviet CPD represented an enormous step towards the reconstitution of competitive politics, but the absence of party choices and the limits to campaigning hardly allow this to be reckoned Russia's 'founding' election. Much the same can be said about the Russian republican elections in March 1990, although the subject now at least was Russia proper. The absence, indeed, of a founding election immediately following the change of regime in August 1991 and the disintegration of the USSR later that year had an enormous impact on the shape of Russia's struggling democracy, retarding party development and allowing a state system to consolidate itself relatively insulated from popular control. The Russian elections of December 1993 were in effect the founding elections; but they did not entail a change of government and were held according to no stable set of rules; the electoral law was imposed by decree rather than legislative consultation. Russian democracy has not had a founding election, and this is yet another indicator of the hybrid nature of Russian democracy.

Electoral politics, however, limited the choices of the regime system and, however imperfect the procedures, determined the nature of Russia's emergence from communism. While the elections might have been flawed, the commitment to electoral politics precluded some of the harsher options. Chinese-type authoritarian modernisation was excluded once perestroika legalised political contestation. Gorbachev's own attempts to control the transition within the framework of 'managed democracy', retaining a leading although modified role for the Communist Party, shattered under the impact of electoral defeats and the emergence of parliamentary assemblies legitimised by the popular vote. Gorbachev's own refusal to accept the electoral challenge when taking on the post of Soviet president irremediably weakened his legitimacy, whereas Yeltsin's clear victory in the Russian presidential elections of June 1991 gave him the popular mandate to face down the coup attempt and ultimately to challenge Gorbachev himself.

Early votes, however, were constrained by external factors: in 1989 by the Party apparatus; in 1990 the elections were partial in that the Russian parliament was far from sovereign; in June 1991 the Russian president was formally subordinated to All-Union structures; and the December 1993 elections were held in the wake of a political cataclysm with a large swathe of the political spectrum excluded. Only in December 1995 were all the elements of a free election in place, governed by an electoral law passed by parliament and within the framework of a stable constitutional order. But by that time the ability of elections to change the political order had been severely constrained by the provisions of the new constitutional order.

Genuine electoral politics in Russia emerged gradually out of a distinctive mix of quasi-elections and referenda. Votes between 1989 and 1993 had a plebiscitary character in that they focused more on the very nature of the new political order than simply the renewing of the personnel of an existing system, the distinction noted earlier between 'constitutional' and 'normal' politics. The direction of Russia's development is still not assured and it is this very factor that prompted the regime system to place limits on the ability of elections to achieve a change of course. The powerful presidency in Russia discounted strong parties and weakened the role of parliament. The very stress on strong executive power, however, could be self-defeating, and a change of president may signal not only a change of government but a change of regime as well.

Electoral politics also have a less tangible effect by becoming the main form of social contestation, reducing the typically Russian contest of ideological absolutes. The old struggle between 'Westernisers' and 'Slavophiles' was echoed in the tension between 'Atlanticists' and 'Eurasianists', while the binary structure of politics was reflected at first in the struggle between 'democrats' and 'partocrats', and later between 'democrats' and 'red-browns'. Elections, moreover, act as the primary form of political mobility, bringing new people into political life; people who in one form or another reflect real social interests.[76]

Numerous theorists seek to understand elections, in post-communist societies and elsewhere.[77] The classic approach is to suggest that voting behaviour is associated with socioeconomic divisions and interests, but this can hardly be applied (yet) to Russian society. Simplistic rational choice theory would suggest that governments that deliver the goods get rewarded, whereas those held responsible for poor economic performance (on a national or personal level) get punished. In Russian conditions this would mean that any government for the forseeable future would be deeply unpopular. More nuanced approaches seek to incorporate belief systems and political commitments into voting behaviour, the role of negative or 'protest' voting, as well as the problem of 'tactical' voting.

The elections of December 1993 and 1995 belied the optimism of those who saw postcommunist Russia in terms of a unified democratisation process. The already tenuous concept of parliamentary government was further discredited. The rise of nationalist sentiments in 1993 and of neo-communist restorationism in 1995 reinforced national democracy as the predominant ideology of the regime. Although the majority of patriotic and nationalist movements were marginalised in October 1993, their ideas appeared to triumph. Zhirinovskii's impressive vote in December 1993, and to a lesser extent in 1995, revealed the degree to which support for charismatic personal leadership is structured into Russian politics. Yeltsin had based his challenge to the communist system and Gorbachev personally on a distinctive mix of democratic slogans and personal courage. Now the mantle of charismatic leadership appeared to be slipping from Yeltsin to Zhirinovskii, representing a new tide of popular dissatisfaction and a new wave of insurgency. Just as Gorbachev had given birth to the Yeltsin phenomenon, so now Yeltsin engendered his challenger.[78] Zhirinovskii's constituency to a degree overlapped with Yeltsin's, attracted by the politics of protest. Earlier ballots offered simple alternatives, greatly simplifying the political choices facing the voter: communism or democracy; Soviet power or Yeltsin's democracy; the continuation of reforms or the renewed dominance of the old managerial classes; the president or Congress; Yeltsin or Khasbulatov. In December 1993 the external threat to democratic transformation, the image of the enemy as it were, was for the first time absent. The Russian people, paradoxically, created this danger from within the democratic process itself. The strong vote for the CPRF in December 1995 and for Zyuganov personally in June 1996 suggests not only disaffection with the reform process but a larger alienation from the post-August 1991 political order.

Post-communist elections in Russia might well reflect the immaturity of the Russian electorate and its susceptibility to demagogic promises, but they also reflect a more profound institutional immaturity of the democratic system and of political and social processes in their entirety. Crisis appears to be the normal state of Russian politics, and institutional reorganisation typical of the system. As for society, the revolutionary implications of the fall of communist power and the change in property relations has not yet given birth to a stable new class or ordered hierarchy of elite privileges and societal values. The whole concept of 'support' appears friable and susceptible to rapid changes; and by the same token, 'opposition' to a large degree cannot be taken as a stable political position but a reflection of temporary antipathies. Although taking full advantage of the benefits conferred by incumbency, Yeltsin's re-election in July 1996 reflected more than electoral manipulation but the emergence of a solid constituency in support of the new order – or at least, opposed to the restoration of the old.

6   Remaking the state: the legislature

Men are in public life as in private, some good, some evil. The elevation of the one, and the depression of the other, are the first objects of all true policy.

Edmund Burke[1]

The birth of parliamentarianism in Russia has been tortuous. Three times in Russian history a legislature has been dissolved by force: on 9 July 1906 Nicholas II used troops to dissolve the First State Duma, only two months after its convocation; the long-awaited Constituent Assembly met for only one day on 5 January 1918 and was forcibly prevented by the Bolsheviks from reconvening the next day; and on 21 September 1993 Yeltsin ordered the dissolution of the Russian Congress of People's Deputies (CPD) and the Supreme Soviet. In addition, the Second State Duma was dissolved on 3 June 1907, the Soviet CPD, established amidst so many high hopes by Gorbachev during 1988–89, was prematurely terminated in September 1991, and its Supreme Soviet followed into the dustbin of history by the end of the year. The first two pre-revolutionary State Dumas were dissolved prematurely (the First, as noted, by force), the Third (1907–1912) lasted its full term, the Fourth was brought to a sudden end in February 1917, and none were marked by conspicuous success in bringing executive authority under effective control.

The 'Fifth' State Duma elected on 12 December 1993 was the first legislature in modern times to see out its full term. This and successive Dumas were faced by similar problems. Russia appeared inhospitable soil for parliaments and the question remained: was parliamentarianism, with its associated culture of compromise, proceduralism, legalism and alternativity, something alien to Russian political culture and traditions; or did the earlier failures betoken no more than the traumas of a difficult birth, like the overthrow of Germany's parliamentary republic in 1933 (a country apparently equally hostile to the conventions of parliamentary life), before a genuine parliamentary system could at last be firmly rooted in a viable constitutional order? The problem of remaking the institutions of the Russian state will be examined in this chapter and the next.

PROBLEMS OF STATE-BUILDING

Administrative weakness was one of the heaviest legacies that the old regime bequeathed to the new.[2] Administration was subordinated to the Communist Party apparatus and even lacked the basic responsibility of recruiting its own civil servants; this was managed by the Party's nomenklatura system. The soviets were primarily political bodies and were never designed to be effective instruments of administration. Their bloated memberships met rarely in plenary session while the actual administrative work was carried out by their executive committees (*ispolkoms*) guided by the local Party organisations, the all-powerful *obkoms* at oblast level, *gorkoms* in the cities and towns and the *raikoms* in urban and rural districts. Gaidar noted that 'The plenitude of power of the bureaucracy inevitably leads to the complete destruction of the organisation of the work of the state.'[3] The Soviet regime was polymorphous, with little distinction between political, social or economic institutions. T.H. Rigby coined the term 'mono-organisational socialism' to describe this system in which all levels of social activity were controlled by the Party.[4] The weakness of governance was both cause and consequence of the parallel rule of the Communist Party, which gave a semblance of unity and direction to Soviet administration while ensuring that the state (narrowly defined) did not become an autonomous political force in its own right.

Interwoven like a double helix, the collapse of the Communist Party to a degree also entailed the collapse of the state. The political reforms from 1988 precipitated a crisis of authority and deprived the administrative system of its accustomed rules and leadership. It soon became clear that Soviet institutions could not be reformed but had to be thoroughly remade. But in the meantime Russia was constantly in danger of sailing into what former president Lech Wałęsa in Poland called the 'Bermuda triangle' between a weak presidency, a fractured parliament and an ineffective government.

Building democratic institutions must be at the heart of any democratisation process, but this was relatively neglected in the first post-communist years as attention focused on economic transformation. Compared with the other post-Soviet states, it was both easier and more difficult for Russia to establish the institutions of an independent state. Russia inherited the buildings, staff and networks of the defunct Soviet Union, but this itself caused problems because it inherited the attitudes, bureaucratism and inefficiencies of the old regime whereas the other republics could start with a relatively clean page. Just as Lenin in the early years of Soviet power attributed the defects of the new regime on holdovers from the old system, so too the new government in Russia had a ready object on which to place responsibility for its own inadequacies.

The weakness of institutions put the premium on individuals, and post-communist administrative and legal structures worked only fitfully. Political power was diffused, and state building in Russia was impeded by the struggle between numerous centres of power, the presidency, the Congress and the Supreme Soviet, the government and regional authorities. The creation of presidential rule under Gorbachev had failed to overcome the crisis of executive power, and this was also the case in post-communist Russia. Even as they formally gathered more and more powers, Gorbachev and Yeltsin found that their directives were not implemented and their authority waned.

PARLIAMENT: TAKE ONE

Following the 1991 coup the ebbing of the simple conflict between the communist 'centre' and the insurgent 'democrats' revealed structural weaknesses in the organisation of legislative power and exposed a crisis in relations between executive and legislative authority. The Russian legislature elected in March 1990 was designed neither to choose nor to control a government, let alone act as the supreme source of sovereignty. It did not have effective means to fulfil customary parliamentary functions like approving and overseeing budgets and legislation. The absence of the separation of powers worked both to the legislature's advantage, in that it had direct control over about half of state expenditure, but also to its disadvantage, as in its weak control over the executive.

Up to 1992 the Russian legislature was an accomplice to its own marginalisation: it voted to establish a presidential system at the Third CPD in April 1991, adopted the Law on the President at the Fourth on 24 May, and granted the presidency emergency powers to drive through reform by decree at the resumed Fifth Congress in November 1991. With the appointment in November 1991 of a non-party 'government of reforms', what came to be called a 'cabinet of specialists', parliament was deprived of the right of detailed oversight over the work of the government. Although decrees and the appointment of key ministers required parliamentary approval, the legislature effectively lost control over policy and the government. Up to the Sixth Congress in April 1992 parliament largely acceded to the process of self-marginalisation.

Parliament's 'marginalisation', however, was of a special type; the increased powers of the presidency were always clearly envisaged within the context of parliamentary supremacy. The Law on the President, for example, drafted by Shakhrai, insisted that 'the president does not have the right to dissolve or suspend' the Congress or Supreme Soviet, he or she was to report at least once a year to the Congress, and their decrees were not to infringe existing legislation.[5] The extraordinary powers of the president were always regarded as temporary, so that when at the height of the struggle in 1993 parliament deprived the president of these powers they were doing no more than what they were entitled to.

Sharpening differences over economic policy and state construction gave rise to the emergence of a 'rejectionist' front, those united by their opposition to the breakup of the USSR, radical economic reforms and Yeltsin's entourage. Their positive programme was unclear and reflected divergent interests, but a common hostility to the new order represented by the August regime was enough to unite them in opposition to Yeltsin. At the same time, although independently, Khasbulatov and his colleagues sought to reverse the marginalisation of parliament as an institution, leading to profound political crisis at the Sixth and succeeding Congresses. At that Congress, for example, Khasbulatov condemned the cabinet's 'attack on democracy' and the dismissive attitude by ministers towards representative institutions.[6]

The crisis of governance derived not so much from the personal qualities of the new leaders, the social context of the new politics or even long-term factors like the weakness of liberalism in Russia. More immediate political factors allowed the emergence of a type of dual power and ultimately provoked a constitutional crisis that led to bloodshed in the streets of Moscow in October 1993.[7] There remained a fundamental 'constitutional' crisis because the 1978 Russian constitution was heavily amended after 1990 and ended up granting both the executive and the legislative branches supreme state power.[8] Russia was *de jure* a parliamentary republic but *de facto* became a presidential republic. The balance between executive and legislative remained a matter of political struggle rather than constitutional law. The president's extraordinary powers were temporary and subject to the approval of parliament. Parliament itself enjoyed extensive powers under the existing constitution and, increasingly dominated by rejectionist groups, was able to block the executive's initiatives for constitutional change and economic reform.

The Congress of People's Deputies and the Supreme Soviet

The hesitant advance towards democracy of the perestroika years encumbered Russia with an unwieldy and largely unworkable parliamentary system. Russia was the only post-Soviet republic to retain the cumbrous two-tier legislative system for the elections of March 1990 (see chapter 5). The Russian Congress was made up of 1,068 constituencies, of which 168 (15.7 per cent) were national-territorial and 900 (84.3 per cent) were territorial. The Congress was to meet twice a year to legislate on the most important constitutional and other issues. With a two-thirds majority the Congress could alter the constitution, ratify changes in the name of the republic and cities, and change the powers of the presidency.[9]

The Congress selected a smaller Supreme Soviet, the body properly known as the parliament, to examine current legislation and debate policies. By September 1993 the Supreme Soviet contained 248 voting members and 138 non-voting members working in committees and commissions, and thus a total of 384 officially worked in parliament on a permanent basis, although about a quarter of Supreme Soviet deputies were inactive. All Congress deputies over a five-year period were to have the opportunity of becoming members of the Supreme Soviet, but this did not work out in practice. In the three years of the Russian parliament it was renewed only twice, at the Sixth Congress in April 1992 and again at the Seventh in December 1992.[10]

The Supreme Soviet was divided into two chambers with equal rights; the Council of the Republic headed at first by Nikolai Ryabov, and a smaller Council of the Nationalities chaired by Ramazan Abdulatipov, a deputy from Dagestan and a former central committee secretary responsible for nationality issues. Because of the smaller pool of deputies on which it drew, almost all the deputies from the national territories entered the Supreme Soviet. Each Council had its own commissions and in addition there were twenty-one committees of the Supreme Soviet, which played an active part in policy formation, holding hearings on various issues and amending legislation.

The Supreme Soviet was headed by the chairman, a first deputy chair (Sergei Filatov until January 1993 and then Yurii Voronin to October 1993), and three deputy chairs. With Yeltsin's election as president in June 1991, the chairmanship became vacant. Yeltsin's former ally Khasbulatov was the main candidate, but he encountered stiff opposition at the Fifth Congress in July 1991;[11] he was associated with the ethos of the old Party system and considered to have an abrasive personality. Having won his spurs during the coup, at the resumed Fifth Congress Khasbulatov was finally confirmed as 'speaker' (his favoured term for the post) on 28 October 1991 with 559 votes.[12] Khasbulatov's election did not put an end to Yeltsin's conflicts with the Russian parliament, and indeed intensified them as Khasbulatov, an economist by profession, sought to modify the government's economic reform programme and to defend the prerogatives of parliament – and his own.

The Presidium of the Supreme Soviet consisted of some forty members, the speaker and his deputies, and the heads of commissions and committees, and became a powerful body in its own right. It had its own commissions dealing with such questions as citizenship and Russians abroad, and some ten departments dealing with administrative and legal matters and the like. The Presidium increasingly acted as a substitute for the policy initiatives coming from a party-based legislature. It was a classic Soviet body, and inevitably tended to substitute (*podmena*) for the functions of plenary sessions and commissions of the Supreme Soviet as a whole. Khasbulatov's power was derived from the Presidium's right to issue decrees (*postanovleniya*), buttressed by his own right to issue directives (*rasporazheniya*), which he used, for example, to establish his own 5,000-strong unit of armed forces subordinate to himself alone. Already by the Sixth Congress in April 1992 Khasbulatov was accused of making the Presidium 'a mute machine for rubber-stamping illegal decrees'.[13] Yeltsin accused the Presidium of blocking many of his radical reforming bills. The Presidium emerged as a bastion of the old nomenklatura,[14] and the prestige of the Supreme Soviet as a whole fell sharply, both as an institution and in the personal ratings of its members.

The 1990 election was not so much one-party as non-party, and almost every deputy represented a party unto themselves. The demise of the CPSU enhanced the role of the factions in parliament, a process that contributed to party formation but from the roof down. The discipline that had failed in the CPSU was not transferred to other parties, and party discipline as such largely disappeared. The absence of a multiparty system, in this parliament and its successor, was reflected not only in the weak links between parliamentary factions and the parties to which they were nominally subordinate, but also in the arbitrary relationship between individual deputies and the faction to which they belonged. Party or factional discipline counted for little, and deputies joined and left caucuses at will. Deputies were a 'mass', weakly organised in constantly changing groups, hence the difficulty of maintaining a stable majority for any long-term policy.

More important than group affiliation was occupation and social status. Over three-quarters of deputies when elected in 1990 were functionaries of one sort or another and only 22 per cent were from the free professions and workers. The dropping of set norms meant that the proportion of manual workers fell sharply, but, contrary to the claims of the communist conservatives, this benefitted less the intelligentsia (apart from in Moscow and some other big cities), but senior administrators.[15] In 1990 78 per cent of the deputies worked in managerial structures,[16] only fifty-one (5%) were workers and peasants actually employed in factories and farms, while 179 (17%) were intelligentsia employed in the liberal professions.[17] The real winners were not even high Party officials but senior administrators in ministries, regional *ispolkoms* and other agencies. The state nomenklatura, created by the Party, came into its own.

The social composition of the CPD was to cast a long shadow over the parliamentary politics of post-communist Russia; the key to voting patterns was its social and occupational structure. In the dying days of the old regime part of the old administrative elite aligned with the so-called democrats against the communist centre, allowing Yeltsin to be elected chairman of parliament in May 1990, but once that centre disappeared after August 1991 this unnatural alliance broke down and the democrats found themselves a shrinking minority.[18] As long as politics was refracted through the one-dimensional struggle between 'communists' and 'democrats', the lower and middle echelon of managers were willing to support the 'democrats', but when more complicated choices emerged deputies from the middle and lower managerial levels migrated into the conservative camp.[19] The democrats lost their majority from the centre and the Yeltsinite reform process entered the doldrums.

The self-definition of anti-communist as democrat, moreover, did not withstand the fall of communism. The personal qualities of many 'democratic' candidates in the March 1990 elections were obscured by their anti-communist rhetoric, and the whole process of candidate selection on the democratic side appeared random in the extreme, whereas the apparatus at least advanced experienced managers and officials. The democratic deputies as a group were marked by a lack of professionalism, the absence of organisational and ideological unity, personal ambition often taking the form of blatant and unprincipled careerism, and a susceptibility to the good life. The majority of the Congress had a vested interest in maintaining the administrative structures inherited from the communist regime, and thus entered the ranks of the 'conservatives'. Their aim initially was not so much to overthrow Yeltsin's government as to shackle it and to prevent the radical reconstruction of the past. No majority could be found in parliament that could work with the president to generate a set of common principles of government.

Genesis of a tragedy

Conflict between parliament and the presidency became endemic: personal factors played their part but structural factors were primarily responsible for the constitutional crisis that became a crisis of the state. As soon as the Supreme Soviet reconvened after the coup on 19 September 1991 it opposed the president's appointment of heads of administration and criticised government policies. The democrats at this time retained the whip hand and were no less critical of the president than the conservatives were to be later. There were some grounds for their criticisms, in particular the nomenklatura roots of appointments to the presidential apparatus, but their inability to establish a working relationship with the executive undermined their ability to withstand the conservative shift later.

Khasbulatov allegedly used his control over scarce resources and privileges, like foreign trips and offices, to reward his supporters and make life uncomfortable for his critics. Already in January 1992 he had launched the first of his many broadsides against the 'shock therapy' approach to economic reform, condemning 'anarchical, uncontrolled price rises' and insisted that 'We are fed up with experiments.' He antagonised members of parliament as much as he did the president. The main charge against him was that instead of allowing parliament to act as an impartial forum for debate, he turned it into his own power base. Deputies claimed that he regularly exceeded his authority, others accused him of authoritarian methods of rule, and a growing number called for his replacement.[20]

If we see Khasbulatov as a purely negative figure then all seems to fall into place, but the picture is not quite so clearcut. Why did parliament itself, despite criticisms, fail to remove Khasbulatov? Did they see in him the best defence for their own privileges and powers, or did he effectively take a principled stand in defence of parliamentary prerogatives? Despite an undercurrent of disappointed expectations (Khasbulatov had hoped to be nominated Yeltsin's running-mate in the June 1991 presidential elections, and later anticipated becoming prime minister), the relationship between Khasbulatov and Yeltsin was not entirely adversarial. Khasbulatov defended the unity of the Russian state and took an extremely critical approach to the aspirations of Russia's republics for sovereignty, let alone independence. His criticisms of neo-liberal economic policies raised important issues, while his defence of parliamentary rights was both coherent and legitimate, albeit, some suspected, not always sincere. Khasbulatov, moreover, up to late 1992 ensured that the majority of presidential legislation passed through parliament, with over 800 normative acts, including 200 laws, being passed by the Supreme Soviet in its first four convocations; and he blunted some of the extreme criticisms of Yeltsin. The two men were in frequent communication until relations were finally ruptured in December 1992.[21] Khasbulatov claimed to represent the centre to achieve consensus and balanced reformist legislation.[22]

The president himself failed to build consensus in parliament, not meeting with the leaders of the democratic movement for several months after the coup, and appeared to forget their earlier efforts on his behalf. Yeltsin's own rash and often ill-considered assaults on Congress narrowed the scope for compromise. The principles of parliamentary and presidential government are both equally valid, but the tragedy for Russia was that both were being pursued with equal vigour at the same time: like two trains approaching on the same track, the collision would be disastrous for both.

While Khasbulatov certainly sought to turn the Russian parliament into his personal power base, the main reason for the crisis of legislative power in Russia was structural, primarily the legacy of the anti-parliamentarian essence of Soviet power and then, during perestroika, the incompetent approach to institutional reform. In establishing a powerful Congress Gorbachev hoped to balance the powers of the Communist Party; but the disappearance of the latter left the field clear for the former. The structure of parliament meant that it was an anti-parliamentary parliament, unable to work like a 'normal' representative and legislative body. The constitution, although heavily amended, still gave enormous powers to parliament, but the August 1991 settlement prescribed no institutional way to fulfil this role. The biannual Congress, as the 'highest state authority' enjoyed enormous powers and when in session could alter the constitution by a simple two-thirds majority, including depriving the president of his powers, or indeed, if they dared, abolishing the presidency entirely.[23] As long as the Congress wielded the enormous power to amend the constitution at will, and as long as the floor of the Supreme Soviet could be manipulated by the Presidium (which emerged as a type of parallel government) and by the speaker, no real parliamentary politics could emerge.

The distinctive feature of the crisis was that while policy initiative lay with the presidential side, control over implementation and administration lay with parliament. This dualism was reflected in the very nature of the struggle, with parliament by necessity reduced to blocking measures: they had the power to impede presidential initiatives but lacked the power to develop policies – hence the growing irresponsibility of the Supreme Soviet's actions. The Congress and its Supreme Soviet were in the classical position of power without responsibility, but their power was essentially negative. Parliament failed to become an effective working body, with most of its legislation not direct-acting but requiring further regulations and decrees, offering enormous scope for the bureaucracy to hinder or to profit from them. The rejectionists, moreover, took full advantage of the moral and political collapse of the democratic challenge, intensifying the crisis of power at all levels.

The conflict only gradually assumed the dimensions of a general crisis of power. At first Yeltsin grudgingly tolerated a degree of legislative oversight over his actions. He accepted the Supreme Soviet's repeal in November 1991 of the presidential decree imposing a state of emergency on Chechen-Ingushetia, but he overruled attempts by parliament to force the local elections due on 8 December 1991. Parliament's reversal of Yeltsin's decree of 19 December 1991 merging the Ministries of Security and Interior was allowed to stand. Parliament procrastinated over passing laws on such critical issues as privatisation, land reform and ownership, bankruptcy and the new constitution, and passed illiberal legislation on such issues as exchange controls. Rejectionist deputies opposed the reformers' reliance on economic aid from the West and sought more government intervention to preserve Russian industry, and in general were wary of the 'cosmopolitan' democracy that was allegedly being introduced into Russia. Khasbulatov became increasingly critical of the president's wide powers and sought parliamentary control over the government including the right to veto government appointments and policies.

Meetings of the Congress were times of high drama. Attempts by Yeltsin to propitiate the rejectionists on the eve of the Sixth Congress in April 1992 by removing the ministerial status of two of his key supporters, Burbulis and Shakhrai, failed; Yeltsin's sacrificial tactic did not work then or later. The Congress failed to adopt a new constitution, placed even stricter controls over the progress of reform, and restricted the purchase and sale of land.[24] The Russian CPD appeared to be going the same way as the old Soviet Congress, acting as a brake rather than the motor of reform. Following the Sixth Congress Yeltsin threatened to hold a nationwide referendum on the new constitution, for the early dissolution of parliament (its term was due to end in March 1995) and new elections. A referendum was allowed if one-third of Congress deputies or 1 million members of the public asked for one, but even if Democratic Russia had collected the required signatures, the Supreme Soviet would still have had to agree to call a referendum. Thus there was stalemate and no legal way in which Yeltsin could dissolve Congress and call new elections.[25] In recognition of this Yeltsin rejoined the parliamentary process of drafting the new constitution, rather than holding a referendum and imposing his own.[26] Yeltsin, however, remained convinced that the Congress had outlived its purpose: 'In my opinion, it is an artificial, supra-parliamentary entity. Its very existence is a permanent basis for disrupting the balance between the legislative, executive and judicial branches'.[27]

Yeltsin's emergency powers had been granted for only 1 year and were due to expire on 1 December 1992, thus the prelude to the Seventh Congress (1–14 December 1992) was if anything more tense than before the Sixth. On 28 October 1992 Yeltsin banned parliament's security force, responsible to Khasbulatov for the defence of the White House but which had been used in an attempt to enforce parliament's claims to the *Izvestiya* print works. Yeltsin was already considering a forceful resolution of the conflict by declaring direct presidential rule;[28] he also sought to broaden his support in Congress by forging an alliance with the centrist Civic Union, which claimed the allegiance of up to 40 per cent of the deputies. Once again he hoped that the sacrifice of some of his closest supporters would appease his conservative critics. On 25 November the minister for information, Mikhail Poltoranin, was dismissed, and the next day the post of State Secretary, held by the deeply unpopular Burbulis, was abolished. Yeltsin also sacrificed Yegor Yakovlev, the chairman of the 'Ostankino' Commonwealth television company, Galina Starovoitova, presidential adviser on nationality issues, and Arkadii Murashev, one of Yeltsin's fellow coordinators of the Interregional Group of Deputies in the old Soviet parliament and now head of Moscow's police.

Yeltsin's attempts to postpone the Seventh Congress failed, and its 1,040 deputies duly met on 1 December amid growing threats that it would try to remove the government. Divided into fourteen factions and with the balance of the 'marsh' having tilted even further towards the conservatives,[29] the reformers faced a formidable task. Yeltsin's opening speech was directed to the centre by promising a mixed economy with more scope for an effective state sector, the prevention of deindustrialisation, more support for Russia's scientific and technological potential, and he even promised the continuation of the old system of state orders, detested by the neo-liberal reformists. He demanded that the legislature forego their legislative duties and concentrate solely on amending and ultimately replacing Russia's constitution.[30] In his opening address Khasbulatov argued that the president's attempt to portray the struggle as one for or against reform as 'nothing but primitive propaganda' and instead the choice was between two models of the market economy, with Khasbulatov condemning Gaidar's reforms for having ignored the social costs of reform: instead, he favoured the Scandinavian model of a social market economy and insisted that Congress and the government were 'doomed to cooperate'.[31]

Yeltsin conceded that the four key ministers (foreign, defence, security and interior) should be confirmed by parliament, in addition to the existing convention that the prime minister had to be approved by parliament. Despite Yeltsin's concessions, the Congress on 9 December refused to confirm Gaidar as premier, with 486 votes against and 467 in favour. Gaidar could have limped on as acting prime minister until April 1993, but his position would have been severely weakened and for a second year Russia would have been without a fully entitled premier. Above all, a constitutional amendment passed by Congress stipulated that any attempt to dissolve the Congress would automatically deprive the president of his authority. Yeltsin was incensed, having made major concessions yet having received nothing in return. His hopes of a liberal–centrist alliance with the Civic Union came to nothing, and at the Congress the majority of Civic Union deputies voted with the opposition to limit presidential powers. The centre of Russian politics appeared to have disappeared.

On 10 December Yeltsin forced a showdown. In a short but threatening speech, he called for a referendum to be held in January 1993 to decide who should have power, the president or parliament. He argued that the conservatives in the Congress had impeded the reforms, insisting that 'What they failed to achieve in August 1991, they decided to repeat now and carry out a creeping coup', and he condemned Khasbulatov's personal role: 'The constitution, or what is left of it, is turning the Supreme Soviet, its leadership and chairman, into all-powerful rulers of Russia. They are rising above all bodies of executive power but as before are not accountable for anything.' In a bitter assault he fumed: 'It is no longer possible to work with such a Congress. The walls of this hall have blushed from endless insults, from the filth that swamps this Congress due to the sick ambitions of bankrupt politicians.'[32] Yeltsin's attempt to deprive the Congress of a quorum by calling his supporters to a meeting in a neighbouring chamber failed, and only some fifty-three left, leaving nearly 800 to continue work. The 'power ministers' had stayed, and indeed the security (Barannikov), defence (Grachev) and interior (Yerin) ministers pledged support for the constitution and political neutrality.

It was this act of parliamentary defiance in defence of the prerogatives of the legislature that led Travkin to argue that 'practical proofs of the birth of a normal civil society are beginning to appear',[33] while *Rossiiskaya gazeta* talked simply in terms of 'the birth of civil society'.[34] On 11 December Congress passed a resolution that emasculated Yeltsin's proposed referendum, passing a constitutional amendment which banned any plebiscite that could result in a vote of no confidence in any high state body, or which could lead to its dissolution before its term of office had expired. Under the auspices of the chairman of the Constitutional Court, Zor'kin, a deal was brokered on 12 December in the form of a nine-point agreement, to be accepted in full or rejected. A referendum was to be held in April 1993 on the adoption of the new constitution, with contentious points to be placed as options, and in the meantime the existing balance between executive and legislative was to be maintained. Nominations for the post of premier were to be put to the Congress for a non-binding popularity poll, and the president would nominate one of the three most popular figures for the premiership.[35] After consultations with the factions and some complex voting Chernomyrdin replaced Gaidar as prime minister. He immediately announced that 'I am in favour of deepening reforms, but not the impoverishment of the people', and 'I am for a market economy, for reforms, but not the bazaar.'[36]

Russia appeared to have entered a vicious circle in which it could not have elections before the adoption of a constitution, but could not adopt a constitution before elections. It would be a simplification to interpret the conflict as one between a 'communist' parliament and an executive power inclined to the autocratic. Burbulis saw the root of the conflict between parliament and government in that 'the Soviet system of representative power is no longer suitable for the current level of development of society'.[37] Deputies, he argued, spent far too much time acting as lobbyists for particular interests rather than working on national questions. The weakness of party politics meant that parliament itself as an institution took on a monolithic role as an actor in politics rather than as the vessel in which politics was conducted. In other words, politics was displaced into struggle between institutions rather than by consensual processes within them. Without changes to the structure of legislative power there could be no stable political development.

The end of the Supreme Soviet

Fears of the instability that the referendum planned for 11 April 1993 might cause, led some, like Travkin, to call for its abandonment. Leaders of the country's twenty-one republics warned that the referendum could lead to 'an uncontrollable struggle for power' and tear the country apart,[38] and both Khasbulatov and Rutskoi feared that the referendum could unleash chaos in Russia's unstable conditions. Yeltsin began to consider alternatives, and on 9 February he proposed bringing elections forward a year, so that parliamentary elections would take place in 1994 and presidential ones in 1995.

Following desultory negotiations between Yeltsin and Khasbulatov, the Eighth Congress met on 10–13 March 1993 but failed to sanction the referendum or to establish the framework for the adoption of a new constitution. The Congress stripped Yeltsin of many of the powers granted to him earlier to implement economic reform: he was deprived of the right to issue decrees with the same force as parliamentary laws; to appoint presidential envoys or heads of administration; or to appoint government ministers without the approval of parliament. The government was granted the right to submit legislation directly to parliament (bypassing the presidency), a privilege that the Soviet government under Pavlov had sought not long before the coup. The presidency emerged limited and damaged by this bout with Congress.

The unstable compromise reached at the Seventh Congress was now comprehensively repudiated. In the last months of the old parliament Khasbulatov in effect organised an insurrection against Yeltsin and sought to use the combined forces of an eclectic rejectionist front to propel him to power. He now proposed the establishment of a parliamentary republic at the centre and the restoration of the power of the soviets in the localities. Khasbulatov declared himself in favour of the restoration of a new form of Soviet power in which local executive authorities would be subordinated to local soviets which would in turn be subordinated to the presidium of the Supreme Soviet.[39] The president would have been reduced to a figurehead, and the head of the legislature would in effect have been chief executive.[40] Khasbulatov had long advocated the municipalisation of soviets to turn them into effective bodies of local self-government,[41] but this was taking his earlier ideas much further. On trips to the provinces he urged local soviets to resist the executive authorities, and by April 1993 he was boasting that he had restored Soviet power in the regions, and he soon tried to restore Soviet power in the centre as well. The Khasbulatovite programme ultimately sought to establish a type of post-communist soviet power: 'soviets without Bolsheviks', as the Kronstadt insurgents of March 1921 put it.

Parliament's challenge left Yeltsin facing a conundrum, and as usual in a crisis he resolved on decisive action. In a broadcast on 20 March he announced a referendum for 25 April and the imposition of 'special rule' that would have freed him from legislative restraints, a declaration that was clearly unconstitutional. Despite the suggestion of a forceful resolution to the crisis, when the decree was published on 24 March it made no mention of the dissolution of Congress or the suspension of parliament. Zor'kin's attempts to mediate this time came to nothing, having discredited himself by rushing to condemn Yeltsin's 'special rule' before even having seen the decree. The Ninth Congress, called in response to Yeltsin's announcement, nevertheless met on 26 March in an atmosphere of extreme crisis. A meeting between Yeltsin and Khasbulatov on 27 March appeared to provide a solution by stipulating early presidential and parliamentary elections in autumn 1993. However, Congress on the next day angrily rejected the deal, and turned against Khasbulatov himself, with some 300 deputies voting for his resignation, and the vote to impeach Yeltsin fell only seventy-two short of the required two-thirds majority. Khasbulatov's own room for manoeuvre had been drastically reduced, and the final day of the Ninth Congress on 29 March was marked by the passage of numerous acts stripping Yeltsin of his remaining powers.

Despite strong support for pre-term elections in the referendum of 25 April 1993, the rejectionists refused to allow parliamentary elections and the crisis deepened. While the result weakened Khasbulatov personally, the Supreme Soviet was increasingly radicalised by the conflict, and parliament as a whole over-estimated its strength, interpreting concessions as weakness. The dismissal of Barannikov as security minister was reversed by the Presidium on 28 July, although the Constitutional Court ruled that parliament in this case had exceeded its powers. Liberal deputies suggested that Barannikov had been providing parliament with incriminatory material to use against its opponents in the anti-corruption campaign. The Supreme Soviet reduced its quorum to 50 per cent so that it could quickly reassemble in a crisis.

The politicisation of the struggle between parliament and presidency meant that the endemic constitutional crisis had been transformed into an overt political struggle for power. The extreme right, made up of extremist Russian nationalists and imperial restorationists, allied with the extreme left, neo-Bolshevik and Soviet rejectionists, to defeat the centre. The evidence that the parliamentary leadership engaged in a premeditated attempt to seize power, however, remains circumstantial; the accumulation of weapons suggests a degree of planning, but could have been defensive. Over the summer Khasbulatov and Rutskoi toured the provinces, hoping to garner support. On a visit to the Far East Rutskoi declared that within two months he would be president. During a visit to Orël and Bryansk he insisted that an end to the confusion had to be made during the autumn, suggesting that the Congress would call for simultaneous pre-term parliamentary and presidential elections; he announced that an alternative policy programme was being developed that would allow the rebirth of Russia from the regions up.[42] More importantly, it is clear that parliament was planning to emasculate presidential power. Isakov, head of parliament's committee for constitutional legislation, proposed yet new amendments to the constitution that would have established a 'parliamentary autocracy', subordinating the government and individual ministers to its control and reducing the president to a mere figurehead.[43]

Parliament now openly sought to sabotage the government's economic reforms in a particularly vicious revival of the 'war of the laws' that had marked the fall of the Soviet regime. Yeltsin's decree of 8 May 1993 accelerating privatisation was suspended on 20 July by the Supreme Soviet and referred to the Constitutional Court to rule on its legality.[44] His attempts to modify the recall of Soviet-era banknotes by the Central Bank in July 1993 was vigorously resisted by the Supreme Soviet; a resolution on 9 July 1993 declaring that Sevastopol in the Crimea was part of Russia threatened war with Ukraine. Above all, Yeltsin in early September vetoed the Supreme Soviet's hyper-inflationary budget and restored Gaidar to take charge of the economy.

Interpreting the results of the April referendum as a renewed popular mandate, Yeltsin went on the offensive and sought to break the impasse by convening the Constitutional Assembly in June 1993, a tactic (as we have seen) that was only partially successful. The draft of a new constitution was completed in July, but its adoption was blocked by some regional leaders. Yeltsin's failure on 18 September to convert the Federation Council into a fully fledged consultative-advisory body to replace parliament's existing Council of Nationalities triggered the final crisis.[45] On that very day Khasbulatov escalated the personal vendetta by accusing Yeltsin of being a common drunkard. Since the referendum Russian political life had descended to mutual mud-flinging amid accusations of corruption, a process encouraged by Rutskoi himself.[46] By a presidential decree of 1 September 1993 both Rutskoi and first deputy prime minister Shumeiko, who had been trading insults, were suspended pending investigations into corruption.[47] The inner life of parliament itself had similarly degenerated, with a regime of fear against all of Khasbulatov's opponents. The more far-seeing deputies had already resigned their mandates, with Travkin leaving soon after the April referendum, and with former allies of Khasbulatov like Ryabov migrating towards the presidential camp. Parliament appeared unable to respond to the changes taking place in Russian life.

The October events

Finally, on 21 September 1993, Yeltsin took the dissolution option. Presidential decree No. 1400 'On Gradual Constitutional Reform in the Russian Federation' dissolved the Supreme Soviet and the CPD, whose powers were to be transferred to a new Federal Assembly. The existing Federation Council was to be vested with the functions of the upper chamber of the Assembly, while elections to the new lower chamber, the State Duma were to take place on 12 December 1993. One of the reasons for Yeltsin's action was the failure of the Constitutional Assembly to adopt the new constitution, and it was now ordered to agree a final version with parliament's own Constitutional Commission (nominally headed by Yeltsin himself) by 12 December.[48] The Constitutional Court was urged not to meet until the Federal Assembly began its work, but in the event ten out of the fourteen judges condemned the presidential decree.[49]

The rejectionists greatly overplayed their hand, especially given the results of the April referendum. Khasbulatov and the deputies who supported him did not realise quite how detached they had become from popular opinion, and when they issued the call for the masses to come to defend the White House in September 1993, instead of the expected crowds a rather desultory few thousand assembled. Support for the parliamentary rejectionists was fragmented, and within parliament itself the picture is confused. Representatives of thirteen out of the fourteen factions remained in parliament, but it is clear that the number of deputies in the White House was falling sharply, some attracted by the promise of jobs in the presidential system and by generous retirement payments. The Tenth CPD was hastily convened, but while some deputies attended, the Congress lacked a quorum (the required number was swiftly decreased) since, among other reasons, Yeltsin had deprived them of free travel.

Even during the phoney rebellion between 21 September and 3 October the parliamentary leadership was divided. According to some reports, Abdulatipov claimed at a meeting of regional representatives in St Petersburg on 27 September that many deputies were prepared to jettison Khasbulatov and open negotiations with the presidential team.[50] Negotiations did take place under the aegis of Patriarch Aleksii II in the Danilov monastery, and by 1 October agreement had apparently been reached between the presidential negotiators led by Filatov and the parliamentary team led by Sokolov and Abdulatipov. However, that evening Khasbulatov's deputy, Voronin, arrived and apparently deliberately sought to drag out the talks to allow more time for the formation of armed detachments in Moscow.[51] In the event, the remaining deputies in the White House rejected the agreement that would have restored some services to the building in exchange for giving up arms.[52]

Khasbulatov had long been courting regional leaders, but with mixed success. At the St Petersburg meeting, attended by representatives of forty regional and republican soviets and nine representatives of heads of administration, a declaration was adopted calling for simultáneous presidential and parliamentary elections by the end of 1993, the so-called 'zero option'.[53] This approach, supported by presidential wannabees like Yavlinskii and presidential has-beens like Gorbachev, was sharply rebuffed by Yeltsin in a television broadcast on 27 September. He insisted that simultaneous elections would cause a power vacuum, arguing that 'Dual power is very dangerous, but absence of all power is doubly so', and confirmed that presidential elections would be held on 12 June 1994.[54]

In only four oblasts (Amur, Belgorod, Bryansk and Novosibirsk), could Yeltsin not count on the support of either the soviet or the head of administration (which in most cases he himself had appointed).[55] The governor of Novosibirsk, Vitalii Mukha, offered the Supreme Soviet an alternative home and on 29 September hosted an emergency conference of Siberian soviets, attended by deputies from fourteen out of the nineteen Siberian regions. The presidential candidate of June 1991, Aman Tuleev, the chairman of the Kemerovo regional soviet, once again placed his distinctive mark on national politics by calling for the formation of a Siberian Republic on the basis of Tomsk, Novosibirsk and Kemerovo regions and the Altai Territory.[56] The delegates threatened to block the Trans-Siberian railway, withhold taxes and establish a Siberian republic if Yeltsin did not withdraw his dissolution decree. At a meeting on 30 September representatives of sixty-two out of Russia's eighty-nine republics and regions, mostly from soviets, called on Yeltsin to lift the blockade on the White House.[57] The general tendency for regional leaderships to use the crisis to advance their own interests was clear.

Heavy-handed attempts to impose controls over the media during the crisis were condemned on 28 September by Gleb Pavlovskii, one of the heads of the Postfaktum independent news agency. He criticised the government's instructions ordering state-run radio and television not to report the negative reactions from regions and republics, the president's declining popularity in the provinces, or to make much of attempts to find a mediated solution of the crisis by independent politicians.[58] The army leadership in the shape of defence minister Grachev declared their neutrality and their unwillingness to be drawn into political conflict. At this stage, declarations of neutrality served Yeltsin well. Andrei Kokoshin, the first deputy defence minister and the only civilian defence minister, insisted that there was no evidence of active support for parliament in the army, but just in case warned of the extreme penalties for any commander who deviated from Defence Ministry orders.[59]

In the event it was the army that saved Yeltsin's fortunes. Violent demonstrations on Sunday 3 October soon gave way to insurrection, with armed marauders from the White House seizing the Mayor's office in the old Comecon building opposite. If at that point they had turned west and marched on the Kremlin they may well have been able to seize power, instead the insurgents turned north into the suburbs to seize the Ostankino television centre. Here they encountered stiff resistance from the Interior Ministry forces defending the building, and got locked into a firefight lasting several hours. By the evening Yeltsin had returned to the Kremlin from his dacha, and then spent a large part of the night urging the military commanders to crush the insurgency. Having learnt the pitfalls of intervening in domestic political disputes, the military leadership was wary but finally agreed to take action, although a military force was only assembled with considerable difficulty and drew on numerous units and the Alpha security force. By dawn on 4 October the White House was ringed by tanks and by the afternoon the rebel leaders headed by Rutskoi and Khasbulatov had surrendered and were incarcerated in the Lefortovo gaol. According to official statistics, 146 people died in the fighting.[60]

The exit from communism had bequeathed Russia with a new type of dual power as parliament and president struggled for control over policy and government. Continued allegiance to the slogan of 'all power to the soviets' encouraged Congress to undermine all purposeful activity by the government, while the executive authorities increasingly ruled as if there was no parliament. The amended 1978 constitution had become a mix of democratic and traditional elements, with a large section, for example, second to none in its evocation of classical liberal rights, but this was balanced by sections reiterating the commitment to the politics of Soviet power. Thus the principle of 'the defence of the constitution' could mean different things to different people, just as the process of drafting the new constitution itself reflected not only genuine differences of principle but the struggle between different elite groups to control the process. The interpenetration of questions of principle and the struggle for power was the hallmark of the confused but increasingly polarised struggle between the executive and legislative up to October 1993. By that time the constitutional crisis had become a political crisis and increasingly threatened not only the cohesion of the polity but the integrity of the country as well.

The struggle was not exclusively one between two branches of power, the executive and the legislative, but was waged within parliament itself. On the one hand, the so-called democrats were, for various reasons, unable to sustain an independent challenge within parliament and were thus forced to rely on presidential structures, a shift which made democratic reform in Russia a technocratic project rather than something with an organised mass base. On the other hand, an alternative movement coalesced around the 'rejectionists', supported by perhaps the majority of deputies who rejected the dissolution of communist power, the disintegration of the USSR and the onset of radical marketisation. The conflict between these two groups was only gradually transformed into a struggle between institutions, with the rejectionists reluctant to give up their power base in parliament or their control over the constitutional process.

While formally the Supreme Soviet might have had legality on its side, it lacked political and popular legitimacy. It was almost completely devoid of institutional bases of support, having alienated in turn important interests like the media and the armed forces, quite apart from public opinion. The only serious forces that rallied to parliament's cause were the section of the Constitutional Court supporting Zor'kin's position, and about half of the regional soviets, and even then their support was highly qualified. The majority of Russians believed that political legitimacy lay with the democratically elected president and not with parliament. As Sergei Kovalev, the former head of parliament's human rights committee and later chairman of the Commission on Human Rights under the Russian presidency, put it, the president 'made an unconstitutional yet equitable step based not on the letter of the law, but on the fundamental principle of right'.[61] Vladimir Orlov in *Moscow News* put it equally strongly when he argued that there was 'a force above the constitution, the force of the people'.[62] Vera Tolz sums up: 'Regardless of what the constitution says, many Russians believe that real political legitimacy resides with the democratically elected president and not with the congress.'[63]

Others, however, suggest that there was an alternative to 21 September. They insist that the presidential team deliberately misread the results of the April 1993 referendum and refused to see that the message was for both sides to reach agreement. Yeltsin's political style was very different to Gorbachev's and was based on destroying opponents completely and expelling them irreversibly from the political arena. This war to the death first meant Gorbachev's political annihilation, then Khasbulatov's and Rutskoi's, but in the event cleared the space and prepared the conditions for Zhirinovskii and Zyuganov. Yeltsin was not a consensus politician nor an institution builder but held presidential structures in a constant state of precarious reorganisation; thus not allowing them to assume an identity, or political stance, of their own. His failure to establish an effective working relationship with parliament was hardly surprising given his failure to work even with his own mass support in the Democratic Russia movement.

The Russian October of 1993 can be seen, for good or ill, as completing the revolution of August 1991. Neither the banning of the Communist Party nor the dissolution of parliament were strictly speaking constitutional acts, but while deficient in legality they clearly commanded a high degree of popular legitimacy. While there are certain similarities between Yeltsin's act and that of president Fujimori in Peru in his *autogolpe* (self-coup) of April 1992, perhaps a better analogy is with De Gaulle's démarches from 1958 leading to the end of the parliamentary Fourth Republic and the establishment of the presidential Fifth Republic. Bitterly divisive though De Gaulle's acts may have been in the political community, the referendum of September 1958 showed overwhelming popular support (about 80 per cent of voters) for the new presidentialist constitution.

In Russia, however, the violent dénouement to the conflict irreparably damaged Yeltsin's reputation and undermined the legitimacy of the new constitutional order. Since the August 1991 coup Yeltsin had appeared to many as too much of a destroyer, a *soi-disant* democrat employing Bolshevik methods to destroy Bolshevism. Democratic Russia naturally supported the regime, but there was no great outpouring of support for Yeltsin's dissolution of parliament. Rather than the mass demonstrations typical of Yeltsin's insurgent phase against the communist regime, only some 10,000 gathered in his support outside the Moscow Soviet on Tverskaya on 26 September. Polls suggested that while 43.2 per cent supported his decree of 21 September (it was opposed by 29.6 per cent), only 20.2 per cent supported the blockade of the White House while 58.1 opposed it, and only 19.4 per cent supported the storming of the parliament building, an act condemned by 60.2 per cent.[64] Whereas the parliamentary side required positive commitment, apathy and neutrality worked to the president's advantage, but alienation is not a good basis on which to build a political system.

PARLIAMENT: TAKE TWO

The 1993 constitution abolished the two-tier system of Congress and Supreme Soviet and created a bicameral Federal Assembly: the upper house, the Federation Council, made up of 178 representatives from Russia's 89 federal components; and the lower house, the State Duma, with 450 deputies. The establishment of the Federal Assembly marked a decisive break with Soviet traditions. The constitution clearly outlined the functions of the two chambers of parliament, with the powers granted to the Assembly balanced by countervailing powers of the executive.

The Federation Council (FC)

Whereas the two chambers in the old Supreme Soviet, the Council of the Republic and the Council of the Nationalities, were in effect two parts of a single unit, often meeting together and with a single presidium, the Federal Assembly is a genuinely bicameral body. The State Duma and the Federation Council are located in different buildings and meet separately, except for ceremonial occasions. The FC allows the direct representation of the components of the federation in the parliamentary system and acts like the Senate in the USA, with two representatives apiece from Russia's 89 components, one each from the executive and legislative branches (article 95.2). It is responsible not only for the nationalities question, the prerogative of the old Council of Nationalities, but bears equal responsibility for the monitoring of regional issues. In terms of parliamentary procedures, the rights of the republics and regions have indeed been equalised.

Yeltsin's plan to convert the unelected Federation Council created in August 1993 into the upper chamber of parliament was opposed even by his own supporters, and soon after the October events he announced simultaneous elections to both houses of the Federal Assembly. The first 2-year convocation of the FC was elected in open competition in the December 1993 elections. Electoral associations were largely irrelevant and the great majority of members elected (108 out of 178) were independents. Dominated by elites from the regions and republics, the FC brought together many experienced and serious politicians, including many presidents of the republics and regional governors. The FC acted as an effective counterweight to the Duma and was able to moderate conflict between the president and the lower house.

The FC shares the legislative role with the Duma, with a majority in both houses required for most bills to become law. If the president vetoes a bill, a two-thirds majority is required to override the veto. Certain legislative functions are exclusively the preserve of the upper house (article 102.1), above all matters affecting the republics and regions; approval of internal border changes; confirming presidential decrees; imposing a state of emergency or martial law; the use of armed forces outside the Russian Federation; scheduling presidential elections; impeachment of the president, and certain judicial functions including (on the president's initiative), ratifying and removing from office the Procurator-General, appointing justices of the Constitutional, Supreme and Supreme Arbitration Courts, and overseeing federal laws adopted by the State Duma.

Bills are usually drafted by committees of the Duma and then, if passed by a simple majority, are sent to the FC where, if receiving 50 per cent support they become law when signed by the president. In case of disagreement a reconciliation committee is established. The question of equality of rights between them does not arise since the two bodies have different functions, a major advance in the development of constitutional order in Russia. However, certain functions that might properly be considered the prerogative of the Duma, like the right to introduce a state of emergency or the decision to send troops abroad, are granted by the constitution (article 102) to the FC rather than to the Duma as a result of the convulsions of 1993.[65]

The first convocation of the FC by and large supported the Yeltsin administration, voting for the Social Accord Treaty in April 1994 and giving critical support on other issues. The selection of Vladimir Shumeiko, a close presidential ally and a member of Russia's Choice, to chair the first convocation, helped moderate conflicts. Since the majority of deputies were employed elsewhere, however, absenteeism was high and it was often difficult to gather a quorum. Whereas Duma deputies customarily spend three weeks in four in parliament and a week in their constituencies (if elected as single-members), it is the other way round for members of the FC who usually bear major responsibilities in their constituencies. The work of the upper house demonstrated the irrelevance of party labels, and appeals for support had to be couched in the language of regional interests.

The constitution requires an upper house for the Duma to be able to act as a law-making body, but delays in adopting a law on constituting the Federation Council threatened to undermine the validity of the 1995 Duma elections. According to the constitution (article 95.2), the FC 'consists of two representatives from each member of the Russian Federation; one each from the representative and executive bodies of state power', but the detailed procedure for 'forming' the FC was to be regulated by federal law (article 96.2). The notion of 'forming' (*formirovanie*) allows varying interpretations, including election, delegation or appointment.[66] The upper house in Germany, the Bundesrat, is appointed, but the Duma argued that this was unsuitable for Russian conditions and insisted that the Federation Council should remain an elected body. But should the elections be open to anyone, or should the heads of administration and the legislatures be elected and then automatically made members of the FC? The majority of heads of administration at that time were not elected but appointed by the president, while about half of the local legislatures were filled by appointees of the executive authorities.

The controversy lasted right up to the December 1995 elections. The legislative committees of both houses supported the electoral variant, and although a law to this effect was passed on 27 July it was vetoed and a second version was adopted on 11 October 1995. At that time 66 out of 89 regional governors and presidents of republics were presidential appointees. Yeltsin sought to delay regional and republican elections until after the presidential elections, and in concession to this the final law adopted by the Duma on 5 December 1995 allowed the postponement of gubernatorial elections for up to one year. According to the new law the Federation Council is formed from the governors (heads of administration) and legislative heads from each of Russia's eighty-nine components. Those republics with bicameral assemblies (like Karelia and Yakutia) were forced to choose between their two speakers. The governors were to be popularly elected by December 1996, although twelve exceptions were made allowing elections in December 1995. A candidate wins if they gain 50 per cent plus one of the vote; if not, the contest goes to a second round between the two leading candidates.[67] Members of the FC are full-time officials in their own regions or republics and thus have little time to devote to Federation Council matters. To compensate, the FC's apparatus was strengthened to increase the throughput of legislation.

The second convocation of the FC elected the former Politburo member Yegor Stroev as its new chairman on 23 January 1996. He sought to strengthen Russia's federal system while improving the work of the FC itself, in particular by addressing the problem of poor attendance. Stroev had become a member of Russia Our Home's leadership in May 1995, having been elected governor of Orël oblast on 11 April 1993 and winning a seat in the FC in December 1993 with 80 per cent of the vote.

The State Duma

The lower house, the State Duma, is elected every four years and consists of 450 deputies. The State Duma elected in December 1993, however, lasted only 2 years, on the grounds that the pace of change was too rapid for a long parliamentary term. The accompanying debate over the new electoral law sought to draw on world experience. The simple first-past-the-post system, as practised in Britain, was considered unfair, and a mixed territorial and party system, as applied in Germany, Georgia and Lithuania, was adopted for elections in 1993 and 1995, with half the Duma elected by a proportional party-list system and half from single-member constituencies.

The first task facing the Fifth Duma was to establish its own working practices, leading to the charge that it spent more time dealing with its own affairs than those of the country. It adopted a law on the status of deputies, the Duma's budget, regulations (*reglament*) on its work and on secretarial and other support for deputies.[68] Article 97.3 of the new constitution insisted that 'Deputies to the State Duma work on a professional permanent basis' unless engaged in teaching, scientific research or work related to the arts; the transitional arrangments for the Fifth Duma, however, allowed ministers to remain MPs. The Duma met in plenary session for only two days a week, and the other three were devoted to work in the committees. Duma committees (there were twenty-three in the Fifth Duma, twenty-eight in the Sixth) are divided among factions according to what is known as portfolio agreements. The victors of the 1993 elections, the LDPR, gained the chairmanship of the geopolitics committee, whose productivity was close to nil, while Yabloko's Mikhail Zadornov at the head of the budget committee proved able to rise above factional interests and steer through important legislation in both the Fifth and Sixth Dumas. It is in the committees that acts are discussed and amendments proposed, work that is invisible to the general public until it bears fruit in legislation. While much legislation passes through on the nod in Western parliaments, in Russia each paragraph tends to be the subject of heated debate by the Duma as whole.

The candidate from the APR, Ivan Rybkin, was elected chair of the Fifth Duma, with the support of communists and the LDPR, but in contrast to his predecessor, Khasbulatov, he turned out to be a fair and non-partisan speaker. Learning from bitter experience, the constitution does not envisage the post of speaker as the organiser of parliament, and neither does it provide for a presidium. The presidium has been replaced by a committee which manages general organisational affairs; and the powers of the speaker were drastically reduced. Rybkin, however, gained greatly in authority, although his attempts at impartiality were condemned as betrayal by some of his former communist colleagues. His supple leadership played an important part in facilitating cooperation and in making the Duma an important element in the decision-making process.[69] The majority of communist deputies themselves, however, had become 'parliamentarianised', and communists became one of the most effective parliamentary factions.

The distinction between factions and groups is important: a faction is formed by parties crossing the 5 per cent threshold (eight in the 1993 elections, four in 1995); whereas deputy groups, enjoying the same rights as factions, can be formed on an *ad-hoc* basis as long as (according to rules adopted in January 1994) a minimum of thirty-five deputies join. This allowed the large number of deputies elected as independents in single-member constituencies to combine, although some joined the established factions. In January 1994 the New Regional Policy group attracted sixty-seven newly elected deputies from the constituencies (where over half were elected as independents), and even attracted deputies from established factions, in particular from Russia's Choice.

The political characteristics of the new assembly recalled those of the old one. The proportional system had been introduced to tie deputies to the emerging party system by imposing an element of discipline on their behaviour. The intention had been to 'parliamentarianise' the embryonic parties and at the same time to stimulate their development.[70] These aims were only partially fulfilled. While the shifting mass of weakly differentiated factions lacking effective leadership might have gone, many of the new factions and groups were poorly organised. The LDPR's unity broke down once Duma politics got under way, and some of the party's MPs began to see Zhirinovskii as more of a liability than an asset and some of its local organisations sought to distance themselves from the party.[71] Party factions and groups remained fluid with considerable movement between them, with a quarter of Gaidar's faction deserting him in the Fifth Duma, while Yabloko lost a fifth of its members.[72] Only the CPRF faction developed a sense of cohesion, and thus contributed to the emergence of a rudimentary sense of party discipline in voting.

The Duma is at the heart of the legislative process, drafting and endorsing laws and issuing resolutions (*postanovleniya*), but a variety of bodies are granted the right to initiate legislation, including the government, the Federation Council and the president (article 104), who was also granted the right to issue laws by decrees. The constitution does not specify the relative superiority of legislative acts or decrees, but world practice favours the former. An absolutely crucial provision allows the Duma and the FC to override a presidential veto or decree if both houses can gather a two-thirds majority. For a bill to become law a simple majority of the Duma and then of the Federation Council is required; budgetary and taxation laws also require the approval of the government. Bills are then passed to the president and if within fourteen days he or she vetoes it, it is then sent back to parliament and can only become law if passed by two-thirds of the deputies in both chambers. The Constitutional Court adjudicates contradictions between parliamentary legislation and presidential decrees.

The Duma's prerogatives include the initiation of impeachment proceedings against the president, endorsing the president's choice of the prime minister, declaring an amnesty (the president retaining the right for pardons), and calling for a vote of confidence in the government as a result of which the president can either change the government or dissolve the Duma. A parliamentary amendment on 14 April 1995 requires a faction to collect a minimum of ninety votes before tabling a no-confidence motion in the government. The Duma's oversight functions of the budgetary process are relatively limited, simply adopting the budget as a whole. In parliamentary systems the government is chosen by parliament and held accountable to it, but other than endorsing the president's choice of prime minister the Duma has little to say in the formation of the government and cannot dismiss specific ministers, let alone the prime minister. The State Duma has the right to reject two presidential nominees for prime minister, but if it rejects them a third time then the president can dissolve the Duma, a right that cannot be exercised in the first year after parliamentary elections (see chapter 7). Urgent constitutional amendments include increasing the Duma's control over the budgetary process and its oversight of the government.

In November 1993 the president's press officer, Vyacheslav Kostikov, had suggested that irrespective of the results of the elections there was no reason to change the prime minister.[73] Despite the constitution's stipulation that the head of the government is nominated by the president, the State Duma must give its consent and normal parliamentary practice, albeit in an attenuated form, asserted itself to ensure some correspondence between the composition of the government and the political complexion of the Duma. Lacking a majority in parliament the reformists after December 1993 were forced to cede their positions. Gaidar had earlier been most insistent that Yeltsin dissolve the old parliament and hold legislative (but not presidential) elections, but instead of gaining a firm legislative base for his reformist government it was Gaidar who was forced to resign.

For the first time Russia had the possibility of creating a genuine parliament. Virtually all the deputies had completed higher education and worked in parliament on a full-time basis. The new legislature became an effective professional parliament and not simply a decorative adjunct to presidential politics and party struggles. The Duma proved capable of independent initiatives, but its powers were limited, though in February 1994 it exercised its questionable right to pardon those involved in the events of 3–4 October 1993 and in the 1991 coup. Despite Yeltsin's protests, Rutskoi, Khasbulatov and others were released from gaol, and an end was put to the whole affair. The Chechen war exposed the limits of the Duma's powers, and its divisions. The crisis starkly revealed the changed balance of power between the executive and the legislative, and factional differences prevented the passage of a no-confidence vote on the government. Attempts to bolster the legislature's control over military action within Russia failed, and in March 1995 the Duma dismissed the human rights commissioner, Sergei Kovalev.

Formally, the Duma lacks the right of interpellation (the calling of ministers to account in writing) but the work of ministers has been monitored through the committee system and the Duma voted to devote the last hour of every Friday to examine the work of ministries. It also lacks sufficient powers to monitor the implementation and observance of the laws it passes, without which legislative activity becomes meaningless. Nevertheless it began to undertake these duties, and in its first session held some sixty parliamentary hearings, many of the resulting recommendations being adopted by the ministries concerned or incorporated into decrees and laws. Thus, despite the limited rights formally granted by the constitution, parliament's oversight functions grew. For the first time since 1991 a budget was adopted in December 1995 before it was actually due to come into effect. In its 2-year convocation the Fifth Duma passed 461 draft laws, 282 of which were signed into law by president Yeltsin. Three out of the twelve constitutional laws were adopted (on Referendums, on the Constitutional Court, and on the Supreme Arbitration Court), while a sixth of the laws concerned economic matters. More than 500 partly drafted laws were referred to the Sixth Duma, which held its first meeting on 16 January 1996.[74]

The 1993 constitution provided an effective environment for political stabilisation, marginalising extremism and facilitating compromise and consensus.[75] Although it was a dangerous business to be a deputy in Russia, with three murdered in the first year of the Fifth Duma,[76] politics became increasingly parliamentarianised as parties focused on fighting elections and on the legislature; the virulent rejectionists (many of whom were elected to the Duma) were sidelined. The new cohort was in a better position to play a stabilising role in the regions, with many of the most influential politicians, together with representatives of social and political movements, now directly involved in parliament. In his press conference of 22 December 1993 Yeltsin committed himself to working closely with the new assembly,[77] and by and large he kept his promise, assisted by G. Satarov, the presidential adviser responsible for relations with the Duma. A core of experienced legislators now emerged determined to avoid the fate of earlier legislatures. Elected for a 2-year term in December 1993, it appeared that deputies had no sooner learnt how to become effective parliamentarians than their term ended – hence the many calls for the postponement of the 1995 legislative elections. In the Fifth Duma's final session on 22 December 1995 Rybkin read out a letter from Yeltsin praising the lower house for furthering Russia's transition 'to civilised parliamentarianism'.

The Sixth Duma contained 157 members of the old Duma (35 per cent), 49 per cent of the new convocation had been legislators at various levels before, fifty-two had worked in various executive branches, fifteen had previously been members of the Federation Council, and 29 per cent came from Moscow.[78] Although the CPRF did remarkably well, winning 157 seats in the new Duma (see appendix 2.6), the pro-communist bloc with 45 per cent of the seats failed to obtain the two-thirds required to overturn a presidential veto. The CPRF faction reflected the age profile of the party as a whole, with over one-third over 50 years of age and another 6.5 per cent over 60; workers accounted for no more than 7 per cent.[79] There were fears that a CPRF-dominated duma would entail constitutional paralysis, with attempts to restore the soviets, denounce the Belovezha Accords, resurrect the USSR, put Yeltsin on trial, revoke international treaties and introduce censorship.[80] The communist Gennadii Seleznev, a deputy speaker in the Fifth Duma and from January 1995 a secretary of the CPRF's Central Committee, was elected chairman of the Duma but refused to suspend his party membership, although he claimed he would work on behalf of the Duma as a whole and concentrate on improving its functioning. From the moderate wing of the CPRF, Seleznev noted that Russia could learn from the Chinese model of economic reform and argued that the Swedish model of socialism was applicable to Russia.[81] Shokhin from the Russia Our Home faction was elected first deputy speaker and four other deputy speakers were chosen. Committee chairmanships were divided not only between the four factions crossing the 5 per cent threshold but also the three groups formed in the new Duma.[82] The CPRF headed nine committees, the three other factions four apiece, and the rest among the three other groups.

PARLIAMENTARIANISM AND RUSSIAN POLITICS

In the transition from communism the articulation of interests and group concerns far exceeded the abilities of the political system to aggregate them.[83] The fate of the old parliament clearly demonstrated the difference between 'democratisation', a process in which the political and economic bases of democracy are established, and 'democracy' itself, which by and large can concern itself with the defence of rights and the formal pursuit of contestatory politics. The bracketing of the process from the purpose suggests that a different set of rules apply to each, a course fraught with danger. The Bolshevik regime itself was ostensibly nothing else but a means to an end, but ultimately its self-preservation became the end itself.

The use of undemocratic methods to establish democracy raises many of the classical issues about the extent to which a democratic order has the right to defend itself. The Nazi Party was banned in post-war Germany, and other countries have legislated against incitement to racial hatred or the violent overthrow of the state. While there are undoubtedly dangers in the recourse to unconstitutional acts, the resolution of the crisis of dual power during September and October 1993 by forceful means did necessarily mean a setback for the growth of parliamentarianism in Russia. Many, indeed, would argue that the opposite is the case, and that the removal of the Soviet-style parliament and the establishment of the Federal Assembly opened the door to the emergence of Western-style parliamentary politics and the rule of law.

After October 1993 some of the structural sources of conflict between parliament and the presidency were eliminated. The Russian parliament between 1990 and 1993 acted as a permanently functioning constituent assembly, passing hundreds of constitutional amendments, while the president in turn issued hundreds of *ukazy*, modifying Russia's legal space at will. The multi-tier legislature in Russian and Soviet history has typically been designed to limit popular sovereignty, and now its abolition and the creation of a bicameral assembly represented a major advance towards democracy in Russia. The abolition of the Supreme Soviet's Presidium, which had in effect become an alternative government, now gave the concept of the separation of powers institutional form. Whereas deputies in the old Supreme Soviet veered towards irreconcilable opposition, politics in the new Duma set up a drift towards the political centre. The redistribution of powers between the branches of government at least established a viable political system and eliminated the source of some of the earlier conflicts. The strong presidency now had a juridical basis to it, while the emergence of a strong prime minister gave greater flexibility to executive power and allowed a separation of functions within the political system. Above all, the removal of the constitution as a weapon in political struggle allowed political stabilisation.

The adoption of the constitution inaugurated a new period in the development of parliamentarianism in Russia. Yeltsin's alleged strategy for a 'controllable democracy' in Russia[84] was only partially successful. The new legislature, in contrast to the old Supreme Soviet, is clearly now the junior partner, but fears that the new legislature would be a 'pocket' parliament proved exaggerated. The legislature has not been converted into a branch of the executive; nor can it claim the prerogatives of the executive. The Duma was able to carve out an important role for itself *despite* the formal provisions of the constitution but *within* the constitution's framework. The constitution, moreover, does not regulate in detail the relations between the executive and the legislative branches of government; these very ambiguities potentially allow the development of a viable parliamentarianism in Russia. It is as destabilising for legislatures to have too much power as to have too little, and only history will tell whether the balance established in 1993 is a viable one.

7 Remaking the state: the executive

A constitution is the property of a nation, and not of those who exercise the government.

Thomas Paine[1]

A qualitatively new stage in Russia's history began in 1991, the attempt to find a viable form of post-communist government. The victory of the Russian 'shadow state' over the Soviet system in August 1991, followed swiftly by the demise of the Communist Party and the disintegration of the USSR, established the conditions for rebuilding government on new principles. While the democrats might have come to power, it was not clear whether democracy itself had triumphed. The challenge now was to institutionalise the new political order by forging instruments of executive authority that were both accountable to a legislature and operated within the rules of law overseen by an independent judiciary and regulated by a constitution. Almost none of this existed amidst the rubble of the Soviet regime, but very soon a powerful executive was reconstituted that overshadowed not only the legislature but the very democratic gains that it claimed to advance.

THE PRESIDENCY

The academic debate over the relative merits of parliamentary and presidential systems of government is far from over, but in Russia the issue is far from academic. Advocates of parliamentary government, of the sort practised in Britain or Germany, stress that it encourages democratic forms of conflict resolution; the development of lively party systems; the clear formulation of alternative policy choices; the constant scrutiny of government and public administration; flexibility in the timing of elections if the government loses its majority or the confidence of parliament; and allows mistakes to be corrected and extremes to be tempered. They level three main arguments against presidential systems: over-dependence on the personality of the leader often giving rise to unpredictability; the way that they undermine the development of party systems; and the limits placed on the formulation of clear policy choices and alternative governments.[2]

Presidentialists counter by insisting that parliamentary rule is a luxury afforded only to stable societies. As an anonymous Yeltsin aide put it, a parliamentary republic is 'unsuited for our severe social-climatic conditions'.[3] In the immature post-communist democracies, the argument goes, the attitudes and elites from the past were too strong, the tasks too urgent, the aggregation of interests too fluid, and the social bases for party systems too amorphous to allow parliamentary government. Partisans of presidential rule stress the need for a strong executive (the 'strong hand') to overcome overt and covert resistance in the transition to new forms of political and economic life. The sheer number of parties could not compensate for their organisational weakness and lack of influence in society, and the development of parliamentarianism was hesitant and contradictory. In these circumstances only a strong presidency could provide effective leadership to drive through the necessary reforms. In Russia, moreover, as Yeltsin noted in April 1992, the very unity of the country was at stake and could best be preserved by a strong executive.[4]

Presidential and parliamentary forms of rule, however, do not necessarily have to be exclusive. Earlier drafts of the Russian constitution had favoured a mixed system along the lines of the quasi-presidential system in France, where the president is directly elected by the people and the prime minister has to command a parliamentary majority. The French president is elected by popular mandate and conventionally enjoys the right to formulate foreign policy and aspects of domestic policy, but the government requires a majority in parliament and thus also enjoys a popular mandate. Such a civilised compromise, probably the optimum variant for peaceful political development in Russia, is not altogether foreclosed. Developments in Russia, moreover, were only part of a larger trend towards the strengthening of executive authority throughout the region. Belarus in spring 1994 was the last of the post-Soviet states to establish an executive presidency, while Hungary and the Czech Republic were the main examples of parliamentary systems in Central Europe. Rudimentary party systems, faction-ridden parliaments, and grave economic and social crises appeared to justify the strengthening of executive power elsewhere.

The emergence of presidential rule

A presidential system emerged in the last Soviet years to compensate for the decline of the CPSU and the weakness of parliament.[5] Despite the resurrection of the revolutionary slogan 'all power to the soviets', the revived legislatures failed to live up to expectations. The constitutional amendments of 1 December 1988 made the USSR CPD the highest power in the land, and following the elections of March 1989 Gorbachev was elected chair of the new body and the basis of his rule began to shift from the Party to the new legislature. On the very day that the Communist Party officially lost its monopoly on power on 14 March 1990, the powers of the presidency were strengthened. A national executive presidency independent of the legislature was established, and Gorbachev was elected to this post in an uncontested ballot by the CPD on 15 March 1990. His refusal to face national elections undermined the legitimacy not only of the post but marked the point where his credibility as a democratic reformer was fatally damaged. Presidential powers were increased during the course of the year, and at the Fourth USSR CPD in December 1990 the shift to presidential power was completed by the transformation of the old Council of Ministers into a more limited 'cabinet', with the prime minister and ministers nominated by the president and accountable to him.

The powers of the prime minister remained limited and the executive powers that were more properly the prerogative of the government were devolved to the Supreme Soviet's Presidium. While the powers of the presidency were greatly increased, the powers of the Soviet legislature were not correspondingly diminished. A new type of dual power emerged that was inherently unstable but manageable as long as the chairmanship of parliament was in safe hands. The chairman of the Soviet Congress, Luk'yanov, however, betrayed Gorbachev in August 1991, and later, after much the same system was reproduced in Russia, the struggle between the presidency and parliament dominated the first phase of Russia's independent statehood. When Yeltsin became chair of the Russian Supreme Soviet in May 1990 he gained executive authority but his powers were firmly subordinated to the legislature. The trajectory towards parliamentary rule, designed initially to compensate for the declining power of the CPSU, was intercepted by the emergence of presidential systems rooted in the newly 'empowered' legislatures but naturally striving to increase their own powers at the expense of the legislatures that had given them birth.

The presidential option looked increasingly attractive as a means to overcome the crisis of reform in Russia. At the First CPD between May and June 1990 all factions united in favour of a strong leadership, and with Yeltsin's election to chair the Supreme Soviet a significant step was taken towards the development of the presidential system in Russia. In 1990 the Russian parliament passed some 150 acts affecting virtually every aspect of Russian life; even so, Yeltsin insisted that the crisis of executive power remained acute.[6] His conservative opponents began to have second thoughts over the merits of a presidential system, but were outmanoeuvred, by the opportunity offered by Gorbachev's referendum of 17 March 1991 on the 'renewed Union'. As noted (pp. 12–13), a second question was added to the ballot in Russia asking 'Do you consider necessary the introduction of the post of president of the RSFSR, elected by universal suffrage?' Russians voted by the same margin for the Union and a directly elected president of Russia.[7]

At the Third (Emergency) Congress Yeltsin, in one of those reversals of fortune that mark his career, turned the tables on those who had sought to curb his powers and emerged with a mandate for a strengthened presidency. On the opening day, 28 March 1991, Gorbachev tried to enforce his ban on marches by introducing troops into Moscow, but popular defiance showed him where power really lay, and soon afterwards he signed the Novo-Ogarevo 'nine-plus-one' agreement with Russia and the other republics. For the Congress and Yeltsin, the day proved decisive. The conservative bloc 'Communists of Russia', with their allies in the 'Rossiya' faction (together comprising about half the deputies), tried to keep the question of the presidency off the agenda. The unpopularity of the Soviet government (headed by Pavlov), and the increasingly stark conflict between allegiance to the unitary CPSU and aspirations for Russian sovereignty and statehood, led to a break in communist ranks. The Afghan war veteran and noted patriot, Rutskoi, defected and formed his own 'Communists for Democracy' faction. The balance now shifted in Yeltsin's favour, and not only were the proposed constitutional changes affecting the powers of the presidency accepted and arrangements made for elections on 12 June, but the Congress, on its last day, 5 April, accepted Yeltsin's surprise demand for immediate powers to issue presidential decrees within the framework of existing legislation to hasten economic and political reform in Russia.

The necessary amendments were made to the constitution at the Fourth CPD on 22 May 1991. The principle of the division of powers was ratified, and executive and judicial branches of the state were to be formed. The new president, elected for no more than two consecutive 5-year terms, could not be a deputy or a member of a political party. He or she would head the executive branch and would be the highest official in the land, but was obliged to report to the Congress at least once a year. The president had the right to issue binding decrees and to suspend decisions of executive bodies if they contradicted the constitution or Russian laws. Both the Supreme Soviet and the Congress, however, could revoke presidential decrees, although the actual voting procedures to do this were not specified. The Congress could impeach the president by a two-thirds vote on a report by the Constitutional Court issued at the initiative of the Congress itself, the Supreme Soviet, or one of its chambers.[8] Thus the extensive powers of an executive presidency were enshrined in law, but so too were a number of slow-acting time bombs.

The session also adopted a law on the election of the president, and after an intense two-week campaign the first direct elections for Russia's presidency were held on 12 June 1991 (see appendix 2.3). The former prime minister, Ryzhkov, was the most serious challenger to Yeltsin, standing as the candidate of the establishment and receiving the support of the Communist Party apparatus and the media. His programme appealed to the stability and order of the Soviet system, a system that was palpably unstable and disordered. Bakatin stood for the more liberal side of the communist establishment, the side represented by Gorbachev's reformism. Though he had established his liberal credentials when minister of the interior before being replaced by Pugo in late 1990, Bakatin's poor challenge was yet another indication of the low esteem in which Gorbachev's reform communism was held. Zhirinovskii was apparently a joke candidate, with his wild nationalistic rhetoric and populist promises of instant wealth, yet his strong showing revealed the volatility and alienation of the electorate. General Al'bert Makashov had already made a name for himself at the founding congress of the CP RSFSR in June 1990, when he had assailed Gorbachev's record both at home and abroad. Aman Tuleev was the chair of the Kemerovo oblast soviet and posed as the defender of local autonomy and controlled economic reform.[9]

Yeltsin's decisive victory, polling 57 per cent of the vote and thus winning outright in the first round,[10] endowed his presidency with a popular legitimacy that Gorbachev's had lacked and helped him withstand the August coup. Instead of the largely ceremonial presidency, as in Czechoslovakia and Hungary, Russia found itself with an executive presidency on the American model. Victory gave Yeltsin freedom of manoeuvre in relations with parliament and allowed him to confront the CPSU. But, as with the Soviet parliament earlier, while the authority of the presidency had increased, the powers of parliament had not correspondingly decreased.

Following his inauguration on 10 July Yeltsin issued a flurry of presidential decrees, including the reappointment of Silaev as prime minister and the appointment of a number of ministers to the Russian government, the creation of a presidential administration, and a renewed onslaught against the CPSU by banning political parties from executive bodies. Yeltsin's heroic resistance to the coup seemed to justify the growth of presidential power, and the hastily reconvened Supreme Soviet in August granted him emergency powers to deal with the situation. He was granted yet more powers by the reconvened Fifth CPD (28 October–2 November 1991), including the right to reorganise the government, but now attempts were made to define the legal relationship between the president and the Supreme Soviet to avoid presidential power turning into dictatorship. On 2 November 1991 the Congress gave him the power for one year to appoint ministers and pass economic decrees without reference to parliament.[11] On 6 November Yeltsin assumed the post of prime minister, in addition to his other responsibilities, and placed himself at the head of a 'cabinet of reforms' (see below), with the RSFSR Council of Ministers now officially called the Russian government.

While defending strong executive authority, Yeltsin's entourage recognised the need for some separation of powers to avoid a return to a new form of despotism which would once again exclude Russia, as they put it, from 'civilised society'.[12] The idea of 'delegated legislation', in which a government is allowed to rule for a time through decrees with the force of law, is used by democratic states in times of emergency (see also O'Donnell's notion of delegative democracy, p. 164). On these occasions, however, the legislature usually establishes limits to the emergency powers, overseen by a constitutional court, and a set period which can only be renewed with the assent of parliament.[13] In Russia after the coup no such stable system emerged; the expanding powers of the presidency were at first delegated by parliament but thereafter were converted into a self-sustaining presidential system. The appeal to the logic of the struggle against Bolshevism, already seen during the insurgency phase in the form of 'wars of the laws' and declarations of sovereignty, perpetuated the Bolshevik legacy of administrative arbitrariness.

When in opposition Yeltsin had assaulted the old system with a hybrid programme encompassing a populist critique of the privileges of the power elite, an appeal to social justice, economic reform, the restoration of Russian statehood, and the radicalisation of democratic change. Once in power, however, he tempered these demands and demonstrated that he had outgrown his populist phase. No longer the challenger but the incumbent, Yeltsin soon came to rely on the instruments of the state rather than the mass politics of the street, though on occasion he was not averse to using the crowd. Yeltsin soon freed himself from the popular movement that had brought him to power.

While this meant that Yeltsin remained a free agent politically, it also suggested a failure to ensure an adequate institutional framework or political constituency to support the presidency. He failed to consult Democratic Russia over the choice of Rutskoi as his running mate for the presidential elections, nor did he consult with them over the formation of his government. Gorbachev had discovered earlier that strengthened presidential power is no guarantee of effective government. Gorbachev had ended up working in a vacuum, and the same fate threatened Yeltsin if he built up his personal authority to the detriment of institutions and mass political structures. However, while both presidencies faced similar problems, there were two great differences: first, by contrast with Gorbachev, Yeltsin had a popular mandate and represented the expressed aspirations of the people for a new system; and, second, there was no obvious individual, movement or ideology to challenge Yeltsin's authority.

Even before the coup Yeltsin had prepared a series of decrees strengthening presidential power, and these were swiftly implemented in the following months. Executive authority became more independent of the legislature, though it remained constrained by law and regulated by parliament within the framework of 'delegated legislation' and what we have termed authoritarian democracy. Many questions remained, however, including the limits to presidential power. Would a strong executive encourage the development of democracy in society, or would it act as a substitute for popular democratic organisation? Would not the 'strong hand' inevitably take on aspects of the Bolshevism which it sought to extirpate, and perpetuate rather than overcome traditions of authoritarianism and arbitrariness?

These fears appeared to be justified by the strengthening of presidential powers following the defeat of the Supreme Soviet in October 1993, a process formalised by the adoption of the constitution later that year. Many functions of the old legislature, including some of its committees and commissions, were incorporated into the presidential system and yet another massive impetus was given to the inflation of the presidential apparatus. By the same token, some of the conflicts that had formerly taken place between the two institutions were now played out within the presidential system itself. Presidential powers were enormous, including certain legislative and judicial functions. The Russian presidency began to take on the features of the Tsarist or Soviet systems, with weak prime ministers, a minimal separation of powers and with politics concentrated in the person of the monarch in their court or on the Politburo and its Central Committee apparatus. Once again an unwieldy concentration of power took place, marked by corruption and inefficiency.

The presidential system in Russia evolved rapidly, discarding bodies and creating new ones with bewildering rapidity. Below we shall look briefly at some of the main institutions since 1991.

The vice-presidency

The country has not been fortunate in its choice of vice-presidents. Gorbachev's confidence in Yanaev proved singularly misplaced, and the latter went on to act as the figurehead for the coup of August 1991. Yeltsin, too, came to rue his choice of Rutskoi as vice-president. Rutskoi, a retired air force colonel who had been shot down in Afghanistan, retained close links with the military establishment. Yeltsin had chosen Rutskoi as his running mate in the 1991 presidential elections in the belief that he could influence the vote of democratically inclined Russian communists, patriots, and reform-minded elements in the military and industrial establishments. Later Yeltsin's team would claim that Rutskoi contributed little to their victory.

Rutskoi's role in the governing team was ambiguous both because of his ambitious personality and because of the novelty of the institution. Even in the United States with a 200-year history, the role of the vice-president, apart from such duties as chairing meetings of the Senate and joint sessions of Congress, changes with the personality of each incumbent. Rutskoi had hoped after the coup that his party (the 'Communists for Democracy' group that after the coup became the People's Party of Free Russia) would form the basis of the new administration and that he would play an active executive role. On 17 November 1991 he had been assigned a number of responsibilities in the presidential administration, focusing on internal security matters and, to a lesser degree, on economic reform, yet his advice fell on deaf ears, and within a month he had become estranged from Yeltsin and isolated from the administration. Rutskoi was excluded from Yeltsin's inner circle of advisers, and was not on good terms with the presidential staff.

Rutskoi, who as vice-president might have been expected to owe Yeltsin a debt of loyalty, became one of his most bitter opponents. He challenged Yeltsin's economic reform policies and urged a more militant line over the defence of the rights of Russian minorities in other republics. He revealed his contempt for the radical reformers in the new government by calling Gaidar and his reform team 'boys in pink trousers', and he insisted that the monopolies should be broken up before prices were raised. To provide Rutskoi with some more positive occupation, Yeltsin on 12 February 1992 gave him responsibility for overseeing the reform of the farm sector, and in addition from September he was given special responsibility to oversee the fight against organised crime. Throughout 1992 he tried to maintain a fragile independence, but by the time of the April 1993 referendum Rutskoi was in open opposition to the president, and when Yeltsin decreed the dissolution of the Supreme Soviet in September 1993 Rutskoi was sworn in by the opposition as president.

Given the sad history of this institution it is not surprising that the December 1993 constitution abolished the post. In the event of the president becoming incapacitated their duties are to be carried out 'temporarily' by the prime minister, and new presidential elections must be scheduled within three months (article 92.2). The acting president is forbidden 'to dissolve the State Duma, to schedule referendums or to submit proposals on amendments to the Russian constitution or on revising its provisions' (article 92.3).

The presidential administration and advisory bodies

The administration of the president was officially established on 5 August 1991 to oversee regional and republican administration. On 13 September a group of experts was established to analyse socio-economic problems, and on 12 December a State–Legal Directorate (GPU) was formed to prepare the decisions of the president.[14] A State Council (Gossovet), named after the highest consultative body in the Russian Empire between 1810 and 1917, was established on 19 July 1991 as a consultative body responsible to the president to examine presidential decrees, to formulate priorities for government policy and to exercise a degree of control over presidential power.[15] As with many earlier institutions, under Gorbachev, the State Council was no sooner formed than abolished, in this case on 30 November 1991 when it became the Presidential Consultative Council.[16] This had a somewhat similar role to the State Council but, following protests from parliament, with a lower status and less autonomy. This, in turn, in February 1993 became simply the Presidential Council.

Chaired by the president, its thirty-odd membership included an eclectic list of the great and the good dominated by writers, academics and some politicians. The Presidential Council represented the best in Russian intellectual life but played a marginal role in detailed policy formation. The Council as a whole, for example, opposed intervention in Chechnya but was overruled by the Security Council. In January 1996 a number of prominent members resigned, including Gaidar, academician Sergei Alekseev, the journalist Otto Latsis and Sergei Kovalev, who at the same time resigned from his post as head of the presidential Human Rights Commission in protest against Yeltsin's use of force to resolve problems, the secrecy surrounding state administration, ignoring of public opinion, and personnel changes. The same charges had been made against Gorbachev earlier, and indeed the shift of the intelligentsia from Gorbachev to Yeltsin between 1990 and 1991 played an important part in the dissolution of the old regime.

Yeltsin's main councillor, Burbulis, had headed the State Council and in the space of eighteen months changed his job title five times.[17] Burbulis had taught 'scientific communism' in Sverdlovsk[18] when Yeltsin had been *obkom* first secretary there, and together both negotiated the rough passage through the democratic insurgency to the Kremlin. Having led Yeltsin's personal campaign staff in the presidential election of June 1991, Burbulis remained one of his closest advisers, taking on also the post of first deputy prime minister in late 1991, and was often represented, justifiably, as some sort of *éminence grise* behind the new regime. He was one of the main architects of the first stage of the democratic transformation in Russia: the CIS had in part been Burbulis' idea, and he was also a strong advocate of Gaidar's shock economic policies. He became the target of bitter hostility, especially from parliament, and despite his protestations was gradually marginalised,[19] until dismissed from all his substantive posts on 26 November 1992.

In the first period Yeltsin relied on two main groups, the so-called 'Sverdlovsk mafia' made up of Yeltsin's former associates from the Sverdlovsk Party organisation, and a group of younger economists around Gaidar. Both groups owed their positions entirely to Yeltsin and were thus dependent on him. The presidential administration was headed at first by Yurii Petrov, formerly Communist Party chief in Sverdlovsk. Petrov was accused by the democratic forces of obstructing reforms, and in January 1993 was replaced by Sergei Filatov, formerly Khasbulatov's deputy in parliament. Filatov, a man marked by personal integrity and impeccable democratic credentials, was clearly uncomfortable in the hothouse atmosphere of intrigue swirling around the presidency. His replacement as chief of staff on 15 January 1996 was the former nationalities minister, Nikolai Yegorov, who had been the president's representative in Chechnya from November 1994 to February 1995, during the most intense stage of the fighting. The appointment of the hard-line Yegorov indicated the strengthening of Korzhakov's position, long opposed by the liberal Filatov. Oleg Lobov, another key figure in Yeltsin's entourage who ran his inner secretariat and later became secretary of the Security Council, was formerly Petrov's deputy in Sverdlovsk.[20] Lobov was assisted by Lev Sukhanov and Viktor Ilyushin, who checked all documents before they got to Yeltsin. In the first period all key decisions went through these men, arousing enormous hostility from those excluded from this charmed inner circle.[21] Ilyushin remained the central figure at the heart of the Yeltsin administration, wielding enormous infuence over policy. The emergence of a shadowy half-world focused on the presidential chief of security, Korzhakov, has been noted earlier. As Yeltsin physically began to wane, the role of the presidential entourage appeared to become all the more prominent.

The Security Council (SC)

A Russian Security Council was established soon after Yeltsin's election as president in June 1991. It was then designed mainly as a consultative body as part of the presidential apparatus and operated in parallel with the government. When he took over direct control of the cabinet in November 1991 Yeltsin dissolved various structures that shadowed the government, including the SC. The Law on Security of 5 March 1992 reconstituted the SC as a body chaired by the president and with four other permanent members (the vice-president, prime minister, the first deputy chair of the Supreme Soviet, and the secretary of the SC, who was to be appointed by the president with the agreement of the Supreme Soviet). A law of 4 April 1992 restricted the Security Council to seven broad functions, including the drafting of basic policy guidelines and determining the key issues facing the president. Apart from Yeltsin, Rutskoi (until the vice-presidency was abolished) and Gaidar (until replaced by Chernomyrdin), membership included Filatov until January 1993, when replaced as first deputy chair of the Supreme Soviet by Yurii Voronin, and Yurii Skokov, who was SC secretary until 11 May 1993 when he was briefly replaced on 11 June by Yevgenii Shaposhnikov until Oleg Lobov took over later in the year, and numerous other members called on an *ad-hoc* basis with discretionary voting rights. In June 1996, as noted, Lebed was appointed SC secretary.

In April 1992 the Sixth CPD forced Yeltsin to resign as prime minister, and at the same time Burbulis and other allies resigned their government posts. This encouraged Yeltsin to strengthen presidential structures, especially in the field of security and foreign policy. By a decree of 3 June the SC was reformed to draft an annual report as the basic programmatic statement for executive bodies, and to draft decisions.[22] The SC's jurisdiction was significantly broadened by a presidential decree of 7 July 1992, allowing it to issue orders to heads of ministries and local governing bodies, as well as controlling the activities of organisations involved in implementing the council's decisions.

Skokov had long been associated with the defence industries and he was now given the right to coordinate the work of the executive branch.[23] The SC was likened to the Politburo of old, though Skokov denied any such role, arguing that on the contrary, the SC was a constitutional body which 'guarantees the president the opportunity of carrying out his functions in administering the state, in elaborating measures to protect the interests of society, the state and the individual'.[24] The SC effectively limited the powers of the government and parliament. The July decree called for each decision of the SC to be accompanied by a presidential decree and Skokov was given special powers to ensure their implementation, while all ministries and local officials were called upon to fulfil its decisions. The functions of the SC steadily grew: on 8 October 1992 an interdepartmental commission headed by Rutskoi was established to combat crime and corruption; the secretariat of the Council of Heads of Republics (established on 23 October 1992) was allocated to the SC; and in December 1992 an interdepartmental commission to coordinate foreign policy was established under the SC and chaired by its secretary.

The strengthened Security Council appeared to be the core of that long sought for 'strong hand', the authoritarian political structure that could manage the system in the transition to a market economy. Yeltsin's chief political adviser, Stankevich, argued that the SC would become the main strategic decision-making body in Russia.[25] Skokov sought to create a power base by forming permanent local security councils in the regions, made up of former obkom officials and the directors of the largest plants. Opponents accused the SC of replicating Communist Party structures by fusing executive and legislative power, setting the agenda and controlling information to Yeltsin. The SC was accountable neither to parliament nor to the government and to some it appeared that Yeltsin had created the instrument of his own downfall.[26] By early 1993 however (and probably not accidentally in the light of these warnings), the SC was increasingly marginalised by the rejuvenated presidential administration, now managed by Filatov, and Skokov himself was dismissed as secretary and the SC declined in importance.

Following the October 1993 events the SC was brought under the exclusive control of the president and its membership changed.[27] According to the 1993 constitution, the president 'forms and heads the Security Council' with its status to be defined by federal law (article 83.g). The amended Law on Security stipulated that the SC was subordinate to the president and chaired by him, and its decisions were to be issued in the form of presidential decrees and instructions. The SC had no independent political standing other than as an instrument of presidential rule. Like the Politburo of old, the SC usually took decisions not by a majority vote but by consensus, thus avoiding individual responsibility by its members.[28]

The SC's job was to prepare presidential decisions in the sphere of security, but security soon took on a rather broad definition. During the Chechen war the SC emerged as an important centre of power, by this time bringing together not only the president, its secretary (Lobov), but also the prime minister (Chernomyrdin), the foreign minister (Kozyrev), and the heads of the 'power ministries'.[29] It was the SC that on 29 November 1994 (and confirmed on 7 December) resolved to use force against Chechnya (probably at Grachev's instigation), a decision taken by voting rather than by the usual consensual procedure.[30] Lebed's appointment as SC secretary in June 1996 was followed by a significant expansion in its role, becoming the focus (much to prime minister Chernomyrdin's chagrin) of Yeltsin's rejuvenated presidency. A decree on 10 July charged the council with defending Russia's vital interests in the social, economic, defence, environmental and informational spheres.

The presidency according to the constitution

The new constitution is built around the principle of a strong federal presidency, granting it extensive powers in naming governments, introducing legislation and making policy. This version, it might be noted, scaled back some of the powers granted the executive in the Sobchak–Alekseev version. The president is the head of state and the 'guarantor' of the constitution (article 80), elected for a 4-year term with a maximum of two terms (with the upper age limit of 65 now dropped) (article 81), and was assigned numerous powers. The president nominates the prime minister and can chair cabinet meetings, proposes to the State Duma the director of the Central Bank, nominates to the Federation Council members of the Constitutional, Supreme and Supreme Arbitration Courts, and also nominates the Procurator-General. The president is also head of the Security Council, confirms Russia's military doctrine, appoints the commander-in-chief of the Armed Forces, and 'exercises leadership of the foreign policy of the Russian Federation' (article 86). The president is granted the right to introduce a state of emergency and suspend civil freedoms until new federal laws are adopted. Equally controversial is the presidential right to issue binding decrees that have the power of law but which do not have to be approved by parliament.

Impeachment was made extremely difficult, requiring a ruling on a demand by a duma commission, set up with at least 150 votes, by both the Supreme and Constitutional Courts to be confirmed by two-thirds of both the State Duma and the Federation Council, and was to be initiated only in the event of 'treason or commission of some other grave crime' (article 93.1). The president was granted the right to veto State Duma legislation and in extreme circumstances to dissolve it (article 109, and see pp. 152–3); if the Duma rejects the president's nomination for the post of prime minister three times, it is deemed to have dissolved itself. The post of vice-president, as noted, was abolished and in the event of the president's incapacity power is transferred to the prime minister. The government was subordinated to the president and, formally, did not have to represent the majority party or coalition in parliament (see chapter 6).

The government is appointed by the president and responsible to him or her. Like the Tsar according to the 1906 constitution, who reserved to himself responsibility for foreign policy, control of the armed forces and the executive, the 1993 constitution gives the president control over such matters as foreign and security policy. Typical patterns of Soviet politics were also replicated, above all the emergence of a multiplicity of informal bodies which aggrandised power irrespective of constitutional provisions. Russia's presidency in effect began to act as a duplicate government, with the functions of ministries often shadowed by agencies under the presidency, and the role of the cabinet itself was in effect usurped by the presidency. The 1993 constitution formalised this development by granting direct presidential control over four key areas: security, defence, home and foreign affairs. The office of prime minister therefore exerts only partial control over its own ministers, and is deprived of control over the so-called 'power ministries'.

The new constitution sought to prevent a repetition of the conflict between executive and legislative authorities that had so nearly destroyed the Russian state. A strong and largely irremovable president was to act as the focus of stability, while the government was largely removed from the control of parliament. The problem of presidential systems, however, is their rigidity; it is almost impossible to change the president in mid-term without bringing down the regime itself. Parliamentary systems, on the other hand, allow more flexibility in forming governments and in responding to popular moods. This perhaps, is precisely what the advocates of presidential government have been trying to avoid. Presidential government in post-communist Russia is based on the notion of *choicelessness* in the so-called transition. The Bolshevik formula had been 'one class, one party, one ideology' and in early post-communist Russia this appeared to become 'one policy, one leader'. The politics of reform mimicked the future-oriented politics of the old regime, although there is a qualitative difference in their orientation.

The presidential features of the constitution attracted much criticism. Zor'kin argued that the leading role of the Communist Party had been replaced by the one-man rule of the president, while Rumyantsev argued that the constitution gave legal form to the seizure of power.[31] For Victor Ilyukhin this was a 'constitution for the fascist future', while E. Volodin saw it as inaugurating 'the banana republic of Russia'.[32] A joint declaration of party leaders insisted that the constitution 'restores the authoritarian system in the Russian Federation'.[33] The actual operation of the new system of constitutional power, however, revealed that the constitution did not establish virtually unchecked executive power, as its critics had suggested would be the case. Yeltsin sought to rule with the consent of the Federal Assembly, and for the first time the legislature worked as a genuine parliament. With another president, however, the restraints on authoritarian rule might prove inadequate. Lacking a tradition of democratic institutions and conventions, a developed party system or a firm social basis for liberal politics, the adoption of the constitution suggested that democracy in Russia would be built from the roof down.

THE GOVERNMENT

Executive power in Russia is exercised by the president and the government, a dual executive system with an unclear relationship between the two. The French constitutional axiom that 'The president presides and the government governs' has little place in Russian thinking. Like its Soviet and Tsarist predecessors, the government is largely restricted to managing the economy. The constitution (article 80) endows the president with control over foreign and security policy as well as the main direction of domestic policy, and it is this article that provides the juridical basis for presidental rule. While Yeltsin's was an activist presidency, deciding routine matters on a daily basis, a more distanced relationship between the two branches could be envisaged.

Government by confusion

Silaev had been appointed Russian prime minister in June 1990 in succession to the party apparatchik and Gorbachev ally, Alexander Vlasov, and Russia now began to devise its own economic policies as the seamless web of the old Party-state began to unravel. By August 1991 Russia had 20 ministries and 21 state committees. The despised Soviet prime minister, Pavlov, became one of the leaders of the coup, and afterwards no new Soviet premier was appointed. Instead, on 26 September 1991 Silaev resigned the Russian premiership to head the new Inter-Republican Economic Commission, in effect becoming prime minister of the USSR. This was obviously an unsatisfactory situation, with unclear leadership in both the USSR and Russia leading to delays in taking crucial decisions. The Western powers at this time were quite justified in complaining that they did not know with whom to deal in Moscow, even though they favoured the continuation of the USSR in order to maintain a single economic and political space and to minimise the dangers of conflicts and the proliferation of nuclear weapons.

Yeltsin's relationship with the government up to November 1991 was equally uneasy, and even before the coup Yeltsin had restricted the scope and independence of Silaev's administration. The Russian premiership was left vacant until on 6 November 1991 Yeltsin himself assumed the post, reflecting perhaps his fear that the job might fall into the hands of a rival. Yeltsin's declaration that he would take responsibility for the implementation of reforms himself was nevertheless a courageous step, since it meant that he would be held directly responsible for the hardships to come, but it allowed him freely to use presidential decrees to drive forward the economic transformation. The constitutional status of the Russian government, however, remained ambivalent. As long as Yeltsin had been chairman of the Supreme Soviet there appeared to be no problem with the government's subordination to the Russian parliament. Once a strong presidency had emerged, however, and in the absence of a new constitution, conflict was bound to arise as Yeltsin sought to remove the government from legislative control.

To accelerate reforms the Fifth CPD allowed the presidency to form a government with only minimal legislative accountability in November 1991. Yeltsin gained the right to appoint his own cabinet, and ministers did not have to gain parliamentary approval.[34] The constitutional situation nevertheless remained unclear, and it was Khasbulatov's attempts to move the pendulum back in the direction of parliamentary oversight of the government that led to the struggles at the Sixth Congress against Gaidar's reformist cabinet and to the full-blown constitutional crisis at the Seventh and later Congresses. The struggle between the presidency and parliament squeezed the government as an instrument of executive authority.[35] The Russian government drew its authority from the president, and the emergency powers granted Yeltsin meant a relatively low degree of parliamentary oversight.

Only in November 1991 did an effective Russian government emerge when Yeltsin appointed a team of radicals to create a 'government of reforms'. On 11 November he divided Russia's twenty-four ministries into four blocks, taking under his own wing responsibility for defence and internal affairs, and appointed five deputy prime ministers: Burbulis as the first deputy prime minister, Gaidar with responsibily for economic affairs, Shakhrai as the legal adviser, Alexander Shokhin with responsibility for social affairs, and Mikhail Poltoranin as minister of information. The core of the cabinet was drawn from a group of academics close to Burbulis. Chief among them was Gaidar, 35, the minister for finance and economics who had worked with Yavlinskii and Shatalin, authors of doomed economic reform plans in the Gorbachev era, but who took a more marked neo-liberal free market line. Gaidar had been a Senior Research Fellow at the Institute of Economics, from where he brought several colleagues into the government, including Shokhin and the radical energy minister, Vladimir Lopukhin, as well as the foreign trade minister, Peter Aven, who were accused by their opponents of being theoreticians who did not understand how society actually worked. Soon afterwards Russia took over all the USSR ministries and enterprises on its territory, and the scene was set for a radical attempt at social transformation.

Gaidar now launched a radical economic reform programme, promulgated largely by Yeltsin's decrees rather than through the more cumbersome and increasingly hostile Russian Supreme Soviet. Yeltsin's strategy from late 1991 was directed towards 'a policy of breakthrough', shock therapy in the economy and marginalisation of conservative forces in parliament.[36] The 'government of reforms' launched a wave of decrees which began to break down the old economic administrative-command system and to build up the new. Above all, from 2 January 1992 the long-awaited liberalisation of prices at last began, accompanied by enormous prise rises, inflation, and falling living standards (see chapter 12). Despite fears that the reforms would provoke popular discontent, the first year of economic reform passed with remarkably little public protest. The reforms, however, were bitterly criticised by the majority in parliament, Khasbulatov personally, and vice-president Rutskoi. Yeltsin supported his government through all this, but left himself room for manoeuvre if the parliament or people suggested a serious crisis of legitimacy. When he sensed that popular acceptance of the reforms was reaching breaking point, he adjusted the tiller.

Such an adjustment took place during May–June 1992 when pressure from the conservatives and the industrial lobby forced Yeltsin to undertake a government reshuffle. Industrialists had criticised Gaidar's government for failing to extend government credits to failing enterprises or to soften the social impact of reform.[37] Yeltsin appointed three former state directors to key ministries, including Chernomyrdin, who became a deputy prime minister and took over responsibility for the energy sector from the academic Lopukhin, who had antagonised many in the industry. Chernomyrdin had been appointed minister of the Soviet gas industry in 1985, and in 1989 he became chairman of the new state company, Gazprom. Shumeiko, formerly director of the giant Krasnodar measuring instrument factory, was brought in as one of the two first deputy prime ministers. Yeltsin on 15 June 1992 signalled his determination to continue on the path of radical economic reform by appointing Gaidar acting prime minister (pending confirmation by parliament). At the same time the radical reformer Anatolii Chubais, the head of the State Property Committtee (GKI) responsible for privatisation, was promoted to become a deputy prime minister, thus strengthening Gaidar's hand in the cabinet. A 'government of deputy prime ministers' emerged as Yeltsin sought to broaden the social and political support for reform policies.

The government reshuffle in mid-1992 did not put an end to the pressure for a change of course, and increasingly, for a change of government. Rutskoi called for a reorganisation of the government in which the current 'theoreticians' should be replaced by 'people with practical knowledge'.[38] Travkin, at the time one of the leaders of Civic Union, called for Yeltsin to change the government's economic course or resign. He insisted that Yeltsin had been mistaken to dissolve the USSR, denied that the nomenklatura was impeding reform, and asserted that Yeltsin's decrees 'do not fit into our life'.[39]

Although Russia has only half the population of the former USSR, its government bureaucracy is no smaller. By September 1992 Russia had 137 central ministries and departments, compared to 85 in the former USSR. At that time some thirty ministries and committees were abolished, although in effect they were simply reorganised. The massive industry ministry in late 1991 had absorbed most of the branch ministries, and now once again was to be broken up into a State Committee for Industry and four branch committees with virtually the same powers as the ministries abolished a year earlier. In addition to Gaidar there were nine deputy prime ministers, each responsible for a cluster of ministries.[40] According to Shumeiko's draft Law on the Council of Ministers presented to parliament in September 1992, the president retained the right to appoint and dismiss the prime minister, the deputy prime minister, and the ministers themselves, but candidates were to be vetted by the appropriate committee of the Supreme Soviet and approved by parliament as a whole. The draft failed to please Khasbulatov, however, and he insisted that 'the development of parliamentarianism was the path to democracy'.[41] On 13 November 1992 parliament adopted a modified version of the law giving Congress control over ministerial appointments, granting parliament the sole right to nominate ministers, and subordinating key ministers (like that of foreign affairs) to parliament. This indeed was the basis for a parliamentary republic.

The struggle to control the government came to a head at the Seventh Congress. Gaidar's uncompromising stance and the failure of Yeltsin's desperate attempt to take the confrontation between executive and legislative to the country led to the fall of Gaidar on 14 December 1992, though not to the immediate dissolution of the reforming cabinet. The new premier, Chernomyrdin, in Khasbulatov's words, 'was not so much a new horse as an old charger'. Chernomyrdin, although committed to more state intervention in the economy, retained the majority of the liberal advocates of 'shock therapy'. Yeltsin, indeed, cut short a visit to China on 19 December 1992 to save the reformists, stating 'The master must return to restore order.' Boris Fedorov at this time was given overall responsibility for financial policy, and Chernomyrdin soon retreated from attempts to regulate prices and to save industry by pouring in money, which only stimulated inflation. Talk of 'an invisible coup' proved exaggerated.[42]

Following the elections of December 1993 Chernomyrdin placed his stamp on the government. Gaidar, Fedorov and some other reformers resigned and Agrarians and others joined, yet the government retained a broadly reformist course. In effect, a 'coalition' government was formed, but a distinctively Russian type of coalition where posts were divided not through discussions between parties but between specific individuals.[43] The constitution does not oblige the president to appoint the prime minister from the largest party able to gain a majority in parliament; nevertheless, the president had to be sensitive to the balance of forces in the Duma to avoid his government suffering defeats in votes of no confidence. Two ministers were from the Agrarian Party, and there were even overtures towards the CPRF to contribute ministers.

The political evolution of Russian government was in full swing even before the Chechen crisis, taking on more of a conservative and nationalist colouring. The government reshuffle in November 1994 saw leading reformers marginalised and the resignation of others. Shokhin resigned in protest at the appointment of Vladimir Panskov as finance minister, while Chubais became a deputy prime minister for the economy. The privatisation committee was taken over by a much more lukewarm privatiser, Vladimir Polevanov, who threatened the renationalisation of the energy, defence and aluminium sectors. Polevanov was soon sacked, but the perception of Russia's reforms under threat remained: the humanitarian internationalism that had been such a marked feature of policy since Gorbachev's time now gave way to a more assertive Russian state nationalism.

This tendency was further strengthened following the strong communist showing in the December 1995 elections. Chernomyrdin remained prime minister even though his Russia Our Home party had gained only 10 per cent of the vote, but the government further changed its complexion. Kozyrev resigned as foreign minister on 5 January, as did Shakhrai as a deputy prime minister, both preferring to keep their Duma seats. Chubais, the last member of the 'government of reforms' (responsible for the economy) resigned on 16 January 1996. The modernising industrialist Vladimir Kadannikov, the former head of the Volga Car Plant (VAZ) in Togliatti, joined the government as first deputy prime minister. As for the extension of coalition government, Chernomyrdin argued that 'I am in favour of a government that consists of professionals because a government is not a political body.'[44]

Government, prime minister and parliament

Government in Russia consists of the chair of the government (the prime minister), a variable number of deputy prime ministers, usually responsible for a bloc of ministers, and federal ministries, generally with portfolios. Twice in 1992 Yeltsin sought to instil some order into executive power (12 May and 30 September), but the absence of a central administration serving both the presidency and the government undermined these and other initiatives. In addition, bodies like the Security Council appeared at times to usurp the role of the government; a decree of May 1992 ordered the Ministry of Justice to register the normative acts of the ministries, and a high proportion were found not to be legal although that did not stop their implementation. The basic problem, however, is that cabinet government is much more difficult to achieve in a presidential than in a parliamentary system. In the USA the post of prime minister is dispensed with altogether, and the president chairs cabinet meetings. In France the president has the prerogative to appoint or dismiss the prime minister as long as the latter has the support of parliament, and it was a rudimentary version of this system that emerged in Russia. The government was responsible both to parliament and to the president, but the precise balance of accountability remained unclear.

Russia is not a parliamentary republic but neither is it fully a presidential one in the classical sense. The Public Chamber of the Constitutional Assembly on 30 October 1993 agreed to adopt the version sponsored by Filatov that the prime minister would be appointed by the president with the consent of the State Duma. This version was opposed by Sobchak, chair of the Public Chamber, who argued that this would 'sharply strengthen the position of the president, placing him higher than the figure of a constitutional monarch'.[45] According to the constitution the prime minister takes over in the event of the president being incapacitated. The premier forms his or her cabinet, which is then to be approved by the president, and the two share a great deal of executive authority. In America the president is head of the executive, whereas according to article 110.1 executive power in Russia belongs to the government, but the head of the government works within the framework of presidential power. A hybrid 'tripartite' system emerged in which the government acts as a relatively autonomous centre of political authority in its own sphere, the president sets the overall direction of policy, while the Duma acts in a supervisory capacity and the ultimate source of public accountability by 'keeping the trust of the government', passing votes of no-confidence and confidence.

A no-confidence vote in the government can be initiated by a Duma deputy at any time, but the signatures of one-fifth of all Duma members are required for a motion to be placed on the agenda. A motion of no-confidence is adopted by a simple majority of total Duma membership (article 117.3), which then sets in train a complex process of confrontation. The president has two choices: either accept the motion, dismiss the government and nominate a new prime minister for the Duma's approval; or disagree with the Duma. If within three months the Duma once again expresses its lack of confidence in the government, then the head of state can either sack the government or dissolve the Duma by ordering new elections. The threat of dissolution is at the centre of presidential power, protecting the government and restraining the Duma out of fear of provoking elections. Article 109, however, modifies the dissolution option by stating that article 117 cannot be activated to dissolve the Duma in the year following its election or in the six months before a presidential election. This would imply that in its first year or before a presidential election the Duma could dismiss one government after another with impunity, only having twice to vote a motion of no-confidence and not even having to wait three months between the two votes.

The dissolution option can be activated in a second manner, this time on the initiative of the government itself. The prime minister can ask the Duma for a vote of confidence; if the Duma fails to pass a vote of confidence in the government, the president must either dissolve the Duma or dismiss the government, a decision that must be taken within seven days of the vote.

Despite its reduced powers under the new constitution, the Duma has proved able to define its own agenda. The coalition government in a rudimentary way reflected the parties and some of the main concerns of the Duma. In particular, strategic allies were sought among the parties in the Duma that would make governance possible, in particular by offering ministerial portfolios to parties that were apparently in opposition to the government itself (e.g. the Agrarian Party). This did not prevent the Duma holding a vote of no-confidence in the government following 'black Tuesday' (a sudden fall in the value of the rouble on 11 October 1994), and again on 21 June 1995 in protest against the Budennovsk crisis (when hostages were seized by Chechen guerrillas). Chernomyrdin countered by tabling a confidence motion, which if not passed would have led to either the Duma or the government falling within a week. Threatened by imminent dissolution, a second vote of no-confidence on 1 July failed (just) to pass, and thereupon Chernomyrdin withdrew his confidence motion.

The prime minister is appointed by the president and endorsed by the State Duma and is in principle accountable to both – in principle because parliament's checking is rather limited. If the president's nomination is three times refused by the Duma it is automatically dissolved and the president's choice is confirmed (article 111). This is the second path whereby the presidential dissolution option can be triggered. The Duma's right to veto a nomination has been removed; but it can be assumed that in most circumstances a president would change the candidate after the previous candidate was rejected twice. A prime minister's resignation is tendered to the president rather than to the Duma. It is incumbent upon the prime minister to tender his or her resignation following presidential elections, but is not after parliamentary elections.

Soviet law since 1988 had stipulated that those who took up government posts were to resign their parliamentary seats, a principle reaffirmed by the 1993 constitution. Deputies cannot simultaneously be employed in the government or hold paid jobs in any field except teaching, scientific research and culture in general. Once the 2-year transitional period ended in 1995 the principle was rigorously applied and nineteen deputies elected from the party-lists resigned their seats. Kozyrev, elected to parliament from a single-member constituency in Murmansk, was forced to choose between resigning from the cabinet or giving up his legislative seat. The idea that ministers cannot simultaneously be MPs was designed to maintain the separation of powers, but the bizarre rule (applied also in France) undermines the ability of parties to form a government, weakens the solidarity which binds together the governing party in countries like Britain and Germany, inhibits the Duma's ability to question ministers on a daily basis, and weakens the government's capacity to explain its policies in parliament.

The unclear relationship between the political complexion of the Duma and the composition of the government is probably not sustainable in the long-term, and the most logical resolution of the problem is for the government to require a parliamentary majority. Of course, given a fragmented and divided Duma with no stable majority, this would be problematical; the architects of the 1993 constitution took precisely this problem into account in drafting the articles on the relationship between government and parliament. The relationship between the president and prime minister could not but be based on trust if effective governance was to be pursued. However, Yeltsin at times treated his prime minister, Chernomyrdin, in a remarkably off-hand manner. The cluster of deputy prime ministers allowed on occasion for one or another to usurp the prime minister's role. Government by confusion remained an enduring feature of post-communist Russian politics.

THE STATE REMADE

The attempt to remake the Russian state was bound hand and foot by old bureaucratic institutions and traditions. The 'new' state was a peculiar hybrid: on the one hand, adapting old state structures to new conditions; and, on the other, introducing genuinely new ideas and approaches.[46] It is the unstable balance between these two elements that caused so many problems in the first post-communist years and gave rise to 'a contradiction between the content and form of state power'.[47] The democratic state-building slogans of the insurgency phase up to August 1991 were soon trampled underfoot in the rush for power and privileges when the old order fell. After the coup the Russian state absorbed the detritus of the Soviet regime but failed to pursue a consistent policy of state renewal.

Reform of public administration in Russia was yet another important element in the total transformation of society launched from 1991, and suffered from many of the problems afflicting political and economic reform. The problem of weak administrative structures was compounded by the absence of an effective (let alone honest) civil service and professional central and local government administrators. Civil servants were forbidden to participate in business by a law of 22 March 1991, yet many continued their business activities.[48] A General Directorate to train senior *cadres* for the civil service (known as Roskadry) was established by a decree of 28 November 1991, accompanied by plans to introduce competitive entrance exams and the like. The Institute of Management in Moscow was transformed into a new Civil Service Academy, designed to train a new generation of professional government employees. A professional civil service reflecting civil society rather than acting as an administrative instrument of executive authority only slowly emerged. Bogged down in elite conflicts and institutional turf wars and lacking a solid professional core of modern administrators, reform in this sphere proceeded as contradictorily as in most other areas.

The political system formalised by the 1993 Constitution reflected numerous conjunctural factors. A constitution, ideally, reflects a popular consensus around certain principles and values, whereas this constitution contained elements that reflected only the concerns of a particular time and the interests of a particular group. One of the substantive criticisms of the 1993 constitution is its lack of balance in the separation of powers between branches of national government. However, it is not clear how the question of balance can be resolved, since 'balance' is something derived from the alignment of social and political forces and in new states is essentially contested.

In Russia a cabinet system coexisted with a presidential one, with the constitution effectively making the president head of government. This can be characterised as a bifurcated executive system: on the one hand, the president and his or her apparatus working from the Kremlin; and on the other, the prime minister and the government, based primarily in the White House (formerly the Supreme Soviet building) and Old Square (previously the headquarters of the Central Committee). By 1 October 1995 the seventy-three federal ministries, state committees,

committees and services employed some 30,000 people; 5,000 officials (excluding technical staff) were employed by the president's office and 2,000 by the cabinet secretariat; while federal agencies in the regions employed an astonishing 364,000, double the 187,000 for the whole USSR in 1990.[49]

The opposition claimed that the centre of political gravity had returned once again to the Kremlin, which now adopted many of the institutions and functions of the Politburo of old. The presidency had its own security service, its own Security Council apparatus and much more besides. Vitalii Tret'yakov, the trenchant editor of *Nezavisimaya gazeta*, argued that 'It is a constitution for presidents in general and for president Yeltsin in particular.'[50] Rumyantsev noted that 'When the president personally formulates foreign and domestic policy, one can say that the monarchical principle outweighs the democratic principle in the constitution.'[51] Konstantin Lubenchenko went even further in claiming that the constitution not only gave an overwhelming advantage to presidential power but actually 'codifies the existence of a totalitarian state that controls all spheres of the life of society'.[52]

The transplantation of a French-style presidential system to Russian soil took authoritarian forms. Parliament lacked the right to exercise normal legislative control over the government, in its formation and its activity; the separation of powers was now institutionalised but unbalanced. While the constitution embodies the principles of liberalism, it is predicated on the assumption that the strong president will also be a liberal. In the event of this not being the case the authoritarian elements embedded in the constitution will come into contradiction with its liberal provisions.

8   The politics of pluralism

Our object in the construction of the state is the greatest happiness of the whole, and not that of any one class.

Plato[1]

We are now in a position to reflect more broadly on the nature of post-communist political development in Russia. We will begin by examining the ambiguities in Russian pluralism, the social nature of the transition, and the emergence of a quasi-democratic regime system of rule, and conclude with an examination of the role of personalities in general and Yeltsin's place in particular in post-communist Russian politics.

RUSSIAN PLURALISM

The political system was marked by the following features. First, although formally the presidency had gained enormous powers, its authority and powers were fragmented; the presidential system itself was prey to factionalism and competing policy lobbies. Second, the fractured nature of political authority allowed the 'power' and political ministries, the only bodies with the bureaucratic muscle to do so, to devise and pursue their own agendas and policies, often in contradiction with officially proclaimed policy. Third, the government was relatively marginalised, concerned mainly with the economy. Fourth, while parliament emerged as an effective legislative agency, its political influence was relatively weak because authority had been transferred to the presidency and the government. Fifth, the numerous political parties did not yet add up to a viable multiparty system. In short, a modified bureaucratic politics model clearly applies to post-communist Russian politics.

While the political situation remains fluid the emergence of a distinctive Russian 'power elite', a structured pattern of interest and pressure group politics, can be identified. The political and economic spheres remain relatively distinct and the tendency for regional leaders to combine public office with private business has declined, but at the same time there has been 'a revitalisation of power exerted by former nomenklatura members and an activation of previous social networks'.[2] In addition to and often part of the reconstituted nomenklatura elite, the economic reforms saw the emergence of powerful financial-industrial groups who appeared to become the main arbiters of power struggles in Moscow. The policy gulf between new entrepreneurs and traditional state managers was gradually eroded as the rudiments of a financial and trade market system emerged. While few now oppose integration into the world economy, most favour government support for native industries and businesses through policies of national capitalism. The distinction between the regional political and managerial elites, which during the fall of communist power looked particularly salient, gave way to the recognition of common interests.

Post-communist Russia was dominated by a shifting pattern of coalition politics reflecting the fractured pluralism of society. The weakness of parties meant that no efficient mechanism existed to channel popular feelings into legislative affairs, or then to support parliamentary politics in society; this weakness, however, was compensated by the growth of a dense network of interest and pressure groups. The mere existence of numerous interest and other groups, however, does not automatically betoken a pluralistic system. Despite some 15,000 interest groups in America, power is allegedly concentrated in what president Eisenhower called 'the military industrial complex' and C. Wright Mills 'the power elite'. In Russia the problem of the genuine pluralisation of politics and the dispersal of influence, if not power, is all the sharper and Dahl's model of a polyarchy of countervailing interests is not yet applicable.

Bureaucratic state socialism undermined the autonomy and scope for reciprocal interaction of groups in society, and the practice of pluralistic politics was limited to interest groups like the military, industry and agriculture competing for scarce resources allocated by the central administrative system. Links were primarily vertical, between a group and the government, rather than horizontal, between groups themselves. The old regime had maintained a very high degree of monopoly over the distribution of the social and political goods of society, and pressure groups and lobbies emerged out of the power structures of the regime itself. Government at the centre and the localities was in certain respects not much more than a general committee for coordinating the affairs of sectoral interests generated by the system itself. Social groups and interests were patterned into a relationship of dependence on the party-state. This dependence had begun to erode as the system itself began to decay, and the rudiments of a pluralistic society were emerging even within the carapace of the old society, but this was a type of sectoral or departmental pluralism rather than a pluralism originating in society itself.

The new pluralism, therefore, bore the stamp of its provenance under the old regime. Vertical links were replicated as struggling enterprises sought credits, and privatisation was in part an attempt by the state to divest itself of direct budgetary responsibility. Groups that had been strong under the old regime found themselves strategically placed to take advantage of the new conditions. Sectoral groups lost their strategic location at the heart of governmental structures but retained privileged access to decision-making. Groups like the military, the heavy industry or agricultural lobbies were no longer part of the system itself but gained a corporate identity within the new system, something achieved with outstanding success by the Ministry of Oil and Gas (Minneftegazprom), which in 1989 became the state concern 'Gazprom' and some major oil companies. Outsider groups now fought their cause on a more level playing field and gained greater scope for independent lobbying, but the development of a genuinely pluralistic system was distorted by the predominance of corporate interests, once again part of a new power elite. The breakdown of the old system revealed the degree to which Soviet society had become fractured, and groups, no longer constrained by the party and the security apparatus, began to carve out fiefdoms for themselves and exerted direct pressure on parliament and local assemblies. In post-communist conditions the concept of the 'revenge of the nomenklatura' means the ability of strategically placed groups to take advantage of the new freedoms to consolidate themselves. A pseudo-pluralistic system emerged.

The multiparty system in Russia developed in the interstices of political life; parties were only one of the forms in which post-communist politics was structured. Parties were rivalled by social associations like trade unions and business organisations, and there were also various organised but not necessarily institutionalised social forces such as the 'mafia' or elements of the old nomenklatura. Various pressure groups emerged to promote specific causes and interests, and the common complaint against MPs was that they had become lobbyists for particular interests rather than representatives of the general good. Khasbulatov's parliament became a forum for unrestrained lobbying, but in both the old and the new parliament deputies openly acted on behalf of special interests. The absence of either a law in general concerning lobbying, or detailed parliamentary procedures to regulate it, meant that the scale of the interpenetration between political elites and special interest groups is hard to quantify.

There was an enormous growth of divergent social and economic interests but their ability to be represented at the political level was unequal. Some groups had privileged access and greater resources to make their voice heard, while others, above all those dependent on the state budget like teachers and health workers, let alone pensioners and unskilled workers, were forced to return to the politics of the streets and strikes. Corporate interests remain the most effectively organised. Vol'skii's RUIE, one of the elements of the Civic Union, acted largely as a pressure group for the industrialists who, having lost the privileged access to the ministries that they had enjoyed in the past, turned to parliamentary lobbying. The Russian United Industrial Party, sponsored by Vol'skii was established in April 1995 to achieve direct representation in the Duma. The unity of the industrialists should not be exaggerated, with deep regional and sectoral divisions. The new elites are by no means homogeneous, with divisions between industrialists and entrepreneurs, with the former on the whole for state subsidies while the latter favour macroeconomic stabilisation, a stable currency, low inflation and so on.[3]

Even the traditional elites were forced to find new ways of advancing their interests and their special interest lobbying became increasingly professional. One form was the formation of so-called 'elite clubs' like the Reform Club 'Interaction' (*Vzaimodeistvie*), Club-93, VIP-Club, the Council for Foreign and Defence Policy and Yurii Petrov's Club of Realists, where their members could meet behind closed doors and share their views. Entrepreneurial groups sought to influence elections but found that support for various apparently sympathetic candidates and groups gave little return on their 'investment' once in parliament. Openly oppositional groups, like Sergei Kurginyan's 'Constructive Unity' (*Soderzhatel'noe edinstvo*), sought not to influence the regime but to improve the quality of the thinking of the patriotic opposition. All of them, however, suffered from the failure of different elites to talk with each other, and thus the politics of pressure and lobbying was as fragmented as the party system it shadowed.[4] As the 1995 elections approached, groups like the 'Russian Business Round Table' considered direct participation in the elections.[5] These attempts failed miserably and none of the numerous business groups crossed the 5 per cent threshold in 1995.

A NOMENKLATURA REVOLUTION?

The transition was in many respects an incomplete revolution, with profound continuities in elite structures and political practices. If the collapse of communist power in 1991 was something akin to an 'abdication', whereby the regime relinquished power without much of a struggle, the elite structures at the heart of the old regime did not by any means renounce their advantages. So-called 'outsiders', like dissidents, had little chance of coming to power, and in Russia (like most other post-Soviet states) even nationalists found the path of political insurgency blocked by the consensual (if not negotiated) pattern of political transition that left much of the old system in place, losing *only* the obviously politically dysfunctional political apparatus of Party rule and the intellectually obsolescent claim to be 'building socialism'. Shorn of this political and intellectual incubus, which far-seeing elements even within the system had long realised to be antithetical to the effective development of the polity and society, the old elites forged an alliance with the new authorities and thus secured themselves a place in the new order. In contrast to Germany after the Second World War, where its traditional order had been destroyed by defeat and Allied intervention, it was out of the old Soviet order that the new Russia was born. The democratic insurgency soon ran into the sands of this stubborn socio-political reality.

The late Soviet years were marked by the bifurcation of elite structures between a Party elite and a nascent middle class, and, more specifically, the final Gorbachev years saw the accelerated divergence between Party and state officialdom, with the latter beginning to distance itself from the communist regime. The anti-communist revolution thus entailed only a partial transformation of the social order: certain groups ascended, others fell, but most adapted to the new regime. The losers were the old Party apparatchiki, the military top brass, and the military-industrial complex as a whole. However, many of these, particularly the regional elites, were able to make the transition with relatively few losses, and much of the old nomenklatura did very well by converting their privileges into material assets, often in the form of real estate and stakes in enterprises through nomenklatura privatisation. Clearer winners were the new class of entrepreneurs and those who had been able to use civic activity as a path of upward social mobility, often as a substitute for economic initiative. The nomenklatura, strictly speaking, refers not only to former Party officials (the apparatchiki) but to the top managers and administrators, who went on to become elected regional deputies and from whom most governors were drawn.

In the late Soviet era the term 'mafia' took on broad meaning, encompassing the fused political and semi-criminal priviligentsia. Telman Gdlyan's book *Mafia of the Lawless Times* exposed the luxurious life-styles of the Party mafia in the Soviet Far East and Moscow.[6] Even before the coup the nomenklatura elite adapted to post-communist forms of social organisation as they valorised or 'capitalised' their assets, converting privileges enjoyed by custom into property defended by right. Top Party officials, for example, crossed over to take positions in the state apparatus, assisted by Gorbachev's aide, Boldin.[7] The old elite transformed intself into the new by shifting from Party to state posts, creating economic structures subordinate to the party, and by joining emerging independent commercial organisations where they exploited personal contacts and knowledge of the system. State assets, in theory owned by everyone but concretely owned by no-one, were privatised to become personal assets; ownership (or lack of it) had proven to be the Achilles heel of the old system, and now became the cornerstone of the new. The late Soviet 'mafia' imperceptibly became part of the class of 'new Russians', those able to take advantage of emerging opportunites and the lax legal framework to enrich themselves. It is for this reason that Govorukhin describes post-communist Russia as 'the great criminal revolution'.[8]

Under late communism nepotism and patron–client relations undermined the political criteria of elite recruitment in the nomenklatura system. The political elite began to degenerate into a social class, perhaps one of the most economically useless in history. As Milovan Djilas had long ago noted, the Party fostered a class which grew at its expense and began to transform itself into a traditional oligarchy.[9] Under the carapace of the declining communist regime a vigorous network of informal relations emerged directed towards gaining benefits of the system, a phenomenon identified by Zvi Gitelman as constituting a 'second polity', paralleling the 'second economy' of 'really existing socialism'.[10] The 'new class', as Djilas termed it, eventually outgrew the system that had given it birth. August 1991 can thus be seen as the revolt not of society but of a rebellious section of the old elite against the tutelage of its progenitor, the communist system, and in this scheme of things there was no room for popular democratic mobilisation or anything more than superfical decommunisation. One section of the elite was politically expropriated by another representing the emerging economically based class system. The decapitation of the Party in 1991 did not destroy these networks of communication and patronage but forced them to adapt to a more open environment and new rules of operation. From this perspective it was no longer a question of the new society bearing the deformations of its tragic birthpangs, but that the new society *was* the old society in a new guise.

The post-communist regime system emerged out of the old nomenklatura system and in its way represented the reconstitution of late Soviet forms of rule – but without the CPSU. Regional Communist Party bosses, as Hough described them in his classic work *The Soviet Prefects*, performed numerous functions, few of them directly connected with politics but mostly associated with lobbying for resources, getting supplies for local enterprises, and in general managing local labour and wage funds.[11] Party, state and economic management overlapped, with all responsible positions being filled exclusively through the nomenklatura appointments system. With Gorbachev's attempts to restrict the Party more narrowly to the sphere of politics, some of the more far-sighted party officials shifted over to state posts to join the economic managers already heavily represented in the ranks of the local soviets and their executive bodies – and continued to do what they had always done but in new ways.[12]

Democratic institutions need a stable class structure to sustain them, and in many respects a post-communist psychosocial order was already highly developed within the framework of the communist system. One of the reasons commonly given for the failure of the 1991 coup was that sections of the old elite were already becoming incorporated into the new. A post-revolutionary settlement was already in the making in which the second echelon of the office-holding nomenklatura were turning themselves into capitalists and officials of the new order. It is hardly surprising that they were unwilling to jeopardise their chances by defending the crumbling old order. In other words, the old political class saw its best hopes of survival by transforming itself into a new social elite.

But what is the nomenklatura and is it still valid to use the term?[13] Should we continue to call the demobilised army of officials and administrators by their old name? After all, over half a decade has passed since someone was last appointed by recommendation of a department of the Central Committee. The temptation to continue to use the term, however, is great; words give substance to abstractions and make the intangible real, but ultimately the term will become increasingly anachronistic. In the post-communist context the concept of the nomenklatura is less of a precise occupational category than a way of identifying a broad social class. The academic Dmitrii Furman, for example, talks of the nomenklatura as 'a vast network of personal relationships and clans'.[14] This encompasses the former Party bosses, enterprise managers, officials of the old regime and many more who were formed in the same school and recognise certain common interests, irrespective of whether they called themselves democrats, patriots or whatever. The transformation of the Politburo member into the president, the oblast Party secretary into the mayor, the criminal entrepreneur into a businessman, all suggest not so much the formation of a new elite as the *reformation* of the old. It is this, among other things, which gives Russia's current social transformation its hall-of-mirrors quality.

This elite dominates many of Russia's regions and republics, and indeed some of the other successor states. In this context the August regime's refusal to sanction purges of the nomenklatura through lustration laws and the like, as demanded by the radical democrats, makes more sense. There is a normative element to the 'self-limiting' nature of Russia's democratic transition, the attempt to bring an end to the cycle of violence and retribution characteristic of Russian history, but more prosaic concerns also play their part, the need to draw on the skills of the old elite, to secure their loyalty to the new dispensation, and, above all, to preserve the gains of the reformed old/new class.

Despite the hopes of the activists of the democratic insurgency during 1989–91, after the coup Yeltsin concentrated on economic reform at the expense of democratic renewal, and remarkably little decommunisation took place. This had never been part of Gorbachev's strategy, and even though Yeltsin's programme in the insurgency phase was permeated by an anti-communist rhetoric, this was not translated into purges against the communist elite. There was remarkably little turnover in the regional and local elites, and in 1994 82.3 per cent of senior administrative staff and legislators were still made up of former nomenklatura officials.[15] According to Kryshtanovskaya, 75 per cent of the new political elite and 61 per cent of the new business elite comes from the old Soviet nomenklatura. The businessmen mostly came from the Komsomol (38 per cent) and from the old economic bureaucracy (38 per cent). She notes the central role played by a small number of banks favoured by the government in unifying the new elite in the wake of the collapse of the old system.[16]

While the 'democrats' were disappointed by the absence of significant decommunisation, experience suggests that their political activists were often incompetent administrators, and so by necessity the Yeltsin regime was forced to rely on the old guard. This however, is only a partial explanation: far more importantly, Yeltsin forged a strategic alliance with the old administrative elites by choice to secure a social base to his own rule and at the time to free himself from dependence on any particular constituency, the democrats included. Thus the refusal to hold elections in the aftermath of the August coup, when the democratic wave was surging strongly, can be understood as part of Yeltsin's strategy to consolidate his alliance with regional and central administrators. Stability took precedence over deepening the anti-communist revolution.

The option was only possible because of the virtual self-destruction of the commanding heights of the political system during the August putsch: Yeltsin's ban on the CPSU was no more than the *coup de grâce*. Yeltsin decapitated the political leadership of the old regime and placed himself at the head of its elite hierarchy. The Party was destroyed as a functioning political organism and its administrators in the regions, now firmly ensconced in the local soviets, were free to forge new alliances. The confiscation of the CPSU's property allowed local soviets to dispose of these assets as they saw fit, an important factor in buying their allegiance to the new system. This analysis, of course, leaves out the important question of political preferences, and the residual tension between the new regime in Moscow and the provincial elites was an important factor shaping post-communist politics in Russia. The main point, however, is that the regime's self-image, as a progressive reforming government in the centre combatting the conservative inertia of the regions, greatly simplifies the true state of affairs. The establishment of presidential envoys (see chapter 12) was one way that the centre sought to ensure compliance from the regions and reflected the tensions.

Corporate clans combining new financial entrepreneurs with some of the traditional industrial and administrative elite represented an enormous concentration of resources. Not only did they sponsor parties and politicians who could represent their interests, in a certain sense they became the functional substitute of political parties. The concept of the 'party of bosses' (*partiya nachal'stva*) was used to describe administrative and state economic managers who not only enjoyed important positions in the country's management structures but who entered politics in their own right and who, without being affiliated to any particular party, enjoyed considerable electoral successes.[17] They continued to exercise significant political influence in the centre and in the regions. To many observers Chernomyrdin's Russia Our Home party was created to channel this spontaneous development and incorporate it into the existing alignment of political forces. The 'party of bosses', however, was a phenomenon larger than Russia Our Home, and, indeed, was often in opposition to the 'party of power'. The assumed ally of the 'party of bosses' was the CPRF, but it would be a mistake to suggest an overwhelming identity of interests. The marketising and modernising part of the nomen-klatura elite, who had accepted the end of communist rule earlier, were natural allies of Chernomyrdin's Russia Our Home rather than the CPRF, fearing the new upheavals that would attend the return to power of radical rejectionists. The 'party of bosses' disliked Yeltsin's regime, but the alternatives were worse.

The notion of a 'party' of bosses is misleading insofar as its existence militated against the creation of autonomous parties: its very existence reflected the anti-political traditions of the Soviet regime. Although the rapid advance of privatisation reduced the role of state economic managers, in many respects the directors of privatised enterprises (depending on the form chosen) remain relatively shielded from market forces – for the time being at least. Those who definitely operate in market conditions, like bankers, commodity traders, traders and the like, are not included in the 'party of bosses' and gravitated towards the more radically pro-market parties like Russia's Democratic Choice. In this context it might be noted that some genuine parties, however different their political convictions, might well find a common interest in opposing the 'pseudo-politics' represented by the 'party of power' in defence of a commonly constituted political space. However odious the policies espoused by some of the parties on the Russian political scene, as long as they remained within the framework of constitutional politics they contributed to the structuration of political debate in Russia.

The post-communist class system in Russia is represented schematically in Table 5. While the political shift from a communist to a nominally democratic order could be achieved fairly swiftly, there could be no such direct transition in the social sphere. The emergence of the unofficial or shadow system inhibited the transformation of the old officialdom into a democratic class system, acting as a barrier and in many cases a vale of tears for those trying to make that transition. In other words, between the old elite and the new class system there lay a whole series of social networks that derived from the past but at the same time looked to the future. In social terms, there could be no simple leap from the past to the future. Between the official mono-class system and the democratic meritocratic class system lay a third system entirely, a feature typical of post-communist societies.

The new capitalists are a thoroughly syncretic and heterogeneous class, including outright

Table 5 The class structure of post-communist Russia

Official: *Nomenklatura*, operating according to command principles. After August 1991 the old class of communism is reformed to become one element of the new class of democracy.

Unofficial or shadow system: Based on patronage and client relations, bribery, the second economy, black market mechanisms, allied often with criminal elements and corrupt sections of the cooperative movement. The official system began to merge with this shadow class to create the politico-economic 'mafia' or the criminal bourgeoisie. To capitalise on their political advantages they asset strip their old contacts and knowledge; a political class becomes a degenerate economic class.

Democratic class system: Based on meritocracy, market and competition, officialdom becomes a civil service.

---

criminals, the mafia, shady dealers from the black economy and the cooperative sector, officials from the KGB and the old Party structures, the corrupted new democrats 'grabbing' (from *prikhvatizatisiya*, a pun on *privatizatsiya*) as fast as they can for the limited period they find themselves at the trough and, occasionally, some genuine new entrepreneurs. The priviligentsia only gradually turned into a middle class. The proto-bourgeoisie converted its power and privileges into property and rights, and they were aided in this endeavour by the state. Just as under communism, politics came first in the sense that the new class was consolidated as a result of an exercise of political will rather than emerging as a spontaneous process of class formation. Tensions remained between the political elite and the emerging new bourgeoisie, yet both realised that they had a fateful dependency on each other.

The old elite metamorphosed into a new one, but at the same time a multiplicity of new elite structures emerged. The scale of elite fragmentation is a matter of some controversy: the American diplomat Thomas Graham in late 1995, suggested that Russian government was an oligarchy in which political and economic power was held by narrow cliques.[18] The structure and context of elite politics changed as recruitment became more open and caste-type and politically driven methods of recruitment (typical of the nomenklatura system) were undermined. The new Russian elite, however, is still far from representative of society at large, with the old Party-state and managerial structures greatly over-represented.

While the notion of a nomenklatura revolution reflects important elements of Russia's current social and political transformation, it is far from revealing of the whole truth. Although there was some popular mobilisation, notably between 1989 and 1991 with marches, meetings, strikes and flag-waving, this was not a genuine popular revolution and not even a negotiated revolution, with the orderly transfer of power from a ruling group to an organised opposition. The transition can be characterised as the consensual and evolutionary political self-transcendance or self-transformation of an unviable order into one more consonant with the modern age. A defunct ruling class shakes off the ideology and structures which stifled its development and, emerging from the chrysalis, takes wing, legitimised by the language of democracy and the market but neither democratic in conviction nor prepared to submit to the free play of market forces. The democratic insurgency can thus be seen as an auxiliary in the struggle between elites, to be dispensed with when no longer required. This does not mean that Russia's democracy is no more than a masquerade, or that its rudimentary market system is no more than a convenient mechanism for the new class to enrich itself, but it does suggest the flawed hegemony of the new historical order.

THE REGIME SYSTEM

The tension between the weakness of the Russian state (characterised by the poor reach of the judicial authorities, fiscal confusion, inept administration, and the like) and the hypertrophy of the state apparatus encouraged the emergence of what we have dubbed the 'regime system'. The elimination of the political monopoly of the CPSU in Russia was not replaced by multiparty governance as such but by a regime system in which power was concentrated in the instruments of executive authority in an unstable relationship with legislative power and popular movements. The pluralism of the system is not in doubt; what is questionable is the degree to which open democratic forms of adjudicating these interests have been institutionalised. The factors which inhibit the development of a multiparty system are not necessarily the same as those which hinder the development of a functioning democratic system, but one way or another the fate of democracy depends on the integration of the new political forces into the system of government.

While the main structural features of the old system have disappeared (the one-party state, the command economy, the ubiquitous security system), elements of what Rigby called 'bureaucratic crypto-politics' have continued in a new form, but now joined by a number of public policy spheres – the presidency, parliament, the media, business, and the like. Thus the regime system limited the scope of politics but cannot be defined as full-blown authoritarianism – the syncretic mix of authoritarian, corporatist, liberal and democratic elements we have characterised as authoritarian democracy.

In weakly established democracies a leader can become so strong that he or she can ignore those whom they are meant to represent. O'Donnell characterises these countries as having 'delegative' rather than representative democracy with the electorate allegedly having delegated to the executive the right to do what it sees fit for the country.[19] Thus a government emerges that is 'inherently hostile to the patterns of representation normal in established democracies' by 'depoliticising the population except for brief moments in which it demands its plebiscitary support'.[20] A large· literature deals with questions of the efficacy and justification of delegative democracy in the context of the developing world, focusing on questions like the function of authoritarian institutions in economic policy-making and the related issue of the role of democratic representation and representative institutions. The evidence suggests no clear conclusion that authoritarian forms of modernisation (as in Taiwan or Singapore) are more effective than democratic societies, and indeed contemporary thinking highlights the increasing costs associated with authoritarian policy-making.[21]

The technocracy versus the partocracy had long been a standard theme of Soviet politics.[22] The CPSU performed numerous functions in the management of the economy and the polity and, while not representative, it nevertheless claimed to be acting on behalf of the society in achieving certain common goals. In its final period, as utopian aspirations gave way to more mundane forms of legitimation, the party sought to ground its rule in the achievement of improved standards of living in what Breslauer called 'welfare-state authoritarianism'.[23] The collapse of the Soviet system put an end to that particular debate over whether the system could evolve into a de-ideologised social-democratic polity.

The allure of authoritarianism, however, did not disappear, and after August 1991 elements of technocratic rule were re-established, if not always by technocrats themselves, to sustain the rule of the 'government of professionals' in the name of reform. The restoration of economic rationality took precedence over democracy and equity. The new pluralism encouraged a form of horizontal bargaining, particularly in the economic sphere, that gave rise to a form of mimetic pluralism that stimulated the development of parties and political movements but incorporated them not into full-blown corporatism (the polity was too fluid for that) but into the soft authoritarianism of the regime system. This 'softness' permeated the institutions of the new polity. The Civic Union, for example, was a classic corporatist organisation, representing both workers and management in industry, and trade unions and enterprise managers often found common cause against outside agencies.

Solzhenitsyn explicitly sought to make the corporatist representation of economic and professional interests a substitute for classic liberal forms. Democratic proceduralism and elections were to be based not on party or ideological standpoints but parliament was to consist 'of representatives of social strata and various professions'.[24] The tendency was towards a distinctive form of corporatism, seeking to coopt groups into a shifting reform consensus and stressing the role of experts and practical people in a technocratic reform project. After August 1991 Yeltsin had hoped to establish some form of post-communist corporatism in Russia in which all the supporters of reform would enter 'a single political bloc'.[25] Yeltsin's reform coalition, however, soon disintegrated and he found himself increasingly under pressure from the centre and the right. The weakness of organised liberalism revealed by the 1993 and 1995 elections undermined the precarious balance of his presidency and he found himself increasingly reliant on the old elite.

The informal movement origins of most parties left its stamp on the nascent party system. Civil society type 'anti-politics' was typical of the insurgency phase, marginalising political parties as instruments of mobilisation and political communication.[26] The experience of earlier revolutions, moreover, demonstrates that it is difficult to institutionalise the aspirations of the politics of insurgency, and more effective (often authoritarian) forms are established that 'betray' the revolution while at the same time maintaining its core principles. It now appeared that the anti-communist democratic revolution had to be 'saved' at the expense of sacrificing some of its participatory and spontaneous forms. This was the function of the regime system of government, much strengthened after 1993.

The relative independence of government from both parliamentary oversight and party control and its interweaving with the presidential system gave rise to 'regime politics', occupying the space between an ill-formed state system and a rudimentary civil society. Executive authority, from the president down to the district prefect, became largely independent from political organisations or representative institutions, and thus ultimately from the citizenry. The link between the outcome of elections and the formation of a government was tenuous. Parliament was less a lawmaking body (with presidential decrees having the force of law) than a representative assembly. The unstructured and fragmented party system played little part in the formation of policy or in the composition of executive authorities, while parliament itself was to a degree marginalised. The powerful corporate actors of earlier times took up new forms of lobbying to preserve themselves. The military and industrial interest groups, entrepreneurs and financiers, exerted a disproportionate influence on government, but a rudimentary form of countervailing powers often diluted their influence. It is for this reason that the term 'regime system', suggesting a fairly flexible, reasonably open and politically determined system of rule, is used in preference to the application of some form of corporatist terminology, a term that would give a misleading impression of a stable alliance between political groups and particular interest, professional or pressure groups.

There were weaknesses in the position of the August bloc in which reformist sections of the old elite allied with liberal Westernisers. One of these is the absence of a sustained strategy for reform, limited always by concern not to threaten their own interests and to shift the costs of reform on to others. Conflicts between sections of the nomenklatura over the spoils of privatisation, disputes over export licences and the like, gradually undermined the limited hegemony of the new class. The widespread popular resentment against the bureaucracy-turned-bourgeosie undermined the credibility of attempts to achieve democratic political legitimacy.

It might be noted that post-war Japan has also been characterised by a form of regime politics, institutionalised until 1992 by the dominance of the Liberal Democratic Party (LDP) in the Diet and by innumerable informal links with business and other constituencies. A comparison with pre-1989 Italy is also useful. Even the much-vaunted French presidential system is riven by problems and gave rise, according to one observer, to 'the death of politics' under president Mitterrand, marked by the centralisation of government, the fusion of administrative and political elites, the dominance of the head of state and the corresponding marginalisation of the prime minister and the cabinet, and above all by the etiolation of parliament.[27]

These international comparisons put into perspective 'culturalist' interpretations of post-communist Russian political development. While Russian traditions, and in particular the legacy of institutional confusion and arbitrariness, played an important part in forming the mental world of those who shaped the post-Soviet system, these traditions on their own are an inadequate explanation for these developments. Reissinger *et al.* have proposed, in a different but equally fruitful context, what they call a 'political economy' perspective which stresses 'the evolving concrete material interests of different members of society during a time of rapid change'.[28] Factors like intra-elite conflict and the political economy of economic reform, as much as inherited cultural norms, shape post-communist political development. Inherited elites seek to maximise their economic advantages in a time of dramatic opportunities, but equally they seek to underwrite their gains in the political sphere; legal guarantees on their own at a time of 'revolution' (if that, indeed, is what Russia is engaged in) are barely worth the paper on which they are written. Thus the regime system has emerged as a function of the poor differentiation between politics and economics and as a response to the political needs of the dominant groups in post-communist Russia. As the revolutionary tide ebbs and legality becomes consolidated, when the dangers and opportunities of a time of emergency give way to customary and 'normal' politics, then one can assume that the regime system will give way to a more demonstrably democratic system.

PERSONALITIES AND REGIME

The weakness of institutions and parties in post-communist Russia accentuated the role of individuals and enhanced the role of leadership. The absence of stable constitutional structures or a neutral administrative system focused politics on leaders and officials at all levels. In the broader system, as we have seen, the transformation of the nomenklatura politocracy into a meritocratic civil administrative system was no simple matter. The lack of people with administrative and independent political experience forced the new regime to rely on the old generation.

In contrast to some East European countries, the first generation of 'democratic' politicians in Russia came largely from the old system. Very few of the new political elite emerged out of the dissident movement, an indication of just how effectively the KGB had marginalised dissent. It might be noted that even an anti-communist dissident background did not guarantee liberal politics in power, as the Georgians under Zviad Gamsakhurdia discovered to their cost. The main source was the old Communist Party bureaucracy and associated institutions. Gorbachev had been an apparatchik, albeit a relatively enlightened one, having spent his whole working life as an administrative official in Komsomol and Party offices. Yeltsin, in contrast, had worked as a specialist in the building industry, and only later became a full-time Party official, and indeed one of the most powerful as first secretary of Sverdlovsk obkom. Yeltsin himself drew on the old elite, appointing people like Skokov and Lobov to key posts, arguing that the abolition of communist structures absolved rank-and-file communists of their links and allowed them to join other parties.[29] Under the old regime the most active and able joined the Communist Party, out of conviction or careerist considerations, or both. Thus the last generation of Bolsheviks comprised a large part of the first generation of so-called democrats, and the spectacle of former apparatchiki mouthing democratic platitudes was not always a pleasant one. The generation of 'perestroika democrats' often shared many of the attitudes of the regime against which they had come to fight but which had originally nurtured them.

Another source of recruitment for the new democratic elite was academic life, many members of which had also been members of the CPSU. Popov, Sobchak, Rumyantsev, Khasbulatov, Gaidar and many more had spent time teaching and researching. Not only had Burbulis been a Party member for 20 years but had also taught Marxist-Leninist philosophy, a profession that Vladimir Lysenko had also pursued before becoming one of the leaders of the Republican Party. Out of 64 deputies to the Russian Congress elected from Moscow in spring 1990, 59 had been educators. Rutskoi's jibe that the Gaidar team was made up of junior research fellows was countered by Gaidar's riposte that they had been senior researchers.[30] Military figures also played a prominent part in the post-communist political mix. Rutskoi had been an air force colonel, and the Defence Ministry under Grachev remained a bastion of uniformed officers.

A new cohort of politicians from various walks of life, including the new business community, only gradually emerged. The role of research centres ('think tanks') has been extremely important as a base for political leaders, in or out of office, in a distinctive mix of knowledge and power. The Gorbachev Foundation gave Gorbachev a political home, the Strategiya foundation gave Burbulis a sanctuary, while the Centre for Economic and Political Research (EPIcentre) provided a base for Yavlinskii and gave Yabloko's policies some scholarly credibility.

The high degree of political elite continuity in Russia stamped the politics of the transitional period. Yeltsin was in many respects a typical product of the old system, which had been characterised by the use of authoritarian methods. As he himself admitted, 'I was brought up by this system. Everything was impregnated by administrative-command methods of leadership, so I behaved in the same way.'[31] Whereas Gorbachev had been a stable and known quantity, Yeltsin for many remained an enigma whose politics and personality appeared to be in a constant state of self-creation. In fulfilment of his vow at the 28th Party Congress in July 1990 Yeltsin remained aloof from party politics, and from his own supporters in Democratic Russia, the organisation that had provided organisational muscle in his struggle for power. Yeltsin's own entourage was primarily drawn from two sources: above all former partocrats and administrators, motivated not by ideas but by ambition and self-interest, who adopted the language of democracy but tended to work in the traditional 'commandist' manner; and 'romantic democrats' who fell to the squabbling that had marked the democratic camp in opposition. The two streams came into conflict, and the romantic democrats soon faded away.[32]

The behaviour of the 'democrats' in power aroused the criticism of the liberal intelligentsia. Yakovlev in December 1991 warned that 'Our society is travelling further and further away from the democratic path of development', and many other critics were equally dismayed by the undemocratic features of the new regime. Furman argued that Yeltsin was creating an authoritarian populist regime based on an anti-communist and Russian chauvinist ideology, and that the intake of functionaries had led to the '"communisation" of democracy from within'.[33] Many suspected that while the ideology had changed, the social nature of the regime and the old authoritarian style had not. A Democratic Russia leaflet in March 1992, for example, characterising the nature of the post-coup regime, argued that 'Power fell into the hands of the August bloc, the alliance of the democratically elected Russian leadership headed by Yeltsin and a large part of the nomenklatura', and that under the cover of the radical reforming rhetoric they sought to consolidate their power. While the 'rules of the game' had changed, the relationship of the authorities to society remained the same, hence an independent civic movement should be established as an opposition to the August bloc.[34] According to Afanas'ev, 'popular power' (*narodovlastie*), characterised by the absence of the separation of powers, the claim to be acting on behalf of the people, the echoes of traditional *sobornost*, all undermined the development of genuine democracy.[35]

According to this view, the democratic revolution had been hijacked by the old functionaries and, ultimately, by the power-hungry Yeltsin himself. In this context the notion of 'democratic consolidation', commonly applied to other transitions, takes a peculiar form in Russia.[36] This is hardly surprising since the 'democratic revolution' took place in a country with barely established borders, no clear sense of its national identity and interests, an incoherent political system, an economy undergoing radical transformation and collapse, and with its very statehood in question as regional and republican elites sought to take advantage of the weakness at the centre to consolidate their own (often undemocratic) power.

A new political order emerged in Russia, based on a distinctive social relationship with the former elite and regional forces (the 'August bloc'), but its democratic features are tempered by the political characteristics of the regime system noted above. In this context it is not surprising that the concept of 'democrats' was confused, it not being clear why a particular group should claim a monopoly on the term when in many respects they were indistinguishable, say, from moderate patriots. The very concept of democracy became an element in intra-elite power struggles and lost much of its allure to society.

THE YELTSIN PRESIDENCY

For good or ill, Yeltsin will go down in history as one of the great figures of the twentieth century. Although to contemporaries he appeared a flawed personality, too ready to sacrifice principle in the pursuit and retention of power and rather too partial to demotic pursuits or an ill-considered appeal to the people, his stature may well rise as his achievements are placed in historical perspective. He aroused the profound distrust of sections of the intelligentsia, both domestic and foreign, and of the common people, burdened by the erratic course of reform, but equally gained the loyalty of those committed to a vision of a democratic Russia integrated into the international system, at the same time maintaining its own traditions. His charisma and leadership were indeed flawed, but in a distinctive way reflected the ambiguities of the country itself.

The fall of the communist regime in August 1991 was followed not by the consolidation of democratic institutions but by their subversion by the rise of a largely autonomous form of presidential rule. Many have argued that elections in late 1991 might have broadened the democratic consensus, stimulated the development of a party system, and renewed parliament and thus avoided later conflicts. Instead, Yeltsin concentrated on economic reform at the cost of institution building, and thus set in train a process whereby the reforms themselves lacked solid public or political support and he found himself locked into a futile conflict with his erstwhile allies in parliament. The goal of stability was raised above electoral accountability, but in the event achieved neither order nor democracy.

Presidential power appeared to undermine not only the authority of parliament, but popular participation as well. Post-coup politics were marked by the gradual disempowerment of Russia's citizens as they were deprived of the elections, referenda, the marches and so much else that had characterised the last years of Gorbachev's rule. Local soviets were to have been elected in December 1991, but by threatening to resign Yeltsin was able to postpone the elections. Burbulis stressed after the coup that the main problem was to establish a system of vertical executive power, a process that the elections would not assist. The strong presidency, he argued, ensured full-blooded statehood for Russia, and the soviets 'could become a major obstacle to the course of reform' because of their composition, purpose and structure.[37]

Democrats warned in increasingly apocalyptic tones that a creeping coup was in progress.[38] Not only had elections been suspended, but Yeltsin distanced himself from his erstwhile supporters in the 'democratic' camp. Unlike De Gaulle, who on returning to power in 1958 proceeded to build a Gaullist party, Yeltsin failed to institutionalise his support in the form of a mass organisation, appealing instead to 'the people' as a whole. His democratic supporters were aggrieved that they had lost contact with him amid fears that the presidential system was turning into a dictatorship. Afanas'ev was critical of the concentration of powers in the executive branch, while Gleb Yakunin and Ponomarev complained that none of the president's administrators came from Democratic Russia.[39] They condemned the way that Petrov used his control of Yeltsin's private office to decide whom he saw and what he read. In late May 1992 Shakhrai complained that 'honest people' could not work under such conditions, and resigned from the presidential team because 'I simply didn't want decisions actually made by Petrov and Skokov to be attributed to me.'[40]

The opposite danger was equally palpable, the collapse of central authority altogether. Thus after the rough ride at the Sixth Congress in April 1992, when parliament tried to curb presidential powers and modify the government's policies, Yeltsin sought even greater powers in order to bolster the position of his government and economic reform team led by Gaidar. Yeltsin's rule by decree (*ukaz*) bypassed parliament but did not markedly improve the efficacy of government. Executive lawmaking usurped the legislative prerogatives of parliament, retarded any effective separation of powers and inhibited the development of the rule of law because of the inherent arbitrariness of this form of governance. Talk of a second coup at that time appeared ill-founded. Yeltsin had firm control of the army, parliament was divided, there was no base of popular support for an alternative programme.

On 4 June 1992 Yeltsin announced that he would not seek a second term once his current 5-year period of office ended in June 1996, when he would be 65. He insisted, however, that he would not resign during the current term, though many doubted that he could survive in office for the full 5 years. In addition, health worries dogged him allied with concern over an alleged increasingly serious drink problem. In his press conference of 21 August 1992 Yeltsin expressed confidence that there was no force in the country capable of launching a serious challenge to his power.[41] His popularity, however, continued to fall and it soon became clear that Yeltsin had squandered the enormous political capital accumulated in the struggle for Russian statehood and during the coup.[42] Like the system itself, Yeltsin was a hybrid figure, both democratic and authoritarian.

Yeltsin's rule was nothing if not controversial. From the first his presidency was denounced as authoritarian, later accompanied by accusations of corruption. Yeltsin's suspension and subsequent banning of the Communist Party and the expropriation of its property did not appear to herald a glorious beginning to Russia's democratic era; neither did attempts to manipulate the media. Many of those who left Yeltsin's elite denounced the mercenary and chaotic atmosphere in the Kremlin's corridors of power. These included Yeltsin's press secretary, Pavel Voshchanov, the former Procurator-General, Aleksei Kazannik, the former ministers Nikolai Fedorov, Sergei Glaz'ev, Ella Pamfilova and Boris Fedorov, quite apart from the former vice-president Rutskoi.[43]

There were indications of the 'Gorbachevisation' of Yeltsin, sacrificing liberals, surrounded by representatives of the nomenklatura, capitulating to their demands and apparently allying with them as Gorbachev did during the hardliner's 'winter offensive' of 1990–91. Rather than relying on the democratic movement, Yeltsin instead began to concentrate on intrigues within the ruling elite. Like Gorbachev, Yeltsin could turn into an obstacle to his own reforms. Also like Gorbachev, there were two sides to Yeltsin: the radical reformer condemning the privileges and political corruption of the old nomenklatura; and the apparatchik who had himself climbed the slippery pole and was thoroughly imbued with the ethos of the old regime. These two sides were in constant tension, with the democratic aspect emerging in times of adversity, and the authoritarian in times of success.

By 1993 Yeltsin had lost much of his authority and his final showdown with parliament damaged his reputation. While the destruction of his enemies in parliament and the adoption of the presidentialist constitution represented a personal triumph for Yeltsin, his victory was pyrrhic since the enhanced powers granted by the constitution were offset by the blow to his authority delivered by the elections of 1993 and 1995 and the murderous war in Chechnya. It soon became clear that, deprived of its reformist rhetoric, the Yeltsin presidency was severely weakened. Even though Yeltsin insisted that the reforms would not be derailed, he was forced to make concessions to the new balance of power. Despite attempts to maintain the technocratic nature of the government, elements of coalition were broadened. From early 1996, moreover, Yeltsin appeared to capitulate to hardline demands, sacking reformist officials and the like, in a desperate bid to jettison what he considered political liabilities in the presidential election.

The Chechen war exposed the chaos at the heart of Russian governance, and in particular in the institutions of the presidency. Yeltsin's decision-making style was revealed as secretive, arbitrary and unpredictable and influenced by shadowy figures in his entourage; many feared that Yeltsin's inner circle was able to manipulate him to further their own interests. The SC emerged as a body like the Politburo of old, secretive yet extraordinarily powerful and removed from any form of public accountability. The crisis hastened the realignment of Russian political life. Yeltsin's status as a leader with a vision of the future for the country was weakened and his legitimacy as a democratic leader eroded. His erratic and unpredictable leadership style, with long absences from public view and unsteady appearances, led to a sharp decline in his popularity, with more than half of those polled in late February 1995 calling for his resignation.[44] Like Gorbachev earlier, the credibility he had gained as leader of reforms was undermined. The war thus accelerated the political realignment of the country, with Yeltsin now disowned by his former 'democratic' supporters as he appeared to return to his communist roots. The democratic movement lost its illusions about Yeltsin as their protector and now sought to root liberal democracy in popular aspirations and support. Their slogan now was 'For democracy but without Yeltsin'.[45] The widening gulf between Yeltsin and the liberals was compensated by an increasing dependence on the former Soviet nomenklatura, despite his reiterated commitment to the reform process. He appeared to have completed his political trajectory to end where he had begun, supported now by the former communist elites and regional bosses.

Despite the sharp decrease in his popularity, the general flatness of the political scene led many, and not least in the presidential entourage itself, to believe that Yeltsin could win a second term in the presidential elections of June 1996. A vast class of office-holders had been spawned by the Yeltsin presidency, and many stood to loose by a change of leader. Their hopes, however, were cut short by Yeltsin's rapid physical deterioration, with a heart attack (myocardial ischaemia) in July and a second in October 1995 that weakened him both physically and politically. Skokov noted that Yeltsin had 'failed as a president' and 'exhausted his abilities in the post', but his 'ego' prevented him from admitting this.[46] Yeltsin had failed to groom a 'crown prince', and the replacement in case of emergency, prime minister Chernomyrdin, was no friend of Yeltsin's Kremlin companions. Yeltsin's illness threw into sharp relief a system that had weakened parliamentary oversight of the executive. However, when it came to a run-off between Yeltsin and a communist nationalist challenger, Yeltsin won, especially since the Duma was already in the hands of the opposition.

Yeltsin's inclination to rule by decree independently of organised interest groups and parties in society was reinforced by circumstances, above all the absence of a stable presidential majority in parliament. This reinforced the administrative 'regime' nature of his rule, eschewing populist appeals while foreclosing democratic openings. His rule did not become authoritarian populist but worked within the framework of what we have described as authoritarian democracy. By occupying the centre ground of Russian politics with his own type of authoritarianism, Yeltsin denied the ground to his opponents. The degeneration of this relatively benign form of 'enlightened despotism' into some uglier form of dictatorship could not be excluded, especially since there was a tendency to dismiss those with an independent mind from Yeltsin's entourage. One of the main reasons for Yeltsin's political longevity was that it was not clear who or what could replace him or his regime. In this sense he did become irreplaceable: against the communist hardliners there had been Gorbachev and the reform communists; against Gorbachev there had been Yeltsin and the democrats; while against Yeltsin there were various rejectionist forces that could spell peril for Russia and the world. However flawed Yeltsin might be, the alternatives appeared worse: 'Whatever we say of Yeltsin, even in his condition [having recently suffered his second heart attack], he is still the only guarantor of democracy and the irreversibility of economic reform.'[47] This was a verdict reiterated by the voters in June–July 1996.

Yeltsin appeared to be a better opposition politician than one with a strategy in power. Adam Michnik's critique of Wałeşa can be applied with equal force to Yeltsin; Michnik argued that Wałeşa was a charismatic figure who was necessary at a time of crisis but disastrous once a democracy had been established.[48] Voshchanov noted that Yeltsin remained a populist, in the sense that 'He always says what people are waiting to hear and always leaves as everybody's favourite.' He argued that Yeltsin's refusal to set up his own party was based not only on political considerations, the refusal to be categorised as serving the interests of a particular political group, but also for personal reasons, the refusal to share his success with any other leader. Moreover, despite Yeltsin's condemnation of the privileges of the old elite, he enjoyed all the trappings of power inherited from Gorbachev, and indeed added to them.[49] Most dangerous of all, Yeltsin had created a power system that concentrated enormous power in the hands of one individual – and who could predict how these powers would be used by his successors?

Yeltsin himself could not easily be characterised. He was an intuitive politician acting on the basis of his own judgements. He listened but did not always act according to the advice of his associates. This gave him the reputation of being rash, but meant that he was not the prisoner of any particular political or social interest. He explicitly tried to be president of all the Russians, and while this could be seen as lack of principle, it also provided some focus to a bitterly divided society. Yeltsin, however, failed to consolidate his own support and alienated politicians in the centre who in normal circumstances would have been his natural allies. He tried to use the presidency as an autonomous, almost Bonapartist, force standing above the contending political currents. If his rule became authoritarian, he tried to make it benevolent and relatively liberal. Despite the many justified criticisms that can be made of Yeltsin's presidency, his rule did not become hostage to any particular interests and the rudiments of a market economy and a democratic polity, however distorted, emerged. The absence of cohesive parties cutting across religious, ethnic and regional lines meant that conflict remained raw and unmediated and increased pressure on the president to provide a firm hand. Yeltsin turned out to be a statist rather than a populist, and, perhaps as a legacy of his communist past, was careful to work through established bureaucratic channels, albeit short-circuiting them on occasion, reflecting the arbitrariness that was also a feature of Bolshevik rule. The Yeltsin presidency was marked by the consolidation of liberalism but not of democracy.

Part III

Federalism, nationalism and regionalism

9 Federalism and the state

It should now be clear: Russia in the forseeable future cannot be simultaneously united and democratic.

Yevgenii Yasin[1]

The Russian Empire grew through a process of overland expansion: rather like the United States, it occupied relatively empty territories across a vast continental mass, a type of colonisation (unlike that of Britain in India) that is largely irreversible. The emergence of these two continental states has overshadowed the traditional nation-state and each, as de Tocqeville foresaw, seemed 'called by some secret design of Providence one day to hold in its hands the destinies of half the world'.[2] The major difference, however, between the two is that whereas the United States some 200 years ago devised an effective political system and a sturdy relationship between individual states and the federal authorities, Russia is still in the process of building a viable relationship between the centre and the localities.

THE ETHNO-FEDERAL LEGACY

Defeats in war and the fall of Tsarism in 1917 allowed several nations to leave the Russian empire. The aspirations of Poland and Finland to independence went largely unopposed; whereas Ukrainian independence was precarious and was undermined as soon as the Bolsheviks won the Civil War of 1918–20. Earlier declarations in favour of 'the right of nations to self-determination', notably in Lenin's 1916 pamphlet of that name, were modified in January 1918 by Stalin, the people's commissar of nationalities, to be 'a right not of the bourgeoisie, but of the working masses of the given nation'.[3] National liberation was subordinated to the class struggle. The Bolsheviks once again 'gathered the lands' of the historical Russian state, but based on the new principle of 'socialist internationalism'. Autonomous national independence movements were crushed, as were varieties of 'national communism', but a state was recreated that reflected Bolshevik views of national self-determination, the principle of territorial autonomy for specified ethnic groups with the formal right to 'self-determination up to and including secession'. In practice, of course, in keeping with the Marxist view that economic modernisation would make national differences redundant, national aspirations were firmly subordinated to the imperatives of socialist construction, as defined by the Bolsheviks themselves.

The principle of federalism was only grudgingly acknowledged, and then only partially implemented. While Lenin in his 'Declaration of the Rights of the Toiling and Exploited

People', prepared for the Constituent Assembly in January 1918, called for 'a federation of the Soviet Republics of Russia', the RSFSR constitution adopted in mid-1918 contained no effective federal elements. The consolidation of Bolshevik rule over Ukraine and the conquest of Armenia, Azerbaijan and Georgia over the period 1920–21 necessarily intensified the debate over the structure of the state. Stalin proposed the 'autonomisation' plan to reduce the newly conquered states to the status of Russia's existing autonomous republics (Tataria, Bashkiria, Kazakhstan and Turkestan). Lenin, however, concerned by the chauvinist and arrogant behaviour of Bolshevik officials in Transcaucasia, on 26 September 1922 rejected the autonomisation plan in favour of the creation of a new federation, and as a first step the three Transcaucasian republics were federated into one.

The Union Treaty of 30 December 1922 creating the USSR brought together four Union Republics: the RSFSR, Ukraine, Belarus and the Transcaucasian Soviet Federative Socialist Republic; together with 26 autonomous areas, 22 of which were in Russia. The first Soviet constitution of January 1924 was marked by a centralising ethos, with Russia's governing institutions mostly converted into the corresponding USSR body. The policy of *korenizatsiya* (indigenisation), however, adopted by the Twelfth Party Congress in 1923, sought to root Soviet power in native elites and encouraged the use of indigenous languages, but by the early 1930s state policy had changed to renewed Russianisation. By 1991 the number of Union Republics had risen to fifteen: three emerged as a result of the disintegration of the Transcaucasian Federation (Armenia, Azerbaijan and Georgia); five Central Asian republics were created as a result of carving up the territory of the RSFSR (Kazakhstan, Kyrgyzstan, Tajikistan, Turkmenistan and Uzbekistan); and four had been incorporated into the USSR during the Second World War (Estonia, Latvia, Lithuania and Moldova). Thus the Soviet Union that died in December 1991 was a very different one from that born in 1922.

Russia, too, had changed, and the country that in 1991 became the 'continuer' state to the USSR was far smaller than in 1922, having donated territory to Ukraine and the Central Asian republics.[4] The geographical area of the RSFSR under Soviet power had decreased both in absolute and in comparative terms: if in 1922 the RSFSR comprised 94.7 per cent of the territory of the USSR, by 1991 this had fallen to 76.2 per cent. In terms of size, the USSR had become rather more a union of equals, divided up into fifty-three different types of national-territorial units: 15 Union Republics and 38 autonomous republics, oblasts and okrugs. Why some of the autonomous areas should have become Union Republics, and others not, remains a source of bitterness for areas such as Tatarstan to this day. There was, moreover, a considerable disparity between the historical and the actual ethnic borders between the peoples.

This distinctive form of national-territorial federation was intended neither to promote the emergence of ethnically pure nation-states nor, on the contrary, to allow the emergence of multinational 'nations' within the framework of the ethno-federal areas: they were seen as no more than a transitional stage in the long-term goal of complete state unity, passing through an initial stage of 'coming closer' (*sblizhenie*) to result ultimately in complete fusion (*sliyanie*), on a world scale if possible. In the meantime, however, rather than being a union of equal and sovereign peoples, Soviet federal policy was based on a strict hierarchy of nations, with some privileged to have a state in their name, while other ethnic groups failed to qualify for the honorific of 'nation' and instead were called 'nationalities' (*narodnosti*). While the 1989 census listed 128 nationalities, only 68 formally made up the 53 ethno-federal units. Ethnic Russians made up just over half (50.78 per cent) of the Soviet Union's 290,938,469 population in July 1990. They were followed by Ukrainians at 15.45 per cent, Uzbeks at 5.84, Belarusians at 3.51 and Kazakhs at 2.85 per cent (see Table 1). The official language was Russian, but the country was host to over 200 languages and dialects, at least eighteen of which had more than 1 million speakers.[5]

For most of the period the Soviet national-state system maintained a precarious balance and survived because some other force, namely the CPSU, exercised real power. Declarations of republican sovereignty and the Russian Decree on Power unwittingly accelerated the destruction of the Soviet state, although their main target had been the communist regime which had sat uncomfortably above them all as some sort of sixteenth republic. While a viable post-communist federation or confederation might have been feasible,[6] in the event the destruction of communism was accompanied by the destruction of the Soviet state. Tsipko noted that 'Ironically, the putschists have helped through the plans of the most radically-minded divisionists.'[7] While the coup may have destroyed the final shreds of legitimacy of attempts to 'renew' the communist system, its effect on reconstituting the Soviet state, while devastating in the short-run, was less conclusive in the longer perspective. The disintegration of the USSR did not destroy the idea of a historical and national core to a multinational state centred on the territories of the former USSR. This was a view shared not only by the most irreconcilable Soviet and Russian nationalists, but also by a broad swathe of democratic opinion and Gorbachev himself.[8]

Russia itself replicated on a smaller scale some of the features of the USSR. As we saw in chapter 2, at the time of the last census in 1989 Russia included 31 ethno-federal components (16 autonomous republics, 5 autonomous oblasts (provinces) and 10 autonomous okrugs (regions): the titular nationality comprised an absolute majority of the population in 8 and a comparative majority in 3,[9] and in the other 20 ethnic Russians were in the majority (see Tables 2 and 3). In the 16 autonomous republics the titular nationalities comprised only 42 per cent of the total population; in the autonomous oblasts 22 per cent; and in the autonomous okrugs only 10.5 per cent, largely as a result of the heavy in-migration of Russians and other peoples.

The area of the RSFSR occupied by autonomous territories increased from 40.7 per cent in 1922 (27.7 per cent in the 1989 borders) to 53.3 per cent in 1989, but only 16.7 per cent of the total population lived in what had become thirty-one ethno-federal components.[10] Out of a total RSFSR population of 147.02 million in 1989, 119.87 million (81.53 per cent) were ethnic Russians: of these, 108.06 million (73.5 per cent of the total RF population) lived outside ethno-federal units; while 11.8 million (8.03 per cent) lived within the national-state territory of some other nationality. The 9.8 per cent of ethnic Russians in the Russian Federation living in the ethno-federal territories of others make up 45.7 per cent of the population of these areas (see Table 2). The nearly 12 million ethnic Russians living in ethno-federal territories, moreover, constitute a source of potential Russian nationalist mobilisation. The total population of the forty-one nationalities with their own or sharing ethno-federal areas is 17.71 million (12.05 per cent of the total population of the RSFSR), but of these only 10.32 million (7.02 per cent) live in their own titular federal unit.[11] Ethnic Russians make up the overwhelming majority of the country's population but find themselves in the anomalous position of not having an ethno-federal area of their own – hence the calls by some nationalists either for its establishment or for the abolition of the territories of ethnic minorities.

The formal status of the autonomous republics and oblasts changed as they declared their sovereignty, and at the same time often changed their names. The constitution was amended on 15

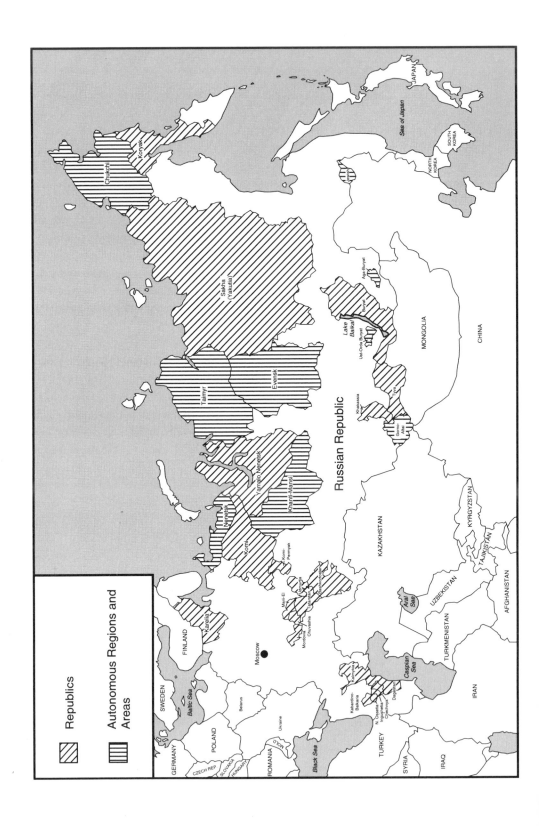

December 1990 to delete the word 'autonomous' in the title of Russia's sixteen republics, and they simply became 'republics forming part of the Russian Federation'. On 3 July 1991 the Supreme Soviet elevated 4 of the 5 autonomous oblasts (Adygeya, Gorno-Altai, Karachai-Cherkessia and Khakassia) to the status of republics and they were removed from the jurisdiction of the krais to which they were formerly subordinate.[12] This brought the number of republics to 20, leaving only the Jewish autonomous oblast. The number of republics rose to 21 when on 4 June 1992 the Supreme Soviet split the Chechen-Ingush republic into two. This brought the number of Russia's federal components to eighty-nine (see constitution, article 65.1). The twenty-one national republics comprise 15.2 per cent of the population and 28.6 per cent of Russia's territory.

There were numerous anomalies in Russian nationality policy. Why should some peoples have a 'republic' and others not? In Russia thirty-three national groups have some sort of territorial home, excluding Russians and some of the less numerous peoples, though some lived in great communal dwellings like Dagestan. Another sixty-three peoples live in Russia without a national home. Equity would suggest that all should be on an equal footing, irrespective of whether they have a republic in the 'near abroad' (7.8 million compatriots of the titular nationalities in the fourteen former Union Republics live in Russia, including 4.4 million Ukrainians); or in the 'far abroad' (821,000 Germans), Koreans (107,000), Poles (95,000), Greeks (92,000), Finns (47,000) and a few other peoples; or Jews who have a nominal homeland abroad (Israel) and one in Russia, Birobidjan, in the inhospitable Far East where 1.7 per cent of Russian Jews live comprising 4.2 per cent of the total population of the area. By contrast, over 90 per cent of Yakuts, Tyvans, Kabards and Balkars live in their republics, while at the other extreme a two-thirds of Tatars and Mordvins and nearly half of Chuvashis and Maris live outside their titular republic, a total of 9.7 million people living outside their nominal republics (see Table 2).[13]

As the USSR disintegrated the ethno-federal republics were drawn into the struggle between the Union and the republics. In the Law on the Delimitation of Powers between the USSR and the Subjects of the Federation of April 1990 Gorbachev gave Russia's autonomous republics the right to join any new Union Treaty on terms equal with the Union Republics. The elevation of the political status of Russia's republics was later rejected by Yeltsin as a threat to Russia's territorial integrity.[14] Instead he sought to rebuild Russia on the basis of a civic identity and loyalty to a democratic Russian state. As we shall see, he was willing to renegotiate the relationship between Russia and its republics and championed the achievement of sovereignty from below on condition that they remained loyal to the Russian state.

The complexity of minority issues in Russia is daunting. The rich diversity of Russian ethnic composition means that much of the population has multiple identities with overlapping ethnicity, religion, culture and language. As noted, the 1989 census identified 128 ethnic groups, although sixteen had a population of less than 5,000. There are twenty-six groups among the peoples of the North alone, ranging from the Nentsy numbering 34,200 to the Entsy at 200. At the same time, the table demonstrates the overwhelming predominance of the ethnic Russians at 81.5 per cent of the population, followed a long way behind by the second largest group, the Tatars at 3.75 per cent. Soviet statistics probably underestimated the number of Jews, and probably the number of ethnic Germans and Poles as well.

While there remains a devastating potential for Russia to split up, the figures above suggest a complex picture that differs in several respects to the nationality problems of the USSR. The majority of Russia's republics lack a clear demographic basis to aspirations for independence,

Figure 4(a) The regions and republics of European Russia

and, to date, a trigger mechanism for disintegration has been lacking in Russia. However, territories where the titular nationalities are the strongest can be found on the borders of Russia: in the North Caucasus the Islamic bloc of Dagestan, Chechnya, Ingushetia, Kabardino-Balkaria, together with Buddhist Kalmykia and Christian North Ossetia; and in the Far East Tyva on the borders of Mongolia, and Agin okrug. The Volga and Kama republics form a single contiguous territory in the centre of Russia (see Figure 7a), but in Chuvashia and Marii-El, Russians make up a clear majority. In Tatarstan Tatars comprise 48.5 per cent of the population and Russians 43.3 per cent, but only a third of all Volga Tatars live in Tatarstan. The independence of some of the republics at the margins of the Federation, like Chechnya or Tyva, might not destabilise the fragile unity of the country; whereas the secession of a

Figure 4(b) The regions and republics of European Russia

republic in the heartlands, like Tatarstan, could stimulate a snowball effect tearing the unity of the Federation apart.

Woodrow Wilson was asked during the Versailles peace conference in 1919, 'Does every little language have to have a state all its own?' The answer for the USSR in 1991, as in Eastern Europe in 1919, appeared to be 'yes'; whereas in Russia today a somewhat different dynamic operates – or so the leadership believes. In America it proved impossible to achieve Theodore Roosevelt's dream of no longer having Italian-Americans, Hispanic-Americans, Anglo-Americans but only Americans, whereas the problem in Russia is rather different for historical reasons. The Bashkirs, Tatars and others were long established, and in many cases predated the arrival of the Russians themselves; but at the same time existence of Tatar-Russians, Bashkir-Russians and so on is an established fact. This is reflected in the two terms used to denote 'Russian' in the language: *Rossiiskoe* means 'of Russia', used adjectivally, giving rise to the noun *Rossiyanin*, a citizen of Russia of whatever ethnicity; whereas *Russkii*, the noun, denotes those who are ethnically Russian.

The *korenizatsiya* policy of the 1920s had contributed much to the development of the national consciousness of the peoples of Russia, and in particular had consolidated national cultures and scripts. From the 1930s onwards, however, schooling in native languages was reduced and the policy of national development reversed. With the collapse of the Soviet regime, policy returned to that of the 1920s, with the difference that the earlier nation-building was now accompanied by state-building; for many peoples the restoration of national symbols and culture was not enough and they now sought full-blooded statehood. The USSR had denigrated the nation in favour of class and could always stop centrifugal tendencies by invoking the principle of class unity, which justified the maintenance of the integrity of the state. Without this safety net, Russian state policy in the post-communist transition had to be rather more wary in unleashing minority nationalist passions.

The Russian leadership from 1990 sought to prevent the 'Balkanisation' of Russia. The central question was to define a new relationship between the many peoples of Russia and the reborn Russian state. The ethno-federal legacy left a heavy burden, with political inequalities not only between regions and national areas, but between the autonomies themselves. The sixteen autonomous republics in the RSFSR had had their own constitutions but (in contrast to the Union Republics) no right of secession, whereas the five autonomous oblasts and the ten autonomous okrugs had no constitutions and even fewer rights to self-government. This legacy of inequitability in national relations needed to be remedied; some peoples sought to become nations in their own right, and tried to do this within the framework of traditional ideas of statehood. It is clearly impractical, however, for all 128 peoples in the Russian Federation to achieve statehood; instead, the emphasis for the majority has moved from 'national self-determination', taking the form of state-building, towards forms of national-cultural self-development. The rediscovery of national identity is at the same time the remaking of this identity in post-Soviet conditions where *all* societies face a crisis of values. For Russia to remain together its regions and peoples will have to become part of a shared political community, and indeed part of a national market and single economic space, to compensate for the limitations that will necessarily have to be placed on aspirations to statehood.

The division of Russia into national areas, therefore, did not 'solve' the national question but exacerbated it. The question of national development, instruction in native languages and so on, cannot be reduced to the question of statehood since so many people live outside 'their' state (an argument the rejectionists make about the USSR as a whole). Not only do a large proportion of people with their own titular republic live outside their nominal area, but the national areas themselves are home to many other peoples (primarily Russians). Russians, however passively they behave, by the mere fact of their presence are perceived as a threat to native languages and traditions, representing an ever-present danger of cultural assimilation. In most areas, however, Russians never considered themselves the bearers of an imperial creed but sought to escape hardship at home, to find work and better wages, or were deported involuntarily. The absence of counter-mobilisation to the nationalism of some of the titular nationalities is striking, but the strong vote in 1993 for Zhirinovskii in some of the national areas revealed ethnic Russian fears.[15] Just as in the elections to the First and Second Dumas in 1906 and 1907, where the greatest support for Russian nationalist parties came in the fiteen *gubernii* of the Pale of Settlement and border areas with mixed populations, so too in the elections for the 'Fifth Duma' in December 1993 strong support for Zhirinovskii's nationalism came from areas of mixed settlement. Parties that opposed the ethnocratic territorial organisation of the country gained.

The constitution now recognises all territories as multinational, guaranteeing equal rights for all of Russia's citizens irrespective of where they find themselves. The problem, however, arises when it comes to the question of collective rights. While all the peoples of Russia have the right to national and cultural development, the political form in which this can be expressed remains ambiguous. Russia is considered a state of all of its citizens, irrespective of their nationality, but the ethno-federal legacy of the Soviet period is difficult to reconcile with this conception. The ethno-federal system itself remains a potent element stoking the fires of inter-ethnic conflict (although it is neither a sufficient nor a necessary condition for such conflicts). Attempts, however, to separate the national question from the problem of territorial autonomy would in the short run only precipitate conflict. Of all the poisoned chalices bequeathed by the Soviet regime, ethno-federalism was perhaps the worst.

TOWARDS A NEW FEDERALISM

Just as the old USSR had been an incomplete federal system, so within Russia itself federalism was only partial. The RSFSR had been made up of a number of autonomous republics and regions, but the rest of the country lacked federal representation. The system was a mixed ethno-federal and unitary one and thus very different, say, from the United States where representation is federal-territorial from the entire country. How was Russia to move from an ethno-federal system to a genuine federal-territorial system in which *all* of Russia's territories were subjects of federation?

Towards the Federal Treaty

Learning from the fate of the USSR, which had responded too late to the problem of nationalism, the First Russian CPD in May 1990 decided that the Russian federal system should be renewed; the Declaration of State Sovereignty of 12 June 1990 recognised 'the need for a significant extension of the rights of the autonomous republics . . . and regions of the RSFSR'; and the Supreme Soviet Presidium on 17 July proposed a timetable for a Federal Treaty. A draft was ready for the Third CPD to adopt in March 1991, but the vigorous anti-federalist lobbying of a group of deputies meant that it was returned to be redrafted. The fourth draft of the USSR Union Treaty, published three days before the coup, made provision for a Russian treaty to regulate its own international relations, and the disintegration of the USSR and the problems confronting the adoption of the new Russian constitution placed even more of a premium on achieving an agreement to prevent the disintegration of the Russian Federation.

The debate focused on what was to be the subject of the Russian federal system? If only national-territorial areas, then what about regions like Yenisei, and even more, what about peoples without territory? Sakharov had suggested making all 53 Soviet national-territorial units subjects of federalism in his draft constitution for the Union of Soviet Republics of Europe and Asia, though it was not clear why 53 republics should represent some 130 peoples, especially when ethnic boundaries did not coincide with the national ones and where the titular nationalities were often in a minority in the republic that bore their name. Gorbachev simply confirmed the rights of the fifteen existing Soviet Union Republics as the subjects of the proposed Union Treaty, and in effect washed his hands of their own internal minority problems. The debate over the new federal treaties reflected the struggle between two different visions, one focusing on individual rights in a democratic state, while the other prioritised national rights loosely identified with the existing ethno-federal regions.

The declarations of sovereignty of the Union Republics of the USSR was accompanied by declarations of sovereignty by the national areas of Russia. Russia declared its state sovereignty on 12 June 1990, and a month later, on 20 July, North Ossetia declared itself a union republic, albeit as part of Russia. Karelia on 9 August declared its sovereignty but did not change its status, while Khakassia on 15 August unilaterally raised its status to an autonomous republic. On 29 August Komi and on 30 August Tatarstan declared themselves sovereign, followed by Udmurtia on 20 September and Yakutia on 27 September.[16] What these declarations meant in practice remained to be discovered, but it soon became clear that a declaration of sovereignty by no means signalled its achievement. Russia's autonomous republics sought to join Gorbachev's Union Treaty process in their own right, an idea at first supported by Gorbachev to undermine Yeltsin's power base even if it meant the destruction of the Russian Federation – he has still not been forgiven for this. In this context it is less surprising to find that the autonomous republics that were most active in seeking sovereignty were also those that most actively supported the putschists in August 1991, with the leaderships in Tatarstan, Kabardino-Balkaria and Chechen-Ingushetia actively supporting the SCSE.

It was on a visit to Tatarstan in August 1990, following his election as chairman of the Russian parliament, that Yeltsin declared 'Take as much independence as you can', and he went on to suggest that if this meant secession from Russia, then 'your decision will be final'. In Bashkortostan soon after he once again urged the local authorities to 'take as much power as you can swallow'.[17] In his speech to the Fifth CPD on 28 October 1991 Yeltsin argued that 'The process of self-determination of peoples, which began even before the revolution of 1917 but which was interrupted by crude force for many decades, is now entering its decisive phase. A new national consciousness is forming in the Russian people that is democratic in its very essence.'[18] It was all very well to urge local sovereignty in a bid to counter Gorbachev's overtures to Russia's republics, but how was this 'freedom' and 'self-determination' to be institutionalised, and would it be democratic and compatible with the unity of the state? Yeltsin was to find that the nations of Russia, which under the Soviet system had enjoyed various degrees of formal autonomy, now tried to convert their rights into genuine powers. While the Karelians, the Dagestanis, the Buryats and the Yakuts sought to extend their autonomy to control resources on their territory, the Chechens and certain groups in Tatarstan sought outright independence.

One of the concrete manifestations of sovereignty was the 'presidentification' of Russia's republics, once again following the example set by Yeltsin himself. Tatarstan led the way, electing a president on the same day as Russia (12 June 1991). By the end of 1991 presidents had been chosen in Kabardino-Balkaria, Marii El, Mordovia, Chechnya and Tyva, and with other republics moving in the same direction. Tatarstan had moved the furthest in translating its declaration of sovereignty into practice, having chosen not only a president but also a new name (formerly Tataria) and a coat of arms, and sought economic sovereignty through establishing its own bank and bringing former Union enterprises under its own jurisdiction. The only other republic to have set on the same path was Chechnya. The key issue everywhere was control over local property, natural resources and budgetary matters, especially taxation.

In the struggle to shape a new post-Soviet federalism 'democrats' argued that 'The choice is either the creation of a democratic state with guarantees to all the peoples of the federation of the right to self-determination, and protection of this right, or disintegration in accordance with the same former USSR scenario.'[19] They insisted that Russia could avoid the fate that had befallen the USSR only by granting full autonomy to the republics, whereas statists responded that it was this logic that had led to the break-up of the USSR. Instead, they insisted that since the ethnic borders of Russia only roughly corresponded to the existing borders, and because every single region of Russia was multi-ethnic to one degree or another, rights should be individual rather than national. While reactionaries revived the Whites' Civil War slogan of Russia 'united and indivisible' (*edinaya i nedelimaya*), the principle was shared by most of Russia's new leaders, although they were divided over how this could be achieved.

Galina Starovoitova, Yeltsin's main adviser on nationality issues, sought to manage nationality issues without violence, and placed her hopes on the development of an effective federal system but in the meantime argued in favour of giving the republics a free rein so as not to provoke conflict. Nationality policy in the early period was criticised for constantly reacting to crises rather than developing consistent principles, and her departure in October 1992 signalled a hardening of attitudes. In the long-run the aim was the transition from the national to the territorial organisation of the federation, but in the short-term the State Committee for Federalism and Nationalities under Shakhrai insisted that national self-determination was to be dependent on two other principles of international law, human rights and the inviolability of borders. The Committee's policy according to Shakhrai was based on a number of principles: the equality of all people's living in the federation; the genuine development of federalism in Russia; the depoliticisation of nationality policy; reliance on the legally formed authorities in the components of the federation, whether the centre liked them or not; the indisputable priority of political methods in resolving national conflicts; accepting the link between economic and nationality policy; and consistency in nationality policy.[20]

In practice Russian policy sought to preserve the cohesion of the Russian Federation by such means as maintaining the neutrality of the federal centre in inter-ethnic conflicts, placing a moratorium on border changes, banning the creation of new federal components through the division of existing units, assisting the stabilisation of political elites in the republics by advancing moderate nationalists, managers and entrepreneurs to leadership positions, and preventing the fusion of state and mafia-criminal structures in the national areas.[21] The government was unable to implement some of these principles but their enunciation helped restrain centrifugal trends.

An alternative federal policy was adopted by the Supreme Soviet's Council of Nationalities. Its chairman, Abdulatipov, argued that the revival of the national life of the peoples of Russia was an essential part of the formation of civil society and the establishment of a legal state: 'We consider national rebirth as the combination of the national idea with general human interests and democratic principles.' He insisted that in a multinational society the state should not stand above the various ethnic groups, and he condemned those who sought to replace the national principle by the territorial one. He agreed that the priority was individual human rights, but this should not infringe national rights. In the larger context, he noted that the cornerstone of policy was the 'Russian question', the 25 million Russians in the near abroad who had lost their motherland, and warned that Russia could not be indifferent to infringements on their rights.[22]

Federalism has a long history in Russia. It has been argued that the treaties signed between the Tsar and the governments of peoples entering the empire, like the Caucasian khans and Central Asian emirs, contained provision for a division of powers between the centre and the locality, the hallmark of federalism. Various national areas of the old empire had certain rights and privileges, with local self-government and limits to the rights of Tsarist *chinovniki* to meddle in local affairs. These early elements of federalism were undermined during the centralising and unitarist period of the second half of the nineteenth century, as the supranational principles of Tsarist imperial statehood began to give way to a nation-building statism, yet did not disappear entirely. The Bolsheviks had at first condemned the concept of federalism, but were soon forced to incorporate it in their state-building, however, as we have seen, federal forms were undermined by a unitary practice. In drafting Russia's new constitution Yeltsin insisted on three key principles: that human rights were to be guaranteed throughout Russia, including the republics; the unity of Russia must be maintained; and the constitutions of the republics should not contradict the Russian constitution.[23]

The major obstacle to adopting the constitution was disagreement over what was to be the subject of federation. The draft of October 1991 weakened the old ethno-territorial division of Russia by proposing two forms of representation: ethno-federal from the *republics*, which would not necessarily be the same as that from the existing autonomous republics; and federal-territorial, as in the USA or Germany, from *zemli* (lands, or in German *Länder*). A highly regionalised Russia was to emerge with some forty units, the republics and the zemli (whose relative status remained controversial), and all of Russia for the first time would become a subject of the federation and not just specified ethnic parts.[24] The project tried to finesse the arguments of those who called for the ethnically Russian parts to separate from the national minorities to create a Russian autonomous republic, but the draft appeared to satisfy neither wing. On the one hand, it was attacked for undermining the unity of the country by conferring extensive rights on the titular republics, and indeed for infringing the rights of Russians living in them. On the other hand, the attempt to equalise the rights of republics and lands was interpreted as an attack on the privileges of the former. The draft represented a move away from the traditional Soviet absolutisation of the ethnic dimension in state building, which had granted statehood to all sorts of ethnic groups to whom the principle was often alien and pointless, but having tasted statehood the ethno-federal territories would not give it up without a struggle, especially when Yeltsin and his associates had used the rebirth of statehood so effectively in their own struggle against the communist regime.

The October 1991 draft constitution asserted that Russia existed as a multinational state that had come into being over the centuries. The draft reflected the view that Russia was a constitutional rather than a treaty federation, that the state sovereignty of Russia as a united state only needed to find a constitutional and federal form rather than being formed through contracts with its members. This did not exclude the signing of a Federal Treaty between the republics of Russia and the state as a whole, but did not give the republics the right of secession since they were already part of a pre-existing Russian state. Thus the draft condemned the treaty path to a new constitution, which would have given all the subjects of the new federation the choice whether to join or not. According to Rumyantsev, this would not only have caused endless conflicts but it would also have denied that Russia was *a priori* already a 'sovereign state created by the peoples historically living in it'.[25] Russia had never been a treaty federation (unlike the USSR) and therefore none had the right to secede and neither would they be given a choice of whether to join. Tatarstan, Tyva and Chechen-Ingushetia had never formally signed to join the RSFSR or the USSR, and were now bitter that they would not be given the option of entering the Russian Federation as signatories of a new treaty.[26]

Post-communist Russian state-building was thus caught between three principles. The first suggested that all national-territorial formations should be abolished in their entirety, and that Russia should become a unitary state and be divided into simple administrative regions like the Tsarist *gubernii*, a view advanced by patriots and even more vigorously by nationalists like Zhirinovskii. The other view absolutised the federal principle and sought to divide Russia into fully-fledged republics and *zemli* with equal rights. The third view, advanced by the leaders of Russia's republics, sought to maintain the existing hierarchy of federalism, with the ethno-federal units at the top. The 1991 draft constitution took the second path and weakened the ethno-federal principle in favour of a de-ethnicised federalism. This led to protests in the republics by advocates of the third path, and later versions of the constitution made concessions in form to the national elites in the titular republics while equalising the content of the new federalism. The special status of national republics was retained but the rights of Russia's regions were enhanced.

This balance between privileges and rights was enshrined in the Federal Treaty, signed on 31 March 1992 and ratified by an overwhelming majority of the Sixth CPD on 10 April.[27] The Treaty recognised three types of federal subjects: 20 (now 21) national-state formations (formerly autonomous republics) as sovereign republics within the Russian Federation; 57 administrative territorial areas (krais, oblasts, as well as the cities of Moscow and St Petersburg); and 11 national-territorial areas (autonomous oblasts and autonomous okrugs). All had equal rights and obligations, but the republics were allowed the attributes of statehood: their own constitutions and laws, their own elected Supreme Soviets (parliaments), supreme courts, and, if they so wished (which most did), presidents.[28] With the elevation in 1991 of four autonomous areas to the status of republics the total had risen to 20, and of these, 18 signed the Treaty. Tatarstan, which had earlier voted for self-rule, and the Chechen Republic, which had declared independence from Russia in November 1991, refused to sign. Tatarstan insisted on a separate bilateral treaty between itself and Russia as equal sovereign states. Bashkortostan had threatened not to participate but at the last moment agreed to sign when granted additional budgetary rights.[29]

The Federal Treaty did not signify the creation of a new state, Abdulatipov insisted, since such a state had existed already for centuries, and neither did it denote the transformation of the state into a federation, since Russian statehood had long contained elements of federalism, but was an attempt to define the powers of the federation and its subjects.[30] In contrast to the old Soviet constitution, the Treaty did not grant the republics the right to secede but bound them together while granting greater powers and freedoms. The Treaty was not intended to act as a substitute for the constitution, and instead was incorporated, with some amendments, into the constitution as a special section. Moscow retained the right to control defence and security and to set federal taxes while the signatories now gained some control over natural resources and formalised their borders. They could now also conduct foreign trade on their own. The extent of their control over natural resources and the right to levy taxes remained unclear and caused endless conflicts later – including a joint declaration by the presidents of Bashkortostan, Tatarstan and Sakha (Yakutia) that the federal authorities ignored the legitimate rights and interests of the republics.[31]

Once again a form of ethno-federalism was confirmed in Russia despite hopes to avoid this route. The new Russian federalism now developed on a constitutional-treaty basis, though much remained to be done. The local and national constitutions had to be amended to take into account the new agreements, numerous national laws had to be changed and the rights of the non-national areas had to be given a juridical foundation. It appeared absurd to retain three different types of subjects of federation, yet 'asymmetrical federalism' might well be the only basis on which the Russian Federation could survive. Yeltsin had earlier favoured the division of Russia into some 8–10 large regions to avoid nationality clashes and separatism, and Rumyantsenv had favoured the division of Russia into zemli and republics with equal rights. This had been opposed by the national republics who wanted more rights in *comparison* with the Russian oblasts, even though they were gaining extensive rights in comparison with the past. The national republics were united on this, irrespective of their ethnic composition. Karelia, a republic in which the titular nationality made up only 10 per cent of the population, sought exactly the same rights as Tatarstan or Tyva with much larger proportions of the titular nationality. Behaviour was defined by status rather than ethnic composition: in a different way this was confirmed by the rise of regional separatism.

The Federal Treaty did not put an end to debates in Russia about the form of its federalism. Questions of property and taxation remained vexed, the fundamental question over whether Russia should be a regional rather than an ethno-national federation had not been resolved, and an unstable hierarchy of federalism had been established. The twenty-one republics were endowed with the appurtenances of a state, but the others were not. Tatarstan's constitution affirmed that it was a state 'associated with Russia',[32] and the constitutions of some of the other republics (namely Tyva, Karelia and Yakutia-Sakha) declared the primacy of local laws over Russian ones.[33] The struggle between executive and legislative power in Moscow allowed the regions to ignore presidential decrees and legislative acts and weakened economic links. In 1993, for example, Moscow collected only 40 per cent of the tax revenues due to it from the regions and republics,[34] and over two dozen refused to pay the centre their federal tax obligations. The confusion allowed considerations of short-term advantage to predominate over juridical principles of unified and equal state-building for all of Russia.

The new federalism in the constitution

Drafts of the constitution had encouraged the aspirations of Russia's republics for sovereignty while at the same time limiting these aspirations, a tension still not satisfactorily resolved. Strengthened by his victory in October 1993, Yeltsin took a more assertive line towards the regions and republics of Russia and in effect reneged on what he had been forced to concede during the struggle with parliament. In particular, the word 'sovereign', which a number of republics had adopted to describe themselves, was struck from the constitution on the grounds that one state could not have two sources of sovereignty. The constitution adopted on 12 December 1993 finally gave legal form to Russia's federal system.

The rights of Russia's 21 republics, 6 provinces, 49 regions, 2 cities (Moscow and St Petersburg) with regional status, and 11 autonomous areas were significantly equalised and made subject to the laws and decisions of federal authorities. The principle of 'asymmetrical federalism', the keystone of the Federal Treaty, was in principle abandoned. No longer were some subjects of the federation 'more equal' than others – at least in theory. While the provisions of the Treaty were reflected in the new constitution, the text itself was no longer bodily incorporated to underline the principle that Russia is a federation based on a constitution and not on a treaty.

The constitution regularised the hybrid federalism that had been emerging in Russia based partly on national areas (like Belgium and India) and partly on areas lacking any national significance (as in Brazil, Germany and the USA). This mix of national and territorial federalism was accompanied by declarations (article 5) on the equality of all the subjects of the federation, when in fact they had greatly differing rights. The republics, for example, have their own constitutions, governments, parliaments, presidents and other attributes of statehood denied the territorial formations; the latter, however, have the right to issue their own charters. Indeed, the adoption of the constitution marked yet another step away from the old Soviet primacy given to the ethno-federal organisation of the state, a principle that was largely meaningless when the CPSU acted as the universal coordinating force, but which threatened to tear Russia apart in its absence. The new document sought to prioritise civil over collective ethnic rights, and at the same time tried to prevent ethnic differences becoming the foundation of local or central statehood, a development that could only exacerbate centrifugal tendencies.

Claims that Yeltsin was trying to restore a unitary state, however, were exaggerated. His aim was more modest: to restore the viability of the state and put an end to the dangerous game in which the excutive and legislature during their confrontation vied with each other to promise most to the localities. Regions and republics were now guaranteed significant areas of autonomy as long as their legislative acts did not contradict the Russian constitution or federal laws. The long-standing dispute between republics, on the one hand, and between regions and territories, on the other, began at long last to be settled, although debates over Russia's state structure were by no means over. Any attempt to abolish the ethno-federal republics would provoke massive resistance and probably precipitate the break-up of Russia.

Moscow instead sought accommodation with the republics and enshrined the principle of asymmetrical federalism in a series of treaties with them. In a departure from the principle enunciated in the constitution, the signing of the treaty between Tatarstan and Russia on 15 February 1994 suggested that Russia was indeed a treaty rather than a constitutional federation. The treaty affirmed Tatarstan's right to have a constitution, tax system, foreign policy and foreign trade policy. By the end of 1995 a total of nine treaties had been signed between Moscow and individual republics granting generous tax concessions, control over natural resources and other advantages. These ethno-federal units are less than fully fledged nations, and with their heterogeneous populations it is difficult to see how most can be; at the same time they are less than full-scale states recognised in international law. It is this ambiguous status that makes them such uncomfortable members of the Russian Federation; a discomfort exacerbated by the exclusion suffered by the hundred-odd other nationalities living in the country (including ethnic Russians) who do not have republics to their name. To balance the situation special treaties delineating competencies were signed with a number of regions. On 12 January 1996 a bilateral treaty granting extensive economic rights was signed between the federal centre and Sverdlovsk, the first such act with a federal subject without the status of a republic. A treaty with Kaliningrad region laid the basis for a free economic zone there. By June 1996 23 subjects of the federation had signed power-sharing treaties with Moscow. Thus the regions, like the republics earlier were granted quasi-autonomous status.[35]

The struggle over the constitution and Federal Treaty was only one aspect of finding a new political framework for the conduct of relations between the peoples of the Russian Federation. While fears about the disintegration of the Russian Federation might have abated, they have not disappeared. The constitution achieved what Rumyantsev had long advocated, namely the limitation of the sovereignty of Russia's republics; yet he now suddenly became the defender of the rights of the republics.[36] Meanwhile, support for a return to the *guberniya* principle, whereby Russia would be converted into a unitary state and divided into administrative units and the principle of ethno-federalism abolished, continued to grow.[37] The advocates of 'gubernisation' insisted that a unitary state was not necessarily a centralised one, and pointed to the example of France where regional devolution has eroded Napoleonic centralism. In Spain since the death of Franco in 1975 a hybrid type of federalism has emerged with the devolution of authority to seventeen self-governing provinces; but the lack of historical identity of some of the regions suggests elements of 'false federalism'.

The pressures that had led to the disintegration of the USSR might not end there, and there were fears that they might destroy the Russian Federation itself. The lines of fracture in Russia run not only along ethnic lines but also along regional-economic lines. The radical economic reforms launched in late 1991 in the short-term threatened to undermine the country's unity as regions sought to protect themselves,[38] but Gaidar insisted that the development of a national market would halt the tendency towards autarchisation within Russia and create incentives for greater integration.[39] The lack of support for separatism in the 1993 and subsequent elections indicated that reports of the imminent demise of the Russian Federation are exaggerated. The comparison with the USSR is misleading because the dynamics of Russian politics are very different; there are powerful centripetal trends that check the tendency towards disintegration.

10 Nationalism and Russia

In these days of doubt, in these days of painful brooding over the fate of my country, you alone are my rod and my staff, O great, mighty, true, and free Russian language! If it were not for you, how could one keep from despairing at the sight of what is going on at home? It is inconceivable that such a language should not belong to a great people.

Ivan Turgenev[1]

One of the unique features of West European civilisation was the emergence fairly early on of territorially sovereign states whose relations were regulated, at least after the Treaty of Westphalia in 1648, by a rudimentary system of international law. These sovereign states in time evolved into nations based on principles of popular sovereignty in which the nation was considered to consist of a broader political community expressing the political will of all the people. In the Eastern half of the continent, however, the concept of nation retained a primordial ethnicised content whereby an individual was a member of an ethnic community irrespective of their will. The nation was a community relatively independent of politics, allowing several culturally based nations to coexist within a multinational state. Russia offered a third approach to the idea of nationhood where ethnicity and participation were subordinated to the ethics of state survival itself. From 1991 Russia unambiguously adopted the West European model, much to the disappointment of its nationalists and patriots.

Soviet policy had simultaneously maintained separate national identities, above all through the notorious 'point 5' of Soviet passports where individuals had to state their ethnic identity (chosen from either the maternal or paternal line, but once entered forever irrevocable), and crushed any but the most formal political expression of that identity. The Soviet regime had been shockingly careless about generating a substantive sense of 'Soviet' nationality, limiting itself to abstractions about 'eternal friendship' between peoples united in an 'indivisible union'.[2] The Russian Federation is no less of a multinational state than the USSR had been, with some 27 million non-ethnic Russians living in a state consisting of 128 recognised nationalities, and the place of ethnic Russians themselves in the new order remains contested. Russia embarked on a distinctive type of nation-building on the foundations of a fractured sense of community and an unclear definition of national identity. How can we understand post-communist nationalism, and can a polity be built in Russia combining democracy and patriotism?

NATIONALISM IN THE DEMOCRATIC REVOLUTION

When the long-awaited revolt of the nationalities against the Soviet state came, it was led by Russia, something few had anticipated. Nationality politics once again entered the mainstream of political discourse as communist internationalism gave way to a 'renationalisation' of politics. Russia's struggle for sovereignty, however, was both national *and* democratic, elements that did not always sit well together. Russia's rebirth as a sovereign state took a national form but did not adopt the classic exclusive forms of nationalism. 'Nationalism' as such is something largely alien to the Russian tradition, where the focus has historically been on maintaining the state. Klyamkin noted that 'Nationalism has not taken root in the Russian mentality, and contrary to the West, is perceived by Russians with suspicion.'[3] Patriots in the Slavophile tradition consider nationalism yet another Western invention, like Marxism, come to snare the poor Russians.

From the perspective of power politics, Russia was the greatest loser at the end of the Cold War. The fall of the USSR undermined the principles on which Russians had defined themselves as a state for centuries. The Bolshevik experience had lasted a mere 74 years, but its fall shattered the statehood (*gosudarstvennost*) that had emerged in the course of a millenium. Russia had lost territory before when in 1918 Poland and Finland gained their independence, though parts of their territory were regained by Stalin during the Second World War. The separation of the Central Asian republics also did not affect Russia's core perception of itself, having only conquered the area in the late nineteenth century and then bound it loosely to Russia. But the alienation of Ukraine, and to a lesser degree Belarus, struck at the very heart of Russian self-identity. It was in Ukraine that the Russian state arose and here were born many of Russia's greatest writers: Nikolai Gogol in Poltava, Anna Akhmatova in Odessa and Mikhail Bulgakov in Kiev. The former editor of *Moscow News*, Len Karpinskii, observed that 'Millions of Russians are convinced that, without Ukraine, it is impossible to speak not only of a great Russia but of any kind of Russia at all.'[4] It came as a shock for Russians to have to start thinking about Ukraine as a separate country, a shock that the English survived when most of Ireland and the homeland of some of the greatest 'English' writers such as Jonathan Swift and George Bernard Shaw achieved independence.

Ukrainians, however, insisted that the Russian state drew its provenance not from Kiev but that after the devastation of the Mongol conquest had developed as a new state separate and distinct from the earlier Kievan Rus'.[5] As the French discovered during the decolonisation of Algeria, it is not always easy to determine what is the core and what is the periphery. On the Eurasian land mass, with weak natural frontiers, historically shifting borders and centuries of migration and intermarriage, this is an even more intractable problem. The separation of Algeria or Ireland did not strike to the very heart of the identities of France or Britain, but Russia appeared to lose part of its heart. Those on the 'wrong' side of borders after 1991 were liable to develop a form of *pieds noirs* nationalism, and those on the 'right' side could become prey to revanchism and neo-imperialism.

The disintegration of the USSR and the threats to the integrity of Russia itself placed enormous strains on the democratic experiment in Russia. Democracy and the attempts to rejoin Western civilisation in the popular mind began to be equated not only with economic hardship but the destruction of the state itself. The writer Alexander Zinoviev had already argued that perestroika was an unmitigated disaster.[6] Now others began to argue that democracy itself was a comparable disaster for Russia.[7] The USSR had reformed itself out of existence, and now there was a danger that Russia would go the same way.

In broad terms there are two approaches to the national question in post-communist Russia. Tsipko dubbed the two restorationists and divisionists, while Roman Szporluk wrote in terms of a distinction between 'empire savers' and 'nation builders' in the USSR.[8] The empire savers sought to maintain the dominance of Russians over non-titular nationalities, whereas the nation builders sought to achieve Russian statehood with regard to what had been the Soviet centre. In contemporary Russia the distinction is highly misleading, not only because the centre has disappeared but also because 'imperial' thinkers precisely emphasise the supra-ethnic element of national identity; even the nation builders, in their determination to preserve the unity of the Russian multi-ethnic state, are to a degree empire savers. The divisionists sought to destroy the empire and the hypertrophy of the centralised state, but gradually came to appreciate the dangers implicit in their anti-statism. Neither of the two groups had a monopoly on democracy, and indeed in many areas overlapped, and neither was the national idea the preserve of any one group; the liberals and the democrats, too, rather belatedly came to take seriously the problem of Russian national self-identity.

Patriots and nationalists argue that the destruction of the USSR does not necessarily mean the end of some sort of multinational state, but while patriots hope for the voluntary reconstitution of some sort of supranational union, nationalists use the language of threats and sanctions to create an entity which privileges Russians as the core of an imperial identity. Both agree that the borders bequeathed by the Soviet regime are arbitrary, with the many adminstrative changes in territories reflecting political expediency rather than ethnic, historical or linguistic realities. Neither the Russian empire nor the USSR, of course, had been nation-states in the conventional sense, but neither were they, according to the patriots, empires in the colonialist sense. Beissinger stresses the ambiguity in the distinction between states and empires, with the Tsarist empire in particular representing 'a confused mix of empire and state-building'.[9]

Following the fall of the USSR the patriots were unable to sustain a distinctive political identity and found themselves united with the nationalists on a range of issues; the distinction between them (discussed in greater detail below) was blurred so we can in most cases talk of national-patriots. Both agreed with Travkin that the disintegration of the USSR had been an unnecessary disaster that overshadowed all later developments in Russian politics.[10] Both were concerned to defend the 25 million 'Russians' who suddenly found themselves 'abroad' because of the break-up of the USSR. The Russian patriotic and nationalist movements were the main counterweight to the liberals and democrats, and as time passed were to gain in influence. But it was an open question whether the more introspective form of patriotic reawakening, which was compatible with a liberal state, would predominate or the more aggressive nationalist movement that was far more willing to work with neo-communists and other rejectionists and which typically condemned liberalism and all its works.

The divisionists in Democratic Russia and elsewhere welcomed the disintegration of the USSR as representing the break-up of the Russian empire, artificially delayed for so long by the Bolshevik imperialism of a new type. The rejectionists, on the other hand, were appalled to see the non-Russian republics split away from what they argued was a historically constituted entity. The basic disagreement between the divisionists and rejectionists was over the question of the degree to which the territory of the USSR represented a recognisable political and human community. The restorationists stressed the ties of language, culture and economy, but above all the sheer scale of human intermingling. They drew on the community-building achievements of the old Russian empire, which had been able to incorporate different cultures and peoples without destroying their cultural and civilisational identities; a very different type of empire to those of Western Europe, the patriots insisted. The USSR's accelerated industrialisation had further mixed up peoples, which together with its ir-responsible approach to borders meant that the fate of the peoples of the former USSR could no longer be separated. Just at the moment when the pseudo-federal system could have taken on a genuinely federal form, the whole experiment was shattered.

The divisionists, however, insisted that the patriots and nationalists underestimated the extent to which the Soviet Union had ceased to be a political community in any recognisably modern sense even before the August coup. It was not just the struggle against the old regime that had taken on a national colouring; nationalist aspirations predated the Soviet regime and were to outlive it. Soviet hopes for the rapprochement and ultimate merging of nations foundered on the rocks of national identity, the liberals insisted. A concept of community, despite the intense propaganda about the emergence of a post-nationalist community of Soviet peoples, had never really developed.

Russia did not have an empire; it was an empire, although towards the end it became more classically a colonial power both in internal and external aspects. The USSR had been an empire-state, like the Bismarckian Second Reich and the Habsburg empire, based not on the colonial model of a subjugated people but rather a system in which all came under the tutelage of an abstract principle incarnated in the guise of the collective emperor, the Party. While Russians were over-represented in All-Union institutions, giving the Soviet Union the appearance of a Russian empire, the ethno-federal system had, as it were, become increasingly ethnicised but not federalised by the advancement of national elites to positions of power in their respective republics. Since the death of Stalin it was not clear whether protest against the system used the language of nationalism, or whether nationalist movements in the old regime had no other option but to become movements against the system itself. In the last years of perestroika the rise of nationalism was used as a battering ram against the communist system and, perhaps unavoidably, the old state as well. Democracy and nationalism were not opposed but complementary in the anti-communist revolution; only under conditions of post-communism did a contradiction emerge between the two.

In most countries the nationalist revolt against communism preceded the democratic revolution, but in Russia it was the democratic insurgency against communism that made possible the rebirth of the nation. As far as the liberals were concerned, it was clear that democracy and empire in the old USSR were incompatible, but the disintegration of the empire was not a sufficient, though probably a necessary, condition for the emergence of democracy. Only the republics appeared to be appropriate vessels in which democratic institutions could be constructed. The commitment to democracy was an intrinsic part of the movement for national rebirth, and this perhaps made the democratic project in Russia rather more resistant to nationalism than in some other post-communist countries. Nevertheless, liberals gradually came to appreciate the importance of national identity in the state building endeavour. A de-ethnicised democracy did not necessarily mean a denationalised one.

Unlike the leaders of Ukraine or other post-communist states, the democratic government of Russia was not automatically the beneficiary of the positive attributes of nationalist integration and laboured under the burden of being identified with the loss of the 'empire', of territory and of national purpose. The democrats insisted that while the borders might be historically nonsense, they reflected political realities and should not change. The Russian authorities found themselves in the position of having to generate a new and smaller national identity for what in effect was a new state built on the rump of one of Europe's oldest. The Russian state-building endeavour itself became the centre of a new Russian national identity as the government struggled to maintain the unity of the republic. Thus one of the most important shifts in post-communist Russian politics took place, namely the defection of part of the liberal camp to patriotic positions.

A distinctive national democratic tendency began to take shape joined by such figures as Rumyantsev, Lukin, Stankevich, Boris Fedorov and many more. The new patriots insisted that they could provide an alternative to the 'vulgarised version of the "Russian idea"', which stressed the cult of the state and of Russia as a Great Power, and which associated the idea of empire and state. They insisted that 'only a democratic Russia could be great', a greatness which lay 'not in force but in truth, not in material power but in nobility of spirit'. The growth of chauvinism would only provoke the persecution of Russians in other CIS states, and then turn back on Russia itself in the form of refugees and migration.[11] Liberal patriots tried to prove that not all manifestations of Russian identity were right-wing and sought to retrieve the national idea from the domination of the nationalist rejectionists, with their inability to understand the aspirations of the peoples of Russia for elements of sovereignty, their crude threats to the other former Soviet republics and their hankering for the restoration of the old USSR.

As an exercise in state-building the USSR proved a failure. The Bolsheviks tried to transform an empire into a state, and failed. Some parts were simply unassimilable, especially when Stalin's greed reincorporated parts, like the Baltic republics and Galicia (Western Ukraine around Lvov), that would later lead the struggle that destroyed the Soviet empire-state. The creation of fifteen post-Soviet states can be seen as the completion of the process of national emancipation that had taken shape in the nineteenth century, yet the problems associated with nineteenth century nationalism have still not been resolved. The aspiration for ethnic states, which reached its apogee in Hitler's Germany, was one of the outcomes of the struggle for national liberation against the great empires of the past.

The relationship between national consciousness and state consciousness is ambivalent. In contrast to Eastern Europe and some other republics of the USSR, in Russia, Ukraine and Belarus state consciousness preceded the development of an articulated national consciousness. The period of 'declarations of sovereignty' in 1990 reflected above all the aspirations to reborn statehood; the development of nationhood in the Slavic republics came later and was to a degree the consequence rather than cause of the struggles of 1989–91. In Russia state consciousness developed fairly rapidly, whereas the development of a sense of nationhood is still rudimentary and remains contested. In Western Ukraine national consciousness was far in advance of that of the Eastern part, with its large Russian population. In fairly compact and historically constituted republics like Georgia and Estonia, however, the absence of a strong division between state and national consciousness was to cause many problems following independence. Citizenship rights were too often confused with ethnic identity and the struggle for national survival continued even when the fight for reborn statehood had been won.

State-building took three contrasting forms: democrats struggled for inclusive and equal citizenship for all peoples living on a particular territory; nationalists privileged titular groups in various types of ethnicised nationalism; while what can be called bureaucratic (or nomenklatura) nationalism reflected the distinctive legacy of the Soviet dissolution. The first form, democratic (civic) or inclusive nationalism, stresses equal citizenship for all the peoples of whatever ethnic origin living in a particular territory and willing to accept the constitution. This would entail, for example, an Estonia for all those living in Estonia without privileges for ethnic Estonians. The stress is on statehood rather than nationhood, with universal citizenship for all those living in a particular territory. Of course, laws making the language of the titular nationality the state language privileges native speakers, fluent in job applications and favoured in appointments to the new state administration, yet this can be considered one of the inevitable penalties of a world divided into nation states, a form of social organisation that might well have exhausted its potential.

Within the old system ethnic divisions coincided with power relationships; the best jobs were on the whole reserved for Slavs. Yet the struggle against the nomenklatura system was only marginally a struggle against the dominance of ethnic Russians. At the very least, Ukrainians and Belarusians had the same opportunities as Russians, and the national elites thoroughly consolidated their positions in the national republics during Brezhnev's long rule. The obverse of this argument is that there is no group comparable to the *Volksdeutsche*, who after the First World War perceived themselves as having fallen into a subordinate status in the newly independent countries carved out of the Austro-Hungarian empire. From this stemmed, in part, the Second War. In the former USSR no equivalent '*Volksrussen*' emerged, despite the efforts of nationalists to create such a group. A large proportion of the Russians in the Baltic republics voted in favour of independence, and after independence many in Ukraine continued to occupy high office and the majority, while perhaps regretting the loss of easy ties with the other republics (as indeed ethnic Ukrainians did themselves), soon came to terms with thinking of themselves as Russian Ukrainians.

The question, unfortunately, could not be resolved quite so easily, and in the post-USSR, as in former Yugoslavia, the previously hegemonic nations, Russia and Serbia, represent distinctive problems, while nationalists in the other republics often confused desovietisation with derussification. Democratic nationalism is not always able to salve wounded national pride in either the hegemonic or the other successor republics. The whole issue of protecting the rights of one's nationals abroad is fraught with danger: in the 1930s it was Hitler's claim to defend the Sudetan Germans in Czechoslovakia that led to war; Serbia's claims on behalf of its compatriots in Croatia and Bósnia caused untold suffering in the ensuing wars; and Russia, too, began to extend guarantees to its ethnic compatriots who suddenly now found themselves 'abroad'.

The second form is ethnicised or exclusive nationalism, which stresses blood ties and ethnic homogeneity. In Estonia, for example, this would suggest a republic for ethnic Estonians and the exclusion of Russians living on the territory. In conditions of post-communism this was understandable, particularly in the Baltic republics. The Soviet regime after the war had pursued a policy of Sovietisation, including the construction in Latvia and Estonia of large industrial facilities drawing in workers from other parts of the union, above all Russia. This was part of a deliberate attempt to dilute the national consciousness of the area, which had resisted Soviet occupation so bitterly during the first Soviet occupation of 1940 and again after the restoration of Soviet power after 1944. Sovietisation here took the form of Russianisation of the society (if not the Russification of the titular nationality itself) in linguistic and demographic terms; hence desovietisation later took on a derussianising hue.

The third main form is nomenklatura nationalism, particularly evident from 1990 when local communist regimes tried to maintain power by appealing to national feelings. This was the case in Serbia, where the old Communist Party led by Slobodan Milosevic renamed itself the Serbian Socialist Party but retained its monopoly on power by appealing to Serbian national pride and stimulating a sense of grievance. In Turkmenistan the old party boss Saparmurad

Niyazov transformed himself into a post-communist nationalist leader, as did Islam Karimov in Uzbekistan. The most spectacular transformation was of Leonid Kravchuk in Ukraine, who changed from being the persecutor of national aspirations in the communist system to the proponent of a vigorous state-building endeavour as the old regime crumbled. In the Russian republics, also, there was no shortage of nomenklatura nationalists, in particular in the North Caucasus and the Volga.

'Communist nationalists' in the former Union Republics discouraged ethnicised nationalism, fearing nationalist mobilisation as a threat to their own powers. In Kazakhstan, Nazarbaev was a reluctant nationalist, and indeed more of a patriot who tried to strengthen the powers of a modernising state to withstand Kazakh nationalists and native democrats. Nazarbaev strengthened his own power in order to inhibit the emergence of a divisive ethnicised nationalism. To a degree also in Ukraine the fear of ethnic conflict encouraged authoritarian government, and this was the case in many of Russia's internal republics. From Moscow's perspective, nomenklatura nationalism appeared to be the lesser evil compared with exclusive ethnicised nationalism. While Zhirinovskii's nationalism was to a degree ethnicised, privileging ethnic Russians, that of the CPRF and people like Prokhanov was 'imperialist', in the sense that they favour a supranational identity for Russia.

Different types of nationalism are not necessarily mutually exclusive, and indeed democratic and ethnicised nationalism are, at their best, complementary. The rediscovery of national identities, language and culture is an essential element of democratic state-building, for Russians as much as other peoples. While the recovery of a people's past is by definition exclusive, the pluralism and equal citizenship written into most post-communist constitutions allows communities to develop their own culture while not threatening the rights of others. The attempt of ethnic Russians to restore the fabric of their devastated past does not necessarily threaten other peoples sharing Russian national territory or their newly independent neighbours. Often the discovery of one's own culture only enhances respect for others; as Friedrich Engels had long ago observed, 'The Poles are never more internationalist than when they are at their most national.'

Nationalism in the anti-communist revolution therefore has a dual character; both integrative and supportive of state-building and political order (with or without democracy), and divisive, when ethnicised or exclusive nationalism is used by elites or oppositional forces to gain power and to preserve what they see as threatened national identities. In Russia, in the 'romantic' first phase of its post-communist history at least, a democratic and inclusive nationalism predominated as state-building took precedence over nation-building. While the potential for degeneration into bitter inter-communal conflict cannot be discounted, comparisons with Yugoslavia should be treated with care. There are significant differences in political dynamics, above all the effective destruction of the old communist elite as a coherent political force, the channelling of conflict into political forms (as in the struggle for the constitution and the Federal Treaty), and the lack of ethnicised political mobilisation of Russians themselves.

THE RUSSIAN NATION AND NATIONALISM

For much of its history Russia did not have a nation as such. In 1721 Peter the Great had declared Russia an empire to elevate the grandeur of the country and his throne, but even before that the country had not had stable institutions of nationhood. The very existence of

Muscovy was bound up with dynastic politics and its sense of nationhood was only embryonic. Occupied by the Mongols from 1240 to 1480, Russia had been torn away from Europe and ever since preoccupied with national defence. Russia had lived as an empire, but a distinctive one since it lacked the characteristic division between a metropolis and a periphery. The state had become the central element in Russian national identity in the struggle against the Mongols and then in the drive to 'gather the Russian lands' around Muscovy. The development of the Russian state thoroughly confused the concepts of empire and nation: many different nations lived together within the framework of imperial institutions and law, and it was far from being the 'prison-house of peoples', as Marx had inadequately dubbed the Russian multinational empire. Only under Alexander III in the 1880s had there begun a serious retreat from imperial supranational policies to build a Russian nation through the Russification and assimilation of peoples.

Lenin had been hostile to Russian nationalism, considering it almost by definition as chauvinistic. Within months of the Bolshevik revolution he began a ruthless attack on the cradle of Russian national identity, the Russian Orthodox Church, and by the late 1920s the official church had compromised with the atheist state in what was called Sergianism, after the capitulation of Patriarch Sergei to the secular authorities in 1927. The policy of indigenisation (*korenizatsiya*) during the 1920s, which sought to redress some of the imbalances of Tsarist nationality policy by advancing national elites to positions of power in the non-Russian areas, was inherently anti-Russian. Stalin's collectivisation destroyed the peasantry, the backbone of the Russian nation and the source of its most profound spiritual and cultural traditions, and the purges destroyed the old intelligentsia, the source of the brilliant age of cultural achievement from the middle of the nineteenth century.

A new Soviet intelligentsia was born, and at the same time concessions were made to the form if not the content of Russian identity and history. Stalin increasingly used Russian nationalism as a way of relegitimising the Soviet system, especially during the Second World War, which in the USSR was known as the Great Patriotic War, but at the same time gutted it of any cultural or historical dynamism. The complaints of the other republics against the Union centre were often directed against Russia, with whom the Union was understandably and often deliberately confused. As we saw in chapter 2, to the other republics (and to a certain extent to Russians as well), Soviet power was synonymous with Russian power. Russians predominated in positions of authority, especially in the central apparatus of government and party, and the Russian language and culture buttressed their position. The USSR appeared as a 'Russian' empire in a new guise.

Russia's identity, however, was dissolved in that of the USSR, and, as the peripheral republics, was ruled by Soviet Moscow in a neo-colonialist manner. The development of Russian national consciousness and statehood was inhibited. Russia itself was less shielded against central policies than perhaps any of the other republics, and its social and economic welfare was neglected; its educational level was among the worst of any of the republics, and its standard of living was in the middle range. The physical decay of Russia's towns and countryside was evidence enough of the lack of economic and social privileges.

Unlike the 'national liberation' movements in the other republics of the USSR, Russian anti-communist movements were not necessarily anti-imperialist or ethnically based. Russia had never achieved a developed sense of itself as a nation-state and no distinction between empire and nation were considered necessary in Russian thought, since Russia by destiny was considered to be an imperial nation. Even the Slavophiles of the nineteenth century did not advocate a retreat from empire, although they recognised the burden that it imposed. Only from the 1960s, as part of so-called dissent, did a rediscovered sense of anti-Soviet and anti-imperial Russian national identity and consciousness begin to take shape.[12] Solzhenitsyn was one of the first to argue that Russia was paying too high a price for empire, an empire moreover that was only pseudo-Russian, insisting that Russia was squandering the resources it needed for its own regeneration. He stressed that the heart of the Soviet system was an ideology based not on a people but on an abstract utopianism interpreted by a political party, and warned against the destruction of the Russian people while arguing that minority groups should be allowed to secede from the USSR.[13] He urged the regime to abandon communist ideology, insisting that only if it did so could it save the people, and probably itself too. For his pains, in 1974 he was sent into exile. Igor Shafarevich argued that in their attempts to undermine so-called 'great Russian chauvinism', the old regime had generated and sustained an innate Russophobia.[14] The new Russian nationalists were sustained by a profound sense of the crisis in which the Russian nation found itself, a crisis marked by the weakening sense of Russian identity, the loss of Russian national traditions, the destruction of the countryside, and Russia's lack of status within the USSR.

During the 'stagnation' period under Brezhnev an official Russian nationalism flourished to buttress the decaying regime, but this nationalism was used to support Soviet colonialist imperialism both in relation to the non-Russian Soviet republics and abroad. Early on in Brezhnev's regime two members of the Politburo, Dmitrii Polyanskii and Alexander Shelepin, were dismissed for allegedly promoting the Russian nationalist cause and defending Russian national interests. By 1973, however, Alexander Yakovlev, then a high official in the CPSU's Central Committee, was sent into 'exile' in Canada for his vigorous denunciation of renaissant Russian nationalism. The regime tolerated a Russified Soviet nationalism to compensate for the declining appeal of Marxism-Leninism.

Already, towards the end of the Soviet regime the distinctive features of patriotic and nationalist tendencies in Russian national thought had begun to emerge. The patriotic trend stressed Russia's spiritual traditions, the revival of Orthodoxy, and the need to act as stewards of Russia's environment in harmony with the many peoples who share the Eurasian land mass. The nationalists espoused a far more aggressive view, stressing Russia's imperial role as the 'gatherer of the lands', and drawing on the national Bolshevik tradition of Nikolai Ustryalov in the 1920s and the Eurasianist thinking of the time which proclaimed Russia's separateness from the West and its destiny to dominate the Eurasian landmass. They emphasised the need for military power, rule over the non-Russian peoples and contempt for the decadent West.[15] The Soviet regime could make common cause with the second but was profoundly at odds with the first.

The distinction between patriots and nationalists is one drawn by patriots themselves. Patriots draw on the 'soil-bound' (*pochvennik*) tradition of Slavophilism and stress the existence of a historically constituted supranational community on the Eurasian land mass in which all the various peoples had broadly been able to pursue their own destinies even when incorporated into the Russian empire. While Russians might be an 'elder brother' to some of the peoples, with a particularly rich culture and destiny, all the various cultures had an equal right to their development. This 'imperial' approach is supranational and stresses the rights of individuals and communities rather than nations. The nationalists, however, stress precisely the development of state structures exalting the ethnic Russian nation and defend a type of colonialist relationship with other peoples and its neighbours. Nationalists consider the Soviet regime, with its crude 'Russification' policies and its power politics, in a more favourable light than the patriots, and hence are more willing to ally with Soviet nationalists and rejectionists. Pozdnyakov insists that patriotism, love of the motherland and one's people, has nothing in common with nationalism.[16] In his view 'Nationalism is the last stage of communism, the last attempt of an outdated ideology to find in society support for dictatorship'.[17]

The tension that was apparent throughout the Soviet era, and which divided the 'dissident' Russian national movement in the Brezhnev years, continues to this day. On the one hand, the gosudarstvenniki (statists) argue that a strong Russian state is the central feature of the very existence of the Russian people, and thus 'national Bolsheviks' from the 1920s made their peace with the Soviet system as the recreator of the Russian empire. Today this tradition is reflected most vigorously in the pages of Prokhanov's paper *Zavtra* (before October 1993 *Den'*), arguing that for centuries the Russian multinational state has been engaged in a struggle to defend 'the Russian idea' against cosmopolitanism, freemasonry and Zionism, and as Dostoevsky had suggested earlier, Russia should turn its back on the decadent and insidious West and seek its destiny in the East (the Eurasian option). On the other hand, the *vozrozhdentsy* (a term that can loosely be translated as 'revivalists') condemned the Soviet state and Marxist ideology for having subverted the true nature of Russian statehood and culture, and insist that only the cultural and moral revival of the Russian people, based on the values of Orthodoxy, can save Russia. Solzhenitsyn is firmly in this tradition, insisting unequivocally: 'The time has come for an uncompromising *choice* between an empire of which we ourselves are the primary victims, and the spiritual and physical salvation of our own people.'[18]

The contradiction between the two faces of Russian national thinking (the term nationalism here is misleading) was marked during perestroika. The regime sought to use nationalist (statist) opinion to undermine the democratic movement and the patriots (the revivalists), irreconcilable opponents of the communist (if not Soviet) regime. Russia's patriotic rebirth was perceived as one of the main enemies of communism and thus the authorities tried to discredit it. The extremist Pamyat' nationalist organisation, peddling a hysterical concoction of anti-semitism with assaults against freemasons, foreigners and democrats, was probably sponsored (and certainly tolerated) by the KGB to discredit the independent movement in general and Russian patriotism in particular. The influence of Pamyat', however, was over-estimated and they gained few votes in the elections of spring 1990. In a typically ambiguous way Gorbachev sought to coopt some elements of Russian national rebirth to buttress the regime. The Orthodox Church in 1988 was allowed to celebrate the millenium of Christianity in Russia with great pomp; the representation of non-Russians in the Politburo was decreased to one (Shevardnadze), republican Party leaderships were purged to eliminate some of the corruption and Russians given a greater role in Kazakhstan, Turkmenistan and Uzbekistan; and the scheme (bitterly opposed by Russian patriots) to divert Siberian rivers to Central Asia was cancelled.

Following the elections in March 1989 the struggle intensified for Russia to become a fully fledged republic within the USSR, with the full range of republican institutions and social organisations. Between the patriots and the nationalists the democrats now emerged as advocates of a distinctive form of denationalised Russian statehood. These 'democratic statists' sought to reassert Russia's political institutions and sovereignty in the struggle against the communist regime and the Soviet centre. The Russian nationalists now became alarmed, since while they supported the rebirth of Russia they considered that this should take place only within the framework of a (decommunised) union, insisting that Russia was the historic core of a multinational community. The nationalists, and indeed some of the patriots, soon realised that the struggle for state sovereignty by the many peoples that made up the USSR threatened the existence of the larger community, and indeed of Russia itself, and thus even then made a tacit alliance with conservatives within the communist regime itself in order to preserve the Union. The nationalists condemned the Union Treaty on the eve of the coup, as in the letter that Zyuganov helped draft 'A Word to the People', the manifesto of the coup, and fought the hardest for a renewed Union afterwards. Zyuganov's brand of communist nationalism later became one of the dominant trends in the CPRF.

The fall of the USSR forced a redefinition of Russian identity: Russia had never been a nation state, and it was now not a question of appealing to tradition but of creating a new national identity. One of the issues dividing patriots, nationalists and democrats was the question of how much of the Russian past was 'usable' in the present. Tsipko asked 'if the formation of a new Russian statehood is unavoidable, which historical foundations should it be built on?'.[19] Russia did not really have a choice between 'empire' and 'nation' since by its very nature there would be imperial elements in its national identity, not necessarily from any acquisitive urge but by its sheer size, demography and history.[20] The patriots sought to maintain the Union (by democratic means), and even sections of the reborn democracy could not reconcile themselves to the smaller nation state form of Russia, while the nationalists openly espoused the reintegration of the former Soviet Union, irreconcilably denouncing the Belovezha Accords creating the CIS.

Theories of nationalism are based on the idea of the nation. But what is the Russian nation and how can it be identified? It can be associated with the Russian language and therefore with Russian speakers (*Russkoyazychnye* or *Russofony*). This immediately raises a number of problems. What about the large number of Russian-speakers in the former Soviet republics outside Russia? Are they part of the Russian nation? Alternatively, the Russian nation could be determined by ethnicity. Only ethnic Russians (*Russkie*) could be considered part of the Russian nation. But what about the 19 per cent of the inhabitants of Russia who are not ethnic Russians; and how is one to establish the difference, for example, between an ethnic Russian and an ethnic Belarusian? How does one define ethnicity? Is the Soviet definition of ethnic Russians as 'having Russian parents' acceptable? What about those of mixed parentage?

The Russian nation can be identified through religion. For some scholars, like Edward Keenan, the Orthodox church stands as the 'only authentically Russian national institution'.[21] But Russia since the sixteenth century has contained significant numbers of Muslims, and today a number of the Federation's republics (in particular along the middle Volga) are reviving Islamic culture and institutions. What about the Jews; what is their nationality? In addition, in a secular society, how many Russians today are practising Orthodox Christians? The Russian nation can be identified more broadly with its culture, but this again raises a number of problems: for example, the writer Nikolai Gogol is quintessentially part of Russian culture yet he was of Ukrainian provenance. Finally, the Russian nation can be defined through its common history. This is the path taken by the Eurasianists who argue that 'the peoples of the old empire possess a common past that preceded both Tsarism and Soviet communism'; for them the Russian nation encompasses 'that vast stretch of continental land from the Carpathians to the Pacific'.[22] This is probably too broad a category to be of much operational significance since reliance on a single definition blurs precisely the problems in establishing the contours of the national community.

While it is hard enough to define the Russian nation, the associated question of national identity is even more intractable. The new identity is torn between four distinct approaches which, while not exclusive, determine the nature of the new polity. The first is the restoration of an imperial role. The debate over Russian national identity is overlain and complicated by the problem of the Soviet Union. While most neo-communist movements (like the CPRF) use the language of militant Russian nationalism, their relationship with 'genuine' Russian national thinking is ambivalent: Russian statism is not necessarily the same as neo-Soviet imperialism. Movements like Zhirinovskii's LDPR are essentially proto-fascist and openly display their irredentism and contempt for democracy, adopting an avowedly 'imperial' stance on the disintegration of the old Union. The solid vote for the LDPR in parliamentary elections reflects the disenchantment of those who equate democracy with disintegration and loss of national prestige. Henry Kissinger has warned that Russian nationalism could be translated into a desire to return to a position of dominance over the other republics.[23]

The second approach focuses on ethnicity, on loyalty to ties of blood and kinship. The nation (defined here as an ethnic community) is not necessarily coterminous with state: the Russian (like the Hungarian) state today is smaller than the Russian nation, whereas in most of the other fourteen post-Soviet republics the state is larger than the nation. The ethnic definition is opposed by democrats, patriots and nationalists alike (the latter appealing to imperial supranational traditions), although claims to defend Russians 'abroad' contain elements of ethnicised nationalism. The nomenklatura nationalists in places like Tatarstan are careful to check claims to ethnic exclusivity made by the titular nationality. Thus the dynamics of post-communist Russian politics differ from those in Yugoslavia, but there remains a devastating potential for ethnic conflict.

The third approach stresses the development of a cultural community, the view that the core of Russian national identity lies not so much in its imperial traditions but in religio-cultural features. One of the most sophisticated exponents of this view is Dmitrii Likhachev. Born in 1907, Likhachev was a witness to the revolution and its sufferings. Arrested in 1928 he spent 6 years in the notorious Solovki camp, a former monastery on an island in the White Sea which Lenin in 1920 converted into a prison.[24] Likhachev survived and pursued a life of scholarship in his chosen field of philology. He traces the interaction between Russia and Europe and stresses that Russian culture is part of European culture in general, opposing the myth of Russian exceptionalism and supporting pan-European development. At the same time, he extolls the elements that make Russia Russia, and above all the Orthodox Church and its liturgy, though he opposes theocratic versions of Russian destiny. Contrary to much writing in the political culture vein, he insists that an ethos of individualism had been growing since at least the seventeenth century to temper the traditional collectivism of Russian society. Respect for tradition, he insists, should not entail the 'mechanical imitation of what has ceased to exist'. Praising patriotism, he condemns nationalism as a pathology parasitic on genuine love of one's motherland, and in particular he denounces Great Russian nationalism and anti-Semitism.[25]

The cultural definition of Russian statehood is also fraught with dangers; it is not clear how any version of cultural homogeneity, defined even in weak terms of a dominant tradition, is possible in a country marked by such ethnic diversity. In relation to other groups the old messianism about Russia's leading role and the cultural mission of Orthodoxy, formulated at the end of the last century by V. Solovyev and others, can appear threatening. An inverted form of this messianism was used by the Bolsheviks to sustain the idea of the universal proletarian revolution emerging out of Russia, and the struggle for democracy on occasion became a new form of traditional messianism. While Russian cultural ethnocentrism plays an ambiguous role in the new Russian state, multiculturalism expressed in state forms may lead to the disintegration of the country. Nation-building is an essential element of the modern state-building project.

The fourth approach argues precisely that the loss of Russia's imperial role and the fragmented sense of Russian nationality can be compensated by the establishment of a new identity based on the civic institutions of revived statehood. The major obstacle to the development of a civic national identity is the emergence and consolidation of national elites in the autonomous republics and regions of Russia, and the persistence of the 'greater Russia' idea. Nevertheless, Russia has a unique chance of forging a new national identity not despite but because of the catastrophic failure of the old system; there is no choice but to start again. The civic approach to Russian national identity and the democratic statist approach to rebuilding the country became the dominant ideology of the government after August 1991. This stressed civic responsibility, the rebirth of Russian statehood governed by law, a democratic and inclusive form of nationalism, and good relations with all the other resurgent nationalisms both within and beyond Russia.

Yeltsin pursued a differentiated policy towards the national question, exploiting the power of Russian patriotism in the struggle against communism, notably during the coup, but resisting nationalist demands. In an unabashed appeal to civic nationalism in January 1991 Yeltsin argued that 'Russia, the legal successor of a great state which has existed for centuries' was now being reconstructed. All the nations of Russia should live according to the basic principles of 'human dignity, rights and individual freedoms'. The basic attainments of human civilisation 'like the market, a state based on law, democracy, the mechanisms of social partnership, pluralism', should all be implemented in Russia, he insisted, but here 'they will be filled with original content and embellished with bright, new colours'. 'Today, the war of the state against its citizens, which lasted for decades in Russia, is ended'.[26] He promoted aspirations to Russian statehood and democratic forms of nationalism but did not compromise with exclusive forms of ethnicised nationalism and refused to exploit the grievances of Russians abroad to broaden his own political base. Excoriated by the national-patriots, he remained the president of all citizens in Russia and refused to proclaim himself the militant defender of Russians abroad, as Milosevic had done in Serbia.

A post-imperial civic identity began to emerge but it was increasingly challenged. The civic approach was found wanting because of its failure effectively to incorporate patriotic themes, and Russia's apparent inexorable decline. Calls for the restoration of empire, territory, prestige and order gained ever more adherents, as witnessed by the strong showing for the LDPR in 1993 and again in 1995, now joined by the rejectionist CPRF. A post-imperial Russian patriotism emerged in the late Soviet years and after the coup focused on remaking a Russian nation-state based on economic liberalism, democratic constitutionalism and oriented towards partnership with the West and integrated into the global economy. This, however, was challenged by a more introspective form of hybrid nationalism drawing on Russian and Soviet traditions and extolling Russia's dominance in Eurasia and its separateness from the West.

The weakness of organised liberal blocs left a profound political vacuum which various nationalist and patriotic groups sought to fill. The anti-Soviet democrats appeared to have believed that the destruction of the old system would be enough to create a new one, and thus lacked a serious programme of political and economic reforms for Russian conditions. The patriots advanced a set of alternative conservative values that were perhaps more in keeping with Russian traditions: nationality (*narodnost*), fairness (*spravedlivost*), patriotism and statehood (*gosudarstvennost*), accompanied by such notions as spirituality (*dukhovnost*) and morality (*nravstvennost*), as part of the reinterpretation of the 'Russian idea' which rejected the liberal emphasis on materialism, the democratic emphasis on individualism and the reformers' emphasis on Westernisation. Post-communist Russian patriotic movements, however, found themselves locked into a dialectics of extremism. The excesses and hysteria that marked much of the thinking of the national-patriots during the transition period inhibited the development of constitutional patriotic conservatism.

Russian national thinking contains various strands, and even those antagonistic to the West are not necessarily incompatible with some form of democratic law-based state. In contrast to most of the states of Eastern Europe, in Russia the national issue only rose to prominence on the political agenda *after* the democratic revolution, whereas elsewhere the struggle against communism had simultaneously been *sui generis* forms of decolonising national liberation struggles. Public opinion was therefore democratic before it became nationalistic. At the same time, the 'nationalism' of the dominant nationality is a much more amorphous phenomenon than that of the smaller nations, torn between patriotism, nationalism and Sovietism. While Russians did not become Soviets in quite the same way that the English became British, the challenge facing Russia (and Britain and France earlier), was to achieve self-liberation from imperial ambitions and messianism.

THE CHECHEN WAR AND THE REPUBLICS OF RUSSIA

Russian and Cossack forces in 1817 began their advance from the north and west on the Chechen plain, establishing the fort of Groznaya ('formidable') in 1818. Ten years later the great Caucasian war broke out, confronting the Russian empire with one of its greatest military challenges. The Chechens wavered in their loyalty to the last leader of the Caucasian forces, the Dagestani Avar Imam Shamil, but they were brought back into the fold by the occasional terror campaign. After the surrender of Shamil in 1859 Chechnya remained an uncomfortable member of the Russian empire. Under the onslaught of Marxist atheism in the Soviet period, 'Sufism absorbed the de-formalised, but nonetheless still vibrant faith into its informal networks.'[27]

The North Caucasus remains a source of troubles for rulers in Moscow. Over fifty peoples occupy the Caucasian mountains and foothills from the Black Sea to the Caspian, organised into seven republics in Russia and two (Abkhazia and South Ossetia) in Georgia (see figure 10). Political divisions, however, have been largely superimposed upon peoples who define themselves in terms of clan, village and extended kinship group. The political divisions, moreover, are to a degree arbitrary, with the North Ossetians separated from their Southern compatriots, the Kabards (from the Adygei group) joined in one state with Turkic Balkars, while natural associates, the Chechens and Ingush were split apart. The 4.7 million North Caucasians differ in language and ethnicity, but they have many features in common. They are predominantly rural societies sharing codes of honour and culture, and, with the exception of the Christian Ossets, they are Sunni Muslims. There are at least thirty areas of inter-ethnic tension in the Caucasus.

The Chechens led the way in challenging the sanctity of intra-Russian borders and the integrity of Russia itself. In 1928 mosques had been closed and the use of Arabic, a vital

Figure 5 The North Caucasus

element in intercommunal discourse, banned. In 1936 Stalin joined the Chechen republic with the neighbouring Ingush, and in 1944 both peoples were deported to Central Asia on the grounds of collaboration with the Germans during their occupation of the North Caucasus. Among the deported was the young Ruslan Khasbulatov, who later became speaker of the Russian parliament. In 1957 Khrushchev allowed them to return to their homeland, but the burning sense of Chechen resentment was not allayed. 'Chechnya' as such, however, is an abstraction: the third of the republic North of the Terek river is not historically Chechnya, having been taken from Stavropol Krai to compensate Chechen-Ingushetia for the loss of Prigorodnyi *raion* to North Ossetia after the war; and the rest of the republic is home to some 400 villages each with its own leader and over 100 *teips*, as the Chechen clans are known, in a shifting pattern of alliances and feuds.

On 27 November 1990 the Chechen-Ingush Supreme Soviet, headed by Doku Zavgaev (until September of that year also Party first secretary in the republic), adopted a declaration of state sovereignty. With his support the Chechen National Congress, an informal advisory body made up of clan elders and excluding much of the urban population, had met in Grozny between 23–25 November 1990 and elected Major-General Dzhokhar Dudaev, on leave from his air force unit stationed in the Baltic, chairman of its executive committee. In March 1991 Dudaev resigned his commission and settled with his family in Grozny. On 5 September the National Congress executive committee met to consider the implications of the coup and, declaring (falsely) that Zavgaev had supported the putschists, deposed the Supreme Soviet.[28] Following a wave of unrest stimulated by Dudaev, destroying Moscow's attempts at mediation, he wrested power from the legal authorities.[29] The subsequent unilateral declaration of independence enjoyed far from universal support, and the clearly illegal and rigged parliamentary and presidential elections of 27 October 1991, which saw Dudaev gain 90 per cent of the votes cast (63 per cent of the total electorate),[30] were no more than a way of formalising his coup. Thus began a process that some feared would emulate the break-up of the USSR earlier.[31]

Dudaev had served in Estonia, and indeed married a Russian there, and his bitter and almost irrational anti-Russianism appears to have been imbued during his time in the air force and says much about the effectiveness of political education in the Soviet military. This was not a case of Isaiah Berlin's 'bent twig' theory, which argues that nationalism rises when the twig of ethnic identity is bent by oppression and wanes when the pressure is relieved, but arose out of the distinctive pathology of Soviet nationality politics. In addition, after years of persecution by the Soviet authorities, the clans (*teip*) re-emerged, each based on a group of families and bound by mafia-style codes of honour. Dudaev secured the support of the highlands teips against the more prosperous lowlanders in the north, he was opposed by resident non-Chechens, by the small Chechen intelligentsia and found little support in the traditionally Cossack areas north of the River Terek.

Moscow's initial response was tempered by the spirit of liberalism that permeated the barricades of August 1991. Yeltsin's imposition of a state of emergency in the region in November 1991 was rejected by the Soviet Interior Ministry, which judged that the use of force would lead to unnecessary violence, and was overturned by the Russian parliament on 11 November 1991. Yeltsin now had 3 years to get used to Chechnya's *de facto* secession, although the republic's independence was not recognised by any state. The imposition of an economic blockade accelerated the descent of the republic into anarchy.

Dudaev was allowed to consolidate his hold on the republic and to arm himself, largely with the armaments left by the retreating Soviet Army from late 1991. He imposed his rule by military methods, using armed force to dissolve the Chechen parliament in June 1993. While the insurgency was partly a national liberation struggle against an alien oppressor, a large proportion of the population (Russians and ethnic Chechens alike) were united in sullen hostility to rule by a group of adventurers. Dudaev's rule lacked domestic legitimacy, shifting power from the urbanised, educated and Sovietised elites of the lowland areas to the lesser developed and traditionally more anti-Russian and anti-Soviet groups of the southern highlands. One oppositional group after another was crushed. Chechnya (having separated from the Ingush Republic in 1992) soon became the centre of arms, narcotics and money laundering operations as it spiralled into lawlessnes.

A strategy of patient economic and political pressure might well have achieved the desired result of returning Chechnya to the fold of the Russian Federation. Throughout the spring and summer of 1994, however, the covert war launched against the regime, managed by the Federal Counter-Intelligence Service (FSK) led by Sergei Stepashin, proved singularly ineffective. The extent of support for anti-Dudaev groups is difficult to assess but it is clear that opposition to the regime did not automatically translate into support for its opponents, while it is axiomatic that collaboration with Moscow tended to consolidate rather than erode support for Dudaev. Following the failure of Umar Avtorkhanov's oppositional Provisional Council to take Grozny in October 1994, the FSK was given a free hand to overthrow Dudaev. The FSK was allowed to recruit soldiers from regular military units without even informing their commanding officers. It was the capture of some of these clandestine forces following the disastrous failure of their assault on Grozny on 26 November that precipitated the full-scale invasion by regular forces on 11 December. The new Russian parliament no longer had the power to stop the bloodshed.

Many factors precipitated what soon came to be known as the 'Second Caucasian War'.[32] By summer 1994 the conflict between the regime and its opponents, concentrated in the Nadterechnyi raion bordering Stavropol krai, had escalated into a full-scale civil war. The endemic divisiveness of the Chechen opposition and the failure of the Provisional Council to dislodge the Dudaev regime meant that Moscow could not expect proxies to do its work. There was widespread concern, probably exaggerated, that Chechnya provided the base for banditry and mafia-type organised crime throughout the Federation, and in particular Moscow. The hijacking and taking of hostages in Stavropol and Krasnodar krais involved Chechens, and it appeared that the instability in the republic was a dagger pointed at Russia itself.

The fear of the 'domino effect' of Chechnya's independence on other republics and regions is unlikely to have played much of a role in the timing of the intervention since the federal system in Russia had stabilised considerably following the adoption of the constitution. More important was the need to secure rail and road communications with Dagestan and the Transcaucasian republics. Above all, Moscow sought to regain control of the Chechen section of the Caspian-Black Sea oil pipeline, running from Baku to the Russian port of Novorossiisk, with a branch running into Ukraine. The pipeline from the huge Tengiz field in Kazakhstan runs north of the Caspian and joins the Baku-Novorossiisk line at Grozny, where important oil refining and other energy installations are located. Additional pipelines from the Central Asian oil and gas fields are planned, and Russia sought to ensure that they took the Russian route rather than through Iran and Turkey to the Mediterranean. The timing of the war might well also owe something to Yeltsin's sagging popularity, propelled by the belief that a 'short, sharp war' could restore his fortunes. In the event, the savagery and intractable nature of the war undermined Yeltsin's democratic credentials.

The 'party of war' in Moscow apparently believed that regular forces could achieve a swift victory, or, as defence minister Grachev put it when ordering the ill-fated tank assault on New Year's Eve, Grozny could be taken 'in two hours by a regiment of paratroopers'. Instead of a *blitzkrieg* offensive Russian forces faced house-to-house fighting in Grozny, and only on 19 January was the presidential palace taken. The war was marked by military ineptitude on a grand scale and broke almost every rule in the book of modern warfare. The costs of the war in terms of suffering and destruction were enormous. Liberals in Moscow had long argued that attempts to remove the secessionist Chechen leader by force would lead to high casualties and an Afghan-like guerilla war against an implacable *mujahadeen* foe. The operation, moreover, used indiscriminate force and failed to distinguish between armed fighters and the civilian population.

According to Sergei Yushenkov, the chair of the Duma's defence committee and a resolute opponent of the use of force in Chechnya, Russia's military intervention had 'assumed the scale of a crime against humanity'.[33] The report by the presidential human rights commissioner, Sergei Kovalev (a veteran dissident campaigner for human rights), reported that the civilian death toll had reached 24,000 by the end of February.[34] At that time the Russians admitted to losing over 1000 troops (though the true toll is probably much higher) while the Chechen staff reported losing about 3,500 fighters, but once again the real figure is probably much higher. Even after the presidential palace in Grozny was captured and the city occupied, lootings, beatings and torture were common as the federal forces sought to disarm the population and to 'reimpose constitutional order'.

The war revealed not so much the shortcomings of the new constitution but the failure of the Yeltsin regime to abide by a document that it had itself imposed on the country. A domestic military operation was launched without declaring a state of emergency or imposing martial law, thus avoiding parliamentary scrutiny. According to article 87.2, martial law could only be imposed in the event of aggression against Russia, while a state of emergency had to be approved by the Federation Council and the State Duma (article 88). Without either, the Russian authorities did not have the right to use arms or disrupt communications networks. In addition, the president did not have the right to use the Russian Army for tasks for which it was not intended, and attempts to suspend aspects of the law of 24 September 1992 'On Defence' were probably illegal. The conduct of the operation, moreover, violated international human rights agreements. The Geneva Convention of 12 August 1949 and the supplementary protocols of 1977 limit ways in which wars can be fought and guarantee the rights of the civil population if they do not actively participate in fighting. The Russian forces used indiscriminate violence against the civilian population. The Constitutional Court, however, resolved later that the war had been legal.

What sort of constitutional order can ever be imposed on the 'liberated' territories is unclear. Nikolai Semenov, the former first secretary of the Grozny Communist Party city committee, headed the interim Russian-supported administration in Chechnya and his deputies were all members of the old Soviet establishment. Moscow sought to counter Dudaev's ethnicised nationalism with nomenklatura nationalism. Marred by violence, gubernatorial elections were nevertheless held on 17 December 1995 and despite a low turnout Moscow's appointee (and the former leader of the republic), Zavgaev, was elected. The Kremlin refused to negotiate with Dudaev but entered into negotiations with some of his commanders. Once committed to military means of resolving the Chechen problem Russia had to fight to a negotiated conclusion: to withdraw prematurely would lead to loss of face and perhaps precipitate other secessionist crises. Thus Russia tried to avoid Gorbachevite capitaluation to the insurgency, as in Afghanistan, but this did not necessarily mean physically occupying the highlands. Chechen insurgents continued the war from the mountains, seizing hostages in Budennovsk in summer 1995 and in Dagestan in January 1996, leading to major crises in Moscow. Dudaev's death in April 1996 made possible substantive talks, and the ceasefire brokered on the eve of the presidential elections marginalised the Chechen factor in Russian politics, especially since no one else appeared to have a solution to the problem.

The larger question however remains unanswered: was the war in Chechnya a result of *conjunctural* factors (the declining Yeltsin presidency, geoeconomic concerns in the North Caucasus and the Caspian, and the like, including a healthy dose of errors and stupidity); or did it reflect a more profound *structural* transformation of Russian politics, the adoption of a militant Eurasianist stance of aggressive centralised state-building at home and the assertion of a neo-imperialist Great Power ideology abroad by a revanchist elite representing military-industrial and security interests? Elements of both probably contributed to the war but the central question in certain respects is not the war itself, but the manner of its conduct. For this, short-term conjunctural factors can be held firmly responsible.

The 1993 constitution provided for the development of a form of 'asymmetrical federalism'. The signing of the bilateral treaty between Moscow and Tatarstan in February 1994 allowed a flexible relationship between the two parties and brought their relationship within the constitutional process. This relative stabilisation in centre–periphery relations was jeopardised by the use of force in Chechnya. The crisis revealed the constitutional limits to the powers of the Federation Council in a presidential system, leaving both regional and republican leaders angry and frustrated and looking for more potent forms of institutionalising their power. The long-term impact of the Chechen crisis may well be attempts to change the structures of the Russian federal state, above all altering the balance between the executive and legislative branches. Rather than enhancing the unity of the Russian Federation, the Chechen war probably contributed in the long-run to centrifugal pressures; in particular, the fact that Chechnya was a Muslim country alienated opinion in other Muslim republics.[35] However, with the exception of Ingushetia, whose president Ruslan Aushev found himself in the front line and unequivocally condemned the war, the Caucasian republics adopted an ambivalent position. Most of their leaders were members of the old-style Soviet establishment and feared that they would be the first to be swept away by any popular mobilisation in support of Dudaev. The Chechen case is unique, a country whose very identity was bound up with the notion of resistance to Russia. While five of the North Caucasian republics border independent Georgia and Azrbaijan, the other four are unlikely to seek secession. For most of the other republics secession would entail enormous difficulties, and even Tyva, located on Russia's borders, would find communications through Mongolia difficult. Most of the republics are not economically viable, with 90 per cent of the Tyvan budget, for example, provided by federal funds, and have heterogeneous populations.

There were in effect two wars in Russia from late 1994, one in Chechnya and the other in Moscow for the soul of the reform process. It is still too early to write off the liberal and democratic changes in Russia or to dismiss the enormous transformation that has taken place since the onset of Gorbachev's reforms. The Russian government was faced by multiple crises and contradictory demands in formulating a nationality policy for the peoples of the Russian Federation. The analogy between these republics and those making up the former Soviet Union is not quite accurate. The titular nationalities of the republics in Russia, like the Yakuts in Sakha and the Chuvash in Chuvashia, are minorities in the republics that bear their names. Moreover, they are economically much weaker and as enclaves in Russia their trade and industries are thoroughly part of the larger economy. The destinies of their peoples had long been bound up with Russia; but Russia's destiny, too, was now bound up with theirs.

11 Regional and local politics

> While examinations of Kremlin politics cover many of the significant events, however, they do not tell the full story of the transition toward democracy in Russia.
>
> Robert W. Orttung[1]

Russia's regions vary in population, size and structure, occupational patterns, in orientation and dependency towards Moscow, and above all in their values. Regional government is becoming increasingly diverse and no single approach can cover the enormous heterogeneity in Russian provincial life. Some regions remain bastions of 'conservatism' (e.g. Ulyanovsk) resisting attempts to impose change from the centre; others (like Tambov) after the victory of a communist in the December 1995 gubernatorial elections sought to restore Soviet power; yet others (like Nizhnii Novgorod) have been in the forefront of political and economic reform; while all have taken advantage of the weakness of the centre to seize powers and a degree of sovereignty that in certain cases poses a threat to the continued existence of the Russian state itself. Within the localities themselves at least five institutions have competed since the coup: the regional governor (often called the head of administration), the presidential envoy, the heads of the oblast and city councils, and the city mayor.

In chapter 8 we discussed the importance of the nomenklatura elites in the localities, but the degree to which local politics is factionalised and divided along various lines of interest and allegiance should be stressed. In these circumstances pressure from Moscow to pursue often unpopular reform policies encountered not so much resistance as fell into the general web of paralysis and ungovernability that characterises so much of the Russian state today. Local government and regional politics remain confused, although certain patterns have begun to emerge. In particular, the trend towards strengthening executive authorities in the localities, the emerging alliance between technocrats and the former nomenklatura, increased differentiation between regions with respect to the speed of economic reform, and the striving for regional autonomy. The attempt to re-establish vertical structures between the centre and the localities has been accompanied by the growth of numerous horizontal structures between the regions. The fate of the democratic experiment in Russia will be settled as much in the regions as in the central institutions of the state.

THE ORGANISATION OF POWER

The last years of the Soviet regime were marked by a general crisis of executive authority, with decrees being launched into a void and remaining unimplemented. Nowhere was this more noticeable than in local government, and in particular in the provinces of Russia. The disbandment of regional and district committees of the Communist Party removed one of the last institutions that had at least tried to implement decisions. The post-Soviet state sought to find a way of filling this vacuum in governance with a system that was both effective and democratic, but opted for the former whenever there was a conflict with the latter.

The elections of March 1990 allowed the democrats for a time to sustain a majority in the city soviets in Moscow, Leningrad, Ryazan, Sverdlovsk, Sakhalin oblast and a dozen or so more. Elsewhere the old system survived, with soviets in the republics and regions dominated by the nomenklatura, in particular the directors of the large state enterprises and collective farms. The election of anti-establishment candidates was hindered by the under-representation of urban areas in comparison to rural districts, it taking about four times as many votes to elect an urban than a rural candidate.[2] Not a single oblast, krai, republic or okrug soviet had a clear democratic or anti-establishment majority. Local elites withstood the electoral challenge by screening out democratic candidates in the nomination stage, manipulating the local media, running prominent elite candidates out of the glare of publicity in rural constituencies, and foisting lesser-known officials on local workforces.[3] The traditional establishment dominated in rural areas where they maintained their control over information networks, but one reason for their victory could quite simply be that they were more astute politicians than their democratic opponents.[4] The establishment's response in urban areas was more mixed and by the time of the fall of Soviet power in August 1991 had begun to adapt to the challenge of reform.[5] The Russian regions in the last days of the old regime presented a rich mosaic of struggle and change which continued in new forms into the democratic era.

Despite the disbandment of the Party following the coup, former communists remained in positions of authority at the local level. Communist officials, indeed, who found themselves unemployed often took up important posts in local state administration.[6] It was for this reason that Yeltsin sought to ensure the continuation of reform in the localities by imposing a system of executive controls over local authorities. Already in May 1991 Yeltsin had ordered local deputies to monitor the progress of land reform in their constituencies, a programme where local bureaucracies were the most obstructive.[7] On 14 August 1991 he appointed Valerii Makharadze to the new post of Russian state inspector at the head of the presidential control administration, responsible for ensuring the implementation of legislation.[8] And on 21 August the Russian parliament established the post of head of administration at the regional level (krais, oblasts, autonomous regions and districts) to lead the corresponding executive authorities as the successors to soviet executive committees. On that day the president was granted yet more powers to monitor the activity of soviets, and leaders in four regions (including Tambov) were dismissed for acquiescing in the coup.

Following the coup Yeltsin sought to consolidate executive power by appointing presidential envoys (*predstaviteli prezidenta*) to the localities.[9] The envoys were likened to the Bolshevik system of commissars, who monitored the political reliability of former Tsarist officers in the Red Army during the Civil War and imposed the will of the government in the localities. The decree of 22 August 1991 stated that envoys were to ensure that local legislation was compatible with national laws, and could recommend the dismissal of local officials who undermined national policy, and they were to analyse the situation in the localities and to report back to the president. Envoys could impose presidential decrees directly, avoiding the local bureaucracies. Rather contradictorily, they were enjoined not to interfere in local administration or to issue orders covering the given territory.[10] Separate instructions limited the powers of the presidential envoys in the national republics of Russia.[11] The state inspector was to oversee the work of the representatives as well as coordinate the work of local executive bodies.[12] Yeltsin clearly hoped that the presidential envoys would be able to work in harmony with local administrations while at the same time relying on the support of local democratic movements to place pressure on recalcitrant administrations. The aim was to introduce a reforming element from outside and to establish a supervisory authority that could act as an autonomous presidential vertical chain of authority. A total of sixty-six had been appointed by late 1992.[13] The vague formulation of their powers soon rendered them largely ineffective, and in any case the process of elite reconsolidation meant that many came to terms with the existing establishment.[14] The age of ideological warfare in Russia's regions was a remarkably short one.

At the same time Yeltsin tried to ensure effective local governance by appointing one official in each region the head of administration, referred to as governor (*gubernator*) at the regional level since their role was consciously modelled on Tsarist Governor-Generals.[15] In a few cases, as in Nizhnii Novgorod, Moscow and St Petersburg, the governor was also the presidential envoy. The governors were directly appointed rather than being locally elected and thus sat uneasily at the head of the local soviet bureaucracy, with whom they were supposed to work in partnership. Most appointed governors were not the existing heads of oblast or krai executive committees, leading to numerous conflicts where the local soviets sought to have their own chairman appointed governor. Several governors, moreover, were former Party officials, leading to vigorous condemnation by the democrats.[16] Regional governors in turn appointed heads of administration in cities and districts, who displaced the old soviet executive committees (*ispolkomy*) headed by chairmen who hitherto had been the senior executive figure in the district.

Regional government remains part of the state system, whereas lower-level administration was separated from the state (see below). The struggle between executive and legislative authority at the centre was reflected locally. The localities duplicated the national power system, with a 'government', for example, created in Moscow with its own premier. The Supreme Soviet 'Law on *Krai* and *Oblast* Soviets and Administrations' adopted on 5 March 1992 defined the functions of soviets and executive bodies in favour of the former; territories and regions were to have a charter establishing the constitutional basis for local authority; but the details of the financial and economic powers of regional government remained vague.[17] The Federal Treaty also acted as a normative act specifying the powers of the oblasts and the cities of Moscow and St Petersburg. These acts did little to resolve the crisis of local power, and the local soviets and the administrations appeared to operate according to two sets of laws: those of the Russian Supreme Soviet for the soviets; and presidential decrees and executive orders for the mayors and administrative bodies.[18] It was not clear to whom mayors were subordinate, the Russian president (through the presidential envoys), parliament or the local soviet. A system of dual if not triple power emerged. The conflicts were particularly bitter in Moscow, but while tensions between mayors and soviets were endemic it was possible, as in Nizhnii Novgorod and St Petersburg, to establish an effective working relationship.[19]

Expectations that regional and local heads of administration would have to subject themselves to the test of popular approval in the elections designated for 8 December 1991 were disappointed when on 1 November 1991 the Fifth CPD in its decree 'on the organisation of executive power in the period of radical economic reform' postponed them to December 1992 and granted the president the right to appoint heads of administration. Yeltsin did however concede that new heads of administration would have to be approved by the corresponding soviet and Russian MPs from that territory.[20] Not surprisingly, many turned out to be the current oblast leader or even former Party leaders, leading to accusations from the radicals that Yeltsin was betraying the democratic revolution by allowing old apparatchiki to retain power.[21] Democrat warnings of 'the revenge of the nomenklatura' were perhaps exaggerated since it was not clear where else one was to find a pool of professionalism and experience; certainly not from among the democrats themselves.

Regional government remained marked by chaos and corruption. The presidential control administration sought to monitor the work of administrations both ideologically, to ensure loyalty to the president, and technically, above all to ensure probity and financial order. The new head of the control administration, Yurii Boldyrev sought to make the administration more neutral, neither for nor against the president, and to de-ideologise the role of the presidential envoys. He insisted that in the struggle against corrution yet more regulation was not the answer but higher wages and firm procedures in the localities. Many abuses, he noted, stemmed from officials combining administrative posts with entrepreneurial activities. Corruption could not be justified by arguments about the necessary evils of the primary accumulation of capital, because that way would lie the Latin American path of development.[22] According to some estimates, three-quarters of the thousand-odd organised criminal groups were protected by state or managerial structures, police bodies included.[23] The prevailing criminalisation of the provinces squeezed out honest entrepreneurs, and the mafia even began to prepare candidates for elections. The police could do little, arguing that current laws restricted them, while the presidential representatives proved an inadequate mechanism to prevent corruption and to ensure effective local administration. Instead, by mid-1992 Yeltsin turned to the Security Council, and its secretary Skokov was invested with more powers to establish local commissions of the Security Council to oversee the work of local administration. Boldyrev himself fell foul of intrigues among the presidential staff, having secured the dismissal of some regional heads of administration for corruption who happened to be presidential allies, and when in March 1993 his attempts to investigate the corruption in the Western Group of Forces in Germany was blocked by the president, he was forced to resign.[24]

From July 1991 regional and local soviets were required to form a 'small soviet' one-fifth the size of the full complement of deputies, thus duplicating the national pattern of the CPD electing a smaller Supreme Soviet. The presidiums of the soviets, which had coordinated their work, were made redundant and in most places abolished. The small soviets were selected from the larger soviet, which retained general supervisory functions, with the small soviet acting as a working legislature. In Yekaterinburg the number was reduced from about 100 to 30, and in Moscow a small soviet (duma) of 99 was chosen in January 1992.[25] In Moscow conflicts continued, but in most places the small soviets proved to be effective working bodies, often chaired by the local head of administration. Politics was kept to a minimum as a new ethos of administrative reason gave rise to an ideology of rule by 'professionals'.

The heads of administration added a critical dynamic of change in the localities, but they remained hampered by the local soviets which were too large, unwieldy and ultimately irresponsible.[26] The local authorities, especially in the rural regions, were considered strongholds of conservatism and this rather undemocratic system appeared the only way to force through the reforms. Following the coup Yeltsin had the option of holding elections to replace some of the more conservative figures in local government, yet the results might well only have confirmed them in office with a renewed legitimacy. Yeltsin therefore took another option, imposing heads of administration from the centre to dismantle the old Party-state machinery and the command economy. What he lost in democratic legitimacy he hoped to gain in effectiveness. The central problem, however, remained: strengthened executive power on its own could not work in the absence of effective democratic procedures and the rule of law, and the restructuring of the institutions and powers of local government to avoid ambiguities. In the long run Yeltsin's approach proved counter-productive, and the opposition, notably communists, won many of the governorships in the regional elections in the year from December 1995. In Tambov, in particular, the wheel turned full circle as a communist was elected in December 1995: the Morton's fork of democracy now skewered the reformist leadership in Moscow.

Local authorities were caught in the crossfire between president and parliament. By early 1993 Yeltsin had issued over 2,000 decrees while the Russian parliament had issued 3,400 acts in one form or another, many contradicting the former. While Yeltsin tried to transcend the soviets, Khasbulatov and the Russian parliament tried to municipalise and turn them into genuine bodies of local government. The heads of administration, the presidential envoys, and the chairs of the local soviets all vied with each other for the dominant voice in the localities. Even after the end of dual power in October 1993 the incoherence of the government's regional policy remained a constant theme. A draft regional policy devised by the Nationalities Ministry, for example, was rejected by the government in December 1995 on the grounds that the document failed to present a unified governmental policy, only policies for individual sectoral ministries.[27] There was no consensus on how to restore central authority; and the MP Sergei Mitrokhin argued that 'at present the government simply does not have a regional policy'.[28]

REGIONAL POLITICS AND REFORM

Local elites had been consolidating their positions since at least Brezhnev's 'stability of cadres' policy. In the national republics it was relatively easy for former communists to turn into nationalists and rule through functionally different but structurally similar forms of power. The regions of Russia, however, could not legitimate their struggle for greater local autonomy by appealing to national traditions but had to find political and economic arguments. Decentralisation and regionalisation appeared to be the answer to the numerous problems of the localities, yet the authorities in Moscow had spent decades combatting the sin of *mestnichestvo* (localism), and this tradition would not disappear overnight. The destruction of the administrative-command system led to the weakening of central authority and the *de facto* decentralisation of power. Regions sought to take advantage of Moscow's weakened grip to gain control of their own economic and political resources, yet this on its own was no substitute for a constitutional redivision of powers.

The first years of independent Russian government saw a marked differentiation between regions in the speed and scale of reform, but this only exacerbated existing differences. Despite the Soviet regime's commitment to regional equalisation, there were marked disparities in the level of economic development and standards of living, with the national areas tending to be at the bottom of both scales. The traditional agrarian regions tended to lag behind in reform, whereas the areas approaching post-industrial types of development raced ahead.[29] The development of a genuine capitalist national market would encourage a type of unity from below, whereas the regions which pursued a slow model of economic reform tended towards economic autarchy and often political separatism; by mid-1992 twenty-three regions had placed some form of customs regime on the movement of goods.[30]

To many it appeared that while the coup may have failed in the centre, it was triumphant in the regions and localities. This certainly was the view propounded by the president, hence numerous attempts to subordinate local executives to central institutions and to replace the former leaderships. Above all, the establishment of presidential envoys was designed to ensure local compliance with central policies.[31] This embryonic pro-consular system alarmed Yeltsin's erstwhile 'democratic' supporters, if only because he did not appoint more of them to these positions:[32] In October 1993 the powers of the presidential envoys were reduced and those of heads of administration increased.

While suggestions of a 'quiet coup in the provinces' and the 'revenge of the nomenklatura' contain important elements of the truth, especially in the context of the emergence of the regime system of rule discussed in chapter 8, there are important countervailing forces. The regions had a latent democratism that sought to find institutional expression, and indeed, resistance to the imposition of strong executive rule was not always an expression of conservatism but often reflected a genuine attempt to establish new democratic procedures to replace communist rule. While conflict between executive and legislative power in the localities was common, it was not universal. The reduction of subsidies and political control from the centre forced the localities back onto their own resources, and encouraged liberals, bureaucrats and managers to work together to save their region.

Numerous organisations were created to bring regions and towns together, with a wave of regional associations being established from late 1990, mostly following the borders of the corresponding economic region. Russia has eleven economic regions, each closely tied to the national administrative system.[33] In his presidential campaign of June 1991 Yeltsin had argued for the division of the country into some 8–10 large economic regions, and the idea had been incorporated into the October 1991 draft Constitution in the form of zemli. At the Fifth Congress in November 1991 Yeltsin supported the attempt of neighbouring regions to unite to create larger units in the Far East, Siberia, Urals and so on.[34] The creation of regional associations was supported by Moscow to counter-balance the sovereignisation of the former national autonomies and the regional separatism of oblasts and krais.[35]

The Siberian Association (*Sibirskoe soglashenie*) was established on 2 October 1990 and brought together all nineteen administrative regions of East and West Siberia. It was the most effective in integrating regional and nationality politics. The borders of some of the associations changed in order to correspond more closely with the local definition of the region rather than the economic definition taken from the Soviet state planners. The most effective associations were those most distant from the centre – the Far East, Siberia and the Urals – where regionalism was infused with the separatist spirit that had already been evident at the time of Russia's earlier disintegration during the Civil War.

Centrifugal tendencies thus affected not only the titular nationality areas, but also some of the ethnically Russian parts of the federation where there were increasingly strident demands for economic, and even political, autonomy. The most important regional movement affected Siberia and the Russian Far East; Siberian deputies came together in a congress in Krasnoyarsk on 27–28 March 1992 and some went so far as to call for separation. Deputy B. Perov of the Tyumen oblast soviet urged that 'the congress should adopt a manifesto on independence, declare itself the supreme authority in Siberia and at the same time dissolve on the spot all the colonial organs of Russian power'. The vice-chairman of the Kemerovo oblast soviet, V.

Figure 6 Siberia and the Russian Far East

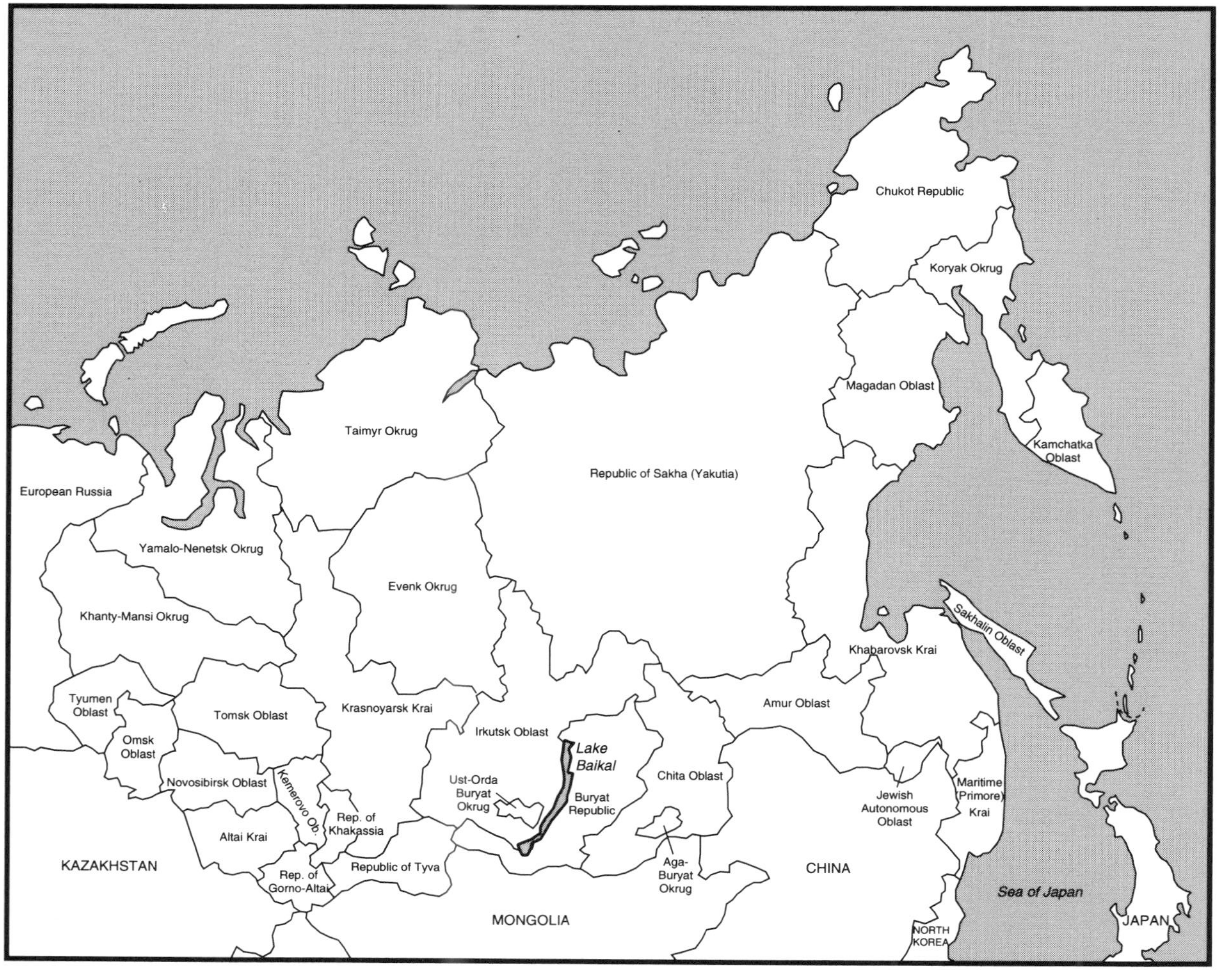

Streligov, declared 'We can manage without Russia, but Russia cannot manage without us.' The final resolution stopped short of these actions, but voted almost unanimously for the motion proposed by a deputy from Tomsk to demand that the Russian Supreme Soviet and the president 'take urgent and comprehensive measures for the decolonisation of Siberia'.[36] A meeting of the Siberian Association on 15 July 1992 once again demanded greater control over Siberia's rich natural resources, the right to conduct foreign trade directly, and an end to what they called the colonial exploitation by Moscow.[37]

The traditional Soviet system of planning had given priority to vertically integrated branches of the economy run by ministries, and had paid very little attention to questions of regional development (or, indeed, environmental issues). In Siberia the emphasis had been on extractive industries and energy supplies, at the expense of developing a local manufacturing base, infrastructural development or food supplies. In exchange for the 'export' of industrial raw materials, either to the rest of the country for processing or abroad for hard currency, Siberia had to import most of its food, machinery and consumer goods. In the long-running 'East-West' debate the advantages of developing regional industrial complexes in Siberia were contrasted to the availability of skilled workforces, good transport and close proximity to markets in European USSR, and indeed the bulk of investments went to republics like Ukraine and Belarus. The collapse of the centralised supply system threw Siberia's dependency into sharp relief, and various regions were forced to resort to barter, such as coal for machinery between Moscow and Kemerovo. While energy prices remained depressed, the price of machinery rose many-fold. Production of Siberia's oil fell by some 20 per cent in 1992, and gold production by some 40 per cent.[38] Thus there were powerful economic factors, generated by the distorted pattern of Soviet development, fuelling demands for autonomy in the post-Soviet era.

The distinction between the two parts of Siberia (East and West) and the Russian Far East became stronger as their regional identies were given free rein and the reform processes followed different trajectories. Regional associations sought to promote the economic development of their regions, but more overtly political aims soon came to the fore.[39] The Federal Treaty addressed some of their concerns for greater local autonomy, but the pressure to transform regionalism into separatism remained strong. The new economic relationship between the centre and the regions remained contested, but from Moscow's perspective Siberia and the Far East were far too important for Russia's economy as a whole to be allowed to go their own way. A new balance between regional and national concerns had to be found.

In most parts of the country initiatives by the local authorities to achieve economic reform had not come to much and instead the main initiative came spontaneously from entrepreneurs from below and Yeltsin's government from above. However, some successes had been achieved by the governor in Volgograd oblast, Ivan Shabunin, while in Ryazan the leader of the city soviet, Valerii Ryumin, tried to implement radical economic reform. In St Petersburg, the capital of Russia from Peter the Great's time to 1918, economic reform was accompanied by the attempt to rediscover its identity as the capital of the North-West region.

It was Nizhnii Novgorod, however, that became the exemplar of 'reform from below'. The reformist team was led by Boris Nemtsov, a 32-year-old physicist appointed oblast governor by Yeltsin in September 1991, working closely with his appointee as mayor of the city, Dmitrii Bednyakov. They were advised by the economist Yavlinskii in the development of a regional economic programme that saw rapid privatisation through the open auction of municipal property (and later of large state enterprises as well) and marketisation of the local economy.[40]

Instead of entering into confrontation with the local soviets, Nemtsov established a 'co-ordinating council' that brought together executive and legislative authorities in a common attempt to find solutions to common problems.[41] Opposition came not so much from so-called conservatives but from radical democrats 'slighted at not having received posts in the new administration'.[42]

A study of Khabarovsk krai in the Russian Far East demonstrated that on its own a devolution of power would do little to improve regional administration, which found itself with almost anarchic powers as local executive, legislative and judicial authorities clashed. Regionalism appeared to be a cover for the old elite to consolidate its power free from interference from Moscow, taking advantage of the chaos to grab the spoils attendant upon the dismantling of the Soviet state. The area was marked by 'confusion, inefficiency, political corruption, and philosophical malaise'.[43] The collapse of the Party-state system provoked the decline of governance in its entirety. Almost no new public housing had been built, yet local officials squandered millions of roubles on palatial residencies for themselves. Most had been chosen in the semi-democratic elections of March 1990, and were well aware that they would not be re-elected in new elections and therefore strove to exploit their provisional hold on power. The fall of the Communist Party and the KGB removed the system of external restraints which had at least limited corruption, and the absence of a new democratic ethos and oversight meant that a gaping moral vacuum opened up to accompany the administrative chaos. Presidential power could not hope to replace immediately the sophisticated system of Party rule.

In a manner typical of Russian post-communism, rather than sharing power the two main local bodies, the 250-strong Khabarovsk krai soviet and the Khabarovsk krai administration, fought for power. The governor clearly considered the local soviet and its chairmen to be illegitimate, since they had been elected during the Soviet period, while the local soviet and its chairman considered the governor an imposter foisted on them by Moscow. The situation was not helped by the presidential representative, with a small staff monitoring the activity of the other two bodies yet offering little positive in the way of legislative initiative. In the centre and the localities, power tended to drift from institutions to individuals with inadequate safeguards against the corruption of power and with no one accountable for anything.

No effective separation of powers had taken place, and instead chronic confusion reigned. The transition from the administrative-command system to a functioning democracy was hampered by the postponement of elections, the weakness of the judiciary (with a poorly staffed Public Prosecutor's office still used to dependence on the authorities), and above all by confusion in the governmental system itself and the weakness of implementation mechanisms. Old patronage networks continued to operate, while there was a great shortage of competent officials to operate in the new conditions. The social basis for a democratic regime appeared to be lacking, with few lawyers, a minuscule business class, an intelligentsia devastated by Stalinist mass murder and Brezhnevite persecution, and with social relations corrupted by the pervasive criminalisation. The attempt to impose a democratic system by undemocratic methods in the absence of democrats appeared indeed as yet another utopian project dreamed up in Moscow. In contrast to Poland and Czechoslovakia, where Solidarity and Charter 77 acted as the kernels of alternative power and ideological systems, in the USSR perestroika had been launched by a storm of decrees and orders from above, and only in certain areas, like the big cities, the coal-mining regions and some of the anti-Moscow union republics, did civil societies take shape from below.[44] In most of Russia's regions there had been minimal mobilisation, apart from a brief flurry of activity at the time of the coup, and thus few new structures or individuals had emerged to replace the old. The political parties were weak or non-existent, and the majority of the population apathetic. The regions of Russia were characterised not by the rebirth of politics but by political stagnation.

This is a deliberately extreme presentation of the case: elements hold true throughout Russia, but in most areas countervailing pressures are emerging and the picture is more complex. For example, the extent of political mobilisation during the last years of perestroika was probably greater than suggested here; the robustness of the nascent parties in the regions is often underestimated; and the vitality of the local press and 'society' (*obshchestvennost*) should not be under-rated.[45] The 'provinces' became increasingly attractive places to live, and the long-term population drift from the country to the towns began to be reversed.[46] The oblast capitals became the focus of revived cultural and social life, drawing on regional traditions to begin the process of developing civil society from below. Only when this process matures can we begin to talk about democracy in Russia.

While perhaps not as developed as in the big cities, the outlines of a multiparty system began to take root in the regions. A survey of fifty presidential envoys on 30 November 1992 asked about the most influential parties in their regions. Democratic Russia (Yakunin, Ponomarev) was recognised in 26 regions; the DPR (Travkin) in 22; the Russian Communist Workers' Party (Anpilov) in 19; the People's Party of Free Russia (Rutskoi) in 13, and so on for 23 parties, though the first three were recognised as being influential more often than all the rest put together.[47] The strong regionalisation of most parties meant that while the local organisation might bear the same name as the central one, there were often great differences in policies. Many envoys noted that the strength and influence of parties in the regions was insignificant, although of course some of their most active leaders could make their influence felt as individuals, especially if appointed to positions of authority. Most regions, however, had a reasonable spectrum of political parties, however small, including usually some home-grown ones and in particular those concerned with local environmental issues. The two main groups, Democratic Russia and the DPR did have quite sizeable organisations (up to 250–300 members) in about half of the regions.

The survey revealed that of 141 top party or state figures (obkom or *gorkom* first secretaries and chairmen of soviet oblast executive committees, *oblispolkom*) before August 1991 in 50 regions, 124 remained in the locality. Of these, 33 or about a quarter remained in the political elite, 45 joined the state sector and 46 went into the private sector.[48] The most effective survivors were oblispolkom chairmen (20), whereas only thirteen party leaders managed to find a niche for themselves in the new political system. Thus the anti-communist 'revolution' allowed many former communists to adapt to the new structures. The large proportion joining the private sector illustrates the political flexibility of the old elite, and possibly their ability to use old contacts to new purposes, in particular personal enrichment.

Even before the coup the Communist Party was losing power, but the most able or the most farsighted of the apparatchiki were shifting over to posts in the local state system. In Yaroslavl, for example, the lack of experience of anti-establishment figures elected to the city council meant that in most cases the executive and old elites still dominated. Following the coup the struggle between old and new elites continued, but in a new form since the establishment no longer had the ideological or organisational resources of the Communist Party behind them. Local soviet leaders were suspicious of the presidential envoy, asking as elsewhere 'Who elected him?'.[49]

THE REGIONS IN RUSSIAN POLITICS

In schematic terms recent Russian politics can be characterised by a sucession of dualities: Gorbachev's Union against Yeltsin's insurgent Russia; Yeltsin's executive authority against the insurgency of Khasbulatov's parliament; and then, following the October events, it was the turn of Russia's regions and republics to be counterposed to the federal authorities in Moscow. This conclusion, however, would be misleading, despite the attempts by politicians to 'play the regional card' against Yeltsin's regime in Moscow. The sheer diversity of Russia's hinterland, the tensions between the republics and regions, jealousies between the regions themselves, precluded the emergence of a coherent second axis in regions against Moscow.

The regions of Russia claimed more autonomy and the right to forge foreign economic relations. The Yenisei republic in the heart of Siberia was a case in point, as well as the Far Eastern region, long-neglected by Moscow and used as a security zone, and even regions like the Urals and the Kuban. Regions and republics exploited the struggle between the presidency and the old legislature to extend their prerogatives. The 'regionalisation of reforms' promised by Gaidar suggested that Moscow would no longer interfere so directly in local economic affairs.[50] The struggle in Moscow between Congress and president, however, accelerated the process of regionalisation without reforms. In Mordovia, for instance, in April 1993 the republic's newly confident conservative Supreme Soviet abolished the post of president (held by a popularly elected Yeltsinite) and took on the plenitude of power itself, something that the Congress in Moscow would no doubt liked to have done. Yeltsin, no doubt, learnt from the example of President Kirsan Ilyumzhinov of Kalmykia, who abolished all representative assemblies in the republic, claiming that 'We are the first territory to dispense with soviet power.'[51]

A 'Union of Governors of Russia' was established at a meeting at the Kremlin with Yeltsin and Burbulis on 17 November 1992,[52] and appeared to be an attempt to diversify the structure of Russian government to use the republics as a counterweight to the recalcitrant Congress. This appeared to be the purpose of the Council of Heads of the Republics established on 15 October 1992, bringing together the leaders of the twenty-one republics in Russia as a consultative and coordinating body chaired by the president. Yeltsin sought to use the Council to postpone the Seventh Congress, and it appeared that it could become a parallel structure outflanking parliament, especially since it was sponsored by the Security Council led by Skokov. The Council insisted that the Federal Treaty would have to be a constituent part of the new constitution and that Russia's nationality policy had to be devised within its framework.[53]

The dissolution of the Russian Congress in Autumn 1993 opened a new phase in regional politics. The December 1993 elections revealed the political geography of Russia to be fractured along several axes, with divisions between metropolitan areas and the countryside, and between the north/north-west and the south/south-west. The main base of communist support was in the Central Black Earth region to the south-west of Moscow, whereas the LDPR's strongest support was in the new Russian border areas (especially in the south) and those in proximity to national conflicts. While Moscow and St Petersburg are distinguished by the greatest concentration of people who have benefitted from the reforms and hence supported democratic platforms, the south-western part of the country, including regions like Voronezh with a strong concentration of military and engineering plants, was closer to Zhirinovskii and the communists. Voters above the 55th parallel (on which Moscow stands) on the whole supported reformist positions, while those below tended to support the repackaged nomenklatura elites. The European north was predominantly industrial, while the south was more rural and agricultural. The pattern, however, was not consistent, with the reformers maintaining their support in the capitals, parts of the Urals, the north (especially Arkhangel'sk oblast) and parts of the Far East (Khabarovsk krai), but losing areas that were traditionally sympathetic to them, in particular some of the industrial centres of the Urals and some regions in Siberia.[54]

The Federal Treaty of 31 March 1992 sought to make all the subjects of the federation, whether they be republics or regions, equal in a juridical sense, yet the new republics of Russia were granted more of the attributes of statehood and more economic powers than the regions.[55] The 1993 constitution proclaimed the political equality of Russia's regions and republics, and yet continuing differences in prerogatives provoked a new round of conflicts. Although both documents stressed that Russia's eighty-nine federal components were equal, in practice some were more equal than others. The twenty-one republics appeared to be at the top of the pyramid, followed by the krais, oblasts and autonomous oblasts, with the autonomous okrugs at the bottom (see chapter 3 of the constitution). In contrast to the republics, the powers of the remaining sixty-eight subjects of the federation appeared residual, sharing certain listed powers and enjoying other unspecified prerogatives not conflicting with the national state (article 76.6), but there was no mention of any detailed regulatory or financial powers that they could exercise independently. Republics can elect presidents and adopt constitutions, while regions often had governors imposed by Moscow and adopted 'charters'. Regions sought to narrow the difference, while republics fought jealously to preserve the differential.

The centre concluded treaties with some of the republics (Tatarstan, Bashkortostan) and some regions, but inequalities remained in the distribution of federal budget revenues. At the same time, many regional leaders, like Eduard Rossel, the chairman of the Sverdlovsk oblast Duma, complained that the centre failed to respect the provisions of the constitution demarcating the responsibilities of the centre and the localities.[56] The centre, apparently, placed obstacles in the way of regions adopting their charters, either arguing that they failed to conform to the constitution (as in the case with Orenburg) or 'losing' it in the Kremlin's corridors (as happened with Sverdlovsk).

The federal law demarcating the division of powers and property between the federal authorities was the subject of fierce conflicts between the supporters of federalism and the supporters of unitarism. Mayor Sobchak of St Petersburg emerged as a strong federalist, insisting that Russia's regional policy should be based on the maximum decentralisation of power and that the historical legacy of unitarism should be abandoned. The federal authorities, however, insisted on the supremacy of the constitution and federal laws throughout Russia's territory and the impermissability for members to change their status. Afraid of centrifugal pressures, the centre moved sharply away from Yeltsin's old slogan of 'take as much sovereignty as you can swallow' towards a more classical centralised policy.

The balance of power between the regional dumas and governors remained unclear. The decree of 9 October 1993 proposed radical changes to local assemblies:[57] they were to be reduced in size from the old 2–400 to some 15–50 deputies, who were to be full-time legislators; the legislatures in the republics, however, tend to be larger with some 100–130 deputies. The decree of 22 October 1993 gave the new regional assemblies (usually called dumas, with a few sticking with the traditional name of 'soviet') the right to pass laws, something denied the old regional soviets. At the same time, however, the decree gave local governors, many of whom were appointed by Yeltsin, a great deal of authority over the new regional parliaments. Local laws were not to contradict federal laws, presidential decrees or governmental instructions. The localities are allowed a wide degree of discretion in their electoral systems, and the republican leaderships in particular take full advantage of this (by districting in favour of rural areas and so on) to ensure compliant assemblies. Local administrative officials can also run in local elections, and with their greater resources they tend to overshadow parties; similarly, managers of local enterprises and farms dominate local assemblies. Local elites remain in power. Although two-fifths of deputies now have to be full-time legislators, the centre only fitfully enforces this rule. Decentralisation on its own does not lead to democracy; regional democracy remains flawed.

There remains a tension between the processes of 'republicanisation', the attempts by national areas to raise their status and achieve sovereignty, and 'regionalism', the attempts of one or more territories to gain greater autonomy within the Russian Federation. Some regions converted themselves into republics. Between April and July 1993 Vologda, Chita and Sverdlovsk oblasts and Primorsk krai declared themselves republics within the federation, but only Sverdlovsk oblast declared itself a fully fledged republic.[58] A major grievance was the difference in the share of taxes allowed to be kept by the region in comparison with neighbouring republics. Regional aspirations for greater autonomy were limited in most cases by financial dependence on Moscow, although some budgetary decentralisation was achieved, with a marked growth in the proportion of income and expenditure passing through local budgets. Regional budgets cover a growing percentage of expenditure on health, education, culture, arts and so on.[59]

On 9 November 1993 Yeltsin prohibited the attempt by Sverdlovsk oblast to transform itself into the core of a Urals Republic encompassing six oblasts, and at the same time sacked the regional governor, Rossel. In response the latter declared that he would stand for election as governor of the republic, and in the event was returned to the Federation Council in the December 1993 elections. His chance to retake the governorship came later, and in elections in August 1995 (elections that Yeltsin tried to ban), Rossel easily beat Yeltsin's appointee, Aleksei Strakhov. Despite attempts to portray him as a separatist, Rossel insisted that he advocated no more than genuine decentralisation to the regions, arguing that this was the only way that the federation could survive intact. To further this aim, in September 1995 he established his Transformation of the Fatherland party. He called for the introduction of regional taxes and the abolition of the redistribution of collected taxes among Russia's regions, something that alienated regions in receipt of central subsidies;[60] while his plans to equalise the rights of all components of the federation alienated the republics.[61] The problem would not go away, however, and on 28 November 1995 the governor of Khabarovsk oblast, Victor Ishaev, called for the establishment of a 'Far Eastern Republic.'

The end of the democratic insurgency in August 1991 had been accompanied by a moratorium on elections in the regions and localities. Following the crushing of the legislature in Moscow, Yeltsin issued a number of decrees dissolving local soviets and stipulating that new elections should be held for reconstituted regional assemblies. On 22 October 1993 he called for local and regional elections to be held between December 1993 and the following spring, but his decree established only the broadest of 'basic guidelines', allowing the regional authorities (in most cases the governor), enormous discretion in establishing detailed electoral arrangements. In St Petersburg Sobchak imposed residency and occupational restrictions on voting rights in the election to the new fifty-member assembly, leading to an outcry,[62] while in Tula the governor so simplified procedures that he simply gave himself the right to appoint deputies to the oblast soviet.[63] The vote in 6 out of 23 constituencies to the Yaroslavl' oblast soviet and 7 out of 22 constituencies in the city were declared invalid because turnout fell below the required 25 per cent.[64] Later, some two dozen regions abolished a minimum turnout because of the difficulty of exceeding the 25 per cent threshold.

The regional assembly elections at last extended the democratic revolution to the mass of the people in the localities. Democracy, however, led to the result that the reformers had long feared, namely the consolidation of rejectionist forces in the regions. In one of the first local elections, held in Penza on 30 January 1994, 40 out of 45 seats in the oblast assembly went to former Communist Party functionaries and the nomenklatura elite despite the presence of a large number of representatives of the liberal professions and new entrepreneurs among the 180 candidates, with the results allegedly skewed in favour of the more conservative rural areas.[65] On 17 September 1995 Yeltsin once again suspended the local electoral process, decreeing that regional governors be elected in December 1996 (that is, after the presidential elections due in June 1996), and legislatures only in December 1997. Later, twelve exceptions were made to allow regional elections in December 1995 and Moscow's mayoral election on 16 June 1996. The number of presidentially appointed administrative heads gradually decreased.

The government, as noted, was often accused of not having a regional policy. In certain respects, this worked to the good and allowed a rich variety of different forms of regional politics to emerge; the attempt to impose a single regional policy might well have strengthened centrifugal forces. While arbitrary and incompatible tax regimes, for example, were a burden, the relatively *laissez-faire* regional policy allowed regional elites to adapt to local circumstances.

LOCAL SELF-GOVERNMENT

The chaos of Soviet administrative practice was nowhere more marked than in local government. Under Khrushchev and later there had been repeated attempts to 'enhance the role of the soviets', but they had all failed because of the lack of political or economic autonomy. Unable to tap into the resources of local industries (especially if they were involved with the defence sector), local government was burdened with political responsibility but lacked autonomous control of funding and resources. Local authorities found it difficult to take over control of housing and planning land use, and large sectors of local life remained under the control of enterprises or their parent ministries.

Power in the Soviet Union had not only been centralised but it had also been displaced from elected local authorities (soviets) to a parallel hierarchy of Communist Party committees and soviet executive committees (*ispolkomy*), with the latter subordinated not only to the soviet at its level but also the *ispolkom* at the level above (hence the term 'dual subordination'), and in many cases to local branches of state ministries as well.[66] Party organisations were chiefly concerned with ensuring plan fulfilment, and local needs were subordinated to this overriding task.[67] During perestroika a broader agenda of improving local government was introduced. The revolutionary slogan of 1917, 'all power to the soviets', was revived, but this itself obstructed the genuine municipalisation of the soviets: the notion of 'all power' ran contrary to the separation of powers.

Local self-government refers to the political and managerial activities of local authorities in municipalities and raions below the level of oblast government. Amendments to article 138 of the old constitution on 24 May 1991 introduced the concept of 'local self-government' for districts, towns, boroughs and villages, replacing the ispolkom responsible for local administrative services with a 'local administration' and its 'head of administration' responsible to the soviet. Local soviets could now take a critical attitude to the head of administration and other officials in the local administration (article 147).

These provisions were incorporated into the long-awaited 'Law on Local Self-Government in the RSFSR' of 6 July 1991. In a crucial departure from Soviet practice (which postulated the unity of the state from top to bottom), local self-government was defined as an autonomous entity and not part of the state system (in contrast to regional government). The law provided for the popular election of a head of administration for a 5-year term who was to provide leadership in local administration but would be responsible to a soviet, also popularly elected for 5 years. The respective functions of mayors and councils (which were to have no more than 100 deputies) were spelt out in detail but in places overlapped, creating a permanent source of conflict. The law, which applied to city soviets and below, extended the autonomy of local authorities in setting budgets and taxation, control over land use and the local economy, and gave them greater powers over municipal property in the transition to the market economy. The provisions of the law were to be implemented following the election of mayors and local councils on 6 December 1991, but, as we have seen, following the coup local elections were postponed and the law was modified.[68] In particular, heads of administration were appointed rather than elected, and further changes in 1993 modified the whole basis on which budgets were organised.

Local authorities are torn between the increasing demands made of them and their limited resources. Traditional Soviet patterns remain in that local government remains responsible for a far wider range of activities than is typical in the West; responsibility for the whole local 'communal economy' includes not just housing, trading standards and the like, but also production and ensuring supplies of food and consumer goods. Amidst the general collapse local mayors have tried to maintain services not properly within their domain, and have levied local taxes to maintain them.[69] Since the local finance base remains so weak local authorities have been driven to desperate stratagems to fund their activities, including the seizure of resources intended for the centre or an appeal for subsidies from the government. Whether out of traditional commitments to local welfare or as acts of political survival, local authorities have tended to subsidise local services and supplies, thus, whether deliberately or not, impeding the marketisation of social relations and, also coincidentally, undermining attempts at effective central fiscal management.

Local revenues traditionally came primarily from sales taxes rather than any system of rates or local taxes on individuals and enterprises, although this has now changed. Cutbacks in central funding further disrupted city services, and as enterprises became more independent from their parent ministries from the late 1980s their parlous finances and growing concern for profits meant that they were less inclined to subsidise local services, and thus the local authorities found themselves even more short of money.[70] Moscow was hit particularly hard; under the old regime as the capital of the Union and a showcase Soviet city it was subsidised by central government, with transport losses and capital expenditure coming from federal funds, but in 1991 the city was ordered to pay its own way, leading to price rises and the commercialisation of some services. Today each level of local government negotiates with the level above it for the share of revenues it can keep, with the regions responsible for collecting taxes and then passing the money upwards – if they are so minded. As the federal tax inspectorate became more organised many of the loopholes were closed. One of the major possible sources of funds, the privatisation of housing and trade, was lost. After endless conflicts, Moscow agreed to the government plan to give most apartments away free. All the sitting tenant had to do was pay a small registration fee, and the flat became their own. Most of the 'small privatisation' of the retail trade in Moscow did not go through auctions, which would have raised more money, but through buy-outs by the shop's workers and the like.[71]

Instead of the fall of the old regime opening a new chapter in local government, it appeared that the problems were only exacerbated.[72] The institutional structure of the soviets themselves was a key factor inhibiting the development of effective policies. Soviet adminstrative theory had extolled the virtues of fused executive and legislative authority, part of the Marxist tradition of commune democracy to have 'working bodies, both executive and legislative at the same time'. As long as the CPSU was able to 'coordinate' the work of the local soviets and the executive committees, the system worked relatively smoothly. But without the guiding hand of the Party, conflict became endemic. In Moscow and Leningrad there were conflicts between the chairs of the soviets and the chairs of the executive committees (ispolkom), that is, the heads of the administrative side of things. The dominant Democratic Russia caucus in Moscow was torn by factional infighting, and Popov and his associates on the presidium at the time had nothing but contempt for the factionalism and pettiness of many of the democratic deputies.[73]

The tendency to strengthen executive power at the national level was duplicated in the localities. In an extended paper 'What is to be Done?' of late 1990 Popov stressed the need for a thorough reorganisation of the structure of local government. Like Yeltsin at the national level, so Popov at the local advocated the creation of dynamic and strengthened executive authority, in the form of popularly elected mayors.[74] Plenary sessions of the city soviet were to be held only once a year, while policy was to be made by a smaller duma selected by the full soviet, by the ispolkom and by the mayor, who would be able to veto duma decisions. The raion soviets were to be downgraded to purely consultative bodies.[75]

Some of this was achieved before August 1991, and the rest afterwards. On 12 June 1991 Popov and Sobchak were elected mayors of Moscow and St Petersburg, respectively. The concept of an elected chief executive is alien to the British political system but is more familiar to Americans. The creation of the mayorality in Moscow was accompanied by the establishment of a system of prefects who represented the mayor in ten newly established prefectures that were superimposed on the thirty-three old boroughs (raions); the boroughs themselves were broken up into 124 new 'municipal districts' based on district housing boundaries;[76] the buildings and property of the old raion soviets and their executive committees were taken over by the prefects. Executive authority separated itself from the legislative, not only institutionally but also physically, with Popov taking over some floors of the old Comecon building opposite the Russian White House, and Sobchak in St Petersburg moved the mayor's office into the old Communist Party headquarters, the Smolny.

Like Yeltsin, Popov insisted that 'without strong executive authority reforms will not be implemented in Russia'.[77] He resigned in June 1992, still complaining that he did not have enough powers to implement the necessary reforms, especially the privatisation of businesses and housing. Popov argued that the weak democratic movement in Russia faced the same dangers as after the February revolution of 1917: 'At that time democrats could find no way of overcoming the old and establishing the new and the road to dictatorship was opened.' He called for privatisation and entrepreneurism, and strong executive power; the main task was to overcome 'the final legacy of the totalitarian regime, the all-powerful soviets at all levels, and to elect normal representative bodies'.[78] Others, however, saw Popov and his 'reformer' friends as the main threat to democracy. The chairman of the Moscow city soviet, Nikolai Gonchar, was scathing of Popov's confrontational style, arguing:

> The mayor's office needs an image of an enemy so as to justify the economic collapse that is occurring. Once the Communist Party was out of the picture, the only remaining contender was the democratically-elected city council.[79]

The attempt to achieve accelerated change from above threatened political stability in conditions where the conflict between executive and legislative authority in the centre and the localities had become endemic. Although apparently elected with a democratic majority, the Moscow soviet had proved unable to formulate effective policies or to work with the local executive authorities led, in the first instance, by Popov, and then by Yurii Luzhkov. The Mossoviet and the mayor's office were locked in bitter conflict that tended to paralyse city management. But as with the national parliament, it would be simplistic to portray the struggle as one between an enlightened administration and a conservative soviet. The nature of this 'conservatism' has to be analysed, and it appears a far richer critique of the neo-liberalism, impetuosity, intolerance and sheer incompetence of the administration than might appear at first sight. Gonchar, for example, was indeed a leftist, not of the neo-communist tendency but of the Western social-democratic sort to be found in town halls throughout Europe.[80]

Following the October 1993 events the whole structure of local soviets was swept away. Yeltsin on 7 October ordered the dissolution of rebel soviets and soon afterwards all village and town soviets, but not regional or republican ones.[81] On 27 October 1993 he ordered elections to reorganised local councils in Moscow, St Petersburg and the other sixty-six regions and areas,[82] to be held between 12 December 1993 and March 1994.[83] Thus Yeltsin fulfilled his promise to put an end to the Soviet era. However, Yeltsin did not order elections in Russia's twenty-one 'ethnic' republics, although the decree recommended that these republics re-organise their legislatures and hold elections, and the majority agreed to do so. The new legislative bodies were to be much reduced in size and to become professional bodies made up of full-time deputies. The new councils, now often called dumas, were to be elected for 2 years and to have between 15 and 50 deputies;[84] they were to be purely representative bodies, losing their earlier administrative-executive character.[85] In Moscow the elections on 12 December 1993 were for a new thirty-five member Duma, now displaced from its grandiose building on Tverskaya Street.[86] As with the national legislature, so too the Duma's new charter, devised by Luzhkov, emasculated the new assembly in an attempt to avoid the old conflicts, giving the mayor the power to veto its decisions and even to dissolve it. The Duma was to be largely non-political and to concern itself with the administration of the city.[87]

The reform of local government was particularly divisive and ultimately the constitution allowed scope for considerable local variations: as article 131.1 put it 'Local self-government in urban and rural settlements and other territories is exercised with due consideration for historical and other local traditions. The structure of local self-government bodies is autonomously determined by the population.' Among the rights of local authorities were the management of municipal property and local budgets, the levying of local taxes and duties, the protection of public order, and also the resolution of 'other questions of local importance' (article 132.1).

Solzhenitsyn and other patriots advanced the *zemstvo* alternative.[88] This advocates the 'gubernisation' of local government, becoming part of a single unitary state system but with a great degree of local decentralisation. They argued that this would overcome the tangled skein of overlapping authority and encourage participation in local affairs. The usual way of achieving popular participation, however, is through political parties, but these were held in contempt by Solzhenitsyn and his friends.

In August 1995 a new Law on Local Self-Government was adopted by the State Duma, part of the continuing attempt to structure political space in Russia. The debate over the law was influenced by the Council of Europe's Charter on Local Government, and the text was amended to take into account Western standards. The constitutional right to devise local government bodies was confirmed, thus surrendering the principle of uniformity, as was a degree of control over local resources and taxation. Relations between local legislatures and executive authorities were clearly defined, as were the functions of the local authorities, including ensuring the implementation of laws and social policy. Municipal charters were to be adopted by local assemblies, but these were to conform to the broad rights allowed by the regional authorities over local government. Regions themselves, as earlier established by the constitution, were to adopt their own charters. Local elections were to have been held within six months of the adoption of the law, but as usual they were postponed. While regional agencies were jealous of the powers granted local government, the latter were also faced by encroachments on their prerogatives by federal institutions. Central government ministries in post-communist Russia appeared as difficult to bring under local control as their Soviet predecessors had been.[89]

THE UNITY OF THE STATE

The reorganisation of local government strengthened the powers of the executive at the expense of the legislative, and thus the conflicts at the national level were duplicated in the localities. In the first stage of Russia's transition it proved impossible to combine administrative rationalisation and conversion to the market economy with elections, open government and greater democracy. Indeed, democracy was relegated by other items on the agenda, yet the strengthening of executive structures suffered from a 'democratic deficit' that undermined not only their legitimacy but also their effectiveness. Attempts to take the politics out of local and regional government will probably ultimately be futile as the regime system of government disintegrates.

The struggle at the centre between executive and legislative powers fuelled demands for ever more autonomy from the regions. Gorbachev had promised 'a strong centre and strong republics', and Yeltsin's policy of 'a strong centre and strong regions' appeared to be leading towards much the same result, although in Russia integratory and centrifugal trends appear evenly matched. The main question became the level at which integration would take place, and the centralisation typical of Soviet politics was reproduced in the localities. As the reforms took hold Russian regional politics became increasingly heterogeneous as it became clear that the threat to the unity of the republic came not only from the nationality areas.

Comparisons between the disintegration of Yugoslavia and Russia have often been drawn but are in many respects misconceived. In Yugoslavia it was the communist regime that held the state together and once that was gone there were no historical, cultural or institutional foundations strong enough to hold the country together. In Russia, however, the unity of the state has been the central feature of the last 500 hundred years. As we have seen above, the post-communist regime has sought to find ways of institutionalising this unity, but has only been partially successful in this endeavour. The establishment of the Federation Council in December 1993 gave regional elites a powerful hold on the national decision-making process and provided a focus for a common political discourse.

The attempt to impose 'reform' on the regions revealed a fundamental flaw in the post-communist Russian polity, namely the failure by the Yeltsinite regime to understand the legitimate political status of its interlocutors. In other words, the centre tended to perceive the regions as being in some way in a pre-political state, 'with traditional elites and institutions incapable of grasping the meaning and implications of democracy, and as such have to be disciplined through a combination of violence and economic subsidies, just as under communism'.[90] The struggle for democracy itself became the disciplinary discourse. It was not quite like under communism, however, because 'the centre' as such was a shifting and mobile interplay of various forces and by no means shared a single ideology. Even its formal commitment to democracy was tempered by the explicit recognition of contingent 'reasons of state' in its dealings with the regions. It was precisely at the time of the Chechen war, when his links with the 'democrats' were effectively ruptured, that Yeltsin turned to find support among the regional leaderships – and reforged his ties with the Soviet-era regional elites.

Attempts to maintain the unity of the state primarily by administrative means were counter-productive, the more so when outright violence was used, as in Chechnya. Russia could only be kept together by political means, by a constant process of political negotiation and accommodation. Such a policy appeared to work in Tatarstan, and was the only viable approach to Russia's regions and localities. This does not mean that Russia has to retain precisely the same borders as today: some territories might leave (Chechnya), and some might try to join (South Ossetia); but if these changes are achieved by political means they will not threaten the unity of the state. Neither does it assume that Russia has to remain a relatively centralised state. In fact, it might be argued that unity could be more effectively assured through devolution within the framework of a genuinely federal separation of powers, or even a strongly decentralised unitary state like France, and even more so, Spain.

Part IV

Economy and society

12　Transforming the economy

Gaidar's reform secured macroeconomic change, namely the destruction of the old economy. It was a wildly painful break, surgically crude, with the rusty grinding sound of pieces of old parts and mechanisms being ripped out together with the flesh, but the break occurred. Most likely, it simply could not have happened any other way. We had virtually nothing to work with apart from Stalin's industry, Stalin's economy, adapted to the present day. And its make-up dictated precisely that sort of a break: over the knee. The system was destroyed in the same way that it was created.

Boris Yeltsin[1]

The fall of the Berlin Wall might have ended the political division of Europe, but it exposed the economic one. Two Europes still faced each other, one relatively prosperous, the other confronted with the legacy of a failed economic experiment. By some reckonings the Soviet Union in 1991 was comparatively as far, if not further, behind the leading Western countries as Russia had been in 1913. Soviet socialism had never found an effective economic policy, and indeed it could be argued that revolutionary socialism by definition cannot have one since it rejects many of the basic laws of modern economic development. The Soviet system stormed into the industrial age but failed to respond to the challenges of post-industrialism. Only under Gorbachev was the assault against the market tempered, but the search for a distinctive socialist economics was not abandoned. Only after the August 1991 coup did economic reform give way to the marketising transformation of the entire system. There is no single optimal path of transition and the question of sequencing, the relative priority between stabilisation, liberalisation, privatisation and restructuring, has still not been resolved.[2]

THE ROAD TO THE MARKET

Russia contributed 61 per cent of the USSR's GNP, and even before the coup had begun to disengage itself from the Soviet economy. Already on 3 September 1990 the prime minister, Silaev, had outlined the Russian government's programme which envisaged a speedy transition to the market, but recognised that this would be impossible without coordination among all the republics. The programme, which ran to over a thousand pages, advocated a new structure to replace the ministries for separate industries – an inter-republican economic council. Despite its length, the proposed programme was marked by the absence of governmental unity, personal conflicts and the lack of clear criteria for implementation.[3] By November 1990 the Russian parliament had passed laws on agriculture and began devising its own economic reforms; the Russian government unilaterally cut by 80 per cent its 1991 budget contribution to the Soviet treasury. However, the period up to August 1991 was marked by frustration as Russian programmes came into conflict with Soviet ones, and the economic crisis only worsened. With the fall of the Soviet government the Russian economics team inherited a yawning budget deficit, a mountain of roubles accumulated as a result of years of monetary and fiscal laxity, and a debilitating system of price controls. The result was empty shops, low labour productivity and rampant inflation.

The lack of clarity over what exactly was the subject of economic reform, Russia or the Soviet Union, continued to impede progress after the coup. The Inter-Republican Economic Committee headed by Silaev, with Yavlinskii one of its key advisers, sought to maintain an integrated economy. Their efforts led to the signing of an economic treaty on 8 October 1991 in Almaty by eight republics.[4] The treaty stressed private ownership, free enterprise and competition, and committed the republics to marketisation and restricted government interference. They were forbidden unilaterally to take control of shared property or to put up trade barriers between themselves. The rouble was to be the common currency, but members were allowed to have their own currencies if it did not harm the rouble.[5] The treaty in essence repeated the provisions of the rejected Shatalin/Yavlinskii 500-day plan of August 1990, but in the new circumstances of independent states it did not really offer viable measures to deal with the economic crisis. The main problem was that it dealt with the external aspects and not with the root causes of crisis in each of the republics. Hopes for a federal reserve banking system, an economic arbitration court and all the other trappings of a federal union were probably unrealistic given the obstacles to maintaining political union. The independent republics, led by the Baltic republics, instead began putting up customs posts. Ukraine declared that it would establish its own currency, the hryvna, and in the meantime launched the coupon, and other republics considered taking similar measures.

The break-up of the Union dislocated regional patterns of economic specialisation and destroyed the national market. The vertically integrated Stalinist economy had encouraged the manufacture of goods in gigantic plants in an attempt to benefit from economies of scale, and the production of key items for the whole USSR were concentrated in a limited number of plants. When some pharmaceutical plants were closed during 1989–90 because of their high pollution levels, they soon had to be reopened because they were the sole suppliers of items necessary for medicines. However, a debate continues over the extent of economic dependency between the republics, with suggestions that this was exaggerated by Gorbachev and his associates in their attempt to prove the desirability of the Union.[6] A study of the Baltic republics, for example, argued that their dependence on the rest of the Union was not as critical as had been thought, and certainly nothing that normal economic contracts could not cover.[7] It has been estimated that the disruption of trade with CIS countries contributed 10 per cent to Russia's overall economic decline in the early 1990s.[8]

The CIS documents signed in Belovezha and Almaty in December 1991 were vague on economic integration. The paradox emerged that the republic with the greatest potential for independent economic development, Russia, remained the most committed to a larger economic unit. Russia provided nearly 67 billion roubles in subsidy to the other republics in 1989, and in 1988 was the least dependent on trade with the other republics. Russia sold its energy and raw materials relatively cheaply, and paid for consumer goods at inflated prices, and it stood to gain most from a shift to the use of the dollar in inter-republican trade. The desire of the other republics for economic separation was politically motivated, though in the long term they were probably right to believe that they could manage their own resources and enterprises better than distant Moscow could under the old regime. They feared Moscow's domination in whatever shape it came, benign or malign, subsidy or exploitation. Only the Central Asian republics sought to maintain the old links since they were clear net beneficiaries of subsidies from Moscow, but even they soon sought to forge new links with their regional neighbours.

The Soviet legacy to Russia was a heavy one indeed. The structural reorganisation of the Russian economy took place against the background of a sharp decline in real incomes and production, the latter falling in the USSR as a whole by 17 per cent in 1991, and in light industry, hit hardest by the cuts in imports, output fell by 40 per cent.[9] In comparison, in 1932, the hardest year of the Great Depression in the USA, GNP fell by only 14 per cent. In Russia national income fell by about 5 per cent in 1990 and 9 per cent in 1991.[10] Pavlov's government had been marked by fiscal and budgetary anarchy and rising budget deficits. This was made worse by local authorities refusing to contribute to republican funds, and republics reneging on commitments to the Union budget, in particular the central stabilisation, pension and social security funds. Credits were received from the State Bank, which in turn only encouraged the printing presses to work faster even though increases in the money supply required parliamentary approval. The problem of the USSR foreign debt burdened the transition, having risen to $77 billion ($60 billion to Western creditors and $17 billion to Asian and East European countries) by late 1991.[11]

Chubais stressed the long-term nature of the economic crisis in the USSR, marked by the sharp decline in growth rates from the mid-1970s, the growth of debt money and budget deficits. The anti-alcohol campaign and its attendant revenue losses was only one element in a larger crisis in which enterprises and ministries took advantage of the chaos of perestroika to obtain cheap investment funds from the central budget. The problems, therefore, were 'only the summit of a prolonged socioeconomic structural crisis connected with the decay of the centrally planned economy'.[12] In the early 1990s the structural crisis turned from a latent to an actual one.

The financial crisis reached catastrophic proportions, and this more than anything else hastened the demise of the USSR. The Soviet inflation rate quadrupled in 1991, reaching some 700 per cent by the end of the year. The chairman of the State Bank Victor Geraschenko warned in early December that only enough funds remained for a few days' of expenditure, a crisis precipitated by the Russian parliament's objections to the Bank's policy of printing money to meet commitments.[13] Yeltsin agreed to bail out the Union government, but at the price of a tough budget strategy and the transfer of the Soviet Ministry of Finance to Russian jurisdiction. On 20 November the process was accelerated when Yeltsin in effect took over all the remaining Union economic ministries, disbanding several of them, and bringing under Russian control all strategic natural resources.[14] Thus Russia, despite itself, was forced to take over Soviet economic institutions, but was in danger of finding itself in the position of responsibility without power since little that was positive could be done until there were new budget laws, effective taxation, credit and monetary policies.

SHOCK THERAPY AND BEYOND

Jeffrey Sachs, the adviser to the Bolivian and Polish governments and the leading advocate of 'shock therapy', now moved on to Moscow. The theory behind 'shock therapy' is that countries plagued by years of planning, state ownership and bureaucracy have to be jerked into the mainstream of market reforms. This is to be achieved by the rapid liberalisation of prices, removal of subsidies, expenditure cuts and severe reductions in money supply. The result in Bolivia, Poland, Russia and elsewhere has been an immediate explosion in prices, a rapid rise in unemployment and a steep fall in production. The aim was for goods that had previously been hoarded to find their way back to the shops and for queues to decrease, deterred by the high prices if not eliminated by the sufficiency of goods. Higher prices would encourage production, and a revived private sector would gradually bring supply and demand into line. Price rises would then stabilise, and the economy would then begin to move out of recession.[15]

The theory was condemned by the veteran economist John Kenneth Galbraith as 'simplistic ideology'. He argued that the neo-liberal reliance on the market to the exclusion of any major role of the state was primitive economics.[16] Shock therapy places intolerable strains on the economy and society and companies that in other conditions might have fought their way to viability are forced to close for lack of liquidity. The fall in production is matched by spiralling prices and the population sees its savings disappear and endures yet more suffering. Living standards, already low, plummet, and tight budgetary constraints mean that there is a lack of funds to provide adequate social security for the growing army of the unemployed and needy. The sheer speed of the transition intensifies the suffering and the whole fragile tissue of democratic institutions is placed under almost intolerable strain. In comparison, it took Germany 10 years to move to a market economy after the war, and Britain retained price and other controls into the 1950s. Even Thatcher did not dare to remove rent controls, and it took over a decade to privatise some 5 per cent of the British economy from the early 1980s.

The many different approaches reduce to two different philosophies of the transition to the market. One urged the need for 'shock therapy' and a 'big bang' on the Polish model and insisted that only in this way would vital Western assistance be forthcoming. They drew the conclusion from Gorbachev's reforms that half-measures are often worse than none. The other line, advocated by the democratic opposition like Yabloko, centrists and so-called con-servatives, proposed a slower route with controlled price rises, demonopolisation, gradual privatisation and assistance to enterprises. Russia's road to the market began with a vigorous 'big bang', but then began to draw on elements from the second school.

Gaidar stresses the initially disastrous conditions in Autumn 1991 for reform in Russia: grain reserves would last barely four months, foreign currency and gold reserves were exhausted, and a lack of credit-worthiness. The old system was completely paralysed and the new one did not work. In these conditions, he insisted, all talk about a soft, evolutionary approach to reform was meaningless. His strategy was based on a three-year programme: in the first, the deficit would be eliminated, queues eliminated, and the rouble made convertible; in the second, price rises would be halted and the currency strengthened; and in the third economic growth could be anticipated from private savings and private investments. Un-fortunately, he did not have 3 years but only 11 months, and the softening of policy led to continued price rises combined with a fall in output. Those countries which had three years of consistent reform, like Poland, Estonia, Albania, the Czech Republic, Latvia and Lithuania saw rises in production. Those countries which sought to preserve elements of the old system saw record falls: in 1994 output fell by 26 per cent in Belarus, 25 per cent in Kazakhstan and 23 per cent in Ukraine. Thus the problem in his view was not that Russian reforms were pursued too dogmatically, but that they were pursued without consistency and firmness.[17]

Gaidar's political position was always exceptionally weak; appointed deputy prime minister in charge of economic policy on 7 November 1991, he became first deputy prime minister on 2 March 1992, acting prime minister on 15 June 1992, and was dismissed on 14 December 1992, although he briefly returned to the economics portfolio in late 1993. Despite this, he was the architect of the first stage of Russia's economic reforms. His policy was marked by a commitment to traditional International Monetary Fund (IMF) precepts including a balanced budget, the reduction of inflation, cutting back subsidies, exposing the domestic economy to the world market and raising energy prices.[18] He and his neo-liberal allies tended to idealise neo-classical economic theory and denigrated the role of the state and other regulatory institutions of contemporary capitalism.[19]

As the USSR moved towards oblivion Russia drew up a fully fledged independent economic policy, and Yeltsin outlined his proposals to the Russian CPD on 28 October 1991. The programme included: (1) economic stabilisation based on tight monetary and credit policy, strengthening of the rouble (although one of the major problems was the influx of roubles from the former union republics), and he mooted the idea of a separate Russian currency to protect the republic's economy; (2) price liberalisation; (3) privatisation and the introduction of a mixed economy with a growing private sector, accelerated land reform; (4) reorganisation of the financial system, tight control of budget expenditure, reform of the tax and banking systems.[20] Yeltsin's programme promised 'to stabilise the situation' and then to 'begin the process of rejuvenation', and he admitted that the measures would be unpopular but expected there to be an improvement by autumn 1992. Thus he outlined a programme for radical changes in both ownership and management of the Russian economy that drew much on the Polish experience of shock therapy.

On 1 November the CPD granted Yeltsin wide powers (valid until 1 December 1992) to be used to promote reform. Presidential decrees on such matters as banks, property and land reform, taxation, currency and so on were to be submitted to the Russian parliament, and if not rejected within seven days they became effective otherwise they were to be discussed by parliament within ten days.[21] On 6 November Yeltsin reorganised the government, stating that for the duration of radical economic reforms the president would also act as head of the 'government of reforms' himself. On 7 November Burbulis was appointed first deputy prime minister, Gaidar took over responsibility for economic policy, and Alexander Shokhin was nominated to become another deputy prime minister responsible for health, labour and employment, education, culture, social protection and science and technology. A new Russian Council of Ministers with twenty-three ministers was appointed, and the country prepared itself for yet another grand attempt at social engineering.

In late 1991 wage limits were lifted, restrictions on foreign economic activities eased, minimum wages set, all customs barriers introduced by individual regions of Russia banned, VAT set at 28 per cent, guidelines for privatisation in 1992 adopted, and much else besides. Then on 2 January 1992 came comprehensive price liberalisation, with prices freed from administrative control on about 90 per cent of retail prices and 80 per cent of wholesale prices. On 29 January the restrictions on trading, established in the 1920s, were lifted and soon kiosks sprouted on the streets of towns. Ambitious targets were set to reduce the budget deficit, which by some estimates reached one-fifth of GDP in 1991, and to achieve a balanced budget by the end of the year. Monetary policy was tightened, and attempts made to bring the flood of roubles under control. Bread, milk, vodka, medicines, rents, public transport and the price of some utilities remained controlled, and from March 1992 local councils had the right to impose local controls as long as they paid for any subsidies. From May 1992 energy prices were increased, but because of political fears not to anything approaching world levels as demanded by the IMF.

The January measures were a mixture of price liberalisation and price reform, raising prices rather than letting the market find a natural level balancing supply and demand. Demand was damped down by what for most Russians were exorbitant prices, but too little was done to free the supply side of the economy, with only desultory moves towards privatising the retail sector. Reforms to price structures appear to have operated mainly in one direction, price increases. Consumer price inflation rose sharply, by 245 per cent in the first month, January, alone before falling back to 10 per cent in August;[22] at which point the government's attempt to resolve the problem of inter-enterprise arrears stimulated a new wave of inflation, rising to a monthly 25 per cent by the end of the year. By November 1992 prices had risen 22-fold, whereas wages had only increased 10-fold.[23] An incomes policy had been an essential element of shock therapy in Poland, but in Russia the government considered wage controls politically unfeasible and in effect it was unnecessary since the wage-price spiral was not the central element fuelling inflation. Within a month the amount needed to keep a family afloat tripled and the percentage of wages spent on food rose dramatically from 22.4 per cent in December 1991 to 88.3 in January, but by July this had fallen to 35 per cent.[24] The impact of the price rises was cushioned by savings and accumulated goods, but these were soon exhausted; the wiping out of savings, indeed, became one of the most bitter charges against Gaidar economics.

Shock therapy leads to a sharp drop in manufacturing production. In Poland industrial output fell by 37 per cent from 1990 before beginning to pick up in late 1992, but was worse in Russia because shock therapy was applied to an economy already in very deep recession. Industrial output in Russia plummeted by 20 per cent in 1992, compared with a fall of 11 per cent in 1991. Production was hit by the tight squeeze on investment in order to avoid the traditional waste of resources on inefficient investment projects. The aim of the first period is to destroy the old inefficient system rather than to construct anything new.[25] In Russia, in conditions of extreme monopolisation, instead of firms cutting prices to compensate for falling demand, they cut output and raised prices. Between 1990 and 1995 GDP fell by some 50 per cent, compared to a cumulative fall of some 31 per cent in US GNP during the Depression.[26] Despite the temptation to blame shock therapy for this fall, countries (like Ukraine) which sought a 'soft landing' into economic reform witnessed far greater falls in output. In Russia, moreover, despite the halving of industrial output, real disposable incomes doubled.[27]

The reorganisation of management of the economy far exceeded changes in ownership, and indeed appeared once again, as in the Soviet economy of old, to be on a carousel of administrative reform. The new Ministry of the Economy headed by Andrei Nechaev absorbed the old general ministries like Gosplan and Gossnab, the state supply system abolished in January 1992. The Ministry of Industry took over the two dozen branch industrial ministries, now called departments within the ministry. Some of the ministries were turned into concerns, trusts, associations and so on, but still closely tied to ministerial departments. The whole system, moreover, in 1992 appeared paralysed, with factories waiting for orders from ministries in Moscow that no longer existed. In late 1992 there were plans once again to disaggregate the departments and to reform them as ministries. Moreover, the whole system was permeated by corruption in which managers often looked to their own interests rather than those of their enterprises, and sought ways of profiting from the crisis by transferring ownership to themselves and associates on the cheap, or by purloining foreign currency income.

The Russian budget deficit was running at about 15 per cent of GDP by mid-1992, and the tendency was for it to rise as the government was forced to ease its public sector spending restrictions and to raise state sector wages. A $6 billion stabilisation fund for the rouble could not be used effectively until the rouble exchange rate settled at a realistic market rate. Fears of a social backlash meant that energy prices were raised only five-fold in April 1992 despite the demand of the IMF to raise them to world levels. On one of Yeltsin's periodic tours of the country in late May 1992 the dangers of an immediate full price liberalisation of energy prices was brought home to him. On his return on 30 May 1992 he sacked his radical energy minister, Lopukhin, and replaced him by Chernomydrin, chairman of Gazprom, the state-owned gas company. He thus fulfilled his promise at the Sixth CPD to replace some of the young academics in his government with professionals.

If one source of opposition to the liberal policies of Gaidar came from the industrialists, another came from oppositional democrats. Yavlinskii insisted that it was a mistake for the government to liberalise prices before privatisation and competition had been introduced. A third source of opposition came from parliament. Already on 2 April Khasbulatov delivered a speech to parliament in which he criticised the governments's economic policies and urged a 'correction to the reforms' by the reintroduction of administrative controls over prices, and various tax benefits to enterprises and households.[28] Economic policy was at the centre of discussions at the Sixth CPD (6–21 April 1992), and a resolution adopted on 11 April appeared to restrict the reforms to such an extent that the government offered its resignation. In the event, the Congress resolution on 15 April gave critical support to the course of reform but called for a medium-term strategy covering the stage following shock therapy.[29] Despite the victory of Yeltsin's line, the reforms continued to lack a solid parliamentary base and Gaidar's policies, and the man himself, were subject to perpetual sniping.

Tight monetary and fiscal policies were pursued to restrain inflation and to stabilise the value of the rouble against international currencies. A cash crisis arose because of inflation and parliament's refusal to allow the government to print sufficient money. Millions of government employees, in mid-1992 still some 90 per cent of the workforce, went unpaid because of the lack of banknotes. The major problem, however, was the arrears accumulated by firms that were unable to sell their goods; by June 1992 huge debts had been run up between companies, primarily between the old state industries and the military-industrial complex, amounting to the staggering total of more than a trillion roubles (£5.5 billion). Debts arose because they could not sell goods to consumers, who had no spare cash, and because they had been unwilling to sack workers or to cut down on overheads, but above all because they in effect gained credit by not paying for goods received. The Russian Union of Industrialists and Entrepreneurs (RUIE) and parliament insisted that the Central Bank should extend them credit, but the Gaidar government equally forcefully refused. The government hoped that the companies would shed staff and become efficient enough to sell goods that people wanted at prices they could afford. The by-product would be unemployment and bankruptcies, but for the reformers this was a necessary price to pay for economic efficiency. If the firms were bailed out the result, Gaidar insisted, would be hyperinflation, continued shortages and a useless rouble. However, the government reshuffle of June 1992 led to concessions to the industrial lobby in the form of writing off debts and by increased monetary emissions, which doubled between June and October: the government was caught between the millstones of inflation and unemployment.

Gaidar's policies were challenged by the alliance of neo-communists and nationalists in parliament and the centrist industrialists outside. The RUIE was largely made up of the directors of the large state enterprises who favoured a slower pace of reform and more government subsidies. Many of them were monopolies and they took advantage of the liberalisation to raise prices and cut production, the opposite of what the reform policies were meant to achieve. Some of them also opposed privatisation, since this would deprive them of their power. Their argument that post-communist countries did not need a mass input of capital, but that the government should establish the conditions for business to be able to function, had a certain logic. The key element was for Russia to enter world markets, in particular for its highly sophisticated arms industry but also for those with saleable goods.

The centrist challenge to neo-liberal policies finally succeeded when on 14 December 1992 Chernomyrdin replaced Gaidar as prime minister. While most of the radical 'government of reforms' remained, a change of tack was promised with more credits for state industry, and on 5 January 1993 limits on profits on some consumer goods and services were announced in an attempt to keep prices down, along with the reimposition of price controls on some essential goods to fulfil the promise that the democratisation of society would not be accompanied by the impoverishment of the people. However, the government's new chief economic strategist, Boris Fedorov (who had resigned from the Soviet government in December 1990 complaining of its timid economic reforms), insisted that the plans were impractical, and they were in effect shelved.[30] He insisted that price controls were not the way to combat inflation, which in December 1992 had risen to 25–27 per cent a month. In 1992 inflation accelerated from an annual 90 per cent to 1,450[31] and in early 1993 was close to crossing the critical 50 per cent a month threshold marking the beginning of hyperinflation.

In the event, Chernomyrdin's economic policy did not differ all that much from Gaidar's. The policy of tight credit and monetary policy was restored, and indeed in addressing parliament on 28 January 1993 Chernomyrdin insisted that because of accelerating inflation he had no alternative but to make financial stabilisation and the strengthening of the rouble his priorities, and he warned that this could not be achieved by administrative means. However, cabinet divisions meant that doubts remained over how long the policy would be maintained. The gains of shock therapy were in danger of being lost in the struggle between parliament and president; only with the resolution of the political conflict in late 1993 did economic policy gain overall coherence. The Fifth Duma from 1994 proved receptive to the logic of centrist economic reform, and in December 1995 for the first time since 1991 adopted a budget before it was due to come into operation.

The 1993 constitution granted the Central Bank of Russia (CBR), previously subordinated to the Supreme Soviet, a degree of independence from the legislature. It was allowed to determine the money supply within the framework of a commitment to the stability of the rouble. Its director was to be hired or fired by the State Duma, but only on the president's recommendation. Thus the CBR gained some room for manoeuvre, above all from parliament, but enjoyed nothing like the degree of independence enjoyed by the Bundesbank or the Federal Reserve Bank in America. Few restrictions were placed on capital flows in and out of the country.[32] By 1995 almost all the other republics had introduced their own currency. The final demise of the rouble zone following the CBR's currency reform of July 1993 at last gave Russia effective monetary and credit control, and when combined with a more market-oriented monetary policy, a more transparent budget and good relations between the CBR and the government, Russia's prospects for financial stabilisation improved. Its financial markets developed rapidly, providing a sensitive feedback mechanism for macroeconomic decisions, but the scene was marked by a rollercoaster of booms and busts. A notable low point was 'black Tuesday', 11 October 1994, when the rouble lost over 20 per cent of its value, largely as a consequence of an earlier loosening of monetary policy and, it was suspected, because of machinations by bankers. The rouble swiftly recovered its value but its vulnerability was exposed and between September 1994 and January 1995 it lost half its value. By late 1995 the rouble was effectively stabilised within a dollar corridor. While hyperinflation was avoided, inflation remained a problem, falling from 18 per cent in January 1994 to around 5 per cent in July before once again rising to 18 per cent in January 1995 and falling to 3.2 per cent in December 1995. The major problem, however, was to achieve full rouble convertability, without which Russia would attract little foreign investment because of difficulties in repatriating earnings, given the natural limits to barter or countertrade.

The whole reform package depended on the West in the form of a moratorium on debts and stabilisation funds. Debt relief released valuable foreign currency to finance imports and stabilise the currency. By April 1992 a package of IMF assistance totalling $24 (£13.5) billion in the first instance had been agreed, of which some $6 billion was for a stabilisation fund to support the rouble. Before releasing the funds the IMF insisted on the implementation of the second phase of the economic reform programme, the freeing of energy prices, further tightening of monetary and fiscal policies and the encouragement of private ownership. Russia gained full membership of the IMF and the World Bank on 27 April 1992, after some debate over the size of Russia's quota in the IMF which sets its capacity to borrow, and thus became eligible for the promised $24 billion. In return for IMF funds Russia had to reduce its budget deficit, cut credits to loss-making enterprises, establish the legal framework for private ownership, reform the farm and energy sectors, service debts to the West and establish a unified exchange rate for the rouble. However, the struggle against inflation and cuts in factory subsidies and defence spending were jeopardised by the vigorous rearguard action against Gaidar's reforms in parliament. Russia found itself simply unable to comply with IMF demands and even Yeltsin had reservations about the full-scale IMF restructuring plans. On being asked about the dangers of a 'social cataclysm' on 28 April 1992, he insisted 'We do not intend to work to the direct dictation of the IMF. We do not share the views of this organisation on everything and we will stick to our point of view.'[33] In the event Russia received little of the economic assistance promised by the Group of Seven (G7).

Standby loans are a crucial element in providing a source of non-inflationary financing. The negotiation of a $6.25 billion (£4 billion) IMF loan in early 1995 was conditional on the government holding down inflation, reducing the budget deficit and cutting back on central bank credits to loss-making state industries and collective farms. The IMF insisted that the budget deficit be kept to 7.7 per cent of GNP, but the Chechen war and associated costs strained a budget already under severe pressure. Although direct credits to state firms had been phased out from 1994, subsidies continued to flow to agriculture. Russian welfare payments and salaries in the state sector are calculated as multiples of the minimum wage, set by the Tripartite Commission established by presidential decree in January 1992 but influenced by the Duma. In the event, the budget adopted by the Duma on 24 February 1995 envisaged a deficit of only 8 per cent of GDP. The way was thus paved for the loan to be agreed on 10 March 1995, although unusually tight conditions were imposed. Russia agreed to eliminate budget imbalances, liberalise foreign trade, simplify tariffs and scrap tax exemptions for big businesses; and talks were opened with foreign creditors over the rescheduling of Russia's foreign debt, now totalling $120 billion, one-third of which was held by the Paris Club of government creditors.[34]

A presidential decree of 15 November 1991 and later measures decisively broke with the old state monopoly on foreign trade by liberalising foreign economic relations, and regulating flows by tariffs rather than quantitative restrictions. Trade patterns changed dramatically, with a shift away from the former Soviet markets towards Western Europe; in 1994 Russian trade with the EU was worth almost double that with the CIS. In 1995 foreign trade turnover at $113 billion represented a 21 per cent increase over 1994, with exports to non-CIS countries rising by 28 per cent to $59 billion, while exports to the CIS fell 3.5 per cent to $12.4 billion. Russia ran a healthy foreign trade surplus ($31 billion at that time).[35] The trade structure, however, was unbalanced, consisting mainly of energy and raw material exports and the import of consumer goods.

Chernomyrdin's government continued the economic reforms while trying to maintain sound fiscal and monetary policies. In 1994 the government launched yet more initiatives to advance the economic reforms focusing on a renewed attempt to achieve macroeconomic stabilisation; a new phase of privatisation in industry and agriculture; and a vigorous effort to improve the climate for foreign investment. The key factor here was the availability of investment resources, both domestic and foreign; the decline in the rate of investment had far exceeded the decline in output during the first three years of radical reform. In 1995 Russia's GDP fell by only 4 per cent and it appeared that the worst was over as far as macroeconomic stabilisation was concerned and that a return to economic growth could be envisaged.

PRIVATISATION AND ENTREPRENEURSHIP

Changes in ownership structure proved remarkably resistant to change. In the first nine months of 1991 only forty-five large enterprises were privatised in the whole of the USSR, and in Poland, too, the privatisation of industry had taken a year to begin, though shops and other small properties had been disbursed fairly swiftly. As Poland and other countries discovered, it is very difficult to privatise large plants, not only because of the lack of capital, but the structure and product range of companies is often not only obsolete but, with the huge military sector in Russia, very difficult to orient towards the market. Foreign investors, even when encouraged, were not keen to take them over because of their poor economic performance.

The Soviet economy, moreover, was the most monopolised in the world. Up to a third of all industrial enterprises were absolute monopolies, producing goods that no other company in the USSR produced. Not only in production but also in the sphere of management, in trade and supply, in research and development, the system was characterised by 'the "super-monopolism" of state power'.[36] Denationalisation would have to be accompanied by demonopolisation to stop privatisation simply transforming state monopolies into private ones. As in Britain, however, privatisation tended to precede the break up of monopolies, and in most cases simply achieved the transfer of a state monopoly into the private sector where they could impose punitive charges on captive customers. Monopolies, however, affected only certain industries, and overall the concentration of industry is not that much greater in Russia that in the United States. The problem in Russia is 'the missing fringe of small firms', in capitalist countries the source of technical innovation, competition and job creation.[37]

The main purpose of privatisation is to break the dependence of enterprises on the state budget. Subsidies and relatively easy access to bank credits fuelled inflation and undermined the credibility of the whole reform programme. However, privatisation is as much a political act as economically expedient, the destruction of the old monopolies and their corporate dependence on the state not only begins to create a capitalist market but also entails the destruction of the associated bureaucracy. For Chubais, the deputy prime minister at the head of the State Committee for the Administration of State Property (Goskomimushchestvo, GKI), responsible for privatisation, the programme was designed to create a new class with a stake in property and thus make society less susceptible to political demagogy. In his address to the nation on 19 August 1992 Yeltsin described privatisation as the 'ticket to a free economy'. Private property was considered the basis of a civilised society and the foundation on which democracy could be built.

The aim of privatisation was to overcome the amorphousness of the whole notion of property and to personify it in the form of concrete owners or known corporate agencies. The abstraction of 'state property' was to be overcome and a new class of property owners created. The presidential decree on the Privatisation of State and Municipal Enterprises in the RSFSR of 29 December 1991 set ambitious targets for privatisation, but little was said about demonopolisation.[38] The Government Programme of Privatisation of June 1992 was the main document outlining Russia's privatisation programme:[39] all small enterprises (the 200,000 enterprises with up to 200 employees, most of whom were owned by local or municipal authorities) were to be sold through competitive auctions, commercial tender competitions or lease buy-outs; large enterprises (with 1,000 to 10,000 employees) were to be transformed into joint-stock companies (corporatised), after which their shares were to be sold or distributed according to the provisions of the mass privatisation programme; medium-sized enterprises could adopt either the direct sale or corporatisation method. Three main approaches were available for disbursing the assets of joint-stock companies. The first was for collectives to receive up to 25 per cent of non-voting shares free, and another 10 per cent of voting shares at a discount, while managers could buy up to a fifth of voting shares for a nominal sum. The second option was for workers and managers to purchase 51 per cent of normal shares in closed sales. The third option applied only to medium-sized enterprises and allowed a managing group to privatise an enterprise while ensuring solvency and employment for at least one year; the managing group could buy 30 per cent of voting shares, while 20 per cent was sold to workers and managers at preferential terms.[40] Strategic and defence enterprises, utilities and those with over 10,000 employees could only be privatised, if at all, with the government's approval.

In addition, in August 1992 the government began to issue privatisation vouchers with a nominal value of 10,000 roubles. Citizens were given investment coupons, that is registered securities enabling them to buy shares or management shares at preferential rates of the 6,000 medium and large companies earmarked for corporatisation in 1992 and privatisation in 1993. The coupon method does not create additional capital or strengthen the management of companies, but it symbolised the advent of 'popular capitalism': Russia now has the highest number of shareholders in the world. Chubais favoured direct auction privatisation, despite criticisms from the opposition that this would allow the 'mafia' to buy up enterprises, combined with voucher sales. A more radical approach to privatisation was advanced by neo-liberal 'romantic marketisers' like Larisa Piyasheva (who advised Popov on Moscow's strategy of low-price giveaways to existing employees), who proposed the transfer of all types of enterprises free to worker collectives, with the purchase of part of the property if it was especially profitable.

Much of the debate over privatisation focused on the issue of equity. If state enterprises had earlier belonged to the people, then how was their formal ownership now to be translated into real ownership? The argument that enterprises should be given to their workers was flawed since those in viable enterprises would benefit far more than those in the service sector or bankrupt plants. The debate was often couched in terms of equity versus efficiency, though some, like Professor Richard Layard of the London School of Economics and an adviser to the Russian government, argued that giving away shares combined both efficacy and equity and would at the same time build up popular support for the reforms.[41] Anders Aslund, another adviser, favoured the most rapid disbursement of state assets to establish a critical mass early on in the reform process.[42] Milton Friedman, however, insisted that ownership meant not only assets but also liabilities, and that old illusions would be perpetuated if the first step on the road to the market was giving people something for nothing instead of having to provide something in return.[43] The giving away of state property to workers might well undermine both efficiency and equity since those who did not work in a state enterprise or had retired would be at a disadvantage, and the value of enterprises in any case varied sharply.[44]

Privatisation turned out to be a highly complex affair in which genuine problems were compounded by an almost obsessive fear of foreign penetration of the economy allied with the attempt to avoid the Soviet mafia buying up land and enterprises with their ill-gotten gains. Moreover, the typically heavy-handed bureaucratic approach to privatisation smothered local initiative. In one respect, however, privatisation was easier in Russia than elsewhere since the process was little affected by reprivatisation, the restitution of property. Russia's former owners were for the most part dead, and their heirs scattered to the four corners of the earth. Changes in property relations took a number of forms, of which outright privatisation was only one. The other options were leasing arrangements, worker-management schemes, the so-called 'nomenklatura privatisation' whereby managers and former political officials took the best of the state enterprises, and the creation of new businesses. Leasing, holding companies and the like appeared to be at best a half-way stage, a type of pseudo-privatisation.

Gaidar admitted that privatisation would be 'a heavy, long process',[45] but in the event it proved one of the more sucessful policies. By September 1994 some 100,000 enterprises had been privatised and over 80 per cent of the industrial workforce were in privatised enterprises.[46] The privatisation of small businesses was more or less complete in regions like Nizhnii Novgorod, Ryazan, Irkutsk and Khabarovsk, and of the enterprises subject to voucher privatisation, 24,000 were corporatised and 15,000 privatised by that time.[47] By 1995 29 per cent of the housing stock had been privatised. The aim was to make the transition to the market economy irreversible by creating a class of property owners while at the same time making firms more efficient and market-oriented. In addition, rapid state-sponsored privatisation sought to pre-empt factory directors from appropriating choice parts of the state economy. The majority of privatised enterprises were not sold to the public but in workforce elections, encouraged by their managers, voted for the option that allowed staff to buy 51 per cent of the stock at a fixed price. Rather than outside owners coming in and shaking out factories and sacking staff and managers, control remained within the factory gates. The relatively successful voucher privatisation was followed from mid-1994 by a second stage focusing on key aspects of enterprise restructuring and with more emphasis on private sector development, including the transition to cash privatisation, the attempt to achieve more efficient corporate management, and the accelerated development of securities markets and legal reforms. Enterprises were now encouraged to raise investment resources on the open capital market, and at the same time cash auctions and investment tenders for stakes in the newly privatised companies and for blocks of shares held by the state in privatised enterprises accelerated.

Vigorous attempts were made to attract foreign investment, and by mid-1994 it appeared that capital flight had been seen to be reversed as foreign portfolio investment rose.

One of the complaints of the directors was that they were committed to providing a range of social facilities such as creches, housing and hospitals which they considered a form of hidden taxation on their enterprises. These non-productive assets were in theory to be transferred to the local authorities, but they too (as we have seen) lacked the resources to maintain them. Because of the sheer size of the country with great regional variations, and the enormous press of other demands on the central leadership, local authorities played a key role in the privatisation process. However, they had little incentive to do so since they received only 50 per cent of the proceeds from the sale of municipal enterprises, and 10 per cent from the sale of regional and federal enterprises.[48] The Moscow authorities, moreover, insisted on control over privatisation in the city, and even safeguarded for itself the right to renationalise enterprises in the capital.

Privatisation was open to all sorts of frauds known collectively as 'nomenklatura privatisation'. Speculative dealers, above all former functionaries, stood to benefit unduly from the process since they could exploit their insider knowledge, contacts, and above all liquid assets. They could take advantage of their strategic position to buy the best shares in the best companies. The most common method was for managers to hive off the most profitable parts of an enterprise and then to lease or sell them to private companies with themselves as directors, which they then applied to register with the local authorities. The semi-privatisation of Gazprom, which allegedly made its former head Chernomyrdin a very rich man, was only the most spectacular example of insiders taking advantage of new opportunies. Underworld operations could also take advantage of the sell-off to launder illicit earnings into legitimate businesses. To prevent nomenklatura privatisation the state committee for anti-monopoly policy, a body independent of the government, vetted all company registrations valued at more than 50 million roubles. The anti-monopoly legislation was relatively ineffective and pursued with a singular lack of vigour, and demonopolisation tended to take spontaneous rather than planned forms.[49]

While nomenklatura privatisation aroused widespread public envy and hostility, and to a degree undermined the legitimacy of the whole privatisation process, it could be regarded as no more than a distinctively Russian form of spontaneous privatisation and an adaptation to new conditions of the customary rights that had developed during Brezhnev's rule. From this perspective there was nothing to stop formal legislation sanctioning these informal processes; but this, perhaps, was to take too benign a view. The vast majority of the population had been lumpenised, deprived of property, and in these conditions the attempt to conduct a radical economic reform and privatisation without strict controls by the executive and judicial authorities allowed a small group of economic managers and nomenklatura capitalists to seize the lion's share of state property. There is an element of carpet-bagging capitalism in post-communist Russia, interested in short-term gains and asset-stripping the beached monstrosities of the old communist economy. Lax fiscal and political controls in the first stage of marketisation allowed 'rent-seeking' to develop, defined by Aslund as 'any activity designed to exploit a monopoly position or to gain access to government subsidies, as opposed to profit-seeking in a market with competitive firms'.[50] Many of the anti-marketeers insisted that a distinctive type of 'comprador capitalism' was emerging.[51] It is probably impossible to eliminate corruption altogether from the process of privatisation; certainly, early American capitalism did not emerge with clean hands. It will take several years at least for effective regulatory mechanisms to emerge. It was this element that so aroused the hostility of the opposition, and the CPRF in the Sixth Duma took the battle over privatisation into a new and more bitter phase. Chubais was confident, however, that privatisation was now deeply embedded in society and would require a revolution once again to extirpate it.

The government's industrial policy was rudimentary, veering between very high interest rates for certain industries and very low (in effect, given inflation, negative) interest rates for energy, agriculture and defence industries. No real policy had been devised for the selective support of enterprises and industries. Denationalisation is usually accompanied by bankruptcy laws allowing previously subsidised but unprofitable companies to go to the wall; in September 1991 for the first time a mine in Donetsk was declared bankrupt, unable to pay its debts and the banks unwilling to extend further credits.[52] Thus began the process of hardening the budget, but the bankruptcy law only came into effect in March 1993 and remained remarkably toothless, above all because creditors had little incentive to recover their claims.

The creation of new businesses began to change the shape of Russian ownership, although the roots of many in the shadow economy perpetuated the links between business and crime. Some 80,000 businesses were created in 1991, though not all were new in the strict sense but represented the privatisation or changes in the legal status of existing enterprises. These businesses included about 9,000 joint-stock companies, 227 concerns and 123 consortia, some 1,300 commercial banks and 110 exchanges.[53] The first commodity exchange was formed on 4 April 1990,[54] and by early 1992 there were some 400 in Russia dealing with everything from metals to money, acting as a substitute for the old centrally controlled distribution system bringing buyers and sellers together. The largest was the Moscow-based Russian Commodity and Raw Materials Exchange, dealing in goods ranging from electronics to aircraft. The business ethics of some of the commodity exchanges, however, were on occasion questionable.

Following the adoption of the Law on Co-operatives of 26 May 1988 the number at first increased rapidly, but their contribution to the economy did not meet the expectations of some of their most ardent partisans such as the chair of the All-Union Association of Cooperatives, Vladimir Tikhonov.[55] Some turned into other types of businesses, and most worked closely with state enterprises, and indeed many were formed by these enterprises, to supply and sell their goods more effectively than the unwieldy state firms. Relatively few cooperatives were genuinely commercial businesses started from scratch by entrepreneurs to meet the needs of the market.[56]

At first wary of foreign direct investment (FDI), especially in larger firms, the Russian government later sought to attract foreign investors. For this a strong legal and financial system was required, as well as a reasonably stable political environment. Joint ventures had been the great hope of the Gorbachev years, yet they too failed to live up to expectations. By the end of 1991 there were some 2,600 joint ventures registered in Russia, employing some 135,000 people, the great majority of whom were Russians.[57] They were producing over 7 per cent of all computers, 10 per cent of the telephones and a growing proportion of shoes.[58] Another channel, however, was represented by the thirteen free economic zones that had been established in Russia by the end of 1991, encompassing some 18 million people, 12 per cent of the total population of Russia.[59]

The great challenge facing Russia was to restore the microeconomic tissues of an entrepreneurial and active society. Many new ventures were created, and Russians appeared to take to the market with more gusto than business acumen, and the enormous amount of 'air selling' (*torgovlya vozdukhom*), deals in imaginary goods by imagined syndicates, gave an impression of much more business activity than there really was. The lack of business ethics was symbolised by large-scale software piracy. Copyright laws were ignored as video and audio cassettes, books and records, were all copied without licence in a manner reminiscent of Asian countries in their capitalist infancy. The skills learnt in bringing out *samizdat*, the illegal publishing of so-called dissident material during the communist occupation, were now applied to the nascent capitalist economy. The absence of an effective banking system and contract law and the presence everywhere of street hawkers and market hustlers, robber taxi drivers and organised crime, gave birth to the image of the 'Wild East', a riotous free-for-all on the fringes of the emerging market. The fear remained, however, that the fully fledged market would not emerge, and that this anarchic hustling and criminalised market operating in the interstices of the bureaucratised system would actually *be* the market in Russia.

AGRICULTURE

The legacy of the Soviet regime was particularly heavy in agriculture. Since Stalin's decision to launch forced collectivisation in 1929, Soviet agriculture had suffered a 'permanent crisis'.[60] This crisis was marked by low productivity of land and workers, gross wastage, and food shortages that on occasion reached famine levels, as in Ukraine in the early 1930s and again in 1946. Average crop yields between 1975–90 were a third of those typical in America, and much of what was grown was squandered since it could neither be harvested nor stored correctly. Some 80 per cent of potatoes spoil during harvesting, and then over a half of what is left rots in storage; the USSR lost as much grain as it was later forced to purchase from abroad, 30–40 million tonnes.

The lack of good farm machinery meant that 66 per cent of work was carried out by hand. The shortage of housing and socio-cultural facilities in the villages gave rise to an extraordinary internal migration in which 27 million people left the villages for towns in the twenty years from 1965, thousands of villages lay deserted, and others were populated only by the old and infirm. In many areas the proportion of the population employed in agriculture had fallen to 5–10 per cent, giving rise to a great shortage of labour and a corresponding absence of rises in production. One of the speakers at the founding congress of the USSR Peasants' Union in June 1990 vividly summed up the situation when he argued that for decades the agrarian sector of the economy had been 'treated as a type of internal colony out of which resources were pumped for the development of towns and industry'.[61] Agrarian relations had been refeudalised and a distinctive type of new serfdom emerged.

Under the Soviet system there had been an integrated national economy but not a national market. The system had been marked by absurdities with little regional specialisation, and indeed each region tried to become self-sufficient in basic foodstuffs irrespective of climatic conditions and soil types. The collapse of the state distribution system in the absence of a national market actually increased attempts to achieve regional self-sufficiency. Traditional policies underpriced agricultural products leading to shortages, partially remedied by the price liberalisation of 1992 which cut back excess demand for agricultural products. In principle, commercial farms should respond to higher prices by increasing supplies, but the poor transport infrastructure, underdeveloped storage and retail networks, lack of credit and equipment, all inhibited the development of the market in foodstuffs.

Agrarian reform was therefore high on the agenda in the transition from communism and was an essential element in the restoration of private property and market forms of economic coordination.[62] However, the concept of agrarian reform is ambiguous, and can mean a simple redivision of land between different proprietors and users with the emphasis on the development of private ownership (land reform in the narrow sense), or it can mean the reorganisation of agrarian relations in their entirety, affecting not only land ownership but the whole structure of the agro-industrial complex. Both the first and the second scenarios would be long and hard in Russia.

Those who looked to the Chinese model of reforms soon learnt that there was one fundamental difference between the two countries. Whereas in China 70 per cent of the population still live in the countryside, in Russia the total was 38 million, less than a quarter of the population. In these circumstances the privatisation of land was a particularly difficult issue, and here a multilayered (*mnogoukladnoe*) approach was essential. It would have meant repeating earlier mistakes if now, instead of forcing people into collective (*kolkhoz*) or state (*sovkhoz*) farms, new policies forced them out. All types of agricultural activity had a part to play in post-communist Russian agriculture; the aim was not so much privatisation as marketisation.

The attempt to transform peasants into farmers, as under Stolypin, faced numerous obstacles, not least of which was the reluctance of the mass of the peasantry to lose the traditional support of the collective farm. Land is but one component of agriculture, and the private farmers, lacking seeds, equipment and credit, faced an uphill struggle for survival. The absence of a land market giving farmers the right to buy and sell land inhibited the development of private farms. The Law on the Land passed by the Soviet CPD in March 1990 refused explicitly to endorse the concept of private property in land, but it marked a considerable advance in accepting 'lifelong ownership, with the right of bequeathal' (article 3) as long as the land was used 'for family smallholdings, personal cultivation' and so on (article 20).[63] The collective and state farm system was not challenged.

In late 1990 and early 1991 the Russian parliament laid the legislative basis for agrarian reform in Russia. Yeltsin's government was committed to the break up of the collective and state farms and the creation of a system of small private ones.[64] On 23 November 1990, once it had become clear that the 500-day programme would not be implemented, parliament pushed ahead with its own radical economic reforms and abolished the state monopoly on land and endorsed private agriculture. Farmers were for the first time allowed to employ labour, regarded as exploitation by the old regime, and were exempted from taxes for 5 years. In December 1990 a law granted the ownership of land to anyone willing to use it for agricultural production for 10 years, and thus the collective-state farm system began to be dismantled. The presidential decree of 27 December 1991 on land reform ordered the mandatory transfer of land from collective and state farms to new forms of property rights including private farms. Collective-state farm managers were liable to large fines if they failed to allocate land within the predetermined time to individual farmers who left the old structures. Loss-making state-collective farms were to be abolished, while all the rest were to be reorganised either by division into private farms, forming producer cooperatives or joint stock companies, or some combination of these. The farms had until 1 March 1992 to register their plans and by 1 January 1993 to implement them. Regional land reform committees and local authorities were to monitor the progress of land redistribution and to overcome resistance.[65]

Land remained outside the purview of the nationalisation programme outlined above. Rutskoi, at first responsible for agrarian reform, admitted his ignorance of agricultural matters and was ambivalent towards land privatisation, if not towards agrarian reform as a whole.[66]

The Agrarian Union in the old parliament became the core of the Agrarian Party of Russia (APR), and their leader, Mikhail Lapshin, advocated gradual reforms that would not undermine social stability; in other words, they defended the old collective farm system. While the radical reformers sought to extend the rights of land ownership and to abolish restrictions on use and resale, this was opposed by the APR on the grounds that land would be bought up, probably by mafia-type organisations with spare cash for speculative purposes, squeezing out genuine farmers. The Sixth CPD on 16 April 1992 retained the 10-year ban on the resale of land and placed limitations on land entitlement. Democratic Russia collected a million signatures to hold a referendum on the land question. The Seventh CPD eased some of the restrictions on land entitlement, reducing restrictions on land sales to 5 years, and following the defeat of the Supreme Soviet, Yeltsin on 27 October decreed a free market in land, marketising Russian agriculture and ending the separation between agriculture and the rest of the economy that had existed since Stalin's collectivisation in 1930.[67] The 10-year moratorium on land sales was revoked and the system of compulsory state purchases of agricultural produce ended. The market in land remained constrained, however, and the issue remained controversial in the 1995 elections.

Under the old regime the state farms were centrally managed, like the rest of the economy, and managers were not free to decide on the choice of crops and types of animal husbandry that were best suited to local conditions. Instead, managers had to obey commands coming from Moscow and the local Party satraps. Not surprisingly, a great number were in effect bankrupt, kept afloat by generous subsidies from Moscow. The key element now was for the farms to gain their economic independence and to find genuinely profitable lines of activity. One of the options for the collective and state farms, commonly practised in Hungary and the Baltic, was to transform themselves into joint-stock companies, and for some to be reorganised into something like the Danish and Dutch producer's cooperatives. Marketing for smaller concerns could be assisted by processing and distribution cooperatives, popular in both France and Italy. Above all, a land bank like the Credit Agricole in France was essential.

The international trend is towards larger farms, so a radical shift to small farms in Russia could well reduce its comparative advantages. In market conditions a large proportion of state and collective farms could well turn out to be efficient economic enterprises. A model that could combine both competitiveness and equity was sought. General parcelling of the land into smaller units applied only to unprofitable farms, the more successful ones were better equipped with machinery and other means of production than private farms, but were now threatened by the withdrawal of preferential supplies of scarce fertilisers, agrochemicals, feedstuffs and machinery.

In contrast with the Baltic republics and the Western marches of the Soviet Union, the great mass of Russia had never known a system of consolidated family farming. Before 1929 peasants in effect owned land, but in the form of strips governed by the commune and subject to periodic redistribution. After 1991 the aim was not to reprivatise or reconstitute the family farm system, but to build it from scratch and thus to complete what Stolypin had tried to achieve when he was prime minister between 1906 and his assassination in 1911. The obstacles facing the independent farmer, however, were formidable. Not only did they lack tools, seeds, fodder, breeding stock and so on, but they also faced hostility from the collective farms and in many cases from the villagers themselves.

The number of peasant farms in Russia rose from 31,000 in October 1991 to 258,119 in July 1993 cultivating a total of nearly 11 million hectares, mostly in European Russia and particularly in the Volga and North Caucasus regions.[68] The size of land-holding varied across the country depending on the type of land, with larger holdings in the non-Black Earth Volga valley, and smaller holdings in the north, although the average was 40 hectares (100 acres). The Association of Peasant Farms and Cooperatives (AKKOR), the main body representing private farmers founded in January 1990 with government help, fought hard for the private ownership of land. Its attempts to achieve a market in agricultural land, despite the adoption of a new Land Code in July 1995, were blocked by people like Nikolai Komov, the head of Roskomzem (the government's Land Resources and Tenure Committee), who insisted that the land market should be based on leasing.

The tight monetary policy from September 1993 led to the end of advantageous credits for private farmers. The number of private farm failures increased sharply and by late 1994 more farms were being disbanded than being created; a third of the 283,000 farms remaining in November 1995 lacked a tractor and were severely under-capitalised. They employed an extraordinary 1.5 million people, some 18 per cent of the total agricultural labour force, but produced only 6 per cent of total output.[69] According to Rutskoi only a very small proportion produced food for the market rather than just for themselves.[70] The lack of credit and impediments to a market in land provoked the danger of land parcelling, the creation of farms that in the long-term would prove unviable since land could not be bought to create more viable units. Dissatisfaction with government policy led to the creation of the Union of Landowners in December 1994, led by AKKOR's president Vladimir Bashmachnikov, with directly political functions; affiliation with Russia Our Home in the 1995 elections reflected the weak political base of rural liberals.

Agriculture faced enormous price increases for machinery, livestock and other inputs; a new type of 'scissors crisis' emerged because of the growing disparity between agricultural and industrial prices. Output fell by at least a third, labour productivity collapsed, the infrastructure of rural social life (schools, hospitals and the like) fell into disrepair and rural incomes declined. Payments for deliveries were often delayed, credits were denied while investment for agricultural infrastructure dried up. Not only had the window of opportunity for radical agrarian reform been missed but the deteriorating condition of the sector strengthened conservative parties and discredited radical economic reform in its entirety. The result was the strong showing of the APR in the December 1993 elections, a protest vote largely transferred to the CPRF in December 1995. The Yeltsin regime had clearly failed to build a political constituency in the countryside for agrarian reform and had managed to alienate even its natural supporters.[71]

Agrarian reform entailed a revolution in the countryside, and was resisted not only by the agricultural bureaucracy but also by a rural population accustomed to the security provided by the traditional neo-feudal agrarian system. The most active people had long ago been killed or moved to the cities. The collective and state farms were the centre of local life and the population, with its pensioners, agrarian specialists, local schools, and much else, all depended on the network of social and economic relations that centred on them. Take away the farm, and the village society and economy was in danger of collapse. Here, too, nomenklatura privatisation was common, as farm directors, the great majority of whom had been communists, sold land to the local elite but resisted distributing it to their own peasants, though attitudes slowly changed under pressure from the centre.

The structure of village society is not susceptible to easy generalisation, but certain groups can be identified. They include dynamic families, often with leadership or technical experience in the old collective-state farm system, able to run an independent farm; single village pensioners dependent on the collective-state farm; village school graduates who might be deterred from migration to the cities as unemployment rises and thus look for opportunites closer to hand; a large group of lumpenised and usually alcoholic farm workers; a growing reverse migration of urbanites returning to the land; city dwellers with relatives in the countryside; demobilised soldiers who made up a large proportion of private farmers; and refugees or migrants from the 'near abroad'. Thus agrarian society is far more complex than some standard descriptions of a drink-sodden brutalised mass, and there was enough human potential to create an independent peasantry – given the right technical and political conditions.

Agrarian reform was therefore a highly complicated question, with the central problem being how to maintain production while simultaneously conducting a major sociopolitical revolution in the countryside. Numerous problems remained, such as the optimum level of tax rates, the problem of forming a land market and the development of mortage credit on land. Reform, moreover, was accompanied by a sharp deterioration in the terms of trade between town and country; prices of industrial goods rose far faster than agricultural produce. Despite the diversion of some 27 per cent of the federal budget to the needs of agriculture in 1995, grain deficits continued. The disappointing harvest of 63.5 million metric tons in 1995 (down from 81 million in 1994) reversed the trend for grain imports to decline, from 35 million tons in 1991 to 11 million in 1993 and 3 million in 1994. Environmental factors also play their part. Against the background of the devastating environmental damage caused not only by the wasteful and irresponsible Soviet pattern of industrial development but also by the supreme Bolshevik disdain for the earth itself, its forests, waters, land and air, the revival of Russian agriculture was faced with a heavy legacy. While there is now a general awareness that agriculture has to maintain the natural and social environment, there is less agreement on how this is to be achieved.

EVALUATION OF RUSSIAN ECONOMIC REFORM

About a dozen fully fledged macroeconomic programmes between 1992 and 1995 were derailed because of political instability; economic reform staggered forward in response to short term crises and needs. The notion of shock therapy strictly speaking applies only to the first months of 1992, and thereafter lax money supply undermined economic stabilisation until the tight money supply policy of 1994–95 forced down inflation – and living standards. Despite the tendency to view developments through apocalyptic spectacles, and given the appalling starting conditions and the lack of a coherent reform programme this is understandable, Russia has nevertheless made significant advances on the road to a market-based economy.

The first years of Russia's economic transformation were difficult but not catastrophic. Prices multiplied by 2.6 in 1991 and 1992, by 9.4 in 1993, by 3.24 in 1994, and in 1995 by only 2.31. Overall, in the period of reform prices had increased by 4,800.[72] Living standards fell (although during 1992–93 real incomes more or less kept pace with inflation, but following the tight money policy during 1994–95 fell by 8 per cent in 1995); goods faced problems of demand rather than supply; inflation was on a rollercoaster of rises and falls; the budget deficit remained large but was gradually brought under control when it stopped being funded by monetary emissions; some foreign capital was invested in Russia but was dwarfed by capital flight; investment by 1995 had fallen to 25 per cent of its 1990 level; industrial production fell by unprecedented percentages but gradually bottomed out (falling by only 3 per cent in 1995 compared to 21 per cent in 1994); the fall in overall GDP also slowed down (falling 4 per cent in 1995 compared to 15 per cent in 1994); inequalities increased sharply but income differentials had stabilised by late 1995, with the richest 10 per cent earning thirteen times more than the poorest 10 per cent; unemployment rose (though not as fast as predicted); and the rouble continued to depreciate. Critics point to the large black economy and the associated difficulty of collecting taxes, the emergence of rentier capitalism and the priority of merchant capital over industrial production, and the problem of monopolies. In agriculture there was only a limited development of competitive market forms, and the state continued to pour in subsidies. In industry privatisation tended to change the form but not the content of enterprise behaviour and failed to stimulate consistent enterprise restructuring. Privatisation allowed an already privileged class to consolidate its position by the transformation of public goods into private wealth. Whole sectors of the economy were criminalised, often with the connivance if not the participation of the government agencies designed to regulate them. Ellman notes that shock therapy as a survival programme had been remarkably successful, as a liberalisation programme there had been some positive results, but as a stabilisation programme it was a failure.[73]

Aslund, however, stresses the enormous achievements of the Russian economy in the last few years. The military-industrial complex acted as less of a brake on the marketisation of the economy than the CBR and the old state managers, and the total fall in the standard of living did not exceed 10 per cent – and this at a time of dramatic economic transformation. Aslund argues that the effect would have been better if 'shock therapy' had been pursued with even more vigour, removing export and price controls and ending the rouble zone. As it is, the privatisation process masterminded by Chubais, in his view, transformed the country.[74] Shops are heavily stocked with a broad range of domestic and foreign goods; the shops themselves, now mostly in private hands, have become more attractive and queues have largely disappeared, although prices, even when adjusted for inflation, are much higher than in the past. Privatisation of much of the housing, shops and services had transformed the individual's relationship to property, but agrarian reform moved slowly. Although the first stage of industrial privatisation was nominal, it prepared the way for the structural transformation of the second phase. Even the dramatic falls in production should be placed in context. While official figures from Goskomstat, for example, up to 1995 continued to show a decline in industrial output, they did not take into account private production. The large new private sector created by the reforms was simply not taken into account by official statistics. An upbeat assessment came in the OECD's country report for Russia in 1995:

> The role of the state in controlling the economy has been vastly reduced, domestic prices and foreign trade have been extensively liberalised, and monetary and fiscal policy is increasingly moving towards operational standards typical of market economies.[75]

A structural transformation of the economy had taken place, with cuts in defence spending, the rise of a vigorous financial services industry and the growth of the service sector, rising from 33 per cent of GDP in 1990 to 50 per cent in 1994; for the first time since Stalin's industrialisation production of services exceeded production of goods. The reforms gained a self-sustaining character, having learnt by doing some of the rudiments of the operation of a market economy. Powerful interests were now bound up with the continued marketisation of the economy, including some 40 million shareholders as well as a vigorous new class of entrepreneurs. The process, however, required political stability, a clear legal framework and the development of self-regulatory mechanisms to avoid the endless repetition of the scandals and excesses of the early reform years.

The measure of success was the stimulation of economic activity, the modernisation of the structure of industry, competitiveness on world markets, rising living standards, a stable and convertible currency, and budgetary stability. The bill for inefficiency was no longer to be paid by the consumer but shifted back to the monopolist industrial structures, forcing them to reduce excessive costs and increase production. This remained to be achieved, giving rise to no shortage of critical analysis. Marshall Goldman, for example, explains 'why economic reforms in Russia have not worked'. Shock therapy in his view failed to stimulate the supply side of the Russian economy and instead sucked in imports. Rather perversely, he holds the absence of a dynamic entrepreneurial class responsible (together with political infighting) for the failure of the economy to take off;[76] but where was this entrepreneurial sector to come from in Russian conditions if not through a dynamic (albeit painful) breakthrough into market relations? Russia is not China (with a huge peasant economy geared to the market), and neither is it Poland or Hungary, which even before the fall of communism had vigorous entrepreneurial sectors. Russia, in this sense, was indeed an economic *tabula rasa*, but one already distorted by powerful shadow networks of economic exchange.

Yeltsin insisted that the great achievement of shock therapy had been the change in popular attitudes, the weakening of the dependency syndrome and an awareness that the transition to the market was now, after so many false starts, for real and that new opportunities existed.[77] In a vigorous defence of his policies on the anniversary of the coup Gaidar condemned all the forces holding back the reform process, the military-industrial complex, the farm lobby, and the professional economists and others calling for subsidies and protectionism. He insisted that the reforms were on course and that 'the market has started to work'. Indeed, he argued that the development of the market was the only force that could keep the country together.[78] Gaidar's policy focused on four key principles: the government would not return to the state distribution of resources; it would not print money to revitalise the economy; it would not freeze prices or wages; and it would not interfere with the market establishing the exchange rate between the rouble and the dollar.[79] At the Seventh CPD on 2 December 1992 Gaidar argued that his greatest achievement was to have launched reform in a country stifled by more than 70 years of communism, and the predicted mass unrest had not taken place.[80]

Attitudes had indeed changed, and even the CPRF did not support a return to the command economy and accepted a role for foreign investment. There had been little public protest, and the level of strikes was below that of 1991. The administrative allocation of goods and services had been abolished and a genuine market had emerged. After years of suspicion the international financial community and the industrialised West committed themselves to support Russia's economic reforms, despite shortcomings and reverses.[81] Russia began to be reintegrated into the world economy, hosting the 'G8' summit in spring 1996, and the idea of regional and national specialisation had at last been grasped. While shortages remained, the sharp fall in demand (rather than increases in production) allowed an increase in stocks and the warnings of famine that had been common in 1991 disappeared. Monopolisation of the economy remained but it was increasingly bypassed. The decline might have bottomed out and taken on a sectoral character, marked by continued decline in some industries but by growth in light industry and consumer services.

Much was made of the unsalubrious 'primary accumulation of capital' phase of early Western capitalism: Russia, it is argued, is only experiencing a delayed version. If this is the case, the best policy would be sound money, minimal and simple laws, straightforward regulation and basic taxes to unfetter Russian entrepreneurism and allow it to race 'ahead of our Western form of corporate capitalism, which has grown flabby and slow. It is possible to imagine a future of Russian capitalism that asserts itself in the early 21st century as the envy of the world'.[82] However, the law of uneven development would suggest that stages are not repeated but jumped, and while capitalism was new to Russia, it was not the early stages of capitalism that Russia needed. The structure of modern capitalism as a world system has changed radically.

Russia may find itself locked into a type of comprador capitalism in which small elites with external links exploit resources to the benefit of foreign capital rather than developing a solid indigenous industrial and commercial structure. Russia had great difficulties in establishing an adequate market environment because of structural and cultural factors. In conditions of high transaction costs in a market plagued by corruption, banditry, political opportunism and fiscal instability, entrepreneurs sought to maximise immediate returns to the detriment of long-term investment. Rather than trading acting as the nucleus and source of capital for a productive market economy, it might end up as the substitute for a genuine market system. Rather than acting as a motor of development, the system may become endemically corrupt in the manner of some Third World countries, and find it very difficult to break out of the cycle of misdevelopment.

The modernisation of Russian industry involves not only the creation of a national market and regional specialisation to overcome the vertical centralisation of Soviet planning, but also overcoming the problem endemic to mature industrial powers, that of old 'rustbelt' industries. Even if Russian economic reforms were successful, the problem of the old coal and steel industries would remain, affecting in particular the Kuzbass in Siberia (Kemerovo region) and the Urals. In the short-term regional fragmentation accelerated, exacerbated by the uneven embrace of market relations. Existing regional imbalances in standards of living and incomes were exaggerated, and prices varied greatly even between neighbouring towns. Land reform was most effective in the south, whereas in the north and the non-Black Earth regions they marked time. The great majority of new businesses and joint enterprises were to be found in Moscow, St Petersburg and Nizhnii Novgorod, whereas traditional industrial areas, quite apart from the political complexion of the regional leadership, found it difficult to adjust to competitive market conditions. An area like Udmurtia, with three-quarters of its workforce employed in military enterprises, could not survive without state orders and subsidies, and a rapid transition to the market was out of the question.

The radical economic programme bitterly divided the political scene. Early fears that the RUIE and its allies in the Civic Union and other corporate associations would compel the government to modify its policies appear to have been exaggerated. Enterprise directors were split between a moderate group favouring an intensification of radical reform, and a conservative bloc calling for a change of course.[83] Representatives of the industrial lobby in the government were not able substantially to influence policy,[84] and, indeed, appear to have 'gone native' and become converts to liberal economics. Managers were split by industry and by responses to changing circumstances; some sought to exploit the new opportunities, while others still hoped for government subsidies. One of the candidates for the premiership in December 1992, Vladimir Kadannikov, gave a ringing endorsement of Gaidar's reforms on behalf of industrialists and the 150,000 workers in his semi-privatised Volga Car Plant

(VAZ);[85] while the Agrarians in Chernoymyrdin's government lobbied hard for soft subsidies to agriculture.

Opponents of shock therapy argued that Russian conditions differed from elsewhere, lacking an effective distribution system, commercial banks or a labour market. Price liberalisation in these circumstances would lead to economic slump. They insisted that the lifting of price controls and subsidies should have been preceded by building institutions and the demonopolisation of the economy. Gaidar responded by arguing that while price liberalisation was an instantaneous act, privatisation was a long-term process, and the two could not be placed in a situation of fatal dependence. While it was easy for Gaidar's opponents to make the populist claim that his reforms were impoverishing the people and that the monopolistic production system should have been dismantled before freeing prices, neither in Russia nor in any other post-communist country has a genuine alternative economic programme been described in detail. The Civic Union's programme for the transition, which included price controls and other residues of the planned economy for the 'stabilisation period', were almost certainly incompatible with the transition to a market economy, and so too were the economic policies of the CPRF.

Yevgenii Yasin, director of an independent research institute advising the RUIE and from November 1994 economics minister, accused Gaidar of a 'lack of reality', failing to realise that in a country dominated by monopolies the lifting of price controls would simply allow managers of state enterprises to raise their prices. Yasin became economics minister in November 1994 whereupon he modified his views. In an extensive analysis Yavlinskii poured withering criticism on Gaidar's reforms, but the most significant feature of the critique was the absence of any positive alternative.[86] Gaidar's team was described by the economic writer Selyunin as the first qualified government in his lifetime.[87] Shatalin, the director of the International Institute of Economic and Social Reforms, warned that Russia could lose half of its industrial production and become a raw materials supplier for the developed world. He insisted that it was tragedy for Russia that Gaidar had chosen the liberal rather than the socially-oriented model of the market economy, since the latter was more suited to Russian conditions.[88]

It was these arguments that Khasbulatov deployed at the Seventh CPD.[89] In response to Khasbulatov's argument that the choice lay between the 'Americanisation' of the economy or more socially-oriented Scandinavian social-democratic approaches, Gaidar riposted that the choice lay between becoming a developed economy or a Third World one.[90] His arguments were to no avail, and parliament replaced him by Chernomyrdin who put an end to talk of shock therapy and sought a more regulated path to the market economy although he, too, broadly followed the course laid out by Gaidar. The room for economic manoeuvre for post-communist governments was very limited indeed, and while all realised that there was no way back, the attempt to salvage something from the past could be as dangerous as destroying the past in its entirety. Even the communist faction in the Sixth Duma realised that there could be no return to the command economy, but their industrial and social policies threatened to prolong the trauma of economic transition indefinitely.

The command economy in the Soviet Union disintegrated before the communist system itself. Russia was faced by an awesome legacy of economic mismanagement, mismodernisation and decay. The question of economic transformation was a question of what sort of Russia was to emerge from the shell of communism. No longer did Russia set itself up as an alternative model but sought to join global processes of economic interdependence, but found that there was no single model of the market economy. Russia and the other post-communist societies had to feel their way forwards on the edge of a precipice in the dark. The cold rationalism of shock therapy imposed enormous strains on the economy and society, and its benefits, like a stable currency and improved productivity, appeared elusive. However, no other economic programme provided a coherent alternative. The political system survived the various crises, and indeed gradually socialised the population into acceptance of the market. The lesson of the reform experience in Eastern Europe, however, appeared to be that while drastic economic liberalism might be necessary in the first stage, it had to give way to strategies aimed at stimulating growth and combining macroeconomic stabilisation with microeconomic enterprise viability and national development. Amid the endless debates, however, one thing was clear: the fate of democracy in Russia and the stability of the international system depended on the successful economic transformation of Russia.

13 Social transformation

No society can surely be flourishing and happy, of which the far greater part of the members are poor and miserable.

Adam Smith[1]

Democracy is as much a social and cultural project as a political one: it cannot be built in the air, in the minds of intellectuals and politicians, but needs to be rooted in society itself. As Solzhenitsyn put it: 'Stolypin believed that it is impossible to create a state governed by laws without first having an independent citizen: social structure precedes any political programme and is a more fundamental entity.'[2] After 74 years of the Soviet regime the social basis for democracy in Russia, while not absent, was weak. As Shakhrai, the state legal adviser at the time, put it: 'We have no middle class of property owners upon which to build a stable government. If I have something to lose: my work, my apartment, my family, my dacha, my car, my savings, then I will be a support for the state and of a stable social stratum. Unfortunately, our society has not progressed to that stage yet.'[3] The basic principle of the reformers was, to quote Solzhenitsyn again, that 'there can be no independent citizen without private property.'[4]

SOCIAL STRUCTURE

In Russia democracy came before the development of a bourgeoisie, and as Barrington Moore long ago observed, 'No bourgeois, no democracy.'[5] The existence of a substantial middle class is no guarantee of democracy, as Germany discovered in the inter-war years, but to date there has been no liberal democracy without a capitalist social structure. A traumatised and propertyless society jeopardised the building of democracy in Russia, and the weakness of social organisations, like trade unions and professional bodies, undermined effective political institutions. While the concept of transition refers properly to political change, Russia entered a period of accelerated social transformation affecting all aspects of class and elite relations, the family and social groups. The marketisation of social relations undermined not only the achievements, however rudimentary, of the Soviet welfare state, but also challenged the whole network of existing social relations and cultural values.

While the events of August 1991 were dramatic and came to symbolise the fall of the old regime, the Soviet system had already undergone a long decay since at least the death of Stalin in 1953. The old authority system underwent significant evolution, and at the same time an embryonic new pattern of social relations began to emerge. The protracted degeneration of the old system itself became a factor in shaping the new order as features like patronage networks, corruption and clientilism became endemic. The long transition allowed morbid systems of social irresponsibility to become firmly lodged in the body social as a pseudo-civil society regulated not by law but by the anti-law of customary practices took shape. The emergence of powerful criminal networks in the lee of decaying Party authority, the evolution of the political nomenklatura appointments mechanism into a corrupt social phenomenon, the development of a shadow economy preyed on by protection rackets and living off the inefficiencies of the state economy, all this and more shaped the social subject of the transition.

The 74 years of the Soviet regime had churned society as if it had gone through a concrete mixer. Tatyana Zaslavskaya argued that instead of the social structure having become simpler, it had in fact become more complex than comparable capitalist societies. Groups, classes, elites, workers, peasants, and indeed whole peoples, were displaced, mixed up and thrown down. Instead of the organic growth of social complexity and differentiation over a more or less steady pattern of development, the USSR had telescoped decades of modernisation (and an ideologically driven pattern of mismodernisation at that) into just a few years. Social ties today show great signs of instability; the very fabric of society has been torn and the process of healing will take decades. As Lech Wałeşa observed, 'It is very easy to make fish soup out of a bowl of goldfish, but it is very difficult to get a bowl of goldfish out of fish soup.'

The old regime recognised three great groups in society depending on their relationship to property and the means of production: the two classes of workers and peasants and the stratum of the intelligentsia. The ranks of the working class had increased rapidly, rising from some 1.7 million in Soviet Russia in 1920 to 45 million in 1989. Stalinist industrialisation had seen the growth of the working class, the accompanying cultural revolution the emergence of a Soviet technical intelligentsia, while collectivisation destroyed the peasantry as a class and encouraged a mass exodus to the towns. From the 1950s to the 1970s an average each year of some 1.7 million people fled the devastated countryside to seek new opportunities in towns.[6] In the early 1990s 26 per cent of the population lived in rural areas, a proportion that began to rise as life in the cities became tougher for certain sections of the population, above all pensioners. By 1989 out of a total Soviet population of 284.5 million there were 117.24 million (41.21 per cent) workers and employees, 19 per cent of whom were employed in agriculture and forestry.[7] Russia began its post-communist journey with a higher proportion of its workforce in state employment than most other republics. By the end of 1991 the non-state sector in Russia (including collective farms) contained 23 per cent of the total employed population and the share of total employment in the private and individual sector rose rapidly from the 2.7 million (2.3 per cent) in late 1991.[8]

The kneading of Soviet society and the political controls inhibiting the development of group activity led many observers to talk of the 'lumpenisation' of society. Indeed the word *lumpen*, in Marxist terminology designating the declassed and lumpish masses below the proletariat, became one of the standard terms to describe post-communist Russian society. The symptoms were social apathy and political passivity, but the defining feature was the lack of property and hence the lack of a stake in society. Workers, peasants and indeed intelligentsia had all allegedly been lumpenised, cast adrift in Soviet society and prey to demagogy and jealous of the success of others. Lumpenisation entailed a type of negative egalitarianism in which society was levelled down to the lowest common denominator, distinguished not by equality of opportunity but by an equality in poverty impatient of complex solutions.[9]

Table 6 Population of USSR, Russia and some Russian republics

Year	Total population (million)	Of whom			
		Urban		Rural	
		million	%	million	%
USSR					
1979	262.4	162.9	62	99.5	38
1989	286.7	189.2	66	97.5	34
Russia					
1979	137.6	95.4	69	42.2	31
1989	147.4	108.4	74	39.0	26
1990	148.0	109.2	74	38.8	26
Tatarstan					
1979	3.4	2.2	63	–	–
1989	3.6	2.7	73	–	–
Buryatia					
1979	0.9	0.5	57	–	–
1989	1.0	0.6	62	–	–
Yakutia					
1979	0.8	0.5	61	–	–
1989	1.1	0.7	67	–	–

Source: For USSR, *USSR: Facts and Figures Annual*, edited by Alan P. Pollard, vol. 15, 1991 (Gulf Breeze, FL, Academic International Press, 1991), p. 498; for Russia, *RSFSR v tsifrakh v 1989g.*, (Moscow, Finansy i statistika, 1990), p. 21; for republics, *Izvestiya*, 28 April 1989, *Pravda*, 29 April 1989.

DEMOGRAPHY AND WELFARE

Russia suffers from a severe demographic crisis (see Table 7). Natural population increase has been falling for at least a quarter of a century, reflecting the pattern common to most developed industrial societies where planned parenting has seen a dramatic decrease in the size of families. In Russia the fall in the number of women in the primary childbearing age group, the lack of confidence in the future, increased levels of stress in a changing society and declining living standards provoked a sharp decrease in the fertility rate (the average number of children born to a woman between the ages of 15 and 50), falling from around 2 from the 1960s to the late 1980s to less than 1.4 in 1993.[10] The average family has not two but one child, thus falling below the level of natural reproduction of population levels. In 1960 the RSFSR had seen a natural population growth of 2 million,[11] in 1985 749,500; whereas in 1992, for the first time since the war, there was negative natural population growth as deaths outnumbered births by 190,000.[12] In 1994 the population declined by 920,000,[13] a fall that was offset by inmigration from the former Soviet republics, but the total population still fell by 124,000. By 1995 it appeared that the demographic situation had stabilised; the rate of natural increase (births over deaths) changed from −5.9 per 1,000 in 1994 to −5.5 in 1995.

The average Russian family lacks the clear predominance of either the male or female side; it is increasingly nuclear as the tradition of living with parents and grandparents wanes; and it is often childless or one-child. Children tend to be economically dependent on their parents for longer than in the West because of housing shortages, low wages and other labour market inflexibilities. Changing perceptions of morality have given rise to an exceptionally large

Table 7 Births, deaths and natural movement of Russian population (thousands)

Year	Births	Deaths	Growth
1960	2,782	886	1,896
1970	1,904	1,131	773
1980	2,203	1,526	677
1985	2,375	1,625	750
1990	1,989	1,656	333
1992	1,598	1,805	−297

Sources: *Naselenie SSSR, 1988* (Moscow, 1989), p. 40; *Demograficheskii ezhegodnik 1991* (Moscow, Goskomstat, 1992), p. 55; *Moskovskie novosti*, no. 49 (5 December 1993), p. 6.

proportion of marriages being provoked by the pregnancy of the bride, and it is these marriages that prove to be the most unstable, with the child almost always staying with the mother. If in 1960 12 out of every 100 marriages ended in divorce, by 1990 an extraordinary 42 out of every 100 marriages failed.[14] Fewer than a quarter of divorced women enter into a second marriage within 10 years of divorcing, thus millions of children live in one-parent families without the benefit of the father's influence, and usually without any male role models at all.[15]

The decline in the birth rate, falling by 13 per cent in 1992, was accompanied by a dramatic rise in the mortality rate; the death rate from unnatural causes alone rose in that year by 8 per cent.[16] The infant mortality rate (for children up to the age of 1) reached 17 per 1000 in 1992, much higher than the average for developed countries.[17] It was these sort of figures which provoked the national-patriots to argue that Russia was victim of planned genocide, that democracy was no more than a Western plot to undermine the very genetic basis for Russian life.[18]

The starkest symptom of the social crisis was the declining life expectancy of Soviet men, ranked 54th out of 56 countries that supplied data in 1989. Average male life expectancy fell from 65 in 1986 to 63.5 in 1990, and then fell dramatically to 57.3 in 1994.[19] Female life expectancy was higher but had also declined to 71.1, giving an average life expectancy in Russia of some 65 years compared to 75.5 in America (72 for men and 69 for women). There is a marked variation within Russia, with life expectancy in rural areas in general lower, and with regional disparities, with the situation worst in the Far East and Eastern Siberia, and best in the North Caucasus and the Volga region. There are also differences between the old Soviet republics, with the highest life expectancy in 1990 in Armenia at 68.4 years for urban residents, and the lowest in Turkmenistan at 60.6.

There are many reasons for high Russian male mortality, ranging from the rising number of workplace and traffic accidents, the prevalence of heart disease, a high suicide rate (rising from 39,150 in 1990 to 61,886 in 1994),[20] and violent deaths (rising from 16,000 to 26,000 over the same period).[21] High rates of tobacco addiction and the instability of family structures play their part. One of the main factors, however, is alcohol abuse, with *per capita* consumption in Russia for the first time exceeding that of France in 1993. Between 1986 and 1994 alcohol consumption rose from 11 litres per head of population to 14.5; while deaths directly caused by alcohol (per 100,000 of population) over the same period rose from 9.3 to 37.8.[22] Gorbachev's anti-alcohol campaign of 1985-87 had dramatically misfired, encouraging the production of low-grade moonshine liquor (*samogon*), and the abolition of the centuries-old state monopoly on vodka production in 1992 (as part of Russia's commitment to economic liberalisation) saw prices fall dramatically.[23] In 1995 the vodka monopoly was reimposed in a desperate attempt to avert the social catastrophe. The deeper causes of Russia's alcohol dependence, however, still have to be treated, with some arguing that it was a response to the authoritarianism of society and its profound inequalities, while others, like the sociologist Igor Bestuzhev-Lada, insisting that the system itself was responsible for alcoholism, and that the only cure was the democratisation of society and the development of a citizenry responsible for its own actions.[24]

The higher death rate for men led to a sharp gender imbalance, with 9.2 million more women than men in Russia's population of 148.5 million by early 1993. The age structure was also imbalanced, with 29.1 per cent of the population at that time above working age. There are some 37 million pensioners in Russia today, and there are plans to raise the retirement age, currently 60 years for men and 55 for women. For every 1,000 people of working age, there are 770 non-working (pensioners and children under 16).[25] The nearly one-third of Russia's population who are pensioners are an important factor in electoral politics, tending to be more keen on casting their votes on election day and allegedly taking a more conservative approach than the rest of the population, which under Russian conditions means voting communist.

Advocates of the 'strong hand' argued that democracy might have to be sacrificed to allow market liberalism to develop: a more accurate formulation suggests that it was the welfarism of social democracy rather than democracy *per se* that was sacrificed in the transition to a market economy. Budgetary constraints forced a retreat of the frontiers of welfarism, but in the long-run the aim was to divert resources to productive investment and industrial modernisation. The reformers were divided over the degree to which the inevitable hardship resulting from economic reform should be compensated: how generous should the system of social provision be to protect the weaker sectors of society?[26] At one extreme were the neo-liberals Piyasheva, Pinsker and Nikolai Shmelev, who accepted that economic reforms would inevitably entail a high social cost. They advocated complete deregulation and minimal controls on the free market and condemned rationing systems as distorting the operation of the market: on the other side, Civic Union insisted that full-scale free market economic policies could not be applied to Russia in its fragile state. Yeltsin's government steered a middle course, seeking to maintain a minimum threshold of welfare benefits but imposed cuts in the general level of social provision. Repeated promises to inject a 'greater social content' into the reforms were defeated by the equally harsh imperative of financial stabilisation.

The onset of market relations exacerbated the housing crisis inherited from the Soviet Union. According to official statistics, in Moscow alone in 1994 there were 30,000 homeless people, but the actual figure may well have exceeded 100,000, while in Russia as a whole some 4 million were estimated to be homeless.[27] Out of a population of some 8 million in Moscow, some 8 per cent still live in communal flats – *kommunalki* – in which numerous tenants share the kitchen and bathroom.[28] Their number is declining, however, as tenants are moved out and the apartments are converted into large and highly desirable flats.

Soviet health care had always been lamentably underfunded, despite attempts during perestroika to improve the situation. The USSR spent only about 3.6 per cent of its GNP on health care, half that of most West European countries and a third of the sum spent in the United States. The reforms had undermined already low wages, and the provision of medicines and equipment became even more sporadic. Following the fall of communism funds devoted to health fell to 1.8 per cent of the Russian budget in 1994, and traditional shortfalls and inequalities in the standard of provision were exacerbated.[29] Standards of hygiene were never very high but now deteriorated further, while staff were demoralised by low pay and lack of resources and medicines. For all but the richest, standards of health care fell sharply, a decline dramatically illustrated by the outbreak of cholera and diptheria across Russia.[30] Cases of infectious diseases increased sharply, with tuberculosis once again prevalent in the majority of Russia's regions. The breakdown of mass immunisation was one of the main factors allowing diptheria to return, while the spread of cholera was facilitated by antiquated water and sewage systems.

Only a small proportion were the 'winners' in the transition, while the vast majority in the short-term saw their incomes shrink and their job security eroded. In his speech to parliament on 25 September 1992 Gaidar admitted that 30 million people lived below the poverty line; but the whole notion and the appropriate level of such a 'line' has been much debated. In Russia it is based on level of household income required to maintain a minimum level of consumption, but the actual income in many families is often hidden from the authorities and as the tax system began to bite was usually understated, quite apart from wide regional variations. Real income did not fall dramatically in the first years of liberalisation because of inflationary budgetary emissions, but the imposition of a tight money policy saw real incomes fall by 13 per cent in 1995. On average in 1995 a quarter of the population had incomes below the poverty line but the number had fallen during the course of the year from 49.4 million in January (33 per cent) to 28.9 million in December (20 per cent). Income stratification also slowed, with the richest 10 per cent of the population gaining 27 per cent of the country's total income, while the poorest 10 per cent had only 2.5 per cent, with 63 per cent of the population earning below average incomes.[31]

While the USSR had a highly developed system of social security benefits it was inappropriate for a market-based economy, quite apart from being extremely wasteful. Budgetary constraints alone forced a radical overhaul of the social security system to target it towards low income groups and to improve the social safety net. While 'Benefit programs must provide security but at the same time discourage dependence on the state', the optimum balance is something that eludes most developed societies let alone the former communist states.[32] The main thrust of reform is to lessen direct dependence on the state budget by developing employer insurance schemes with employee contributions for health, pensions and unemployment benefits.[33]

The Ministry for Social Welfare, headed by Pamfilova from November 1991, played a key role in neutralising opposition to the hardships caused by reform. The ministry was responsible for the more vulnerable sections of society, the aged, invalids, large and single families, refugees and the homeless. Pamfilova admired the German model of social welfare which gave assistance when required but at the same time discourages dependency. She insisted that despite the price rises Russia would not be swept by violent social unrest: 'The Russian people are wiser than the politicians. They quickly spot a lie and don't fall for cheap provocations.'[34]

WAGES AND UNEMPLOYMENT

The transition to the market economy meant changing the whole social landscape. Enterprises under the old system were not only production units offering pay, but also provided food, housing, holidays, medical and childcare. Local authorities, short of money themselves, could take over only a fraction of these responsibilities. The economic reforms challenged what the Chinese called the 'three irons' of the Maoist era: the lifelong job, lifelong wage and lifelong

Table 8 Employment in the state and non-state sectors

Type of employment	1990		1991		1992	
	Million	*%*	*Million*	*%*	*Million*	*%*
State sector:						
State enterprises	61.3	82.4	55.6	75.3	49.4	68.1
Social organisations	0.6	0.8	0.7	1.0	0.5	0.7
Consumer cooperatives	1.5	2.0	1.5	2.0	1.5	2.1
Collective-state farms	4.0	5.4	4.0	5.4	3.4	4.7
Non-state sector:						
Joint ventures	0.1	0.1	0.1	0.1	0.2	0.3
Leased enterprises	2.8	3.8	5.6	7.6	4.8	6.6
Share-holding societies	0.2	0.3	1.1	1.5	4.0	5.5
Economic societies	0.1	0.1	0.8	1.1	3.1	4.3
Other cooperatives	2.6	3.5	2.5	3.4	2.1	2.9
Private activities	1.2	1.6	1.9	2.6	3.5	4.8
Total:	74.4	100.0	73.8	100.0	72.5	100.0

Source: Sheila Marnie, 'How Prepared is Russia for Mass Unemployment?', *RFE/RL Research Report*, vol. 1, no. 2 (4 December 1992), p. 45.

position. This was balanced by the 'iron ricebowl', a minimal but secure standard of living. Marketisation now challenged the traditional pattern of work, wages and job security.

Money wages in the Soviet Union by 1991 had fallen far below even the miserly rate of neighbouring countries.[35] Khasbulatov stressed that the Soviet state had been a super-exploiter, giving only 7 to 15 per cent of the labour value back to the worker in the form of wages, whereas under capitalism workers received 60–70 per cent.[36] The economist Matlin argued that the Soviet government had long been waging an economic war against its own people, a war which had intensified during perestroika. By 1991 surplus value reached 210 per cent of wages, rising from 126 per cent in 1985 and 102 per cent in 1908 under the allegedly exploitative Tsarist regime. The methodology on which these figures are based can be disputed, but the trend is clear: late communism was twice as exploitative as late Tsarism. Matlin argued that 'The political revolution of August [1991] should be followed by an economic revolution, dismantling the state monopoly of the means of production.'[37]

Economic reform imposed new hardships and provoked the further pauperisation of society. The prices of goods, including basic foodstuffs, began to approximate world levels, yet the average monthly pay remained at absurdly low levels. As the economic reforms began to bite, money wages tended to fall even lower in relative terms and wage differentials increased sharply as the transition to the market sharply exacerbated social inequalities. Shock therapy was accompanied by growing inequality, with the incomes of the richest 10 per cent rising from five times those of the poorest 10 per cent in 1991 to thirty-five times in 1995.[38] Those with access to foreign currency and goods, or employed by a successful cooperative or company, could become relatively rich very quickly, while those tied to a state wage and pensions saw their position further undermined. The economic reforms initially depressed standards of living and made the monetary measure of household wealth even more arbitrary than before.

The old system of subsidised housing, transport, childcare and much else had rendered the money wage part of income relatively less important,[39] but now the end of generalised subsidies meant that money wages had to cover far more of individual needs. Access to quality health care, pre-school facilities and even education now increasingly had to be paid for. The government found itself trapped, since wage rises could only be met by increasing budget expenses in the form of subsidies, and this would only return the whole process to square one. Yeltsin was forced to negotiate a tortuous path between the pressures of the IMF for financial stabilisation, on the one hand, and the ability of the Russian people to endure yet more hardship on the other. He took a middle path, and the dash for the market was tempered by attempts to cushion some of the painful effects of the transition for vulnerable groups by ensuring at least a survival income.[40] Miners in the Kuzbass region of Siberia and elsewhere threatened industrial action at various times, and fear of working class protest clearly influenced budgetary priorities; this was to a degree self-defeating since increased wages without commensurate rises in productivity only fuelled inflation.

Despite claims that the USSR had beaten the problem of unemployment in the 1930s, and concerns over labour shortages in the 1980s, unemployment had in fact been disguised by endemic overstaffing in Soviet enterprises leading to the low labour productivity typical of the extensive model of economic development. The structure of the Soviet labour force, while broadly corresponding to trends elsewhere, nevertheless revealed a disproportionately high number engaged in manual labour, some 50 million out of a 133 million-strong labour force (with another 7 million involved with the armed forces). Until the RSFSR Law on Employment of 19 April 1991 it was a crime not to work.[41] For most of the Soviet years there had been a relatively free movement of workers, but there had not been a labour market as such. Shokhin argued that the labour market was made up not only by those changing jobs but by all those involved in social production. He argued that the anticipated dramatic rise in unemployment was misleading since many would be between jobs and would not register as long-term unemployed, and there was huge latent pool of labour mobility, if not unemployment, in the over-staffed and inefficient plants. The key question was how long they would be between jobs, and the capacity of the private and cooperative sectors to absorb the new reserves of labour.[42]

Shokhin was proved right, and while unemployment increased its scale was less than some of the more apocalypic predictions had suggested, although for a society unaccustomed to any official unemployment the phenomenon itself was shocking. On 1 January 1996 2.3 million people (3.1 per cent of the working population) were registered as unemployed, an increase of 690,000 over the previous year, while some 5.9 million people (8.1 per cent) were jobless.[43] The scale of 'hidden unemployment', however, is difficult to estimate but must have affected another ten million. The official unemployment figures, moreover, have been much criticised by bodies like the International Labour Organisation who condemned the bureaucracy involved in registering with the Federal Employment Service.[44] Unemployment was worst in Ivanovo oblast, dominated by the crisis-ridden textile industry predominantly employing women, where joblessness is five to six times higher than the national average. Unemployment was also particularly high in Ingushetia, Norilsk in the Far North, timber and logging towns, and previously secret defence industry towns.[45] Long-term unemployment also rose, with those without a job for over a year trebling in 1994 to 7 per cent. Women and young people were particularly affected by long-term joblessness.

While the conventional view attributes the lack of mass unemployment to the lack of restructuring, changes in the structure of employment, with shifts to new and more dynamic sectors of the economy, may well have absorbed labour surpluses. The anticipated catastrophic rise in unemployment, moreover, was averted by weak or non-existent bankruptcy laws and the reluctance with which enterprises shed staff, especially in small towns with only one enterprise. In the military-industrial electronics factories of Zelenograd, for example, not far from Moscow, enterprises with perhaps 6,000 workers remained idle while a handful made toys with electronic components. Wages ultimately were paid by state subsidies, acting as a huge form of hidden unemployment benefit. With the end of the Soviet regime it might have been thought that the army of bureaucrats, some 80 per cent of whom were women, would become redundant, but the Russian administrative apparatus continued to burgeon.

New placement and retraining schemes were launched, the benefits system simplified, and Russia's 2,300 employment exchanges run by the Federal Employment Service began to be modernised and the 10,000 staff were retrained to cope with the influx of 'customers'. The emphasis was on developing an effective placement service, retraining for displaced workers, and financial incentives to employers to take on hard-to-place workers.[46] Many of those who lost their jobs felt no need to go to a labour exchange since they could find jobs on their own, but as the traditionally taut labour market became much slacker demand increased for the range of specialist services provided by such centres.[47]

LABOUR AND TRADE UNIONS

One of the key questions of the democratic transition in Russia was how the working class was to be integrated into the post-communist political order. The old gulf between workers and intellectuals had been partially bridged as the new Soviet technical intelligentsia had emerged, but independent labour politics had been delegitimised and incorporated, like the women's and youth movements, as part of Soviet 'transmission belt' politics in a monstrously bureaucratised trade union movement. In the post-communist era the whole notion of class politics was in bad odour because of its association with the discredited Soviet regime, and this was reinforced by fears of the lumpenisation of society in general and the working class in particular. This was offset, however, by the experience of Solidarity in Poland and the miners' strikes in the USSR. The discipline and political sophistication of these reborn labour movements indicated that fears of lumpenisation had been exaggerated.

On 11 July 1989 the first major strike of the Kuzbass and other miners demonstrated that perestroika was no longer simply a revolution from above but had now to accommodate itself to worker activism from below.[48] The miners' strike, moreover, swept away any residual belief that the CPSU was in any serious way a party of the working class. A year later these same miners staged an avowedly political strike calling for the resignation of Ryzhkov's government and for radical reforms. These strikes demonstrated that the nascent workers' movements, at least in this area, were fighting not for any renewed form of 'the dictatorship of the proletariat' but for a broad democratic programme.

Numerous new unions soon emerged.[49] The first was the Independent Miners' Union (NPG) established in Donetsk in October 1990, but later it was plagued by divisions and financial scandals. The main process, however, was for old unions to rename themselves and to try to adapt to new conditions, now without state subsidies, compulsory membership and stripped of some of their social functions. The leadership of the new unions were often the same as the old Soviet ones. Several trade union groupings were established but by far the largest was the Federation of Independent Trade Unions of Russia (FNPR), the successor to the old Soviet trade union organisation (VTsSPS) created in March 1990, with some 60 million affiliated members out of a total Russian labour force of 72.5 million organised in forty All-Russian unions.[50] The FNPR perpetuated the traditions of the old union movement, including collective membership of whole industries, covering managers as well as workers. At first chaired by Igor Klochkov, it protested against attempts to impose a wage freeze, insisting on 'market wages for market prices' and demanding guarantees that minimum wages would not fall below subsistence levels, and fought for a minimum wage indexed to the cost of living.[51] While broadly supportive of the Russian government's attempts to transform the economy, they insisted that this should not primarily be at the expense of working people.[52] One of the largest trade union organisations was the Moscow Federation of Trade Unions (MFPS), claiming the affiliation of thirty-nine unions with 5.7 million workers; another active union was Sotsprof, which originally called itself socialist but later simply called itself a 'social' trade union and supported Yeltsin's dash for the market. The General Confederation of Trade Unions (VKP) sought to act as an umbrella organisation throughout the CIS but remained embryonic.

In keeping with his corporatist instincts Yeltsin sought to work with the labour unions, and effectively integrated the FNPR into the regime system. The idea of social partnership was formalised by the establishment in January 1992 of the Tripartite Commission on the Regulation of Social and Labour Relations, bringing together organised labour, management and the state, with the brief to review and set wage levels and to mediate in labour disputes, which helped establish the system of quarterly indexing of minimum wages and pensions.[53] In the face of labour activism and wage demands the government usually capitulated, but the price of labour peace was a strained budget.

Soviet trade unions had traditionally distributed social security benefits and payments for medical treatment. The government now took over many of these functions, including the crucial Social Insurance Fund, and only the wealthiest of the unions could continue to provide subsidised holidays or nursery and other facilities for working parents. Much of this now became marketised, often priced beyond the reach of a large part of the population. Unions no longer received subsidies from the government or employers. One problem was the unclear juridical position, with antiquated Soviet legislation on the statute books and unclear Russian laws to regulate their status. A far more profound problem facing unions, however, was their shifting social and political role, lacking credibility in the workplace and in society at large.[54]

Opponents of shock therapy had long argued that Yeltsin's government would be swept away by a tide of popular dissatisfaction, led by organised labour. In the event, despite the hardships, popular opinion did not harden against Yeltsin's reforms, partly because unemployment had not yet taken on a mass character. The independent trade unions, like the NPG led by the deputy Victor Utkin, tended to support Yeltsin. The largest successor trade union organisation, the FNPR, was holding its congress at the time of the dissolution of the Supreme Soviet; Klochkov had earlier joined the Civic Union, and he now threatened a general strike and bitterly condemned Yeltsin.[55] In the event, as dissolution began to turn into insurrection, the FNPR, together with the VKP, sharply condemned the parliamentary leadership of Khasbulatov and Rutskoi, approved Yeltsin's restoration of law and order, and then summarily dismissed Klochkov and replaced him by Mikhail Shmakov, the head of the MFPS. The FNPR's newspaper, *Rabochaya tribuna*, was allowed to continue publication.[56]

Unions were now faced with the novel task of defending the interests of their members. Popular responses to marketisation were more muted than anticipated by those who warned of a 'social explosion', but there was nevertheless an undercurrent of economic strikes. The FNPR launched a week of action from 21 October 1991 to ensure that the interests of workers were not forgotten in the transition to the market. In the Kuzbass in late October 1991 100,000 health workers went on strike in protest against worsening conditions in hospitals, poor pay and conditions, and lack of medical supplies,[57] and in April 1992 another strike by some of the 4 million health workers threatened the reforms. Miners, once Yeltsin's strongest supporters, by 1995 once again took industrial action against arrears in wage payments, caused largely by delays in delivering state subsidies. Much of Russia's coal industry is inefficient and unprofitable necessitating subsidies to the tune of 40–45 per cent.[58] Plans to close some eighty mines by the year 2000 provoked a new round of protests; the attempt to close only 4 out of 26 mines in the Russian part of the Donbass led to strikes,[59] and elsewhere, especially in the Far North and East, closure of mines would lead to the death of entire communities in which Russia's 800,000 miners are employed. Economic liberalisation severely weakened the bargaining position of workers and relative wages fell sharply.

Trade unions were transformed from instruments of the state to instruments of collective bargaining. Employers, however, were less effective in transforming themselves into effective bargaining partners, long having been merely cogs in the larger chain of command to the ministries. The RUIE was unable to transform itself into a representative employers' organisation. Major challenges, however, faced the union movement, above all to transform themselves from bureaucratic state agencies to the organisational core of the labour movement.[60] The FNPR to many represented no more than part of the political nomenklatura, allied to the enterprise directorate and more interested in elite-level intrigues than the membership; it is for this reason that a number of unions, often calling themselves 'free' to distinguish themselves from the old-style unions, were established, and in contrast to the old unions did not allow members of management to join.[61]

Classic struggles emerged in workplaces, with employers sacking workers for attempting to establish independent trade unions, arguing that the existing FNPR network was sufficient, although the latter more often than not sided with the management against the workers they claimed to represent. Not surprisingly, trade unions did not figure significantly in workplace life and according to polls were trusted by only 13 per cent, partially trusted by 25 per cent and distrusted by 36 per cent.[62] The Moscow intelligentsia on the whole kept itself well apart from the struggle for free trade unions, while political parties at first had almost no role to play in labour struggles. New labour legislation considered by the Duma would severely restrict the right of workers to strike; while newly privatised enterprises often sought to eliminate organised labour altogether from the workplace. In short, the labour struggles that had accompanied the rise of Western industrial society and which led to the recognition of a range of union rights were once again being re-enacted in Russia.

GENDER POLITICS

The functionalist analysis of women in three roles, as workers, mothers and homemakers, is standard when studying Soviet society. The Bolsheviks considered that gender inequality would be overcome if women were absorbed into social production, children's upbringing and daily life socialised, and a socialist camaraderie established in relations between the sexes. In the early 1930s the separate women's departments (*zhenotdely*) in the Party were closed and the 'women's question' was declared resolved. The 'thaw' of the 1950s and 1960s revealed that the question was far from over, and later analysis revealed that on all the main indices of social achievement and psychological freedom women were at a disadvantage compared to men.[63]

The participation rate of women in paid employment was one of the highest in the world at around 90 per cent. In the period of extensive economic growth the proportion of women in the Russian workforce peaked in the 1970s at 53 per cent, but as the economy began to shift to a more intensive form of development the proportion fell to 52 per cent in 1987[64] and by 1990 was down to 48 per cent and will no doubt continue to fall as economic reform leads to high female unemployment. Women made up 60 per cent of Soviet specialists with higher and secondary special education, constituting 58 per cent of all engineers, 67 per cent of doctors, and up to 91 per cent of librarians. Even though half a million women in the USSR were directors of enterprises, institutions and organisations,[65] there was both vertical and horizontal professional segregation. Within the workplace the usual 'glass ceiling' on promotion was in place; the higher one went in an administrative or professional hierarchy, the lower the proportion of women. Women predominated in less qualified work and nurturing professions and received on average a third lower wages than men.

Women are the losers in Russia's new transformation. As workers, women are made redundant before men and often with worse benefit rights. The average unemployed person in Russia is a woman with higher or specialised education in the 35–40 age group with one child.[66] Women, who had traditionally made up half of the Russian workforce, account for 75 per cent of the officially unemployed; three out of every four people who lost their jobs in 1993 were women.[67] Wages in the highly 'feminised' professions, moreover, fell below the living minimum leading to strikes by teachers, health care workers and textile workers. Post-war Soviet economic development drew on women instrumentally, as the last great reserve army of labour (together with the peasantry), but as soon as labour shortages gave way to labour surpluses, the alleged emancipatory benefits of paid employment were soon forgotten and the other two roles of women, as mothers and homemakers, were once again stressed. The low birthrate had already prompted Gorbachev to argue that the Soviet regime's attempt 'to make women equal with men in everything' by putting them to work on construction sites, offices and factories had been at the cost of 'their everyday duties at home – housework, the upbringing of children and the creation of a good family atmosphere'. The strategy therefore was 'to make it possible for women to return to their purely womanly mission'.[68]

But as homemakers, too, women are under enormous pressure.[69] The lack of housing, alcoholism and the stultifying social atmosphere placed the Soviet family at risk, with a high divorce rate, but whether the appeal to the traditional values of the patriarchal family is an adequate response may be doubted. The division of labour in homes remains traditional, with women doing most of the domestic chores and taking primary care of children.[70] Thus the well-known phenomenon of the 'double burden': a full shift at paid work and then several more hours of unpaid work looking after the home and queuing for goods. Loss of a job at least reduces one of the burdens, but in the transition to the market this was accompanied by a profound reorientation of women's identities in the mass media, suggesting that it was somehow 'unfeminine' to be active professionally and politically.

It was also accompanied by a rapid deterioration of the social facilities used by women. The fall of communism led to the destruction of social services like childcare and pre-school nurseries, or their commercialisation, placing them far beyond the reach of average families. While women had earlier been forced to work, the birth of a child now usually meant giving up paid work altogether. The electoral bloc Women of Russia noted that 3 million single women in Russia had to rely on their earnings alone; their wages had declined relative to men's: if earlier, women's wages were nearly 70 per cent of men's, by December 1993 they had declined to about 40 per cent; they were also concerned about maternal and infant mortality and high levels of illness.[71]

As citizens, too, women have largely disappeared from national leadership. Under the old regime quotas were reserved for women, and they comprised from one-third of the total deputies (in national) to one-half (in local) soviets; one-third of the deputies elected to the eleventh convocation of the USSR Supreme Soviet (1984–89) were women, but the partial removal of quotas led the proportion elected to the USSR CPD in March 1989 to fall to 15.7 per cent.[72] With the complete abolition of quotas in the March 1990 elections to the Russian Congress the proportion of women fell to just 5.5 per cent.[73] However, the trend was reversed in the December 1993 elections, largely due to the efforts of the Women of Russia electoral association which won 8.13 per cent of the party-list vote.[74] The proportion of women in the Federal Assembly rose to 10.8 per cent, but this figure masks the disparity between the Fifth Duma, where women comprised 13.1 per cent of the total (58), and the Federation Council, elected on a first-past-the-post system where women appeared to be at a disadvantage, resulting in only 5.1 per cent of women.[75] The Women of Russia bloc was a unique attempt in Russia for a women's party to appeal directly to women as a specific constituency.[76] The bloc, however, failed to breach the 5 per cent threshold in 1995, leading to a fall in women's representation in the Sixth Duma to 46 (10.2 per cent).[77]

It would be misleading to suggest that women were simply passive victims of the transformation. Opportunities for women to participate in the rich socio-political life of post-communist Russia, in the new political parties, trade unions, business life, protest movements and human rights groups, increased as much as for anyone else. Even here, though, women were under-represented, especially in leading bodies. A strictly numerical approach does not always reflect reality, and there is no doubt that qualitatively women played an important part in the democratic movement, however, as in the West, women tended to be absent at the point where decisions are taken: 'Where there is power there are no women; where there are women, there is no power.'[78] Some women, like Ekaterina Lakhova, the head of the Women of Russia Duma faction, took an active part in issues like renewing Russia's Family Code (regulating marriage and family matters).

Women's interests are weakly articulated in the political system because, among other things, women's organisations are weak. The fall of the Soviet regime led to the dissolution of some of the old bureaucratic women's organisations. The Soviet Women's Committee, however, survived with the new name of the Russian Union of Women and kept its lavish headquarters, but without subsidies it was forced to take up commercial activities; it was one of the main sponsors of the Women of Russia bloc. A women's movement began to take shape at the grass roots, but there were numerous social and political factors inhibiting a strong separate women's movement in Russia. If the social democrats of the past had argued that 'the women's question' was just one aspect of the emancipation of labour as a whole, so in the post-communist transition the emphasis has been on the achievement of democratic and citizenship rights for all. Women's activity was channelled into the struggle for democracy, just as once before it had been subordinated to the struggle for socialism. Rather than building strong collective organisations, women in post-communist Russia have tended to adopt individual strategies. This may well reflect what has been called the 'escape from forced emancipation' typical of Soviet-type systems, marked by an allergy to public engagement.[79]

The problem of gender differentiation did, however, generate three main forms of women's political activity. The first was the development of numerous local associations and pressure groups which campaigned for various measures or focused on particular issues. Brutal conditions for conscripts and the horrors of the Chechen war stimulated Lyubov Lymar's Soldiers' Mothers of Russia and similar organisations. The second form was involvement in some of the existing women's organisations to try to turn them from bureaucratic structures of Soviet power into genuinely responsive organisations not only *for* women but also *of* women. The third was the attempt to create genuinely independent new structures. One of these was the Centre of Gender Studies of the Academy of Science, established in early 1990 and directed by Anastasiya Posadskaya, which analysed demographic and social problems of women in Russia and acted as a link between Russian and Western feminists. However, despite the direct threat posed by marketisation to women (in economic, social and identity terms), there was no upsurge of a politicised women's movement in Russia. Posadskaya noted that state policies were still designed *for women* and not programmes of *women themselves*.

As in other spheres, the question remained whether the 'modernisation' of Soviet women would necessarily repeat Western patterns, or whether Russian modernity might differ in significant ways from that prevalent in the West. Why should sexual identity become gender identity?[80] The question is often raised of Russian women's own consciousness of their own interests in the three spheres mentioned above (work, motherhood, family) and as individuals or part of a feminine community. In refusing to adopt Western criteria of feminism, had they in some way internalised their own subjection, or was their refusal to adopt Western ways of thinking a reflection of a deeper cultural difference between Russia and the West?

THE ENVIRONMENT AND DEMOCRATISATION

Marxists traditionally looked upon nature as a resource to be plundered in the service of humanity. Holloway notes that 'Land, air, and water were as much victims of Stalin's ruthless policies as the people of the Soviet Union were. "We cannot expect charity from nature," Stalin said. "We must tear it from her."'[81] The environmental movement had played a central role in popular mobilisation during perestroika, and indeed throughout the communist era environmentalists had acted as a residual source of social consciousness and responsibility. The outstanding plant biologist Academician Nikolai Vavilov, for example, had tried to defend the autonomy of science against the depradations of Trofim Lysenko, but had failed and was arrested in June 1940 and died of starvation soon after.[82] He was not alone, and the courage of the earth scientists prompted Douglas Weiner to describe the discipline as 'the Gulag of freedom'.[83] In a certain sense the biologists and allied disciplines of the Soviet period can be described as the kernel of civil society waiting for more propitious circumstances to germinate.

These better times proved to be Gorbachev's perestroika. A multitude of environmental groups emerged who insisted that communism had been as much an environmental disaster as it had been a political and economic one.[84] A study by Goskomstat, the State Statistics Committee, revealed that an average of nearly 100 million tons of pollutants were discharged into the environment annually in the 5 years to 1991.[85] Commercial felling of forests at some 2 million hectares a year far exceeded the replacement rate, which in taiga conditions in any case is very slow. The indiscriminate use of chemical fertilisers and pesticides laid waste great tracts and contaminated rivers and ground waters; the deserts of Dagestan and Kalmykia had increased from 15,000 to a million hectares in a generation; in the Arctic tundra overgrazing had led to the loss of 40 million hectares of pasture (an area larger than Germany); the wildlife of Eastern Siberia has been devastated by factory pollution; the level of the Aral Sea is falling by one metre a year; the closed Caspian Sea was filling with poisons; Lake Ladoga (Europe's largest lake near St Petersburg) is dying from nitrate and phosphate poisoning; on the high seas the USSR had systematically lied about slaughter of a large part of the world's protected whale population, dumped nuclear waste into the Sea of Japan, and dumped seven nuclear submarines and an ice-breaker, six of them in the shallow sea around Novaya Zemlya between the Barents and Kara Seas, north-east of Murmansk; and the sad list could go on.[86] The cumulative effect of these disasters had a devastating effect on public health.

Nikolai Vorontsov had been the first non-communist Soviet minister, given responsibility for the environment in 1989, and he increased spending on environmental protection to 1.3 per cent of GNP. But this had little impact on the gross pollution of most industrial cities, with the worst affected like Kemerovo, Bratsk and Norilsk exceeding by ten times permitted levels of air pollution.[87] Alexei Yablokov became the minister for the environment in the new Russian government, a man who had long fought for environmental causes and had been the first chair of the Soviet branch of Greenpeace. Russia faced a daunting task in overcoming the disastrous environmental legacy of the old regime. The loss of biodiversity was matched by the human health hazard posed by the crisis, and Yablokov calculated that 20 per cent of the country's population lived in ecological disaster zones and another 35–40 per cent in ecologically damaged conditions.[88]

It was clear that the money required to deal with this ecological catastrophe was not available. Even more tragically, Russia faced the dilemma shared by other post-communist countries, namely the balance to be drawn between environmental policies and the costs in economic and job terms. It was all very well to advocate the closure of environmentally hazardous plants and industries, but how would the economic losses be covered, and where would the new jobs for those made redundant come from? Who would pay for the closure of the giant pulp and paper mills threatening Laka Baikal in Southern Siberia, the deepest freshwater lake on Earth containing one-fifth of the world's fresh water and home to 1,500 plant and animal species, 1,200 of them found nowhere else in the world? The main form of industrialisation in Siberia was resource extraction, and with the acute pressure for foreign currency, logging of the fragile taiga forests, half of the world's coniferous forest and over one fifth of all forest (being twice as large as the Amazon rainforests), was set to increase. Korean, Japanese and American firms increased their presence despite the resistance of local authorities and the native peoples, and who would police environmental laws, prevent the erosion of soils and silting of rivers, prevent the loss of animal habitat and make up the losses in hard currency earnings for raw timber exports?[89]

The disintegration of the USSR jeopardised Soviet environmental and conservation legislation as each republic sought maximum advantage for itself, leading, for example, to the return of sea fishing of sturgeon in the Caspian, banned in 1962 by the Soviet Ministry of Fisheries.[90] The collapse of the Soviet economy, however, had a beneficial environmental impact, as plants closed and industrial activity declined, but deindustrialisation is hardly a long-term solution to the crisis. The tension between environmental security and economic well-being is an acute one in countries in economic crisis.

The issue was particularly acute concerning nuclear power. The explosion at the Chernobyl reactor on 26 May 1986 was dreadful proof of the dangers of nuclear technology in the hands of an irresponsible state.[91] The USSR had fifty-three nuclear power stations operating in 1991, most of a primitive design lacking concrete container systems. The presence of such a dome at the RBMK-type Chernobyl power plant might have contained much of the radiation released following the explosion. In republics like Russia, Ukraine, Lithuania and Armenia nuclear power played a crucial part in the energy balance. In 1993 Russia had twenty-eight nuclear power stations supplying 11.8 per cent of the country's energy needs (18.9 GWe – Gigawattts electric), while Ukraine's fifteen supplied 25 per cent (13 GWe). Ukraine suffered from chronic energy shortages, amassing enormous debts to Russia for oil and gas deliveries, and insisted it could not close the remaining two working reactors at Chernobyl (which supplied 7 per cent of Ukraine's electricity) until the West helped pay for alternatives, like a gas-fired power station. In Armenia the Metzamor station was taken off line in March 1989 in the wake of the December 1988 earthquake, but returned to active service in 1995. Thus while many reactors should have been closed on environmental grounds, to have done so would have left cities cold in the harsh winters. The energy shortage, exacerbated by falling output of oil, gas and coal, led Russia's powerful 'Minatom' agency in December 1992 to propose an increase in nuclear power output to 37 GWe by 2010 by completing unfinished plants and constructing new ones.[92] Yablokov called the plan 'unacceptable from the legal, ecological, economic and political points of view',[93] but the severity of the energy shortfall was such that there was no guarantee that his warning would be heard, especially since nuclear power was a smaller component of Russia's energy balance than in many developed Western states.[94]

The legacy of past nuclear irresponsibility, however, was one that could not be avoided. The problem of radioactivity was the greatest single catastrophe afflicting the country. Some 8,000 people had died as a result of the Chernobyl explosion, and contamination affected large parts of Ukraine and 40 per cent of Belarus – provoking movements for national independence – as well as sixteen regions of Russia. There were fears, moreover, that the sarcophagus containing the damaged Reactor 4 at Chernobyl was in danger of disintegrating.[95] In Moscow itself leakage from nuclear plants and research institutes made certain parts of the city extremely dangerous. Some 600 miles of the Yenisei downriver from Krasnoyarsk-26 were heavily contaminated since in the past water from the cooling towers in a military plant producing plutonium went straight into the river. The legacy of atmospheric nuclear tests still affected parts of Siberia downwind of the Semipalatinsk test site in Kazakhstan. An explosion in tanks containing nuclear waste in 1957 at the Chelyabinsk-40 installation cast radioactive materials over a wide area, and another explosion at Kyshtym near Chelyabinsk in 1976, kept secret for 20 years, contaminated a large part of the Urals. Everywhere there were Chernobyls waiting to happen, in old nuclear power stations and secret nuclear factory towns like Chelyabinsk-65.

The fall of communist power did not resolve the environmental crisis but made possible analysis of its scale. At the same time a whole series of new problems arose concerning conditions of marketisation, weak state power and energy shortages.[96] The Russian government was conscious of the relationship between economic transformation and environmental factors, adopting a Law on Protecting the Environment on 19 December 1991,[97] and sought to develop cooperation with the other CIS states on environmental policy.[98] The Law on Specially Protected Natural Areas, finally signed into law by Yeltsin on 14 March 1995, was the cornerstone of measures to regulate the protection and use of specially protected areas. Russia already had strictly protected Nature Reserves (*Zapovedniki*), established some 70 years ago, National Parks (set up in 1983), Special Purpose Reserves (*Zakazniki*), Nature Monuments, and some others, and the act now introduced a new type of protected area, Regional Natural Parks (analogous to State Parks in the USA). The act drew a clear distinction between the federal and regional level of protected areas, a particularly important delineation at a time of privatisation, with the Zapovedniki and National Parks to remain federal property, while the Zakazniki were under regional control.[99] The Zapovedniki were the heart of Russia's conservation policy and biological diversity, whereas some of the other areas were virtually 'paper parks', encroached upon by the increasing number of small landowners, farmers and herders, quite apart from the pressure of mining, logging and other business interests.

The revival in environmental awareness was reflected by the convocation of the First All-Russian Environmental NGO Conference (30 May–1 June 1995), organised by the Socio-Ecological Union, with some 350 representatives from numerous environmental bodies, including the semi-official All-Russia Society for Nature Conservation. The conference represented the first serious sign that 'society' was once again organising in conditions of reform to place environmental concerns at the head of the agenda. Delegates agreed to coordinate their work more closely to achieve the provision enshrined in the constitution (article 42) that 'Each person has the right to a decent environment', and within that framework discussed a strategy for sustainable development in Russia and established a coordinating committee for future actions.

One of these was collective representation at the official National Congress on Nature Conservation (2–5 June 1995), a belated response to Russia's commitment at the Rio de Janeiro world environmental congress to 'sustainable development'. The purpose of the Congress was to approve the official 'Concept for Sustainable Development' devised, of all people, by the Ministry of Economy, that included such ideas as 'transition to sustainable development can occur only with a restart of economic growth and increase of efficiency in economic production'. The document was rejected by the Congress and the NGOs were to be represented on the committee devising a new draft.[100] At the Congress the minister for environmental protection Victor Danilov-Danilyan publicly pledged himself to establish a Department of Zapovednik Management to take over full control for the management of these areas. The Ministry's past neglect had come in for much criticism, with environmental funds consolidated into general budgets, and the whole system coming alarmingly close to collapse.[101]

Democratisation thus acts as a two-edged sword in the field of environmental politics. On the one hand, it makes possible the relatively honest appraisal of environmental problems, allows the mobilisation of lobbies and groups, and promotes public participation in legislative acts. On the other hand, powerful new corporations and business lobbies emerge to exploit natural resources, private entrepreneurs encroach on protected areas, the capacity of the state to regulate and implement environmental programmes weakens, and the resources available for conservation and rehabilitation decline. The Russian case demonstrates clearly, however, that environmentalism is not the preserve of affluent Westerners[102] but concerns a large and growing constituency from all walks of life.

Part V

Foreign policies

14　Foreign policy

Russia's misfortune lies in this: Russia and Europe live in different historical times.

G. P. Fedotov[1]

The fall of communism overshadowed perhaps an even more epoch-making event, the disintegration of a geopolitical unit that had lasted some 500 years and in comparison with which the reign of communism had been a mere interregnum. The whole geopolitical and strategic balance not only of the post-Second World War era but of the whole epoch since the Congress of Vienna in 1815 came to an end. Russia's long climb from local, regional, continental and then to global power appeared suddenly to have been dramatically reversed. The dissolution of communism ended one set of problems associated with global confrontation in the Cold War, but the disintegration of the Soviet Union raised no less epochal issues. Would the inherent instability of Russo-European relations for the last 400 years give way to a new partnership? Would the new Russia be able to define a post-imperial and post-communist national identity and integrate into global economic and political processes? What sort of 'normality' was normal for Russia?

The definition of foreign policy to a large degree depends on the self-definition of a country itself, and Russia had to find itself and come to terms with its revived national identity before any coherent foreign policy based on 'national interest' could be defined. The interdependence of foreign and domestic policy under Yeltsin was closer than ever before as Russia sought a favourable international climate to ensure economic assistance and to facilitate its reintegration into the international system. In the first period Russian foreign policy was thoroughly 'domesticated', with domestic reform taking priority over any remaining global ambitions, but gradually the outlines of a more 'balanced', or as others would put it, a more assertive if not aggressive policy took shape. Despite a multitude of obstacles a sophisticated and multifaceted foreign policy emerged committed to contemporary principles of international relations (as outlined, for example, in the UN Charter), but this policy was threatened by domestic political instability and the rise of an assertive nationalism.

THE DEVELOPMENT OF RUSSIAN FOREIGN POLICY

Russian foreign policy developed rapidly and passed through five main stages. Each was marked by contradictory goals that imbued policy with what we shall call an 'essential ambiguity', often reflected in what appeared to be irresolution and muddle. We use the term 'essential' because the conflicting aims were structured into the very situation and could hardly be avoided if a complex policy was to be pursued, and 'ambiguous' because they reflected the profound and unresolved (and probably unresolvable) civilisational and geopolitical choices facing Russia. The very concept of 'choice' in these circumstances may be too stark because Russia, by its very position and history, will inevitably have multifaceted if not contradictory foreign policies, many of whose elements might appear to be incompatible, but which reflect the real needs of particular circumstances.

1 The emergence phase: before the coup   Even before the coup the outlines of an independent policy had emerged, yet the problem of defining Russia's interests as distinct from those of the USSR had not been resolved. Yeltsin's election to chair the Russian CPD on 29 May 1990 and the Declaration of Russian State Sovereignty on 12 June set the scene for a debate over Russia's national interests and over the shape of its foreign policy. Already by October two central principles had emerged: that Russia would seek friendly relations with the other Soviet republics in a renewed union; and that Russia wished to return as an autonomous force in world politics, defending its status as a Great Power but at the same time seeking 'to occupy a worthy (*dostoinoe*) place in the community of civilised peoples of Eurasia and America'.[2] Whether these aims were compatible remained to be seen.

A separate Russian diplomatic service was re-established in October 1990, and in November Andrei Kozyrev was appointed foreign minister. From 1974 to 1990 Kozyrev had worked in the Directorate of International Organisations in the Soviet Ministry of Foreign Affairs (MFA), and thus it is not surprising that he later placed so much emphasis on international institutions. He argued that Russian policy would no longer be based on ideology or messianic ambitions but common sense and the realistic evaluation of concrete needs. He developed new approaches to international issues, even though policy, in this area as in most others, remained in Yeltsin's hands. Russia's first independent acts reflected the blurred distinction between foreign and domestic policy, namely the signing of treaties with Ukraine on 19 November, Kazakhstan on 21 November and with Belarus on 18 December 1990. The treaties recognised the signatories as sovereign states and declared that their relations would be based on principles of equality, non-interference and the renunciation of the use of force, and that they would establish diplomatic relations with each other. Soviet and Russian foreign policy began to diverge as Russian diplomacy sought to facilitate the radical transformation of society and to defend what came to be seen as Russian national interests separate and distinct from those of the Soviet Union. During Gorbachev's visit to Japan in April 1991, for example, Yeltsin made it clear that the USSR could not negotiate a return of the four disputed Kurile Islands without consulting Russia.

Yeltsin's defence of the concept of a sovereign and independent Russia, presented so eleoquently during his presidential campaign in June 1991, however, was conceived within the framework of a renewed Union. Russia sought not the disintegration of the Union but its transformation on the basis of a renegotiated treaty, retaining a system of collective security, a coordinated foreign policy, and the maintenance of a common economic, transport and migrational space. To this end Russia took an active part in the nine-plus-one negotiations for a new Union Treaty and was committed to signing the documents on 20 August when the coup intervened. Russia's assertion of an independent foreign policy, therefore, was considered compatible with a renewed Union with its own federal government. This is a classic example of the 'essential ambiguity' of Russian policy since it was difficult to see how mutually exclusive claims to sovereignty could be reconciled within a single state.

2 The establishment phase: between the coup and disintegration, August to December 1991 The nine-plus-one process was ruptured by the events of August 1991 and never really gained credibility thereafter, despite Gorbachev's last ditch attempts to transform the USSR into a Union of Sovereign States (see chapter 1). The tension between decaying Soviet and embryonic Russian foreign policies provoked only confusion and frustration.

Following Shevardnadze's resignation as Soviet foreign minister on 20 December 1990 Alexander Bessmertnykh had been appointed in his place, but during the coup he had wavered. He in turn was replaced by Boris Pankin, the former ambassador to Prague and one of a handful of Soviet envoys who denounced the putschists without hesitation. Pankin notes the atmosphere:

> In those days the common obsession that gripped our entire leadership was with the idea of becoming a 'civilised state'. The issue of being patronized or humbled did not arise. In fact giving advice to the Soviet Union was a pastime that had been positively encouraged by the highly sociable Shevardnadze, who in all his contacts with the West seemed more ready to be polite and accommodating than to stand firm.[3]

Pankin, however, proved to be only a temporary appointment, and although he fought to defend the Soviet MFA and modified some of the cuts imposed on its personnel, he was accepted neither by the Soviet foreign policy establishment nor by the emerging Russian Foreign Ministry. The Soviet MFA began to wither away despite attempts to 'democratise' its ruling collegium and its reorganisation into a Ministry of External Relations after merger with the Ministry of Foreign Trade.

Conflicts between the USSR and Russia were not only institutional but also over policy. Russia influenced the decision in September 1991 to remove the Soviet training brigade from Cuba, the decision to halt arms sales to Afghanistan on 13 September, and the restoration of diplomatic relations with Israel on 24 October 1991, 24 years after they had been broken off following the Six Day War of 1967.[4] Yeltsin's state visit to Germany, hitherto Gorbachev's keenest supporter, in November 1991 sought to secure economic assistance for Russia's own promised reforms, and at the same time was a clear signal that Russia had returned to the international community as a power in its own right.

The reappointment of Shevardnadze on 19 November 1991 as minister of external relations represented Gorbachev's last desperate attempt to restore his crumbling authority. Shevardnadze made no secret of his view that Gorbachev bore much responsibility for the coup. Since his resignation he had founded the Foreign Policy Association and become co-chair of the Democratic Reform Movement. He now hoped to use his good relationship with the American secretary of state, James Baker, to convince Washington to support Gorbachev's attempts to keep the Union together. The overwhelming Ukrainian vote for independence on 1 December 1991, however, signalled the end of the USSR and opened up a whole new geopolitical situation in Eurasia.

By the end of the year Russia had swallowed up the Soviet state. On 18 December 1991 Yeltsin brought the Soviet diplomatic service under Russian control, and on 22 December the Soviet foreign and defence ministries were abolished. The Soviet Ministry of External Relations was merged with Russia's, and Shevardnadze once again left political office until he entered the cruel political fray in his native Georgia. Yeltsin placed himself in direct control of the Russian Foreign Ministry, and Burbulis took over routine operations.[5] Russia inherited the mantle of responsibility and sought international recognition for its new status by being acknowledged as the primary successor state. It was recognised as the 'continuer' state, taking on responsibility for Soviet treaties and obligations and above all for the Soviet strategic arsenal (see chapter 16).

3 The 'romantic' phase, January 1992–February 1993   Freed from the burden of the Union, Russia re-entered the world stage and by January 1992 had already been recognised by 131 states. Addressing the Russian MFA on 27 October 1991, Yeltsin set two main aims for Russian policy: to secure favourable external conditions for domestic political and economic reforms; and to overcome the legacy of the Cold War and to dismantle confront-ational structures.[6] Both policies were laced with ambiguities: to what degree would economics (economic reform at home and integration into the world economic system abroad) be placed above national interests, however defined; how would this Atlanticist orientation be compat-ible with Russia's Great Power status; and why was nothing said about forging a new relationship with the former Soviet states? Questions such as these have led to this period of Russian foreign policy being dubbed 'romantic', allegedly excessively pro-Western at the expense of Russia's own interests and at the price of the neglect of its own 'backyard' in the CIS.

National-patriots, centrists and democratic statists alike were to varying degrees sceptical about the viability of the Soviet successor states, and insisted that Russia should direct its policy far more actively towards them. Post-communist Russian nation-building was pro-foundly influenced by the problem of the 25 million Russians (however defined) who had suddenly found themselves 'abroad', and the defence of their rights and status permeated domestic politics. The Russian leadership was hesitant to adopt ethnicity as a factor in inter-state relations and thus allegedly abandoned their compatriots abroad; but by the same token the sanctity of the new international borders and the sovereignty of the new states was acknowledged. This did not, however, prevent the blurring of the distinction between domestic and foreign policy when discussing relations with the former Soviet states, especially when Russian strategic interests were concerned. The widespread use of the term *blizhnee zarubezh'e* (near abroad) for the former Soviet republics suggested that these countries were somehow in a different category from genuinely foreign countries.

Kozyrev noted that 'the second Russian Revolution unfolded in a favorable foreign policy setting',[7] and proceeded on the assumption that military force was no longer relevant as an instrument of policy. This view, which turned out to be premature, allowed the military to make the running in the near abroad, as the foreign ministry all but abdicated responsibility in the area. Kozyrev on several occasions condemned the military and the 'party of war' (in particular, General Lebed in Moldova).[8] With the onset of a deep Western economic recession in the early 1990s and Germany's preoccupation with its new Eastern territories, the international environment deteriorated. Western funds became more limited, and in any case the bulk went to the 'old' Eastern Europe (above all Hungary, Poland and the Czech Republic). Whether justified or not, there was a palpable sense of disappointment in Russia as early hopes of a rapid transformation with Western help evaporated.

4 The reassertion phase, from March 1993   Post-communist Russian foreign policy is marked by continuity in strategic goals, but a turning point in tone and to a lesser degree in substance took place towards the end of 1992 and into early 1993. The opposition condemned Kozyrev's alleged servility and 'romantic' obsession with the West and his failure to formulate an effective policy towards the former Soviet republics. As far as the national-patriots and centrists were concerned, allegiance to the principles of a cosmopolitan liberal universalism threatened Russia's very existence as a state. Russian policy began explicitly to assert a hegemonic concept of its 'vital national interests' in the near abroad, coupled with a reassertion of Russia's Great Power status in the world at large. It was at this time, Pavel Baev notes, that 'geopolitics successfully replaced communist ideology as the conceptual basis for Russia's foreign policy'.[9] This brought the concept of *realpolitik* firmly back into the lexicon of foreign policy discourse, displacing the idealistic universalism of the Gorbachev years. Russia might well be a post-imperial state, but this did not mean that it had no interests to defend.

Already in March 1992 Stankevich and other proponents of an active post-imperial Russian foreign policy sponsored a Russian Monroe doctrine, defining the whole area of the former Soviet Union as one vital to Russian national interests.[10] This approach was further developed in August 1992 in the first 'Strategy for Russia' report of the Council for Foreign and Defence Policy (CFDP), established by Sergei Karaganov, the deputy director of the Institute of Europe. The document argued that Russia's interests were not necessarily the same as the West's, and indeed, that the gap between the two would probably increase; and as a corollary, the focus of Russian policy should shift from the West to the near abroad from whence the main challenges to Russian security would come. Thus the document advocated an 'enlightened post-imperial course' that could balance the relationship with the West and Russia's concerns in the near abroad.[11]

In a speech to the Civic Union conference on 28 February 1993 Yeltsin for the first time made explicit Russia's claim to have a 'vital interest in the cessation of all armed conflicts on the territory of the former USSR', and appealed to the UN 'to grant Russia special powers as the guarantor of peace and stability in this region'.[12] In April 1992 the new line was formalised in the unpublished 'Foreign Policy Concept' drafted by the Security Council, which once again declared Russia to be the guarantor of stability in the former Soviet Union. While the international community was reluctant to endorse Russia's special role, it was unwilling to intervene itself and thus *de facto* Russia was granted a free hand to impose its own order in the post-Soviet space – with the important exception of the Baltic states.

Kozyrev's own position evolved, with his enemies accusing him of a chameleon-like opportunism to maintain his post, usually involving uncritical support for Yeltsin. Kozyrev sought to combine two principles that according to some were mutually exclusive. On the one hand, he sought to 'guarantee the rights of citizens and the dynamic socio-economic development of society'; on the other, he insisted that Russia was 'a normal Great Power, achieving its interests not through confrontation but through cooperation'.[13] By late 1993 Kozyrev had adopted a more sharply defined empire-saving strategy, insisting that Russia had the right to intervene to prevent the country 'losing geopolitical positions that took centuries to achieve'.[14] Alarmed by the apparent appeal of Zhirinovskii's nationalistic rhetoric in the December 1993 elections, much of the Russian political elite incorporated some of his ideas into their own programmes. The attempt to make Russia a democracy *and* a Great Power became the central principle of Russian policy from early 1993, but these aims (typical of the essential ambiguity characteristic of Russian policy) appeared increasingly incompatible.

As far as Kozyrev was concerned, Russia could be a democratic post-Cold War Great Power pursuing a non-ideological definition of national interests that might sometimes entail elements of competition with the West. This tough approach was vividly manifested in Kozyrev's refusal in November 1994 to sign documents already agreed with NATO concerning the Partnership for Peace (PfP) programme in Brussels. Attempts by the West to delegitimate the pursuit of Russia's 'normal' Great Power interests by forever raising the spectre of a revival of the Cold War, according to Yeltsin a month later at the Budapest summit of the OSCE in December 1994, threatened to lead to the emergence of a 'cold peace'.[15] It was at this time that Kozyrev left the Russia's Choice faction in the Duma when they condemned the war in Chechnya. He became a proponent of the reconstituted ideology of power, but this did not mean the abandonment of all of his earlier views and he remained committed to a viable relationship with the West. Despite his partial conversion to a Great Power ideology, his critics continued to characterise his foreign policy as confused and amateur.[16]

Kozyrev's new-found statism not only undermined his credibility as a liberal but also damaged his ability to function as foreign minister. At home his stand was widely interpreted as yet another manoeuvre to stay in power, while abroad his credibility, already undermined by the indeterminacy of Russian policy in the Bosnian war, imbued Russia's foreign policy with a damaging unpredictability.[17] National-patriots and neo-communists denunciations were roused to fever pitch by his weak response to the threat of Nato expansion and the bombing of Serb positions in Bosnia in August 1995. Despite his alignment with 'pragmatic nationalists' Kozyrev remained committed to a constructive relationship with the West, refusing to accept that the latter remained the threat it had been during the Cold War. In the December 1995 elections Kozyrev retained his single-member seat in Murmansk; faced with the choice of leaving the foreign ministry or giving up his seat, he chose the former and on 5 January 1996 resigned. Thus a distinctive era in Russian foreign policy came to an end.

5 The new pragmatism   His replacement as foreign minister was the head of the Foreign Intelligence Service, Yevgenii Primakov. A specialist on Middle Eastern affairs, Primakov had risen high in the former regime, holding senior positions in the academic world and becoming a candidate member of the Politburo. He had been Gorbachev's envoy to the Gulf from 1990–1 charged with averting war with Iraq. Although foreign policy is a presidential prerogative, the change of ministers inevitably changed the tone and modified the substance of policy. While seeking to maintain good relations with the West, Russia would now reassert its position in China, the Far East and with its traditional allies in the Middle East. A pragmatic politician, Primakov nevertheless took a substantive view of Russia's national interests and insisted that the country was a Great Power.[18] His four priority tasks for Russian foreign policy were to create the external conditions to strengthen Russia's territorial integrity, to support integrative tendencies within the CIS, to stabilise regional conflicts (above all in the former USSR and Yugoslavia), and to prevent the spread of weapons of mass destruction. Primakov had been highly critical of the West, and thus his appointment signalled Yeltsin's attempt to achieve consensus with his critics in the Duma. Communists and nationalists in the Sixth Duma, indeed, welcomed his appointment.

The phases discussed above were marked by excesses: in asserting Russian autonomy the first undermined the viability of the USSR; the second precipitated the collapse of the USSR by reducing Gorbachev to little more than a figurehead; the third exaggerated dependence on the West; the fourth in reaction failed to build a stable and predictable relationship with the world at large; while the fifth endangered the very real achievements of Kozyrev's foreign policy in normalising relations with the world at large.

THE STRUCTURE OF POLICY-MAKING

Soviet diplomacy had traditionally had two faces: one focused on the professional diplomats in the Soviet MFA and was characterised by traditional expertise in negotiation techniques, conflict management and the like; the other, inspired by the residual internationalism of the socialist system, was organised by the Communist Party's International and other departments. Shevardnadze had limited the prerogatives of the latter and by the end of perestroika foreign policy had firmly shifted from the Party to the state and was concentrated in the hands of the specialists in the Soviet MFA. Already by August 1991 the Party organisation had been abolished in the Russian MFA, and the merging of the Russian and Soviet MFAs in late 1991 was accompanied by the 'de-ideologisation' of the new ministry. This was designed above all to improve its professionalism and to ensure that the ministry worked to defend Russia's national-state interests. The cause of international revolution was officially pronounced dead.

The Russian MFA inherited buildings and diplomatic staff from the old regime. Kozyrev moved into the luxurious offices in the foreign ministry building on Smolensk Boulevard and set about rebuilding the Russian diplomatic service. Up to 1991 about two-thirds of Soviet embassy staff abroad were also on the payroll of the KGB.[19] The Russian MFA was restructured to reflect the new priorities of foreign policy. The traditional confused system of administrations (*upravleniya*) and sections (*otdely*) were replaced by a more ordered and hierarchical system of *departament*, *upravlenie* and *otdel*. Thirteen departments (*departamenty*), overseen by deputy ministers, 9 functional administrations (*upravleniya*) and 3 services were initially established. The old regional administrations were transformed into 7 *departamenty*: Europe, North America, Central and South America, Africa, the Near East, the Asia-Pacific region, and South West Asia. There were also departments for International Organisations and Global Problems of International Humanitarian Assistance, and Cultural Cooperation. The departments dealing with information and the press were significantly upgraded.[20] Of particular significance was the creation in the period April–May 1992 of a *departament* for relations with CIS countries, a belated recognition of the importance of this area of what had now become foreign policy, but also an attempt to pre-empt the claims of those who demanded a separate ministry to handle CIS affairs.

All the deputy ministers were new appointments, and most of the next level down (heads of *departamenta*) were Kozyrev appointees too, marked by their relative youth, degrees in higher education and liberal political outlooks. Despite allegations that the Soviet MFA had been vastly over-staffed, in terms of numbers there was little difference between the old and the new. In December 1991 the Russian MFA had a staff of 240, but this soon expanded to about 3,200 in October 1992, not much less than the 3,700 in the Soviet ministry in November 1991. Staff had to reapply for their jobs and professional competence came second to loyalty to the new regime as the criterion for selection. Some of the bright new young – and inexperienced – department heads in the new Russian ministry resisted the absorption of Soviet staff even though the old ministry, for all its faults, represented a pool of professional expertise. Conflict was fuelled by a profound distrust of the older generation of Soviet diplomats, especially if they had been active communists. Many of the most experienced diplomats were either dismissed or for various reasons refused to serve the new Russian authorities, doubting their competence, some capitalised on earlier contacts to set up businesses, and some non-Russians went to join the diplomatic services of their own republics. The work of reorganising the ministry was completed by Autumn 1992, marked by the influx of 'fresh democratic forces' whose professional competence was sometimes questioned. Above all, the 'arrogance of youth' in the ministry was reflected in the inability to accept independent analysis and the rupturing of the links (so much strengthened under Shevardnadze) with the academic community.[21]

By decree in February 1992 Yeltsin subordinated the 'power' and 'political' ministries to the presidency, bringing the MFA and the ministries of defence, internal affairs, security, justice and some others firmly under his control.[22] Numerous presidential agencies and advisory groups were spawned to formulate the main lines of foreign and security policy and to supervise the current work of the ministries, reducing the foreign ministry to not much more than a specialist executive agency. Even though Yeltsin in November 1992 made the MFA responsible for coordinating Russia's foreign policy, confusion remained as individuals and institutions sought to pursue their own foreign policy agendas.

Relations between the MFA and the Supreme Soviet before October 1993 were particularly strained. Presidential supremacy in the field of foreign policy was challenged by the constitution of that time, with articles 104, 125 and 121.5 granting the CPD the exclusive right to 'determine the foreign and domestic policy of the Russian Federation', while the role of the president and government remained vague. Parliament sought to defend its constitutional prerogatives in the foreign policy sphere and increasingly devised autonomous policies of its own. Khasbulatov condemned the failure to give Russia 'a dignified place commanding respect in the world community',[23] while Vladimir Lukin, chairman of the Supreme Soviet's and later the Duma's foreign policy committee, with an interval as Russian ambassador to America, was harshly critical of Kozyrev's policies, condemning him for his alleged excessive pro-Westernism and failure to develop a coherent policy towards the former Soviet republics. Lukin's temporary replacement at the head of the committee, Yevgenii Ambartsumov, was no less expansive in interpreting the role of parliament in foreign affairs, in particular in propounding a Russian Monroe Doctrine according to which 'the entire geopolitical space of the former Soviet Union [is] a sphere of vital interests'.[24]

The events of late 1993 dramatically altered the institutional context of Russian foreign policy. The 1993 constitution put an end to policy dualism and confirmed the president's pre-eminent role. Article 80.3 baldly states that the president 'determines the basic guidelines of the state's domestic and foreign policy': article 80.4 stipulates that he or she 'represents the Russian Federation within the country and in international relations'; and article 86 specifies that the president 'exercises leadership of the foreign policy of the Russian Federation' (86a); conducts negotiations, signs international treaties (86b); and instruments of ratification (86c), and accepts letters of diplomatic accreditation (86d). The president decides membership of the Security Council, chairs its sessions and is the final arbiter of Russia's military doctrine. The president, in consultation with parliament, nominates ambassadors, and has the right to appoint and dismiss members of the government, including those responsible for foreign policy. The government's powers over foreign policy are limited, being authorised only to implement measures for 'the realisation of the foreign policy of the Russian Federation' (114.1e). In other words, it is intended to do little more than to implement policies coming from the presidency. The work of the MFA in the new conditions was formulated by a presidential statute of 14 March 1995, subordinating it to the president but delegating to it 'the development of the general strategy for Russian foreign policy'.[25]

This was reflected in the reduced foreign policy role assigned to parliament. Formally, the State Duma's functions are restricted to approving or rejecting international treaties (article 106d), while the Federation Council authorises the use of Russian troops abroad (102.1d). Both issues could prove controversial. Parliament's foreign policy role, however, is broader than the above would suggest. Above all, the committee system ensured that foreign policy issues remain firmly within the purview of deputies. The FC's committees for foreign affairs, CIS affairs, and security and defence policy are complemented by the Duma committees for foreign affairs, defence, security, CIS affairs and links with compatriots, and, in the fifth Duma as a sop to Zhirinovskii, a special Committee for Geopolitical Affairs. The anti-Western majority in the Fifth Duma, and even more so in the Sixth, forced foreign policy to adopt the language of struggle between Russian and Western interests. The resulting espousal of Russia as a 'Great Power' meant that 'ideological dogma had priority over commonsense'.[26]

Many other organisations play their part in the foreign policy process. In addition to the domestic security agencies and the Foreign Intelligence Service, the Security Council took an active foreign policy role. A decree of 16 December 1992 created the Interdepartmental Commission for Foreign Policy (ICFP) of the Security Council, headed at the time by Skokov, with enormous powers to coordinate the whole field of foreign and security policy.[27] The SC was charged with developing in concrete form a concept of Russia's national interests, special strategic policies and strategies for dealing with crises in the 'near abroad'. This work was carried out in the SC by 'interdepartmental commissions', consisting of representatives of governmental ministries and agencies, including a Commission on Foreign Policy headed until the autumn of 1994 by the deputy foreign minister A. Adamishin. However, while all the structures for effective policy-making were in place, the general 'absence of executive discipline' in the country and the 'weakness of the whole power machine', as the deputy secretary of the SC, Lieutenant-General Valerii Manilov put it, meant that not much was achieved.[28] Above all, SC staff did not supervise the flow of documents addressed to the president, without which it could not control the everyday activity of government agencies.[29]

With the creation of the Russian Ministry of Defence in May 1992 older Soviet patterns of rivalry between the foreign and defence ministries re-emerged. Kozyrev insisted on the primacy of the foreign ministry, and warned (unsuccessfully) against the military becoming an autonomous force in areas such as Trans-Dniester.[30] On several occasions, as in Abkhazia and elsewhere, it appeared that Russia had two foreign policies, an official presidential one and another pursued by the military. Yeltsin's debt to the military following the October events only increased their scope for independent initiatives.

The country was marked by the proliferation of non-governmental 'think tanks', lobbying pressure groups, pseudo-academic research institutes established by retired or dismissed politicians, and money-making ventures launched by institutes of the Academy of Sciences to augment the meagre funds available from the state. By far the most important, however, was the Council for Foreign and Defence Policy, founded in June 1992 'as a public organisation of politicians, entrepreneurs, civil servants, media figures and academics whose purpose is to support the development and implementation of strategic conceptions for the development of Russia, its foreign and defence policies'.[31] In the words of its director, Karaganov, its task was to coordinate the contending proposals to create 'a stable political centre in the country'.[32] Membership ranged across the political spectrum, including Vol'skii, Yulii Vorontsov (adviser to Yeltsin on foreign affairs), Andrei Kokoshin (first deputy minister of defence), Lukin, Vladimir Petrovskii (deputy secretary-general of the United Nations), Yavlinskii and many more to total some fifty people in May 1994. Its first report (noted above) called 'A Strategy for Russia',[33] strongly influenced the evolving debate over Russia's foreign policy and place in the world, while its second report in May 1994 had even greater resonance (see below).[34]

In contrast to the Soviet era, and indeed even under Gorbachev, policy-making was now a much more open and pluralistic process. Some regional and republican leaders (in particular Tatarstan and Chechnya) also sought to sustain foreign policy initiatives, but their scope for this was limited by the Federal Treaty of 31 March 1992, which had unequivocally reserved to the federal authorities responsibility for foreign policy, and by the 1993 constitution. The MFA in December 1994 established a Consultative Council of Russian Federation Subjects on International and Foreign Economic Relations to coordinate local initiatives. Primakov sought to curb international freelancing by regional elites, institutions and social forces sought to influence policy through lobbying, press campaigns and other normal features of pluralistic politics. However, the politicisation of foreign policy had some negative consequences as crude representations of complex foreign policy decisions became part of domestic political struggles, adding yet another layer of unpredictability to Russian foreign policy.

Despite the new pluralism, in certain respects post-communist Russia reproduced Soviet, if not Tsarist, patterns of foreign policy-making. Once again the government was reduced to executing policies decided upon by the Tsar, Politburo or president, with its functions largely focused on economic issues. Decision-making in the Soviet system might have been cumbersome, with foreign-policy decisions coordinated between the relevant ministries, Central Committee departments and the KGB, but at least Soviet policy was marked by consistency. Russian policy, however, was marked by a lack of coordination and often contradictory purposes. In its second policy statement 'A Strategy for Russia', the CFDP was bitterly critical of the fragmentation of foreign policy-making:

> None, even the most elementary strategy for the defence and realisation of the national interests of the country, can be implemented under the present condition of the institutions intended to formulate and implement it . . . Each official enjoys the freedom to have his own policy. This situation not only weakens the position of the country but also disgraces it. This is one of the most difficult challenges for Russian foreign policy.[35]

Although foreign policy prerogatives were concentrated in the hands of the presidency, the presidential apparatus itself was divided into competing factions seeking to influence Yeltsin.[36] The presidential system included a number of analytical centres and presidential assistants for foreign policy, with Dmitrii Ryurikov a longtime adviser on foreign policy to Yeltsin, together with academic specialists like Karaganov, Migranyan, Satarov, Emil Pain, Leonid Smirnyagin and Dmitrii Volkogonov. Whatever their merits, these advisers could not substitute for a solid bureaucratic structure combining expertise with the ability to control decision-making and implementation. Although a 'presidential' foreign policy system might have been established, effective control over formulation and implementation remained with the ministries. The foreign, defence and intelligence ministries represented concentrations of information, expertise and experience, and with their own policy agendas. Thus the erratic jerks in Russian foreign policy reflected not only conceptual shifts but changes in the relative weight of various governmental agencies.

The creation of the Foreign Policy Council on 26 December 1995 represented an attempt to overcome the fragmentation of Russian foreign policy. The new council, chaired by the president and with a secretariat, includes the ministers of foreign affairs, defence, foreign trade, CIS affairs, and finance, as well as the heads of the Federal Security Service, Foreign

Intelligence Service, Federal Border Service, and the president's foreign policy aide. The council's main task was to monitor the implementation of foreign-policy decisions made by the president and reflected Yeltsin's attempt to concentrate foreign-policy decision-making in his own hands, in an effort to impose order on the chaotic Russian foreign policy process. The changes since 1990 have been dramatic, yet the behaviour of institutions appears to have taken on a life of its own, increasingly impervious to changes from above.

THE DEBATE OVER FOREIGN POLICY

By late 1991 Russia had lost much of the territory for which it had fought for centuries. Peter the Great's defeat of the Swedes at Poltava in 1709 gave Russia access to the Baltic ports, and in particular Riga. Catherine the Great's defeat of the Ottoman Turks gave Russia access to the ports of the Black Sea, above all Sevastopol in the Crimea. Victory in the Second World War gave the USSR an extended security zone reaching as far as Berlin. Russia's military-strategic expansion now not only ended but collapsed, and the 'gathering of the lands' went into reverse as the rump Russian state in the West was reduced to not much more than Muscovy under Ivan the Terrible in the sixteenth century. From an imperial point of view, the collapse of communism and the disintegration of the USSR was a defeat for Russia. It lost its warm-water ports in the Baltic republics, and now had to rely on Kaliningrad, separated from Russia by Lithuania, St Petersburg, which was not really a natural harbour, and the ice-bound ports of Murmansk and Arkhangel. The retreat from the Baltic and the Black Sea pushed Russia eastwards away from Europe and the Middle East and back into the Eurasian heartlands. It is against this background that the debate over Russian foreign policy unfolded. In this section we will briefly indicate some of the issues and contending views.

From ideology to interests and back

Russian foreign policy under Yeltsin was predicated on a post-imperial and democratic relationship with the world at large and with the successor states, but how was Russia to respond to the West's *de facto* marginalisation of Russia in the international system or to the alleged infringements on the civic, and on occasion, the human rights of the Russian-speaking populations in some of the post-Soviet republics? What were Russia's national interests, and what form would their espousal take in the international system? Would Russian foreign policy indeed become something new, as Kozyrev promised, or would traditional Great Power and Russian imperial traditions reassert themselves?

Gorbachev's foreign policy, adroitly managed by Shevardnadze, was conducted within the framework of what was called the New Political Thinking (NPT). Russian foreign policy continued some of its concerns, such as ending political and military divisions, reintegration into the world community and the demilitarisation of foreign policy, but at the same time qualitatively new issues emerged. Russian foreign policy differed sharply from the compromises of the Gorbachev era, which had tried to maintain the status of the USSR as one of the two superpowers, and Russia's ambitions were now more modest. It no longer made sense to talk of the de-ideologisation of foreign policy, of a world divided into 'two camps', however interdependent, or of the conflict between the social systems of capitalism and socialism.

Now, more than ever before, there was a blurred distinction between domestic and 'foreign' policy. Foreign policy was a field over which domestic politics was fought, but while various interests sought to exert their influence, policy remained firmly in the hands of the president and his ministers. The challenge now was to redefine Russian national interest in the new geopolitical circumstances of the post-Cold War world and the disintegration of the USSR. But before national interest could be established, the nature of Russia itself had to be defined. The interests of a national democratic state would be very different from a neo-imperial Russia, and it would be hardly appropriate to talk of the national interests of a Russia dissolving once again into the principalities of the fourteenth and fifteenth centuries. Did Russia have constant geostrategic, political or ideological interests, and what social groups could mould a new Russian national interest?[37] Pre-revolutionary imperial messianism, whereby Russia had not only a military but also a spiritual mission to bring enlightenment to neighbouring peoples and the world, and the Soviet Union's self-definition as the harbinger of international socialism, were repudiated. Russia's national identity began to be reformulated as a state rather than as an empire. But even some of those who accepted the birth of a nation insisted on the retention of Russian universal values, threatened allegedly by the rush to embrace the West, and that Russia retained a 'mission' if not a messianic purpose.[38] The debate in essence was over a new ideology of foreign policy for Russia.

A distinction should be drawn between national and state interests, and indeed national interests may well be opposed to those of the state.[39] In contemporary foreign policy, it is state interests that predominate over those of the nation, yet in post-communist countries the distinction remained blurred. Estonian nationalists and extreme Russian patriots sought to identify the interests of the state with those of a particular national group. Talk of the 'national interest' in a multinational state could be misleading and some suggested that the term 'fundamental interests' might be more appropriate.[40] Mythical ideas of the homogeneity of national interests overlook the conflicting interests of contemporary civil society, and indeed the ability of nationalists and communists to subsume conflicting social interests into a single plane of national struggle testifies to the relative under-development of civil society in Russia. Pozdnyakov goes so far as to argue that national interest and state interest are identical.[41]

At the centre of the debate over Russian foreign policy was the attempt to define Russia's relationship with Western civilisation and strategic concerns. Failure to deal with this question in 1917 led to the fall of the Provisional Government. Russia's subservience to the West, above all in honouring its commitments in the Great War, allowed it to be pressured by the French into launching the disastrous Galician offensive in June 1917. The national-patriots from 1991 accused Yeltsin's government, too, of selling Russia's interests short by kowtowing to the West, begging for assistance and alienating Russian lands and islands. A new Russian isolationism emerged, warning against 'over-Westernisation' and the 'Americanisation' of foreign policy. They stressed the need for native (*samobytnyi*) traditions and questioned the need for Russia's 'return' to Europe and reintegration into the world economy. The dominant centrist view, however, can be formulated as 'the road to our future passes through the West but does not stop there': joining the world but on Russia's terms, not as a supplicant but as an equal, retaining Russia's own identity and defending its interests.

Opinion divided over whether Russia constitutes a separate civilisation or whether it is no more than a variant of 'world civilisation', usually considered synonymous with the West. The emergence of a 'new Eastern Europe' of Ukraine and Belarus separating Russia from the rest of Europe stimulated the 'Eurasian' tradition in Russian philosophy, and indeed the tension in Russian national identity can be interpreted in the light of a struggle between Atlanticists and Eurasianists.[42] The latter shared Dostoevsky's view that Russia should concern itself with dominance in Asia rather than dreams of European integration: 'In Europe we are hangers-on and slaves, but in Asia we walk as masters.' The old debate resurfaced between the Westernisers, oriented towards Western values and Russia's integration into European processes, and the Slavophiles, stressing Russia's native traditions and distinct culture. Tibor Szamuely argues that before the revolution and again today Russian thinkers:

> would not have accepted the idea of the Russian past having been just a part of a single, uniform, homogenized European experience . . . . Whether they gloried in this difference and strove to perpetuate it, like the Slavophiles, or yearned for a decisive break with tradition, like the 'Westernisers', all alike recognised that Russia had merely been in Europe, but not of it.[43]

Likhachev takes issue with Szamuely's view that Russia is the only European country that 'owed virtually nothing to the common cultural and spiritual heritage of the West'.[44] He insists that Russia was part of European development, owing its religion and much of its culture to Orthodox Christianity and borrowing early concepts of statehood from the Scandinavians.[45]

Eurasianists argue that Russia is not part of European civilisation but represents a separate and distinct civilisation of its own acting as the 'balance holder' between Europe and Asia.[46] They deny the need for Russia to integrate into Europe, arguing that it had never shared a common civilisation.[47] The Eurasianists revived the geopolitical school of thinking, developed by Halford Mackinder in the early part of the century, according to which Russia encompasses most of the 'geographical pivot of history', acting as the balanceholder in the World Island.[48] As far as they were concerned, Russia was a bridge between Western and Eastern civilisations. The modern Eurasianists, drawing on the thinking of their predecessors in emigration of the early 1920s, question uncritical pro-Westernism and advocate a reorientation of policy towards the countries of the former Soviet Union. Stalinist xenophobia, in their view, had given way to a condition that Krizhanich had already diagnosed in Russia three centuries earlier: 'Xenomania (*chuzhbesie* in our language) is an obsessive love of foreign people.'[49] Sergei Goncharov, a researcher at the Far East Institute, noted that:

> today, we are moving away from total confrontation with the West toward an equally total fraternisation. In the process, we sometimes overstep the bounds of reason in our desire for alliance . . . . The idea of the primacy of human rights is being turned into an absolute as zealously as the earlier concept of 'class interests' was.

He advocated a policy of 'rational egoism' that placed the success of domestic reforms over any other considerations, even though this might lead to measures that displeased the West.[50] Eurasianism thus represented the moderate face of the Russian rejection of the West.

Of all the Slavophiles Peter Chaadayev was the most pro-European, a sympathy accompanied by a denigration of Russia. In his first *Philosophical Letter* he wrote 'We do not belong to any of the great families of humanity, to either the West or the East, and have no traditions of either. We exist outside time'.[51] It was this attempt to emulate the West by vilifying Russia that so incensed sections of society following the fall of communism. Pozdnyakov, one of the leading exponents of Eurasianism, pointed out that no sooner had the socialist utopia died out than a host of new ones sprang up to replace it, including '*mondialiste* Westernisers whom Russian national traditions tell nothing whatever – are pushing Russia into Europe', and he insisted that 'it would be very wrong and, in fact, dangerous to forget that Russia's history, the history of the formation of our society and state, differs *entirely* from that of Western Europe'.[52]

The debate over Eurasianism is essentially a debate over paths of development and the principles of political and economic reform. Zagorskii stresses, however, that the concept of the West is no longer confined to Europe or America but includes Japan, South Korea and other newly industrialised countries, none of whom had renounced their own civilisations but had become part of the synthesis of global civilisation. The concept of Russia as a bridge is therefore meaningless, since links between Germany and Japan could quite happily bypass Russia. Eurasianism is a bridge leading nowhere.[53] The debate, however, clearly signalled, as Mark Frankland has observed, 'that the natural relationship between Russia and Europe is more likely one of rivalry than of unbroken cooperation'.[54]

Drawing the line

The liberal-democratic view dominant in the first post-communist period was firmly oriented towards the West and the global institutions of the post-war world.[55] Kozyrev's reforms in the foreign ministry were buttressed by Burbulis's predominance over much of the presidential administration, while the defence and security establishments were disoriented by the failure of the coup. The liberals soon came to terms with the smaller Russia, and tried to develop a new Russian statehood with a definition of the national interest that focused on domestic economic and political transformation, release from the burden of empire and economic entanglement with the near abroad, and international integration based on the global division of labour, international competitiveness and openness to the international financial system. They tried to develop good relations with the former Soviet republics but within the framework of Russia's national security interests rather than any larger concept of Russia's hegemonic role in post-Soviet international affairs, and supported the development of peaceful integration through CIS institutions.

Russia's attempt to formulate a new international doctrine took place in a relatively benign international environment, with no direct threats to its integrity and no global threat of the sort that had derailed the democracies in the 1930s. This did not, however, prevent the emergence of a rejectionist movement in both domestic and foreign policy. The first meeting of the CFDP on 2 July 1992 warned of a growing anti-government alliance, including disaffection in the army and the military-industrial complex.[56] Kozyrev found himself at odds with other sections of the government, for example, with the Ministry of Defence over arms sales to potentially unstable countries like Iran and Libya. The liberal line in foreign policy was under threat, and already on 30 June Kozyrev had warned of the possibility of another coup, this time led by national-patriotic forces rather than by communist conservatives.[57] Kozyrev presented a vigorous defence of his policies to the Russian parliament on 22 October 1992:

> There is a danger that our discussion on foreign policy will become something other than the search for the best way of realising the interests of the country. Under the cover of slogans like 'the third path', 'Eurasianism', 'enlightened patriotism' (very similar to socialist patriotism) the democratic path of development ... is questioned, the choice of transforming Russia into a democratic country and an equal member of the community of democratic states of the world.

Kozyrev defended a 'democratic programme for the rebirth of Russia as a Great Power'.[58]

He had long resisted the formulation of Russia's foreign policy in a single document, reminiscent of the codified and ideologically correct programmes issued by the CPSU in its heyday, and the fact that work continued in this direction indicated the weakness of his grip on the foreign policy process. Like Gaidar, Kozyrev was an intellectual who came to his post with clear theoretical preferences and convictions that took time to temper in the real world of policy-making. His first attempt to formulate Russia's foreign policy concept in spring 1992 summarised the liberal-democratic line: economic recovery, human and civic rights, democracy, reintegration into the world economy, and Russia as a new model Great Power concerned with global economic, environmental and nuclear security in a community of democratic states. This version was contemptuously rejected by parliament in July 1992 on the grounds that it was too vague, too pro-Western and failed to identify Russia's national interests or to formulate a scale of priorities.[59] The alternative programme issued by the CFDP stressed good relations with Western Europe and China, and placed rather less emphasis on the American relationship. It took a pessimistic view of Russia's immediate economic prospects, and talked in terms of Russia's geopolitical encirclement which could be mitigated by pursuing an 'enlightened post-imperial integrationist course' towards the former Soviet republics, many of which enjoyed only a 'weak historical legitimacy' in terms of borders, ethnicity and economic development.[60]

The MFA's revised version of its document on 1 December 1992 took a more assertive line on the Russians-abroad question, and although still committed to international integration and human rights, began to move away from the vague universalism of Gorbachev's NPT towards a more focused attempt at formulating the principles of Russian policy. It took a positive view of Russia's economic integration into the international community and supported a global rather than a continental strategy for Russia.[61] The document's stress on 'partnership' with the United States, based on 'adherence to common democratic values', was attacked by the Russian ambassador to the United States, Lukin, who condemned those in Moscow who were guilty of 'romantic, infantile pro-Americanism'.[62]

In a series of speeches Stankevich, at the time political adviser to the president, argued that a commitment to 'universal human values' was too weak a platform on which to build a foreign policy, and instead called for a Russia that could combine elements of democracy, patriotism, Great Power interests (*derzhavnosti*), and national consensus while avoiding narrow nationalism and xenophobia.[63] He hailed the concept of patriotism as something that could save Russia, and insisted that Russia was no longer an empire, concentrating on external expansion, but should develop as a state in which its resources were mobilised for economic and cultural development.[64]

The national-patriotic view contained elements of Pan-Slavism, a movement that gathered force in the second half of the nineteenth century with congresses in Prague (1848) and Moscow (1867), with unsuccessful revival attempts at meetings in Prague (1908) and Sofia (1910). The Poles had never been attracted by Pan-Slavism, and Czechs like Milan Kundera insisted that Central Europe had always been part of Western Europe and forcefully excluded Russia from the shared European cultural experience.[65] Pan-Slavism had few answers to the general cultural crisis of post-totalitarianism, and wherever it was revived, as in Serbia and the fringes of Russian political life, represented a nostalgic representation of a world of Slavic brotherhood that had never existed.[66]

In an attenuated form, however, the revival of the Slavic idea influenced the development of foreign policy. Solzhenitsyn proposed a Slavic commonwealth of Russia, Ukraine, Belarus and North Kazakhstan,[67] and elements of this proposal were incorporated into the original idea proposed by Burbulis for the CIS. The idea of the Slavic commonwealth failed because of objections by the Islamic republics and Ukraine's fear of becoming locked into an eastward-looking alliance. Russia tried to transform the relationship with Central and Eastern Europe (CEE) into one of partnership, and the Bulgarian president Zhelyu Zhelev insisted that 'decades of communist power did not succeeed in destroying the historical Orthodox and Slavic feelings that bring together the Bulgarian and Russian people'.[68] Declarations of sympathy for Serbia in the Yugoslav wars were based on the alleged commonality of interests based on a shared religion and ethnicity. Solzhenitsyn remained consistent in his views, advocating a retreat from Tajikistan and the recognition of Chechen independence, once the traditional Cossack territories north of the Terek river had been reincorporated into Stavropol krai.[69]

The national-patriots were divided on most issues but on one thing they agreed: that Russia should remain a Great Power. As far as they were concerned 'Russia's entry into the civilised world community', as Yeltsin described the aim of Russian foreign policy,[70] should not be at the expense of Russia's national interests. Many of them refused to accept that the unity of the Slavic peoples of the former USSR was irrevocably broken, and thus looked to some unit larger than what they considered to be the incomplete national units of the successor states. Their arguments, often incoherent in detail, are primarily important because they reintroduced the language of truculant nationalism into Russian political discourse. They succeeded in shifting the terms of debate away from the 'romantic internationalism' of the Gorbachev and early Kozyrev years into a general sense that 'Russia is fated to be a Great Power'; though how and why this should be the case was never adequately explained.

The theme of the betrayal of Russia's national interests featured in the attack by the historian Natalya Narochnitskaya's on Kozyrev's foreign policy when she bewailed Russia's loss of territories. She urged that Russia should revoke the CIS treaty and try to reunite the former Soviet republics.[71] Like the CPRF and other rejectionists, she suspected that the West's policy of keeping Russia democratic was in fact a policy to keep Russia weak. This is the way that they interpreted Zbigniew Brzezinski's argument that Western assistance should be based on a policy of strengthening the non-Russian republics and ensuring that Russia remained a post-imperial power.[72]

The democratic wave of 1988–91 gradually gave way to a more assertive sentiment. The resignation of the liberal first deputy foreign minister Shelov-Kovedyaev, who had sought to devise a post-imperial relationship with the CIS, in October 1992 was a sign that Yeltsin was giving way to domestic pressures. While Russia did not take over the attitudes of the USSR it did begin to see its interests as paralleling those of the Soviet Union. In his rather bizarre speech to foreign ministers at the CSCE conference in Stockholm on 14 December 1992, Kozyrev outlined in a mock speech the hardline policies that were to be expected from Russia if the conservatives came to power. He spoke of a 'Helsinki' Europe split into two, with the European Union taking responsibility for order in the West while in the 'Eastern zone' Russia would assume unique responsibility for conflict management where CSCE norms would not be fully applicable. The former Soviet republics would 'immediately have to enter into a new federation or confederation, and on this we will have tough negotiations'.[73] Although this was meant to be taken as a warning of what *might* happen if hardliners came to power in Moscow, much of this, paradoxically, was implemented later by Kozyrev himself.

The concept of the 'national interest' in government thinking evolved. Yeltsin insisted that 'the main task facing Russia is to emerge from the deep quagmire of crisis and to change to a life that will enable us and other peoples to live and work normally'.[74] Kozyrev added that 'the "supertask" of Russian diplomacy in all areas is to make the utmost, concrete contribution to the improvement of the everyday life of Russian citizens'.[75] In other words, the aims of foreign policy were subordinated to the needs of domestic reform, undermining the autonomy of foreign policy. He was committed to a genuinely internationalist conception of human rights as the central pillar not only of post-communist Russian foreign policy but as a universal process of the late twentieth century: 'The realisation of human rights in our country is inseparable from our policy to integrate Russia into the global family of democratic states.'[76] As far as Kozyrev was concerned, this programme would hasten economic recovery and the revival of Russia's Great Power status, this time, allegedly, as a 'normal Great Power'.[77]

The view that Russia should be a Great Power did not go unchallenged. The journalist Oleg Moroz argued that earlier attempts to become a superpower had given Russia nothing except futile wars in Korea, Vietnam and Afghanistan. He argued 'It is time for us to give up our primitive habit of puffing up our cheeks and making a first-rank power of ourselves. . . . Whether we want to or not, we are now forced to admit that by all criteria Russia is a second-rank power. . . . In terms of importance, we should take our place somewhere between Egypt and Colombia, and sit there quietly.'[78] Not many were prepared to accept such a radically minimalist view of Russia's status, especially when armed with nuclear weapons.

Russian foreign policy developed against the background of a debate over the structure of international relations itself in the late twentieth century. The democrats espoused a normative approach, insisting that ethical and moral considerations had an important part to play in international affairs.[79] They were attracted by the concept of world society, and sought to integrate Russia into the existing system of international institutions. The national-patriots held to a more traditional view, stressing the primacy of the national interest in a 'realist' world in which foreign policy was determined by the power of states. The neo-communists incorporated patriotic themes into a programme that sought not only to reconstitute the Soviet Union but to reassert its superpower status: the realities of power rather than the pursuit of justice dominated the thinking of the centrists. But whose power? The realist pursuit of alleged national interests in an international system dominated by nation-states now had to be tempered by a world covered by a multitude of international non-governmental and governmental international organisations. The unravelling of Stalin's 'hyper-realist' foreign policy ultimately led to the collapse of the USSR as the Baltic and other forcibly incorporated republics took their revenge. The lesson appears clear: there is nothing more unrealistic than brute realism.

Russia was torn between remaining a *status quo* power or becoming a revisionist power. It had been the greatest loser in the territorial settlements of the Soviet years and was thus potentially a revisionist power. In addition, a type of 'Versailles syndrome' emerged whereby the democrats were alleged to have betrayed Russia's national interests in the exit from communism, above all in signing the Belovezha Accords that consigned the USSR to the dustbin of history. As with Britain earlier, the loss of empire is accompanied by the search for a new role.

RUSSIA AND THE WORLD

Russia's foreign policy is constrained by geopolitical factors. The sheer size of Russia means that it is faced with a multiplicity of regional issues, and in certain respects it has as many foreign policies as it has neighbours. In particular, Russia was forced to define a new relationship not only with the world at large but also with the former members of the 'indissoluble' USSR. The emergence of fifteen independent republics onto the world stage ranks as an event of unparalleled historical importance, shifting the balance of power on the Eurasian landmass and altering the global system of international relations. The very concept of the 'near abroad', as noted, suggested some sort of intermediate status between sovereign statehood and traditional dependence. Russia was linked by centuries of political and human contacts with these new states but now had to find new forms of interaction.

In its relations with the former Soviet republics Russia, unlike the hardliners under Gorbachev, refused to use the large Russian populations as a lever against the new leaderships. Russia recognised the existing borders and stated clearly, for example, that it accepted the territorial integrity of Ukraine and consistently viewed the problems of Crimea as an internal Ukrainian matter. Alleged discrimination against Russian populations was raised in fora like the OSCE and the Council of Europe, but the use of more robust methods was rejected. This accommodating line, which at its most extreme interpreted every assertion of Russian interests as a revival of an imperial mentality, drew increasing criticism on the grounds that even a democratic and post-imperial Russia had legitimate national interests. Centrists insisted that Russia should take a firmer line towards the CIS states, while Lipitskii, chair of the People's Party of Free Russia, urged a complete reorientation of Russian foreign policy away from its Western focus towards former Soviet and Soviet bloc countries.[80] The development of a more assertive foreign policy was interpreted by some of Russia's neighbours as the recrudescence of traditional imperialism. However, this 'neo-imperialism' (if indeed it can be called that) was based on a position of weakness rather than strength. The second report of the CFDP warned, however, that Russia's neighbours were on the whole even weaker, giving rise 'along with the general growth of nationalism in Russian public opinion and political circles to a growing sense of Russia's imaginary omnipotence'.

A thin line separated security-building along Russia's borders and the revival of neo-imperial ambitions. Kozyrev insisted that Russia had no choice but to involve itself here in conflict-management, including the use of force for peace-keeping: 'For Russia this kind of "isolationism" would entail millions of refugees and chaos along the perimeter of the southern borders.'[81] Russian policy, however, tended to be reactive. If indeed the issue of 'Russians abroad' was primary and Solzhenitsyn's idea of a Slavic union had any resonance, then one would have anticipated that Russian policy would have concentrated on areas where Russians were concentrated, notably Eastern Ukraine, Crimea and Northern Kazakhstan, whereas in fact Russia made no attempt to use the issue of Russia's right to split the countries and absorb contested areas. Any attempt to do so, as Emil Pain (a member of the Presidential Council) warned, would provoke a permanently destabilising legacy of hatred in the residual states.[82]

The reassertion of Russia's special interests in the former Soviet republics, considered a covert form of neo-colonialism by its critics, was regarded relatively benignly by the West. Not wanting to get involved in complex disputes, the West by default allowed Russia a relatively free hand. There were limits, however, to Western indifference, and it was clear that direct Russian intervention in the Baltic republics or Ukraine would be a matter of international concern. The line, indeed, was narrow between Russia's 'legitimate interests' in the near abroad, and a revived imperial policy. At what point would a Western response be triggered, and what form could it take? Those in the West, like Brzezinski, who took a critical attitude towards Russia's role in the near abroad almost invariably saw Ukraine as a counter-balance to a Moscow-centred Western policy. Indeed, the inter-war language of 'buffer states' was soon dusted off, and the notion of a *cordon sanitaire* against 'Russian expansionism' was not far away. The American journalist Robert Seely, for example, asserted that 'an independent Ukraine is a natural buffer between Russia and the central European states', and in the spirit of the post-ideological Cold War mentioned above went on absurdly to argue that Ukraine could be 'a more reliable source of support for the international order than Russia'.[83]

Russia was recognised as the continuer state to the USSR, taking over responsibility for its treaty obligations and enjoying the privileges of the old state. Russia became the residual legatee of all the authority that was not devolved to the other republics. A vivid manifestation of Russia's dissolution in the Union was that whereas Ukraine and Belorussia as well as the USSR took seats in the UN as founding members (according to a deal agreed with Stalin in 1945), Russia had been left firmly in the cold. Now Russia took over the USSR's seat as one of the five permanent members of the UN Security Council, giving it a right of veto.

The fall of Soviet communism allowed the global hegemony of the single remaining superpower, but at the same time it removed any purpose to this predominance. The Soviet MFA had long been torn between 'Americanist' and 'Europeanist' tendencies, and while during perestroika European policy had been revived, the concentration on America in the old game of superpower politics remained. Reflecting the shrinkage in Russia's global weight, it was only natural that Russia focused more on the European aspects of its foreign policy, although care was taken not to neglect other spheres and the relationship with America remained crucial. The meeting in Vancouver in April 1992 between Yeltsin and Clinton was the first ever 'superpower' summit devoted not to overcoming confrontation but to economic issues. Yeltsin's visit to Washington in June 1992 dispelled the lingering reservations that characterised Soviet-American relations even at their best and marked the confirmation of Russia's status as a partner in world affairs. The signing of the 'Charter for Russian-American Partnership and Friendship' at that time noted that the 'welfare, prosperity and security of a democratic Russian Federation and the United States of America are closely linked'. In his address to Congress on 17 June Yeltsin drew a thick line under the past, insisting that communism, 'which spread everywhere social strife and brutality, which instilled fear in humanity', had collapsed never to rise again. He insisted that Russia had made 'its final choice in favour of a civilised way of life, common sense and the universal human heritage'. For good measure, he stressed that 'The freedom of America is now being upheld in Russia.'[84]

Points of tension, however, remained in Russia's relations with America. The lack of coordination between Russia's aggressive arms sales and foreign policy led on several occasions to conflict, as over the proposed sale of submarines and nuclear power technology to Iran and cryogenic engines to India. The economic depression in the final period of Bush's term in office and his weak leadership meant that the euphoria of the end of the Cold War was not translated into effective policies to assist the rehabilitation of Russia and other post-communist states. Plans to expand Nato to CEE countries (see chapter 15) and the war in Yugoslavia brought Russia's apparent national interests into confrontation with those of the West. Nevertheless, despite calls for more attention to be devoted to the other post-Soviet republics, America focused on a 'Russia first' policy.

The primacy of superpower dialogue over specifically European policy towards Russia gradually faded. But Europe itself was divided, with tensions between the French ambition to create a European presence on the world stage, German concerns about insecurity on its eastern borders, and Britain's insistence on the primacy of Nato and support for the expansion of the

EU to CEE in the hope that 'widening' would undermine the 'deepening' of EU integration. The EU's concentration on deepening integration through the Maastricht process, a treaty that significantly raised the threshold of the *acquis communautaire* (the body of Union law), made it more difficult for the Eastern European countries to meet membership criteria.

The European direction of Russian foreign policy was repeatedly stressed by the Yeltsin administration, but was only fitfully implemented. At a press conference in Paris on 17 April 1991 Yeltsin stressed that Russia could 'play a unique role as a bridge between Europe and Asia and that it can contribute towards extending the area of European cooperation, particularly in the economic field, from the Atlantic to the Pacific'.[85] Russia's economic weakness inhibited the development of this programme, but its openness to the international economy gradually bore tangible fruit. Russia's links with the EU were strengthened, but this was to be a long and hard road. Rather than imposing sanctions the West signalled its displeasure with the conduct of the Chechen war by putting pressure on the political elite by suspending moves towards Russian integration into Western institutions. The EU delayed the signature of a trade and cooperation agreement, while the Parliamentary Assembly of the Council of Europe suspended membership procedures.[86] The head of the Council of Europe, Daniel Tarschys, insisted that as long as Russia ignored 'basic rules and standards' of human rights it would be inappropriate for Russia to join.[87] However, following the fair elections of December 1995 Russian membership was approved on 25 January 1996 on the grounds that 'integration is preferable to isolation'. Russia on 28 February became the 39th member of the Council of Europe. A dramatic reorientation in Russia's trade patterns took place, shifting from Eastern to Western Europe, with the EU by 1993 becoming Russia's biggest export market.[88] It was understood, however, that Russia's entry into the EU would not be considered in the forseeable future.

Policy towards what had formerly been known as 'Eastern' Europe was now subsumed into larger European policy, as indicated by the single department for Europe in the MFA. During 1989–90 these countries shrugged off their Sovietisation; and relations between them and Russia began on a new footing. Even as the USSR declined, Russia had been pursuing a distinct East European policy of its own marked by common democratic aspirations. Yeltsin's first official visit to the region was to Czechoslovakia in May 1991 in which he moved far beyond Gorbachev's 'regret' over the invasion of the country in 1968 and instead called it a 'gross mistake and interference in Czechoslovakia's internal affairs'. On 29 August 1991 Kozyrev condemned the armed intervention in Hungary in 1956 in equally harsh terms. By appealing to common values and laying to rest some of the ghosts of the past, some of the traditional Russophobia of the region began to dissipate.

Relations had to be rebuilt with the former bloc countries (sometimes called the 'middle abroad'), but once the immediate question of the withdrawal had been resolved, relations, both economic and political, languished. After 42 years of a less than glorious career, the Council for Mutual Economic Assistance (Comecon) formally ended its mortal existence on 28 June 1991. In 1989 Comecon countries accounted for nearly half of Soviet trade, but from 1 January 1991 mutual trade was conducted in hard currencies at world prices, leading to a collapse of economic relations. New forms of economic interaction had to be found since Russia was the main provider of much of the oil, almost all the natural gas and the greater part of other natural resources to the region. Russia unreservedly accepted the complete sovereignty of these states, but the legacy of mistrust remained and as long as the outcome of democratic reforms in Russia

Figure 7 Central and Eastern Europe

hung in the balance, the nervousness of the former satellite countries was understandable. As far as the Central European and Balkan countries were concerned, the security vacuum that had opened up from the Baltic to the Black Sea should be filled by the rapid expansion of Nato to the east, but this, as we shall see in the next chapter, threatened precisely to alienate Russia and provoke the security crisis that it was designed to overcome.

One of the greatest challenges to Russia's liberal foreign policy arose over policy towards the conflict in the former Yugoslavia. Russia followed UN policy in Bosnia despite the condemnation by rejectionists in parliament and elsewhere who insisted that Yeltsin and Kozyrev had 'betrayed' its traditional ally by failing to use its veto in the Security Council to block anti-Serbian resolutions. The Yugoslav wars forcefully raised the dilemma in Russian foreign policy: would alliance with the West (the Atlanticist approach) take precedence over Russia's traditional Great Power interests in the Balkans based on notions of Pan-Slavism and commonality of religion and ethnicity? Kozyrev vigorously defended his policies, rejecting the notion of the 'Slavic factor' in its approach to the Yugoslav crisis, and warned that the division of Europe into Slavic, Germanic or Francophone areas would return Europe to before 1914 in which yet another Serbian crisis could threaten war. The pursuit of a foreign policy based on ethnic or religious considerations could destroy Russia where millions of Orthodox Slavs lived with millions of Muslims and other faiths.[89]

Russia's political support for the Serbs, however, reflected the pressure from the national-patriots at home, and endowed Russian policy in the Balkans with a fatal incoherence; not only did Russia gain no benefit from its Balkans policy, but exposed its weakness. Russia had simply been bluffing in its Balkan policy, a ruse soon exposed as its limited influence over Serbia was revealed, and thereafter Moscow was no longer considered a key player in peacemaking, although it was not altogether ignored. The Russian envoy, Vitalii Churkin, played a positive role in the Bosnian crisis, helping to broker the Sarajevo cease-fire in February 1994, but Russia's membership of the contact group gave it little leverage once decision-making was pre-empted by Croatia's restoration of sovereignty over Serb-held Western Slavonia and Krajina. The journalist Aleksei Pushkov noted Russia's complete marginalisation in the crisis and condemned the MFA's failure to develop its own policies in the region. He insisted that more than the fate of former Yugoslavia was being resolved but the future diplomatic shape of Europe, and in the new European order Russia had lost its position.[90] Both the European powers, and Russia, were marginalised by the forceful entrance of the USA into the Bosnian crisis in 1995 and the transfer of peace-keeping operations from the UN to Nato.

Following the fall of communism the 'Asianist' orientation of Russian policy gained in importance. Fear over the fate of the under-populated and isolated eastern regions of the country, sharing a long border with China, remained a top concern. The major obstacle to Russia's integration in the affairs of the Asia-Pacific region, now that the fear of communism was lifted, was its own weakness and economic disintegration, ethnic unrest and separatist tendencies. In contrast to the rapid development of the Pacific region as a whole, the Soviet Far East remained backward and under-developed. Under Gorbachev economic and political ties with China and other Pacific countries had begun to improve, and the massacre in Tiananmen Square on 4 June 1989 did not fundamentally alter the new Sino-Russian relationship and mutual trade grew rapidly. The Chinese road of authoritarian modernisation combining political conservatism and economic radicalism attracted many in Russia. During Yeltsin's visit to China in December 1992, and confirmed on his second visit in 1996, numerous military and technology agreements were signed on arms sales, military cooperation and the modernisation of some of the 256 factories built by the Soviet Union in the 1950s.

The conflict over the Kurile Islands, called by Japan the Northern Territories (Habomai Islands, Iturup, Kunashir and Shikotan Islands), occupied by the USSR since 1945, threatened Japan's participation in international funding for Russia's reforms, though Japan remained Russia's third largest trading partner. The Russo-Japanese Treaty of 1855 placed Sakhalin Island under joint control, but in 1875 Russia gained control over the whole island in exchange for the Kurile Islands. The Treaty of Portsmouth in 1905 ceded Southern Sakhalin to Japan in exchange for Russia gaining the Southern Kurile Islands. Southern Sakhalin was known as Karafuto until it was annexed by the USSR at the end of the Second World War, and at the same time the USSR reoccupied the Southern Kurile Islands, leaving Japan with nothing. An agreement in 1956 stipulated that the USSR would return two of the four disputed islands. Public opinion in the islands themselves suggested that at least a third would be willing to come under Japanese sovereignty if the terms were right, but public opinion in Russia opposed any territorial concessions. In 1991 Yeltsin proposed a five-stage approach to the question; a recognition that the problem existed; then Russia would declare the islands a free economic zone, where the Japanese would be given preferential treatment; the demilitarisation of the islands, entailing the closure of the many Russian bases; and fourth, agreements would be reached between Japan and Russia on economic, trade, social and cultural issues. These four stages would take some 20 years, and by the fifth stage new leaders would appear who would be able to cut the Gordian knot.[91] In the face of what appeared to the Russian side as total Japanese intransigence, despite pressure by national-patriots and the military leadership, after half a decade no more had been achieved than recognition that the problem existed.[92]

In contrast to difficult relations with Japan, Russia inherited and maintained India as the main partner and ally in Asia. A treaty on friendship and cooperation signed in January 1993 sought to build on Soviet–Indian ties but at the same time to make them mutually beneficial by discarding the old logic of exclusive geopolitical alliances; relations with the Third World starkly posed the question of how to define the 'national interest'. The 'burden of achievement' in Central Europe, the costs of supporting 'client states' from Cuba to Vietnam, and the disastrous war in Afghanistan, all undermined the Soviet consensus on foreign policy that had underlain its drive to become a global superpower. During perestroika the NPT allowed universal humanistic concerns to challenge the old view that international relations represented the class struggle on a global scale. The theoretical basis for Soviet support for Third World revolutionary states was undermined by the view that development was now seen as having to precede socialism, rather than socialism being the key to unlocking development. The vigorous debate over Soviet Third World policy resulted in Soviet disengagement under Gorbachev.[93] Soviet troops were withdrawn from Afghanistan in February 1989, and the traditional relationship with Cuba became much more strained. Solzhenitsyn called these countries 'insatiable squanderers of our wealth',[94] and Soviet aid to Afghanistan, Angola, Cuba, Ethiopia, Kampuchea and Mozambique was cut.[95] Disengagement became a rout, but as its own policy became more assertive Russia once again sought to reforge old alliances.

BECOMING A 'NORMAL GREAT POWER'?

Gorbachev had begun the hard task of providing the Soviet Union with a more sophisticated foreign policy by diversifying its orientation. Soviet foreign policy, perhaps necessarily, given the nuclear dynamics of the Cold War and later the needs of economic assistance, retained the form if not the content of traditional superpower politics. Russia, however, while asserting its Great Power status and despite its nuclear arsenal, had no ambition to assume the burdens of superpowerdom. Russia's identity and national interests would be forged not in global struggle with the West but in developing a new political and economic order at home. The shapelessness of the Russian state, however, gave birth to a rather amorphous foreign policy; the redefinition of national interest proved to be an open-ended process in which the struggle between liberal and national-patriotic approaches to foreign policy reflected the larger struggle over the strategy for development and over Russia's own identity and place in the world.

Kozyrev stressed the distinction between 'the normalisation of relations with other countries and normal relations with them', noting that Gorbachev had begun the first task but it was up to Russia to complete the second. At the heart of the new foreign policy was the idea of Russia as a 'normal Great Power', one 'that does not rely on threats (like the USSR) but at the same time knows how to live in a world that is not conflict-free'.[96] The notion of Russia as a Great Power, however, would inevitably alarm its neighbours, while the idea of 'normality' in this context acted as a normative acknowledgement of acceptable forms of behaviour but at the same time could not be anything but ambiguous.

Empires had fallen before, but never one armed with nuclear weapons. While a strong Soviet Union had been a threat to the rest of the world, a weak Russia was equally dangerous because of the damage it could do itself and its neighbours. It has indeed been argued that Russian foreign policy took on the characteristics of the 'tyranny of the weak', threatening economic and military anarchy if it did not receive substantial assistance from the West and was not accepted into global economic structures.[97] From the Russian perspective, however, things looked very different. Sergei Rogov, the Deputy Director of the Institute of the USA and Canada, noted that 'Today the country has no enemies, but neither does it have reliable allies capable of and prepared to render support in trying times. The promises of large-scale aid from the IMF and the World Bank, which gave rise to many painful internal economic measures, in reality turned out to be purely token sums.'[98] As far as he was concerned, Russia had failed to achieve a 'civilised' divorce with the former Soviet states, giving rise to a zone of instability around Russia, and neither had it been able to defend its status as a Great Power. It was Zhirinovskii's appeal to wounded national self-consciousness that had proved successful in the 1993 and 1995 elections.

There were four major conditions for a stable post-Cold War Europe: that the economic Berlin Wall dividing the post-communist countries from their prosperous neighbours was overcome; that the successor states to the USSR continued on the path of democratic modernisation and did not come into conflict with each other; that a militant nationalism did not re-emerge in Germany or Russia, in the former based on economic strength and in the latter on economic weakness; and that a place was found for Russia in the post-Cold War security order that did not threaten its permanent exclusion from Europe. None of these conditions could be guaranteed, and the tendency to impose a post-Cold War settlement on Eastern Europe and beyond rather than renegotiating the basic structures that could sustain the peace, provoked resentment and threatened to undermine the peace itself. The CPRF played forcefully on fear that the West sought to impose a 'new world order' on Russia, while Lukin insisted that the West through the Partnership for Peace programme sought to rupture Russia's remaining links with the former Soviet republics in the sphere of security. In his view the future of Europe depends on 'the "Europeanisation" of Germany and the democratisation of Russia'.[99]

From 1990 a separate Russian foreign policy emerged, but as time passed it appeared that more and more elements were borrowed not only from the Soviet Union but also from the pre-revolutionary era. The question of continuity was posed in ever sharper forms as foreign policy evolved away from the so-called 'liberal universalism' of the early period towards a more vigorous assertion of Russian Great Power national interests. There was no consensus, however, on what precisely constituted Russia's national security and other interests: the liberals saw them as lying in close ties with the West and peace with its neighbours; the centrist groupings sought greater reliance on indigenous economic and military resources to buttress a rather broader vision of Russia as a Great Power; the national-patriots envisioned Russia as a type of superpower in regard to its neighbours and in the world at large, to be achieved by restoring aspects of the old administrative-command system; the neo-communists more explicitly sought to re-establish the Soviet system and the Soviet geopolitical space; while Zhirinovskii's crude nationalism promised easy solutions to a disappointed people but threatened Russia's neighbours and provoked once again the image of Russia, whether communist or not, as the permanent enemy. Each vision of Russia's national security interests reflected profound differences in thinking about what it means to be a Russian and what Russia itself means. As long as no new orthodoxy could emerge or be imposed, an instability lay at the heart of Russian foreign policy.

Russia sought to find its place in the world at a time when, unfrozen from the Cold War, international relations is in an unprecedented state of flux. Above all, long-term processes have come to fruition whereby economic strength is a more accurate measurement of power than narrowly defined military power. While America might have welcomed Russia as a bulwark against Japanese or Chinese expansion in Asia, its economic weakness left the country vulnerable. While Moscow was invited as a guest to G7 meetings, full membership could only come with economic recovery. If Russia's economy moves effectively onto market principles and global integration, many of the deeper problems of Russia's identity and place in the world will resolve themselves. Economic weakness undermined Russia's aspirations to become a Great Power.

There remained something very 'abnormal' about the Russian foreign policy process, quite apart from the gulf between its aspirations and capacities. The fragmentation of governance meant that it often appeared that Russia was pursuing several different policies simultaneously. On the one hand, the official line from Kozyrev's MFA sought integration into the Western system on the basis of a commitment to 'Western values', but at the same time the Ministry of Defence and other security agencies appeared to pursue an independent 'neo-imperial' line in the near abroad. Thus Russia appeared to have one foreign policy run by civilians, what Furman called the 'dinner jacket policy', and another conducted by the military, dubbed by him the 'camouflage suit policy', as seen in Georgia, Tajikistan and Azerbaijan.[100] The parliamentary elections of December 1995 marked a new phase in Russian foreign policy but once again inhibited the emergence of a 'normal' relationship with Russia's neighbours and the world at large.

Russia's bluff in the Balkans had been called, tempting the West to do the same over Nato expansion and other issues. Russia's foreign policy was marked by a gulf between rhetoric and capacity, reflecting the struggle between national-patriots and internationalists at the heart of policy-making. The Great Power policy demonstrated that Russian thinking remained rooted in the past and that it had only been partially demilitarised: as Eggert puts it, 'The Russian military bureaucracy, which is not controlled by civil society and has a vague notion of the outer world, is incompatible with the Western one, which is subordinated to a civil society and is well educated.' In its relations with the 'near abroad', too, Russian policy was coloured by the belief that the independence of countries like Ukraine was only a temporary phenomenon, provoking the West to view Kiev as a counterbalance to Russia and inhibiting the establishment of normal Russian relations with Ukraine. While focusing its attention on minor issues, Russian foreign policy often neglected problems of primary importance: 'Instead of pretending to be a Great Power, Russia should rather open its frontiers to ideas and capital.'[101] The development of an aggressive post-democratic foreign policy cannot be excluded. Russia is still far from being a 'normal' Great Power.

15 Defence and security policy

The wolfhound century leaps at my shoulders,
But I am no wolf by blood.

Osip Mandelstam[1]

The USSR had the world's biggest army, with over 4 million men under arms in 1988. The vast majority of its officers (80 per cent) were Russian and some 90 per cent, including almost all senior officers, were members of the Communist Party.[2] In the Brezhnev era the military devoured between 25–30 per cent of GNP.[3] The well-known saying that the USSR did not *have* a military-industrial complex, it *was* one, reflected a frightening truth. Not only were much of the country's industrial resources devoted to military needs, but the system of conscription and patriotic education made the military the cornerstone of national identity. All of this was eroded during perestroika, and the disintegration of the USSR was soon followed by the division of the Soviet armed forces as the newly independent republics created their own military establishments. Russia was burdened with the legacy of Soviet imperial expansion, a bloated defence sector and, perhaps most significantly, a military establishment accustomed to getting its own way, at least in terms of resources. Could a new model of civil–military relations be forged in post-communist Russia, and with it a demilitarised sense of national purpose?

THE END OF THE SOVIET ARMED FORCES

Russia had been reluctant to create its own armed forces yet by early 1992 was forced to embark on this path. With the fall of communism the Soviet Armed Forces were no longer a military threat but a source of social and political instability to the countries that had sacrificed so much to give them birth. Attempts to maintain a single CIS command were soon undermined by the aspirations of republics like Ukraine to create their own armed forces, fuelled by fears that a Russianised Soviet Army could be used to reimpose Moscow's rule. The challenge facing Russia was to disengage its forces from neighbouring countries, to maintain control over the huge nuclear arsenal, and at the same time to reconstruct its own armed forces for new tasks.

What was to be done with the Soviet Army, most of it deployed in Russia and which in ethos and tradition appeared antithetical to the principles of the new democracy? After the coup the General Staff in Moscow was left virtually without a master; there was an army, but no state.[4] Yeltsin at that time sought to gain the allegiance of the high command by promising to keep the army intact, but following the disintegration of the USSR this proved both meaningless and counter-productive as morale and discipline plummetted. Some long-term solution to the problem had to be found; by necessity rather than choice because of the creation of national armies in other republics and the weakness of CIS military structures. Russia ultimately was forced simply to rename the Soviet Army the Russian Army, and thus incorporated the worst as well as the best of the old traditions. Russia was left to deal with the problems bequeathed by the old regime, with forces stationed not only in the former Soviet republics but also in Germany and Poland.

The former Soviet defence minister, Dmitrii Yazov, was implicated in the coup, and his replacement, Yevgenii Shaposhnikov, immediately launched a purge in the ministry.[5] He later became the commander-in-chief of what became known as the Joint Command, formally accountable to the CIS Council of Heads of State but in practice the absence of any effective CIS command mechanism meant that he worked closely with Yeltsin.[6] The Joint Command was responsible for control over strategic nuclear arms, the coordination of military doctrines and the military reforms of CIS states, and the resolution of armed conflicts both within the CIS and along its borders.[7] The Bishkek summit in October 1992 agreed to develop a joint military security concept as well as a new command structure for CIS forces.[8] Countries like Ukraine, however, sought to escape from the old security system centred on Moscow and attempts to maintain the CIS Joint Command as the core of a common security system soon foundered, and on 15 June 1993 it was abolished. Russia sought to bring the nuclear forces outside Russia under its sole control, and expenditure on the multilateral Joint Armed Forces organisation was seen as increasingly pointless. Thus the Soviet armed forces, victorious over Nazi Germany but also destroyers of hope in Budapest and Prague, glorious and monstrous, finally died.

Already in December 1991 Ukraine, Azerbaijan and Moldova had announced the intention of creating their own armies. Alarmed by the imperiousness of the coup leaders in August 1991, who had flouted the dignity of Ukraine and its leadership, Kravchuk in December 1991 declared himself commander-in-chief of all forces on Ukrainian territory, some half a million men. Instead of expelling former Soviet forces (the policy pursued by the Baltic states), Ukraine assimilated the Soviet Army to its own purposes. In January 1992 all forces on its territory were required to take an oath of allegiance to the republic, something done with surprising alacrity by soldiers in the Kiev, Odessa and Carpathian Military Districts (MDs). Some 40 per cent were Russian, and they were faced with the choice of pledging allegiance to Ukraine or returning to an uncertain but in most cases hard future in Russia. A symbol of the irrevocable breakdown of the concept of CIS forces was Ukraine's decision in June 1992 to deport military officers who refused to take the oath of loyalty.[9] Ukraine soon succeeded in establishing Europe's second largest army, with ground forces of 308,000 in 1994.[10]

The Conventional Forces in Europe (CFE) treaty was signed in Paris on 19 November 1990 by the 22 Nato and former Warsaw Treaty Organisation (WTO) nations (the number of signatories later rose to 29). The treaty, ratified by the Russian parliament on 8 July 1992, stipulated that the Russian Army and Navy had to be reduced from 2.8 million men to 2.1 million by 1995 and placed restrictions on the number, type and deployment of weapons and forces: indeed, of all the signatories only Russia (and Ukraine) faced restrictions on where weapons could be stationed on their own territory. Germany is allowed a maximum of 375,000 soldiers by the CFE Treaty, and Ukraine's ratification of the CFE Treaty in July 1992 limited its forces to 250,000.[11]

The successor republics gradually took over their own security and foreign policy. In Russia the problem of ethnicity and divided allegiances played little role since the officer corps was overwhelmingly Russian. The emergence of a Russian national army, however, was retarded by the role played by the Joint Command and by a residual belief that Russia would be the centre of some larger unit. As the republics created their own armed forces, the CIS failed to establish a security structure similar to Nato's. The Collective Security Agreement signed in Tashkent on 15 May 1992 was limited both in scope and the countries involved (see chapter 16). The CIS facilitated the division of military resources between the former fifteen republics, and by mid-1992 seven CIS members plus Georgia began the division of Soviet military assets within the terms of the CFE treaty.

At last Russia decided to have its own army, one of the last CIS states to take this course. Yeltsin's decree on the formation of a Russian Ministry of Defence on 16 March 1992 named himself acting defence minister, and on 7 May he finally ordered the creation of a Russian Army with himself as commander-in-chief.[12] On 18 May General Pavel Grachev was appointed minister of defence. As commander of the Soviet Airborne Forces he had obstructed the plotters in August 1991, and was appointed a deputy USSR defence minister and head of Russia's Defence Committee, having operational command of Russian forces when Yeltsin was acting defence minister.

Hopes that a civilian defence minister would be appointed and that the Defence Ministry would become a civilian department were disappointed.[13] The Law on Defence adopted by parliament after long debate in September 1992 defined the scope of military activity and imposed a strict system of state control over the military, but attempts to enshrine the principle that only a civilian could occupy the post of minister of defence were defeated at the last minute.[14] The first deputy minister, Andrei Kokoshin (responsible for relations with the defence industries and scientific-military policy), was a first-rate academic defence specialist, and indeed the first civilian to be appointed to a leadership position in the armed forces since the 1920s. The majority of appointments to senior posts, however, reflected the predominance of traditionalists: the appointment of Boris Gromov, formerly commander of the Soviet Army in Afghanistan, as deputy defence minister was widely interpreted as a concession to hardliners.[15]

The leadership of the Ministry of Defence pledged to maintain Russia as a military 'Great Power' and to call a halt to the strategic retreat begun by Gorbachev.[16] The transformation of the Soviet Army into a Russian one was not accompanied by the sort of reforms in organisation and mentality that affected the rest of society. Instead, the Russian Army remained a monument to traditional Russian and Soviet values, including a strongly developed sense of self-preservation, its self-ascription as the enshrinement of the highest values of society, its commitment to maintaining Russia as a 'Great Power', and above all a sense of its own superiority *vis à vis* the civil authorities.

THE GREAT RETREAT

The dissolution of the WTO in 1991 and the disintegration of the USSR accelerated the retreat of what had now become Russian forces not only from Central Europe but also from large parts of what had formerly been home territory. In the former East Germany, covering 22 per cent of contemporary Germany, 375,000 troops of the Western Group of Forces remained. By June 1991 all Soviet forces had left Hungary and Czechoslovakia and the last Russian combat troops left Poland in October 1992; in 1993, however, 250,000 remained to be repatriated from

Germany, Poland, the Baltic and Transcaucasia.[17] Finally, 49 years after the Soviet flag had been hoisted over the Reichstag, the last Russian troops left Berlin on 31 August 1994 with due pomp and ceremony (marred only by Yeltsin's extempore performance as conductor).

Russia became the successor not only to the Soviet state, but also to the Russian empire. Russia *de facto* became an imperial power not by choice but by history. How could it shed this burden while maintaining its long-term strategic interests? The definition of these interests, as we have seen, was contested, but Russia's role as a regional power was to some degree thrust upon it by the escalation of regional conflicts. The removal of forces from Moldova, for example, was complicated by the insurgency in Trans-Dniester. An agreement was reached on 10 August 1994 for the removal of all Russian forces from Moldova within three years, but Moscow's struggle with the charismatic commander of the Fourteenth Army, Lebed, led to the precipitate order in 1995 for the dissolution of the army in its entirety, leading to grave concerns over the fate of its equipment and weapons.

The Baltic republics asserted that the enforced stationing of troops on foreign soil was a violation of international law; as long as 'foreign' troops remained the three republics could not feel fully independent. In late 1991 there were some 25,000 former Soviet troops in Estonia, about 60,000 in Latvia and about 40,000 in Lithuania.[18] Negotiations on their removal staggered from crisis to crisis, embittering relations between the new democracies. Grachev in June 1992 argued that the troops could not be withdrawn until housing had been provided for them in Russia, a process that would take several years, neither was it clear who would pay the pensions of the former military personnel living in these republics. The negotiators were caught between extremists on both flanks; in Russia the national-patriots and neo-communists urged Yeltsin to take a firmer line against the Baltic states; whereas radicals there insisted that Russia remove the forces immediately. Up to mid-1992 Russia treated the Baltic forces as a single unit, but at that point indicated that it would be willing to contemplate the speedier withdrawal from Lithuania because of its more amenable approach to citizenship issues.[19] Despite attempts to link military withdrawal to civic rights, the number of Russian troops continued to decline because falling conscription meant that soldiers who had completed their tour of duty were not replaced: by the end of 1992 all but 50,000 of the troops had gone.[20] The removal of troops was completed in Lithuania by the end of August 1993, and despite much over-heated rhetoric the last Russian troops withdrew from Estonia and Latvia by 31 August 1994. Thus the North-West Group of Forces ceased to exist, and Russian troops in Kaliningrad (the Eleventh Army) now came directly under the command of GHQ Land Forces.

The 'great retreat' affected parts of the Russian Federation proper. Following the abortive intervention in Chechnya in November 1991, when some 500 troops were sent and then summarily returned, Russia withdrew its forces from the republic but left behind enormous quantities of *matériel* and arms (which were later used to kill Russian soldiers following the second and more resolute intervention in late 1994). Russia removed its forces from Nagorno-Karabakh, and in May 1992 an agreement was signed with Azerbaijan on the withdrawal of all Russian forces within two years. The relocated troops faced a hard fate in Russia, competing for housing, jobs and pensions with those released by earlier cuts. Many of the 30,000 officers and their dependents withdrawn from Hungary and Czechoslovakia lived in converted barracks while the troops lived under canvas, with many junior officers living below the poverty line. The pitiful plight of forces from CIS countries was graphically illustrated by the case of the 104th Airborne Division, relocated from Ganja in Azerbaijan to Ulyanovsk in 1993. In their 'home' country, the troops were treated almost as invaders and faced difficulties in finding housing and integrating into the local community.[21]

The great retreat encompassed not only the physical return of troops but also a decline in the prestige and morale of the armed forces in their entirety. The military profession was no longer an attractive one, and many officers left for better-paid jobs in the growing private sector. The retreat was accompanied by the erosion of discipline, with many officers taking up entrepeneurial activities to create 'military–commercial clans' specialising in the sale of weapons and equipment. Yeltsin on 21 July 1992 strongly condemned the growth of corruption in the Russian Army, and in particular the illegal sale of military property through underhand deals between the military supply service and commercial interests.[22] Mass demobilisation and desertion, moreover, threatened stability throughout former Soviet territory. By early 1993 there were over 500 illegal paramilitary formations in the CIS, largely composed of deserters from the ranks armed with stolen weapons.[23]

The increased assertiveness of Russian foreign policy was accompanied by attempts to put an end to the retreat. Russia's redefined security policy now sought to keep some military bases in the 'near abroad', regulated by the presidential directive of 5 April 1994 which apparently included the Baltic republics.[24] Following Baltic protests it was later clarified that the Skrunda radar station in Latvia was not classified as a 'military base'. Some twenty-eight bases proper have been identified. Agreement was reached with Georgia for three sites, one at Tbilisi (headquarters of the Transcaucasus Group of Forces) and bases at Akhalkalaki and Batumi for motor rifle divisions. There are two bases in Armenia (Erevan and Gyumri), but none in Azerbaijan although Russia leases the Lyaki early warning radar installation. The view had apparently triumphed that a precipitate retreat from Transcaucasia (and in particular Georgia) would make Russia's hold on the North Caucasus unviable.[25] In Belarus an air force regiment was to remain at Zyabrouka until the year 2000.[26] Some 100,000 men remained in the near abroad, engaged in various peace-keeping operations and in the bases. Some 24,000 soldiers were in Tajikistan alone, policing the border with Afghanistan and maintaining the fragile regime.

DEFENCE CONVERSION

Soviet defence industries had absorbed about one fifth of national income every year since the Second World War. By the last year of perestroika in 1991 nothing much was left of the old Soviet centrally planned economy, but what did remain was overwhelming state ownership and a bloated defence sector. Despite Gorbachev's announcement at the UN in December 1988 of a conversion programme diverting resources to consumer goods,[27] little positive had been achieved. The Russian economy remains one of the most militarised in the world with some 5.5 million industrial and research workers directly employed in defence plants – 24 per cent of industrial employees.[28] According to Mikhail Malei, formerly responsible for the conversion programme, some 35 million people, including families, lived off the military or military-related industries.[29] One-third of St Petersburg's workforce were employed in defence plants, and in some other major industrial oblasts like Saratov or Novosibirsk the proportion is even higher. The huge scale of Russian defence industries and the large proportion of GNP that it represents, the concentration in 'company towns', the regional concentration and the isolation of the defence sector from the civilian economy with little technological spillover, all inhibited attempts to demilitarise the economy.

The term 'military-industrial complex' in fact denotes the most effective part of the Russian economy in which its most technologically sophisticated enterprises are to be found. Defence factories produced not only guns and tanks, but televisions and high technology consumer goods as well.[30] On 20 March 1992 Yeltsin approved the Law on Conversion of Defence Industries which provided a detailed programme for conversion, but left the details for later legislation. Conversion from guns to butter, however, entails large foreign currency costs which can only be earned by arms sales to customers paying in convertible currencies, necessitating large investments in arms factories to maintain competitiveness.[31]

Controls on arms sales were relaxed to provide foreign currency for the hard-pressed exchequer. Throughout the 1980s the USSR sold (or transferred) some $12 billion worth of arms a year, but according to official figures Russia sold only $1.5 billion worth of arms in 1992,[32] a figure that rose to $2.7 billion in 1995, 13.6 per cent of the world's arms market. Russia launched an aggressive campaign of arms sales on the world market not only to gain foreign currency but also to use factories and skills to maximum advantage. An increasingly sharp rivalry developed between Russia and America for a share of the coveted arms market, and became a factor in Russian foreign policy. America had legitimate fears that Russia's desperation for foreign currency encouraged sales to unstable areas, such as submarines to Iran and Sukhoi fighters to China, yet at the same time there was an element of commercial cupidity in America's calculations, as in its apparent attempt to dislodge Russia from its traditional arms market in India and elsewhere. This worked the other way as well, and with the end of the Cold War Russia moved into new markets in Malaysia, Pakistan, South Africa and Turkey.

Government policy was caught between its desire for conversion, on the one hand, and the attempt to maintain the defence capacity of the country and employment, on the other. Only twelve out of 5,000 military factories had stopped producing weapons by late 1992, although military spending in Russia fell to 7.2 per cent of its GNP in 1991[33] and remained between 5–7 per cent thereafter. State arms orders and development funding fell dramatically, and nearly a million defence workers became unemployed and the rest suffered from low wages and loss of morale.[34] Resources devoted to military scientific research fell sharply, while electronic and high-technology industries by 1995 operated at one-fifth of the level of 1991. Investment in military enterprises by that time had fallen to a quarter of the 1990 level, and factories making military equipment survived only by drawing on government credits, which in turn threatened macroeconomic stabilisation. The Russian Army suffered from increasing technological backwardness because of cuts in research and procurements. The conversion programme was envisaged as a long-term programme, leading to the resignation of Malei in August 1993, and was marked by uncertainties over strategy, a lack of funds except from sources (arms sales) that perpetuated the imbalances of Russian industry that they were designed to overcome, and an unclear definition of Russia's own defence needs.

THE NUCLEAR LEGACY

With the fall of communism the instruments of the Cold War became a greater threat to world peace than the systems that had given them birth. Nuclear weapons lost much of their strategic significance but the race to possess them and the difficulty of disposing of them provoked regional rivalries and international concern. In the former USSR they became a source of political instability and nuclear proliferation threatened global security.[35]

The modest cuts envisaged by the Start-1 Treaty of 31 July 1991 were surpassed by a number of proposals later that year. While nuclear weaponry lost some of its political value in East–West relations, among the successor states nuclear issues involved delicate power plays and the management of symbolic relationships. The four nuclear successor republics (Russia, Ukraine, Belarus and Kazakhstan) and the West were in general agreed that nuclear proliferation should be avoided and that Russia should emerge as the only successor nuclear state, but, as usual, the devil is in the details. The Almaty inaugural meeting of the CIS on 21 December 1991 vowed to maintain unified control over nuclear weapons: the president of Russia was granted the exclusive right to use them but only with the approval of the other three nuclear states. Shaposhnikov, as supreme commander of CIS forces, took over control, sharing the firing codes with Yeltsin. This arrangement did not last long, and the day after the decision by the CIS defence ministers on 15 June 1993 to disband the Joint Command, Shaposhnikov was relieved of the 'nuclear suitcase'.

Even if the security of most of the former USSR's 27,000 nuclear weapons, about two-thirds of which were strategic and the rest tactical, were guaranteed, it would take only one to cause a major catastrophe.[36] There were fears that weapons could find their way to nuclear 'threshold' states like Pakistan, Iran, Iraq and Libya. In addition, some 900,000 people were involved in the maintenance of the USSR's thermonuclear arsenal, with perhaps 2,000 people with knowledge of nuclear weapons design and some 3–5,000 with experience in plutonium production or uranium enrichment.[37] Just as defeat in 1945 had allowed America to attract German experts in missile technology, so there were fears that the collapse of the USSR would lead to the proliferation of nuclear technology. The only consolation was that the medium-range weapons had already been destroyed under the terms of the 1987 Intermediate Nuclear Forces (INF) Treaty.

At the December 1991 Almaty meeting Ukraine and Belarus agreed to join the 1968 Non Proliferation Treaty (NPT) as non-nuclear states, and only Kazakhstan hesitated in agreeing to the withdrawal of nuclear weapons from its territory. However, under pressure from an increasingly vociferous pro-nuclear lobby Ukraine later modified its approach, regarding military policy as part of the overall struggle for independence, and thus having second thoughts about unilaterally undermining its bargaining position by renouncing nuclear weapons.[38] The prime minister and from June 1994 president, Leonid Kuchma, had for 10 years been the manager of the world's largest missile plant (Yuzhmash) and insisted that Ukraine had the technical means to maintain its missiles.[39] Ukraine sought political control over the 176 missiles with some 1,200 warheads 'temporarily' on its territory.[40] Both Kazakhstan and Ukraine suspected, probably correctly, that while they had nuclear weapons Russia would negotiate more respectfully with them. The issue damaged Ukraine's standing in the international community. The Lisbon Protocol of 23 May 1992 made Belarus, Kazakhstan and Ukraine partners to the Start-1 Treaty, together with Russia and the USA, and all three pledged to join the NPT as non-nuclear states.[41] By mid-1992 all tactical nuclear weapons had been moved to Russia, but Ukraine and Kazakhstan equivocated over the removal of strategic nuclear weapons. The pro-nuclear lobby insisted that in exchange for surrendering its arsenal Ukraine should receive certain security guarantees. What form these guarantees could take was unclear. Despite misgivings Kazakhstan finally joined the NPT and Ukraine, too, joined as a non-nuclear weapon state on 5 December 1994.

Despite much opposition, the Russian parliament ratified the Start-1 Treaty on 4 November 1992, but already the framework for a much more radical version was agreed at the Bush–

Yeltsin summit in Washington on 16 June 1992. After intense negotiations, the Start-2 Treaty was signed by the two men in Moscow on 3 January 1993. Yeltsin described it as 'surpassing all other disarmament treaties in its scale and importance', while Bush, taking his final bow on the world stage, saw the treaty as marking the definitive end to the Cold War and the start of a 'new world of hope' in which 'parents and children would have a future far more free from fear'. A total of some 17,000 nuclear warheads were to be destroyed, and the American and Russian strategic arsenals were to be cut to between 3–3,500 warheads each by 1 January 2003, less than half the total agreed by the Start-1 Treaty. These cuts of a combined total of some 21,000 strategic weapons would take place in two stages and would include the elimination of all land-based intercontinental ballistic missiles with multiple and inde-pendently targeted warheads (MIRVs), notably Russia's ten-warhead SS-18s, either through straightforward scrapping or through conversion to a single warhead (to a maximum of 90) by adapting the launching pads. Within 10 years the number of submarine-based missiles, the main American deterrent, was to be capped at 1,750. This committed America to destroying about half of its 432 Trident I and II missiles with their eight warheads apiece. Several Russian demands, largely motivated by considerations of economy, were taken into account in formulating the treaty, such as its plan to adapt 90 SS-18 launch pads to take SS-25s, and to convert 105 of its six-warhead SS-19s into single-warhead weapons.

The agreement signalled that the Cold War was truly over, and that arms control had entered a qualitatively new phase with deep cuts reducing the number of superpower ballistic warheads from the peak of 26,331 agreed by the Salt Agreement of 1988 to a little over 6,000 in 2003. Russia broke with the fundamental principle of Soviet military doctrine, namely the need to maintain nuclear parity with the United States. Deterrence as such had ended in 1991 when most missiles had stopped being targeted on each other. It would be a long path, however, from signing to implementing Start-2; not only was there significant opposition in the Duma, which sought to link the issue to Nato enlargement,[42] but the sheer cost of decommissioning placed yet more strain on an over-stretched budget. In a strange reversal of roles some of the funds were provided by the US.

Russia and America have a common interest in preventing nuclear proliferation because, quite apart from the dangers involved, the more countries with nuclear weapons, the less influence for them. The optimum level of their nuclear arsenals, however, remains a matter of debate. Despite the awesome dismantlement costs involved, Russia in 1995 suggested negotiations for a Start-3 treaty that would see a further reduction to some thousand warheads each; sufficient for retaliation, but not enough for a disabling first strike. Faced by the deterioration of its conventional forces, however, Russia became more rather than less dependent on nuclear weapons; the Soviet commitment to no first use of nuclear weapons has been dropped. The central point, however, is that the possession of nuclear weapons on its own does not guarantee a state 'Great Power' status.

MILITARY REFORM AND DOCTRINE

Military reform focuses on two key issues: modernisation, covering technical organisation, equipment and command structures; and professionalisation, developing a new military doctrine, forging a new relationship with the civil authorities and ensuring that the army is not drawn into domestic political disputes or employed in adventuristic foreign policy pursuits. Military reform (and defence conversion, as noted above) was conducted against the background of a severe economic crisis and tight budgets, with sharply reduced defence spending (halving in real terms by 1995), reduced procurement of new weapons and equipment, scrapping of old weapons, and shortages of fuel and spare parts. In 1992, for the first time since the reign of Peter the Great, Russia failed to begin the construction of a single warship.[43] Speaking to the State Duma in November 1994, Grachev claimed that only 40 per cent of the Russian Army's armaments could be classified as modern, a percentage he claimed that would fall to 10 by the year 2000.[44] The loss of technological edge could bar Russia from genuine Great Power status for at least a generation.

The shortage of personnel was a constant refrain. The Law on Military Service of February 1993 was opposed by the military authorities since it reduced the length of military service from 2 years to 18 months and extended exempt categories to cover some 80 per cent of potential draftees. Personnel shortages were caused not only by the high percentage of those due for conscription who were automatically granted deferment (such as those in higher education) or exempted on health or social grounds, but above all by the low number of those actually answering conscription orders. Only 28 per cent of the age group concerned responded to the draft in 1992 and 22 per cent in 1993. Reformers hoped to see the abolition of conscription and the creation of a wholly professional army, an aim conceded by Yeltsin during his re-election campaign in May 1996, but before that in May 1995 he extended the period of compulsory military service from 18 months to 2 years, and ended certain student exemptions.

The quality of those drafted was often low, with little education, poor health and, not infrequently, criminal records. Quite apart from low pay and conditions, the Soviet Army suffered a dreadful record of bullying known as *dedovshchina*. In the second half of the 1980s some 15–20,000 conscipts died 'noncombat' deaths,[45] and in 1991 alone, according to official figures, 5,500 CIS servicemen (mostly conscripts) died through suicide, beatings or accidents, while 98,700 were wounded.[46] In addition, demographic trends, and in particular the extremely low Russian birthrate, made it increasingly difficult to maintain a large conscript army, with ever fewer males reaching recruiting age annually. As a result most units were at best half-manned and the number of officers often exceeded the number of conscripts. The ratio of officers to non-officers is estimated have fallen to one-to-one.

Some saw the solution in the creation of ethnic and regional units, which were traditional for the Russian Army, while others sought to combine this with a purely professional force. A professional army, however, requires higher spending on improved salaries and the like.[47] The introduction of contract service in late 1992 represented a move towards the transition, with 120,000 men recruited in this way in 1993 and another 150,000 in 1994.[48] By 1996 the 270,000 contract soldiers made up an estimated one-third of Land Forces, concentrated primarily in technical and logistic units, while combat units, including those designated for peace-keeping operations, remained severely understaffed.[49] In a typical reversal of policy, Grachev decided by early 1996 to cut the number of army personnel on service contracts by 80,000 as part of the State Duma's decision to reduce the Armed Forces to 1.7 million. The cost of a contract serviceman was at least six times higher than that of a conscript.[50]

In 1991 Russia had 196 divisions, but of the thirty-odd remaining today no more than ten are combat-ready. The precise number of Russian military personnel is difficult to establish because actual presence often diverges considerably from authorised strengths. Grachev was initially in favour of a much reduced force of some 1.5 million, down from three million in 1991, no longer a conscript but a mobile, professional army, but by late 1993 he insisted that force levels should not fall below 2.1 million.[51] By March 1995 he was insisting that numbers should not fall below 1.7 million men from the 2 million enlisted at that time; by 1996 the real figure was probably 1.2 million.[52] Interior Troops (VV), in 29 interior divisions and 15 brigades, now outnumber personnel in the army's Land Forces, while numbers in the police have grown by a factor of 1.5. Their functions have also changed, with fewer engaged in protecting objects and people's security, and more devoted to preventing mass unrest. It is evidence like this that has given rise to the view that Russia has once again become a police state.

The CFE Treaty set strict limits to the number of conventional forces west of the Urals, and placed a ceiling on the number of forces Russia could have on its northern (St Petersburg MD) and southern (North Caucasus MD) flanks.[53] A great deal of Treaty Limited Equipment (TLE) was eliminated by the time the treaty came into force in November 1992, and even more was destroyed in advance of the full implementation of the Treaty in July 1996 when Russia was limited to 1,700 tanks in European Russia, one-sixth of the Soviet total.[54] Moscow sought to revise the treaty, in particular the northern and southern flank limits, on the grounds that it had been negotiated for the USSR and was inappropriate for the security challenges facing an independent Russia whose geostrategic problems had changed so dramatically. Russia hoped to replace the treaty with a more general European arms-control agreement that would limit military research and development expenditure. Above all, Russia requested greater flexibility in the deployment of its forces to meet its new security needs, in particular in the North Caucasus, transformed from a rear MD in the Soviet era to a frontline zone of conflict covering Russia's only access to the Black Sea and the Caspian.[55] The West conceded that the CFE treaty placed severe restrictions on Russia and the limits were revised in late 1995 while the full review in May 1996 gave Russia three extra years to comply.

According to the Russian constitution, defence, like foreign policy, is a prerogative of the president. The president is commander-in-chief of the Armed Forces of Russia, operating through the General Staff. The Security Council is the main military and political body controlling Russia's defence establishment, while the Ministry of Defence is responsible for developing and implementing military, technical and personnel policy. Russia's Defence Ministry liaises through the CIS Defence Council of Ministers where appropriate. The prime minister and parliament can exert considerable practical influence over defence policy through control of budgets and the Duma's defence committee. The status of the armed forces is regulated by the Law on Defence, signed into law on 1 June 1996.

The former chief of the general staff and a noted reformer, General Vladimir Lobov, argued that a 'military doctrine does not exist by itself [but] is part of the overall state doctrine' affecting the economy, science, politics and foreign policy.[56] As Scott McMichael puts it, 'Soviet military doctrine functioned as a virtual surrogate for what the West would call national security policy.'[57] The military doctrine of the Russian Armed Forces took some time to develop: the first draft released in May 1992 was prepared by a team on behalf of the Ministry of Defence and reflected the influence of civilian analysts.[58] It developed the changes introduced into the USSR's doctrine (last revised in 1987), above all in its overwhelmingly defensive orientation, the absence of residual notions of class struggle, and its rehabilitation of the concept of 'national security' and 'national interests'. Some of the old concerns, however, remained, albeit in a new guise, particularly in the notion of 'some states and coalitions' (i.e. the USA and Nato) who still seek to dominate the world. The deployment of foreign troops into countries bordering Russia would be considered a direct military threat, while threats to Russian-speaking populations in other CIS countries might give Russia the right to intervene on their behalf. Russia thus reproduced elements of America's 'backyard' mentality, with its neighbours considered part of Russia's 'sphere of influence'. Russia warned that foreign intervention in any of its neighbouring states, for example Turkey in Armenia, would be considered a direct threat to itself. The stalemate in the struggle between parliament and president meant that this draft was not adopted.

A revised version, called 'The Main Provisions of the Military Doctrine of the RF', was adopted on 2 November 1993.[59] This document was part of Russia's overall security doctrine, and stressed that Russia's vital interests 'in no way involved the security of other states'. The doctrine stressed the need for conflict prevention, the territorial integrity of states, respect for their sovereignty and non-interference in their internal affairs.[60] Learning from the October events, 'separate' military units could now be deployed to support interior troops in internal conflicts or to support border troops in particular cases, provisions utilised to allow Russian forces to intervene in Chechnya. The key change from the earlier draft was the shift in threat perception, now identified as coming from local wars. The Russian Army was to defend Russia's 'territorial integrity', but it was not clear where the borders lay. The new doctrine formalised the view of the former Soviet republics as part of Russia's extended security zone; the army, however, could only move in with the consent of the government involved, but 'consent' (as demonstrated in Hungary in 1956 or Afghanistan in 1979) can be manufactured. The doctrine made no mention of civil or parliamentary control over the military, and had little to say about the role of the army in contemporary Russian society: even though it had tempered some of the postulates of the earlier draft, the doctrine reflected the 'Great Power' thinking of the Defence Ministry. While declaring Russia's peaceful intentions, the doctrine nevertheless revealed an underlying bloc mentality and an insecurity that could provoke a return to hostility to the West.

It was within the framework of the new doctrine that the debate over the requisite structure of Russia's armed forces was conducted. Russia has five services: the three common to most countries, the Air Force, the Navy and Ground Forces, plus two unusual ones, the Strategic Missile Forces (SMF) and the Air Defence Forces (ADF) separate from the other services. Plans to merge the Air Force with the ADF, incorporating possibly the SMF, to create perhaps a new Space Force, was a source of much controversy. The dominant view insisted that the experience of other countries could not be blindly copied since Russia faced distinctive geostrategic challenges in the context of its own history and traditions. The SMF was separate because of the extreme danger posed by unsanctioned actions, requiring exceptionally high skills and discipline in its personnel. The ADF was separate because of the sheer vastness of Russia and the need to have a clear line of command to provide speedy decision-making and responses in case of threat. The military insisted on the need to preserve the advantages of the existing system while carefully making incremental changes in order not to waste scarce resources and undermine the achievements of the past.[61]

Kokoshin argued that a new organisational structure would be developed to accompany the new doctrine, which would abandon the principle of defence along the whole border and instead concentrate on powerful mobile groups. As the minister responsible for military-technical policy, he sought to preserve Russia's potential in the field of military technology, concentrated in some 800 enterprises.[62] As a concession to the generals, the new command structure differed little from the old although Mobile Forces, one of Grachev's pet ideas, hesitantly developed. In 1996 the 'airborne troops reform' was launched whereby they were abolished as a special force and subordinated to local military commands. The five airborne divisions (each with some 6,000 troops) and seven airborne brigades (each of 2,500) had been the core of Russia's rapid deployment forces, and their commander, Colonel-General Yevgenii Podkolzin, insisted that the change would undermine their morale.[63] Others insisted that the Chechen campaign demonstrated that airborne troops had been too lightly armed, while the regular army had the required heavy weapons but lacked the training and tight discipline of airborne forces. It made sense to build the army of the future on an amalgam of the two, and this was the strategy pursued by the head of the Russian General Staff, General Mikhail Kolesnikov.[64]

The new military doctrine sought to give the CIS a military dimension, with Russia acting as a type of garrison state on behalf of the other members. Hitherto responsibility for the defence of the territorial integrity of CIS states had been unclear. However, since the CIS itself was not a military alliance (even though that was one reason for its creation) and the Tashkent treaty states reserved control over their military policy, Russia was premature in declaring that threats to any CIS member state was a threat to itself. Russia nevertheless played an active military role in its unstable southern flank, intervening (overtly or covertly) in Georgia, Azerbaijan and Tajikistan. Its 'peace-keeping' operations, moreover, tended to blur the principle of impartiality or neutrality in disputes (see chapter 16).

The Chechen war raised in the sharpest possible form the need for military reform, revealing low morale, confused lines of subordination, weak political control and confused tactics. The operation was poorly planned and led to enormous civilian and military losses, the city of Grozny was pulverised, and the resort to a military solution when negotiations had not been exhausted suggested a political establishment out of control. The war was marked by staff and planning chaos, with at least three armies involved, and often competing (and even firing) against each other: the regular Russian Army, interior ministry (MVD) forces, and security ministry (FSK) troops. Above all, the shocking brutality of the war affected public opinion profoundly, and despite the alleged support for Zhirinovskii's plans for a 'Last Thrust to the South'[65] polls revealed a strong rejection of neo-imperialist schemes. A survey in April 1995 revealed that 74 per cent were opposed to retaining the Chechen Republic as part of the Russian Federation.[66]

The army as such was only a reluctant accomplice to the war. Since the Chechen campaign was nominally an internal security affair the MVD should have taken charge, but on its own was clearly unable to subdue a whole republic. The regular army, however, accepted responsibility only with reluctance, with Major-General Ivan Babichev arguing that the assault was unconstitutional (a view which the Constitutional Court later rejected), but finally took part in the assault on Grozny. The Defence Ministry Collegium was completely excluded from managing the operation, while the General Staff under Kolesnikov (at least at first) played only a limited part in the operational planning of the intervention, one of the reasons for the confused objectives and the eclectic composition of the assault forces. On 25 January 1995 the MVD's General Alexander Romanov took over operational command but inter-service conflicts continued.

Grachev took advantage of the Chechen crisis to weaken some of his opponents, especially those outspoken in the denunciation of corruption earlier and who now denounced the clumsy intervention. Prominent victims in March 1995 included three deputy defence ministers who had been regarded as paragons of professional dignity and who were in effect dismissed when their posts were abolished: Georgii Kondrat'ev who had led the assault on the White House in October 1993; the popular and authoritative Colonel-General Boris Gromov was appointed the MFA's military expert; and Valerii Mironov, who had long criticised Grachev's mismanagement of military reform. The first deputy commander of the army Colonel-General Eduard Vorob'ev refused to take control of the operation and was dismissed.

In his state-of-the-nation address to parliament of 16 February 1995 Yeltsin was unrepentant but accepted that mistakes had been made. He noted the baleful effects of 'the Afghan syndrome' that had undermined Russia's will to deal with the Chechen crisis earlier, and he noted that 'the reform of the armed forces has been carried out unsatisfactorily' but failed to mention Grachev. The war provoked a reappraisal of decision-making in the military, with plans to remove the General Staff from the control of the defence ministry and to place it under the direct personal control of the president.[67] The Chechen war drained an already exhausted army, diverting reserves from other peace-keeping operations and devouring resources that might have been used to rebuild a more professional and militarily effective force. The decline of the army's combat readiness and military ineptitude in Chechnya weakened Russia's stature in relations both with the former Soviet states and with the world at large. At the Minsk CIS summit in May 1995 states like Kazakhstan and Uzbekistan sought to take advantage of Russia's debilitated condition by taking a more prominent role in adjudicating the Tajikistan conflict. Above all, the war undermined Russia's geopolitical position in the Caucasus, encouraging both Azerbaijan and Georgia to become more assertive. Only on 18 June 1996 was the deeply unpopular Grachev finally dismissed.

SECURITY POLICY AND NATO EXPANSION

In a speech in Berlin on 12 December 1989 James Baker had spoken of 'a new architecture for a new era', a new structure for European and international security. This rather inflexible imagery foreshadowed one of the salient features of post-communist Europe, namely the crisis of the institutions created during the Cold War to conduct and regulate that conflict. While communist Cold War organisations dissolved, those in the West not only survived but sought to expand their roles. Reflecting the larger problem (noted in chapter 14) about the largely unnegotiated nature of the post-Cold War peace, opinion in the West tended towards institutional conservativism, keeping the existing organisations while imbuing them with a new content, whereas Russia became the champion of institutional revisionism, seeking to renegotiate the European security system.

While attention in this section will focus on European security, it should be stressed that all along its southern borders Russia faced multiple security challenges. Russia's broad strategy focused on the attempt to create an extended security zone by direct and indirect intervention in the affairs of the former Soviet states, in Transcaucasia and Central Asia. Whether this security *droit de regard* amounts to neo-imperialism is a matter of considerable controversy. In response, as Alex Pravda notes, some in the West have advocated a policy of 'neo-containment' to undermine Russia's geopolitical hegemony in the region.[68]

In line with its reinvigorated European policy, Russia was an active participant in the web of institutions that was once labelled by Soviet writers the 'all-European process'. This included the CSCE, established in Helsinki in 1975, which with the end of the Cold War entered a period both of deepening and widening. Following the Paris Conference in November 1990 it acquired a headquarters and secretariat in Vienna; a Secretary General (supporting the work of the Chairman-in-Office); a Senior Council; a Permanent Council; a centre for the prevention of conflicts, a human rights commissioner; and an office for free elections (which later became the Office for Democratic Institutions and Human Rights based in Warsaw, specialising in constitution-making). A CSCE Parliamentary Assembly was established in Budapest in July 1992, designed not as a permanent body but to meet on the eve of summit meetings of heads of state to draft resolutions. Russia took over the Soviet seat, and total membership rose dramatically with the accession of the Baltic states in September 1991, all of the former Soviet states in January 1992 except Georgia (which joined a few months later), and with the accession of the post-Yugoslav states the total rose to fifty-three. The accession of the Central Asian states imbued the CSCE with the Eurasian character of Russia itself. It was far from clear, however, whether the CSCE was capable of dealing with the complexity of Eurasian politics.

Expectations that the CSCE would play a growing role in the post-communist world, expressed in the lofty language of the 'Charter of Paris for a New Europe' of 21 November 1990, were disappointed. Despite greater institutionalisation, including a modification of decision-making to allow 'consensus minus one', the CSCE remained but one among many competing institutions.[69] The Americans favoured Nato, whereas the Maastricht Treaty of 1992 envisaged a strengthened role for the defence arm of the EU, the Western European Union (WEU). The CSCE played little part in conflict resolution in Nagorno-Karabakh or in Yugoslavia. Moreover, the hasty widening of the CSCE by the accession of the former Soviet (and Yugoslav) states, some of whom did not meet accepted human rights standards, diluted the CSCE's human rights role. Contrary to the high hopes of 1990, the CSCE failed to become a community for the civilisational integration of Europe and its allies. However, as Zagorskii points out, insofar as the division of Europe was not yet over but had only taken on new forms,[70] the CSCE remained an important forum for the regulation of relations between the eastern and western parts of the Eurasian landmass.

Russian diplomacy sought to strengthen the CSCE, a view outlined by Yeltsin at the Helsinki summit of 9–10 July 1992. This approach was given substance at the Rome meeting of the CSCE Council of Foreign Ministers in November 1993 when Kozyrev called for the CSCE's agencies to be strengthened, for its peace-keeping role to be developed, and greater efforts to link human rights and the rights of national minorities with preventive diplomacy.[71] In an attempt to overcome some of its unwieldy amorphousness, the Budapest Review Conference (10 October–2 December 1994) transformed the CSCE into an international agency, the Organisation for Security and Cooperation in Europe (OSCE). In gaining a stronger institutional framework, however, the OSCE lost some of its original spirit of flexibility and consensus.

Russia's calls for a comprehensive system of collective security based on the OSCE, proposed formally in July 1994, were clearly designed in part to oppose plans for Nato expansion. If the OSCE were indeed to become the main vehicle for post-communist European security, then Nato enlargement would become meaningless. While perhaps never seriously believing that it could become an effective pan-European security organisation, Russia sought to expand the OSCE's political responsibilities and thus diminish Nato's influence and consolidate Russia's influence in European affairs. Despite Russia's equivocations and attempts to 'play' the OSCE 'card', the fundamental question remains unanswered: if there is no longer a security threat from any European power, then why should Nato expand?[72] The subtext to the whole question of Nato enlargement is whether the West was now to be a genuine partner or whether it still represented a threat to Russia – and *vice versa*.

The relationship between Russia and Nato and the question of the latter's expansion to the East (and in particular to the 'middle abroad', the states of Central and Eastern Europe) became one of the most thorny issues in Russia's post-Cold War relationship with the West. With the demise of its old adversary, what was now the point of Nato, and was it possible for Russia to join? While Nato remained the only effective coordinating body for the defence policies of its members, and inhibited the revival of the old balance-of-power politics that had brought war to Europe so often, its future remained in doubt.[73] Nato had always been a defensive alliance, but the problem lay in the definition of the security risks facing Europe. Was Russia part of the problem or part of the solution to European security? And as for Russian membership, a long-term commitment to this end would echo the visionary statesmanship that had brought the EEC into being after the Second World War, as a way of preventing forever war between European powers. The very existence of an expanded Nato would create a permanent source of tension in the centre of Europe; as Kozyrev put it, 'Nato's advance toward Russia's borders cannot but be seen as a continuation, though by inertia, of a policy aimed at containment of Russia.'[74] The renogotiation of European security, with perhaps the launching of a European Treaty Organisation (involving the USA, Canada and perhaps Japan), would prevent Nato itself becoming a threat to European security.

Twice before the USSR had sought, admittedly half-heartedly, to join Nato (Malenkov in the 1950s and Gorbachev in the 1980s), but now the question could be realistically posed. On a visit to Nato headquarters in Brussels in late October 1991 General Alexander Tsalko, deputy chair of Russia's Defence Committee, went so far as to suggest that Russia might join the organisation, initially at consultative level.[75] In late 1994 Boris Fedorov insisted that 'Russia must join Nato', arguing that membership would mean the end of US dominance in the organisation and would counteract Germany's growing power. Russian membership, moreover, would signal the genuine end of the Cold War and further guarantee democratic development in Russia.[76] Even if the principle of Russian membership were to be conceded, numerous economic, military and technical problems would have to be resolved before membership could be taken seriously: however, Nato was adamant that the ties would be far more superficial.

A variety of approaches were devised to combine the extension of Nato influence while not alarming Russia. The Rome summit of Nato in November 1991 established a North Atlantic Cooperation Council (NACC), and on 20 December 1991 it held its inaugural meeting. NACC's membership included thirty-six countries stretching from Vancouver to Vladivostok, including all the members of Nato and the former Soviet republics. The idea was to extend a 'shadow of security' over the region without offering concrete defence guarantees. The relationship of NACC to the CSCE was not clear, though there was some discussion that NACC could be used as CSCE's peace-keeping arm, allowing Nato troops to be used in 'out of area' operations. It made possible the internationalisation of the domestic conflicts of what had been the USSR, helping to regulate relations between the post-Soviet republics, over borders, human and minority rights. The body remained more shadow than substance, however, as demonstrated in its half-hearted attempts to mediate in the Nagorno-Karabakh dispute and its irrelevance in other conflicts.

During his visit to Warsaw in August 1993 Yeltsin had, typically, said 'go ahead' when asked about Poland's prospects for membership of Nato: this stance was rapidly modified on his return to Moscow. Despite some initial uncertainty about its attitude, Russia finally insisted that any expansion would have to meet tough conditions. Russia's objections were not so much a way of keeping Eastern Europe within Russia's security orbit but arose out of the obvious geopolitical consequences of expansion without commensurate commitments. This would amount to the advance of a powerful military alliance in close proximity to its borders (and if Belarus and Ukraine join, then right on its borders) with an unclear purpose. From Russia's perspective, Nato expansion would jeopardise its attempts to have good relations with both Eastern and Western Europe and would in effect signal its exclusion from Europe. As Kokoshin put it, 'The extension of Nato to the East would undermine the attempt to create a Europe-wide security system' and he sought to ensure Russia's special status in relations with Nato.[77] The isolation of Russia and attempts to exclude it from decision-making in Europe could precipitate a post-ideological Cold War, the 'cold peace' that Yeltsin had warned of at the Budapest Summit of the OSCE in December 1994.

Committed to expansion, the dilemma for Nato was how to do so without driving Russia back into hostility. A temporary solution was the Partnership for Peace (PfP) initiative, launched by Nato on 10 January 1994, participation in which would be considered a prerequisite for Nato membership, but would not guarantee it. Whereas NACC was a multilateral body, operating like the OSCE largely by consensus, PfP represented a series of bilateral agreements. By April 1995 twenty-six countries had signed up to the programme, ranging from Albania to Uzbekistan,[78] but although all members were formally equal some were clearly on the fast track for membership, above all some CEE countries. Thus PfP was simultaneously a way of managing Nato enlargement and delaying it. It was not clear whether PfP could indeed become a bridge rather than a barrier across Europe. Russia signed the Partnership Framework Document on 22 June 1994, when Kozyrev conceded that Russia 'had no fundamental objections' to Nato enlargement, but delayed later in signing the associated Individual Partnership Programme.

As the price for expansion, Moscow sought a formal expression to the much-touted post-Cold War idea of a 'strategic partnership' between the West and Russia, a permanent forum for consultation with Nato and a voice in security developments in Central Europe, something that in any case had been emerging within the framework of the OSCE and in the form of bilateral meetings. Russia, moreover, sought guarantees that prevented the forward positioning of nuclear weapons or the stationing of alliance forces in these countries, arrangements that already existed for Norway. The Western powers, however, firmly rejected Russia's attempt to achieve a special relationship with Nato that might allow it to veto eastward expansion, but accepted that it should spring no surprises on Russia. Russia's objections to the integration of the new members into the alliance's military structure, however, appeared to undermine the whole point of joining. Of Nato's sixteen existing members, France for many years was not part of the unified command and Spain is only partly integrated, but for the new members exclusion would weaken Nato's ability to enforce the security guarantees that they sought in membership.

Each crisis in Russia was accompanied by calls for the expansion of Nato, but the risks of expansion were clear. Rather than isolating Russia by pushing the line of confrontation between Poland and the CIS, the West sought to create a European security system encompassing all of Eurasia in which Russia could be a 'partner' but not an 'ally'. The only Russian leader in favour of Nato enlargement was Zhirinovskii, who understood that Russia's exclusion from the new European security order would increase support for his brand of national chauvinism and military revanchism. While Yeltsin and Kozyrev seldom hesitated to use the threat of a nationalist backlash at home as a bargaining counter in negotiations with the West, the threat was not an imaginary one. Sergei Yushenkov, chairman of the Fifth Duma's Defence Committee, suggested on 15 May 1995 that Russia should be given associate membership in Nato on the grounds that this would 'contribute to the formation of a new security system in the framework of OSCE on the basis of existing Nato structures':[79] There are no provisions for associate membership and Nato governments always rejected such proposals. Others insisted that Russia should create its own collective security system within the framework of the old USSR.[80] Kozyrev took the view that 'the deepening of relations between Nato and Russia should become an integral part of the alliance's transformation'.[81]

Post-communist Russia was thus faced with a security dilemma of the first magnitude: the Nato alliance was formed to counter a danger that had disappeared but its continued existence appeared to run counter to Russia's long-term strategic interests. The issue of Nato expansion served to forge an almost unique consensus among all wings of Russian politics. According to Karaganov, 'Nato's plans for expansion mean a potential new Yalta. . . . By accepting the rules of the game that are being forced on her. . . . Russia will lose'.[82] Russia's attempts to renegotiate the post-Cold War order, however, met with little success. Quite apart from the institutional conservatism of the West, Russia's initiatives were often poorly prepared and ill-thought out, as with the rejection by the CSCE Budapest Summit of Yeltsin's plan to establish a European Security Council.

Nato expansion became the defining issue in Russian foreign policy. Nato's bombing of Serb positions in Bosnia in late August 1995 vividly illustrated Russia's marginalisation and raised fears that Russia itself might anticipate the same treatment if it stepped too far out of line. Lebed responded by insisting that if Nato expanded, then Russia should create its own new military bloc made up of the former Soviet republics and other counties that objected to an aggressive Nato on their borders.[83] The prospect of a post-ideological Cold War never looked so real, provoked by the insensitivity of Nato, the narrowness of the ambitions of the East Europeans, and the confused pugnacity of Russia.

CIVIL-MILITARY RELATIONS

Civilian control of the military has been crucial in all previous transitions, notably in Latin America and southern Europe. Even in Spain, the much-admired democratic transition, everything was put in jeopardy in 1981 when some army officers seized parliament. The Soviet regime had created a military machine whose scope was unprecedented in peacetime but had always been careful to ensure Party and state control over the ambitions of the generals. Marxism-Leninism asserted the primacy of the Party over the military but at the same time its view of permanent conflict with capitalism served to justify the maintenance of the huge military establishment and imbued it with prestige. With the dissolution of the regime traditional forms of control disappeared, and at the same time the prestige and morale of the armed forces plummetted. Seemingly interminable political crises gave rise to an un-precedented politicisation of the military, which emerged as a significant political force in its own right, but was not immune to the prevailing spirit of fragmentation.

The armed forces remained loyal to the presidency but potentially they represented the single most destabilising force in the transition. Gorbachev had neutralised the military by continuing high military expenditure, while Yeltsin promised greater professional rewards and ensured the payment of wages despite severe budgetary constraints. Whether the new model of civil–military relations would be enough to isolate the military from politics remained unclear. Defeat in the Second World War had destroyed the military establishments and militarist traditions in Germany and Japan, leaving the civilian state to concentrate on domestic economic development. In Russia the Soviet military establishment remained largely intact at independence in 1991, and it fell to the new state itself to begin the arduous task of civilianising politics. The state itself, however, was in certain respects weaker than the military; as Christopher Donnelly points out, 'large bureaucratic institutions continue to function irrespective of the lack of government. . . . As of mid-1992, the armed forces hierarchy was increasingly determining its own agenda'.[84] The military definition of state security and the militaristic ethos of the ruling class remained to be challenged.

The functional equivalent of defeat in war is humiliation in peace (the Versailles syndrome). As if the great retreat was not enough, the military discovered that involvement in domestic conflicts was extremely damaging. Every intervention acted as a self-inflicted blow on prestige and morale: the Tbilisi massacre of 9 April 1989; the brutal occupation of Baku in January 1990; and the seizure of the television tower in Vilnius and other events in the Baltic in January 1991. The civilian leadership usually retreated behind a cloud of obfuscation and equivocation, while the army was left to explain the corpses. The army's half-hearted involvement in the coup of August 1991 salvaged its pride, but all these events demonstrated once again the dangers of trying to solve the political agendas of others by military means. The military adopted a policy of 'neutrality' in domestic political struggle. General Lobov argued that 'people in uniforms should not engage in party activities, nor in political battles in parliament at any level'.[85] The Law on Defence, moreover, restricts the army to external defence only.

This explains why in October 1993 the army was so reluctant to become involved, and it took several hours of pleading by Yeltsin at the Ministry of Defence to get the military to suspend the formula 'the army is outside politics' and to agree to an assault on the White House.[86] The October events revealed the desperately divided condition of the Russian Army: the force of just 1,700 was drawn from five separate divisions in the Moscow MD; to ensure loyalty tank crews were made up almost entirely of officers, and at least half the infantry were officers or senior NCOs.[87] Already low morale was further undermined by the Chechen campaign, which did little to enhance Grachev's personal standing. A poll of 615 generals and colonels in August 1994 revealed that under 30 per cent trusted Yeltsin, and fewer than 20 per cent had any faith in Grachev, while half said they trusted Generals Lebed and Gromov. As far as their political attitudes were concerned, 80 per cent of these top ranking officers favoured an authoritarian form of government and 64 per cent dismissed Western-type democracy as unsuitable for Russia.[88]

We need to be clear about what is meant by military intervention in politics. For Latsis it means resolute action against the civilian leadership,[89] which has not yet taken place in Russia. The military's involvement in resolving the October 1993 crisis led to much speculation that they would thereafter enjoy a disproportionate influence in policy, whereas in fact the effect was short-lived. The military gained few of the anticipated rewards like increased budgets, an end to personnel cuts and a harder line in the near abroad. Contrary to popular views, as noted, commanders opposed the resolution of the Chechen crisis by military means.

During perestroika the military had become increasingly politicised as the old unity gave way to dissonance of *glasnost* and the rise of republican separatism. The demise of the old Soviet political organs (above all the Main Political Administration) left officers prey to influences from beyond the military. From 1992, however, the reconstituted Russian military authorities fought hard to reverse the politicisation of the army. Measures included the ban on party activity in the ranks, the forced resignation of those actively involved in political life (a dispensation that appears to have been dropped in the December 1995 elections) and the prohibition on army trade unions.[90] Organisations like the All-Russian Officer's Union, registered in February 1992, headed by Vladislav Achalov and Stanislav Terekhov were anti-government, accusing it of indifference towards corruption, dismissing officers for political reasons (above all for criticism of Grachev himself), and for presiding over Russia's military decline.[91] While claiming a membership of 30,000 officers, in fact Terekhov's organisation was minuscule but the armed forces were rife with anti-government sentiments. According to military sociologists in November 1992 only 19 per cent of servicemen supported the government, while its policies were opposed by 56 per cent.[92]

The political views of servicemen are an important factor in electoral politics. According to some estimates there are 1.8 million military personnel; about 7 million members and relatives of service families with the right to vote; some 7–9 million employed in military-industrial enterprises, military research institutes and agencies, with families; some 20–21 million service pensioners and the families of veterans of the Great Patriotic and other wars; and some 2 million Russian Cossacks.[93] Thus the armed forces and related groups make up to 40 million people out of a total electorate of just under 110 million, and this is leaving out of account those employed in the proliferation of other security agencies (MVD, FSB, PSB, etc.) and the Federal Border Service which could well add another 10–15 million people.

The voting pattern of the military in the December 1993 elections remains disputed. According to Yeltsin a third of the soldiers voted for Zhirinovskii's LDPR,[94] but Grachev contested this, insisting that there was no reliable information on military voting patterns.[95] While no global data are available since much voting took place in ordinary polling stations, the evidence suggests that in areas with a high military presence Zhirinovskii's LDPR gained more than average support, reckoned to be in the region of 40 per cent.[96] Another 20 per cent voted for the communists. It is figures such as these that no doubt prompted Yeltsin to seek a reliable armed force under his personal control, hence the expansion of Korzhakov's Presidential Security Service (PSB).

Rather than riding in on a white horse the military vigorously entered the December 1995 electoral race. Having resigned his commission, Lebed joined Skokov's KRO and was placed second on their party list. Skokov had forged strong links with the military when secretary of the Security Council in 1993, and now hoped to capitalise on the revulsion among the officer corps against the venality of political life. General-Lieutenant Lev Rokhlin, commander of forces in Volgograd and veteran of the Afghan and Chechen wars (for which he was nominated a Hero of the Russian Federation, an award he refused to receive) was placed third on the Russia Our Home list. Surveys in 1995 suggested strong support for national-patriotic movements in the forces.[97] The results, however, in December 1995 were disappointing for KRO, failing to cross the 5 per cent threshold, and for the Ministry of Defence, which had hoped to have a strong military presence in the Sixth Duma.

The establishment of parliamentary committees overseeing security policy, and monitoring the budget (and with it military expenditure) marked important stages in the development of civilian control over the military. However, the establishment of political controls primarily requires effective political institutions, and Russia has not yet reached that stage. The other side of the equation, the professionalisation of the military, also requires competent state structures. The absence of the latter encouraged the military itself to enter politics, as witnessed by the large number of soldiers participating in the December 1995 elections. Divided between parties and tendencies, however, 'the military' as such lacked a single voice, and thus diminished the incentive to enter the political arena by forceful means.

Civil–military relations depend to a large degree on relations within the military itself. Like much of Russian life, this proved to be signally faction-ridden. Grachev himself was not popular within the military establishment, considered too dependent on Yeltsin and unable to defend the interests of the military,[98] and was thus always on the lookout for potential challengers. The Chechen war revealed a split between those who out of a sense of professional responsibility had criticised the launching of a bloody campaign when all avenues for negotiation had not yet been explored, and a group who, irrespective of the cost, were willing to pursue the campaign – dubbed the 'party of war'. The 'military opposition' to Yeltsin, if it can be called that, took two main forms: 'the professionals' (Gromov, Lebed, and, potentially, General Andrei Nikolaev, Commander of the Border Troops); and 'the irreconcilables', mainly consisting of retired oficers (including generals Makashov and Achalov, and the ex-KGB officer Sterligov). The appointment of Lebed's ally, General Igor Rodionov, formerly head of the General Staff Academy, as defence minister in July 1996 brought the professionals into the centre of military and security affairs.

Harmonious civil–military relations reflect stable social relations, while social crisis gives rise to tension. The emergence of a Russian Bonaparte would be the natural conclusion of over a decade of political chaos. Military dictatorship was openly canvassed as a possibility by senior army officers. The aim would be not to re-establish communism but to 'restore order' in fulfilment of the 'Pinochet option' for Russia. According to some liberal newspapers, Lebed enjoyed 'a simply unique authority among officers' and was 'in great political demand' in Russian society,[99] some considered him a far more serious potential presidential candidate than either Rutskoi or Zhirinovskii.[100] Asked whether he would respond to the call of 'patriotic forces', Lebed insisted that he would avoid both 'left-radical and right-radical patriots'.[101]

The army had traditionally been the backbone of the Russian state and thus civil–military relations would always be ambivalent. While some saw the Chechen war as the outcome of the militarisation of the Russian state (allied with the security apparatus), the war in practice revealed the enormous divisions within the security, military and foreign policy establishments. Yeltsin's own dominance over security had been enshrined in the new constitution, making the president commander-in-chief, granting him the right to appoint and dismiss ministers and military commanders, to lead the Security Council, to declare states of emergency and war, and in addition placed him in overall control of the Ministry of the Interior, the security services, and the ever-growing PSB. The greater problem, however, was that the military was not subordinated to the state as such but that civilian control came to mean simply bringing the military under the command of the presidency. The Chechen war showed just how dangerous this could be, and there were few checks on the emergence of constitutional praetorianism.

The task now was to forge a modern professional army, a process impeded by Russia's involvement in CIS and domestic conflicts. The more politicised an army, the less professional it will be, as evidenced by the dismissal of the arch-professionals Gromov *et al* during the Chechen war. The course of military reform, moreover, was strongly resisted from within. The abolition of the old political officers gave the military much greater scope for autonomy than before. According to Vladimir Smirnov, a member of the coordinating committee of the 'Soldiers for Democracy' organisation, Yeltsin made a fateful strategic mistake in allowing the army to drift out of control and in delaying the reform of the army and the military-industrial complex. This 'empire within an empire' quickly destroyed all that was good in it and degenerated; illegally selling arms and military equipment, and conducting huge financial machinations.[102]

The Defence Ministry sought to recreate a specifically Russian *ésprit de corps*, but this perhaps inevitably tended towards the patriotic, if not the nationalistic, side of Russian politics. For understandable reasons, the military favoured the preservation of the defence industries and Russia's Great Power status. The military establishment continued to act as an important player in foreign policy, and in particular in relations with the 'near abroad' (as in Trans-Dniester and Abkhazia) and also over relations with Japan. The weakness of central authority meant that the reconstituted Russian military enjoyed considerable autonomy, and allied with the still powerful military-industrial officials, tried to shape policies. The military at times appeared to be making its own policy. The Far Eastern MD, for example, had its own agenda in relations with China, while some regional commanders appeared intent on pursuing their own interests, often associated with the development of various enterprises. This was not so much warlordism as a distinctive form of military capitalism.

This was accompanied, significantly, by an important theoretical shift. Post-communist state-building has returned to Prussian notions whereby 'military force is increasingly considered not only as a necessary attribute of independence, but as a legitimate instrument of policy'.[103] War in Abkhazia, Tajikistan and Chechnya, *pace* Clausewitz, has become a continuation of the policy of national self-affirmation. The first 'Strategy for Russia' report noted that 'The territory of the former USSR will probably become a zone in which military power will play an essential role', and for this the Russian armed forces had to prepare themselves.[104] The age of militarised inter-state relations has not ended. The two halves of Europe live in separate historical times: the Western half in the recent past has waged the greatest wars in humanity's history on a global scale, yet appears complacently to have occupied the moral high ground and delegitimised war as an instrument of policy; while the East is still racked by the volcanic pressures of state and nation-building.

But does this mean that the Yeltsin regime had fallen prey to the influence of the military and returned to the authoritarian and expansionist ways of its predecessors? The answer would appear to be that the military and the Yeltsin presidency had interests in common, but the mere fact that the military could sustain a policy of their own suggests that Russia still has a long way to go before the military can be considered to be under complete civilian control. It will not be easy to shake off Tsarism's militaristic ethos or the USSR's fundamental belief that the central purpose of the state was to prepare for war with the capitalist oppressors. If the military had been considered by some a 'sixteenth republic' in the old USSR, the Russian military is not quite yet a state within the state but it nevertheless exhibits a dangerous degree of independence.

The attempt to sculpt a lean and professional Russian army out of the bloated Soviet defence establishment at a time of economic crisis would inevitably be a long and arduous process. The Russian military was no more immune to the general degradation of public life than any other group. However, by a mixture of inducements and turning a blind eye, the post-communist authorities were able to keep the military out of politics, except when called upon in moments of crisis. Despite its involvement in heavy-handed 'peace-keeping' operations abroad and a radical intervention in domestic politics in Moscow and Chechnya, Lambeth argues that 'The military nonetheless remains a responsible and stabilizing force in Russian society.'[105]

16 Commonwealth and community

A multitude is strong while it holds together, but so soon as each of those who compose
it begins to think of his own private danger, it becomes weak and contemptible.

Niccolo Machiavelli[1]

While the USSR might have collapsed with relatively little violence, the disintegration of the
great empires of the past suggests that the greatest danger comes from conflicts between
successor states and the threat of outside powers seeking to take advantage of the power
vacuum. The arbitrariness of the borders, the intermingling of populations, and a host of
unresolved problems provided fertile ground for conflicts. The ambiguities in Russian policy
towards the successor states, twelve of which including Russia came to be members of the
Commonwealth of Independent States (CIS), was one of the main charges against the liberal
foreign policy of the early post-communist years. The CIS was not itself a state in the
conventional sense and neither was it a subject of international law. Its member states actively
pursued their own independent foreign policies, and tended often to distance themselves from
their former partners. Gradually Russian policy took on a more vigorous aspect, incorporating
the states into an expanded security zone and sphere of vital interests. This chapter briefly
examines the challenges facing state-building in the successor states, the evolution of the CIS,
and analyses the problem of borders and the vexed question of individual and collective rights
in nation and state-building.

PROBLEMS OF STATE AND NATION-BUILDING

Some of the republics had fought for independence, while others had it thrust upon them. All
faced similar problems of reconstructing their economies, creating new systems of state and
legal administration, sustaining viable patterns of accountability and participation, remaking
their national identities and diversifying their foreign policies. Some of the post-communist
nation-states fit quite well Robert Jackson's description of 'quasi-states', owing their existence
to membership of the inter-state system but with few other attributes to sustain their claims
to sovereign statehood.[2] For others, like Ukraine, the achievement of independence in 1991
represented the culmination of a thousand years of complex national development.

Everywhere there was a tension between democracy and nation-building. While in some
areas (the Baltic) the independence struggle can be seen in terms of a national democratic
revolution against both the USSR as a type of empire and against the communist system as a
form of political dictatorship, elsewhere the nature of the independence process is far more

Table 9 Territory and population of former Soviet republics, 1 January 1990

	Territory in thous. Km²	Percentage of USSR	Population in thousands	Percentage of USSR	Percentage growth rate(1)	Percentage urbanised
Former USSR	22,403	100.0	288,624	100.0	0.66	66
Russia	17,075	76.2	148,041	51.3	0.43	74
Baltic:	175	0.7	7,993	2.8	0.59	70
Estonia	45	0.2	1,583	0.5	0.89	72
Latvia	65	0.3	2,687	0.9	0.26	71
Lithuania	65	0.3	3,723	1.3	0.64	68
Moldova	34	0.2	4,362	1.5	0.55	47
Belarus	208	0.9	10,259	3.6	0.58	66
Ukraine	604	2.7	51,839	18.0	0.26	67
Transcaucasus:	186	0.8	15,880	5.5	0.70	56
Armenia	30	0.1	3,293	1.1	0.15	68
Azerbaijan	87	0.4	7,131	2.5	1.32	54
Georgia	70	0.3	5,456	1.9	0.24	56
Central Asia:	3,994	17.8	50,250	17.4	1.57	49
Kazakhstan	2,717	12.1	16,691	5.8	0.94	57
Kyrgyzstan	199	0.9	4,367	1.5	1.79	38
Tajikistan	143	0.6	5,248	1.8	2.72	32
Turkmenistan	488	2.2	3,622	1.3	2.49	45
Uzbekistan	447	2.0	20,322	7.0	2.09	41

Note (1) Percentage growth in population 1989–90.

Source: Economist Intelligence Unit, *CIS: Country Report*, no. 2, 1992, p. 11, modified.

ambivalent. Much of the old authoritarianism was reproduced, and in places (notably Turkmenistan) intensified, in a revived national idiom. It is for this reason that some democrats in 1991 joined nationalists in condemning the disintegration of the Union, fearing that under the guise of sovereignty the peoples of the former USSR would be sacrificed to the ambitions of local nomenklatura elites. Democrats feared that these 'oases of partocracy' represented a danger not only to their own peoples but to Russia as well.[3] The dynamics between democracy and nationalism in post-communist state-building differed in each republic.

The situation after August 1991 was in many respects reminiscent of the world of assertive new nation-states born at Versailles in 1919, and which after much conflict was destroyed by the Second World War. In the inter-war republics of Central Europe democracy was subordinated to the nation-building struggles of the national elites, and while some of the new states retained a formal commitment to democratic institutions, the emergence of a distinctive type of national democracy proved unstable in the long-run. The post-Soviet republics (in particular in Central Asia) reproduced to a remarkable degree the problems of the earlier era, with civic institutions sustained by fragile social bases, tensions between titular and minority nationalities, economies in various stages of under-development, great social inequalities and fundamental questions about the viability of the inherited borders. There are major differences, however, with the international *zeitgeist* of the 1990s favouring democracy, whereas the rise of Mussolini to power in Italy in 1922 endowed authoritarianism of the right with a certain respectability, complementing the increasingly fashionable authoritarianism of the left under the impact of the Great Depression from 1929 and the apparent successes of Stalin's 5-year plans.

In addition, the fragile League of Nations of the inter-war years has now given way to a dense web of international economic, political and human rights organisations, allowing all sorts of strategic interventions to avert or mediate conflicts. The appalling testimony of Bosnia, however, where the serried and quarrelling ranks of the EU, the CSCE and the UN, with honied and ultimately treacherous talk of 'safe areas' and the like, proved unable to stop the Serb killing machine until Nato and the Americans intervened, does not provide grounds for optimism in the efficacy of the new international order. The inter-war experiment of East European democracy and state-building was brought to a summary and brutal conclusion by German expansionism, and today, too, the only guarantee that the post-Soviet republics will be able to continue making mistakes in their own way is that Russia retains a broadly democratic and non-interventionist orientation.

State-building in the successor republics can be examined under four broad headings.[4] The first is the viability of the new state formation and its place in the international system. Only the Baltic republics had recent experience of an extended period of independence, while the Slavic republics had long been subsumed into some larger unit but had various state traditions to draw on. Some of the other states, primarily in Central Asia, were entirely new, as indeed was Russia within its present borders. For most states (like Ukraine and the Transcaucasian republics) the central issue was the revival of earlier traditions of statehood and their amalgamation with often very different modern realities to sustain a viable new national order.

The Baltic republics had no hesitation in joining the mainstream of European development, forging close links with their Scandinavian neighbours, but their proximity to Russia entailed a residual 'Finlandisation', that is, domestic autonomy but restrictions in foreign policy. Russia was adamant, for example, that it would not tolerate their incorporation into Nato and thus, as with Finland during the Cold War, these states enjoyed full domestic and international sovereignty as long as Russia's security interests were respected. For the other states integration in international bodies proved hesitant, with the West wary at first of Ukraine's nuclear ambitions and fearing elsewhere that it would be sucked into local conflicts. The successor states became members of the UN, the OSCE, NACC and international economic agencies (IMF, World Bank and the EBRD in particular). All of this gave international legitimacy to the independent states, but Jackson's notion of 'quasi-states' still clung to the whole process; it would take more than international recognition to transform some of these into viable modern states.

The very existence of the CIS suggested a special community of interests for the former Soviet states, taking priority over whatever new external links the successor states might forge. The Baltic republics, however, refused to be constrained by their former membership of the Soviet Union and resisted any hint of joining, while Ukraine bore CIS membership with the minimum of grace. The CIS played a crucial role in the first period, preventing a total collapse of economic ties and providing a framework for diplomacy between the successor republics. States outside the CIS faced severe problems, with Georgia dissolving into civil war and Azerbaijan facing external occupation and internal insurgency, problems that appeared to subside within the fold of the CIS. Membership, however, did not prevent civil war in Tajikistan and was no guarantee of stability elsewhere. It did, however, establish a framework for peace-keeping operations in Abkhazia, Trans-Dniester and elsewhere.

The second key issue is the tension between political independence and economic viability. With the demise of the rouble zone all states were forced to become fully fledged economic subjects, with their own currencies, customs, membership of international economic organisations and other attributes of economic sovereignty, while at the same time pursuing policies of economic integration with their neighbours and the world. While some countries (like Ukraine) pursued these policies with a marked enthusiasm, others were reluctant economic separatists, and indeed ultimately Belarus and Kazakhstan in 1995 reconfirmed their ties with Russia by forming a Customs Union. All, however, produced goods at a price and quality that found few markets in the world outside and, despite initial hopes for a rapid diversification of economic ties, were forced to restore traditional connections. Those (like Turkmenistan, Kazakhstan and Azerbaijan) with oil and/or gas reserves sought to buttress their political independence by links with Western partners, but the sheer enormity of the stakes in the geopolitics of energy policy served in some cases to undermine the room for manoeuvre of states like Azerbaijan, faced by Russia's refusal to be cut out of either the exploitation or transportation of Caspian oil.

The third issue affecting the viability of the new republics focuses on state-building, the creation of political and administrative institutions. All republics faced the problem of creating new administrative structures since the highly centralised Soviet regime had allowed little scope for republican state governments, ruling largely through the Communist Party. In Kiev, for example, at independence there were no more than 700 ministerial officials to run the affairs of a country the size of France. State-building took place in the most unpropitious circumstances imaginable, with all states suffering severe economic hardship in the first years of independence, but the attempt to trade political stability at the price of delaying economic reform did not work. The absence of serious economic reforms, as in Ukraine until 1994, proved just as destabilising as their implementation, while in Belarus the maintenance of antiquated economic relations provided the framework for president Alexander Lukashenko's populist authoritarianism. Despite fearsome obstacles, most relatively quickly established the rudiments of modern state systems with constitutions, legislatures, presidents and with legal systems usually guaranteeing a range of political rights, including membership of political parties, and defending civic rights like free speech and a free media. There is no doubt, however, that all the new polities were fragile, with the rights proclaimed on paper limited in practice and with government marred by corrupt and inept bureaucracies. Clans that had been strong under communism tended to rule in the new circumstances. The idiom, however, on the whole remained democratic, and in few countries did the political process wither away entirely. While Turkmenistan might be an extreme case of a new personalised paternalism replacing Soviet communism, elsewhere the new polities adapted national traditions and traditional patterns of authority to a novel democratising ethos.

The sheer multiplicity of threats to the new states encouraged the adoption of elements of authoritarianism. The relationship between stability and democracy proved a variable one, and some of the leaders of the new republics indeed considered democracy one of the greatest threats to the political stability of their states. As in Russia itself, the question in the first instance was not so much the development of democracy but the creation of new political orders responsive to the social traditions and political cultures of the republics. As in many post-colonial African states, stability appeared of greater value than democracy; although in the long-run, the absence of democracy itself became a source of instability in Africa and will no doubt do so again in Eurasia.

The fourth issue focuses on nation-building, and in particular the balance to be drawn between the titular nationality and various minorities (which in some cases were nearly majorities). Building nation-states in ethnically heterogeneous areas poses the question of whether the principles of statehood or nationhood should take priority. At its starkest, the emphasis on nationhood threatens the rights of minorities, while statehood means the defence of territorial integrity and universal and equal rights for all irrespective of ethnicity. This on occasion aroused the resentment of a state's titular ethnic group who claimed that not enough was done to rectify historical injustices. Nazarbaev's even-handed approach to ethnic Russians and Kazakhs, for example, led to resentment among the latter that their past subordination was being perpetuated.

Most leaderships sought to avoid alienating ethnic minorities or permanently excluding whole ethnic groups from the institutions of the new states. The problem, however, was deeper, and in the Baltic republics and elsewhere nationality revolutions took place whereby the previously privileged groups, largely Russian in composition joined by Sovietised and Russified national elites, were displaced as a whole new hierarchy of authority emerged. The titular populations predominated in the psycho-social self-definition of the republic's identity. Even the most liberal of citizenship laws could do little to prevent the process of nationality displacement, which in some cases led to the marginalisation of whole ethnic groups in the new hierarchy of political and cultural power in the newly independent republics.

These four factors operated in different ways and with varying intensity in the post-Soviet states. The dissolution of classical empires usually entailed extended periods of instability and war. The disappearance of the Austro-Hungarian empire created a zone of instability in Central and Eastern Europe that in certain respects (Yugoslavia) remains to this day. The withdrawal of Britain from India led to the death of millions at partition in 1947–48, and the conflict between India and Pakistan over Kashmir remains to this day. By contrast, the relatively peaceful disintegration of the USSR can in part be explained by the fact that it was never an empire in the classical sense, with a clearly defined ethnic grouping ruling over subordinate peoples. Perhaps more importantly, the decay of empire began at the centre, and the local elites found power falling into their hands: while demands for national justice in the Baltic republics were accompanied by acts of courage and mass mobilisation, even they could hardly have envisaged that full independence would have been achieved so speedily. With the dissolution of communist power, only Russia could have stepped in to maintain a unified post-Soviet state, and this it resolutely refused to do, and indeed encouraged the independence of others as part of its own liberation as a state from the imperial mentality.

Another factor working in favour of a relatively peaceful outcome of the Soviet collapse is the absence of profound ideological or religious conflicts between the successor states. All were committed, if only in words, to democracy and the market; although by no means all can be considered 'democracies'. In addition, no neighbouring state emerged as a threat to the integrity of the new states. While jostling for influence, the post-Soviet space did not become the arena for the predatory ambitions of foreign powers. The international community, moreover, provided a framework for the peaceful establishment of statehood and the management of nationality issues, economic transformation and nuclear weapons. While the relatively peaceful disintegration of the USSR remains one of the great gifts of history, the stability of the republics and the maintenance of peace cannot be taken for granted.

THE COMMONWEALTH OF INDEPENDENT STATES (CIS)

The CIS did not become the successor state to the USSR, and there is no CIS foreign policy and no CIS 'national interest'. Instead, there are divergent foreign policies in constant uncomfortable interaction with each other. The CIS is not a state in international law, and each member regards economic and foreign policy, and increasingly security policy as well, its own preserve. The first problem was the avoidance of conflict, but numerous other features of the foreign policies of the successor states soon became apparent, including a diversification of economic dependencies, the development of regional alliances and associations in line with traditional cultural affiliations, and the search for protectors and sponsors abroad. The (British) Commonwealth plays a limited role in conflict resolution between states; and an even more marginal role in conflict-resolution within states, as the Nigerian civil war testified. Will the post-Soviet CIS be able to take on a more active role?

Organisation and development

Attempts to create a Union of Sovereign States (USS) in the post-coup period soon came to nothing. The draft treaty of November 1991 still provided for some form of power-sharing between a reconstituted centre and the republics,[5] but the other republics feared that the new centre would recreate patterns of domination; Russia appeared to be assuming the mantle of leadership cast off by the old Union. As we saw in chapter 1, the Ukrainian vote for independence on 1 December 1991 sealed the death warrant for the Union Treaty process, and on 8 December the leaders of the three Slavic republics announced the creation of the CIS.

The CIS played a critical role in managing the transition to independent statehood, yet few of the objectives proclaimed in the CIS treaty of December 1991 were achieved. Commitments to coordinate their foreign policy, to maintain a common economic space, to coordinate transport and communications systems, and to retain open frontiers and guarantee freedom of movement for all CIS citizens were only partially fulfilled.[6] Two opposing views took shape, with the first, supported by Gorbachev, arguing that the CIS should create supranational executive bodies and accelerate integration,[7] while the second defined the CIS as a temporary intergovernmental coordinating and consultative body designed only to provide a civilised mechanism for the 'divorce' of the former Soviet republics.[8] While the CIS registered a 'negative' success in preventing a total collapse of former ties, positive achievements were meagre.

Russia became the 'continuer' state of the USSR in diplomatic terms and in international law, but for the other 'successor' states the term suggested that Russia expected to become the dominant partner. The disintegration of the USSR posed endless questions about the division of assets, capital, institutions and the armed forces. Above all, there was the problem of determining the citizenship of the heterogeneous populations of the new republics (see below). The division of resources proved less of a problem than had been anticipated, and operated on the principle that what was in the republics belonged to them, and what was in Russia belonged to Russia even though both sides might have contributed to its development. As for the division of foreign assets, all the CIS states agreed to exchange their share in return for Russia paying their part of the USSR's foreign debt.

The provisional accords of 8 December 1991 stipulated that the CIS headquarters was to be in Belovezha, the capital of Belarus. The CIS was to coordinate policy through a Council of Heads of State (CHS) and a Council of Heads of Government (CHG), both of which were to meet at least twice a year and the presidency of both councils was to rotate. Individual member states had the right to veto decisions of the councils. In 1992 the councils each met eight times and signed some 275 agreements, though many were of a declaratory nature and lacked

Figure 8 Member states of the CIS

Figure 9 Ukraine

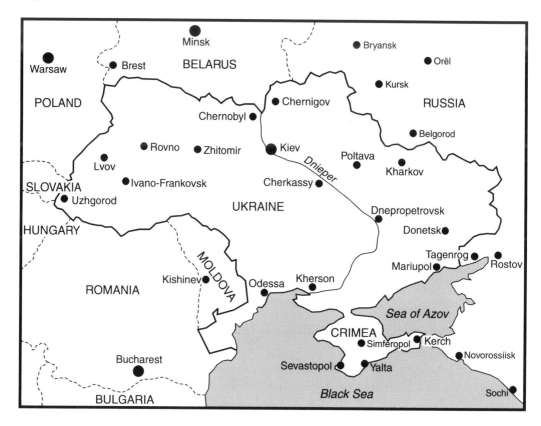

mechanisms for implementation, and about half dealt with military matters. The agreements formalised not the deepening of relations between states but regulated their separation. Early meetings were rather chaotic affairs, but by late 1992 they were better prepared by preliminary meetings of foreign and defence ministers of the member states. According to Kozyrev, meetings of heads of state took on a more productive character as early euphoria over independence gave way to a more sober understanding of the need for reintegration within the CIS.[9] By January 1996 the CHS had met seventeen times.

The CIS is influenced by the way that decisions are taken. Although in December 1991 it was agreed that decisions would be taken by consensus, in practice delegations could easily opt out. The Tashkent summit of 15 May 1992 adopted the formula 'consensus-minus-one', and simple majority voting for procedural issues. Even that proved too restrictive, and any state could simply declare that it was not interested in a particular decision and was thus exempted. Selective participation in signing agreements became standard practice, with only 7 out of 11 member states signing the relevant document on the establishment of the CIS Interparliamentary Assembly at the March 1992 Kiev summit, only six signing the Collective Security Treaty in Tashkent in May 1992, eight delegations approving the 6 July 1992 Moscow Agreement on the status of the Economic Court, and the same with most other accords.[10] The strongest commitment to CIS cooperation was demonstrated by Russia, Kazakhstan, Kyrgyzstan, Uzbekistan and Tajikistan, closely followed by Armenia and Belarus. No agreement was achieved on the imposition of sanctions for the non-observance of treaty commitments.

Figure 10 Transcaucasus

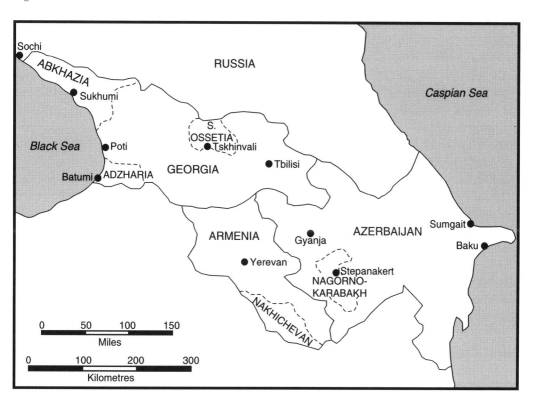

Documents adopted by the CIS were primarily of two types.[11] The great majority fell into the category of *modus vivendi* agreements designed to prevent a total collapse of the infrastructure of the old union. They dealt with such issues as energy, transport, payment of pensions, border forces, customs regulations and so on, and were signed by most of the eleven republics. While possibly contributing in the long-term to an integratory process, in the short term these agreements did little to promote the development of a common space but merely regulated the assertion of national sovereignty and tried to avoid a complete collapse of the old economic area.

The second category consisted of agreements establishing coordinating bodies such as the Collective Security Council, a Council of Defence Ministers, a Customs Council and some two dozen others. Most tried to regulate inter-state economic relations, dealing with such issues as rail transport, statistics, energy, science and technology, and the like. Azerbaijan refused to sign agreements in the defence sphere, and from March 1992 opted out of agreements on coordinating bodies in socio-economic affairs as well. Ukraine was little more enthusiastic about the common institutions of the CIS and, together with Moldova and Turkmenistan, these four states were the most opposed to the institutionalisation of the CIS.[12] They insisted that the CIS was not a suprastate institution.

The CIS was therefore marked by a differentiation process in which three groups of states emerged. The first was a core comprising Russia, Kazakhstan, Kyrgyzstan, Uzbekistan and, until engulfed by civil war, Tajikistan. These countries had been most willing to sign the Union Treaty in 1991 and now signed most agreements, and appeared most devoted to the concept of the CIS evolving into a closer community of nations. Nazarbaev, indeed, urged the creation of a new union, and after the August coup lamented the failure 'to unify the economy while

Figure 11 Central Asia

giving all the states complete independence in matters of foreign and domestic policy'. He argued that 65 per cent of the fall in production in the former union was due to the breakdown of economic ties, and 20 per cent was due to the break up of Comecon and the economic links with Eastern Europe. In his view the absence of a clear mechanism of implementation rendered most of the CIS agreements virtually inoperative, and thus he urged the development of a more concrete unifying principle.[13] Nazarbaev's idea of a confederal union was supported by Gorbachev.[14] A step in this direction would be the creation of the post of General Secretary of the CIS; instead, its Executive Secretary has minimal powers.

The emergence of this core group led some to suggest that the CIS would become no more than a Russian-Central Asian bloc. Indeed, the Eurasianists argued that since Ukraine had driven a wedge between Russia and Europe, Russia should pursue a less Western-oriented policy and concentrate on links with the Central Asian states to ensure Russian predominance in Eurasia. This was in contrast to the Atlanticists, who considered that Russia should aim to join the core states of the industrialised north as quickly as possible, while the Eurasians considered that Russia's natural allies were to be found in the south.[15]

The second group was made up of Armenia and Belarus who were selective in signing agreements and who were wary of the creation of supranational CIS bodies. Belarus supported cooperation within the CIS, but sought to avoid being caught up in a political and military alliance, at first trying to reduce its Eurasian ties but under Lukashenko becoming committed to closer ties with Russia, signing a bilateral treaty on 2 April 1996 committing both sides to integration. Armenia found itself isolated from the heartlands of the CIS and was aggrieved that the CIS had done little to resolve the Nagorno-Karabakh conflict.

The third group was made up of Ukraine, Turkmenistan, Azerbaijan and Moldova. Ukraine made no secret of its desire to become a 'normal' European state, and behaved as though it was embarrassed by Russia's Asian tail dragging it back in geography and time. Ukraine unequivocally opposed attempts to strengthen CIS institutions and fought hard against Russian dominance in the organisation but offered little in the way of a positive programme. Just as Austria and Bavaria had opposed Prussian domination of the German Confederation in the nineteenth century, so too today Ukraine is determined to resist the hegemony of the stronger power and opposes Russian domination in Eurasia. Ukraine thus sought to make the CIS as weak as possible, with no permanent status and a minimal staff, and rejected outright the idea of a unified armed force which Kravchuk considered would infringe Ukrainian sovereignty. At the March 1992 CIS summit in Kiev Kravchuk rejected 14 out of the 19 agreements proposed, and at the Bishkek summit of 9 October 1992 Ukraine signed only 5 out of 15 documents, refusing to sign agreements creating an inter-state television and radio company (Ostankino); forming the CIS economic court; on visa-free movement for citizens within the CIS, and above all objected to the CIS Charter which envisaged suprastate Commonwealth structures. Following the summit, Kravchuk asserted that Ukraine intended to develop exclusively as an independent state.[16]

Turkmenistan adopted an independent stance secure in the enjoyment of its income from its gas fields, its internal stability, and its distance from the conflict in Tajikistan. Azerbaijan and Moldova at first appeared to be temporary members of the CIS, waiting only for an appropriate moment to leave. The 6 July 1992 Moscow summit warned that if they did not ratify the CIS Treaty they would not be admitted to the next summit. On the eve of the Bishkek summit of 9 October 1992 the Azerbaijan parliament voted unanimously against ratification and thus left the organisation.[17] Moldova, too, failed to ratify the Alma Ata accords, but left some room for manoeuvre and continued to participate selectively in the work of the CIS. In the absence of Azerbaijan and Moldova and without Ukraine acting as a counterweight, the CIS was in danger of becoming a Russian backyard.

Negotiations in late 1992 over a revised CIS Charter defining the rights and obligations of member states were riven by disputes over human rights, economic and other issues. At the Minsk summit on 22 January 1993 7 out of 10 members approved the CIS Charter providing for a 'multispeed' CIS, allowing those countries that wished to achieve deeper integration to do so without excluding those who favoured a slower pace. While the CIS remained under-institutionalised, a rudimentary permanent executive body was established in the form of a Coordinating and Consulative Committee assisted by over thirty inter-state, inter-governmental and inter-departmental coordinating agencies covering such issues as foreign policy and the environment. It was clear, however, that a two-tier CIS was emerging.

Despite fears that the whole CIS project might collapse, it soon became clear that it performed certain important functions. Russia, certainly, found it a useful foreign policy instrument, and sought to ensure membership in the organisation. Following the overthrow of Elchibei's nationalist government in 1993, Azerbaijan agreed to rejoin the organisation. Hard on the heels of the debacle in Abkhazia Georgia finally agreed to join the CIS. This brought membership to twelve, with only the three Baltic states outside.

Lacking an effective institutional framework, the CIS was an intergovernmental rather than a supranational body. There was no consensus among the member states over the way that the CIS should evolve. The debate over the CIS Charter revealed basic conceptual differences in attitudes, with one view expressed most forcefully by Kazakhstan stressing the need to establish a more coherent community, while others equally firmly argued that it should be little more than a forum for inter-governmental consultation on specific issues. Differentiation within the CIS indicated its fragmentation but it also suggested flexibility and adaptation to post-Soviet realities. Policy represented less a coherent vision of development than the lowest common denominator of agreement between groups of countries with radically opposed views on its evolution and future.

Security and peace-keeping

The CIS at first provided some form of centralised control over the USSR armed forces but, as we have seen, the republics soon formed their own armies. The Joint Command structure gave way to national armies and the CIS Council of Ministers of Defence took over a coordinating role. The 20 March 1992 Kiev CIS summit recognised the demise of an integrated military structure and took the first steps towards a system of collective security, with joint forces to be established on a case-by-case basis.[18] At the CIS summit in Tashkent on 15 May 1992 the Collective Security Treaty was signed by Armenia, Kazakhstan, Kyrgyzstan, Russia, Tajikistan and Uzbekistan, but the failure of Ukraine and other countries to sign once again revealed the deep divisions. The Tashkent Treaty stipulated that aggression against one of the signatory parties would be considered aggression against them all, but it was less a multilateral military and political alliance than a way of legitimating Russian military assistance to the signatory states.[19] The Tashkent meeting also agreed on the distribution of CFE Treaty limits among the newly independent states. The outlines of a collective peace-keeping force emerged at the 6 July 1992 Moscow summit, followed by a protocol on peace-keeping forces, but the details of collective security initialled at the Bishkek summit on 9–10 October 1992 by nine countries (excluding Moldova and Ukraine) sought to regulate the activities of the Joint Command in peace-keeping operations, but left many questions unanswered.

Acrimony flared at the Minsk summit of January 1993 over the control of strategic nuclear weapons, with Kiev and Almaty reluctant to transfer control to Russia even though all agreed, as discussed in the previous chapter, that Russia would become the only CIS nuclear power in the future. In an appeal to CIS leaders of 17 March 1993 Yeltsin sought to allay the fears roused by his earlier speech to the Civic Union, which had claimed 'special powers' for Russia as the guarantor of security, but countries like Ukraine remained wary and reinforced their reluctance to give up nuclear weapons.[20]

The danger of Russia being drawn into a war against its will was vividly illustrated by Armenia's threats to resign from the Tashkent agreement because of CIS inactivity over Nagorno-Karabakh. In security policy, as in other areas, there was a strong tendency towards bilateralisation, and numerous agreements were signed between Russia and other countries regulating the stationing of troops outside Russia and other issues. The Russian Ministry of Defence increasingly supplanted the Joint Command on security issues that affected not only Russia but the CIS as a whole. Indeed, it was Russia's attempts to maintain its freedom of manoeuvre and frustration at the clumsy multilateralism of earlier agreements that prompted Russia's decision in July 1993 to dissolve the Joint Command.[21] Thus hopes for military integration within the framework of the CIS were dashed, as were plans for standing joint peace-keeping forces. In contrast to Russia's draft Military Doctrine of May 1992, which placed a heavy emphasis on military cooperation within the CIS, the Doctrine approved in November 1993 made only one brief mention of the CIS.

At the CIS summit in Ashgabat in December 1993 a new military coordinating body was established directly subordinate to the CIS Council of Defence Ministers, though the definition of collective security proved contentious. While Russia defined collective security in terms of external threats, Azerbaijan insisted that it should cover threats from one CIS member state against another – obviously directed against Armenia – and in the event the Russian version was adopted and a Council of Collective Security was established. Yet again documents were adopted at the summit in favour of developing cooperation and strengthening trust between CIS members, stressing respect for the sovereignty and territorial integrity of Commonwealth countries.[22] This theme runs as a common thread in CIS meetings, with the adoption of new regulations for the CIS Council of Ministers of Defence by the Heads of State meeting on 15 April 1994 being accompanied by a declaration on the 'Observance of Sovereignty, Territorial Integrity and Inviolability of the Borders of the Member States of the CIS.'

The same meeting reviewed the mandate of Collective Peacekeeping Forces, and by the time of the October 1994 summit of CIS Heads of State, Russia was in effect authorised in the name of the CIS to intervene not only in Tajikistan but in the Transcaucasian conflicts as well. Thus the CIS legitimised Russia's military operations in the former Soviet space, but was unable to establish anything but token collective institutions to control them or collective forces to implement them. Russia increasingly relied on a few key strategic allies (Belarus, Georgia and Kazakhstan, with Armenia and Uzbekistan close behind), and the very notion of common security interests for the whole Commonwealth area was soon abandoned.[23] As a *quid pro quo* for Russia's predominant role in stabilising regional conflicts in the CIS within a broadly collective framework, the other Commonwealth states maintained an eloquent silence during the Chechen war.

The diminished threat of nuclear war or inter-state conventional war is today balanced by the rise of regional conflicts.[24] Russia took an increasingly active role in 'peacemaking' operations, notably in Moldova, Georgia and Tajikistan. Despite the decision to create a CIS peace-keeping force in Tajikistan, Russia's 201st Motorised Rifle Division here acted rather more forcefully than would be expected of mere peace-keepers, patrolling the frontier with Afghanistan and in effect acting as the armed forces of the regime. Yeltsin, indeed, in 1993 announced that Tajikistan's southern border was in effect Russia's too, a position supported by a wide range of liberal opinion in Moscow even though the 'Russian's abroad' question did not operate here – since 1989 most of the 400,000-strong Russian community had fled. Despite attempts to regionalise the peace-keeping forces, with the agreement of 24 September 1993 providing for Collective Peace-keeping Forces to be supplied by Russia and the Central Asian states (excluding Turkmenistan), the latter proved reluctant to provide troops. In Trans-Dniester General Lebed had stabilised the situation, and indeed from 1994 had come into increasingly bitter conflict with the secessionists.

The CIS proved an inadequate forum for the resolution of conflicts and problems besetting the country. It could do little to end the conflict between Armenia and Azerbaijan over Nagorno-Karabakh, the war in Tajikistan or the conflict in Moldova. The crises in CIS states raised the question of Russia's post-imperial peace-keeping role. At first the policy appeared to be one of benign neglect but pressure from the national-patriots and neo-communists, the establishment of a Russian Ministry of Defence, and the sheer multiplicity of challenges in the former Soviet republics meant that isolationism could not be an option irrespective of the urgency of domestic economic needs. The development of the Eurasian option threatened to embroil Russia in regional conflicts and force it to assume the burdens of the old union. Uzbekistan, Tajikistan and Turkmenistan had all been heavily subsidised by Moscow in the past, and now looked for a new framework of support. Russia would gain little from being drawn into the bitter clan struggles of Central Asia, yet could not ignore the instability along its southern borders.

By 1996 Russia had 300,000 troops deployed in various 'peace-keeping' operations in Tajikistan, Moldova (Trans-Dniester) and Georgia (South Ossetia and Abkhazia). Kozyrev admitted that the methods used by Russian forces were unusual for UN operations, but he insisted that they remained true to the UN Charter, everywhere having been invited in by the legal governments and with the agreement of all parties concerned.[25] Kozyrev's argument is technically correct, especially in the context where no one else was prepared to shoulder the burden, but should be seen in the context of the distinction often drawn between 'peace-keeping' and 'peacemaking' (or peace-enforcement); activities that require radically different approaches – or so it is argued. In the post-communist context the distinction cannot be drawn so forcefully, as Nato rather belatedly discovered in relieving the siege of Sarajevo in September 1995. It is true, however, that in its peace-keeping operations Russia was never a neutral third party but resolutely pursued its own perceived geostrategic interests. This did not mean, however, that under the cover of peace-keeping operations Russia actually sought to seize territory. Its aims were simply to secure for Russia a pre-eminent position and to insulate itself from local conflicts, goals that were radically undermined by the Chechen war. Liberals in Moscow indeed asserted that Russia's coercive 'peace-keeping' tactics led 'quite logically to the first bloody war on Russia's territory – Chechnya'.[26]

The CIS thus emerged as a framework for collective security under the aegis of which Russia pursued its own strategic interests and sought to expand its influence. Under the aegis of the CIS Russia restored its position in countries like Georgia and consolidated its position in areas of vital concern to itself (like Central Asia). Attempts by Russia, notably at the 48th session of the UN General Assembly, to get the international community to support these operations failed. However, it would be an exaggeration to argue that the CIS and its peace-keeping operations provided a 'figleaf' under which Russia sought to re-establish imperial control over previously subordinated regions. Russia's ambitions were more modest and went little beyond the attempt to secure a sphere of influence, to dampen down conflicts if not to secure solutions, and to prevent others from entering the former Soviet area. For Kokoshin the priority in Russian policy was to create a system of collective security within the framework of the former Soviet Union, while establishing good relations with Russia's traditional partners beyond this zone of security.[27] This was an aim pursued both by the foreign and defence ministries and provided an essential coherence to Russian policy in this field while retaining the essential ambiguity of Russian foreign policy in general.

Economic integration

Attempts to maintain a single economic space soon crumbled as countries moved towards the market at various speeds. Russia's unilateral plunge into shock therapy in January 1992 found the other republics unprepared. They found themselves using depreciating roubles while suffering from currency shortages, and the rouble zone itself became a source of inflation. The granting of unsecured loans to their enterprises in turn fuelled the inflation in Russia. Russia accumulated large trade surpluses with the other CIS states in 1992, but its attempts to reduce them by imposing various trade and payment restrictions angered the other republics. The tendency towards barter in trade between the republics continued.

To introduce some order into currency affairs an Interbank Coordinating Council on Mutual

Settlements was established at the Bishkek summit of October 1992, though this fell far short of the ambition of those who had favoured an Interstate Emissions Bank. The Minsk summit of January 1993 confirmed the creation of the Inter-state Bank. The Russian Central Bank was still the only body printing money but coordinated policy with the Interbank Council to ensure that the other republics had enough cash. The inter-governmental clearing bank was intended to stop the uncontrolled shift of roubles from one republic to another; only the rouble would be accepted for payment in the zone, though parallel currencies were not forbidden. Six states joined the 'rouble Commonwealth', but the threat remained that Russia would declare the rouble its own currency if the other states failed to clarify their monetary and credit policy.[28] The rouble zone gradually disintegrated as Russia asserted control over monetary policy and the republics launched their own currencies.

At the Bishkek summit of October 1992 a Consultative Working Economic Commission was created to prevent CIS countries bidding against each other in negotiations over oil, cotton and other sales. The summit agreed to establish an economic court to ensure compliance with trade agreements. The CIS countries tried to diversify their markets to gain foreign currency. Russia had occupied Central Asia in the late nineteenth century to ensure a secure source of cotton when supplies were cut off during the American Civil War, but when Uzbekistan tried to sell its cotton on the world market Russia once again turned to America. Whatever its defects, the CIS market was at least known, and the incident illustrates the problems of economic diversification. At the 6 July 1992 Moscow summit Yeltsin noted that some member states had expected to manage without Russia and orient themselves towards the West, but they had experienced difficulties. Central Asian republics who had hoped to enhance their cooperation with their Asian neighbours at the expense of their relations with Russia now realised that the change would not be so easy.[29]

Reintegrative processes in 1993 resulted in the establishment of an Economic Union, but attempts to maintain the rouble zone failed. The CIS summit in Ashgabat in December 1993 saw Turkmenistan joining the Union as a full member, and a single CIS economic system was confirmed. The Customs Union in 1995, the successor to a much weaker agreement by the CIS Heads of Government meeting on 14 March 1992, promised free trade between Russia, Kazakhstan and Belarus. Elsewhere customs barriers began to be established, but the permeability of intra-CIS borders remained.

Bilateralism vs multilateralism

The development of the CIS was marked by the bilateralisation of relations between member states, undermining multilateral attempts to solve problems on a Commonwealth-wide basis.[30] Turkmenistan from the first was sceptical about the value of the CIS, refusing to sign agreements on economic, collective security, financial and other issues, and instead Niyazov relied on bilateral rather than collective agreements. Kravchuk on several occasions insisted that Russo-Ukrainian relations would develop on a purely bilateral basis, while the numerous agreements between Belarus and Russia allowed the former to steer clear of any political or military bloc. Bilateralisation was not altogether incompatible with the existence of the CIS, but this would be a CIS limited to the orderly management of transition to nation-states rather than one committed to finding multilateral solutions to common problems, let alone the attempt to establish a new community on confederal principles.

The bilateralisation of relations reflected the absence of effective regional organisations to mediate between CIS countries. The Collective Security Treaty of May 1992 was the only serious attempt to establish a genuinely multilateral security system, but, despite its aspirations to become some sort of Eastern Nato, performance fell far short of this. While bilateralisation was encouraged by countries like Ukraine which sought a weak CIS, in practice the process was double-edged and raised the danger of the creation of a new union dominated by Russia. Reflecting the highly centralised nature of the old USSR, bilateral relations between the peripheral countries developed slowly and the great bulk of agreements focused on Russia. Links were closest between the core members of the CIS, and agreements on friendship, cooperation and mutual assistance were signed with Kazakhstan, Uzbekistan and Kyrgyzstan. Russia became the centre of a dense web of relationships which rather than enhancing the authority of the CIS began to act as a substitute for it. Russia became the military, economic and political core of a proto-union within the CIS that might at one stage dispense with the CIS altogether and become the kernel of a new 'gathering of the lands'.

The Interparliamentary Assembly was intended to address this problem. Khasbulatov insisted that the CIS was Russia's top priority, arguing that Russian diplomacy had spent too much time courting the West rather than establishing a 'dynamic and coordinated policy' towards members of the CIS.[31] At the first meeting of the Assembly in Bishkek in September 1992 Khasbulatov was elected chairman, and immediately called for the establishment of a common citizenship for CIS states represented in the Assembly.[32] The Seventh CPD on 14 December 1992 ended with an appeal to the parliaments of the CIS states to consider establishing a confederation or some other sort of association for the states of Europe and Asia.

Russia and the CIS

The Commonwealth was fundamentally lopsided due to Russia's sheer size and the fears that this raised in its neighbours, and it was not even clear whether Russian would be the *lingua franca*. The experience of 70 years of Soviet power, using Russification for its own purposes, was hardly a strong basis on which to build a community based on trust. The absence of strong coordinating institutions engendered an atmosphere of constant crisis. Yeltsin on 6 August 1992 announced that Russia would be opening embassies in all the succesor states but the shortage of funds impeded the development of traditional diplomatic relations. Russia tried to avoid the creation of a Russia-Muslim bloc by trying to involve Ukraine, but the latter suspected that Russia viewed the CIS as a mechanism to preserve as much as possible of the old centre, now in a Russian rather than a Soviet guise. Russia tended to view Soviet property and institutions as its own; the other republics had to acquire theirs from scratch. In the army, the diplomatic corps and the foreign trade offices of the USSR Russians had predominated, and with the end of the USSR they transferred their loyalties to Russia. For the other nationalities there could be no such easy transition, and loyalty to an amorphous CIS was no substitute for their own nationhood. Naturally, this gave rise to extreme resentment. At the summit in March 1992 in Kiev Kravchuk warned that the CIS might have to be abandoned altogether.

Russia in 1992 had been hesitant to take the lead in pursuing the integration of CIS states, fearing accusations of neo-imperialism and concentrating on political and economic links with the West, but by 1993 openly espoused reintegration within the CIS framework.[33] Industrialists sought closer union between the CIS countries, and the Civic Union indeed called for the establishment of a collective organ to unify economic, cultural and scientific policy.[34] Under pressure at home and goaded by enthusiastic integrationists like Nazarbaev in Central Asia, together with an awareness that there was no escaping close links with the former Soviet republics, Russia modified its policy and became the main driving force for integration. Already in late February 1993 Yeltsin had called on the international community to grant Russia special powers as the guarantor of peace and stability in the former USSR, and the Security Council's adoption of the document 'Basic Directions of Foreign Policy' in April 1993 reaffirmed Russia's commitment to the unity of the area. Russian foreign policy towards the successor states advanced on three fronts at the same time: the attempt to preserve and strengthen the CIS; the consolidation of relations with the core states in a type of 'Eurasian union'; and the bilateralisation of relations.

Kozyrev from the outset stressed that 'the main priority of Russian diplomacy is the formation of the Commonwealth of Independent States', and argued that 'the viability of the emerging Commonwealth lies in the fact that natural ties will be much stronger than the shackles of the totalitarian system, which in effect made us all prisoners of one huge Gulag'.[35] The countries that led the way in democratic and market reforms would show the path to others, and he rejected the static approach of the CIS as a forum for discussing problems bequeathed by the Soviet regime, but envisaged a type of variable geometry of dynamic relations between the various countries.[36] He successfully resisted attempts to create a separate CIS ministry,[37] a development that would have signalled a shift from Atlanticist to Eurasianist concerns[38] and would have removed the conduct of relations with the former Soviet republics from the liberal MFA. Shelov-Kovedyaev, responsible for relations with the former Soviet republics, insisted that the creation of such a ministry 'would give rise to a new cataclysm in the Commonwealth, since our partners in it would perceive Russia as reckoning their countries as second-rate in comparison not only with "traditional" foreign states but also with the Baltics and Georgia, which are not at all a part of the Commonwealth'.[39] His resignation in October 1992 signalled a hardening of attitudes and the shift of power to the Security Council and other structures of presidential power. Kozyrev and the MFA were seen as the weakest links in the democratic armoury, and hence it was here that the opposition concentrated its fire.

Russian domestic opinion was fundamentally divided over the CIS. National-patriots and some neo-communists regarded it as a fundamentally illegitimate creation. If the other republics had wanted to secede from the Union, then so be it, but there had been no reason for Yeltsin to accede to the dissolution of the Union in December 1991. The secessionist countries, moreover, would then have had no claim to Union property or privileges. Only at the Seventh CPD in December 1992 was the constitution amended to remove the article stating that Russia was part of the USSR. Discussion of the CIS often served as a cover to condemn the disintegration of the USSR: 'Masquerading as a foreign policy issue, it is actually a vehicle for deploring Russia's loss of empire.'[40] Even Yeltsin chided his CIS colleagues, not strictly accurately, at the Kiev summit in March 1992 that it was they and not Russia who had abandoned the USSR.[41] By endorsing the CIS Russia accepted restraints on its freedom of manoeuvre in its relations with the other republics, limitations which enraged the opposition who felt that the interests of Russia as a whole and the rights of Russians abroad were being neglected. They tended to view the creation of the CIS as the denial of Russia's status as a Great Power, evidence of Russia's 'withdrawal into Asia' and alienation of primordial Russian lands. While denouncing the 1991 Belovezha Accords, the CPRF favoured the recreation of the Soviet Union and barely mentioned the CIS in its February 1995 programme.

The threat of Nato expansion prompted bodies like the CFDP to argue that Russia's response should include redoubled efforts to achieve the economic, military and political integration of the CIS.[42] In his decree on CIS strategy of September 1995 Yeltsin stressed that the CIS was a 'priority area' for Russia, although he noted that this should be based on mutually beneficial economic cooperation.[43] While stressing the voluntary nature of CIS integration, there was more than a hint that Russian support for other states would be conditional on them accepting Russia's definition of integration, and that recalcitrant states would not be treated leniently. The decree called for the transformation of the CIS into a fully fledged collective security alliance, the full implementation of earlier security agreements and bilateral agreements on the maintenance of the USSR's security installations. Border controls were to be tightened, and no CIS state should join any military alliances aimed at another CIS state. Thus the CIS is an embryonic counter-alliance to Nato.

Russia emerged as one of the strongest supporters of the CIS because, among other things, it fulfilled a number of essential tasks. It limited the damage caused by the disintegration, and through *modus vivendi* agreements helped avoid the total collapse of economic, infrastructural and human ties. The CIS also legitimated Russia's presence, including the deployment of military forces, in Commonwealth countries. Through the CIS Russia was able to help regulate the conflicts in South Ossetia and Trans-Dniester, though it must be admitted that bilateral approaches predominated. According to the alternative foreign policy programme of the CFDP, the CIS allowed 'the commonality of interests of millions of people who inhabit the space of the former USSR' to be identified. The programme stressed that the CIS contained the potential for the creation of future structures of cooperation between areas 'that were once united in a single Russian state', and in particular they argued that Russia should maintain close relations with Belarus and Kazakhstan, as well as Georgia (at the time not a member of the CIS), because of geopolitical factors and traditional ties as allies of Russia.[44]

Russia was indeed torn over whether it was simply an equal member of the Commonwealth, or whether because of its size and traditions it should act as *primus inter pares*. Ukraine in particular was determined that there would be no new centre, either one created by the CIS itself, or, even less acceptably, if Russia were to claim the honour. Once again the question focused on Russia's foreign policy priorities. If Russia's key foreign policy objective was to prepare to move from the periphery to the core of the world economy, this could only be achieved through natural economic processes and not by diverting scarce resources to unrealistic plans to make Russia the centre of a reconstituted Eurasian union.[45] The definition of Russia's foreign policy depended on the understanding of global processes in their entirety. If one were to accept that the post-Cold War world was defined by the marketisation of world power, in which military and nuclear power had declined in importance relative to economic achievements, then Russia should abandon its military-industrial complex and concentrate on advanced economic modernisation and globalisation and turn its back on the CIS. This was the view of the Atlanticists, but was contested by the Eurasianists.

Prospects for reintegration and the CIS

Without a government or its own armed forces, and with no mechanism to ensure that its decisions were implemented, the CIS was an unloved child of the break-up of the Soviet Union, created hurriedly in December 1991 without prior negotiations over the division of assets, questions of citizenship or the fate of the army. A year later Yeltsin informed the Seventh CPD on 1 December 1992 that many of these issues were less than half resolved.[46] Kravchuk saw the CIS as not much more than a way of achieving a 'civilised divorce', and even Yeltsin's declaration that 'I believe in the Commonwealth' during his press conference of 21 August 1992 did little to restore faith in this hybrid stranger on the international scene. Created in large measure to satisfy Ukraine's desire for sovereignty, Ukraine paradoxically was the most reluctant of CIS partners. The CIS had been formed to keep Russia and Ukraine in a single political space when the attempt to create a new union had failed, but those in favour of greater integration might one day decide to move forward without Ukraine.

The CIS moved neither in the direction of closer economic integration, in contrast to the EU to which it was sometimes compared, nor to tighter security cooperation on the model of Nato. Rather than facing external threats the main danger came from internal conflicts. The coordination of foreign policy and the maintenance of a common economic space were soon forgotten, a common currency zone did not survive, and attempts to maintain a single juridical space throughout the CIS were undermined. Comparisons with the short-lived French Commonwealth, created on the basis of a referendum in 1958 and dissolved two years later, is instructive. However, the independent Francophone countries retain a deep affinity with France, and Russia could hope that it, too, could play a hegemonic cultural role in Eurasia, though it was precisely such aspirations that so alienated countries like Ukraine.

The debate over the future of the CIS was at the same time a debate over the past, and in particular whether the disintegration of the USSR had been inevitable. If the USSR had always been an illegitimate construct, then its dissolution was final and irrevocable; but if the USSR did represent, in however attenuated a form, some primordial unity of the Eurasian land mass, then attempts to recreate some sort of successor body was legitimate and not simply an expression of Russian neo-imperialism. While the CIS consisted of countries with very different cultures and levels of economic development, the main splits did not occur on these lines but because of conflicting elite strategies.

Despite the lack of clarity over the role of the CIS, certain achievements can be credited to it. As Yeltsin pointed out, the CIS was a form of relations between states fated to live together. Many frontiers did not become full state borders, with all the incalculable disruption that would have caused to human and economic relations. The relative transparency of borders was reflected in a type of inter-governmental transparency, with a coordinating group of deputy heads of government established at the Tashkent summit. Integration entails giving up sovereignty, but before being given up it has to be achieved, and this is the phase through which the former Soviet republics are now passing.

BORDERS AND CITIZENSHIP

While a common language, together with a shared history and heritage, is usually considered to lie at the core of a nation, this definition is inadequate when applied to the post-Soviet area. What is the status of Russian-speakers outside Russia? According to the 1989 census 32.8 per cent of the non-Russian ethnic population in Ukraine use Russian as their primary language, in Belarus 31.9 per cent, in Kazakhstan 47.4 per cent, in Latvia 42.1 per cent, and significant proportions in other republics.[47] Table 10 shows that the titular nationality comprises approximately half of the population in Kyrgyzstan, Latvia and Kazakhstan, and between 60–70 per cent in Ukraine, Turkmenistan, Georgia, Uzbekistan, Moldova, Tajikistan and Estonia, and only in Armenia, Azerbaijan, Russia, Lithuania and Belarus exceeds 80 per cent. At the same time, significant populations live outside their nominal republic; one-third of all Armenians, one-quarter of Tajiks, one-fifth of Kazakhs and one-sixth of Russians. Within Russia as well, as noted, there is only a loose correspondence between the republics and ethnic composition.

The natural corollary would be to suggest that in the core areas of the Tsarist empire and the Soviet Union a new nation had in fact emerged, of mixed ethnicity but which on a number of parameters (language, history, cultural orientation and so on) constituted a recognisable community. It is precisely this conclusion that is drawn by the national-patriots and neo-communists in Russia; while liberals at home and abroad have not yet come up with an adequate intellectual response to the problems posed by the sudden disintegration of this community.

Table 10 Nationalities in the republics in 1989 (per cent)

Republic	Population (thousands)	Titular nationality in republic	Russians %	Minor nationalities	%	Other %
Russia	147,386	–	82.5	Tatar	3.8	15
Estonia	1,573	61.5	30.3	Ukrainian	3.1	5
Latvia	2,681	52.0	34.0	Belarusian	4.5	9
Lithuania	3,690	79.6	9.4	Polish	7.0	4
Moldova	4,341	64.5	13.0	Ukrainian	13.8	9
Belarus	10,200	77.9	13.2	Polish	4.0	5
Ukraine	51,704	72.7	22.1	Jewish	0.9	4
Armenia	3,283	93.3	1.6	Azeri	2.6	2
Azerbaijan	7,029	82.7	5.6	Armenian	5.6	5
Georgia	5,449	70.1	6.3	Armenian	8.1	16
Kazakhstan	16,538	39.7	37.8	German	5.8	16
Kyrgyzstan	4,291	52.4	21.5	Uzbek	12.9	14
Tajikistan	5,112	62.3	7.6	Uzbek	23.5	6
Turkmenistan	3,534	72.0	9.5	Uzbek	9.0	10
Uzbekistan	19,906	71.4	8.3	Tajik	4.7	16
TOTAL	286,717					

Source: USSR: Facts and Figures Annual, edited by Alan P. Pollard, vol. 15, 1991 (Gulf Breeze, FL, Academic International Press, 1991), pp. 499–502.

Borders

The borders of the USSR were predicated on an expanding communist world system and in a sense, as Strada points out, they only formally ran across space: essentially, they ran across time.[48] Under Stalin, however, border policy took on a far more instrumental role, and while often formally arbitrary they were part of a conscious design to foster ethnic conflict as part of his *divide et imperare* policy, to make all nationalities dependent on Moscow. The current borders established by the communist regime reflect neither the historical legacy nor demographical realities; but neither would any others – hence the Russian national-patriotic argument that there should be no borders at all. The Russian government rejected the ethnic principle of state-building and sought to find a balance between collective and individual rights while trying to ensure through the CIS that the administrative borders that had now become state frontiers should be 'transparent', allowing free passage for citizens of CIS states. Ukraine, however, objected to the distinction between 'internal' and 'external' borders, and insisted that they all should be considered state borders. There was a gradual hardening of these frontiers, exacerbating problems of citizenship.

There appeared no logical reason why the fifteen Union Republics should be the best state form for the emerging post-communist national communities, and the fall of the old regime was followed by tension as territories sought to make adjustments to the Soviet legacy. There were conflicts in the Trans-Dniester and the Gagauz area of Moldova, the Crimea and Transcarpathia in Ukraine, Abkhazia and South Ossetia in Georgia, civil war in Tajikistan, and many more. The disintegration of the USSR and Yugoslavia revealed the contradiction between the two central principles of the OSCE: the immutability of borders and individual human rights. What if a group of people wished to change the borders and live in a different state? There are no mechanisms available to facilitate the transfer of territory, and history would suggest that border changes are almost always the result of *force majeure*. In addition, there was no clear answer to the problem of reconciling individual rights with the rights of minority groups in any particular territory, the struggle between civic and ethnic identities.[49] The border question became perhaps the single most important symbolic issue in the former Soviet Union. The question acted as a mirror to post-communist politics, testing the readiness of states for democratic and peaceful solutions to intractable problems involving not only territory but questions of national identity and competing truths, if not myths, about the past and present. The issue questioned the very substance of the modern nation-state form of political-territorial organisation.

Soviet borders were intended to be purely administrative divisions and not state frontiers. For this reason, among others, the regime could move the borders arbitrarily and take so little account of ethnic and other factors. When in 1991 these arbitrary lines became state borders, the scene was set for endless conflicts. By late 1991 there were some 168 territorial-ethnic disputes in the former USSR, four times as many as in 1990, and of that figure seventy-three directly concerned Russia.[50] In Central Asia borders were artificial and the states within them may well not survive in their present form. Nearly a quarter of Russia's 61,000 kms of border was not 'formally recognized and specified in any international legal acts'.[51] Rutskoi insisted that the real Russia could not be contained within the borders of the current Russian Federation, though he failed to specify where precisely they should lie or how they could be changed.[52] At the same time, the separation of the peripheral republics exposed what had been the Russian heartlands, and now only 30 rather than the earlier 47 of Russia's 76 primary components lacked external borders. Attempts to strengthen borders, moreover, were fraught with problems. The Russo-Azerbaijani frontier, for example, is straddled by the Lezgin people living in both republics, and for long it did not become a policed state border. With its millions of compatriots abroad, Russia favoured the transparency of borders, though was concerned about the security risk posed by its open frontiers to the south. Drugs and arms smugglers and other criminals took advantage of weak frontier controls. Russia increasingly assisted the CIS republics to police their external frontiers rather than establishing stronger controls on its 'internal' borders.

As soon as a line is drawn on a map the question of secession arises focusing on four main problems: borders and the allocation of territories; the rights of minorities (and in some cases majorities) in the territory that has seceded; the rights of secessionist nationals in the country from which the territory has seceded; and the problem of procedures – how do we know that the leadership of the secessionist territory genuinely reflects the stable wishes of the majority of the population in the territory concerned? All these issues were manifestly present in the case of Chechnya's bid to secede from Russia, but to a lesser extent in some other regions.

The Russian constitution does not envisage the right of secession. One of the few guarantees of stability in Africa had been the declaration by the Organisation of African Unity in 1964 that the colonial borders, however unfair and divisive of 'tribes', should be retained. This principle, despite all the wars, has held to this day, and a similar statute was enacted in Latin America. One of the basic principles of the OSCE is the recognition by member states of the inviolability of each others' borders, a stance which did not help attempts to resolve the Nagorno-Karabakh crisis. During perestroika the principle was extended to the USSR in the affirmation that internal borders were unchangeable, a stand that strengthened the legitimacy of the Union and autonomous republics, even though article 78 of the USSR constitution made provision for changes. It was perhaps less Helsinki and more Karabakh that had confirmed the sanctity of intra-Soviet borders.

But the border question would not go away. The announcement by Yeltsin's press secretary, Pavel Voshchanov, on 26 August 1991 that borders were negotiable if republics became independent drew accusations of Russian chauvinism. Nazarbaev condemned the raising of the question on the grounds that it would make keeping the USSR together much more difficult, but both the border incident, and the earlier threat of sharply raising the price of Russia's oil, were raised out of a 'unifying' impulse, to warn of the consequences of secession. However, the means had undermined the aim, and set alarm bells ringing in the capitals of the other republics. Yeltsin had hoped to make the other republics aware of the price and dangers of seeking full independence, but the plan backfired and accelerated the disintegration of the USSR. Those previously uncommitted now perceived a threat of Russian revanchism, and this helps explain the overwhelming vote for Ukrainian independence on 1 December 1991. Instead of a clear principle becoming the 'guarantor of stability',[53] it became the source of destabilisation.

The Russo-Japanese frontier between the Kurile Islands was the only Russian border not to be recognised in international law, but there were at least twenty frontier disputes that could explode into conflict. Japan made territorial claims on Russia over the Kurile islands, while some revanchist groups in Germany sought the return of the Kaliningrad region. Areas of Karelia and Pechenga were forcibly incorporated into the USSR during the war, but Finland agreed that the borders would only be changed through legal processes and according to OSCE principles.

The major border dispute was with Estonia over lands that had been granted to it by the Treaty of Tartu of 1920, but which had been excluded from Estonia by the Molotov–Ribbentrop Pact of 1939 and after the war incorporated into the Pskov and Leningrad regions of Russia. To many Russians it seemed illogical for Estonia to deny the validity of any Soviet acts, and yet to lay claim to territory on the basis of an act of the discredited Soviet regime, whose arbitrariness in drawing boundaries was well-known. The disputed territory covered only a total of 1,924 sq km (750 sq miles) and contained no major towns and was populated by Russians. Russia was fearful of establishing a precedent, itself having renounced any territorial claims against any of its neighbours. It was not clear why nationalists in Estonia wished to incorporate a Russian area when the country already had problems with the Narva region, the great majority of whose population were Russians. In 1995 the conflict was regularised and Estonia officially renounced claims to the area.[54]

In Russia the possibility of border changes was much debated. Travkin noted that 'The frontiers problem has aways been at its most acute when an empire falls to pieces.'[55] He opposed the revision of borders, and denied that Russia was interested in grabbing land but was 'struggling for national and state survival'. In particular, he insisted that Russia had a duty to defend its nationals living outside its borders, such as in the Trans-Dniester republic, though in democratic ways. Other patriotic groups, like Popular Accord and the Russian National Union, argued that borders could be changed, and recommended a version of the system used to demarcate the border between Poland and Germany in Upper Silesia in 1920–21 where plebiscites were held district by district. The precedent did not augur well since in Silesia most districts voted to return to Germany, yet the region remained with Poland.[56] Hardliners insisted that 'At the present time, relations between CIS states do not lend themselves to regulation by diplomatic means alone.'[57] Kozyrev warned that the demands by the national-patriots to resolve border conflicts by imperial methods, including the use of armed force, would lead to the collapse of the CIS and the emergence of a ring of hostile states around Russia.[58]

Solzhenitsyn in 1991 recommended the retreat of Russian power to defensible borders around the Slavic heartlands (Russia, Ukraine, Belarus and North Kazakhstan). He insisted:

We don't have the strength for the peripheries either economically or morally. *We don't have the strength* for sustaining an empire – and it is just as well. Let this burden fall from our shoulders: it is crushing us, sapping our energy, and hastening our demise.[59]

He noted 'with alarm that the awakening Russian self-awareness has to a large extent been unable to free itself of great-power thinking and of imperial delusions'.[60] The USSR had disintegrated along lines of fracture which did not correspond to those that would be recognised by Solzhenitsyn and others as somehow 'natural', reflecting the ethnic and historical core of a post-imperial Russian state. Solzhenitsyn's belief that the 'irresponsible' and 'haphazard' Soviet demarcation of borders could be corrected by 'panels of experts' and local plebiscites was impractical.[61] The view that Russia could become a genuinely post-imperial state following the adjustment of borders was considered by its neighbours as a typically Russian imperialist approach.

However much borders are moved, there cannot be an exact fit between state boundaries and nationalities. Furman notes that the right of states to inviolable borders contradicts the rights of nations to self-determination. The present borders of Russia and the other republics are absurd, yet, he warned, referring to the tragic precedents of Versailles Germany and today's Serbia, while accepting the present line of the borders means acquiescing in the repugnant acts that had made them so, democrats had no choice but to accept them. Russia found itself in the position of inter-war Germany: 'A large country surrounded by weaker countries with national minorities representing the large country, especially if these national minorities are oppressed (and any national minority may well be oppressed, to a certain extent), is virtually unable to withstand the temptation to use its strength'. He urged that Russia as the most powerful country in the CIS should set an example of a peaceful and humane resolution of border and national issues, up to providing a legal framework for the secession of the Tatars and Chechens, which would then give it the moral right to back minorities in other republics.[62] But what about the rights of the minorities in the secessionist territories? Borders demarcate not only territories but competing truths: they cut across both time and morality.

Citizenship

Up to December 1991 almost all the inhabitants of the USSR had been Soviet citizens; with the demise of the USSR in theory they all became stateless until each republic adopted its own citizenship laws. Russia's first citizenship law of 28 November 1991 granted citizenship to all those resident in Russia or the USSR as long as they registered with the Russian authorities and did not take the citizenship of another state. Dual citizenship was allowed only to those who opted to keep Soviet citizenship. The Russian government declared itself the protector of Russian citizens at home and abroad and banned the typically Soviet practice of depriving people of their citizenship.[63] With the collapse of the USSR a modified version of the law on 6 February 1992 removed the reference to dual Soviet citizenship and allowed any Soviet citizen resident in the USSR on 1 September 1991 to take out Russian citizenship within three years, as long as they had not adopted the citizenship of the republic in which they were residing.[64] A further amendment of 17 June 1993 removed the ambiguities surrounding the Baltic republics and Georgia that had declared independence before 1 September 1991, and allowed residents in other republics to keep their local citizenship while taking out Russian citizenship.[65]

Thus Russia adopted an inclusive citizenship policy, recognising Russian citizenship for millions living outside its borders. Russia, moreover, sought through bilateral treaties to ensure that other states granted the right to dual citizenship. Russia, fearing a flood of refugees, reasoned that its compatriots would be more likely to stay in the other republic if they knew that they could move to Russia at any time. However, attempts to introduce dual citizenship in the other former Soviet republics was not pursued consistently.[66] For the other republics the adoption of citizenship laws was a crucial element in state-building, but at the same time proved bitterly divisive. All the republics, with the exception of Estonia and Latvia (who adopted exclusive citizenship laws) offered citizenship to all those resident on their territory on the day the citizenship law came into effect. Russia's attempt to convince the other republics to allow dual citizenship was resisted for fears that divided loyalties might create a potential fifth column. In Ukraine dual citizenship was regarded as the first step towards renewed union with Russia, and even republics like Kazakhstan and Kyrgyzstan who favoured closer relations with Russia feared that it would undermine new national and civic identities. The struggle continues to turn Soviet citizens into Kazakhstanis, Ukrainians and Russians.

MINORITIES AND RUSSIANS ABROAD

The final years of perestroika were marked by increasingly bitter ethnic clashes: in Nagorno-Karabakh from March 1988, followed by the Sumgait massacres in April; in the Fergana Valley in June 1989, Azerbaijan in January 1990, Dushanbe in February 1990 and Osh in June 1990, to name only a few. The retreat of governance allowed local and regional elites to exploit ethnic grievances, eroding often fragile patterns of coexistence. Once disrupted, especially if accompanied by violence, mutual fears and hostilities fed on each other and made it extremely difficult, even with outside intervention, to restore intercommunal equilibrium. Ethnic disputes usually lie behind the realm of rational politics and are often marked by mutually exclusive claims to historical, territorial or religious justice where compromise is seen as threatening to the very existence of the people in question. In these circumstances adjudication is a hazardous business, especially when outside forces seek to exploit conflicts for their own ends. Macartney in any case long ago noted that the welfare of minorities in these conflicts came third, after concern over general European peace and the stability of states in the European order.[67] The championing of the rights of minorities, in inter-war Europe and today, is often no more than an instrument for revisionist ambitions.

The problem of national minorities in the newly independent republics became a critical one as millions of citizens suddenly found themselves 'abroad'. Some 60 million former Soviet citizens lived outside their nominal republics, 25 million of whom were Russians and 35 million of other nationalities. The sad history of the inter-war years, when large populations of Germans in the Sudetenland, Hungarians in Romania (a problem remaining to this day), Poles in Lithuania (also a current problem), and Ukrainians in Poland, all embittered the triumph of restored statehood after the First World War. The failure satisfactorily to address the question led to the wars in Yugoslavia. In the USSR the idea of a titular nationality in the union and autonomous republics inevitably gave rise to notions of ethnically pure territories. The new states have been called 'ethnocratic' because of the advantages, if only linguistic, enjoyed by the titular nationality.[68] The relationship between national rights and individual human rights was once again posed in the sharpest possible terms. The very definition of nationality is questioned, and while much is made of the contingency of ethnic identity, it is real enough for those on the ground when the issue becomes politicised.

The diaspora problem affects many peoples, including 7 million Ukrainians and 5 million Tatars. The lack of correspondence between Russia and the borders of the post-Soviet Russian Federation, however, means that by far the largest problem in this respect are ethnic Russians. Some 17.4 per cent (25.3 million people) of the total Russian population of the former USSR found themselves in the 'near abroad'.[69] Of these, 11.3 million were in Ukraine, 6.2 million in Kazakhstan, 1.7 million in Uzbekistan, 1.3 million in Belarus, and nearly half a million in Estonia.[70] How were these people to be classified? They were ethnically Russians, but many were willing to take on the citizenship (if offered) of their host republic. Already in his speech of 28 October 1991 to the Fifth CPD Yeltsin was careful to talk of the plight of 'Russian-speakers' in the neighbouring republics, but the patriots insisted on using the term 'Russian citizens'.[71] One way or another, the idea of a larger Russian community,

Table 11 Ethnic Russians and Russian-speakers in Soviet Republics outside Russia in 1989

Republic	Ethnic Russians		Russian-speakers	
	Estimated total	*As % of population*	*Estimated total*	*As % of population*
Estonia	474,000	30.3	544,000	34.8
Latvia	905,000	34.0	1,122,000	42.1
Lithuania	344,000	9.4	429,000	11.7
Moldova	562,000	13.0	1,003,000	23.1
Belarus	1,342,000	13.2	3,243,000	31.9
Ukraine	11,355,000	22.1	16,898,000	32.8
Azerbaijan	391,000	5.6	528,000	7.5
Armenia	51,000	1.6	66,000	2.0
Georgia	341,000	6.3	479,000	8.9
Kazakhstan	6,227,000	37.8	7,797,000	47.4
Kyrgyzstan	916,000	21.5	1,090,000	25.6
Tajikistan	388,000	7.6	495,000	9.7
Turkmenistan	333,000	9.5	421,000	12.0
Uzbekistan	1,653,000	8.3	2,151,000	10.9

Note: The category of Russian-speakers includes non-ethnic Russians regarding Russian as their native language. Since 1989 there has been considerable out-migration of Russians from these republics and thus the figures given above are likely now to have decreased.

Source: Naselenie Rossii. Ezhegodnyi demograficheskii doklad (Moscow, The Centre for the Demography and Ecology of Man, 1993), p. 15.

transcending the apparently arbitrary state borders of 1991, remains a central factor in Russian politics.[72]

There remained the genuine dilemma of how to handle the question of Russians abroad. The OSCE sought to ensure minimum standards in the treatment of ethnic minorities by creating, in summer 1992, an office of High Commissioner on National Minorities and appointed Max van der Stoel to the post. The aim was to achieve early intervention in ethnic disputes, but effective action was inhibited by cumbersome decision-making procedures. The United Nations appeared as ineffective as the old League of Nations in restraining the dictatorships and ethnic terror of the inter-war years. The failure of pan-European institutions in the post-Cold War era is nowhere more apparent than in the failure to internationalise inter-ethnic conflicts or to establish by international treaty a supervisory mechanism to uphold at least a minimal definition of human and civic rights.

The fate of the Russian minorities became bound up with internal Russian power struggles, the issue becoming the main weapon of rejectionists against the August regime. Patriots like Rutskoi insisted that the threat of ethnic violence against Russian speakers justified the maintenance of Russian troops in the 'near abroad', while the generals increasingly used the genuine problem of finding homes in Russia as an excuse to delay withdrawal from newly independent republics. The danger emerged that Russian troops abroad would turn into a police force protecting its compatriots, a prospect that invited endless wars and perpetual instability on Russia's borders. Even more dangerous was the attempt by extremists to establish enclaves of Russian power in foreign states, as in Trans-Dniester. The issue of Russians abroad provided national-patriots in Russia with a powerful weapon with which to attack the government for its alleged indifference to the fate of its compatriots, while sceptics suggest that Russia's allegedly democratic mission to defend the civic rights of Russians abroad was only another ploy to maintain its influence. Ethnic conflicts abroad became a dagger pointing at the heart of Russia's domestic democratic reforms.

Russian policy following the coup lacked consistency and reflected the problems of developing a post-imperial foreign policy. In keeping with the general movement towards a more assertive foreign policy stance, Russian policy hardened. While continuing to reject the use of force and even economic pressure as a means to protect Russian, Russian-speaking and other minorites in the near abroad, Kozyrev noted that the principle of 'non-interference' in the domestic affairs of other states did not apply to the protection of the rights of minorities, and he insisted that Russia would continue to act to protect the rights of Russians abroad.[73] Addressing the Council of Foreign Policy, Kozyrev in early 1995 for the first time accepted that military force might join diplomatic, political and economic pressure as legitimate means of defending Russians abroad. Although Russian forces had been used in Moldova, Tajikistan and Abkhazia, the enunciation of force as an explicit policy option marked a new stage in the evolution of a more nationally centred foreign policy. Kozyrev, however, was careful to distance himself from militant nationalists, condemning their attempts to exploit the issue of Russians living abroad as liable to provoke even greater Russophobia and noting that this 'is the direct path to Russia's isolation or the Yugoslav scenario'.[74]

MIGRATION AND REFUGEES

The late twentieth century has been dubbed 'the age of migration', and indeed the Soviet and post-Soviet experience confirms the view that processes of global change have stimulated a new wave of population displacement.[75] Refugees became a mass phenomenon in the former USSR, with numbers rising from an estimated 422,000 in 1988 to over two million by 1992. By 1994 some two million refugees had entered Russia alone from the former Soviet republics, mainly from areas of inter-ethnic conflict,[76] most of whom settled in south European Russia. Population movement is marked by six major processes: those returning to their homelands from which they had been expelled by Stalin; a broad phenomenon of 'ingathering', the consolidation of ethnic and national groups; Russian outmigration from the former Soviet republics; economic migration; refugees from wars and other disasters; and emigration out of the former USSR altogether.

The category of returnees includes Germans expelled from the Volga at the beginning of the Second World War, Crimean Tatars expelled to Central Asia, and a number of North Caucasian peoples. In their home regions there were few jobs or houses for them. As part of the process of ingathering many Ukrainians and Belarusians left Russia to help rebuild their own countries, while Kazakhs left the war in Tajikistan to return to their homeland. However much the idea is now denigrated, in a feeble and distorted form the Soviet Union had created a new community of peoples, where a Georgian could freely study in Moscow and then go to work in Kiev, and the failure of the CIS to establish common citizenship forced every ethnic group back into the laager of national mythmaking and imagined identities.[77]

As for outmigration, anti-Sovietism had often tended to take the form of anti-Russianism, and now this inglorious tradition took on a new intensity. Russians in Uzbekistan, for example, were now categorised as *pieds noirs* even though many had lived there for generations. The structure of the old relationship between the metroplis and the periphery meant that few of them had learnt Uzbeki; Russian had been the language of higher schools, factories and top level politics as well. Russians made up a growing number of internal migrants between the former union republics. By late 1992 half the Russians of Tajikistan had left, together with one-third from Azerbaijan. Some 3 million ethnic Russians had left the former Soviet republics since 1991, one of the largest migratory movements since the Second World War. While there was undoubtedly some discrimination against them, a survey by the Russian Minorities Research Centre found that only 9 per cent of ethnic Russians abroad expressed concern about their ethnic rights. Economic worries appeared to be a far more potent source of concern.[78]

Economic migration took place both within countries and between them in the former Soviet space. In Russia alone by mid-1994 there were some two million economic migrants forced to move by lack of work and the decline of areas of marginal economic activity. In the six months to May 1994 alone some 500–600,000 people moved out of the Russian Far North and the Far East.[79] We have noted above that the long-term migration from rural areas to the towns has now moved in reverse as city dwellers now head for the countryside. The CIS agreement on pensions provoked an estimated migration of 2 million people to Russia to take advantage of the more generous benefits.[80]

The category of those fleeing actual or implied threats of war and other catastrophes includes so-called ecological refugees, in particular those fleeing the contaminated areas around Chernobyl. Armenians and Azerbaijanis each fled the other's territory, and people sought to escape the wars in South Ossetia, Abkhazia, Trans-Dniester and Central Asia. By February 1992 there were officially 220,000 refugees (overwhelmingly Russians) in Russia, with some 15 per cent of the 300,000 Russians in Chechnya leaving in the year after the coup.[81] The number of Russian refugees from the other republics reached 460,000 by September 1992, with 50,000 arriving in August alone as Russians fled the fighting in Abkhazia, while some

30,000 of the total came from Kazakhstan and 13,000 from Kyrgyzstan.[82] By May 1994 there were 860,000 registered refugees in Russia.[83] Attempts by Russia to sign treaties with other republics regulating the status of Russians were resisted. There were few arrangements for the payment of compensation and so, for example, the Russians who left in a mass exodus from Baku in 1991 received nothing from the Azerbaijani authorities. A treaty with Lithuania, however, provided for the construction by the latter of a settlement for refugees in Russia.[84]

Yeltsin had promised refuge for all Russians who wanted to live in Russia, but in fact Russia was in no position to offer jobs, homes or even passports to the Russians who suddenly found themselves living abroad. Some 9.5 million of Russia's own native citizens were waiting for housing already. Numerous attempts had been made to enact a law on refugees, but none came to fruition and Yeltsin's decree of December 1991 remained the main normative act in this respect. Attempts at resettlement in South Russia were unable to cope with the flood and the status of 'refugee' in Russia remained ambiguous. Only the disabled, pensioners, women and children received food coupons and housing while most refugees were treated as strangers in their own land. They increasingly encountered the hostility of local populations, in particular Cossacks, in the struggle for scarce housing, food and jobs.

Some took the 'exit' option and emigrated from the former Soviet Union, although the number taking this route was lower than anticipated. A total of 2.5 million had left in the four decades after the war, but between 1987–90 alone over a million left.[85] Soviet emigration rose from 39,000 in 1987 to almost 500,000 in 1990, and in 1991 the figure reached 700,000. A study in March 1991 found that 75 per cent of the population had no intention of emigrating, and of the rest 15 per cent thought in terms of a short visit abroad and only 2 per cent firmly considered emigration, which, although a relatively high proportion of the population, in the circumstances is not that high.[86] The liberal foreign travel law (initially passed for the USSR on 20 May 1991 and then adopted by Russia) came into effect on 1 January 1993 and entitled all Russian citizens to a genuine foreign passport, provided they were not on trial, doing military service or privy to state secrets. The new passports were valid for a fixed term, rather than the old documents which necessitated a fresh exit visa for each trip. Rising unemployment at home encouraged many to seek work abroad.[87]

The problem now was to obtain a visa from the host country, which became increasingly difficult as countries feared a flood of Russian economic migrants. In the event the expected mass tide of emigration did not take place. In 1992 some 100,000 Russians left the country, and another 1.5 million were ready to go.[88] The former Soviet Bloc countries of Poland, the Czech Republic, Slovakia, Hungary, Romania and Bulgaria had no visa requirements but tightened restrictions against the hundreds of thousands of Russians who came officially on tourist visits but failed to leave on time. Apart from Jews and Germans, Russians did not leave in great numbers, for various reasons. The Soviet regime had stigmatised émigrés as traitors to the country, and some of this attitude remained.[89]

THE FAILURE OF COMMUNITY?

Historians will long debate whether the disintegration of the USSR was inevitable. With more effective leadership in 1989–91 could some form of confederation have been established? If Gorbachev had focused less on saving socialism and more on rooting a reformed social democratic regime in a renegotiated state, could the community that for good or ill had taken a thousand years to build have been saved? In the short-term the attempt to create a new Union of Sovereign States failed because the elites in the republics did not trust the centre in Moscow and were not ready to give up their own power or to compromise the sovereignty of their republics to form a new union. Yeltsin and his government always argued that they had had no intention of destroying the old Union, but their actions precipitated the latent disintegrative tendencies.

At the same time, although the traditional geopolitical organisation of Eurasia had failed, there remain powerful integrative tendencies. Gorbachev's argument that it would be unwise to dissolve the Union at a time when the European Union was accelerating its own integration was premature. Whereas the EU states began with stable subjects of union, the Eurasian unit that Gorbachev was advocating would have been based on shards that had splintered from what had been in effect a unitary USSR. The republics were convinced that only after the full reconstitution of statehood could reintegrative processes begin. The creation of a Customs Union between Russia, Belarus and Kazakhstan is a powerful reminder of these centripetal trends.

For fourteen of the republics separation from the former USSR was a relatively straight-forward process; for Russia, however, the question of withdrawing from the USSR was far more complex since in certain respects the two were one and the same; at least, this was the way that it looked to the other republics and to many in Russia as well. Thus Soviet troops withdrawing from the Baltic suddenly became Russian troops and returned not to an abstract USSR but to a concrete Russia. Separation from the USSR and its legacy for many republics took the form of weakening their traditional links with Russia. Russia, however, did not go away and the new republics soon discovered that the diversification of economic and foreign policy concerns had to be accompanied by a new relationship with Russia.

How were the post-communist societies and states to interact with each other, and how was their mutual interdependence to become constructive and the legacy of mistrust overcome? The CIS played a valuable part in this, yet its inadequacies reflected the larger problem of establishing national identities and structuring a post-imperial community. A fundamental instability lay at the heart of post-Soviet relations between the republics. Most had gained territory at Russia's expense, and were therefore *status quo* states; whereas Russia had been the net loser out of Soviet administrative reorganisations, and was therefore potentially a revisionist power. The national-patriots in Russia sought to exploit these latent revisionist sentiments, alarming the other republics. The mix of instability in Russian domestic politics, the problem of Russians 'abroad', the presence of what had become Russian garrisons in neighbouring states, and the insecure nationalism of the new states, all made a potentially lethal cocktail of irredentism, ethnic conflicts and war.

Part VI

The struggle for democracy

17 Problems of transition

Time has finally run out for communism. But its concrete edifice has not yet crumbled.
May we not be crushed beneath its rubble instead of gaining liberty.

Alexander Solzhenitsyn[1]

In this chapter we will examine the historical and theoretical problems associated with the
concept of democratic transition, and in the next begin an evaluation of the tribulations of
democracy in Russia. Approaches focusing on modernisation and development are misleading
in suggesting an inevitability in outcomes that can by no means be assumed. The view that
Soviet-style politics could be cast off to expose a nascent capitalist democracy was misleading,
if not entirely erroneous. There *are* profound continuities between the Tsarist, Soviet and post-
Soviet eras in Russia, but at the same time there are enormous disjunctures and discontinuities.
It is precisely the analysis of the dynamics of change and continuity that can reveal the well-
springs of Russian political evolution. Tomorrow's Russia cannot emerge fully formed like
Minerva from the brow of Zeus; but neither is it forever in thrall to its tragic yet glorious past.

THE CHALLENGE OF HISTORY

The speed of the collapse of the communist system took most observers by surprise. When in
1913 the Romanov dynasty celebrated its 300th anniversary, the throne and empire appeared
solidly in place; yet a mere four years later both lay shattered. When Gorbachev came to power
in 1985 the Communist Party and the Soviet system appeared firmly ensconced; and once again
just a few years later communist rule had dissolved and the Soviet Union itself had
disintegrated. Tsarism had been unable to survive the strains inflicted by the Great War, but
in the Soviet case the absence of war made the collapse all the more astonishing. In a time of
peace one of the world's greatest geopolitical powers dissolved politically and disintegrated
territorially. The strain of the Cold War played its part, the attempt to challenge the capitalist
democracies for world leadership and to match their combined military potential, but the
dissolution of the Soviet regime owed as much to its fundamental internal incoherence.
Perestroika exposed the contradictions between the attempt to transcend the market and the
realities of the command economy, the abolition of private property and the luxuriating
privileges of the political elite, the claims to political leadership by the Communist Party and
its own crude manipulations of political decision-making, and above all between the regime's
claims to a monopoly of truth and the mountain of lies on which it rested.

The Soviet regime, like the Romanov dynasty earlier, fell, but what was to replace it? Max

Weber in the early years of this century had been sceptical about the possibility of democracy in Russia, and many today are equally doubtful given Russia's past. The history of reform in Russia provides 'many examples of opportunities missed and reform initiatives wrecked on the rocks of popular indifference or hostility or the resistance of powerful groups in society to the loss of their privileges'. Equally pertinent, given the apparent adaptation of current reforms to traditional patterns, is the observation about 'the ease with which initiatives for change can be sucked into the morass of traditional administrative habits and ways of thinking'.[2] The hopes of the era of 'great reforms' of the 1860s under Alexander II, under pressure from terrorism, gave way to the reaction of the 1880s under Alexander III. The aspirations vested in the February 1917 'bourgeois democratic' revolution which overthrew the monarchy soon gave way to the disappointment of the Provisional Government and the calculated brutality of the Bolsheviks from October of that year. The three main reform periods of the Soviet regime itself, the New Economic Policy of the 1920s, Khrushchev's thaw of the 1950s, and Gorbachev's perestroika, all dissolved into disappointment.

Russia is not the only European country where the passage to political modernity has been traumatic; Weber, it should be stressed, was equally pessimistic about the prospects for democracy in Germany. Studies of the origins and dynamics of the Nazi regime offer a useful comparative perspective on Russian developments. Recent studies have rejected orthodox Marxist interpretations of Nazism as an instrument of monopoly capital, but at the same time the standard liberal view of Nazism as a temporary archaic regression in the onward march of modernisation is equally untenable. Like the Lenin-Stalin regime in Russia, the Nazi state was propelled towards ever more radical measures by its inherent instability.[3] In post-war Germany the alleged 'totalitarian personality' appears to have adapted remarkably swiftly to democratic mores after 1945. But German adaptation has been called into question: as late as 1968 Ralf Dahrendorf demonstrated that high rates of political participation masked a qualitatively flawed political socialisation: 'Democratic institutions are accepted; but they remain external, distant, ultimately irrelevant . . . Democratic behaviour becomes ritualised, a mere observance of external demands, a "duty" of citizenship.'[4] The 'unpolitical German', as Dahrendorf put it, at least made a show of political participation whereas in post-communist Russia reform was thrown onto 'the rocks of popular indifference'. It is usually assumed that the unpolitical character of the German people facilitated authoritarian rule; what then will Russian 'anti-political' tendencies yield?[5]

While most other post-communist countries could aspire to return to some indigenous model of development, however mythologised, Russia's own pre-communist past was both more distant in time and more ambivalent.[6] P. Pestel', one of the leaders of the Decembrist uprising of 1825 (often considered the first blow in the revolutionary struggle for democracy in Russia), advocated a type of 'autocratic modernisation' in which 'Modernisation seemed a far more urgent goal than democracy or human rights.'[7] Russian history demonstrated that every attempt to achieve a 'leap' into modernity in fact only delayed the achievement of the desired modernisation, and indeed, the whole history of Russia from 1825 can be seen as a struggle between the opposed principles of revolutionism and gradualism – and only through gradualism have tangible and enduring achievements been consolidated, like the legal and *zemstvo* reforms of the 1860s. In Russia's last great opening to the West, between 1885 and 1913, industrial production grew at an overall annual rate of 5.7 per cent, and in the four years before the Great War growth reached 8 per cent per annum. In those years Russian wheat exports represented 24.4 per cent of the world market, and rye 34.3 per cent.[8] In politics, too, the standard image of the Tsarist regime as brutal and stifling has been tempered by the idea of the role of 'constrained autocracy' in Russian history.[9]

This was a period of enormous achievements in art and literature, the Silver Age of Russian poetry, a period of brilliant social analysis by religious philosophers like Nikolai Berdyaev, Sergei Bulgakov and Semyon Frank (thinkers who ultimately provided the most sustained rejection of the revolutionism typical of the Russian intelligentsia of that time in the *Landmarks* (*Vekhi*) collection of 1909);[10] and the consolidation of schools of jurisprudence and the emergence of a law-based though not democratic state. A modest form of parliamentarianism had emerged, legal reforms had established elements of a law-based state, and economic growth had brought Russia to the forefront of the European states.[11] It was these achievements that were lauded by Stanislav Govorukhin in his film *The Russia that We Have Lost*, that played to packed houses in 1992 and helped launch his political career. While it was natural to portray the Tsarist era as some sort of golden age in contrast to the age of mass murder that followed, and undoubtedly represented a necessary corrective to the tendentious picture of Tsarism presented by the Soviet regime, the new representation, however, once again failed to explore the tensions in the old society. Eighty per cent of the population, for example, were peasants governed by customary law and relatively insulated from the modernising processes that were transforming the rest of society.

These tensions led to the fall of Tsarism in February 1917 and allowed the Bolsheviks to seize power in October of that year. Instead of moving from autocracy to democracy the 'transition' in 1917 was from Tsarism to communism. Peter the Great's revolution had stimulated the development of what Richard Pipes calls the 'patrimonial' state, where the whole country is an appendage of the monarch.[12] This pattern was reinforced by the communist revolution, and even more than under Tsarism the autonomy of civil associations like trade unions, political parties and public organisations was undermined. The Russian Orthodox Church was humbled and market relations and private property as economic institutions were abolished. Thus in the late twentieth century, when democratisation and economic modernisation were once again on the agenda, their social and institutional bases were even more tenuous than in 1917.

In these circumstances, the conflict between ends and means would once again inevitably come to the fore. Like the socialist revolution of the earlier age, democracy was left hanging in the air until its foundations could be built: the house of democracy in Russia was built from the roof down.

Russia's past is multilayered, and faced with the current challenge of modernisation and democratisation its history is once again being trawled to find elements that can sustain the democratic experiment.[13] Obolenskii argues that Russia's conservatism has deep roots in certain psychological constants of mass consciousness, including anti-personal social attitudes, a social inferiority complex, the lack of moral regulators of social behaviour, and the weak development of a normal work ethic, although even he concedes that there is a countervailing 'syndrome of modernisation'.[14] The view of Russia as eternally reactionary has been challenged by the argument that there were popular and philosophical constraints on autocratic rule.

The political culture approach might suggest that democracy and civil society are somehow alien to Russia. This would be unduly deterministic, and Petro indeed writes of two competing political cultures in the Russian tradition whereby 'democracy, or *narodovlastie* in Russian, had deep roots in Russian history'.[15] Nevertheless, the historical failure of liberalism and democracy to strike institutional and social roots has many later parallels. The two themes that dominate today, the absence of a social basis for democracy and the need for authoritarian government in the transition, were common already in 1917.[16] On several occasions Yeltsin drew the analogy:

> If you are looking for historical parallels, I would compare the present time with the period in which the Provisional Government was in power, especially after June 1917. Despite its many mistakes and faults it sought to establish a democratic republic in Russia. Then the Bolsheviks prevented this and led the country into a bloody civil war. Now, 76 years later, the Russian people has the first real possibility of a free choice of the way forward.

He returned to one of his favourite themes during the insurgency against Gorbachev in the late 1980s, the impossibility of reforming the socialist system: 'we have said farewell to the illusion of giving socialism a human face'.[17] This might well have been true, but the corollary of abandoning an evolutionary exit from communism, of the sort proclaimed but only equivocally implemented by Gorbachev, was a return to the revolutionism that had played such a devastating role in Russian history before.

Yakovlev warned of the parallels between the renewed attempt at democracy in Russia and the catastrophe of 1917, arguing that the new leaders were repeating the mistakes of the February revolution. Gorbachev had failed to use presidential power to secure a de-ideologised politics during perestroika, and once again the 'democratic forces', in Yakovlev's view, 'do not have any extensive programme of civil transformations to withstand the possibilities of authoritarianism'. The new democrats failed to build on and advance the achievements of perestroika, which, in Yakovlev's view, 'managed to overthrow Bolshevism's autocracy, abandon the permanent war against our own people and the war with the people of Afghanistan, and step back from constant nuclear confrontation with the whole world'. Land reform had been delayed and economic mismanagement had plagued both the democracy of 1917 and post-1991. A mere eight months after the overthrow of the autocracy a new and more dreadful enslavement was imposed, a failure according to Yakovlev that sprang from the inability to develop the foundations of democracy. A civic culture based on compromise and dialogue had not emerged, and instead the mass-meeting democracy only reinforced intolerance and 'the bacillus of moral decay'. In 1917 as in the 1990s 'the only path left is to overthrow ourselves, our infinite intolerance towards others, and our pitiful slobbering. Oh, how we hate others for our own laziness, foolishness and ignorance'.[18]

Is post-communist democracy in Russia in danger of going the way of the Provisional Government in 1917? Quite apart from the absence of war and a wholly different external environment, internally the country has changed. When the Russian imperial state collapsed in 1917 it left a semi-industrialised peasant economy, weak civic institutions, a society prey to a disintegrating army, an alienated working class and an intelligentsia tempted by utopian promises of a thorough reordering of society on a non-capitalist basis.[19] By contrast, the collapse of the Soviet state in 1991 revealed a rich network of civic and public associations and a counter-culture, although lacking the legal and social bases of civil society, oriented towards liberal democratic forms of political representation and the restoration of the market. When Soviet authority crumbled there was not the anarchic vacuum that characterised events in 1917 but a shadow society and reborn republican governments ready to take the place of the old system.

The durability of the American and French revolutions (and perhaps the second Russian revolution from 1991) and the ultimate ephemerality of the Bolshevik revolution can be explained by distinguishing between order and stability. Order suggests a sustainable and responsive relationship between the state and society and within the state system, whereas stability denotes a precarious management of order not organically tied to the realities of the polity and society. Thus stability can be imposed but is liable suddenly to fracture under pressure, whereas order suggests a viable polity based on the realities of a given social order. The revolutions in America and France gave birth to new orders that survived wars and restorations, whereas the absence of order (in all senses of the word) in the Russian revolutionary system was palpable. Soviet Russia was characterised by the search for stability through cycles of reform and retrenchment until finally the system was swept away in 1991.

While all countries are prisoners of their history, the history itself usually contains numerous seeds for the future, some of which may lie dormant for centuries. The Russian historical record is not wholly negative, as the partisans of the political culture school of analysis used to suggest, and precedents could be found for traditions of good governance and non-expansionist policies. Russian history was not simply a story of a 'strong state' and 'weak society', but of unique attempts to find a synthesis of the two on the snow-bound Eurasian landmass. There were elements of a 'usable past' in Russian traditions that could generate and sustain liberal and democratic forms of interaction between the state and society.

MODELS OF TRANSITION

During perestroika the linkages between the individual, social groups, the state and society began to be radically transformed. This would at best be a process lasting many years and possibly several generations. Zdenek Mlynar argued that the process of change in what was the Soviet Union had to be incremental: any sudden destruction of the existing system would be extremely dangerous.[20] However, the system did collapse and arguments in favour of incremental change became redundant as Russia entered a period of accelerated political transition and social transformation. The assumption of post-communist rulers is that markets and democratic institutions develop in parallel. Popular support for marketisation, however, was at best ambivalent and, judging by election results, probably hostile, thus exposing the democratic project itself. Warnings about the absence of the social institutions able to sustain democracy remain valid.

The notion of 'transition' suggests the almost inevitable achievement of the desired end, something that in Russian conditions can by no means be guaranteed. The idea of 'transition to democracy' reinterpreted in a liberal guise the old communist historicism that history had a meaning and purpose and that the end point was intelligible to observers. Russia is in a transitional period, but there can be no certainty about the shape of the new polity that will emerge. While the collapse of Soviet socialism had demonstrated the futility of trying to abolish the market and the inadequacies of central planning, and indeed discredited the whole notion of the socialist transcendence of the capitalist social system, the larger question of the new social and political order that would replace it in Russia remains open.

Modernisation and mismodernisation

Modernisation theory was recently vindicated by one of its leading exponents, Lucian Pye, who insisted that it was one of the most effective ways of studying the transition from authoritarian regimes, though warned that democratic outcomes were by no means assured but depended on the outcome of the struggle between national political cultures and the 'world culture' of modernisation.[21] Pye's warning is a necessary corrective to the assumption, so common in 1989, that the fall of the communist regimes would lead to the triumph of liberal values based on economic and political freedom. Indeed, the whole epoch was considered by Francis Fukuyama as representing the triumph of liberalism, warts and all,[22] and Rustow argued that 'A tide of democratic change is sweeping the world.'[23]

Post-communist modernisation theory now takes into account national peculiarities and distinctive types of modernisation.[24] This is not the place for an extended discussion of the concept of modernisation, but it should be stressed that the whole notion of modernity is ambivalent, and the features that distinguish being 'modern' from being 'non-modern' or traditional have been much contested. Modernity takes many different shapes and forms in the modern world, though there may well be a growing underlying convergence (the 'evolutionary universal' noted in the literature) of social formations to create a 'world society'.

Since Peter the Great, Russia has sought to achieve economic comparability with the West but in its own way, and under Sergei Witte and Stalin Russia pursued an early industrial pattern of modernisation based on factories and the extensive exploitation of resources and labour. This continued until the fall of the communist regime despite much talk of the 'scientific-technological revolution'. Some sectors like aerospace and the military-industrial complex did make the transition to late industrial patterns, but on the whole the Soviet economy remained locked into an outmoded pattern of industrial activity based on iron and coal technologies. The post-industrial modernisation current in the West is based on the application of information and bio-technologies, the development of service and knowledge-based industries, the shift to the conservation of resources and nature, and the predominance of the consumer over the producer. The overall lack of modernisation of the Soviet economy and polity gave rise to the systemic crisis at the end of the 1980s.

While the application of modernisation theory to Russia can generate some useful insights, there are limits to its usefulness. Rather than being 'under-developed', the Soviet industrial-isation drive resulted in a distinctive form of 'misdevelopment'. Extraordinary economic achievements coexisted not only with grotesque waste and catastrophic environmental damage but with distinctly inappropriate technologies for the general level of development of the society. Space missions were launched amidst, for example, a people brutalised beyond all measure in Kazakhstan. Factories were built in the wrong place producing goods that people did not want while the queues lengthened. Resources were squandered, and thus the new Russian authorities were not faced with the problem of development as such, but the challenge of redirecting economic activity.

Modernisation in Russia is more than just economic reform, and neither is it identical with the Westernisation of the country. Earlier attempts at modernisation under Tsarism and the Soviet regime endowed Russia with a relatively developed economic and social infrastructure. The real task from 1991, it appeared, was the remodernisation of society to respond to world developments and domestic problems arising from the inadequacies of the earlier patterns of modernisation. Remodernisation entailed the radical reconstitution of society and the values on which it was based. Russia faced a three-fold transformation: the struggle for a civil society; the transition to a market economy; and the reconstitution of national consciousness to overcome both the legacy of imperial thinking at one extreme, and the problem of minority separatism at the other.[25] The rebuilding of political, economic and administrative structures will inevitably take a long time and will be attended by national, social and political upheavals. The modernisation of the economy involves the separation of the economy and the polity and the establishment of a new relationship between the two. The simultaneous transformation of the economy and polity will no doubt be partial and allow enclaves of late modernity to coexist with more traditional parts.

Overcoming the legacy of misdevelopment is no less arduous than trying to overcome under-development, and in certain respects it is more difficult because it entails destroying more of the old to allow scope for new forms to take root. Hence the enormous destructiveness, condemned by the national-patriots, of the first post-communist generation as they tried to eradicate the old system, good and bad alike. Universal childcare, cheap food and housing, and a whole cultural universe were swept away together with command planning and obsolete enterprises. A society that had barely endured the catastrophic upheaval of modernisation under Stalin and his successors were now subjected to a grandiose programme of remodern-isation. Democracy and destructiveness went hand in hand in popular perceptions.

Russia's 'misdevelopment' covered not only the economy but also politics and society. As far as society was concerned, Russia lived simultaneously in the modern world and in a world of preindustrial mentalities that survived perhaps more in Russia than elsewhere, shielded from the restless change and reinventions of modern capitalism by statist and exclusive forms of development. Russia appeared to live in several time-worlds simultaneously, where traditional family patterns, clan relationships and ethnic affiliations coexisted with the modern world of contractual relationships and individualism. In Russia the peasantry, the great repository of national traditions and culture, was destroyed, but just as ethnic communities were sustained by the Soviet form of ethno-federalism and the passport regime, so traditional relations were reinvented in apparently modern forms of social interaction. The Communist Party itself was a modern invention, yet its structures of rule harked back to early modern patterns of political dominance;[26] and the collective farm appeared post-capitalist yet operated according to the all-embracing rules of a distinctive type of primitive feudalism. Social structures therefore had a dual signification; modernising, yet at the same time adapting to a new type of traditionalism.

On the political level misdevelopment meant that Russia's political stage was populated with bodies that carried the same name as those in the West, like political parties, trade unions and so on, but had a very different content. Parliament, too, had to cast off the primitive unanimity imposed by the communist regime, but conflict for the sake of conflict was an equally corrupt expression of political life.[27] The rebirth of politics had to be accompanied by the search for new bases of political consensus. The alternative modernity represented by communism had been demonstrated to be internally incoherent and only sustainable by coercion, and Russia's economic and social misdevelopment now had to be accompanied by a painful process of remodernisation. The speed of the collapse of communist power, however, left the society unprepared and thus borrowing from the West became the norm; but civilisations cannot be borrowed from abroad or transplanted wholesale into existing societies.

The transformation in Russia was predicated on the view that not all capitalist countries were democratic, as the experience of Franco's Spain or Hitler's Germany demonstrated, but all democratic countries were capitalist or at least based on some form of market system.[28] Moore agreed with 'the Marxist thesis that a vigorous and independent class of town dwellers has been an indispensable element in the growth of parliamentary democracy.', summing up his view with the quotation we used in chapter 14: 'No bourgeois, no democracy.'[29] Numerous American political scientists have stressed the connection between democracy and economic growth.[30] In a perverse way, they reiterated Marx's argument that liberalism and private property were two sides of the same coin. The debate on political development of the post-communist countries stressed the need to restore private property to anchor liberal-democratic development in a network of social relationships, and above all in the self-interest of a property-owning class. Classical American social science suggests that a substantial middle class is the bastion of stability, progress and democracy; and post-communist policy was designed to build up such a middle class on the assumption that in Russia it would behave as it did in post-war Western Europe and North America. The liberal-Lockean assumption that the Russian middle class would act with moderation, pragmatism and responsibility may, however, prove unfounded.

Privatisation was intended to overcome the amorphousness of social ownership. In Russia there were very large social groups that were threatened by late industrial development, and even more by post-industrial modernisation. There was no guarantee that privatised property would generate a new bourgeoisie; it might well sustain the old elites and line the coffers of the criminal bourgeoisie, the mafia and comprador capitalists acting as agents for Western capital. Privatisation sought to create a class of share-holder capitalists, but this was far from making a nation of stake-holder citizens.

Questions of leadership and the political conditions necessary for the stabilisation of democratic processes are in the final analysis decisive. Modernisation theorists suggest a strong relationship between socio-economic development and political pluralism, whereas O'Donnell and Schmitter deny the view that a higher level of socio-economic development is a necessary or sufficient condition for the establishment of a pluralistic political system. The more developed Latin American countries like Argentina had until recently failed to stablish stable democratic systems, whereas a less developed country like Peru had, once again until recently, been more successful. The reverse thesis is no more accurate, that political pluralism is a necessary or a sufficient condition for socio-economic development.[31] Thus one of the more cherished illusions of the perestroika years, that Gorbachev's reforms represented the maturation of the USSR's socio-economic development, were placed in doubt.[32] Insofar as generalisations can be made about the relationship between socio-economic structures and political institutions and behaviour, and in each country specific historical and cultural factors have to be taken into account, the post-communist political system is precisely trying to overcome the Soviet social and cultural legacy.

Transition literature's rather linear path towards democracy, while illuminating, is clearly inadequate and needs to be supplemented by analysis of social and class forces. Barrington Moore described three main routes to the 'modern world'; the path of 'bourgeois revolution' that combined capitalism and parliamentary democracy; the reactionary capitalist path that culminated in fascism; and the peasant and/or communist road. The failure of the last two in the twentieth century leaves only the first, though in this respect many are called but few are chosen. The 'modern world' for the great majority and a growing proportion of humanity appears elusive, and the most common path in large parts of the world appears to be under-development (both political and economic) and an inability to reach 'modern society' but to live forever in its shadow. This may be the fate of some of the post-soviet republics, and possibly Russia itself.

Political transition and democratisation

The transition in Russia is often considered part of a global democratic revolution in which dictatorships have found it increasingly difficult to isolate themselves from 'the global trend of intensifying communication and economic integration'.[33] Samuel Huntington has described the current period as the third great democratisation wave in the modern era: with the first lasting from the American revolution until about 1922, when Mussolini's march on Rome set the trend for a decrease in the number of countries that could be considered democratic; the second phase began with the Allied victory and encompassed decolonisation but ran out of steam in the early 1960s, with military takeovers in Latin America and authoritarian regimes coming to power in Africa and Asia; and the current wave began in 1974 with the southern European transitions, continued with redemocratisation in Latin America, and was accelerated by the fall of the communist regimes in the late 1980s and the appearance of the concept of 'good government' throughout the world.[34] Experience would suggest that most seeds of democracy fall on stony ground. Regime change in Latin America has followed a cyclical pattern, and the fall of a regime like the Shah's in Iran did not open the door to democracy.

A large literature has emerged concerning transitions in Latin America, southern Europe and elsewhere. Laurence Whitehead observes that the most successful transitions are those that do not challenge the existing alliance system, and which reinforce existing political and economic links.[35] Events in Eastern Europe, and even more so in the USSR, not only forced the establishment of new security structures and a new balance of power in the region and in the world as a whole, but even questioned existing borders and gave rise to the birth of new states. The transition in Eastern Europe and Russia entailed a total transformation of their socio-economic systems and network of international relations.

O'Donnell and Schmitter demonstrated that no transition to democracy has taken place without major cleavages within the authoritarian regime itself, in particular between 'hard-liners' and moderates.[36] In the context of Gorbachev's reforms there was a four-fold split: the reactionaries, opposed to any major reform but who were marginalised in the middle period of perestroika but staged a comeback as Gorbachev's reforms faltered; the 'conservatives' in favour of moderate and controlled reform which could retain the basics of the old system; the reform communists led by Gorbachev; and the radicals who tried to accelerate the reform process and who soon left the camp of reform communism altogether, leaving Gorbachev to manoeuvre between the conservatives and the renascent reactionaries. By 1990 reform communism had exhausted itself and Gorbachev found himself hopelessly exposed and well-nigh hostage to the conservatives. The room for 'pacts' and other negotiated strategies of regime transition disappeared.

The Soviet transition did however share certain characteristics with the one analysed by Alfred Stepan where the success of the 'liberal' line depended on the presence of a moderate and intelligent opposition, giving critical support to the within-system reformers. This is to the advantage of both, since the moderate opposition can gain at the expense of more radical oppositionists, and the 'liberals' can ward off the assaults of the hardliners.[37] There were major differences, however, since such a model can only work where the regime has a modicum of viability and is able to evolve, whereas the Soviet regime was in an advanced condition of decomposition and the state system itself fractured between the centre and the republics. While the leverage exerted by the liberals with the support of the conservatives was sufficient to neutralise the reactionaries for a time, the whole struggle within the Soviet system was outflanked by the new political pivot based on the republics. The August coup meant the defeat not only of the conservatives, and by implication the reactionaries (though they did not show their hand during the coup), but also of the moderate within-system reformers too, above all Gorbachev himself. The initiative passed to those outside the system who had launched an insurgency against it.

A political transition is about building democratic institutions; but it is about much more than this. The Weimar constitution in inter-war Germany had been a model of democratic institution-building, yet by the early 1930s had palpably failed either to root itself in the affections of the German public and political elite or to provide an effective framework for the solution of social and political problems. Hitler's rise to power in 1933 reflected the devastating role of the irrational in politics and the vulnerability of new democracies to demagogic ideologies.

As decolonisation gathered pace Western social scientists examined the problem of change in authoritarian regimes, the establishment of political order and how democracies achieve stability, questions which have a renewed relevance today with the fall of communist regimes.[38] Several models have been employed which trace the sequence of events that allowed democracies to emerge, notably the study of northern Europe by Dankwart Rustow. State boundaries were established early on in the process but not without numerous wars. The struggle then shifted for dominance within the states, marked by civil wars, coups and internecine warfare until at last, exhausted, the political elites agreed on rules for choosing leaders. It required a few more decades for these rules to be internalised. In what Rustow calls the 'preparatory phase' competing parties are organised on the basis of unresolved class conflict and who struggle inconclusively over issues of meaning to them, but generally abide by the rules of the game. In the 'decision phase' compromises on political participation and procedures are reached, and in the 'habituation phase' politicians and citizens come to accept these procedures.[39]

In post-communist countries the preparatory and decision phases have been reversed, with no prolonged period of struggle and compromise to prepare for democratic means of conflict-resolution. The 74 years of communism in Russia denied the people any experience of competitive, multiparty politics. In certain respects, however, Russia is going through both phases simultaneously, and the country might well now be in the 'preparatory phase' of democracy where the struggles between the centre and localities and between the executive and legislative branches, involving profound issues of constitutional structure, have to date been waged by groups who have broadly-speaking abided by basic democratic norms. Whereas in the 1930s both the left and right condemned what they considered to be the discredited and degenerate rules of parliamentarianism and readily took to the streets, in Russia today the only legitimate source of authority is the law and the constitution, and, however much honoured in the breach, the great majority of political actors claim allegiance to these principles.

In the transition period the very strength of the so-called conservatives, rather than acting as an obstacle to democratic consolidation, can play its part in the institutionalisation of democratic conflict resolution. Studies of transitions suggest that the struggle between well-entrenched forces can either lead to stalemate or force the creation of institutional arrangements to regulate the struggle.[40] This assumes a consensus about the basic 'rules of the game', something that might be threatened by the rejectionists' repudiation of the whole August settlement – the disintegration of the USSR, the market, liberalism, international integration, and so on: but the alternative is civil war. To date, the resurgence of old political elites contending for power through democratic means has balanced the radicalism of the new democratic elites. Both sought to find social constituencies which they could mobilise on their behalf, but the amorphousness of the Russian social formation meant that both the conservatives and reformists were relatively isolated. The temptation remains for maverick political forces, which do not recognise the 'rules of the game', to appeal to one of the few genuinely massive social forces, the lumpen, who would respond to populist slogans. The awareness that both the reformists and conservatives would either have to live together or hang separately facilitated the creation of political consensus at the top, but it would take years for the social basis for the politics of conventions and rules to find its expression in organised social interests and in society at large.[41]

Rustow's question remains valid: 'What conditions make democracy possible and what conditions make it thrive?'.[42] One condition is a stable national and territorial identity, something notably lacking in Russia. The delineation of borders precedes the establishment of democracy, but Russia's very borders remain negotiable. The attempt to develop democracy in the USSR had always been a risky project because of a basic lack of agreement between some national and central elites over the limits of the state. With the disintegration of the USSR it became clear that the vessel for democracy would be the fifteen national states, but in Georgia, Russia and some other republics the debate over borders (both internal and external) is by no means over, threatening the democratisation process in its entirety.

While the literature on comparative transitions is instructive, it is of limited validity for societies emerging not from authoritarian regimes but from totalitarianism, however decayed.[43] The restructuring of political systems is one thing, but the complete reshaping of social and economic structures is another: in terms of urbanisation, educational achievements and occupational structure Russia was already a modernised country. The social, economic and cultural preconditions for democracy are, however, only one aspect of achieving successful change from authoritarianism. There is also the question of political leadership and coalition-building, the problem of defining a political strategy and sustaining it by ensuring that sufficient elite groups can identify with that strategy. In other words, there is a need for a sustainable reform coalition. Gorbachev palpably failed to sustain that coalition and the question remains whether it is possible today.

Globalisation vs nativisation

Jadwiga Staniszkis has identified two main tendencies in the transition: the 'globalists' who favour Westernisation and marketisation; and 'populists' who seek to keep the changes within the bounds of what they perceive as domestic traditions and national interests, retaining a large degree of state control.[44] The question of when a democrat, responsive to popular demands, becomes a populist is a moot one. Russian presidential policy at first fell firmly within the globalist framework but was gradually forced to make concessions to the 'populists' at home. Although formally committed to marketisation and an opening to the West, the pursuit of globalist policies abroad but populist policies at home is an unstable combination that cannot be sustained.

It is useful to compare the democratisation project in Russia with Africa since decolonisation. In Africa there has been a long-term failure to institutionalise the democratic process compensated by the overbureaucratisation of government. At the same time, the states are relatively weak because of their inability to find ways of integrating social structures and interests into the larger state system.[45] Single-party regimes and military intervention were long considered the only antidotes to ethnic conflict and secessionism. At the same time, any ethnocentric or unilinear model of modernisation has to take into account the spontaneous generation of traditional patterns. In Russia the institutionalisation of civic activity appeared to take root very quickly, overcoming political misdevelopment, yet its fragility required an authoritarian carapace for the transition.

The growing class divisions, the emergence of a concentrated monopolistic pseudo-capitalist elite, semi-privatised and state-owned industries allowing as if by sufferance a capitalist sector, and the absence of a strong middle class reminded many of Latin American patterns.[46] There small elites maintained their rule with the occasional intervention of the military when societal and political contradictions became too great. Russia's destiny appeared to be not Western European but an unstable political system built on a corrupt and unequal social system. This model does have some points in its favour, yet the differences between earlier Latin American patterns and the Russian situation are significant. In Russia, in contrast to Latin America, the military had not acted as the midwife of the new polity and therefore lacked the legitimacy to intervene directly in politics. Russia did not have a stable society based on an oligarchic property system developed over the centuries and linked to foreign concerns. The civilian political elite in Russia was able to achieve a relative autonomy from social and military elites, indeed its isolation was part of the problem and necessitated the generation of alliances and patronage systems with the emerging elite structure. Russia generated its own synthesis of tradition and modernity, of old and new elites, of legal-rationality and charismatic rule.

The enormous destructive creativity and creative destructiveness of Western civilisation embroiled all other cultures and civilisations in its expansive dynamism. Other societies either had to find a way of incorporating Western values within a transformed tradition or find that tradition ruthlessly subverted and granted only a pastiche of civilisational independence. Russia had been one of the first to confront the problem, and had spent much of its history inventing strategies to cope with it. After the fall of communism the problem returned with redoubled force. Old debates between Slavophiles and Westernisers, patriots and liberals, were not simply exhumed but re-energised to confront the problems of post-communist Russia, and indeed to respond to universal problems of modernity. The liberals were portrayed as a fifth column hastening the disintegration of Russian civilisation; whereas the patriots painted themselves as the zealots defending the last citadel of the nation's spiritual identity.

The USSR/Russia had little choice but to adapt itself to Western and world patterns of life. In the 1990s the great utopian social experiment conducted in Russia under the flag of democratisation was in effect an attempt at 'recivilising' the country. All the landmarks of the old regime, ownership relations, claims to internationalism, promises of social justice and a whole network of cultural values, were swept away in the tide and a new civilisation was born. The nature of this new order is not yet clear.

18 Democracy in Russia

It is absolutely ridiculous to attribute to the high capitalism which is today being imported into Russia and already exists in America – this 'inevitable' economic development – any elective affinity with 'democracy' let alone with 'liberty' (in *any* sense of the word). The question should be: how can these things exist at all for any length of time under the domination of capitalism? In fact they are only possible where they are backed up by the determined *will* of a nation not to be ruled like a flock of sheep.

Max Weber[1]

The problems facing the Russian transition have now become clear, but their solution remains for the future. It is still too early to know whether the reconstruction of Russia will take longer than the post-war rebuilding of Germany or Japan, but we do know that it will not be any easier. We cannot even be sure what the end point of this new Russian 'time of troubles' will be; liberalism, neo-socialism, or some new type of authoritarianism. In this chapter we will provide a brief assessment of the achievements to date.

DEMOCRACY AND THE RUSSIAN STATE

In the 1990s Russia became caught up in multiple processes of accelerated transition focusing on changes in politics, economics, national identity and culture. The Russian Federation, while in certain respects the successor to the Russian Empire and the Soviet Union, differed from its predecessors politically (in trying to become a democracy), economically (in trying to place market relations at the centre of economic life), geographically (Russia had never existed within its present borders) and civilisationally (joining the international community as an equal). The attempt to change everything simultaneously led to numerous tensions. The challenge of democratisation, for example, entailed the creation of forms of representative government based on popular sovereignty and the rule of law, while the challenge of economic modernisation posed a somewhat different set of challenges whose resolution at times appeared incompatible with democratisation; while the demands of state-building came into contradiction with the principles of national self-determination. The Bismarckian Second Reich in Germany at the end of the nineteenth century had been a Rechtsstaat (law-based state) rather than a democracy, and post-communist Russia took on some of this colouring.

Moore defined democracy as: 'a long and certainly incomplete struggle to do three closely related things: (1) to check arbitrary rulers; (2) to replace arbitrary rules with just and rational ones; and (3) to obtain a share for the underlying population in the making of rules'.[2] The

Russian state very imperfectly achieved these objectives for a variety of reasons. Political demobilisation and problems in structuring political associations was one factor, the hesitant development of democratic state institutions another, while leadership factors were perhaps determining. At the same time, Russia appeared to be a pre-state society in which a pre-political society lived according to its own logic and internal structures. Society appeared to impose its rules on the state, rather than the other way round; while the state itself once again, as so often in Russia's past, increasingly divorced itself from civil society.

Russia's struggle for democracy and statehood took place at a time when the traditional notion of the nation-state itself is facing unprecedented challenges. Our study confirms that the nation-state remains the most important unit of analysis in contemporary international and domestic politics, although it also demonstrates the limitations of an exclusively state-centred view. At the international level the state form is squeezed between globalism (UN, IMF), intercontinentalism (Nato), continentalism (EU, OSCE, Council of Europe), while regionalism operates both at the inter-state level creating cross-national regional identities (Benelux, Turkestan), and at the subnational level in strengthening regional identities within nation states (Catalonia, Bavaria, Volga-Urals, Siberia). The discipline of state borders has been eroded by the proliferation of international organisations, the communications revolution, and the globalisation of entertainment and leisure, while from within, republics, civil associations and economic agencies enter into autonomous relations with the international community.

The slogan of strong 'statehood' (*gosudarstvennost*) was a response to the profound crisis of the post-communist Russian state. The very territory that was to be recognised as Russia remained contested, with part of the political community refusing to accept the finality of Russia's existing borders and claiming special rights to defend the interests of Russians abroad. The consolidation of a state both ruling by law and itself subordinate to the law faced awesome difficulties. The institutional development of the Russian state in the Weberian sense, as an ordered administrative hierarchy able to make decisions backed by force over its entire territory, remained rudimentary. The breakdown of effective vertical structures was accompanied by the growth of localism and regionalism that threatened the unity of the state, while the legacy of ethno-federalism raised doubts whether the new Russian federalism would be strong enough to contain separatist tendencies. The erosion of executive authority itself allowed bureaucratic agencies and personalistic networks a relatively free hand. The emergence of a rich political society found itself weakly integrated into the political institutions of the new polity, and to a degree isolated from social processes and structures. The scale of the economic collapse accompanying the transition jeopardised all the other processes of social and national renewal. The class structure of the transitional period was made up of fragmented social and political groups that provided a very unsure footing for the growth of democratic political institutions and market structures. And, finally, the ambiguity over Russia's own national identity inhibited the development of a stable pattern of international relations.

The collapse of Bolshevik rule gave rise to a vacuum in political programmes. As long as there was a clear opponent in the form of the decaying communist regime the emergent political forces had a popular political platform to hand. Once deprived of this, the limits to the apparently triumphant democratic revolution became clear. For some the obvious alternative was to take up the slogans of ethnic and national superiority, yet the signal fact about Russian political development since the fall of the old regime is the failure of the Russian population to mobilise on national lines. This does not mean, however, that Russian civil society emerged from the communist womb fully formed and civil.

The Hungarian philosopher G. M. Tamás has observed that 'In the former Soviet Union, the suspicion and resentment of government inherent in the rejection of communism unwittingly destroyed the basis for politics itself.' The main enemy, it now appears, was not 'the overbearing, bureaucratized, centralized, tyrannical state . . . but anarchy': the resistance to the old regime and the contempt for its laws now gives rise to resistance to any authority and any laws. The last generation to live under communism conceived of freedom as 'freedom for the individual as a nonpolitical being who is not defined by his membership in the political community'. The basis for citizenship is undermined, and while there remains a romantic attachment to a cultural or ethnic group this new nationalism, according to Tamás, is 'anarchistic and apolitical', not recognizing the idea that 'citizens should work together for a common good, and that in order to achieve that common good, they must be loyal to institutions, that there are political obligations and civic duties that are independent of personal preference and personal interest. . . . People want the "good", but they don't want the "common"', he argues.[3]

Instead of achieving liberal democracy, the break up of the Soviet Union fragmented the single large dictatorship into numerous smaller dictatorships, many worse than the decayed communist regime because of the energy with which they imposed themselves on the population, demanding conformity to communities defined by culture and ethnicity. Shards of the old tyranny took root not only in the new states, but in the institutions and regions of Russia itself. This was no longer the old monolith but the anarchic tyranny of incipient warlordism. Faced by the break-down in the rule of law and civil peace, the rise of criminality, armed security services, regional separatism and so on, the very existence of the state was threatened. As Max Weber put it in an essay in 1915: 'The state claims the monopoly of the legitimate use of violence, and cannot be defined in any other manner. Where this factor is absent, the state is also absent.'[4]

Not only had Russia in certain senses become a 'quasi-state', to use Jackson's term again, but it was also in danger of becoming what could be called a 'quasi-polity', marked by the failure of the state to impose its order over domestic processes. The state lost its effectiveness not only at the inter-state level but also at home. The problem was not helped by the peculiar rootlessness of those arguing in favour of a liberal adaptation to global processes, talking in terms of 'universal human values' and joining the 'civilised world', leaving the language of patriotism and national interests in the hands of nativists of various stripes.

Post-communist Russian politics was thus marked by the struggle between contrasting policies of globalisation and nativisation, although it should be stressed that at many points these views were complementary. For some of the nativists Russian identity was bound up with notions of a strong state, giving rise to the *derzhavnik* (Great Power) tendency, but for other nativists (like Solzhenitsyn and Likhachev) Russian identity was more closely bound up with cultural and social values. At the same time, support for native traditions did not necessarily exclude integration into global economic and social processes. A far more common, and simplified, view, however, is presented by Staniszkis. She takes it as axiomatic that Russian problems of identity and state formation throughout history were resolved through external expansion. The end of the Soviet Union meant that 'real' expansion (military and political conquest) was replaced by symbolic forms (posturing and manoeuvring to defend Russia's status), until the Chechen war meant that this mimicry was abandoned and traditional forms of state-building were restored. Power allegedly shifted from the Atlanticist to the Eurasianist faction.[5]

This argument fails to take into account the powerful countervailing currents in Russian political life. Russian policy often looked confused and contradictory because it *was* confused and torn by contradictory pressures. It is true that Russia's political elites at the centre adopted expansive concepts of military and economic security that encompassed much of the former Soviet territory, but at the same time this policy was pursued on the whole within the formal diplomatic channels available to any power. Russia was notably hesitant about embracing the attempts by Belarus to return to the fold, and Ukraine's suspension of Crimea's constitution in 1995 met with a remarkably muted response consistent with the view that the question was Ukraine's internal affair.

The very balance between security and democratisation appears to have changed. Russia's history since the Mongol conquest has indeed been marked by a dialectic between external security and internal repression, the fear that domestic divisions could lead to external subjugation. While the end of the Cold War has reduced the imminence of the external threat, the sense of a society under siege has not altogether disappeared. Those in favour of authoritarian solutions at home have a vested interest in exaggerating the dangers from abroad. Unlike the earlier Time of Troubles between 1605 and 1613, when foreign powers took advantage of the dissolution of the regime to seize Moscow, the West has been broadly supportive of the Russian regime since 1991; however, a satisfactory balance in Russia's relations with the West has not yet been found. While claims that Russia has unconditionally capitulated to the West and ceded its diplomatic and trading (above all arms) positions are exaggerated, there remains a lack of balance in the relationship that might well provoke the post-ideological Cold War discussed earlier.

Comparisons with the Asian model of development are instructive. Not only have the first stages of industrial development been directed by the state, but the authoritarian political systems placed limits on the democratic process on the grounds that fragile communities required a paternalistic political shield to restrain the destabilising effects of popular participation. Markets require states, but for Russia the major problem was to decide how big the state should be in conditions of economic and political dependency. Most agreed that the overweening socialist state should be diminished, but to what extent should its powers be redirected to strategic planning, discretionary industrial support, infrastructure development, and so on? Attempts to apply a neo-liberal programme anywhere is fraught with dangers, but in Russia, with its long tradition of patriarchal community reinforced by the egalitarian rhetoric of the Soviet regime, it was doubly so. But the problem went even deeper, and just as the institutions and practices of democracy take time to develop, so too the culture of market relations needs time to mature. Christian socialists had long argued that 'The market system has to be guarded by moral values if it is not to play havoc with society.'[6] There are legitimate limits to the scope for markets and the values which inspire them; the pursuit of self-interest and corporate profits cannot be the entirety of society but only part of it.

In contrast to the more developed East European countries like Poland and the Czech Republic, where the 'national idea' united an already existing civil society, in Russia civil society remained amorphous and thus national sentiments were in danger of becoming nationalist. Russia developed as an empire before it became a nation, and even today it is unclear whether a Russian nation as such has developed. How is it to be defined: by ethnicity, by culture, by territory, or some other principle? All remained contested. The weakness of civil society and the indefinability of Russian nationhood once again stimulated the notion of *derzhavnost*, a typically Russian concept denoting the idea of Great Power statehood, in short, the predominance of the state over society.[7]

The events of 1991 undermined two central elements in the country's national identity. The first was the specifically Soviet element, residually acknowledging the force of the Marxist and Leninist critique of capitalism and justifying the Soviet state as a bulwark against capitalist militarism. The disintegration of the geopolitical space of the USSR challenged a second element, the notion of a larger community encompassing Russians, Ukrainians and many other peoples. Whether this should be called the 'Russian imperial' national identity or something more benign remains a moot point. This is precisely one of the issues over which the post-communist Russian national identity remains divided. A specifically democratic identity was undermined because of the countervailing sense of loss of national prestige and the lack of dignity of the new social institutions. Russian nationalism itself remained a fragmented political and intellectual force because of the sheer richness of the Russian national tradition and the multiplicity of often contradictory elements that could be drawn on.

The nation-state was traditionally an inadequate political form for the development of the Eurasian land mass: the steppes, tundra and taiga of Russia and the plains of Central Asia were very different from the market squares, little shops, factories and fields of Western and Central Europe. While the inadequacy of the nation-state model in Eurasian conditions was marked, the alternative supranational model was not clear: the 'imperialist' form would be difficult (but not impossible) to reconcile with democratic aspirations; while the liberal-internationalist type presupposed market-oriented economies and democratic polities.

The development of *gosudarstvennost* took a distinctive form in the post-communist Russia. The regime system of government was entwined with the emerging state and to a degree became a substitute for the state itself. The fall of the regime threatened the survival of the state, with all the major institutions once again placed in jeopardy; the constitution, the presidency, parliament, and the very borders of the state. Yeltsin's regime was based on a shifting 'August bloc' of forces, featuring primarily much of the old nomenklatura elite in the regions and the centre, new corporate interests like the powerful financial-distributive complexes, and the ability to incorporate elements of the opposition while shifting its own ideological base towards more patriotic if not nationalist positions. In this context the gulf between regime and society did not directly threaten the survival of the regime itself.

If the regime substituted for the state, a complex elite system substituted for the development of civil society. The typical political expressions of civil society, like parties, parliament and the rule of law, were subverted by intra-elite negotiations based on personal ties and informal bargaining processes. To prevent intra-elite struggles threatening the elites as a whole a strong leader was required to act as the arbitrator, a role that Yeltsin and the regime system played effectively. At the same time, the legitimation of the regime remained democratic, and democratic procedures like elections were pursued, if only fitfully, and introduced an element of unpredictability into the regime system. Political elites, including much of the communist opposition, accepted the conventions of electoral politics as a means of waging their struggle for a revision of the August settlement. The alternative, as October 1993 demonstrated, was civil war.

The system was relatively stable as long as the various elite interests were balanced, but the very gulf between the regime and society threatened the emergence of a new anti-elite insurgency. The language of this new insurgency would have to rely on populist slogans since both socialism and democracy as protest movements had been tried before in Russia. There could be no return to the old command economy and system of one-party rule, although the attempt to reimpose strict state controls over the economy could return the country to the chaos of 1991. The development of a market economy itself has enormous socio-political implications for the development of civil society, as countries like South Korea have demonstrated. According to modernisation theorists of the 'iron law of pluralism' school, the semi-corporatist regime system thus sows the roots of its own decay.

THE PROSPECTS FOR DEMOCRACY

There is an obvious tension between democracy and order in post-communist Russia. The apparent democratic consensus among the political elite in the early post-Soviet period soon dissolved and gave way to a complex interaction between democratisation and authoritarianism. Agreement on the basic rules of the political game at the fall of communism was undermined by the struggle between Yeltsin and the old Soviet legislature; and doubts over the legitimacy of the new constitution inhibited agreement on the fundamentals of the new political system in which structured political opposition adds to the vitality of the political organism rather than threatening its destruction. The factionalisation of politics, the concentration of power in court attendants and bodyguards, the arbitrary rule of bureaucrats, the growth of corruption and the unpredictability of government suggested that Russia's democratic experiment had run into the sands. In these circumstances a military coup to clear out the augean stables looked attractive to some, but the view that the nascent institutions of Russian democracy had sufficient vitality to cleanse itself remained strong.

Dedemocratisation and Weimar Russia

The internal resources for the stability of most post-Soviet national democracies are probably less than their counterparts in inter-war Europe, but the international environment is not simply benign but positively activist in espousing a set of democratic normative principles. The struggle for democracy, however, will be resolved in the individual states and not by the abstraction we call 'the international community'.

Underlying much of the unease about the accelerated integration into world society and to the market economy was the fear that Russia's 'uniqueness' (*samobytnost*) might be lost. This is a concern shared by the Japanese, Chinese and other major civilisations faced with the apparently relentless tide of globalisation, a phenomenon which to many is no more than another name for Americanisation. These fears in Russia are articulated by Solzhenitsyn and the patriots, the Communist Party and many others who see 'democracy' as a cover for the loss of national identity and subordination to an amorphous cosmopolitanism. Zyuganov explicitly drew on Samuel Huntington's notion of the 'clash of civilisations' superseding the Cold War ideological struggle to justify his defence of 'the Russian idea'.[8] If Bolshevism in Russia was one form of resistance to Western modernity, then his national communism is another.

Rather than 'the transition' inexorably leading to a liberal democracy of the Western sort, by the end of Yeltsin's first term as president there was a growing conviction that the democratic aspirations of the perestroika years and the achievements of the early post-communist period were being undermined. Without the compensation of economic growth, the abuse of power, the corruption and the shabby stratagems to gain state property stood out all the more starkly: 'Corrupt, demoralised, unstable: such a Russia poses a risk to itself and the world.'[9] The moral outrage that had been the hallmark of popular politics during perestroika gave way to political demobilisation. The very concept of democracy appears to have been delegitimised, while the word itself was used as a term of opprobium. The credibility gap between the statements of the leadership and the realities of daily life gave rise to what has been called a 'mistrust culture' and a pervading sense of social nihilism. While socialism in the early Soviet years had been built with enthusiasm, capitalism was now being built with resignation and a sullen sense of betrayal.

In chapter 2 we noted the tension between democracy and reform that gave rise to the 'Morton's fork' of democracy in Russia. Reform became the slogan under which legality and proceduralism was to a degree subverted, but ultimately the democratic movement itself was subverted. The victory of the communist Alexander Ryabov, the former chairman of the regional soviet deposed by Yeltsin after the coup, in the gubernatorial elections in Tambov in December 1995 appeared to bring the democratic insurgency full circle, with the communists now taking advantage of electoral politics to punish the new regime. Gaidar argued that the December 1995 elections had been 'a defeat for Russian democracy'.[10] The Chechen war had already served to divide the democratic camp and to expose the shortcomings of the new regime. The campaign by Sergei Kovalev to bring to the attention of the Russian and world public the human consequences did incalculable damage to Yeltsin's reputation. While supported by the liberals in Russia, Kovalev's criticisms brought abuse from the presidential entourage: Grachev called him 'an enemy of the people' in a grisly reminder of attitudes still prevalent in sections of the Russian elite, while Korzhakov attacked 'unstable liberals who denigrate the idea of human rights'.[11]

The danger of a second coup hung over the democratic reform process in Russia. The long shadow of 1917 emphasised the need for strong state power and warned of the danger from the left, while the destruction of inter-war German democracy provided an equally strong warning of the threat from the right. A constituency for non-democratic authoritarianism and populism clearly existed in the form of disgruntled communists and chauvinistic nationalists, fuelled by economic collapse, rampant inflation, the loss of national identity and by the squabbling of the democrats themselves. The rejectionists considered the Belovezha Accords of December 1991, dissolving the USSR, an act of treason akin to the alleged betrayal of the military by civilian politicians in Germany in 1918–19, and this was gradually woven into the national-patriotic counter-myth. Extremist forces lurked to left and right waiting to take advantage of social unrest and economic dislocation, much as Hitler took advantage of the weakness of the Weimar republic. Before his death in 1920 Max Weber had voiced doubts about the viability of democracy in Germany following the collapse of the Second Reich in 1918, and insisted that Germany needed a strong leader of a plebiscitary or Caesarist type like Bismarck.[12] Commenting on 1917 Weber noted that the Caesarian stamp was ineradicable from mass democracy. The fate of Weimar Germany and the rise of Hitler seemed to bear out Weber's pessimism.

The 'Weimar Russia' scenario, however, should be tempered by the fact that the world of the 1990s was a very different one from that of the 1920s or 1930s, or indeed from the world torn by war in 1917. The growth of economic interdependence, a dense network of human rights legislation and international organisations, all raised the threshold of toleration that extremist reaction would have to negotiate. In addition, for all its faults the Soviet regime had appealed to a form of democratic legitimacy and values that were supportive of democracy, whereas the Wilhelmine Reich had espoused militaristic and elitist values. Neither was it clear what the social basis for fascism in Russia would be. The middle class in Weimar Germany never really accepted 'bourgeois democracy' in the inter-war years, whereas in Russia the nascent middle class and the intelligentsia aspired to live like their counterparts in the West. The analogy with inter-war Germany is instructive but not wholly appropriate. A society that had just freed itself from 74 years of dictatorship was hardly likely to embrace another so soon; the idea of dictatorship remains deeply unpopular among Russians.[13] An anti-totalitarian spirit dominated the country and would probably be enough to thwart the ambitions of a new Napoleon or Hitler – or indeed Lenin.

The comparison between Russia and Weimar Germany is therefore misleading. The democratic government was not foisted on Russia in military defeat but was the outcome of the growth of civic institutions and mentality and arose out of society itself. Historical factors have to be placed in the perspective of current realities of international relations. The norm today is democracy and liberal market systems, whereas in the 1930s Europe was torn between the fascist and communist impulses while capitalism was torn by isolationism and protectionism. The withdrawal from Eastern Europe and former parts of the Soviet empire and the retreat from socialist ideology did leave parts of society disoriented, but the majority were reconciled to the development of a smaller non-socialist Russia. After 1993 politics was diverted into constitutional channels. Despite the loss of territory and the collapse of the comforting certainties of an all-embracing ideology it would be false to argue that liberalism has failed to take root in Russia. Liberalism, though, remains far from hegemonic, challenged by the counter-ideology of statism; and neither is it universal, limited to certain enclaves of globalism in Russia, Moscow, St Petersburg and some other cities.

Authoritarian democracy and the regime system

The presidency was strengthened on the grounds that only strong executive authority could push through the reforms, but, not for the first time, power took on a life of its own and ultimately turned against its creators. The emergence of authoritarian democracy reflected the need to combine political capacity with legitimacy; the establishment of 'strong hand' rule on its own would achieve little, but combined with a claim to democracy it gained in legitimacy and, to a degree, in effectiveness. The early post-communist years were marked by attempts at political stabilisation, the building of institutions of democracy such as political parties, representative institutions, the rule of law, a free press and trade unions, but the political culture of transition politics came into conflict with its aims. The achievement fell far below the aspiration, yet, paradoxically, the application of elements of authoritarian rule through presidential decrees allowed the process of democratisation to proceed, albeit haltingly. Thus a distinctive hybrid form of polity emerged, authoritarian in its instincts and practices, and yet providing scope for the development of democratic norms and conventions. Ultimately the tension between authoritarianism and democracy will have to be resolved one way or the other: it is too early to judge whether this is a transitional phase or the shape of the polity to come.

The hybrid nature of authoritarianism democracy in Russia arose out of the conflict between ends and means and had a dual function: to undermine the old structures of social and political power, while at the same time providing the framework for the growth of democratic forms that could ultimately stand on their own. The second or maturity phase of the democratic revolution is marked by elections, the establishment of the 'civic culture' of toleration and institutionalised conflict over resources and decisions, and a peaceful change of government. Indeed, the MP Vyacheslav Nikonov argued that 'we will only be able to talk of Russia as a democratic or civilised state when the country for the first time in its thousand-year history has a constitutional change of power'.[14] This is still to come, and while politics was reborn in Russia, democratic politics remained rude and unformed.

The institution of the presidency was strengthened to compensate for the absence of more organic forms of social solidarity. The choice appeared to lie between anarchy and authoritarianism, but however much power Yeltsin took, the polity was marked by a crisis of governance as decrees were left unimplemented. Civil society was weak and there were few deep-rooted democratic traditions. The presidency was new and untested, and existed less as an institution and more as an emanation of Yeltsin's own personality. Huntington argued that societies in transition to modernity require firm, if not military, leadership to negotiate the enormous strains placed on society by periods of rapid change.[15] In Russia, however, the 'praetorian' role was fulfilled by the presidency rather than the army, though there was no guarantee that the army would not intervene in certain circumstances. The presidency began to recreate a centre not only for the nation but also for political society, the centre that had crumbled under Gorbachev. The challenge to this 'centre' from Congress and parliament led to a profound constitutional crisis, yet the centre appeared to hold and signs of political and economic stability gradually became evident.

Parliament feared that the strong presidency would act not as a bulwark against unbridled authoritarianism but would itself be the vehicle for that authoritarianism?[16] The October 1993 events once again provoked discussion over the role of authoritarianism in the transition to democracy. Yeltsin's supporters agreed that a coup (*perevorot*) against the constitution had taken place, but argued that this was 'entirely necessary'.[17] Yeltsin himself insisted that strong presidential power compensated for the weakness of democracy 'in a country accustomed to Tsars and leaders, in which defined group interests are not yet clearly established'. However, resisting the calls by some of the intelligentsia for a complete ban on communist and nationalist organisations in the light of their association with the alleged 'red-brown' attempt to seize power on 3–4 October 1993, Yeltsin insisted that they should be allowed to participate in the elections unless the courts demonstrated criminal culpability; otherwise 'we would be hardly distinguishable from the Bolsheviks, who at first banned and then repressed opposition groups because they did not accept Soviet power'.[18]

Communists in the Sixth Duma sought increased social spending, the relaxation of credit and budgetary controls, the elimination of private land ownership, price controls and some nationalisation. They favoured a CIS military and political union, a union with Belarus, control over the press and television, and much more. Is such a programme achievable? It would obviously be opposed by the reformist democrats and liberals, but not only by them. The signal feature of Russian politics by the mid-1990s was the multiplicity of elites structures: resistance would come from financial and industrial concerns and allied centres of power whose interests would be threatened by the reversal of reforms. The August regime was more than a small group of ideologues pursuing a utopian reform programme but now encompassed a variety of social groups whose interests lay in defending the August settlement, if only out of a sense of self-preservation. The *status quo*, however, remains relatively tenuous. As Ludmilla Telen puts it, 'Unfortunately, Russia still lacks a civil society that would digest leftist ideas by turning them from communist into social democratic ones.'[19] In Western Europe it was precisely civil society that drew the teeth of revolutionary socialism and transformed its reforming impulse into evolutionary channels. This does not mean, though, that Russia is ripe for another communist experiment; but it does suggest democracy is by no means consolidated in Russia.

The December 1995 elections marked the emergence of routinised politics, but the confused institutional context in which they were held belied hopes that Russian democracy had become consolidated. Politics was parliamentarianised, but parliament itself was relatively marginal to the operation of the political system. The pseudo-party system was both cause and consequence of the regime system in which political parties were marginal to the operation of governance. While in Japan the regime system focused on one party, the LDP, in Russia, coming out a system dominated by the one-party system for so long, another path evolved focusing on supraparty technocratic government. A coalition of political forces emerged, including the presidency, regional and republican leaderships, the 'power' ministries including the military, privatised enterprises and the governing elite, whose interests were best served by this hybrid system. In the State Duma parties played an important role, but the relative marginalisation of parliament meant that the links with government were weak, while the upper house was based not on party but on regional representation. Just as there was no governing party, so too there could be no official opposition. Instead, the government was faced by a vigorous but inchoate opposition both within the legislature and beyond, elements of which it sought to incorporate through pacts and coalitions.

The regime-based coalition, however, probably only represented a phase in Russian politics, and sources of weakness became increasingly apparent. The radical democrats, for example, had earlier supported the 'strong hand' as a way of implementing radical reform, but their own political marginalisation following the December 1993 elections led them to favour a more party-based system of government. Regime politics was predicated on limited popular political mobilisation, undermining the common notion of 'democratisation' as extending mass democracy through active citizenship. Political parties furthered communication within the elite and mobilised ideological and political resources in intra-elite struggle, undermining the functionalist approach that suggested that certain tasks have to be performed in any society and that parties are responsible for political communication between leadership groups and the people. In post-communist (and, indeed, 'post-modernist') societies, this communicative function is apparently performed (insofar as it is performed at all) by a range of alternative structures, above all social movements and the media. Thus the functions and the very definition of a political party are brought into question.

A STRUGGLING DEMOCRACY?

The disintegration of the USSR was one of the greatest events in European and Asian history. The fall of communism was accompanied by the reversal of the centuries-long Russian process of the 'gathering' of the lands. The nation and the people were left without an ideology and the economy was in free fall. While the transitions in some of the East European countries entailed elements of redemocratisation, the reprivatisation of property and the reliberalisation of social relations as a whole, there was little 're' about Russia's transition, except the rediscovery and recovery of native memory and indigenous traditions and remodernisation. The social, economic and political infrastructure of democratic and liberal systems had to be built for the first time with building blocks that had been thoroughly subverted by the Bolshevik attempt to create an alternative modernity.

From a classical sociological perspective, the institutional basis for Russian politics was different from that prevalent in Western Europe, a difference that predated the Soviet period. Social structures and values differed, marked by distinctive roles played by the military, the intelligentsia, and indeed the peasantry and the working class. Democracy appeared to lack an economic basis and effective social and political institutions, and was thus reversible. The old system had generated a set of social interests whose ability to make demands on the political system only increased after 1991. The traditional 'gate-keepers' of functionalist democratic theory, the political parties and interest groups, remained weak, and the burden of demand fell directly on the government. However, Russia was typical of the post-communist democratisation processes in that the demobilisation of society affected the labour movement as much as any other sector, and there were few demands for an activist participatory democracy.

In post-communist Russia the search for collective identities does not dominate the political process; individualism (of whatever type) appears to have triumphed despite (or perhaps because of) the Bolshevik experience. In many ways Russia is a profoundly stable society, and the new storm of change launched by the democrats after August 1991 can be absorbed by this society like so many other campaigns launched by the Bolshevik regime. Russia is not Germany, and the absence of a clear national identity and purpose in post-communist Russia endowed Zhirinovskii's insurgency with a fundamental lack of focus – for the time being at least.

There are clear signs of a vibrant democratic spirit in Moscow and some other cities and provincial towns, but these represent, as it were, enclaves of democracy in a sea of inertia and conservatism. These islands of democracy, moreover, stood in stark contrast to the gathering power of local elites. Above it all towered the regime system of presidential rule, prey to the vested interests of the old state monopolies and the security apparatus, plagued by bureaucratism and confused decision-making, and inhibiting the emergence of a genuine representative democracy. Society was starkly divided between a relatively small but growing affluent elite who did very well out of the reforms, the so-called *nouveaux riches* or 'new Russians', while the mass of the population lost even the little that they had enjoyed under Soviet rule, above all the sense of security. A stable democracy could only emerge when popular consent for the transformation was achieved by ensuring that its benefits were distributed more equitably.

Rather than focusing on the creation of a market economy, it might have been wiser for the democrats after the coup to have concentrated on constitutional change, new elections and the establishment of a stable and legitimate political framework in which the economic reforms could have been conducted. The attempt to insert the infrastructure of developed capitalism into a society that historically had only relatively weak capitalist development and which had devoted 70 years to extirpating market relations was traumatic. The outcome, according to sceptics, would not be consumer capitalism but a type of comprador capitalism based on monopolies, grotesque inequalities, and a new oligarchy based on the old nomenklatura using its strategic position to filch state property. To the radical democrats, as long as there were no lustration laws, the new democratic institutions were only a veneer over the corrupt structures of the old regime. Russia's democratic revolution was incomplete and its reforms were by no means irreversible. Gaidar warned against the return of communists to power arguing that while there could be no return to the old command economy, it would be 'an elementary matter to return to the situation of 1990–1991, when neither the plan nor the market worked.

Communists will inevitably destroy the market economy as a result of natural traditions, economic illiteracy, the burden of promises, and all this out of the best of intentions'.[20]

The democratic project in Russia was weakened by nationalist aspirations and ethnic tensions, but, contrary to most expectations, withstood the pressures remarkably well and the Balkanisation of Russia was avoided by a mixture of political and economic concessions. The move from imperial or 'socialist internationalist' to national forms of inter-ethnic relations, however, provoked numerous conflicts; certain groups began to argue that there were imperatives higher than democracy, such as keeping the country together and maintaining order, and thus began the ill-fated intervention in Chechnya. The rise of an aggressive nationalist or neo-communist regime in Russia cannot be excluded.

Yakovlev had cast doubts about the success of the democratic project in Russia. Society was too divided and politically and psychologically alienated:

Today we live as if in two worlds. The old Stalinist world, though defeated, refuses to quit the stage, and clings to whatever may serve as a prop. The new world flounders neck-deep in the old structures, and quite often begins to play the game by exactly the old rules. I fear that the spectre of democracy may stalk this country just as destructively as the spectre which has already devastated our land and our souls.

He pointed out that policies were announced and then left unimplemented: 'The boldest decisions remain poised in mid-air – because the old structures persist', and it was for this reason that he supported the strengthening of the executive.[21]

Max Weber had been increasingly pessimistic about the scope for individual self-determination in a world dominated by technical and legal-rational modes of life. Ken Jowitt notes the problem of multiple fragmentation in what he calls the post-Leninist world, and stresses the ambiguities in the political culture:

To put it bluntly: the Leninist legacy, understood as the impact of Party organisation, practice, and ethos, *and* the initial charismatic ethical opposition to it favour an authoritarian, not a liberal democratic capitalist, way of life; the obstacles to which are not simply how to privatise and marketise the economy, or organise an electoral campaign, but rather how to institutionalise public virtues.[22]

The dramatic changes in the economy and polity would be inadequate if the public side of human identity was not also cherished, and a way found to establish a balance between 'ethics' and 'interests'.

The first period of post-communism in Russia appeared to be another time of 'provisionals' (*vremenshchikov*). Everything seemed to be up in the air, laws were passed, resolutions taken, yet little appeared to be done. The only forces with a strengthening social base were the Russian nationalists and statists, and the evolution from democrat to patriot was a path traversed by many in post-communist Russia. The attempt to establish a democracy without democrats and a market without capitalists was fraught with dangers. As Kozyrev noted, 'The dearth of properly qualified manpower for building a civil society makes itself felt not only in governmental and managerial structures but also within the business community.' He insisted that government policy was far from being 'romantically motivated' but that its policy 'aimed at pulling out the roots of the fallen tree of totalitarian rule'.[23] The problem according to the national-patriots was that the democrats were so intent on their destructive task that they failed to allow the healthy new shoots to take hold, and their root and branch destruction of the old system threw away healthy wood with the rotten.

It is still too early to talk of the establishment of a functioning democracy in Russia. The multiparty system is embryonic, the legal system mired in the problems of the past, and elections have been perhaps less than fair. Solzhenitsyn condemned Russia's new 'false democracy' and described Russia's retreat from communism as 'the clumsiest and most painful possible' imposing yet another 'heartless experiment on unhappy Russia'.[24] The very project of democracy did not command universal legitimacy. For many, like Metropolitan Innokenti of Khabarovsk, democracy in Russia was a transitional phenomenon and would in time disappear altogether to be replaced (perhaps in a generation or two) by something more in the Russian tradition of *sobornost*. As far as most national-patriots are concerned, liberal democracy is antithetical to Russian traditions and cannot provide a solution to problems that are distinctively Russian. Its advocacy by the post-communist leadership only served to prove, at least to the satisfaction of these national-patriots, that 'democrats' were alien to Russian traditions, hostile to Russian interests, and servile to the West.

So does Russia have no more than a simulacrum of democracy and a parody of the rule of law? The conventional distinction between democratisation and democracy can perhaps put the question in perspective, although the distinction is fraught with problems. The Bolsheviks, too, sought to build communism as the long-term goal, but in the short-term ethical and moral restraints on the day-to-day conduct of politics were removed. So, too, democratisation can be used to justify all sorts of measures that are antithetical to democracy itself. It is in this sense that democratisation can be best understood in Russia today. While formally remaining true to the ideals of democracy, the day-to-day practice of the August regime subverted the rule of law, undermined the electoral process, marginalised parliamentary accountability and allowed arbitrary patterns of rule and shadowy power groups to emerge – but it did not foreclose the evolution of the polity in a more democratic direction.

The achievements of the regime should not be under-estimated. Ten years after the beginning of perestroika Russia was incomparably more free *and* more democratic than it had been earlier. Although the separation of powers did not take the form of an elaborate system on the American model, powers began effectively to be separated and structured. Although executive authority predominated over the legislative, a rudimentary but unbalanced separation of powers had taken place. The absence of strong parties in parliament did not appear to hamper the legislative process and it was relatively easy to reach the consensus required for the passing of laws. The peaceful change of premiership in December 1992 from a radical neo-liberal to a centrist conservative prime minister, and the changes in government (although not *of* government) achieved following the 1993, 1995 and 1996 elections, indicated the formalisation of procedures for the modification (but not yet transfer) of power. Above all, the non-constitutional parties of left and right were marginalised. Politics came off the streets into a public sphere and was channelled through political institutions.

The greatest achievement of the post-Soviet system in Russia is not the establishment of democracy, a task that will take many years and which in any case is ambiguous, but the restoration of the autonomy of politics, the end of dogmatic and reductionist approaches to power and instead an understanding that political decision-making is an open-ended and contentious process. The restoration of politics means the end of the totalitarian impulse and is the first but essential step on the road to liberal-democracy. The Russian transition was an attempt to provide an institutional framework for pluralism in society, and thus to move beyond the pre-political arbitrariness of Gorbachev's 'socialist pluralism of opinions', and above all to move beyond the wholesale destruction of political institutions and procedures typical of Bolshevism. There are, however, no guarantees that the moment of liberation following the fall of communist power will be anchored in effective democratic institutions and processes. While democratic institutions have appeared, it will take longer for the democratic culture and economic structures that can sustain them to emerge. The easy part was getting rid of the old system; it is much harder to create a new political order and its citizens. Time is indeed of the essence, but not for haste but for habituation, time for the power of convention to assert itself, for toleration to become habitual, for the unwritten rules of convention to impress themselves onto the written word of the constitution.

Democracy has often emerged, as in Germany and Japan, as a result of hardship and catastrophe, in the attempt to overcome a known evil. For Russia, however, the catastrophe has not only preceded but has also accompanied the democratic experiment. Contrary to the hopes of within-system reformers like Gorbachev himself, the Soviet system was not susceptible to evolutionary change but instead suffered a catastrophic breakdown. Very little survived of the externals of the Soviet regime: the system of international alliances; the structure of the state; the organisation of the economy; and the institutions of government. Few institutions were capable of reformation, and most had to be rebuilt from scratch. The new system, however, represented an unstable symbiosis of the old and the new: August 1991 is only a symbolic date and did not represent such a complete rupture with the past as is sometimes suggested. The relatively peaceful transition from communism and incomplete democratisation inevitably meant a high degree of continuity with the old. Thus the impression of dramatic and sudden change in Russian politics masks profound continuities; the forms had changed, but often the content remained remarkably similar. The problem was in determining which elements of the Tsarist and Soviet past would be incorporated into the new order. The defeat of communism in 1991 did not mean the automatic victory of democracy over the Soviet system and network of social relations that it had spawned in its years of power. The attempt of the liberal government in Russia to reshape the social and political order encountered the resistance of existing social and elite groups, and the sheer scale of the problems facing the new regime necessarily led to the reproduction of some of the features of the old.

The general dilemmas facing Russian politics remain unresolved. The eternal question 'What is Russia' has not yet been resolved. While the challenge of globalisation forced something like a consensus to emerge on the need for Russia to integrate into the world economy and international political system, there remained a fundamental incompatiblity between Russia, as a continent-nation and as a distinctive civilisation in its own right, and pan-European and Westernising processes. While Russia was willing to adapt to the imperatives of globalisation, there remains a question over the degree to which these processes are indigenised or nativised, that is, incorporated into the fabric of the new society. While Japan has been very good at nativising what it requires from the international system and rejecting the rest, Russia has tended to veer from one extreme to another, either excessive susceptibility to Western influences (*chuzhbesie*), or angry rejection.

The fundamental problem, it could be argued, is that the post-Cold War order was not negotiated but imposed. The Russian view during 1989–91 suggested that the defeat of communism and the end of the Cold War represented a universal victory, whereas the West tended to view the fall of the Soviet regime as a vindication of all that it stood for and of the institutions that had conducted the Cold War. An imposed peace is usually an unstable one, and instead of negotiations on the shape of the new political order, the West imposed its institutions on the post-communist countries, placing them in the position of supplicants. Since these were the only demonstrably viable institutions there was a natural temptation to proceed in this way, but perhaps more should have been done to involve post-communist countries in shaping the new order.

Russia's democratic experiment began with enormous natural advantages and potential for development, and Russia remains a country of immense natural wealth with a population rich in talents and abilities. The liberal regime faced no coherent mass opposition and it became almost axiomatic, from the Western perspective, that any alternative would be worse. However, an assorted alliance of national-patriots and neo-communists asserted that Yeltsin had exhausted his potential, just as Gorbachev had done earlier, and that it was a time for a builder and healer of society, rather than an eternal oppositionist and destroyer, to take over and pursue a vigorous independent Russian policy. The first post-communist Russian leadership laid the foundations of a new political order in the belief that Russia could only enter world civilisation if it remade its own. But what if there is no world civilisation?

Appendix 1
Chronology

1989

26 March	Elections to the USSR Congress of People's Deputies.
25 May– 9 June	First session of USSR Congress, enthralls the nation.

1990

4, 18 March	Republican and local elections in Russia.
13 March	Abolition of Article 6 of the 1977 Soviet constitution enshrining the CPSU's 'leading role' in politics.
14 March	Gorbachev elected president of the USSR by the USSR Congress of People's Deputies.
16 May– 22 June	First Russian Congress of People's Deputies; 29 May Yeltsin elected Chairman of the Supreme Soviet of the RSFSR by a margin of four votes.
12 June	Declaration of Sovereignty of Russia.
2–13 July	28th Congress of CPSU.
16 July	Declaration of Sovereignty of Ukraine.
27 July	Declaration of Sovereignty of Belarus.
14 November	Appointment of Tass director Leonid Kravchenko to head Gostelradio, signalling assault against glasnost in the mass media.
21 November	Adoption of the 'Charter of Paris for a New Europe'.
27 November– 15 December	Second Russian Congress of People's Deputies, accepts in principle private ownership of land and adopts an agricultural reform programme.
20 December	Shevardnadze issues warning about danger of coup and resigns as foreign minister.

1991

13 January	Fifteen deaths in Lithuania as Soviet special forces storm the television tower in Vilnius.
14–16 January	Barricades in Latvia and Estonia.
14 January	Former minister of finances, Valentin Pavlov, appointed chairman of the USSR Cabinet of Ministers (prime minister).
20 January	Attack by MVD forces in Riga; some 300,000 people in Moscow demonstrate solidarity with the Baltic republics.
19 February	Yeltsin calls for Gorbachev's resignation.

23 February	Hard-line forces of about 100,000 demonstrate in Moscow for firm measures.
24 February	Much larger demonstration in support of Yeltsin.
26 February	Gorbachev's speech in Belovezha denouncing 'pseudo-democrats' for bringing the country 'to the verge of war'.
10 March	Demonstration of 300,000 Yeltsin supporters in Moscow; Yeltsin denounces Gorbachev's 'constant lies and deceptions' and calls for 'a declaration of war against the Soviet leadership'.
17 March	Referendum on the preservation of the USSR; in Russia a second question on the creation of an executive presidency is supported by over half the registered voters.
28 March	Confrontation in Moscow on opening day of Russian Congress, Gorbachev introduces troops into Moscow but 200,000 defy the ban on meetings and support Yeltsin and the creation of the post of President of the RSFSR.
28 March– 5 April	Third (Extraordinary) Russian Congress of People's Deputies convened by conservatives to weaken Yeltsin, in fact Yeltsin turns the tables and gains extra powers for the presidency.
23 April	Novo-Ogarevo '9 plus 1' 'political truce' between Gorbachev and Yeltsin and leaders of eight other republics, agreements signed on joint measures to stabilise the situation in the country, on accelerated transition to the market economy and for a new Union Treaty; in following weeks Yeltsin brings the miners' strikes to an end.
6 May	Russian KGB formed.
21–25 May	Fourth Russian Congress of People's Deputies, ratified constitutional changes strengthening the powers of the presidency and prepared the way for direct presidential elections.
12 June	First direct election of the president of Russia, won by Yeltsin.
17 June	Agreement reached between the '9 plus 1' on the draft of the new Union Treaty.
10–17 July	Fifth Russian Congress of People's Deputies, first stage, fails to elect a Speaker of the Russian parliament to succeed Yeltsin; Ruslan Khasbulatov appointed acting Speaker.
17 July	Gorbachev in London for the meeting of the 'Group of 7', asks for aid.
20 July	Yeltsin's decree banning political parties from state organisations and enterprises.
25–26 July	Plenum of CPSU Central Committee endorses a 'social democratic' programme to be adopted by a full party congress to be held at the end of the year.
29 July	Russia recognises the independence of Lithuania.
4 August	Yeltsin's decree on the departification of state institutions comes into force.
18 August	Two days before the new Union Treaty due to be signed a State Committee for the State of Emergency (SCSE), headed by the vice president Gennadi Yanaev, is established; visit of representatives of the SCSE to Foros in the Crimea where Gorbachev refuses to have anything to do with them.
19 August	Coup launched, tanks enter Moscow; Yeltsin resists and declares coup unconstitutional and calls for a general strike; the White House under siege.

20 August	Mass demonstrations in Moscow and Leningrad against the coup; thousands defend the barricades around the seat of the Russian government and parliament; three die on night of 20–21 August in clash with tanks.
21 August	Coup begins to unravel, Boris Pugo commits suicide and the other members of the SCSE arrested.
22 August	Gorbachev returns to Moscow and finds 'a different country'; emergency session of the RSFSR Supreme Soviet opens and adopts the tricolour flag for Russia; the CPSU suspended in Moscow; Felix Dzerzhinskii's statue in front of the KGB's headquarters in the Lubyanka removed; President Nursultan Nazarbaev of Kazakhstan resigns from the Politburo and decrees the departisation of state institutions; President Akaev of Kyrgyzstan nationalises the property of the republican Communist Party.
23 August	Gorbachev addresses Russian Supreme Soviet, Yeltsin decrees suspension of CPSU throughout Russia and its offices in Moscow sealed.
24 August	Gorbachev resigns as General Secretary of the Central Committee of CPSU; Ukraine declares independence; Russia recognises independence of Estonia and Latvia.
25 August	Supreme Soviet in Belarus declares the republic independent and Chair of the Supreme Soviet Nikolai Dementei replaced by Stanislav Shushkevich; Communist Party of Belarus temporarily suspended.
26 August	Emergency session of USSR Supreme Soviet, Anatolii Lukyanov removed from his post as Chair of the Supreme Soviet, Gorbachev appeals for work on the new Union Treaty to continue; Yeltsin's press secretary Pavel Voshchanov states that the secession of territories could lead to disaster and raises the question of borders.
27 August	Supreme Soviet of Moldova declares the republic independent.
29 August	USSR Supreme Soviet votes itself out of existence; Russo-Ukrainian treaty signed on the inviolability of borders and the creation of temporary inter-governmental structures to coordinate economic policy; CPSU suspended by the USSR Supreme Soviet.
30 August	Similar treaty signed with Kazakhstan; Azerbaijan declares independence.
31 August	Kyrgyzstan and Uzbekistan declare independence.
2–5 September	Emergency session of USSR Congress of People's Deputies; creation of Council of State composed of Gorbachev and the leaders of the republics willing to maintain some sort of union; plans go ahead for a new Union Treaty to create a 'Union of Sovereign States'.
6 September	State Council recognises independence of Estonia, Latvia and Lithuania; coup in Chechnya, Chair of Chechen Supreme Soviet overthrown and Supreme Soviet dissolved, the National Congress of the Chechen People headed by Dzhokhar Dudaev comes to power; Leningrad renamed St Petersburg.
9 September	Tajikistan declares independence.
10 September	Conference on the Human Dimension of the CSCE opens in Moscow; the three Baltic republics join the CSCE.
21 September	In referendum 99.3 per cent of 95 per cent turn-out vote in favour of

Armenian independence, on 23 September Armenian Supreme Soviet declares Armenia independent.

23 September	Communist coup in Tajikistan.
11 October	USSR KGB dissolved and replaced by five separate organisations.
16 October	Levon Ter-Petrossyan elected President of Armenia with 83 per cent of the vote.
21 October	New USSR Supreme Soviet meets without representatives from Ukraine, Azerbaijan, Georgia, Moldova and Armenia.
24 October	KGB abolished.
26 October	In referendum on independence for Turkmenistan 94 per cent vote in favour, on next day the Supreme Soviet declares the republic independent.
27 October	Parliamentary and presidential elections in Chechnya, Dudaev elected President with 90.1 per cent of the votes cast (63.1 per cent of the total electorate).
28 October– 5 November	Fifth Russian Congress of People's Deputies, second stage, Khasbulatov confirmed as Speaker of the Supreme Soviet; Yeltsin outlines accelerated plan for reform.
1 November	Russian Congress grants Yeltsin extraordinary powers to implement radical economic reforms.
6 November	CPSU banned by decree of Russian president; decree on reorganisation of government places president at head of government for the duration of radical reforms.
7 November	Yeltsin's decree imposing a state of emergency in Chechnya lifted by RSFSR Supreme Soviet after Yeltsin admits his 'mistake'.
8 November	Burbulis, Gaidar and Shokhin appointed deputy prime ministers.
14 November	Seven republics support the draft treaty for a 'Union of Sovereign States'.
15 November	A 'government of reforms' created; Yeltsin signs ten decrees accelerating the transition to a market economy in Russia.
1 December	In referendum 90.3 per cent of the 80 per cent turn-out (84.1 per cent of those eligible) vote in favour of Ukrainian independence, and Leonid Kravchuk elected President with 61.5 per cent of the vote; in direct elections the only candidate, Nursultan Nazarbaev, elected President of Kazakhstan; in referendum 97 per cent of the 78 per cent turn-out voted for the independence of the Trans-Dniester Moldovan Republic, and Igor Smirnov elected President; in referendum 88 per cent of turn-out voted for the independence of Gagauz republic, S. Topal elected President; in referendum in Ingush areas of Checheno-Ingushetia 97 per cent of turn-out voted for the creation of a separate Ingush republic within the RSFSR.
5 December	Ukrainian parliament votes to nullify 1922 Union Treaty, proclaiming in effect Ukraine's secession from the USSR.
7 December	The leaders of Russia, Ukraine and Belarus meet in the Belovezha Pushcha in western Belarus and sign an agreement creating a Commonwealth of Independent States (CIS); at the same time they condemn the Union Treaty of 1922.
8 December	Announcement of the Accords in Belovezha on creation of the CIS.

10 December	The agreement on the CIS is ratified by the parliaments in Belarus and Ukraine.
12 December	Russian parliament endorses the creation of the CIS and renounces the 1922 treaty forming the USSR.
12 December	Five presidents of the Central Asian republics meet in Ashgabat and agree to join the CIS.
19 December	Yeltsin's decree on the merger of the Russian Ministries of the Interior and Security into one ministry; the Russian Supreme Soviet annuls this decree on 26 December.
20 December	Inaugural meeting of the North Atlantic Cooperation Council.
21 December	Leaders of Azerbaijan, Armenia, Belarus, Kazakhstan, Kyrgyzstan, Moldova, Russia, Tajikistan, Turkmenistan, Uzbekistan and Ukraine sign the Almaty Declaration on the foundation of the Commonwealth of Independent States, only Georgia and the Baltic republics do not join.
25 December	The RSFSR renamed the Russian Federation; Gorbachev resigns as President of the USSR.
29 December	Overwhelming majority vote in favour of independence of Azerbaijan.
31 December	Official end to the USSR.

1992

2 January	Liberalisation of prices.
23 February	Neo-communists march in Moscow, clash with police.
20 March	Kiev CIS summit, discussed collective peace-keeping while destroying hopes for an integrated military system.
31 March	Signing of Federal Treaty between Russia and eighteen former autonomous republics, and two other treaties for the other administrative divisions of Russia.
6–21 April	Sixth Russian Congress of People's Deputies, endorses with reservations government reform programme; but fails to adopt a new constitution.
29 April	Official announcement that Russia and most other post-Soviet states admitted to IMF and EBRD.
15–16 May	Tashkent CIS summit.
30 May	Viktor Chernomyrdin replaced Vladimir Lopukhin as minister for energy, is appointed deputy prime minister.
1 June	Georgi Matyukhin resigns as chairman of the Central Bank of Russia.
2 June	Vladimir Shumeiko appointed deputy prime minister responsible for industrial administration.
5 June	Mayor of Moscow, Gavriil Popov, resigns; deputy mayor, Yurii Luzhkov, takes over.
11 June	Parliament adopts government's privatisation programme.
15 June	Yeltsin names Yegor Gaidar acting prime minister.
26 June	Minsk summit agrees procedure for exit from the rouble zone.
6 July	Moscow CIS summit.
14 August	Georgian troops 'invade' Abkhazia.
9–10 October	Bishkek summit.
30 November	Constitutional Court announces that it upholds Yeltsin's decrees banning

the CPSU in Russia, but that rank-and-file organisations have the right to exist.

1–14 December	Seventh Congress of People's Deputies; on 10 December Yeltsin's confrontation with Congress leading to deal brokered by Valerii Zor'kin, head of the Constitutional Court.
14 December	Acting prime minister Yegor Gaidar replaced by Victor Chernomyrdin.

1993

3 January	Signing of Start-2 Treaty at Moscow summit of Bush and Yeltsin.
22 January	CIS summit in Minsk attended by leaders of all ten member states, six sign CIS Charter.
10–13 March	Eighth Congress of People's Deputies; stalemate in struggle between parliament and president; Congress refuses to sanction referendum on constitution, strips Yeltsin of numerous powers.
20 March	Yeltsin declares 'special rule' for five weeks and referendum on 25 April to decide question of power.
26–29 March	Ninth Congress of People's Deputies, attempt to impeach Yeltsin fails by seventy-two votes but president stripped of most remaining powers; stiff conditions set for referendum, with a 50 per cent theshold of all eligible voters required.
3–4 April	Vancouver summit between Presidents Yeltsin and Clinton, America commits itself to Yeltsin's vision of reform in Russia.
25 April	Referendum asking four questions: confidence in Yeltsin, support for his economic policies, and whether pre-term presidential and parliamentary elections required.
5 June	Constitutional Assembly meets in Moscow to adopt presidential version of new Russian constitution; agrees however to find compromise with the draft proposed by parliament's Constitutional Commission. The Assembly divides into five working parties to merge the two versions and to discuss the new electoral law. Agreement on basic principles that Russia should be a democracy respecting human rights and private property and governed by the rule of law. Compromise draft sent for ratification to the republics and regions of Russia.
31 August	Last troops withdrawn from Lithuania.
21 September	Yeltsin announces dissolution of the Russian parliament and the holding of pre-term parliamentary elections on 12 December. Parliament goes into emergency session, appointing Rutskoi 'president' and an alternative government is formed, but calls for popular support go largely unheeded except by some regional leaders, hoping to gain maximum advantage from the crisis in Moscow.
24 September	Eleventh CIS summit in Moscow agrees to form an economic union. Azerbaijan rejoins the CIS, and ten members of CIS (excluding Turkmenistan) agree to remove internal trade barriers and to promote the Inter-State Bank as the core of a future currency union.
27 September	Abkhaz forces capture the capital of the region, Sukhumi, and Georgian

president, Eduard Shevardnadze is forced to flee. Reprisals against Georgian citizens begin, thousands of refugees try to escape.

1 October President decrees reduction in number of Duma seats to 450 and promulgates changed electoral regulations.

3 October Demonstrations escalate into armed uprising, with the 'parliamentary' insurgents attacking the Moscow mayor's office and the Ostankino television centre, incited by Rutskoi speaking from the balcony of the White House. Yeltsin returns from his dacha and at 4pm declares a state of emergency.

4 October After a night of appeals by Yeltsin, the military deploys around the White House and by the afternoon the city is back in the hands of the government at the cost of some 146 dead. Khasbulatov, Rutskoi, Barannikov, Dunaev, Achalov, Makashov and twenty-four other 'rebel' leaders taken from the White house to Lefortovo gaol. Publication of *Pravda*, *Sovetskaya Rossiya*, *Den'* and some other papers suspended, and the National Salvation Front, the Russian Communist Workers' Party, Officers' Union, the United Front of Russian Working People and some other 'red-brown' movements suspended.

6 October Yeltsin lifts restrictions on the press; calls for local and regional soviets to be dissolved and for them to be elected on 12 December; Guard Post 'No. 1' at the Lenin Mausoleum removed.

15 October Yeltsin signs decree for plebiscite on the draft constitution on 12 December.

19 October Yeltsin bans a number of parties and movements from participation in the Federal Assembly elections.

22 October Yeltsin decrees new elections for regional legislatures between December 1993 and March 1994, and recommends that the republics reorganise their administrative systems as well.

23 October Georgia joins the CIS as twelfth member.

26 October Yeltsin decrees elections for local soviets in towns and districts between December 1993 and June 1994 and recommends the reorganisation of local government commensurate with his regulations.

27 October Yeltsin signs decree on land ownership removing restrictions on sale and ownership.

28 October Constitution adopted by Sverdlovsk oblast soviet declaring the region the 'Urals republic'.

2 November New Russian military doctrine approved by the Security Council.

6 November Yeltsin approves draft constitution; issues amended electoral regulations.

12 December Elections to the Federal Assembly and plebiscite on the new constitution, which officially came into force on this day.

1994

11 January The Federation Council and the State Duma meet for the first time. Yeltsin addressed the upper house and stresses 'the establishment of Russian democratic statehood'.

14 January Ivan Rybkin elected chairman of State Duma.

16 January Gaidar resigns from the government.

23 February	State Duma grants 'amnesty' to those imprisoned for participation in the August 1991 coup and the October 1993 events; they were released on 26 February by the Procurator-General Aleksei Kazannik despite Yeltsin's opposition, and he resigns.
15 April	CIS summit in Moscow.
28 April	Social Accord agreement signed.
27 May	Alexander Solzhenitsyn returns to Russia after 20 years in exile, lands in Magadan and proceeds slowly by train to Moscow.
21 July	Solzhenitsyn arrives in Moscow.
31 August	Last Russian troops leave Germany, Latvia and (shortly afterwards) Estonia.
22 June	Russia signs NATO's Partnership for Peace Framework Document.
30 September	Yeltsin fails to leave plane to meet Irish premier Reynolds at Shannon airport.
17 October	Murder of *Moskovskii Komsomolets* journalist Dmitrii Kholodov.
26 November	Russian covert operation in Chechnya defeated.
3 December	Georgi Chanturia, leader of National-Democratic Party of Georgia, assassinated in Georgia.
11 December	Russian forces enter Chechnya, start of bloody military campaign to reintegrate the Chechen Republic into the Russian Federation.

1995

1 March	Vladimir List'ev, journalist and head of Russian Public Broadcasting, murdered.
10 March	Human rights commissioner Sergei Kovalev voted out of office by State Duma.
15 March	1995 budget passed by the State Duma.
1 April	Russian Public Television (ORT) starts broadcasting.
14 June	Chechen guerrillas led by Shamil Basaev attack the southern Russian town of Budennovsk.
21 June	State Duma passes vote of no confidence in the government.
1 July	State Duma fails in vote of no confidence in the government.
20 July	Customs Union between Belarus, Kazakhstan and Russia officially comes into force.
11 July	Yeltsin's first heart attack.
12 August	Union of Muslims holds inaugural conference in Bashkortostan.
21 August	Eduard Rossel wins gubernatorial elections in Sverdlovsk.
17 September	Presidential decree setting election of regional heads of administration for December 1996 (with some exceptions) and regional parliaments for December 1997.
19 October	Yeltsin suggests that foreign minister Kozyrev will be sacked as soon as a replacement can be found; within a day Yeltsin backtracks.
22 October	Midnight, deadline for voter signatures in support of electoral associations to be delivered to the Central Electoral Commission.
26 October	Yeltsin suffers second heart attack, hospitalised and much weakened physically and politically.

5 November	Presidential and parliamentary elections in Georgia; Shevardnadze re-elected to a second term.
17 November	CFE Treaty comes into force but Russia allowed three extra years to comply.
6 December	State Duma passes 1996 budget.
17 December	State Duma elections.

1996

5 January	Foreign minister Andrei Kozyrev resigns.
12 January	Bilateral treaty between federal government and Sverdlovsk region, granting extensive economic rights; bilateral treaty signed between Moscow and Kaliningrad region, paving the way for the latter to become a free economic zone.
30 January	Bilateral treaties signed with Kvasnodav and Orenburg regions.
1 February	Yeltsin celebrates his sixty-fifth birthday.
28 February	Russia joins Council of Europe as 39th member.
2 March	Gorbachev celebrates his sixty-fifth birthday; the previous day announced his candidacy for the presidency.
29 March	Quadripartite Treaty signed between Belarus, Kazakhstan, Kyrgyzstan and Russia committing them to closer integration while maintaining their sovereignty.
2 April	Bilateral Treaty of 'union' between Belarus and Russia to establish a common market, coordinated foreign and defence policies and some supranational political institutions, but sovereignty and independence of both states retained.
19 May	First round of mayoral elections in St Petersburg, incumbent mayor Anatolii Sobchak receives 28.8 per cent and former first deputy mayor, Vladimir Yakovlev, 21.8 per cent; since neither won over 50 per cent of the vote a second round required.
2 June	Sobchak narrowly loses second round of St Petersburg mayoral elections with 45.8 per cent of the vote to Yakovlev's 47.5 per cent.
16 June	First round of presidential elections: out of ten candidates Yeltsin comes first and Zyuganov second, but neither gains 50 per cent of the vote so two front-runners go to a second round; Luzhkov overwhelmingly re-elected mayor of Moscow with 89 per cent of the vote.
18 June	Alexander Lebed, who came third in the presidential elections with 14.5 per cent, appointed secretary of the Security Council and national security adviser to the president; defence minister Pavel Grachev sacked.
3 July	Second round of presidential elections: Yeltsin wins with 53.8 per cent of the vote, while Zyuganov gains 40.3 per cent.
9 August	Inauguration of Yeltsin as president for a second term.

Appendix 2

Election results since 1989

APPENDIX 2.1 ELECTIONS TO THE USSR CONGRESS OF PEOPLE'S DEPUTIES (26 MARCH 1989)

There were 2,250 seats, but only 1,500 were contested, the rest (750) were reserved for social organisations. Thus the CPSU was allocated 100 seats, and the CPSU Central Committee drew up a list of exactly 100 (including Gorbachev). Eighty-five per cent of the candidates were communists, whereas in the previous election for the old Supreme Soviet only 71.4 per cent had been communists.

Electoral system

Candidates had to obtain an absolute majority of the votes cast. If none achieved the threshold of 50 per cent, a run-off election was held between the two candidates with the most votes. The second vote usually took place a fortnight after the first ballot.

Results

CPSU 1,931, non-CPSU 319.

In June 1989 the Congress elected a permanent Supreme Soviet of 542 members in which the CPSU gained 475 seats, non-CPSU 67; divided into two equal chambers with 271 seats apiece, the Council of the Union and the Council of the Nationalities.

APPENDIX 2.2 REFERENDUM ON 'RENEWED UNION' AND A PRESIDENCY IN RUSSIA (17 MARCH 1991)

Voters were asked: 'Do you consider necessary the preservation of the Union of Soviet Socialist Republics as a renewed federation of equal sovereign republics, in which the rights and freedom of the individual of any nationality will be fully guaranteed?'. Six republics (Armenia, Georgia, Moldova, and the three Baltic republics of Estonia, Latvia, Lithuania) boycotted the referendum, signifying the *de facto* division of the USSR into at least two parts.

In the USSR 147 million voted (75.4 per cent of the electorate), of whom 112 million (76.2 per cent of turn-out) supported the idea of a 'renewed Union'.

In Russia out of a total registered electorate of 105,643,364, 75.4 per cent (79,701,169) took part, of whom 71.3 per cent (56,860,783) voted 'yes' and 26.4 per cent (21,030,753) voted 'no' (2.3 per cent of ballots were spoiled).

A supplementary question in Russia on a directly elected President gained 69.85 per cent of the vote. Of those who took part, 28 per cent voted against a presidency for Russia and for a renewed Union, 23.4 per cent voted for a Russian president but against the Union, 45.6 per cent voted for a president and for the Union, and 2.1 per cent of votes were spoiled.

Sources: Izvestiya, 26 March 1991, p. 2; *Pravda*, 27 March 1991; M. Gorbachev, *Soyuz mozhno bylo sokhranit'* (Moscow, izd. 'Aprel'-85', 1995), pp. 148–9.

APPENDIX 2.3 FIRST RUSSIAN PRESIDENTIAL ELECTION (12 JUNE 1991)

Turnout

The total number of registered electors was 106,484,518 and turnout was 74.7 per cent. With the exception of Tatarstan, where a boycott of the elections was organised resulting in a 40 per cent turn-out, participation ranged from 65 per cent in Moscow and St Petersburg to 85 per cent in Kursk and Belgorod oblasts. Yeltsin won over 50 per cent of the vote in the first round so no second round was required.

Results

Candidate	Votes cast	%
1. Yeltsin, Boris	45,552,041	57.30
2. Ryzhkov, Nikolai	13,395,335	16.85
3. Zhirinovskii, Vladimir	6,211,007	7.81
4. Tuleev, Aman	5,417,464	6.81
5. Makashov, Al'bert	2,969,511	3.74
6. Bakatin, Vadim	2,719,757	3.42
Invalid votes	3,242,167	4.10
Total votes cast	79,507,282	100.00

Sources: 'Soobshchenie tsentral'noi izbiratel'noi komissii po vyboram Prezidenta RSFSR', *Izvestiya*, 20 June 1991; *Pravda*, 20 June 1991.

APPENDIX 2.4 REFERENDUM (25 APRIL 1993)

Turnout

Out of a total of 107,310,374 eligible voters 69,222,858 actually voted, a turnout of 64.5 per cent. Only Chechnya boycotted the referendum, while in Tatarstan nearly 80 per cent of the electorate ignored the vote, rendering the result there invalid.

Results (in percentages)

	Yes		No		Spoiled ballots
	% of vote	*% of electorate*	*% of vote*	*% of electorate*	
1. Do you have confidence in the President of the Russian Federation, Boris Yeltsin?					
	58.7	37.3	39.2	25.2	2.1
2. Do you approve of the socioeconomic policies carried out by the President of the Russian Federation and the government of the Russian Federation since 1992?					
	53.0	34.0	44.6	28.6	2.4
3. Do you consider it necessary to hold early elections to the presidency of the Russian Federation?					
	49.5	31.7	47.1	30.2	3.4
4. Do you consider it necessary to hold early elections of the people's deputies of the Russian Federation?					
	67.2	43.1	30.1	19.3	2.7

Note: The Constitutional Court ruled that questions three and four involved a change in the Constitution, so that half the electorate would have to vote 'Yes' for them to be binding.

Sources: Rossiiskaya gazeta, 6 May 1993; *RFE/RL Research Report,* vol. 2, no. 21 (21 May 1993), p. 12.

APPENDIX 2.5 REFERENDUM AND PARLIAMENTARY ELECTIONS (12 DECEMBER 1993)

Turnout

Out of a total electorate of 106,170,835, 53,751,696 valid ballot papers were cast, of which 46,799,532 were for the eight groups passing the 5 per cent barrier. The official turnout figure (58,187,755) represented 54.8 per cent of registered voters; only 25 per cent needed to vote for the Federal Assembly elections to be valid.

Referendum on the Constitution

Official figures show that the Constitution was supported by 32,937,630 people, or 58.43 per cent of the vote, thus exceeding the 50 per cent threshold required for adoption; while 23,431,333 voted against it, or 41.6 per cent. Only 30.7 per cent of the total electorate voted for the Constitution, and in seventeen republics and regions the constitution was rejected (*Rossiiskaya gazeta,* 21 December 1993, p. 1; *Byulleten' TsIK,* 1 (12), 1994, pp. 34–8).

Election to the State Duma

Party/bloc	*Party-list*		*Single-member*		*Total seats*
	%	*seats*	*seats*	*no.*	*%*
Russia's Choice	15.51	40	30	70	15.6
LDPR (Zhirinovskii)	22.92	59	5	64	14.2
Communist Party	12.40	32	16	48	10.7
Agrarian Party	7.99	21	12	33	7.3
Yabloko (Yavlinskii)	7.86	20	3	23	5.1
Women of Russia	8.13	21	2	23	5.1
PRES (Shakhrai)	6.76	18	1	18	4.0
DPR (Travkin)	5.52	14	1	15	3.3
Five per cent representation threshold in the party-list vote					

Civic Union	1.93	0	1	1	0.2
RDDR (Sobchak)	4.08	0	4	4	0.9
Dignity and Charity	0.70	0	2	2	0.4
New Names	1.25	0	1	1	0.2
Cedar	0.76	0	–	–	–
Against all	4.36	0	–	–	–
Spoiled ballots	3.10	–	–	–	–
Independents	–	–	–	141	31.3
Postponed	–	–	6	6	–
Total	–	225	225	450	100.00

Note: Out of a total electorate of 106,170,835, 53,751,696 valid ballot papers were cast, of which 46,799,532 were for the eight groups passing the 5 per cent barrier. The top eight percentages in column one refer to the latter figure; the rest to the former, hence the column exceeds 100 per cent.

Sources: *Rossiiskaya gazeta*, 28 December 1993, p. 1; *Byulleten' Tsentral'noi izbiratel.noi kommissii Rossiiskoi Federatsii*, no. (12), 1994, p. 67.

APPENDIX 2.6 STATE DUMA ELECTIONS (17 DECEMBER 1995)

Turnout

Out of a total electorate of 107,496,558 million registered voters, 69,204,820 million (64.44 per cent) participated. A total of 1,320,620 ballots were declared invalid, leaving 67,884,200 valid ballots. Only 25 per cent needed to vote for the Duma elections to be valid. Gubernatorial elections were also held in twelve regions in which 25 per cent of the population live, something that helped inflate turnout figures.

Party/bloc	Party-list		Single-member	Total seats	1993 seats
	%	seats	seats		
CPRF	22.30	99	58	157	45
LDPR	11.18	50	1	51	64
Russia Our Home	10.13	45	10	55	na
Yabloko	6.89	31	14	45	25
Five per cent representation threshold in the party-list vote					
Women of Russia	4.61	0	3	3	23
Working Russia	4.53	0	0	0	0
KRO	4.31	0	5	5	na
PST	4.01	0	1	1	na
DVR	3.86	0	9	9	76
APR	3.78	0	20	20	55
Derzhava	2.57	0	0	0	na
Forward Russia!	1.94	0	3	3	na
VN	1.61	0	9	9	na
Pamfilova *et al.*	1.61	0	2	2	na
Rybkin bloc	1.12	0	3	3	na
Blocs with one MP	–	0	10	10	na
Independents	–	–	77	77	137
TOTAL	100.00	225	225	450	450

Note 1: Although 1.3 million ballots were declared invalid the 5 per cent party-list threshold was calculated using the total number of ballots cast, not only valid ballots.
Note 2: Twenty-five electoral associations received less than 1 per cent of the vote and seven received between 1 and 2 per cent.

Abbreviations: CPRF – Communist Party of the Russian Federation; LDPR – Liberal Democratic Party of Russia; Working Russia (KTR) – Communists–Working Russia–For the Soviet Union; KRO – Congress of Russian Communities; PST – Party of Workers' Self-Management; DVR – Russia's Democratic Choice; APR – Agrarian Party of Russia; VN – Power to the People.

Sources: OMRI Daily Digest, no. 249, Part I, 27 December 1995; *OMRI Daily Digest*, no. 1, Part 1, 2 January 1996; ITAR-TASS, 22 December 1995; *Moscow News*, no. 51 (29 December 1995), p. 2.

APPENDIX 2.7 SECOND RUSSIAN PRESIDENTIAL ELECTIONS (JUNE 1996)

Electoral system

Direct elections without electoral districts. No candidate obtained over 50 per cent of the vote in the first round so the two top candidates went on to a second round held two weeks after the announcement of the results of the first (3 July).

First round (16 June 1996)

Registered voters: 108,495,023

Turnout: 75,587,139 (69.81 per cent)

   Total valid ballots: 74,515,019

   Total invalid ballots: 1,072,120

Results

Candidate	%	Number of votes
1. Boris Yeltsin	35.28	26,665,495
2. Gennadii Zyuganov	32.03	24,211,686
3. Alexander Lebed	14.52	10,974,736
4. Grigorii Yavlinskii	7.34	5,550,752
5. Vladimir Zhirinovskii	5.70	4,311,479
6. Svyatoslav Fedorov	0.92	699,158
7. Mikhail Gorbachev	0.51	386,069
8. Martin Shakkum	0.37	277,068
9. Yurii Vlasov	0.20	151,282
10. Vladimir Bryntsalov	0.16	123,065
Against all candidates	1.54	1,163,921

Note: The percentages are calculated from the number participating in the voting.

Source: Rossiiskaya gazeta, 22 June 1996.

Second round (3 July 1996)

Turnout

To avoid a fall in the turnout between the two rounds the day of the election was shifted from the usual Sunday to a Wednesday, which was declared a holiday. In the event turnout only fell marginally: 74,815,898 cast their votes, representing 68.89 per cent of registered voters.

Result

Candidate	%	Number of votes
1. Boris Yeltsin	53.82	40,208,384
2. Gennadii Zyuganov	40.31	30,113,306
Against both candidates	4.83	3,604,550

Appendix 3

The Russian constitution

We, the multinational people of the Russian Federation,
    united by a common destiny on our land,
    asserting human rights and freedoms and civil peace and concord,
    preserving historically established state unity,
    proceeding from the generally recognised principles of the equality and
        self-determination of peoples,
    revering the memory of our forebears who passed down to us love and respect for
        the Fatherland and faith in goodness and justice,
    reviving the sovereign statehood of Russia and asserting the immutability of
        its democratic foundations,
    seeking to ensure the well-being and prosperity of Russia,
    proceeding from responsibility for our homeland to present and future generations,
    recognising ourselves as part of the world community,
    adopt the CONSTITUTION OF THE RUSSIAN FEDERATION.

SECTION ONE

Chapter 1 Foundations of the constitutional system

Article I

(1) The Russian Federation-Russia is a democratic federative rule-of-law state with a republican form of government.
(2) The names Russian Federation and Russia are of equal validity.

Article 2

The individual and his rights and freedoms are the supreme value. Recognition, observance and protection of human and civil rights and freedoms is the obligation of the state.

Article 3

(1) The repository of sovereignty and the sole source of authority in the Russian Federation is its multinational people.

(2) The people exercise their authority directly and also through bodies of state power and bodies of local self-government.

(3) The supreme direct expression of the authority of the people is the referendum and free elections.

(4) Nobody can arrogate power in the Russian Federation. The seizure of power or the arrogation of powers are prosecuted in accordance with federal law.

Article 4

(1) The sovereignty of the Russian Federation extends to the whole of its territory.

(2) The constitution of the Russian Federation and federal laws are paramount throughout the territory of the Russian Federation.

(3) The Russian Federation ensures the integrity and inviolability of its territory.

Article 5

(1) The Russian Federation consists of republics, krais, oblasts, cities of federal significance, an autonomous oblast and autonomous okrugs which are equal components of the Russian Federation.

(2) A republic (state) has its own constitution and legislation. A krai, oblast, city of federal significance, autonomous oblast or autonomous okrug has its own charter and legislation.

(3) The federal structure of the Russian Federation is based on its state integrity, the unity of the system of state power, the delimitation of areas of responsibility and powers between bodies of state power of the Russian Federation and bodies of state power of the components of the Russian Federation, and the equality and self-determination of the peoples in the Russian Federation.

(4) All components of the Russian Federation are equal with each other in interrelationships with federal bodies of state power.

Article 6

(1) Citizenship of the Russian Federation is acquired and terminated in accordance with federal law and is uniform and equal irrespective of the basis on which it is acquired.

(2) Each citizen of the Russian Federation possesses all rights and freedoms on its territory and bears equal obligations stipulated by the constitution of the Russian Federation.

(3) A citizen of the Russian Federation cannot be deprived of his citizenship or of the right to change it.

Article 7

(1) The Russian Federation is a social state whose policy is aimed at creating conditions ensuring a worthy life and free development of the individual.

(2) In the Russian Federation people's labour and health are protected, a guaranteed minimum wage is established, state support is insured for the family, mothers, fathers, children, invalids and elderly citizens, the system of the social services is developed, and state pensions, allowances and other guarantees of social protection are established.

Article 8

(1) In the Russian Federation the unity of the economic area, the free movement of goods, services and financial resources, support for competition and freedom of economic activity are guaranteed.

(2) In the Russian Federation private, state, municipal, and other forms of property enjoy equal recognition and protection.

Article 9

(1) The land and other natural resources are utilised and protected in the Russian Federation as the basis of the life and activity of the peoples inhabiting the corresponding territory.

(2) The land and other natural resources can be in private, state, municipal or other forms of ownership.

Article 10

State power in the Russian Federation is exercised on the basis of the separation of legislative, executive and judicial powers. Bodies of legislative, executive and judicial power are independent.

Article 11

(1) State power in the Russian Federation is exercised by the President of the Russian Federation, the Federal Assembly (the Federation Council and the State Duma), the government of the Russian Federation and the courts of the Russian Federation.

(2) State power in the components of the Russian Federation is exercised by the bodies of state power formed by them.

(3) The delimitation of areas of responsibility and powers – between bodies of state power of the Russian Federation and bodies of state power of components of the Russian Federation is effected by the present constitution and the Federation Treaty and other treaties concerning the delimitation of areas of responsibility and powers.

Article 12

In the Russian Federation local self-government is recognized and guaranteed. Within the limits of its powers local self-government is independent. Bodies of local self-government do not form part of the system of bodies of state power.

Article 13

(1) In the Russian Federation ideological diversity is recognized.

(2) No ideology may be established as the state ideology or as a compulsory ideology.

(3) In the Russian Federation political diversity and a multiparty system are recognized.

(4) Social associations are equal before the law.

(5) The creation and activity of social associations whose objectives and actions are directed

towards the forcible alteration of the basic principles of the constitutional system and the violation of the integrity of the Russian Federation, the undermining of the security of the state, the creation of armed formations, or the fuelling of social, racial, national or religious strife are prohibited.

Article 14

(1)   The Russian Federation is a secular state. No religion may be established as the state religion or a compulsory religion.

(2)   Religious associations are separated from the state and are equal before the law.

Article 15

(1)   The constitution of the Russian Federation has supreme legal force and is direct-acting and applies throughout the territory of the Russian Federation. Laws and other legal enactments adopted in the Russian Federation must not contradict the constitution of the Russian Federation.

(2)   Bodies of state power, bodies of local self-government, officials, citizens and associations thereof are obliged to observe the constitution of the Russian Federation and the laws.

(3)   Laws are subject to official publication. Unpublished laws are not applied. Any normative legal enactments affecting human and civil rights, freedoms and duties cannot be applied unless they have been officially published for universal information.

(4)   Generally recognized principles and norms of international law and the international treaties of the Russian Federation are a constituent part of its legal system. If an international treaty of the Russian Federation establishes rules other than those stipulated by the law, the rules of the international treaty apply.

Article 16

(1)   The provisions of the present chapter of the constitution form the basic principles of the constitutional system of the Russian Federation and cannot be altered except by the procedure laid down by the present constitution.

(2)   No other provisions of the present constitution can contradict the basic principles of the constitutional system of the Russian Federation.

Chapter 2 Human and civil rights and freedoms

Article 17

(1)   Human and civil rights and freedoms are guaranteed in the Russian Federation in accordance with generally recognized principles and norms of international law and in conformity with the present constitution.

(2)   Basic human rights and freedoms are inalienable and belong to each person from birth onwards.

(3)   The exercise of human and civil rights and freedoms must not violate the rights and freedoms of others.

Article 18

Human and civil rights and freedoms are direct-acting. They determine the meaning, content and application of laws and the activity of the legislative and executive branches and of local self-government and are safeguarded by justice.

Article 19

(1)   All are equal before the law and the courts.
(2)   The state guarantees equality of human and civil rights and freedoms regardless of sex, race, nationality, language, origin, property and position, place of residence, attitude towards religion, convictions, membership of public associations and also other circumstances. Any forms of restriction of citizens' rights on grounds of social, racial, national, linguistic or religious affiliation are prohibited.
(3)   Men and women have equal rights and freedoms and equal opportunities to exercise them.

Article 20

(1)   Each person has the right to life.
(2)   Until its abolition the death penalty can be prescribed by federal law as the supreme penalty for particularly grave crimes against life, the accused being granted the right to trial by jury.

Article 21

(1)   The dignity of the individual is protected by the state. Nothing may be grounds for disparaging it.
(2)   No one must be subjected to torture, violence or other brutal or humiliating treatment or punishment. No one may be subjected to medical, scientific or other experiments without their voluntary consent.

Article 22

(1)   Each person has the right to freedom and inviolability of the person.
(2)   Arrest, taking into custody and keeping in custody are permitted only by judicial decision. An individual cannot be detained for a period of more than 48 hours without a judicial decision.

Article 23

(1)   Each person has the right to inviolability of his private life, individual and family privacy, and defence of his honour and good name.

(2)   Each person has the right to privacy of correspondence, telephone conversations and postal, telegraph and other communications. Limitation of this right is permitted only on the basis of a judicial decision.

Article 24

(1)   The collection, storage, utilization and dissemination of information about a person's private life without his consent are not permitted.
(2)   Bodies of state power and bodies of local self-government and their officials are obliged to ensure that each person has the opportunity to see documents and materials directly affecting his rights and freedoms unless otherwise provided by law.

Article 25

Dwellings are inviolable. No one is entitled to enter a dwelling against the wishes of the persons residing there except in cases prescribed by federal law or on the basis of a judicial decision.

Article 26

(1)   Each person is entitled to determine and indicate his own nationality. No one may be compelled to determine and indicate his own nationality.
(2)   Each person has the right to use his native language and to the free choice of language of communication, education, instruction and creativity.

Article 27

(1)   Each person who is legally present on the territory of the Russian Federation has the right to travel freely and choose his place of stay and residence.
(2)   Each person may freely travel outside the Russian Federation. The citizen of the Russian Federation has the right to return without impediment to the Russian Federation.

Article 28

Each person is guaranteed freedom of conscience and freedom of religion, including the right to profess any religion individually or together with others or not to profess any, and freely to choose, hold and disseminate religious and other convictions and to act in accordance with them.

Article 29

(1)   Each person is guaranteed freedom of thought and speech.
(2)   Propaganda or agitation exciting social, racial, national or religious hatred and enmity is not permitted. Propaganda of social, racial, national, religious or linguistic supremacy is prohibited.
(3)   No one may be compelled to express his opinions and convictions or to renounce them.

(4)   Each person has the right freely to seek, receive, pass on, produce and disseminate information by any legal method. The list of information constituting a state secret is determined by federal law.

(5)   The freedom of mass information is guaranteed. Censorship is prohibited.

Article 30

(1)   Each person has the right of association, including the right to create trade unions to protect his interests. The freedom of the activity of public associations is guaranteed.

(2)   No one may be compelled to join or to remain any association.

Article 31

Citizens of the Russian Federation have the right to assemble peacefully without weapons and to hold meetings, rallies and demonstrations, processions and pickets.

Article 32

(1)   Citizens of the Russian Federation have the right to take part in the administration of the state's affairs both directly and via their representatives.

(2)   Citizens of the Russian Federation have the right to elect and to be elected to bodies of state power and bodies of local self-government, and also to take part in referendums.

(3)   Citizens deemed incompetent by a court and also those detained in places of imprisonment by sentence of a court do not have the right to elect and to be elected.

(4)   Citizens of the Russian Federation have equal access to state service.

(5)   Citizens of the Russian Federation have the right to take part in the administration of justice.

Article 33

Citizens of the Russian Federation have the right to appeal personally and also to send individual and collective appeals to state bodies and bodies of local self-government.

Article 34

(1)   Each person has the right to make free use of his abilities and property for purposes of entrepreneurial activity and other economic activity not prohibited by law.

(2)   Economic activity directed towards monopolization and unscrupulous competition is not permitted.

Article 35

(1)   The right of private ownership is protected by law.

(2)   Each person is entitled to own property and to possess, utilise and dispose of it both individually and together with others.

(3)   No one may be deprived of his property except by court decision. The compulsory expropriation of property for state requirements may be carried out only if full compensation is paid in advance.

(4)   The right of inheritance is guaranteed.

Article 36

(1)   Citizens and their associations are entitled to hold land in private ownership.

(2)   Owners freely possess, utilise and dispose of land and other natural resources provided that this does not damage the environment and does not violate the rights and legitimate interests of others.

(3)   The conditions and procedure for the use of land are defined on the basis of federal law.

Article 37

(1)   Labour is free. Each person has the right freely to dispose of his abilities for labour and to choose a type of activity and occupation.

(2)   Forced labour is prohibited.

(3)   Each person has the right to work in conditions meeting the requirements of safety and hygiene and to receive remuneration for labour without any discrimination and of not less than the minimum pay prescribed by federal law, and also the right to protection from unemployment.

(4)   The right to individual and collective labour disputes utilizing the methods of solving them prescribed by federal law, including the right to strike, is recognized.

(5)   Each person has the right to leisure. Persons working on the basis of a labour contract are guaranteed the working hours, days off and holidays prescribed by federal law and paid annual leave.

Article 38

(1)   Maternity and childhood and the family are under the state's protection.

(2)   Concern for children and their upbringing are the equal right and duty of the parents.

(3)   Able-bodied children who have reached the age of 18 years must look after disabled parents.

Article 39

(1)   Each person is guaranteed social security in old age, in the event of sickness, disability or loss of breadwinner, for the raising of children, and in other cases prescribed by law.

(2)   State pensions and social benefits are prescribed by law.

(3)   Voluntary social insurance, the creation of additional forms of social security and charity are encouraged.

Article 40

(1)   Each person has the right to housing. No one may be arbitrarily deprived of housing.

(2) Bodies of state power and bodies of local self-government encourage housing construction and create the conditions for exercise of the right to housing.

(3) Housing is provided free or at affordable cost to low-income and other citizens indicated in the law who require housing from state, municipal and other housing stocks in accordance with the norms prescribed by law.

Article 41

(1) Each person has the right to health care and medical assistance. Medical assistance in state and municipal health care establishments is provided free to citizens by means of funds from the relevant budget, insurance contributions and other revenue.

(2) In the Russian Federation federal programmes to protect and strengthen the population's health are financed, measures to develop state, municipal and private health care systems are taken, and activities conducive to the strengthening of people's health, the development of physical culture and sport, and ecological and sanitary and epidemiological well-being are encouraged.

(3) The concealment by officials of facts and circumstances creating a threat to people's lives and health entails responsibility in accordance with federal law.

Article 42

Each person has the right to a decent environment, reliable information about the state of the environment and compensation for damage caused to his health or property by ecological offences.

Article 43

(1) Each person has the right to education.

(2) General access to free pre-school, basic general and secondary vocational education in state or municipal educational establishments and in enterprises is guaranteed.

(3) Each person is entitled on a competitive basis to receive free higher education in a state or municipal educational establishment or in an enterprise.

(4) Basic general education is compulsory. Parents or persons in loco parentis ensure that children receive basic general education.

(5) The Russian Federation establishes federal state educational standards and supports various forms of education and self-education.

Article 44

(1) Each person is guaranteed freedom of literary, artistic, scientific, technical and other types of creation and teaching. Intellectual property is protected by law.

(2) Each person has the right to participate in cultural life and use cultural institutions and to have access to cultural treasures.

(3) Each person must display concern for preserving the historical and cultural heritage and look after historical and cultural monuments.

Article 45

(1)   State protection of human and civil rights and freedoms in the Russian Federation is guaranteed.
(2)   Each person is entitled to protect his rights and freedoms by any methods not prohibited by law.

Article 46

(1)   Each person is guaranteed judicial protection of his rights and freedoms.
(2)   The decisions and actions (or inaction) of bodies of state power, bodies of local self-government, public associations and officials can be appealed in court.
(3)   Each person is entitled, in accordance with the Russian Federation's international treaties, to appeal to inter-state bodies for the protection of human rights and freedoms if all available means of legal protection inside the state have been exhausted.

Article 47

(1)   No one can be deprived of the right to have the case against him heard by the court and the judges to whose jurisdiction it is assigned by the law.
(2)   Anyone accused of having committed a crime has the right to have the case against him heard by a court and jury as provided by federal law.

Article 48

(1)   Each person is guaranteed the right to receive qualified legal assistance. Legal aid is rendered free of charge as provided by law.
(2)   Each detainee held in custody and accused of having committed a crime has the right to benefit from the assistance of a lawyer (defence attorney) from the moment of his detention, placing in custody, or indictment respectively.

Article 49

(1)   Each person accused of having committed a crime is presumed innocent until his guilt is proved as provided by federal law and established by means of a legitimate court sentence.
(2)   The accused is not obliged to prove his innocence.
(3)   Any undispelled doubts regarding the individual's guilt are interpreted in the accused's favour.

Article 50

(1)   No one can be tried a second time for the same crime.
(2)   The use of any proof acquired in breach of the federal law is not permitted in the administration of justice.
(3)   Each person sentenced for a crime has the right to have his sentence reviewed by a

superior court as provided by federal law, as well as the right to appeal for pardon or a reduction of sentence.

Article 51

(1) No one is obliged to testify against himself or against his spouse or close relatives, the range of the latter being defined by federal law.
(2) Other instances when the obligation to give evidence is lifted can be laid down by federal law.

Article 52

The rights of the victims of crimes or of abuses of power are protected by law. The state guarantees the victims's access to justice and to compensation for damage caused.

Article 53

Each person has the right to compensation from the state for damage caused by the unlawful action (or inaction) of bodies of state power or their officials.

Article 54

(1) No law establishing or mitigating liability can be retroactive.
(2) No one can be held liable for any act which, at the time it was committed, was not considered to be in breach of the law. If liability for a breach of the law is abolished or mitigated after an act has been committed, the new law is applied.

Article 55

(1) The listing of basic rights and freedoms in the constitution of the Russian Federation must not be interpreted as negating or diminishing other universally recognized human and civil rights and freedoms.
(2) Laws abolishing or diminishing human and civil rights and freedoms must not be promulgated in the Russian Federation.
(3) Human and civil rights and freedoms can be curtailed by federal law only to the extent to which it may be necessary for the purpose of protecting the foundations of the constitutional system, morality and the health, rights and legitimate interests of other individuals, or of ensuring the country's defence and the state's security.

Article 56

(1) Individual restrictions of rights and freedoms can be introduced, with an indication of their extent and duration, in a state of emergency in order to ensure the safety of citizens and the protection of the constitutional system in accordance with federal constitutional law.

(2)   A state of emergency may be introduced throughout the territory of the Russian Federation or in individual localities thereof in the circumstances and according to the procedure provided by federal constitutional law.

(3)   The rights and freedoms contained in Articles 20, 21, 23 (Part 1), 24, 28, 34 (Part 1), 40 (Part 1) and 46–54 of the constitution of the Russian Federation may not be restricted.

Article 57

Each person is obliged to pay legitimately levied taxes and duties. Laws introducing new taxes or detrimental to the taxpayers' situation cannot be retroactive.

Article 58

Each person is obliged to protect nature and the environment and to show solicitude for natural wealth.

Article 59

(1)   The protection of the fatherland is the duty and obligation of citizens of the Russian Federation.

(2)   Citizens of the Russian Federation perform military service as provided by federal law.

(3)   In the event that the convictions or religious beliefs of a citizen of the Russian Federation are at odds with the performance of military service, as well as in other instances as provided by federal law, the citizen has the right to perform alternative civil service as a substitute.

Article 60

A citizen of the Russian Federation can autonomously exercise his rights and obligations in full from the age of 18 years.

Article 61

(1)   A citizen of the Russian Federation cannot be expelled from the Russian Federation or extradited to another state.

(2)   The Russian Federation guarantees the protection and patronage of its citizens outside its borders.

Article 62

(1)   A citizen of the Russian Federation can hold citizenship of a foreign state (dual citizenship) as provided by federal law or an international treaty of the Russian Federation.

(2)   The fact that a citizen of the Russian Federation holds citizenship of a foreign state does not diminish his rights and freedoms or exempt him from obligations stemming from

Russian citizenship, unless otherwise provided by federal law or an international treaty of the Russian Federation.

(3) Foreign citizens and stateless persons in the Russian Federation enjoy equal rights and bear equal obligations with citizens of the Russian Federation, except when otherwise provided by federal law or an international treaty of the Russian Federation.

Article 63

(1) The Russian Federation offers political asylum to foreign citizens and stateless persons in accordance with universally recognized norms of international law.

(2) The Russian Federation does not permit the extradition to other states of persons persecuted for their political beliefs or for actions (or inactions) which are not considered a crime in the Russian Federation. The extradition of persons accused of having committed a crime, or the extradition of sentenced persons to serve their sentence in other states, is performed on the basis of federal law or an international treaty of the Russian Federation.

Article 64

The provisions of this chapter comprise the foundations of the individual's legal status in the Russian Federation and cannot be amended except by the procedure established by the present constitution.

Chapter 3 Federative Structure

Article 65

(1) The Russian Federation is made up of the following components:
the Republic of Adygeya (Adygea); the Republic of Altai; the Republic of Bashkortostan; the Republic of Buryatia; the Republic of Dagestan; the Ingush Republic; the Kabardino-Balkar Republic; the Republic of Kalmykia–Khalmg Tangch; the Karachai-Cherkess Republic; the Republic of Karelia; the Republic of Komi; the Republic of Marii El; the Republic of Mordovia; the Republic of Sakha (Yakutia); the Republic of North Ossetia; the Republic of Tatarstan (Tatarstan); the Republic of Tyva; the Udmurt Republic; the Republic of Khakassia; the Chechen Republic; the Chuvash Republic–Chavash Republic.
Altai Krai; Krasnodar Krai; Krasnoyarsk Krai; Maritime Krai; Stavropol Krai; Khabarovsk Krai.
Amur Oblast; Arkhangel Oblast; Astrakhan Oblast; Belgorod Oblast; Bryansk Oblast; Vladimir Oblast; Volgograd Oblast; Vologda Oblast; Voronezh Oblast; Ivanovo Oblast; Irkutsk Oblast; Kaliningrad Oblast; Kaluga Oblast; Kamchatka Oblast; Kemerovo Oblast; Kirov Oblast; Kostromo Oblast; Kurgan Oblast; Kursk Oblast; Leningrad Oblast; Lipetsk Oblast; Magadan Oblast; Moscow Oblast; Murmansk Oblast; Nizhniy Novgorod Oblast; Novgorod Oblast; Novosibirsk Oblast; Omsk Oblast; Orenburg Oblast; Orel Oblast; Penza Oblast; Perm Oblast; Pskov Oblast; Rostov Oblast; Ryazan Oblast; Samara Oblast; Saratov Oblast; Sakhalin Oblast; Sverdlovsk Oblast; Smolensk Oblast; Tambov Oblast;

Tvear Oblast; Tomsk Oblast; Tula Oblast; Tyumen Oblast; Ulyanovsk Oblast; Chelyabinsk Oblast; Chita Oblast; Yaroslavl Oblast.

Moscow, St Petersburg – cities of federal significance.

The Jewish Autonomous Oblast.

The Aga Buryat Autonomous Okrug; the Komi-Permyak Autonomous Okrug; the
Koryak Autonomous Okrug; the Nenets Autonomous Okrug; the Taimyr (Dolgan-
Nenets) Autonomous Okrug; the Ust-Orda Buryat Autonomous Okrug; the Khanty-
Mansi Autonomous Okrug; the Chukchi Autonomous Okrug; the Evenk Autonomous
Okrug; the Yamal-Nenetsk Autonomous Okrug.

(2)   The admission to the Russian Federation and the formation as part of the Russian
Federation of a new component is carried out according to the procedure laid down by
Federal constitutional law.

Article 66

(1)   The status of a republic is determined by the constitution of the Russian Federation and
by the constitution of the republic.

(2)   The status of a krai, oblast, city of federal significance, autonomous oblast and
autonomous okrug is determined by the constitution of the Russian Federation and the
charter of the krai, oblast, city of federal significance, autonomous oblast and autonomous okrug adopted by the legislative (representative) body of the relevant component
of the Russian Federation.

(3)   A federal law on the autonomous oblast or an autonomous okrug can be adopted upon
submission by the legislative and executive bodies of the autonomous oblast or
autonomous okrug.

(4)   The relations of autonomous okrug forming part of a krai or oblast can be regulated by
a federal law and treaty between the bodies of state power of an autonomous okrug and,
accordingly, by the bodies of state power of a krai or oblast.

(5)   The status of a component of the Russian Federation can be changed by the mutual
consent of the Russian Federation and the component of the Russian Federation in
accordance with federal constitutional law.

Article 67

(1)   The territory of the Russian Federation includes the territories of its components, inland
stretches of water and territorial waters and the airspace over these.

(2)   The Russian Federation possesses sovereign rights and exercises jurisdiction over the
continental shelf and within the exclusive economic zone of the Russian Federation in
accordance with the procedure defined by federal law and the norms of international law.

(3)   The borders between components of the Russian Federation can be amended by their
mutual consent.

Article 68

(1)   The Russian language is the state language of the Russian Federation throughout its
territory.

(2)   Republics are entitled to establish their own state languages. They are used alongside the state language of the Russian Federation in the bodies of state power, bodies of local self-government and state institutions of the republics.

(3)   The Russian Federation guarantees all its peoples the right to retain their mother tongue and to create conditions for its study and development.

Article 69

The Russian Federation guarantees the rights of numerically small indigenous peoples in accordance with the generally recognized principles and norms of international law and the international treaties of the Russian Federation.

Article 70

(1)   The state flag, emblem and anthem of the Russian Federation, the description of these, and the procedure for their official use are established by federal constitutional law.

(2)   The capital of the Russian Federation is the city of Moscow. The status of the capital is established by federal law.

Article 71

The following fall within the jurisdiction of the Russian Federation:

(a)   the adoption and amendment of the constitution of the Russian Federation and federal laws, and the monitoring of compliance with them;

(b)   the federative system and territory of the Russian Federation;

(c)   the regulation and protection of human and civil rights and freedoms; citizenship of the Russian Federation; the regulation and protection of the rights of national minorities;

(d)   the establishment of a system of federal bodies of legislative, executive and judicial power, the procedure for their organization and activity; the formation of federal bodies of state power;

(e)   federal state property and the management thereof;

(f)   the establishment of the fundamentals of federal policy and federal programmes in the sphere of state, economic, ecological, social, cultural and national development of the Russian Federation;

(g)   the establishment of the legal foundations of the single market; financial, currency, credit and customs regulation, monetary emission and the foundations of pricing policy; federal economic services, including federal banks;

(h)   the federal budget; federal taxes and duties; federal regional development funds;

(i)   federal power systems, nuclear power generation, fissile materials; federal transport, railways, information and communications; activity in space;

(j)   the Russian Federation's foreign policy and international relations and the Russian Federation's international treaties; issues of war and peace;

(k)   the Russian Federation's foreign economic relations;

(l)   defence and security; defence production; the determination of the procedure for the sale and purchase of weapons, ammunition, military hardware and other military property; the production of toxic substances, narcotic substances and the procedure for their use;

(m) the determination of the status and protection of the state border, territorial seas, airspace, the exclusive economic zone and the continental shelf of the Russian Federation;

(n) the judicial system; the procurator's office; legislation in the field of criminal, criminal-procedure and criminal-executive law; amnesty and the granting of pardons; legislation in the field of civil law, the law of civil procedure and the law of arbitration procedure; the legal regulation of intellectual property;

(o) federal law relating to the conflict of laws;

(p) the meteorological service, standards and standard weights and measurements, the metric system and measurement of time; geodesy and cartography; geographic names; official statistical records and accounting;

(q) state awards and honorary titles of the Russian Federation;

(r) the federal civil service.

Article 72

(1) The following fall within the joint jurisdiction of the Russian Federation and the components of the Russian Federation:

(a) the guaranteeing that the constitutions and laws of republics, and the charters, laws and other normative legal acts of krais, oblasts, cities of federal significance, the autonomous oblast and autonomous okrugs accord with the constitution of the Russian Federation and federal laws;

(b) the protection of human and civil rights and freedoms; the protection of the rights of national minorities; the guaranteeing of legality, law and order and public safety; the arrangements relating to border zones;

(c) issues relating to the ownership, use and disposal of land, mineral resources, water and other natural resources;

(d) the delimitation of state property;

(e) the use of the natural environment; environmental protection and the guaranteeing of ecological safety; natural sites under special protection; the protection of historical and cultural monuments;

(f) general issues of nurture, education, science, culture, physical fitness and sport;

(g) the coordination of questions of public health; the protection of the family, mothers, fathers and children; social protection, including social security;

(h) the implementation of measures for combating catastrophes, natural disasters and epidemics and the elimination of their consequences;

(i) the establishment of general principles of taxation and levying of duties in the Russian Federation;

(j) administrative, administrative-procedural, labour, family, housing, land, water and forestry legislation, and legislation on mineral resources and on environmental protection;

(k) personnel of judicial and law-enforcement bodies; attorneys and notaries;

(l)   the protection of the primordial habitat and traditional way of life of numerically small ethnic communities;

(m)   the establishment of the general principles for the organization of a system of bodies of state power and local self-government;

(n)   the coordination of the international and foreign economic relations of components of the Russian Federation and the fulfilment of the Russian Federation's international treaties.

(2)   The provisions of this article apply in equal measure to the republics, krais, oblasts, cities of federal significance, the autonomous oblast and autonomous okrugs.

Article 73

Outside the compass of the Russian Federation's jurisdiction and the powers of the Russian Federation as regards the terms of reference of the joint jurisdiction of the Russian Federation and the components of the Russian Federation, the components of the Russian Federation possess state power in its entirety.

Article 74

(1)   The establishment of customs borders, duties, levies, and any other hindrances to the free movement of goods, services, and financial assets is not permitted on the territory of the Russian Federation.

(2)   Restrictions on the movement of goods and services can be introduced in accordance with federal law if this is essential for ensuring safety, the protection of the life and health of people, and the protection of nature and cultural assets.

Article 75

(1)   The monetary unit in the Russian Federation is the rouble. Monetary emission is carried out exclusively by the Central Bank of the Russian Federation. The introduction and emission of other currencies is not permitted in the Russian Federation.

(2)   The protection and the guaranteeing of the stability of the rouble is the basic function of the Central Bank of the Russian Federation which it carries out independently of the other bodies of state power.

(3)   The system of taxes levied for the federal budget and the general principles of taxation and levies in the Russian Federation are established by federal law.

(4)   State loans are issued according to a procedure determined by federal law and are floated on a voluntary basis.

Article 76

(1)   Federal constitutional laws and federal laws which operate directly throughout the territory of the Russian Federation are adopted with regard to the Russian Federation's areas of responsibility.

(2)   Federal laws, and the laws and other normative legal enactments of the components of the Russian Federation adopted in accordance with the aforesaid federal laws, are

promulgated with regard to the areas of joint responsibility of the Russian Federation and components of the Russian Federation.

(3)   Federal laws cannot conflict with federal constitutional laws.

(4)   Outside the compass of the Russian Federation's jurisdiction and the joint jurisdiction of the Russian Federation and the components of the Russian Federation, the republics, krais, oblasts, cities of federal significance, the autonomous oblast and the autonomous okrugs exercise their own legal regulation, including the adoption of laws and other normative legal enactments.

(5)   The laws and other normative legal enactments of the components of the Russian Federation cannot conflict with federal laws adopted in accordance with the first and second parts of this article. In the event of conflicts between the federal law and another enactment promulgated in the Russian Federation, the federal law is to obtain.

(6)   In the event of conflict between the federal law and a normative legal enactment of a component of the Russian Federation promulgated in accordance with the fourth part of this article, the normative legal enactment of the component of the Russian Federation obtains.

Article 77

(1)   The system of bodies of state power of the republics, krais, oblasts, cities of federal significance, the autonomous oblast and autonomous okrugs is established by the components of the Russian Federation independently in accordance with the fundamentals of the constitutional system of the Russian Federation and the general principles of the organization of representative and executive bodies of state power established by federal law.

(2)   Within the areas of responsibility of the Russian Federation and the powers of the Russian Federation as regards the terms of reference of the joint jurisdiction of the Russian Federation and the components of the Russian Federation, the federal bodies of executive power and the bodies of executive power of the components of the Russian Federation form a unified system of executive power in the Russian Federation.

Article 78

(1)   In order to exercise their powers, the federal bodies of executive power can create their own territorial bodies and appoint the relevant officials.

(2)   The federal bodies of executive power, by agreement with the bodies of executive power of the components of the Russian Federation can transfer to them the implementation of some of their powers provided that this does not conflict with the constitution of the Russian Federation and federal laws.

(3)   By agreement with the federal bodies of executive power the bodies of executive power of the components of the Russian Federation can transfer to them the implementation of some of their powers.

(4)   The president of the Russian Federation and the government of the Russian Federation ensure in accordance with the constitution of the Russian Federation, the exercise of the powers of federal state authority throughout the territory of the Russian Federation.

Article 79

The Russian Federation can participate in inter-state associations and hand over to them part of its powers in accordance with international treaties unless this entails the restriction of human and civil rights and freedoms and unless it conflicts with the fundamentals of the constitutional system of the Russian Federation.

Chapter 4 President of the Russian Federation

Article 80

(1)   The president of the Russian Federation is the head of state.
(2)   The president of the Russian Federation is the guarantor of the constitution of the Russian Federation and of human and civil rights and freedoms. Within the procedure established by the constitution of the Russian Federation, he adopts measures to safeguard the sovereignty of the Russian Federation and its independence and state integrity and ensures the coordinated functioning and collaboration of bodies of state power.
(3)   The president of the Russian Federation, in compliance with the constitution of the Russian Federation and the federal laws, determines the basic guidelines of the state's domestic and foreign policy.
(4)   The president of the Russian Federation, in his capacity as head of state, represents the Russian Federation within the country and in international relations.

Article 81

(1)   The president of the Russian Federation is elected for four years by citizens of the Russian Federation on the basis of universal, equal and direct suffrage in a secret ballot.
(2)   A citizen of the Russian Federation who is at least 35 years of age and has been permanently resident in the Russian Federation for at least 10 years can be elected president of the Russian Federation.
(3)   One and the same person cannot hold the office of president of the Russian Federation for more than two consecutive terms.
(4)   The procedure of elections for president of the Russian federation is established by federal law.

Article 82

(1)   At his inauguration the president of the Russian Federation swears the following oath to the people:

In exercising the powers of president of the Russian Federation I swear to respect and protect human and civil rights and freedoms, to observe and defend the constitution of the Russian Federation, to defend the state's sovereignty and independence and its security and integrity, and faithfully to serve the people.

(2)   The oath is administered in a ceremonial atmosphere in the presence of members of the Federation Council, deputies of the State Duma and justices of the Constitutional Court of the Russian Federation.

Article 83

The president of the Russian Federation:
  (a) appoints with the consent of the State Duma the head of the government of the Russian Federation;
  (b) has the right to chair sessions of the government of the Russian Federation;
  (c) adopts the decision on the dismissal of the government of the Russian Federation;
  (d) submits to the State Duma the candidate for appointment to the office of director of the Central Bank of the Russian Federation; raises before the State Duma the question of removing from office the director of the Central Bank of the Russian Federation;
  (e) at the proposal of the head of the government of the Russian Federation appoints and removes from office the deputy prime ministers of the government of the Russian Federation and federal ministers;
  (f) submits to the Federation Council candidates for appointment to the office of justices of the Constitutional Court of the Russian Federation, Supreme Court of the Russian Federation and Superior Court of Arbitration of the Russian Federation and also the candidate for general prosecutor of the Russian Federation; submits to the Federation Council the proposal on removing from office the procurator-general of the Russian Federation; appoints justices in other federal courts.
  (g) forms and heads the Security Council of the Russian Federation, whose status is defined by federal law;
  (h) approves the military doctrine of the Russian Federation;
  (i) forms the administration of the president of the Russian Federation;
  (j) appoints and removes plenipotentiary representatives of the president of the Russian Federation;
  (k) appoints and removes the high command of the Armed Forces of the Russian Federation;
  (l) appoints and recalls, following consultations with the relevant committees or commissions of the chambers of the Federal Assembly, diplomatic representatives of the Russian Federation in foreign states and international organizations.

Article 84

The president of the Russian Federation:
  (a) schedules elections to the State Duma in accordance with the constitution of the Russian Federation and federal law;
  (b) dissolves the State Duma in instances and according to the procedure laid down by the constitution of the Russian Federation;
  (c) schedules referendums according to the procedure prescribed by federal constitutional law;
  (d) submits draft laws to the State Duma;
  (e) signs and promulgates federal laws;
  (f) delivers to the Federal Assembly annual messages on the state of the nation and on the basic guidelines of the state's domestic and foreign policy.

Article 85

(1)   The president of the Russian Federation may use conciliation procedures to resolve disagreements between bodies of state power of the Russian Federation and bodies of state power of components of the Russian Federation, and also between bodies of state power of components of the Russian Federation. In the event of failure to reach an agreed solution he may refer the resolution of the dispute for examination by the appropriate court.

(2)   Pending a resolution of the matter by the appropriate court, the president of the Russian Federation is entitled to suspend the operation of enactments by bodies of executive power of components of the Russian Federation if these enactments contravene the constitution of the Russian Federation and federal laws or the Russian Federation's international commitments or violate human and civil rights and freedoms.

Article 86

The president of the Russian Federation:
(a)   exercises leadership of the foreign policy of the Russian Federation;
(b)   conducts talks and signs international treaties of the Russian Federation;
(c)   signs instruments of ratification;
(d)   accepts the credentials and letters of recall of diplomatic representatives accredited to him.

Article 87

(1)   The president of the Russian Federation is the supreme commander-in-chief of the Armed Forces of the Russian Federation.

(2)   In the event of aggression against the Russian Federation or a direct threat of aggression the president of the Russian Federation introduces martial law on the territory of the Russian Federation or in individual localities of that territory and immediately notifies the Federation Council and State Duma of this.

(3)   The regime of martial law is defined by federal constitutional law.

Article 88

In the circumstances and according to the procedure laid down by federal constitutional law, the president of the Russian Federation introduces on the territory of the Russian Federation or in individual localities of that territory a state of emergency and immediately notifies the Federation Council and State Duma of this.

Article 89

The president of the Russian Federation:
(a)   decides questions of citizenship of the Russian Federation and of granting political asylum;
(b)   confers state awards of the Russian Federation and awards honorary titles of the Russian Federation and higher military and higher special ranks;
(c)   grants pardons.

Article 90

(1)   The president of the Russian Federation issues decrees and directives.
(2)   Implementation of the decrees and directives of the president of the Russian Federation is mandatory throughout the territory of the Russian Federation.
(3)   The decrees and directives of the president of the Russian Federation must not contravene the constitution of the Russian Federation and federal laws.

Article 91

The president of the Russian Federation enjoys immunity.

Article 92

(1)   The president of the Russian Federation begins exercising his powers from the moment he swears the oath and ceases exercising them upon the expiry of his term of office from the moment that the newly elected president of the Russian Federation swears the oath.
(2)   The president of the Russian Federation ceases the exercise of his powers early in the event of his resignation, persistent inability to exercise his powers for health reasons, or removal from office. Furthermore, the election of the president of the Russian Federation must take place no later than three months after the early cessation of the exercise of powers.
(3)   In all instances where the president of the Russian Federation is unable to perform his duties, they are temporarily carried out by the head of the government of the Russian Federation. The acting president of the Russian Federation does not have the right to dissolve the State Duma, schedule a referendum or submit proposals on amendments to and the revision of provisions of the constitution of the Russian Federation.

Article 93

(1)   The president of the Russian Federation can be removed from office by the Federation Council only on the basis of a charge of treason or commission of some other grave crime, filed by the State Duma and confirmed by a ruling of the Supreme Court of the Russian Federation that the actions of the president of the Russian Federation contain the elements of crime and a ruling by the Constitutional Court of the Russian Federation that the established procedure for filing the charge has been observed.
(2)   The decision by the State Duma on filing the charge and the decision by the Federation Council on removing the president from office must be adopted by a vote of two-thirds of the total membership of each chamber on the initiative of at least one-third of the deputies of the State Duma and provided there is a ruling by a special commission formed by the State Duma.
(3)   The decision by the Federation Council on removing the president of the Russian Federation from office must be adopted no later than three months following the filing of the charge against the president by the State Duma. If the decision by the Federation Council is not adopted within this period of time, the charge against the president is deemed rejected.

Chapter 5 Federal Assembly

Article 94

The Federal Assembly-parliament of the Russian Federation is the representative and legislative organ of the Russian Federation.

Article 95

(1)   The Federal Assembly consists of two chambers – the Federation Council and the State Duma.
(2)   The Federation Council consists of two representatives from each component of the Russian Federation; one each from the representative and executive bodies of state power.
(3)   The State Duma consists of 450 deputies.

Article 96

(1)   The State Duma is elected for a term of four years.
(2)   The procedure for forming the Federation Council and the procedure for electing deputies of the State Duma are established by federal laws.

Article 97

(1)   A citizen of the Russian Federation who has attained the age of 21 years and has the right to participate in elections can be elected a deputy of the State Duma.
(2)   One and the same person cannot simultaneously be a member of the Federation Council and a deputy of the State Duma. A deputy of the State Duma cannot be a deputy of any other representative bodies of state power or bodies of local self-government.
(3)   Deputies of the State Duma work on a full-time professional basis. Deputies of the State Duma cannot be in state service or engage in any other paid activity, apart from teaching, scientific or other creative activity.

Article 98

(1)   Members of the Federation Council and deputies of the State Duma enjoy immunity for the duration of their term of office. They cannot be detained, arrested or searched unless detained at the scene of a crime, nor can they be subjected to a body search except as provided by federal law in order to guarantee other people's safety.
(2)   Any question concerning the lifting of immunity is decided by the appropriate chamber of the Federal Assembly upon submission by the procurator-general of the Russian Federation.

Article 99

(1)   The Federal Assembly is a permanently functioning body.
(2)   The State Duma meets for its first session on the thirtieth day after its election. The

president of the Russian Federation can convene a sitting of the State Duma prior to this date.

(3)   The first session of the State Duma is opened by the oldest deputy.

(4)   From the moment that the work of a newly elected State Duma begins, the powers of the previous State Duma are terminated.

Article 100

(1)   The Federation Council and the State Duma sit separately.

(2)   Sessions of the Federation Council and the State Duma are open. In instances stipulated by the standing orders of a chamber it is entitled to conduct closed sessions.

(3)   Chambers may convene jointly to hear messages from the president of the Russian Federation, messages from the Constitutional Court of the Russian Federation and speeches by the leaders of foreign states.

Article 101

(1)   The Federation Council elects from its membership the chair of the Federation Council and his/her deputies. The State Duma elects from its members the chair of the State Duma and his/her deputies.

(2)   The chair of the Federation Council and his/her deputies, and the chair of the State Duma and his/her deputies, chair sessions and control the internal procedures of the chamber.

(3)   The Federation Council and the State Duma form committees and commissions and conduct parliamentary hearings into matters under their jurisdiction.

(4)   Each of the chambers adopts its own standing orders and decides matters relating to the internal procedure governing its activity.

(5)   In order to monitor the implementation of the federal budget the Federation Council and the State Duma form a comptrollers office whose composition and work procedures are determined by federal law.

Article 102

(1)   The jurisdiction of the Federation Council includes:
   (a)   confirming alterations to borders between components of the Russian Federation;
   (b)   confirming a decree of the president of the Russian Federation on the introduction of martial law;
   (c)   confirming a decree of the president of the Russian Federation on the introduction of a state of emergency;
   (d)   deciding the question of the possibility of the utilization of Russian Federation Armed Forces outside the borders of the territory of the Russian Federation;
   (e)   scheduling elections for the president of the Russian Federation;
   (f)   removing the president of the Russian Federation from office;
   (g)   appointing justices of the Constitutional Court of the Russian Federation, the Supreme Court of the Russian Federation and the Superior Court of Arbitration of the Russian Federation;

(h) appointing and removing from office the procurator-general of the Russian Federation;

(i) appointing and removing from office the deputy head of the comptrollers office and half of its staff of auditors.

(2) The Federation Council adopts decrees on matters designated as its area of responsibility by the constitution of the Russian Federation.

(3) Decrees of the Federation Council are adopted by a majority of the votes of the total number of Federation Council members unless some other procedure for adopting a decision is stipulated by the constitution of the Russian Federation.

Article 103

(1) The jurisdiction of the State Duma includes:

(a) giving consent to the president of the Russian Federation for the appointment of the head of the government of the Russian Federation;

(b) deciding a motion of confidence in the government of the Russian Federation;

(c) appointing and removing from office the head of the Central Bank of the Russian Federation;

(d) appointing and removing from office the head of the comptrollers office and half of its staff of auditors;

(e) appointing and removing from office the commissioner for human rights, who operates in accordance with federal constitutional law;

(f) declaring an amnesty;

(g) filing a charge against the president of the Russian Federation to remove him from office.

(2) The State Duma adopts decrees on matters designated as its area of responsibility by the constitution of the Russian Federation.

(3) Decrees of the State Duma are adopted by a majority of the votes of the total number of deputies of the State Duma unless some other procedure for adopting a decision is stipulated by the constitution of the Russian Federation.

Article 104

(1) The right of legislative initiative is vested in the president of the Russian Federation, the Federation Council, members of the Federation Council, deputies of the State Duma, the government of the Russian Federation and legislative (representative) bodies of components of the Russian Federation. The right of legislative initiative is also vested in the Constitutional Court of the Russian Federation, the Supreme Court of the Russian Federation and the Superior Court of Arbitration of the Russian Federation in matters under their jurisdiction.

(2) Draft laws are submitted to the State Duma.

(3) Draft laws on the introduction or abolition of taxes, exemption from the payment of taxes, the floating of state loans, the alteration of the financial obligations of the state and other draft laws envisaging expenditure funded out of the state budget can be submitted only when the government's findings are known.

Article 105

(1)   Federal laws are adopted by the State Duma.
(2)   Federal laws are adopted by a majority of the votes of the total number of deputies of the State Duma unless otherwise stipulated by the constitution of the Russian Federation.
(3)   Federal laws adopted by the State Duma are passed to the Federation Council within five days for examination.
(4)   A federal law is deemed to have been approved by the Federation Council if more than half of the total number of members of this chamber have voted for it or if it has not been examined by the Federation Council within fourteen days. In the event of the rejection of a federal law by the Federation Council the chambers may form a conciliation commission to overcome differences which have arisen, after which the federal law is subject to repeat examination by the State Duma.
(5)   In the event of disagreement by the State Duma with a decision of the Federation Council, a federal law is deemed to have been adopted if at least two-thirds of the total number of deputies of the State Duma vote for it in a repeat vote.

Article 106

Federal laws adopted by the State Duma are subject to compulsory examination in the Federation Council when they concern questions of:
(a)   the federal budget
(b)   federal taxes and levies;
(c)   financial, foreign currency, credit and customs regulation and money emission;
(d)   the ratification and denunciation of international treaties of the Russian Federation;
(e)   the status and protection of the state border of the Russian Federation;
(f)   war and peace.

Article 107

(1)   A federal law that has been adopted is submitted within five days to the president of the Russian Federation for signing and promulgation.
(2)   The president of the Russian Federation signs and promulgates the federal law within 14 days.
(3)   If the president of the Russian Federation, within fourteen days of receiving the federal law, rejects it, the State Duma and the Federation Council re-examine the said law in accordance with the procedure laid down by the constitution of the Russian Federation. If, after repeat examination, the federal law is approved by a majority of the votes of at least two-thirds of the total number of members of the Federation Council and deputies of the State Duma in the wording previously adopted, it is to be signed by the president of the Russian Federation within seven days and promulgated.

Article 108

(1)   Federal constitutional laws are adopted on matters stipulated by the constitution of the Russian Federation.

(2)   A federal constitutional law is deemed to be adopted if it is approved by a majority of the votes of at least three-quarters of the total number of members of the Federation Council and at least two-thirds of the total number of deputies of the State Duma. A federal constitutional law that has been adopted is to be signed by the president of the Russian Federation and promulgated within fourteen days.

Article 109

(1)   The State Duma may be dissolved by the president of the Russian Federation in the circumstances stipulated in Articles 111 and 117 of the constitution of the Russian Federation.
(2)   In the event of the dissolution of the State Duma, the president of the Russian Federation sets the date of elections so as to ensure that the newly elected State Duma is convened not later than four months from the date of dissolution.
(3)   The State Duma may not be dissolved on the grounds stipulated in Article 117 of the constitution of the Russian Federation for one year following its election.
(4)   The State Duma may not be dissolved from the moment it files a charge against the president of the Russian Federation, until the adoption of a corresponding decision by the Federation Council.
(5)   The State Duma may not be dissolved during the period of operation of a state of martial law or state of emergency on the whole territory of the Russian Federation, or within the six months preceding the expiry of the term of office of the president of the Russian Federation.

Chapter 6 Government of the Russian Federation

Article 110

(1)   Executive power in the Russian Federation is exercised by the government of the Russian Federation.
(2)   The government of the Russian Federation consists of the head of the government of the Russian Federation, the deputy prime ministers of the government of the Russian Federation and the federal ministers.

Article 111

(1)   The head of the government of the Russian Federation is appointed by the president of the Russian Federation with the consent of the State Duma.
(2)   A proposal on the candidacy for the head of the government of the Russian Federation is submitted no later than two weeks following the entry into office of a newly elected president of the Russian Federation or the resignation of the government of the Russian Federation or within a week following the rejection of a candidacy by the state Duma.
(3)   The State Duma examines the candidacy for the head of the government of the Russian Federation submitted by the president of the Russian Federation within a week of the day the candidacy proposal is submitted.
(4)   Following three rejections by the State Duma of candidacies submitted for the head of

the government of the Russian Federation, the president of the Russian Federation appoints a head of the government of the Russian Federation, dissolves the State Duma and schedules new elections.

Article 112

(1) The head of the government of the Russian Federation, no later than one week following his appointment, submits to the president of the Russian Federation proposals on the structure of the federal bodies of executive power.
(2) The head of the government of the Russian Federation proposes to the president of the Russian Federation candidacies for the posts of deputy prime ministers of the government of the Russian Federation and federal ministers.

Article 113

The head of the government of the Russian Federation, in accordance with the constitution of the Russian Federation, federal laws and decrees of the president of the Russian Federation, defines the basic guidelines for the activity of the government of the Russian Federation and organizes its work.

Article 114

(1) The government of the Russian Federation:
    (a) drafts the federal budget, submits it to the State Duma and ensures its implementation; submits to the State Duma a report on the implementation of the federal budget;
    (b) ensures the implementation of a single fiscal, credit and monetary policy in the Russian Federation;
    (c) ensures the implementation of a single state policy in the Russian Federation in the sphere of culture, science, education, health, social security and ecology;
    (d) administers federal property;
    (e) implements measures to ensure the defence of the country, state security and the realization of the foreign policy of the Russian Federation;
    (f) implements measures to ensure the rule of law, civil rights and freedoms, the protection of property and public order, and the struggle against crime;
    (g) exercises other powers vested in it by the constitution of the Russian Federation, federal laws and decrees of the president of the Russian Federation.
(2) The procedure for the activity of the government of the Russian Federation is defined by federal constitutional law.

Article 115

(1) On the basis of and in implementation of the constitution of the Russian Federation, federal laws and normative decrees of the president of the Russian Federation, the government of the Russian Federation issues decrees and directives and ensures their implementation.

(2)   Decrees and directives of the government of the Russian Federation are mandatory in the Russian Federation.

(3)   Decrees and directives of the government of Russian Federation, in the event that they are at variance with the constitution of the Russian Federation, federal laws or decrees of the president of the Russian Federation, may be rescinded by the president of the Russian Federation.

Article 116

The government of the Russian Federation surrenders its powers to a newly elected president of the Russian Federation.

Article 117

(1)   The government of the Russian Federation may offer its resignation, which is accepted or rejected by the president of the Russian Federation.

(2)   The president of the Russian Federation may adopt a decision on the dismissal of the government of the Russian Federation.

(3)   The State Duma may express no confidence in the government of the Russian Federation. A decree of no confidence in the government of the Russian Federation is adopted by a majority of votes of the total number of deputies of the State Duma. Following an expression of no confidence by the State Duma in the government of the Russian Federation, the president of the Russian Federation is entitled to announce the dismissal of the government of the Russian Federation or to disagree with the decision of the State Duma. In the event that the State Duma expresses no confidence in the government of the Russian Federation for a second time within three months, the president of the Russian Federation announces the dismissal of the government or dissolves the State Duma.

(4)   The head of the government of the Russian Federation may submit to the State Duma a motion of confidence in the government of the Russian Federation. If the State Duma refuses its confidence, the president adopts a decision within seven days on the dismissal of the government of the Russian Federation or on the dissolution of the State Duma and the holding of new elections.

(5)   In the event of its resignation or the surrender of its powers, the government of the Russian Federation, on the instructions of the president of the Russian Federation, continues to act until the formation of the new government of the Russian Federation.

Chapter 7 Judicial Branch

Article 118

(1)   Justice in the Russian Federation is exercised only by the court.

(2)   Judicial power is exercised by means of constitutional, civil, administrative and criminal court proceedings.

(3)   The judicial system of the Russian Federation is established by the constitution of the Russian Federation and by federal constitutional law. The creation of emergency courts is not permitted.

Article 119

Citizens of the Russian Federation who have attained the age of 25 and have higher legal education and at least five years' experience in the legal profession may be judges. Additional requirements for judges in the courts of the Russian Federation may be imposed by federal law.

Article 120

(1)   Judges are independent and are subordinate only to the constitution of the Russian Federation and to federal law.
(2)   The court, having determined in the course of examining a case that an enactment of a state organ or other organ is not in accordance with the law, adopts a ruling in accordance with the law.

Article 121

(1)   Judges may not be removed.
(2)   A judge's powers may not be terminated or suspended except in accordance with the procedure and on the grounds laid down by federal law.

Article 122

(1)   Judges enjoy immunity.
(2)   A judge may not be subjected to criminal proceedings except in accordance with the procedure defined by federal law.

Article 123

(1)   The examination of cases in all courts is open. Hearing a case in closed session is permitted in circumstances stipulated in federal law.
(2)   The *in absentia* examination of criminal cases in the courts is not permitted, except in circumstances stipulated in federal law.
(3)   Court proceedings are carried out on the basis of the adversarial system and the equal rights of the parties.
(4)   In circumstances stipulated in federal law, court proceedings take place with the participation of jurors.

Article 124

The financing of courts is effected solely from the federal budget and must ensure the possibility of the complete and independent exercise of justice in accordance with federal law.

Article 125

(1)   The Constitutional Court of the Russian Federation consists of nineteen judges.
(2)   The Constitutional Court of the Russian Federation, on the application of the president

of the Russian Federation, the Federation Council, the State Duma, one-fifth of the members of the Federation Council or deputies of the State Duma, the government of the Russian Federation, the Supreme Court of the Russian Federation or the Superior Court of Arbitration of the Russian Federation, or bodies of legislative and executive power of the components of the Russian Federation, resolves cases relating to the compliance with the constitution of the Russian Federation of:

(a) federal laws and normative enactments of the president of the Russian Federation, the Federation Council, the State Duma or the government of the Russian Federation;

(b) the constitutions of republics and the charters of components of the Russian Federation and laws and other normative acts issued by them on matters falling within the jurisdiction of bodies of state power of the Russian Federation or the joint jurisdiction of bodies of state power of the Russian Federation and bodies of state power of components of the Russian Federation;

(c) treaties between bodies of state power of the Russian Federation and bodies of state power of components of the Russian Federation and treaties between bodies of state power of components of the Russian Federation;

(d) international treaties of the Russian Federation that have not entered into force.

(3) The Constitutional Court of the Russian Federation resolves disputes over areas of jurisdiction:

(a) between federal bodies of state power;

(b) between bodies of state power of the Russian Federation and bodies of state power of components of the Russian Federation;

(c) between the highest state bodies of components of the Russian Federation.

(4) The Constitutional Court of the Russian Federation, on the basis of complaints regarding the violation of citizens' constitutional rights and freedoms and at the request of judges, examines the constitutionality of the law that has been applied or is applicable in the specific case, in accordance with the procedure laid down by federal law.

(5) The Constitutional Court of the Russian Federation, on the application of the president of the Russian Federation, the Federation Council, the State Duma, the government of the Russian Federation or the bodies of legislative power of components of the Russian Federation, provides an interpretation of the constitution of the Russian Federation.

(6) Enactments or individual clauses that are deemed unconstitutional lose their force; international treaties of the Russian Federation that are not compatible with the constitution of the Russian Federation are not valid for entry into force or application.

(7) The Constitutional Court of the Russian Federation, on the application of the Federation Council, issues a ruling on whether the presentation of a charge against the president of the Russian Federation of treason or the commission of some other grave crime complies with established procedure.

Article 126

The Supreme Court of the Russian Federation is the highest judicial organ for civil, criminal, administrative or other cases under the jurisdiction of the courts of general jurisdiction, exercises judicial oversight over their activity within the procedural forms laid down by federal law and provides clarification on questions of judicial practice.

Article 127

The Superior Court of Arbitration of the Russian Federation is the highest judicial organ for the resolution of economic disputes and other cases examined by the courts of arbitration, exercises judicial oversight over their activity within the procedural forms laid down by federal law and provides clarification on questions of judicial practice.

Article 128

(1)   Judges of the Constitutional Court of the Russian Federation, the Supreme Court of the Russian Federation and the Superior Court of Arbitration of the Russian Federation are appointed by the Federation Council on the submission of the president of the Russian Federation.
(2)   Judges of other federal courts are appointed by the president of the Russian Federation in accordance with the procedure laid down by federal law.
(3)   The powers and the procedure for the formation and activity of the Constitutional Court of the Russian Federation, the Supreme Court of the Russian Federation, the Superior Court of Arbitration of the Russian Federation and other federal courts are laid down by federal constitutional law.

Article 129

(1)   The Russian Federation Procurator's Office is a single centralized system in which lower-level procurators are subordinate to higher-level procurators and to the procurator-general of the Russian Federation.
(2)   The procurator-general of the Russian Federation is appointed and released from office by the Federation Council on the submission of the president of the Russian Federation.
(3)   The procurators of components of the Russian Federation are appointed by the procurator-general of the Russian Federation by agreement with the Federation components.
(4)   Other procurators are appointed by the procurator-general of the Russian Federation.
(5)   The powers and the organization and procedure of activity of the Russian Federation Procurator's Office are defined by federal law.

Chapter 8 Local Self-Government

Article 130

(1)   Local self-government in the Russian Federation ensures that the population autonomously resolves questions of local importance and the ownership, utilization and disposal of municipal property.
(2)   Local self-government is exercised by citizens by means of referendums, elections and other forms of direct expression of will and through elected and other bodies of local self-government.

Article 131

(1) Local self-government in urban and rural settlements and other territories is exercised with due consideration for historical and other local traditions. The structure of local self-government bodies is autonomously determined by the population.

(2) Changes to the borders of territories where local self-government is exercised are permitted with due consideration for the opinion of the population of the relevant territories.

Article 132

(1) Bodies of local self-government autonomously manage municipal property, formulate, approve and implement the local budget, levy local taxes and duties, implement the protection of public order and also resolve other questions of local importance.

(2) Individual state powers can be vested in bodies of local self-government by law, with the transfer of the material and financial resources necessary to exercise them. The exercise of delegated powers is monitorable by the state.

Article 133

Local self-government in the Russian Federation is guaranteed by the right to judicial protection, compensation for additional expenditure arising as a result of decisions adopted by bodies of state power, and the prohibition of the restriction of the rights of local self-government established by the constitution of the Russian Federation and federal laws.

Chapter 9 Constitutional Amendments and Revision of the Constitution

Article 134

Proposals to amend or revise provisions of the constitution of the Russian Federation can be submitted by the president of the Russian Federation, the Federation Council, the State Duma, the government of the Russian Federation, legislative (representative) bodies of components of the Russian Federation, and also by a group comprising at least one-fifth of members of the Federation Council or deputies of the State Duma.

Article 135

(1) The provisions of Chapters 1, 2 and 9 of the constitution of the Russian Federation cannot be revised by the Federal Assembly.

(2) If a proposal to revise the provisions of Chapters 1, 2 and 9 of the constitution of the Russian Federation is supported by a vote of three-fifths of the total number of members of the Federation Council and deputies of the State Duma then, in accordance with federal constitutional law, a Constitutional Assembly is convened.

(3) The Constitutional Assembly either confirms the immutability of the constitution of the Russian Federation or elaborates a draft of a new constitution of the Russian Federation which is adopted by the Constitutional Assembly by a vote of two-thirds of the total

number of its members or is submitted to a nationwide vote. If a nationwide vote is held, the constitution of the Russian Federation is considered adopted if votes for it are cast by more than one-half of voters casting their votes, provided that more than one-half of voters have cast their votes.

Article 136

Amendments to Chapters 3–8 of the constitution of the Russian Federation are adopted by the procedure envisaged for the adoption of federal constitutional law and come into force after they have been approved by the bodies of legislative power of at least two-thirds of the components of the Russian Federation.

Article 137

(1)   Amendments to Article 65 of the constitution of the Russian Federation, which determines the composition of the Russian Federation, are submitted on the basis of federal constitutional law relating to admission to the Russian Federation, to the formation of a new component of the Russian Federation within it and to the alteration of the constitutional-legal status of a component of the Russian Federation.

(2)   In the event of changes to the name of a republic, krai, oblast, city of federal significance, autonomous oblast or autonomous okrug, the new name of the component of the Russian Federation is to be incorporated in Article 65 of the constitution of the Russian Federation.

SECTION TWO

Concluding and Transitional Provisions

(1)   The constitution of the Russian Federation comes into force on the day of its official publication following the results of the nationwide vote.

The day of the nationwide vote – 12th December 1993 – is deemed the day of the adoption of the constitution of the Russian Federation.

The constitution (Basic Law) of the Russian Federation-Russia, adopted 12th April 1978 with its subsequent amendments and additions, simultaneously ceases to be in force.

In the event of noncompliance with provisions of the constitution of the Russian Federation of provisions of the Federation Treaty – the treaty on the delimitation of areas of responsibility and powers between federal bodies of state power of the Russian Federation and bodies of state power of sovereign republics within the Russian Federation, the treaty on the delimitation of areas of responsibility and powers between federal bodies of state power of the Russian Federation and bodies of state power of krais, oblasts and the cities of Moscow and St Petersburg in the Russian Federation, the treaty on the delimitation of areas of responsibility and powers between federal bodies of state power of the Russian Federation and bodies of state power of the autonomous oblast and autonomous okrugs of the Russian Federation, as well as other treaties between federal bodies of state power of the Russian Federation and bodies of state power of components of the Russian Federation, and treaties between bodies of state power of components of the Russian Federation – the provisions of the constitution of the Russian Federation will prevail.

(2)   Laws and other legal enactments which were in force on the territory of the Russian Federation prior to the entry into force of the present constitution are applied to the extent to which they do not contravene the constitution of the Russian Federation.

(3)   From the day the present constitution comes into force, the president of the Russian Federation, elected in accordance with the constitution (Basic Law) of the Russian Federation-Russia, exercises the powers laid down by the present constitution until the expiry of the term for which he was elected.

(4)   From the day the present constitution comes into force, the Council of Ministers-government of the Russian Federation acquires the rights, obligations and responsibilities of the government of the Russian Federation established by the constitution of the Russian Federation and is thereafter known as the government of the Russian Federation.

(5)   Courts in the Russian Federation administer justice in compliance with the powers laid down by the present constitution.

After the constitution has come into force, the judges of all courts in the Russian Federation retain their powers until the expiry of the term for which they were elected. Vacancies are filled according to the procedure established by the present constitution.

(6)   Pending the entry into force of the federal law laying down the procedure for the hearing of cases by a court with the participation of jurors, the existing procedure for judicial examination of such cases is retained.

The existing procedures for the arrest, holding in custody and detention of persons suspected of having committed a crime are retained until such time as the criminal procedure legislation of the Russian Federation is brought into line with the provisions of the present constitution.

(7)   The first Federation Council and the first State Duma are elected for a 2 year term.

(8)   The Federation Council will convene for its first session on the thirtieth day following its election. The first session of the Federation Council will be opened by the president of the Russian Federation.

(9)   A deputy of the first State Duma can simultaneously be a member of the government of the Russian Federation. The provisions of the present constitution on deputies' immunity as regards liability for actions (or inaction) associated with the performance of official duties do not extend to deputies of the State Duma who are members of the government of the Russian Federation.

Deputies of the first Federation Council perform their duties on a part-time basis.

Notes

1 THE FALL OF COMMUNISM

1 Fyodor Dostoyevsky, 'One of Today's Falsehoods', 1875, in *A Writer's Diary, Volume 1, 1873–1876*, Translated and Annotated by Kenneth Lantz (London, Quartet Books, 1994), p. 288.
2 David Remnick, *Lenin's Tomb: The Last Days of the Soviet Empire* (London, Viking, 1993), pp. 294–5.
3 Mikhail Gorbachev, *Perestroika: New Thinking for Our Country and the World* (London, Collins, 1987), p. 10.
4 This is the theme of E. A. Hewett, *Reforming the Soviet Economy: Equality vs Efficiency* (Washington DC, Brookings, 1988).
5 László Póti, 'The Soviet Reform: Domestic Aspects and Implications for East-Central Europe', in *European Conference on 'Similarities and Differences in the Adaptation of the Countries of Central Europe to the European Community'* (Budapest 28–30 November 1991, Euration), p. 32.
6 E.g. Graeme Gill, 'Liberalization and Democratization in the Soviet Union and Russia', *Democratization*, vol. 2, no. 3 (autumn 1995), pp. 313–36.
7 Neil Robinson, 'Gorbachev and the Place of the Party in Soviet Reform, 1985–91', *Soviet Studies*, vol. 44, no. 3, 1992, pp. 423–44.
8 Póti, 'The Soviet Reform', p. 32.
9 David Remnick, *New York Review of Books*, 17 May 1990, p. 3.
10 Nina Andreeva, 'I Cannot Forego My Principles', *Sovetskaya Rossiya*, 13 March 1988.
11 For a description of these events, see John Morrison, *Boris Yeltsin* (London, Penguin Books, 1991), and for Yeltsin's own view, see *Against the Grain: An Autobiography* (London, Pan, 1991).
12 Estimate by V. Vorotnikov in *Pravda*, 26 March 1990, p. 2.
13 Brendan Kiernan, *The End of Soviet Politics* (Boulder, CO, Westview, 1993), p. 181.
14 L. Efimova, A. Sobyanin and D. Yur'ev, *Argumenty i fakty*, no. 29 (1990), p. 2.
15 *Sovetskaya Rossiya*, 31 May 1990.
16 *Pravda* and *Sovetskaya Rossiya*, 7 June 1989, p. 2; also in John Dunlop, *The Rise of Russia and the Fall of the Soviet Empire* (Princeton, NJ, Princeton University Press, 1993), pp. 16–17.
17 'Deklaratsiya o gosudarstvennom suverenitete RSFSR', *Argumenty i fakty*, no. 24 (16–22 June 1990), p. 1.
18 'Dekret o vlasti', *Argumenty i fakty*, no. 25 (23–29 June 1990), p. 1.
19 E.g. the First Secretary of the Komi Republic (Yu. Spiridonov) and the city Party leader in Kursk (N. Golovin).
20 Ruslan Khasbulatov, *The Struggle for Russia: Power and Change in the Democratic Revolution*, edited by Richard Sakwa (London and New York, Routledge, 1993), p. 222.
21 Khasbulatov, *The Struggle for Russia*, p. 36.
22 *Pravda*, 28 May 1989, p. 1.
23 Gorbachev's most developed attempt to reconceptualise the role of the CPSU appeared in his 'Sotsialisticheskaya ideya i revolyutsionnaya perestroika', *Pravda*, 26 November 1989.
24 Michael Waller, *Democratic Centralism: An Historical Commentary* (New York, St Martin's Press, 1981).
25 The Marxist Platform was published in *Pravda*, 16 April 1990.
26 For an analysis of Gorbachev's attempts to reform the party, see Ronald J. Hill, 'The CPSU: Decline and Collapse', *Irish Slavonic Studies*, no. 12 (1991), pp. 97–119; and also his 'The Communist Party

and After', in S. White *et al.* (eds), *Developments in Soviet and Post-Soviet Politics* (London, Macmillan, 1992), pp. 68–87.

27 *Moscow News*, no. 27 (15 July 1990), p. 5.

28 Hill, 'The CPSU', pp. 113–14.

29 *Moscow News*, no. 24 (24 June 1990), pp. 8–9.

30 *Current Politics of the Soviet Union*, vol. 1, no. 2 (1990), p. 173. At the 26th Party Congress in February–March 1986 membership stood at 18.3 million full and 728,253 candidate members, a total of 19 million, *Izvestiya TsK KPSS*, no. 1, (1990).

31 By 259,605 (1.3 per cent); of these, 136,600 left at their own request, a cumbersome procedure whereby communists had to write a formal letter of resignation and then seek permission to leave from a meeting of the local Party group, *Izvestiya Tsk KPSS*, no. 2 (1989), p. 138, and no. 4 (1990), p. 113.

32 Report of the Central Auditing Commission to the 28th CPSU Congress, *Pravda*, 4 July 1990.

33 Oleg Vite, *Moscow News*, no. 24 (16 June 1991), p. 8.

34 *Izvestiya*, 10 July 1991, pp. 1, 3.

35 *Izvestiya*, 22 July 1991, and for Gorbachev's condemnation, *Pravda*, 26 July 1991.

36 The draft programme was published in *Pravda*, 8 August, *Sovetskaya Rossiya*, 9 August 1991, under the title 'Socialism, Democracy, Progress'.

37 *Sovetskaya Rossiya*, 23 July 1991, p. 1; *Current Digest of The Soviet Press* (henceforth *CDSP*), vol. XLIII, no. 30 (1991), pp. 8–10.

38 For an analysis of the coup, see Richard Sakwa, 'The Revolution of 1991 in Russia: Interpretations of the Moscow Coup', *Coexistence*, vol. 29, no. 4 (December 1992), pp. 27–67; and for a different version 'A Cleansing Storm: The August Coup and the Triumph of Perestroika', *Journal of Communist Studies*, vol. 9, no. 1 (Spring 1993), pp. 131–49. Some of the more useful collections of materials on the coup include *Putch: khronika trevozhnykh dnei* (Moscow, Progress, 1991); *Avgust-91* (Moscow, Izd. politicheskoi literatury, 1991); *Korichnevyi putch krasnykh avgust '91* (Moscow, Tekst, 1991); *Smert' zagovora: belaya kniga* (Moscow, Novosti, 1992); and an account by the investigators V. Stepankov and E. Lisov, *Kremlevskii zagovor* (Moscow, Ogonek, 1992).

39 Mikhail Gorbachev, *The August Coup: The Truth and the Lessons* (London, HarperCollins, 1991), pp. 20–1.

40 *Izvestiya*, 10 October 1991.

41 Boris Yeltsin, 'To the Citizens of Russia', 19 August 1991, *CDSP*, vol. XLIII, no. 33 (1991), pp. 6–7.

42 *Rossiiskaya gazeta*, 9 November 1991, p. 2.

43 See Ivan Bunich, *Zoloto partii* (St Petersburg, Shans, 1992); *Soviet Weekly*, 19 September 1991, p. 5; *Panorama*, BBC TV, 13 July 1992.

44 See Dmitrii Volkogonov, *Argumenty i fakty*, no. 6 (February 1992), p. 4. For the links with the Communist Party of Great Britain, see Nina Fishman, 'Britain: the Road to the Democratic Left', in Martin J. Bull and Paul Heywood (eds), *West European Communist Parties after the Revolutions of 1989* (London, Macmillan, 1994), p. 170.

45 S. Akhromeev and G. Kornienko, *Glazami marshala i diplomata* (Moscow, Mezhdunarodnye otnosheniya, 1992).

46 Remnick, *Lenin's Tomb*, p. xi.

47 Gerd Ruge, *Der Putsch* (Frankfurt, Fischer, 1991), pp. 129, 185.

48 A point made by Pavel Baev, 'Common Security or Common Defence: Options and Choices', *Paradigms*, vol. 2, nos. 1/2 (1991), p. 112.

49 *Moscow News*, no. 37, (1991), p. 1.

50 Gorbachev, *The August Coup*, p. 38.

51 *Moscow News*, no. 37 (1991), p. 1.

52 *Izvestiya*, 7 September 1991.

53 Khasbulatov, *Rossiiskaya gazeta*, 29 October 1991, p. 3.

54 Khasbulatov, *The Struggle for Russia*, p. 223.

55 Boris Yeltsin, *Zapiski prezidenta* (Moscow, Ogonek, 1994), pp. 165–6.

56 *Moscow News*, no. 37, (1991), p. 6.

57 The five Union Treaties were published in *Izvestiya*: 24 November 1990; 9 March 1991; 27 June 1991; 15 August 1991; and 25 November 1991.

58 The idea of something approximating the (British) Commonwealth had first been proposed by Sakharov at the First USSR Congress of People's Deputies in May 1989, and had been promoted by Democratic Russia and Yeltsin.

59 Leonid Kravchuk interviewed in *Kyivska pravda*, 7 July 1995, cited in *Transition*, 11 August 1995, pp. 80–81, where he also notes that the name CIS was suggested by the Ukrainian delegation.

60 *Transition*, 11 August 1995, p. 81.

61 *Rossiiskaya gazeta*, 10 December 1991, p. 1.

62 *Rossiiskaya gazeta*, 24 December 1991, p. 1.

63 A number of books chart the dramatic personal relationship between Gorbachev and Yeltsin, for example *Rossiya segodnya. Politicheskii portret v dokumentakh, 1985–1990* (Moscow, Mezhdunarodnye otnosheniya, 1991), pp. 393–511; *Gorbachev-El'tsin: 1500 dnei politicheskogo protivosostoyaniya* (Moscow, Terra, 1992).

64 The proportion of those supporting Yeltsin to those not supporting him was 69:5, Shevardnadze 52:11, Khasbulatov 48:10, while Gorbachev's proportion was 19:37, *Rossiiskaya gazeta*, 13 December 1991, p. 2.

65 *Guardian*, 28 December 1991.

66 Leonid Gordon is one of the major exponents of the view that a genuine revolution is taking place in Russia, see for example, Leonid Gordon and Natal'ya Pliskevich, 'Lyudi ustali ot nasiliya', *Nezavisimaya gazeta*, 7 December 1991, p. 2.

67 Gorbachev, *Perestroika*, pp. 49–55.

68 Joseph de Maistre, 'Supposed Dangers of Counter-Revolution', in *Considerations on France* (Cambridge, Cambridge University Press, 1994), p. 105.

69 *Vekhi: sbornik statei o russkoi intelligentsii*, (Frankfurt, Posev, reprinted 1967).

70 For a lachrymose analysis of Gorbachev's reforms by the former prime minister, see Nikolai Ryzhkov, *Perestroika: istoriya predatel'stv* (Moscow, Novosti, 1992).

71 *Guardian*, 28 December 1991.

72 A point made by Anatolii Sobchak, *Khozhdenie vo vlasti* (Moscow, Novosti, 1991), p. 269.

73 For a critical analysis of Soviet reformism, see 'Z' (Martin Malia), 'To the Stalin Mausoleum', *Daedalus*, vol. 169, no. 1 (winter 1990), pp. 295–344; and his 'Leninist Endgame', *Daedalus*, vol. 121, no. 2 (spring 1992), pp. 57–75.

74 Abel Aganbegyan, *The Challenge: Economics of Perestroika* (London, Hutchinson, 1988).

75 Alexander Solzhenitsyn, *Rebuilding Russia: Reflections and Tentative Proposals*, Translated by Alexis Klimoff (London, Harvill, 1991), p. 28.

76 Cited in Remnick, *Lenin's Tomb*, p. 202.

77 X (George Kennan), 'The Sources of Soviet Conduct', *Foreign Affairs* (July 1947), pp. 566–82, at p. 580.

2 THE REBIRTH OF RUSSIA

1 Francis Bacon, *The Essays* (London, Odhams Press, nd), 'Of Empire', p. 74.

2 *Rossiiskaya gazeta*, 29 October 1991, p. 1.

3 Edward Allworth, 'Ambiguities in Russian Group Identity and Leadership of the RSFSR', in Allworth (ed.), *Ethnic Russia in the USSR* (New York, 1980), pp. 24–5.

4 Khasbulatov, *The Struggle for Russia*, p. 46.

5 *Soviet News*, 2 August 1989, p. 260.

6 *Soviet News*, 30 August 1989, p. 288.

7 'O mekhanizme narodovlastiya v RSFSR', *Argumenty i fakty*, no. 25 (June 1990), p. 1.

8 *Vestnik statistiki*, no. 10, 1990, p. 72.

9 E.g. 'Slovo natsii', in *Veche*, no. 3 (1981), pp. 106–31; translated as 'A Word to the Nation', *Survey*, vol. 17, no. 3 (summer 1971), pp. 59–63.

10 For a sophisticated version of this argument, see Philip G. Roeder, *Red Sunset: The Failure of Soviet Politics* (Princeton, NJ, Princeton University Press, 1993).

11 *Rossiiskaya gazeta*, 29 October 1991, p. 1.

12 Michel Foucault, 'The Politics of Health in the Eighteenth Century', in *Power/Knowledge: Selected Interviews and Other Writings, 1972–1977* (London, Harvester Wheatsheaf, 1980), edited by Colin Gordon, p. 171.

13 Alexis de Tocqueville, *Democracy in America* (New York, Random House, 1981).

14 See Robert A. Dahl, *A Preface to Democratic Theory* (Chicago, University of Chicago Press, 1956); *Who Governs? Democracy and Power in an American City* (Yale University Press, 1961); *Dilemmas of Pluralist Democracy* (Yale University Press, 1982); *A Preface to Economic Democracy* (Oxford, Polity Press, 1985).

15 Talcott Parsons, *The Social System* (New York, The Free Press, 1951).
16 E.g. G. A. Almond and J. S. Coleman (eds), *The Politics of Developing Areas* (Princeton University Press, 1960); G. A. Almond and G. B. Powell, *Comparative Politics: A Developmental Approach* (Boston, Little, Brown, 1966).
17 S. M. Lipset, *Political Man* (London, Heinemann, 1960).
18 Joseph Schumpeter, *Capitalism, Socialism and Democracy* (London, Allen and Unwin, 1943).
19 G. A. Almond and S. Verba, *The Civic Culture: Political Attitudes and Democracy in Five Nations* (Princeton University Press, 1963); G. A. Almond and S. Verba (eds), *The Civic Culture Revisited* (Boston, Little, Brown, 1980); L. W. Pye and S. Verba (eds), *Political Culture and Political Development* (Princeton, NJ, Princeton University Press, 1965).
20 The political scientist and former adviser to the Central Committee, Alexander Tsipko, distinguishes between 'divisionists' and 'restorationists', *Moscow News*, no. 37 (1991), p. 5.
21 Popular Accord was formed in December 1990 and brought together the Russian Christian Democratic Movement (RCDM), the Democratic Party of Russia (DPR), and the Constitutional Democratic Party (CDP).
22 See, for example, Yelena Bonner and Marina Pavlova-Sil'vanskaya in *God posle Avgusta: Gorech' i vybor* (Moscow, Literatura i politika, 1992), pp. 147–55.
23 *Sovetskaya Rossiya*, 2 October 1991, p. 2; *CDSP*, no. 36, 1991.
24 Cf. Alex Callinicos, *The Revenge of History: Marxism and the East European Revolutions* (Oxford, Polity Press, 1991).
25 A useful introduction to his thinking can be found in Foucault, *Power/Knowledge*, with an 'Afterword' (pp. 229–59) by Colin Gordon on which this account draws.
26 Foucault, 'Two Lectures', in *Power/Knowledge*, p. 83.
27 *Moskovskie novosti*, no. 77 (5–12 November 1995), p. 5.
28 Igor Klyamkin and Andranik Migranyan, *Literaturnaya gazeta*, 16 August 1989.
29 Nursultan Nazarbaev, *Bez pravykh i levykh* (*Without Left or Right*) (Moscow, Molodaya gvardiya, 1991).
30 Gavriil Popov, 'Dangers of Democracy', *The New York Review of Books*, 16 August 1990, pp. 27–8.
31 *Argumenty i fakty*, no. 41 (October 1991), p. 1.
32 *Soviet Weekly*, 26 September 1991, p. 4.
33 Defined by Foucault as 'procedures which [allow] the effects of power to circulate in a manner at once continuous, uninterrupted, adapted and "individualised" throughout the entire social body', 'Truth and Power', in *Power/Knowldge*, p. 119.

3 CONSTITUTIONALISM AND THE LAW

1 James Bryce, *Studies of History and Jurisprudence*, vol. 1 (Oxford, 1901), p. 166.
2 Max Weber, 'Bourgeois Democracy in Russia', in *The Russian Revolutions*, translated and edited by Gordon C. Wells and Peter Baehr (Oxford, Polity Press, 1995).
3 See Lothar Schultz, 'Constitutional Law in Russia', in G. Katkov *et al* (eds), *Russia Enters the Twentieth Century* (London, Temple Smith, 1971), pp. 34–59, esp. pp. 44–7.
4 See Aryeh L. Unger, *Constitutional Developments in the USSR: A Guide to the Soviet Constitutions* (London, Methuen, 1981).
5 Gorbachev introduced these ideas in his speech to the Nineteenth Party Conference on 28 June 1988 (*Izbrannye rechi i stat'i*, vol. 6 (Moscow, 1989), pp. 373–6), and developed them in his Supreme Soviet speech of 29 November 1988, 'K polnovlastiyu Sovetov i sozdaniyu sotsialisticheskogo pravovogo gosudarstvo', *Izbrannye rechi i stat'i*, vol. 7 (Moscow, 1990), pp. 150–75.
6 See L. V. Lazarev and A. Ya. Sliva, *Konstitutsionnaya reforma: pervyi etap* (Moscow, Znanie, 1989).
7 An extended version of this part of the chapter can be found in *Studies in East European Thought*, 1996, forthcoming.
8 *Argumenty i fakty*, no. 47 (November 1990), whole issue; in *Konstitutsionnyi vestnik*, no. 4 (1990), pp. 55–120; a popular edition was published as *Konstitutsii Rossiiskoi Federatsii: proekt s kommentariyami* (Moscow and Krasnoyarsk, newspaper *Svoi golos* and Krasnoyarsk Press and Information Agency, 1991).
9 *Sovetskaya Rossiya*, 19 April 1991; an earlier version appeared in *Sovetskaya Rossiya*, 24 November 1990.
10 *Rossiiskaya gazeta*, 11 October 1991, special section, with an 'explanatory note' on p. 7.
11 Oleg Rumyantsev, 'Zachem nuzhna novaya konstitutsiya', *Konstitutsionnyi vestnik*, no. 8 (1991), pp. 3–7.

12 *Konstitutsionnyi vestnik*, no. 8 (1991), pp. 68–72.
13 *Konstitutsionnyi vestnik*, no. 8 (1991), p. 74; and pp. 84–148 for the revised draft of 24 October.
14 *Rossiiskaya gazeta*, 5 November 1991, p. 1.
15 *Argumenty i fakty*, no. 12, (March 1992), whole issue; republished in *Proekt konstitutsii Rossiiskoi Federatsii: sbornik materialov* (Moscow, Respublika, 1992), pp. 19–81.
16 Vladimir Kuznechevskii, *Rossiiskaya gazeta*, 3 April 1992, pp. 1–2.
17 The Federation Treaty was made up of three separate documents: an agreement (published in *Rossiiskaya gazeta*, 18 March 1992) signed by 18 out of the 20 republics, excluding the Chechen and Tatarstan republics; a document signed by Russia's oblasts and krais; and an agreement with the autonomous okrugs and the Jewish Autonomous Oblast. The Russian Federation was a separate signatory to the Treaty. *Federativnyi dogovor. Dokumenty. Kommentarii* (Moscow, Izd-vo 'Respublika', 1992).
18 *Rossiiskaya gazeta*, 3 April 1992, pp. 1–2.
19 *Konstitutsiya Rossiiskoi Federatsii (proekt): Alternativnyi variant* (Moscow, Novosti, 1992).
20 A. D. Sakharov, 'Proekt Konstitutsii Soyuza Sovetskikh Respublik Evropy i Azii', in *Trevoga i nadezhda* (Moscow, Inter-Verso, 1990), pp. 266–77; also in *Novoe vremya*, no. 52 (1989–90), pp. 26–28.
21 *Nezavisimaya gazeta*, 28 March 1992; *The Independent*, 6 April 1992; *Moskovskie novosti*, 5 April 1992, pp. A6–7.
22 *Moskovskie novosti* (5 April 1992), pp. A6–7. Sobchak insisted that the assertion of Article 1 of the draft (retained in the version adopted in December 1993) that 'the Russian state is a social state' was similar in spirit to the Brezhnev constitution's assertion that 'the Soviet Union is a state of all the people'.
23 *Nezavismaya gazeta*, 28 March 1992.
24 'O proekte konstitutsii Rossiiskoi Federatsii i poryadke dal'neishei raboty nad nim', 18 April 1992, in *Proekt konstitutsii Rossiiskoi Federatsii: sbornik materialov*, pp. 3–4.
25 *Rossiiskaya gazeta*, 16 May 1992, pp. 3–5.
26 By that time seven laws making 340 amendments had been adopted: in 1990 there were 53 amendments and in 1991 29, Rumyantsev in *Konstitutsionnyi vestnik*, no. 15 (March 1993), p. 8.
27 *Konstitutsionnyi vestnik*, no. 13 (November 1992), pp. 25–115.
28 *Konstitutsionnyi vestnik*, no. 13, p. 7.
29 *Nezavisimaya gazeta*, 24 November 1993, p. 2.
30 This version was published as 'Konstitutsiya (osnovnoi zakon) Rossiiskoi Federatsii: proekt' in *Izvestiya*, 30 April 1993, pp. 3–5; reprinted in *Konstitutsionnyi vestnik*, no. 16 (May 1993), pp. 65–108.
31 *Izvestiya*, 13 May 1993, p. 1.
32 *Stolitsa*, no. 22 (132) (1993), pp. 6–7.
33 For example, Marina Shakina, 'Istoriya s konstitutsiei', *Novoe vremya*, no. 23, 1993, pp. 3–5.
34 *Konstitutsionnyi vestnik*, no. 16 (May 1993), p. 202.
35 Shakhrai, for example, argued that it would be legal and constitutional for a Constituent Assembly to adopt a new constitution and declare new parliamentary elections, especially since presidential powers had been relegitimised in the referendum of 25 April 1993, *Izvestiya*, 30 April 1993, p. 2.
36 *Pravda*, 5 June 1993, p. 1.
37 *Nezavisimaya gazeta*, 30 June 1993, p. 1.
38 'Konstitutsiya Rossiiskoi Federatsii: proekt', *Konstitutsionnyi vestnik*, no. 16 (May 1993), pp. 9–64.
39 *Nezavisimaya gazeta*, 26 June 1993, p. 1.
40 'O zavershenii raboty nad proektom Konstitutsii Rossiiskoi Federatsii', Supreme Soviet resolution of 29 April 1993, *Konstitutsionnyi vestnik*, no. 16 (May 1993), pp. 201–2.
41 *Rossiiskaya gazeta*, 3 April 1992, pp. 1–2; *Nezavisimaya gazeta*, 26 January 1993, p. 5.
42 'O sozyve Konstitutsionnogo soveshchanie i zavershenii podgotovki proekta Konstitutsii Rossiiskoi Federatsii', *Konstitutsionnoe soveshchanii*, no. 1 (August 1993), pp. 7–8.
43 *Konstitutsionnoe soveshchanie*, no. 1, pp. 12–20; *Rossiiskie vesti*, 8 June 1993, p. 2.
44 *Moskovskie novosti*, no. 25 (20 June 1993), p. A8.
45 Kronid Lyubarskii, 'Konets sovetskoi vlasti', *Novoe vremya*, no. 24 (1993), pp. 4–5.
46 B. A. Strashun, 'O "smeshannoi" forme pravleniya v proekte Konstitutsii Rossiiskoi Federatsii', *Konstitutsionnoe soveshchanie*, no. 2 (1993), pp. 51–7; and V. E. Chirkin, '"Chistye" i "smeshannye" formy pravleniya: plyusy i minusy razlichnykh sistem', ibid., pp. 57–65.
47 *Konstitutsionnoe soveshchanie: informatsionnyi byulleten'*, no. 1 (August 1993), pp. 109–57; *Rossiiskie vesti*, 15 July 1993.
48 The Assembly envisaged a broad process of consultation, in particular with the subjects of federation,

and a referendum before the draft could be adopted, 'Zakon "O poryadke prinyatiya Konstitutsii Rossiiskoi Federatsii" (proekt)', *Konstitutsionnoe soveshchanie*, no. 1 (August 1993), pp. 155–7.

49 *Izvestiya*, 14 August 1993, p. 1

50 'O poetapnoi konstitutsionnoi reforme v Rossiiskoi Federatsii', *Konstitutsionnoe soveshchanie*, no. 2 (October 1993), pp. 15–19, and see chapter 6.

51 24 September 1993, 'Ob obrazovanii Obshchestvennoi palaty Konstitutsionnogo soveshchaniya', *Konstitutsionnoe soveshchanie*, no. 2 (October 1993), p. 81.

52 *Konstitutsionnoe soveshchanie*, no. 3 (December 1993), p. 7.

53 *Rossiiskaya gazeta*, 10 November 1993, pp. 3–6.

54 Sergei S. Alekseev, *Demokraticheskie reformy i konstitutsiya* (Moscow, Pozitsiya, 1992), p. 4.

55 For an extended discussion of this issue, see Oleg Rumyantsev, *Osnovy konstitutsionnogo stroya Rossii* (Moscow, Yurist, 1994).

56 Cf. Irina Koptel'skaya, 'Konstitutsionnue zakony – novoe yavlenie v zakonodatel'stve Rossii', *Konstitutsionnyi vestnik*, no. 1 (17) (1994), pp. 59–63.

57 *Rossiiskaya gazeta*, 17 December 1993, p. 1.

58 *Financial Times*, 10 November 1993.

59 Yurii Stroev, 'My prodolzhaem', *Konstitutsionnyi vestnik*, no. 17, p. 6.

60 Cf. *Nezavisimaya gazeta*, 30 December 1993, p. 2.

61 For example, Vyacheslav Nikonov, *Nezavisimaya gazeta*, 23 December 1993, pp. 1, 2.

62 See *Novoe vremya*, no. 11 (1993), pp. 42–4.

63 Ralf Dahrendorf, *Reflections on the Revolution in Europe* (London, Chatto and Windus, 1990), pp. 79, 85.

64 Valerii Zor'kin, 'Uroki oktyabrya-93', *Konstitutsionnyi vestnik*, no. 1 (17), (1994), p. 11.

65 Cf. Giuseppe Di Palma, *To Craft Democracies: An Essay in Democratic Transition* (Berkeley, University of California Press, 1990).

66 The distinction is made by Hellmut Wollmann, 'Change and Continuity of Political and Administrative Elites from Communist to Post-Communist Russia', *Governance: An International Journal of Policy and Administration*, vol. 6, no. 3 (July 1993), pp. 325–40.

67 A charge made, for example, by the jurist Aleksei Surikov, *Stolitsa*, no. 22 (132) (1993), p. 7.

68 For example, O. G. Rumyantsev, 'Osnovy konstitutsionnogo stroya: ponyatie, soderzhanie, otrazhenie v konstitutsii', *Gosudarstvo i pravo*, no. 10 (1993), pp. 3–15, and see note 54 above.

69 V. V. Leontovich, *Istoriya liberalizma v Rossii, 1762–1914* (Paris, YMCA-Press, 1980), p. 539.

70 *Moscow News*, no. 46, 12 November 1993, p. 2.

71 'Ob izmeneniyakh i dopolneniyakh Konstitutsii (Osnovnogo Zakona) RSFSR', in *Rossiya segodnya: politicheskii portret v dokumentakh, 1991–1992* (Moscow, Mezhdunar. otnosheniya, 1993), pp. 24–27.

72 Wendy Slater, 'Head of Russian Constitutional Court Under Fire', *RFE/RL Research Report*, vol. 2, no. 26 (25 June 1993), pp. 1–5.

73 *Sovetskaya Rossiya*, 23 September 1993, p. 1. On 30 September the Constitutional Court suspended the membership of three of the judges (one on health grounds), though the other two (Ernst Ametistov and Nikolai Vitruk) had already declared that they would no longer participate in the Court's work.

74 Cf. Robert Sharlet, 'The Russian Constitutional Court: The First Term', *Post-Soviet Affairs*, vol. 9, no. 1 (1993), pp. 1–39.

75 See Robert Sharlet, 'Russian Constitutional Crisis: Law and Politics under Yel'tsin', *Post-Soviet Affairs*, vol. 9, no. 4 (1993), pp. 314–36.

76 *Russkaya mysl'*, no. 4064 (9–15 February 1995), p. 20. Of the 'old' judges, nine had condemned the president's action in September 1993 (Nikolai Vedernikov, Valerii Zor'kin, Victor Luchin, Gadis Gadzhiev, Boris Ebzeev, Nikolai Seleznev, Oleg Tyunov, Vladimir Oleinik and Yurii Rudnik), four had supported the president (Ernst Ametistov, Tamara Morshchakova, Nikolai Vitruk and Anatolii Kononov), while the views of the six newcomers (Vladimir Tumanov, Olga Khokhryakova, Yurii Danilov, Vladimir Yaroslavtsev, Vladimir Strekozov and Marat Baglai, the last to be appointed) remained to be determined.

77 *Moskovskie novosti*, no. 17 (12–19 March 1995), p. 11.

78 Donald D. Barry (ed.), *Toward the 'Rule of Law' in Russia?: Political and Legal Reform in the Transition Period* (Armonk and London, M. E. Sharpe, 1992), p. xvi.

79 Cf. Walicki, *Legal Philosophies of Russian Liberalism*, pp. 165–212. See also Jonathan Sutton, *The Religious Philosophy of Vladimir Solovyov* (London, Macmillan, 1988).

80 Ibid., p. 114.

81 See Barry (ed.), *Toward the 'Rule of Law' in Russia?*, p. 4.

82 Law of 24 October 1990, 'O deistvii aktov organov SSSR na territorii RSFSR', in *Sbornik*

zakonodatel'nykh aktov RSFSR o gosudarstvennom suverenitete, soyuznom dogovore i referendume (Moscow, RSFSR Supreme Soviet, 1991), pp. 16–17.

83 *Moskovskie novosti*, no. 61 (10–17 September 1995), p. 23.

84 *Soviet Weekly*, 24 October 1991, p. 2.

85 E.g. Genri Reznik, *Novaya ezhednevnaya gazeta*, 24 December 1993, p. 1.

86 Albert Motivans and Elizabeth Teague, 'Capital Punishment in the Former USSR', *RFE/RL Research Report*, vol. 1, no. 26 (26 June 1992), pp. 67–73, at p. 71.

87 *Nezavisimaya gazeta*, 13 August 1992, p. 1.

88 Anatolii Kononov, *Soviet Weekly*, 24 October 1991, p. 6.

89 *Moskovskie novosti*, no. 17 (12–19 March 1995), p. 11.

90 See Peter Solomon, 'Limits of Legal Order', *Post-Soviet Affairs*, vol. 11, no. 2 (1995), pp. 89–114.

91 Stephen Handelman, 'The Russian "Mafiya"', *Foreign Affairs*, vol. 73, no. 2 (March–April 1994), p. 90.

92 *Observer*, 11 September 1994, p. 6.

93 Stephen Handelman, *Comrade Criminal: The Theft of the Second Russian Revolution* (London, Michael Joseph, 1994).

94 *Nezavisimaya gazeta*, 21 April 1993, p. 2.

95 *Izvestiya*, 18 October 1994, p. 5.

96 *Nezavisimaya gazeta*, 11 April 1995, p. 1.

97 Some 289 in 1993 and 562 in 1994, *Nezavismaya gazeta*, 11 April 1995, p. 1; *Observer*, 21 April 1995, p. 23.

98 *Moskovskie novosti*, no. 80 (19–26 November 1995), p. 21.

99 *Observer*, 26 March 1995, p. 6.

100 *Observer*, 16 April 1995, p. 21.

101 *Moscow News*, no. 38 (1991), p. 3.

102 Handelman, *Comrade Criminal*.

103 *Soviet Weekly*, 5 December 1991, p. 2.

104 Vadim Bakatin, appointed head of the KGB after the coup, describes the process in *Izbavlenie ot KGB* (Moscow, Novosti, 1992), pp. 197–220.

105 *Soviet Weekly*, 10 October 1991, p. 4.

106 *Rossiiskaya gazeta*, 11 August 1992, p. 4.

107 *OMRI Daily Digest*, no. 8, Part I, 11 January 1996.

108 *Moskovskaya pravda*, 4 September 1992.

109 Victor Yasmann, 'Corruption in Russia: A Threat to Democracy?', *RFE/RL Research Report*, vol. 2, no. 10 (5 March 1993), pp. 15–18.

110 See Alexander Rahr, 'Reform of Russia's State Security Apparatus', *RFE/RL Research Report*, vol. 3, no. 8 (25 February 1994), pp. 19–30.

111 *Nezavisimaya gazeta*, 10 January 1995, p. 3.

112 *Rossiiskaya gazeta*, 28 May 1994, pp. 1, 4.

113 The law 'On Federal Security Service Bodies of the Russian Federation' of April 1995 introduced the name Federal Security Service; and a presidential decree of 23 June 1995 gave details on its implementation.

114 Victor Yasmann, 'Where has the KGB Gone?', *RFE/RL Research Report*, vol. 2, no. 2 (8 January 1993), pp. 17–20, at p.18.

115 *Rossiiskaya gazeta*, 12 August 1992, p. 1.

116 J. Michael Waller, *Secret Empire: The KGB in Russia Today* (Oxford, Westview, 1994), p. 285.

117 *Moskovskie novosti*, no. 9 (5–12 February 1995), p. 6.

118 Solzhenitsyn, *Rebuilding Russia*, p. 29.

119 Gerd Ruge, *Der Putsch* (Frankfurt, Fischer, 1991), p. 153.

120 Gorbachev, *The August Coup*, p. 48.

121 *Zerkalo*, Vestnik Obshchestvennyi Komitet Rossiiskikh Reform, no. 2 (February 1992), pp. 1–2.

122 *Moscow News*, no. 5 (28 January 1993), p. 13.

123 Cf. Geoffrey Best, *War and Law Since 1945* (Oxford, Clarendon, 1994).

124 C. Charles Bertschi, 'Lustration and the Transition to Democracy: The Cases of Poland and Bulgaria', *East European Quarterly*, vol. 28, no. 4 (January 1995), pp. 435–51.

125 Amos Elon, 'East Germany: Crime and Punishment', *The New York Review of Books*, 14 May 1992, pp. 6–11.

126 *Soviet Weekly*, 24 October 1991, p. 2.

127 *Moscow News*, no. 5 (28 January 1993), p. 13.

4 PARTY DEVELOPMENT

1 *Russian constitution*, article 13.1–4.
2 This chapter develops the analysis in my 'Parties and the Multiparty System in Russia', *RFE/RL Research Report*, vol. 2, no. 31 (30 July 1993), pp. 7–15, and 'The Development of the Russian Party System', in Peter Lentini (ed.), *Elections and Political Order in Russia* (Budapest, Central European University Press, 1995), pp. 169–201.
3 Giovanni Sartori, *Parties and Party Systems: A Framework for Analysis* (Cambridge, Cambridge University Press, 1976) and his, *The Theory of Democracy Revisited* (Chatham, Chatham House Publishers, 1987); see also Jean Blondel, *Comparative Government: An Introduction* (Hemel Hempstead, Simon and Schuster, 1990), Part II.
4 See Judith B. Sedaitis and Jim Butterfield (eds), *Perestroika from Below: Social Movements in the Soviet Union* (Boulder, CO, Westview Press, 1991).
5 See Gail Lapidus, 'State and Society: Toward the Emergence of Civil Society in the Soviet Union', in Alexander Dallin and Gail Lapidus (eds), *The Soviet System in Crisis* (Boulder, Westview Press, 1991), pp. 130–47; Victoria Bonnell, 'Voluntary Associations in Gorbachev's Reform Program', also in *The Soviet System in Crisis*, pp. 151–60.
6 Cf. Steven Fish, 'The Emergence of Independent Associations and the Transformation of Russian Political Society', *The Journal of Communist Studies*, vol. 7, no. 3 (September 1991), pp. 299–334.
7 A. V. Gromov, O. S. Kuzin, *Neformaly: kto est' kto?* (Moscow, mysl', 1990), pp. 11–15.
8 E.g. *Neformaly: kto oni? Kuda zovut?*, V. A. Pecheneva (ed.), (Moscow, Izd. politicheskoi literatury, 1990).
9 Vladimir Pribylovskii, *Dictionary of Political Parties and Organisations* (Moscow, PostFactum; Washington, DC, Center for Strategic and International Studies, 1992), pp. 28–32.
10 *Svobodnoe Slovo*, no. 5 (107) (1992), p. 1.
11 See Geoffrey Evans and Stephen Whitefield, 'Social and Ideological Cleavage Formation in Post-Communist Hungary', *Europe-Asia Studies*, vol. 47, no. 7 (1995), pp. 1177–1204.
12 The figure comes from V. N. Berezovskii *et al*, *Partii, assotsiatsii, soyuzy, kluby: spravochnik* (Moscow, RAU Press, 1991), vol. 1 (1), p. 3, with a discussion of classification on pp. 5–9.
13 A survey of 100 political parties and groups is provided by Vladimir Pribylovskii in *Slovar' oppozitsii: novye politicheskie partii i organizatsii Rossii, Analiticheskie vestniki informatsionnogo agenstva Postfactum*, no. 4/5, April 1991.
14 Andranik Migranyan, 'Prospects for the Russian National Movement', *Nezavisimaya gazeta*, 14 November 1991, p. 5.
15 Cf. Michael Waller, 'Political Actors and Political Roles in East-Central Europe', *The Journal of Communist Studies*, vol. 9, no. 4 (December 1993), pp. 21–36.
16 L. Gordon and E. Klopov (eds), *Novye sotsial'nye dvizheniya v Rossii* (Moscow, Progress-Kompleks, 1993), p. 25.
17 Vyacheslav Nikonov, *Nezavisimaya gazeta*, 7 August 1992, p. 5.
18 *Narodnyi deputat*, no. 8 (1992), pp. 96–100, at p. 96.
19 *Izvestiya*, 20 April 1992, p. 2.
20 *Moscow News*, no. 22 (28 May 1993), p. 1.
21 Maurice Duverger, *Political Parties: Their Organization and Activity in the Modern State* (London, Methuen, 1954).
22 The best analysis of the post-communist trade union movement is in *Kto est' chto: politicheskaya Moskva, 1993* (Moscow, Catallaxy, 1993), Part 5.
23 See V. G. Golovin, 'Ekonomicheskie vzglyady politicheskikh partii i blokov Rossii', in *Partii i partiinye sistemy sovremennoi evropy* (Moscow, INION, 1994), pp. 142–71.
24 *Izvestiya*, 24 August 1992.
25 See Yitzhak M. Brudny, 'The Dynamics of "Democratic Russia", 1990–1993', *Post-Soviet Affairs*, vol. 9, no. 2 (1993), pp. 141–70; on the Civic Union, see Michael McFaul, 'Russian Centrism and Revolutionary Transitions', *Post-Soviet Affairs*, vol. 9, no. 3 (1993), pp. 196–222.
26 Khasbulatov, *The Struggle for Russia*, p. 239.
27 Cf. B. I. Koval' and V. B. Pavlenko, *Partii i politicheskie bloki v Rossii*, Vyp. 1 (Moscow, NIPEK, 1993), pp. 11–17.
28 Viktor Aksyuchits interviewed by Mikhail Karpov, *Nezavisimaya gazeta*, 14 November 1991, p. 2.
29 *Izvestiya*, 3 August 1992, p. 3.
30 Alexander Vladislavlev of the Renewal League, *Nezavisimaya gazeta*, 11 July 1992, p. 4.
31 Vladimir Shumeiko, a co-founder of Renewal, in *Moscow News*, no. 24 (14 June 1992), p. 6.
32 *Nezavisimaya gazeta*, 22 July 1992, p. 2.

33 *Segodnya*, 31 March 1994, p. 2.
34 Wendy Slater, 'The Diminishing Center of Russian parliamentary Politics', *RFE/RL Research Report*, vol. 3, no. 17 (29 April 1994), pp. 13–18.
35 Konstantin Medvedev, 'V Rossii vozmozhna smena kursa', *Nezavisimaya gazeta*, 7 December 1991, p. 2.
36 *Obozrevatel'*, no. 2–3 (1992), prilozhenie, p. 21.
37 *Put'*, no. 10 (23) (1992), p. 16.
38 The appeal of the organising committee, *Den'*, no. 41 (69) (11 October 1992), p. 1.
39 *Guardian*, 19 February 1992.
40 A. Orlov, interview with Zhirinovskii, *Sovetskaya Rossiya*, 2 October 1991, p. 2.
41 *Rossiya*, no. 27 (86) (July 1992), p. 3.
42 Vyacheslav Nikonov, *Nezavisimaya gazeta*, 7 August 1992, p. 5.
43 The decree of 23 August 1991 halted the activity of the CPSU; the decree of 25 August confiscated its property; and the decree of 6 November banned the party in Russia. The appeal is in *Konstitutsionnyi vestnik*, no. 13 (November 1992), pp. 221–5.
44 *Konstitutsionnyi vestnik*, no. 13 (November 1992), pp. 226–42.
45 E.g. Sergei Shakhrai, *Moscow News*, no. 22 (31 May 1992), p. 2.
46 *Rossiiskaya gazeta*, 16 December 1992, p. 6.
47 *Guardian*, 8 December 1992.
48 Cf. Arend Lijphart, *Electoral Systems and Party Systems: A Study of Twenty-Seven Democracies, 1945–1990* (Oxford, Oxford University Press, 1994).
49 *Moskovskie novosti*, no. 25 (20 June 1993), p. A9.
50 *Byulleten' Tsentral'noi izbiratel'noi kommissii*, 1 (12) (1994), p. 28.
51 Sergei Mndoyants, Aleksei Salmin, 'Vybor nakanune vyborov', *Nezavisimaya gazeta*, 30 March 1995, p. 3.
52 *Konstitutsionnoe soveshchanie*, no. 1 (August 1993), p. 33.
53 Vera Tolz, 'The Civic Accord: Contributing to Russia's Stability?', *RFE/RL Research Report*, vol. 3, no. 19 (13 May 1994), pp. 1–5.
54 *Izvestiya*, 29 April 1994, p. 1.
55 *Segodnya*, 1 February 1994, p. 2.
56 *Nezavisimaya gazeta*, 22 February 1994, p. 1.
57 *Nezavisimaya gazeta*, 27 May 1994, p. 2.
58 Vera Tolz, 'Significance of the New Party Russia's Democratic Choice', *RFE/RL Research Report*, vol. 3, no. 26 (1 July 1994), pp. 25–30.
59 Interview with Lev Ponamarev, '"Demokraticheskaya Rossiya" nikogda ne stanet sotsial-demokraticheskoi partiei', *Russkaya mysl'*, no. 4046 (5 October 1994), p. 9.
60 *Moskovskie novosti*, no. 77 (5–12 November 1995), p. 6.
61 *Pravda*, 28 December 1993, p. 2.
62 See Richard Sakwa, *The Communist Party of the Russian Federation and the Electoral Process*, Studies in Public Policy no. 265 (Glasgow, University of Strathclyde, 1996).
63 Cf. Martin J. Bull and Paul Heywood (eds), *West European Communist Parties after the Revolutions of 1989* (London, Macmillan, 1994), p. xxiii.
64 *Programma KPRF: Prinyata III s"ezdom KPRF 22 yanvarya 1995 godu* (Moscow, 1995).
65 See, for example, Gennadii Zyuganov, *Derzhava* (Moscow, 1994); and his *Za gorizontom* (Moscow, 1995).
66 *Russkaya mysl'*, no. 4062 (26 January–1 February 1995), p. 20.
67 *III s'ezd KPRF: Materialy i dokumenty* (Moscow, Informpechat', 1995), pp. 84–6.
68 *Independent*, 12 January 1995.
69 Kiril Kholodkovskii, Rossiiskie partii i problema politicheskogo strukturirovaniya obschestva *MEMO*, no. 10, 1995, pp. 77–87.
70 Gleb Cherkasov, *Segodnya*, 9 December 1995, p. 2.
71 NTV 19 December 1995, in *OMRI Daily Digest*, Part 1, 19 December 1995.
72 Anatolii Khimenko, 'Partiinoe stroitel'stvo zamorozheno rossiiskimi "verkhami"', *Nezavisimaya gazeta*, 4 March 1993, p. 2.
73 Alexander Solzhenitsyn, *Rebuilding Russia: Reflections and Tentative Proposals* (London, Harvill, 1991), pp. 54–90, esp. pp. 69–71.
74 Solzhenitsyn, *Rebuilding Russia*, p. 70.
75 *Sovetskaya Rossiya*, 31 May 1990.
76 *Kommersant*, no. 48 (98) (16 December 1991), p. 23. A few groups favoured by Burbulis did get

premises, but Yeltsin's reneging on this promise for the others was yet another reason for the bitter hostility against him of part of the new political elite.

77 M. Steven Fish, *Democracy From Scratch: Opposition and Regime in the New Russian Revolution* (Princeton, NJ, Princeton University Press, 1995).

78 Giovanni Sartori, *Parties and Party Systems: A Framework for Analysis* (Cambridge, Cambridge University Press, 1976), p. 63.

79 *Moscow News*, no. 25 (18 June 1993), p. 2.

80 Ruslan Khasbulatov, *The Struggle for Russia: Power and Change in the Democratic Revolution*, edited and introduced by Richard Sakwa (London, Routledge, 1993), p. 230 and *passim*.

81 The fourteen factions of early 1993 were divided into three broad blocs: the Democratic Centre with 167 members; the centrist bloc of Constructive Forces with 158; and the 'red-brown' alliance Russian Unity with 303. Four factions remained aloof from the blocs: Democratic Russia (48 deputies); Radical Democrats (50); Agreement for the Sake of Progress (54); and Rodina (Motherland) (57), *Parlamentskie fraktsii i bloki*, appendix to *Parlamentskaya nedelya*, 26 March 1993.

82 *Izvestiya*, 24 December 1993, pp. 1–2.

83 Sergei Mndoyants, Aleksei Salmin, *Moskovskie novosti*, no. 67 (1–8 October 1995), p. 6.

84 *Izvestiya*, 24 November 1993, p. 4.

85 *Kuranty*, 6 June 1992, p. 1.

86 *Obshchaya gazeta*, no. 40 (1994), p. 8.

87 *Zerkalo mnenii: rezultaty sotsiologicheskogo oprosa naseleniya Rossii* (Moscow, Institute of Sociology, 1992), pp. 10–11, 7–8.

88 For details of referendum results, including regional variations, see *Rossiiskaya gazeta*, 6 May 1993; Wendy Slater, 'No Victors in the Russian Referendum', *RFE/RL Research Report*, vol. 2, no. 21 (21 May 1993), pp. 10–19.

89 Lyudmila Alekseeva, 'Nesvobodnye profsoyuzy', *Moskovskie novosti*, no. 3 (15–22 January 1995), p. 14.

90 This issue is discussed in the Eastern European context by Sten Berglund and Jan Ake Dellenbrant, 'The Evolution of Party Systems in Eastern Europe', *The Journal of Communist Studies*, vol. 8, no. 1 (March 1992), pp. 148–59, esp. p. 154.

91 *Moskovskie novosti*, no. 75 (29 October–5 November 1995), p. 6.

92 *Independent*, 5 October 1994.

93 Erwin Oberlander, 'The Role of the Political Parties', in K. Katkov *et al* (eds), *Russia Enters the Twentieth Century* (London, Temple, Smith, 1971), pp. 60–84.

94 Cf. Terence Emmons, *The Formation of Political Parties and the First National Elections in Russia* (Cambridge, MA, Harvard University Press, 1983).

95 A. I. Zevelev (ed.), *Istoriya politicheskikh partii Rossii* (Moscow, Vysshaya shkola, 1994); N. V. Orlova, *Politicheskie partii Rossii: stranitsy istorii* (Moscow, Yurist, 1994).

96 Igor' Malov, Maksim Khrustalev, 'Mnogopartiinost'' v Rossii, 1917–1990', *Problemy vostochnoi evropy*, no. 31–2 (Washington, 1991), pp. 79–163.

97 A. Kulik, 'Posttotalitarnye partii v politicheskom protsesse', *MEMO*, no. 2 (1994), pp. 27–38, at p. 29.

98 Kronid Lyubarskii, *Novoe vremya*, no. 7 (1994), p. 12.

99 Cf. Geoffrey Evans and Stephen Whitefield, 'Identifying the Bases of Party Competition in Eastern Europe', *British Journal of Political Science*, vol. 23, no. 4 (1993), pp. 521–48.

100 S. M. Lipset and S. Rokkan, 'Cleavage Structures, Party Systems and Voter Alignments: An Introduction', in *Party Systems and Voter Alignments: Cross National Perspectives*, S. M. Lipset and S. Rokkan (eds) (New York, The Free Press, 1967); see also S. Rokkan, *Citizens, Elections, Parties* (Oslo, Universitetsforlaget, 1970). For an attempt to apply Rokkanian analysis, see Maurizio Cotta, 'Building Party Systems after the Dictatorship: The East European Cases in a Comparative Perspective', in Geoffrey Pridham and Tatu Vanhanen (eds), *Democratization in Eastern Europe* (London, Routledge, 1994), pp. 99–127.

101 Lipset and Rokkan, pp. 50–51.

102 E.g. Nikolai Biryukov and V. M. Sergeev, *Russia's Road to Democracy: Parliament, Communism and Traditional Culture* (Aldershot, Edward Elgar, 1993).

103 E.g. R. Inglehart, 'The Changing Structure of Political Cleavages in Western Societies', in R. J. Dalton *et al.* (eds), *Electoral Change in Advanced Industrial Democracies: Realignment or Dealignment?* (Princeton, NJ, Princeton University Press, 1984).

104 Cf. Richard Flacks, 'The Party's Over – So What is to Be Done?', *Social Research*, vol. 60, no. 3 (fall 1993), pp. 445–70.

105 Francis Fukuyama, *The End of History and the Last Man* (London, Penguin, 1992).
106 Jacques Derrida, *Spectres of Marx*, (London, Routledge, 1994); see also his 'Spectres of Marx', *New Left Review*, no. 205 (May–June 1994), pp. 31–58.
107 Cf. Philippe C. Schmitter, 'Interest Systems and the Consolidation of Democracies', in G. Marks and L. Diamond (eds), *Re-examining Democracy* (London, Sage, 1992), pp. 156–81.

5 ELECTORAL POLITICS

1 Alexander Pope, *Essay on Man*, Epistle 3.
2 See Jeffrey Hahn, 'An Experiment in Competition: The 1987 Elections to the Local Soviets', *Slavic Review*, vol. 47, no. 2 (1988), pp. 434–47; and Stephen White, 'Reforming the Electoral System', *The Journal of Communist Studies*, vol. 4, no. 4 (1988), pp. 1–17.
3 The revised electoral law was published in *Izvestiya*, 28 October 1989.
4 An example of this is given for Yaroslavl' region by Gavin Helf and Jeffrey Hahn, 'Old Dogs and New Tricks: Party Elites in the Russian Regional Elections of 1990', *Slavic Review*, vol. 51, no. 3 (fall 1992), p. 526.
5 Khasbulatov, *The Struggle for Russia*, p. 242.
6 B. N. Yeltsin, in *Chetvertyi s"ezd narodnykh deputatov RSFSR: stenograficheskii otchet*, 21–25 May 1991 (Moscow, Izd. Verkhovnogo Soveta RSFSR, 1991), vol. 1, p. 3.
7 Vitalii Vorotnikov, the outgoing chairman of the RSFSR Supreme Soviet, was elected from Adygeya; Alexander Vlasov, the former RSFSR prime minister who ran against Yeltsin in May 1990 for the post of chairman of the Russian Supreme Soviet, was nominated from Yakutia; and F. Bobkov, formerly Victor Chebrikov's right hand in the KGB, from North Ossetia, although none of them had previously had anything to do with these republics.
8 Philippe C. Schmitter, 'Reflexions on Revolutionary and Evolutionary Transitions: The Russian Case in Comparative Perspective', in A. Dallin (ed.), *Political Parties in Russia* (Berkeley, University of California Press, 1993), p. 31.
9 See Yitzhak M. Brudny, 'The Dynamics of "Democratic Russia", 1990–1993', *Post-Soviet Affairs*, vol. 9, no. 2 (1993), pp. 141–70.
10 For a fuller analysis than can be given here, see Richard Sakwa, 'The Russian Elections of December 1993', *Europe-Asia Studies*, vol. 47, no. 2 (1995), pp. 195–227.
11 'O poetapnoi konstitutsionnoe reforme v Rossiiskoi Federatsii', *Izvestiya*, 22 September 1993, p. 1.
12 *Izvestiya*, 24 September 1993, pp. 3–5.
13 Yeltsin's decree of 11 October allowed the election of the upper house ('O vyborakh v Sovet Federatsii Federal'nogo Sobraniya Rossiiskoi Federatsii'); and the decree of 6 November added yet another clause ensuring that a category of votes 'against all' was added to ballot papers, *Rossiiskaya Federatsiya*, 1 (13), 1993, pp. 7–20; *Moscow News*, 43 (22 October 1993), p. 1.
14 'O provedenii vsenarodnogo golosovaniya po proektu konstitutsii Rossiiskoi Federatsii'; accompanied on the same date by 'Polozhenie o vsenarodnom golosovanii po proektu konstitutsii Rossiiskoi Federatsii 12 dekabrya 1993 goda', in *Rossiiskaya Federatsiya*, 1 (13), 1993, pp. 22–4; *Rossiiskie vesti*, 21 October 1993. The word 'plebiscite' (*golosovanie*) was used rather than referendum.
15 The October 1990 RSFSR Referendum Law stipulated that matters affecting the constitution could be adopted by a simple majority of all registered voters, while non-constitutional matters could be decided by a simple majority of those participating in the referendum. A referendum would only be valid if turnout exceeded 50 per cent of registered voters, *Rossiiskaya gazeta*, 2 December 1990.
16 A trenchant critique of adopting the constitution by referendum was made by Rumyantsev, *Nezavisimaya gazeta*, 24 November 1993, p. 2.
17 These figures have been the subject of considerable controversy, given in *Rossiiskaya gazeta*, 21 December 1993, p. 1 and in full in *Byulleten' Tsentral'noi izbiratel'noi kommissii Rossiiskoi Federatsii* (henceforth *Byulleten' TsIK*), no. 1 (12) (1994), p. 38.
18 *Rossiiskaya gazeta*, 21 December 1993, p. 1.
19 Seven republics voted against the constitution: Adygeya, Bashkortostan, Chuvashia, Dagestan, Karachai-Cherkessia, Mordovia and Tuva; and ten oblasts: Belgorod, Bryansk, Kursk, Lipetsk, Orël, Smolensk, Tambov, Penza, Volgograd and Voronezh, mainly in the Russian south-west where support for the Communist Party was strongest (*Byulleten' TsIK*, no. 1 (12), (1994), pp. 34–8). In Tatarstan the referendum was declared invalid since not enough turned up to vote, but of those

who did 74 per cent supported the constitution, *Nezavisimaya gazeta*, 18 December 1993, p. 1. No vote took place in the Chechen Republic.

20 *Rossiiskaya gazeta*, 25 December 1993.
21 Decree of 11 October, *Rossiiskaya Federatsiya*, no. 1 (13), (1993), p. 17.
22 Ryabov, *Rossiiskaya gazeta*, 11 December 1993, p. 1.
23 Victor Sheinis in *ONS: Obshchestvennye nauki i sovremenost'*, no. 1 (1995), p. 6.
24 Cited by Victor Sheinis in *ONS: Obshchestvennye nauki i sovremenost'*, no. 1 (1995), p. 9.
25 Michael Urban, 'December 1993 as a Replication of Late-Soviet Electoral Practices', *Post-Soviet Affairs*, vol. 10, no. 2 (April–June 1994), p. 128.
26 Yeltsin decreed the increase in numbers to the State Duma on 1 October, 'Polozhenie o vyborakh deputatov Gosudarstvennoi Dumy v 1993 godu', *Rossiiskaya Federatsiya*, 1 (13) (1993), pp. 7–20; *The Political Situation in Russia: Political Parties in Russia*, (Moscow, 'EPIcenter', 1993), p. 26.
27 'Polozhenie o vyborakh deputatov Gosudarstvennoi Dumy', *Izvestiya*, 24 September 1993, pp. 3–5.
28 *Moskovskie novosti*, no. 25 (20 June 1993), p. A9.
29 *Guardian*, 8 October 1993.
30 *Izvestiya*, 4 May 1994, p. 4.
31 *Rossiiskaya gazeta*, 11 December 1993, p. 1.
32 Alexander Rahr, 'The Future of the Russian Democrats', *RFE/RL Research Report*, vol. 2, no. 39 (1 October 1993), p. 4.
33 *Rossiiskaya gazeta*, 14 October 1993, p. 3.
34 *Izvestiya*, 14 October 1993, p. 4.
35 E.g. for the RCDM, *Put'*, 1 (31) (1994), p. 3.
36 *Guardian*, 11 November 1993.
37 *Rossiiskaya gazeta*, 11 December 1993, p. 1.
38 This was the main argument of the commission into electoral fraud led by Aleksandr Sobyanin, *Izvestiya*, 4 May 1994, p. 4.
39 *Segodnya*, 10 March 1994; *Izvestiya*, 4 May 1994, p. 4; *Nezavisimaya gazeta*, 19 July 1994, p. 2.
40 Cf. Wendy Slater, 'Russia's Plebiscite on a New Constitution', *RFE/RL Research Report*, vol. 3, no. 3 (21 January 1994), pp. 1–7.
41 For an analysis of the various figures of registered voters and the differing turnout figures, see Alexander Minkin, *Moskovskii komsomolets*, 11 January 1994, p. 1, and *Pravda*, 28 December 1993, p. 1.
42 Kronid Lyubarskii, *Novoe vremya*, no. 9 (March 1994), pp. 10–13.
43 *Novoe vremya*, no. 7 (February 1994), pp. 8–12.
44 See Mary Cline, 'Nizhnii Novgorod: A Regional View of the Russian Elections', *RFE/RL Research Report*, vol. 3, no. 4 (28 January 1994), pp. 48–54.
45 For Novosibirsk oblast this is argued by Grigorii V. Golosov, mimeo.
46 *Byulleten' TsIK*, no. 1 (27) (1995), pp. 8–14; *Nezavisimaya gazeta*, 21 December 1994.
47 Yurii Vedeneev and Vladimir Lysenko, 'Konstitutsionnye vybory: inogo ne dano', *Nezavisimaya gazeta*, 19 July 1994, pp. 1, 3; 20 July 1994, pp. 1, 3.
48 *Moskovskie novosti*, no. 15 (26 February–5 March 1995), p. 8.
49 *Kommersant-Daily*, 18 November 1995.
50 *Nezavisimaya gazeta*, 16 November 1995.
51 Vyacheslav Nikonov, *Moskovskie novosti*, no. 73 (22–9 October 1995), p. 5.
52 *Moskovskie novosti*, no. 73 (22–9 October 1995), p. 6.
53 *Moskovskie novosti*, no. 75 (29 October–5 November 1995), p. 4.
54 *Moskovskie novosti*, no. 75 (29 October–5 November 1995), p. 7.
55 This is an argument made by Gleb Cherkasov, political correspondent for *Segodnya*, cited in *OMRI Special Report: Russian Election Survey*, no. 8, 21 November 1995.
56 *Moskovskii komsomolets*, 19 December 1995.
57 *Moskovskie novosti*, no. 69 (8–15 October 1995), p. 6.
58 *Moskovskie novosti*, no. 73 (22–9 October 1995), p. 6.
59 *Independent*, 17 October 1995, p. 13.
60 *Moskovskie novosti*, no. 71 (15–22 October 1995), p. 6; *Sovetskaya Rossiya*, 18 November 1995.
61 *The Economist*, 7 October 1995, p. 55.
62 *Moskovskie novosti*, no. 61 (10–17 September 1995), p.5.
63 *Observer*, 1 October 1995, p. 23.
64 *Moskovskie novosti*, no. 61 (10–17 September 1995), p.5.
65 *Moskovskie novosti*, no. 71 (15–22 October 1995), p. 7.

66 E.g. *Moskovskie novosti*, no. 77 (5–12 November 1995), p. 7.
67 *Segodnya*, 27 September 1995, p. 2.
68 The term 'soft' backlash is from Urban, 'December 1993', p. 135, note 19.
69 Dmitrii Ol'shanskii correctly predicted that voter turnout would be in the 60–70 percent range, *Trud*, 16 June 1995, p. 6.
70 Sergei Mdoyants, Aleksei Salmin, 'Pobedit sluchainyi', *Moskovskie novosti*, no. 71 (15–22 October 1995), p. 6.
71 *Moskovskie novosti*, no. 13 (19–26 February 1995), p. 9.
72 *Moskovskie novosti*, no. 44 (25 June-2 July 1995), p. 4.
73 *Moskovskie novosti*, no. 15 (26 February-5 March 1995), p. 8; *The Economist*, 7 October 1995, p. 56.
74 *Moskovskie novosti*, no. 15 (26 February-5 March 1995), p. 8.
75 See for example Stephen L. White, 'Democratizing Eastern Europe: The Elections of 1990', vol. 9, no. 4 (1990), pp. 277–87; Bogdanor, V., 'Founding Elections Regime Change', *Electoral Studies*, vol. 9, no. 4 (1990), pp. 288–94.
76 Cf. Sergei Mdoyants and Aleksei Salmin, 'Dozhivem li do "rytinoi" demokratii', *Moskovskie novosti*, no. 63 (17–24 September 1995), p. 6.
77 These are discussed by Geoffrey Evans and Stephen Whitefield, 'Identifying the Bases of Party Competition in Eastern Europe', *British Journal of Political Science*, vol. 23, no. 4 (1993), pp. 521–48.
78 This is argued by Fedor Burlatskii, *Nezavisimaya gazeta*, 16 December 1993, p. 2.

6 REMAKING THE STATE: THE LEGISLATURE

1 Edmund Burke, 'Causes of Present Discontents', in *Edmund Burke on Revolution*, edited by Robert A. Smith (New York, Harper and Row, 1968), pp. 30–31.
2 See Michel Lesage, 'The Crisis of Public Administration in Russia', *Public Administration*, vol. 71 (spring/summer 1993), pp. 121–33.
3 *Literaturnaya gazeta*, 19 February 1992, p. 3.
4 T. H. Rigby, *The Changing Soviet System: Mono-Organisational Socialism from its Origins to Gorbachev's Restructuring* (Aldershot, Edward Elgar, 1990).
5 'Ob izmeneniyakh i dopolneniyakh Konstitutsii (Osnovnogo Zakona) RSFSR', in *Rossiya segodnya: politicheskii portret v dokumentakh, 1991–1992* (Moscow, Mezhdunar. otnosheniya, 1993), pp. 24–7; for more details, see chapter 7.
6 *Izvestiya*, 12 March 1992, p. 1.
7 See Archie Brown, 'The October Crisis of 1993: Context and Implications', *Post-Soviet Affairs*, vol. 9, no. 3 (1993), pp. 183–95.
8 By mid-1993 the constitution had been amended over 300 times, and the incremental nature of constitutional revision gave rise to numerous contradictions. Chief among them was the vesting of supreme power in both the legislative and executive.
9 Article 104 of the amended 1978 constitution.
10 *Sed'moi s"ezd narodnykh deputatov Rossiiskoi Federatsii: byulleten'*, no. 23 (14 December 1992), pp. 12–13.
11 For Travkin's comments, see *Demokraticheskaya gazeta*, no. 8 (July 1991), p. 2.
12 *Rossiiskaya gazeta*, 29 October 1991, p. 1.
13 *Rossiiskaya gazeta*, 8 April 1992; Dominic Gualtieri, 'Russia's New "War of Laws"', *RFE/RL Research Report*, vol. 2, no. 35 (3 September 1993), pp. 10–15, at p. 14.
14 Report by the analytical centre RF-Politika, *Nezavisimaya gazeta*, 9 July 1992.
15 A. Nazimova and V. Sheinis (*Argumenty i fakty*, no. 17 (1990), pp. 1–2) state that 135 (13.2 per cent) were from the intelligentsia, and 584 deputies (57 per cent) (including 3 top leaders) from top and middle levels of the apparatus and 452 (43 per cent) from other groups.
16 Of these, 228 (22 per cent) were from higher managerial positions in the top ranks of the CPSU, senior ministerial officials, chairs of higher level soviets, and suchlike; 386 (36 per cent) were middle level officials, local party secretaries, leaders of local soviets, military commanders, KGB officials, factory and farm directors; while 213 (21 per cent) came from the lowest managerial tier involved in local management, section heads of research institutes, secretaries of factory party committees, and the like.
17 A. A. Sobyanin (ed.), *VI se"d narodnykh deputatov Rossii: politicheskie itogi i perspektivy*

(analyticheskii otchet o rezul'tatakh poimennykh golosovanii na VI S"ezde narodnykh deputatov Rossiiskoi Federatsii (6–21 Aprelya 1992g.) (Moscow, Organisational Department of the Presidium of the Supreme Soviet of the Russian Federation, 1992), pp. 14, 21–22.

18 According to the declared positions of the factions during the Sixth Congress, some 340 deputies could be considered democrats, 124 in the middle (the so-called *marais* or marsh), and 353 conservatives, but the voting itself revealed that only 240 consistently supported 'democratic' positions, 227 were waverers, and 571 solidly conservative (Sobyanin (ed.), *VI s"ezd narodnykh deputatov Rossii*, pp. 7–8), a balance of forces reflected once again in the voting at the Seventh Congress in December 1992.

19 This is demonstrated for the first four Russian congresses in A. Sobyanin and D. Yur'ev, *S"ezd narodnykh deputatov RSFSR v zerkale poimennykh golosovanii: rasstanovka sil i dinamika razvitiya politicheskogo protivostoyaniya* (Moscow, Informal Analytical Group, 1991).

20 For criticisms of Khasbulatov, see Otto Latsis, *Izvestiya*, 28 August 1992, p. 3; *Nezavisimaya gazeta*, 1 September 1992; Maria Bogatykh, *Rossiya*, no. 36 (94), 2 September 1992, p. 1; Georgi Ivanov-Smolenskii, *Izvestiya*, 3 September 1992, p. 2; interview with Sergei Yushenkov, coordinator of the Radical Democrats faction, *Rossiiskie vesti*, 10 September 1992, p. 2.

21 Author's interview with Khasbulatov, 15 December 1992.

22 This is the argument of his book, Khasbulatov, *The Struggle for Russia*.

23 Article 104 of the amended 1978 constitution, *Konstitutsiya (osnovnoi zakon) RSFSR* (Moscow, Sovetskaya Rossiya), 1991, pp. 32–3.

24 The balance of forces was as follows: some 294 deputies were grouped under the umbrella of the Coalition of Reforms; 170 with the Bloc of Constructive Forces; some 269 independents with another 63 independent-minded deputies in the Sovereignty and Equality faction; and 290 in the oppositional bloc 'Russian Unity', Sobyanin (ed.), *VI s"ezd narodnykh deputatov Rossii*, p. 11.

25 Viktor Sheinis, *Nezavisimaya gazeta*, 23 May 1992, p. 2.

26 *Izvestiya*, 11 June 1992.

27 *Rossiiskaya gazeta*, 30 July 1992, pp. 1–2.

28 Alexander Rahr, 'The First Year of Russian Independence', *RFE/RL Research Report*, vol. 2, no. 1 (1 January 1993), pp. 50–57, at p. 55.

29 Some 267 deputies were grouped under the umbrella of the Coalition of Reforms; 155 with the Bloc of Constructive Forces; some 208 independents with another 51 independent-minded deputies in the Sovereignty and Equality faction; and 359 in the oppositional bloc 'Russian Unity', *Sed'moi s"ezd narodnykh deputatov Rossiiskoi Federatsii: byulleten'*, no. 24 (14 December 1992), p. 15.

30 *Rossiiskaya gazeta*, 2 December 1992, pp. 3–4.

31 *Rossiiskaya gazeta*, 2 December 1992, pp. 3–5.

32 *Rossiiskaya gazeta*, 11 December 1992, pp. 1–2.

33 *Sed'moi s"ezd narodnykh deputatov Rossiiskoi Federatsii: byulleten'*, no. 18 (10 December 1992), pp. 4–5.

34 11 December 1992, p. 1.

35 *Rossiiskaya gazeta*, 15 December 1992, p. 1.

36 *Rossiiskaya gazeta*, 15 December 1992; *Nezavisimaya gazeta*, 15 December 1992.

37 *Nezavisimaya gazeta*, 28 November 1991, p. 1.

38 *Independent*, 10 February 1993.

39 *Pravda*, 4 March 1993.

40 Alexander Rahr, 'Roots of the Power Struggle', *RFE/RL Research Report* (14 May 1993), p. 12.

41 Khasbulatov, *The Struggle for Russia*, pp. 7–8 and *passim*.

42 *Izvestiya*, 13 August 1993, p. 2.

43 *Izvestiya*, 13 August 1993, p. 2.

44 *Rossiiskaya gazeta*, 22 July 1993, p. 1.

45 *Moscow News*, no. 39 (24 September 1993), pp. 1–2.

46 Julia Wishnevsky, 'Corruption Allegations Undermine Russia's Leaders', *RFE/RL Research Report*, vol. 2, no. 37 (17 September 1993), pp. 16–22.

47 *Rossiiskie vesti*, 2 September 1993, p. 1.

48 *Izvestiya*, 22 September 1993, p. 1.

49 *Sovetskaya Rossiya*, 23 September 1993, p. 1. On 30 September the Constitutional Court suspended the membership of three of the judges (one on health grounds), though the other two (Ernst Ametistov and Nikolai Vitruk) had already declared that they would no longer participate in the Court's work.

50 *RFE/RL News Briefs*, 27 September 1993, p. 1.

51 This at least is the view of Yurii Luzhkov, Mayor of Moscow and Yeltsin's strong supporter, *Moscow News*, no. 41 (8 October 1993), p. 4.

52 *RFE/RL News Briefs*, 1 October 1993, p. 5.
53 *RFE/RL News Briefs*, 27 September 1993, p. 1.
54 *RFE/RL News Briefs*, 28 September 1993, p. 2.
55 *Kommersant*, 25 September 1993.
56 *Moscow News*, no. 41 (8 October 1993), p. 8.
57 *RFE/RL News Briefs*, 1 October 1993, p. 5.
58 *RFE/RL News Briefs*, 29 September 1993, p. 4.
59 *Izvestiya*, 29 September 1993.
60 *Izvestiya*, 25 December 1993, p. 1.
61 Sergei Kovalev, *Moscow News*, no. 40 (1 October 1993), p. 2.
62 *Moscow News*, no. 39 (24 September 1993), p. 1.
63 Vera Tolz, 'Crisis as a Form of Political Development', *RFE/RL Research Report*, vol. 2, no. 20 (14 May 1993), pp. 4–8, at p. 6.
64 *Nezavisimaya gazeta*, 30 December 1993, p. 2.
65 The public chamber of the Constitutional Assembly had opposed granting the FC rather than the Duma powers endorsing presidential decrees on a state of emergency, martial law and the deployment of troops abroad, but had been overruled, Viktor Sheinis, *Moscow News*, no. 46 (12 November 1993), p. 2.
66 *Moskovskie novosti*, no. 69 (8–15 October 1995), p. 7.
67 *Nezavisimaya gazeta*, 6 December 1995, p. 1.
68 The *reglament* was devised by a presidential commission chaired by Mikhail Mityukov.
69 For his views, see Ivan Rybkin, *Gosudarstvennaya duma: pytaya popytka* (Moscow, 1994); *My obrecheny na soglasie* (Moscow, Mezhdunarodnye otnosheniya, 1994).
70 N. Shelyutto, 'Osobennosti novykh vyborov', *Rossiiskaya Federatsiya: Obshchestvenno-politicheskii zhurnal* (formerly *Narodnyi deputat*), no. 1 (13) (1993), p. 27.
71 *Izvestiya*, 1 February 1994, p. 3.
72 Ivan Maximov, *Moskovskii komsomolets*, 17 November 1995, p. 1.
73 *Moscow News*, no. 45 (5 November 1993), p. 2.
74 *OMRI Daily Digest*, no. 249, Part I, 27 December 1995.
75 Wendy Slater, 'Russian Duma Sidelines Extremist Politicians', *RFE-RL Research Report* (18 February 1994), p. 5.
76 Andrei Aizderdzis, Valentin Martem'yanov and Sergei Skorochkin, *Moskovskie novosti*, no. 13 (19–26 February 1995), p. 14.
77 *Rosiiskaya gazeta*, 23 December 1994, p. 1.
78 *Nezavisimaya gazeta*, 12 January 1996, p. 2.
79 Ludmila Telen, *Moskovskie novosti*, no. 87 (1995), p. 8.
80 *Izvestiya*, 2 December 1995.
81 *Segodnya*, 18 January 1996, p. 1.
82 The seven factions and groups in January 1996 were the CPRF (headed by Zyuganov) with 149 members, Russia Our Home (Sergei Belyaev) 55, LDPR (Zhirinovskii) 51, Yabloko (Yavlinskii) 46, Russian Regions (Ramazan Abdulatipov and Artur Chilingarov) 42, Popular Power (Nikolai Ryzhkov) 37, and the Agrarians (Nikolai Kharitonov) 35.
83 Alfred B. Evans, Jr., 'Problems of Conflict Management in Russian Politics', *The Journal of Communist Studies*, vol. 9, no. 2 (June 1993), pp. 1–19.
84 *Moscow News*, no. 46 (12 November 1993), p. 1.

7 REMAKING THE STATE: THE EXECUTIVE

1 Thomas Paine, *Rights of Man* (London, Penguin, 1984), p. 191.
2 Cf. Juan Linz, 'The Perils of Presidentialism', *Journal of Democracy*, vol. 1, no. 1 (winter 1990), pp. 72–84; Juan J. Linz and Arturo Valenzuela (eds), *The Failure of Presidential Democracy: Comparative Perspectives* (Baltimore, Johns Hopkins University Press, 1994); see also Arend Lijphart (ed.), *Parliamentary versus Presidential Government* (Oxford, Oxford University Press, 1992).
3 *Demokraticheskaya gazeta*, 12 (15) (12–19 September 1991), p. 3.
4 *Rossiiskaya gazeta*, 8 April 1992, pp. 1–4.
5 See Stephen White, 'The Presidency and Political Leadership', in Lentini (ed.), *Elections and Political Order in Russia*, pp. 202–25.

6 *Moscow News*, no. 25 (23 June 1991), p. 1.

7 Ann Sheehy, 'The All-Union and RSFSR Referendums', *Radio Liberty Report on the USSR*, vol. 3, no. 13 (26 March 1991), p. 23.

8 The law on the presidency is in *Vedemosti S"ezda narodnykh deputatov RSFSR i verkhovnogo Soveta RSFSR*, no. 17 (1991), 512.

9 Michael E. Urban, 'El'tsin, Democratic Russia and the Campaign for the Russian Presidency', *Soviet Studies*, vol. 44, no. 2 (1992), pp. 187–207.

10 For details of the vote, including regional analysis, see D. Yurev, *Prezidentskie vybory* (Moscow, 1991).

11 *Rossiiskaya gazeta*, 31 October and 1 November 1991; *Izvestiya*, 2 and 4 November 1991.

12 *Demokraticheskaya gazeta*, 12 (15) (12–19 September 1991), p. 3.

13 M. Fedotov, *Soviet Weekly*, 24 October 1991.

14 See Eugene Huskey, 'The State-Legal Administration and the Politics of Redundancy', *Post-Soviet Affairs*, vol. 11, no. 2 (1995), pp. 115–43.

15 The core of the State Council consisted of five presidential advisers (also known as state councillors) and the heads of the nine most important ministries.

16 Konstantin Medvedev, 'V Rossii vozmozhna smena kursa', *Nezavisimaya gazeta*, 7 December 1991, p. 2.

17 Namely, state secretary of the RSFSR, secretary of the State Council (19 July 1991), state secretary of the RSFSR (7 April 1992), state secretary to the president (8 May 1992), and finally, adviser without title (14 December 1992), Lesage, 'The Crisis of Public Administration in Russia', p. 129.

18 At the Institute of the USSR Ministry of Non-Ferrous Metallurgy.

19 *Novoe vremya*, no. 34 (August 1992), pp. 14–16.

20 *Soviet Weekly*, 3 October 1991, p. 5.

21 *Demokraticheskaya gazeta*, no. 12 (15) (12–19 September 1991), p. 3.

22 *Rossiiskaya gazeta*, 11 June 1992, p. 5.

23 Alexander Rahr, 'Moscow One Year after the Attempted Coup', *RFE/RL Research Report*, vol. 1, no. 33 (21 August 1992), pp. 1–4.

24 Suzanne Crow, 'Russia Prepares to Take a Hard Line on "Near Abroad"', *RFE/RL Research Report*, vol. 1, no. 32, pp. 21–4.

25 *Trud*, 12 June 1992; see also Yeltsin's interview in *Izvestiya*, 11 June 1992.

26 E.g Shakhrai, *Komsomolskaya pravda*, 18 June 1992.

27 On 20 October 1993 its membership became: Gaidar, Golushko, Grachev, Danilov-Danilyan, Erin, Kalmykov, Kozyrev, Nechaev, Primakov, Fedorov and Shakhrai.

28 See Lieutenant-General Valeri Manilov's interview in *Moskovskie novosti*, no. 23 (5–12 June 1994), p. 11.

29 At that time its membership of fourteen was as follows: Chairman Boris Yeltsin, Secretary Oleg Lobov, Viktor Chernomyrdin (prime minister), Vladimir Shumeiko (chair of the Federation Council), Ivan Rybkin (speaker of the State Duma), Andrei Kozyrev (foreign minister), Sergei Stepashin (director of the Federal Counter-Intelligence Service – FSK), Pavel Grachev (defence minister), Viktor Erin (minister of internal affairs), Andrei Nikolaev (director of the Federal Border Service), Sergei Shakhrai (deputy prime minister), Evgenii Primakov (director of the Foreign Intelligence Service) and Sergei Shoigu (minister for emergency situations) (*Moskovskie novosti*, no. 63 (11–18 December 1994), p. 4). Vladimir Panskov (minister of finances) joined the Security Council in January 1995, *Segodnya*, 17 January 1995, p. 1.

30 *Moskovskie novosti*, no. 63 (11–18 December 1994), p. 4.

31 *Nezavisimaya gazeta*, 4 December 1993, p. 2.

32 *Stolitsa*, no. 50 (160) (December 1993), p. 4.

33 *Pravda*, 19 January 1994.

34 *Rossiiskaya gazeta*, 5 November 1991, p. 1.

35 Sergei Peregudov, *Nezavisimaya gazeta*, 19 February 1993, p. 2.

36 Alexander Rahr, 'Liberal-Centrist Coalition Takes Over in Russia', *RFE/RL Research Report*, vol. 1, no. 29 (21 August 1992), pp. 22–5, at p. 23.

37 *Nezavisimaya gazeta*, 26 May 1992.

38 *RFE/RL Research Report*, vol. 1, no. 3 (31 July 1992), p. 78.

39 *Argumenty i fakty*, no. 32 (August 1992), pp. 1–2.

40 *Moscow News*, no. 42 (18 October 1992), pp. 6–7; *RFE/RL Research Report*, vol. 1, no. 29 (17 July 1992), pp. 70–72.

41 *Rossiiskaya gazeta*, 7 November 1992, pp. 1, 5.

42 Matthew Campbell, 'The Invisible Coup', *Sunday Times*, 20 December 1992, p. 11.

43 Alexander Mechitov, 'Iskusstvo vozmozhnogo', *Moskovskie novosti*, no. 77 (5–12 November 1995), p. 6.
44 OMRI Special Report: Russian Election Survey, no. 13, 12 December 1995.
45 *Moscow News*, no. 45 (5 November 1993), p. 2.
46 See V. B. Pastukhov, 'Stanovlenie Rossiiskoi gosudarstvennosti i konstitutsionnyi protsess: politologicheskii aspekt', *Gosudarstvo i pravo*, no. 2 (1993), pp. 89–96.
47 Pastukhov, 'Stanovlenie', p. 89.
48 S. Filatov, 'Power and Business', *Rossiiskaya gazeta*, 30 December 1992; *Rossiiskie vesti*, 30 December 1992.
49 *Trud*, 27 July 1995.
50 *Nezavisimaya gazeta*, 9 November 1993, p. 1.
51 *Segodnya*, 13 November 1993, p. 2.
52 *Moskovskie novosti*, no. 47 (21 November 1993), p. A13.

8 THE POLITICS OF PLURALISM

1 Plato, 'The Philosopher Ruler', *The Republic*, Part 7, Book 7 (London, Penguin, 1955), pp. 284–5 (modified translation).
2 Peter Kirkow, 'Regional Warlordism in Russia: The Case of Primorskii Krai', *Europe-Asia Studies*, vol. 47, no. 6 (September 1995), p. 923.
3 See David Lane (ed.), *Russia in Flux* (Aldershot, Edward Elgar, 1992), in particular his 'Soviet Elites, Monolithic or Polyarchic?', pp. 3–23.
4 See Evgenii Krasnikov, 'Kluby vmesto partii?', *Nezavisimaya gazeta*, 20 July 1994, p. 2.
5 '"Delovaya elita" idet vo vlast', *Moskovskie novosti*, no. 22 (2–9 April 1995), p. 7.
6 T. Gdlyan and E. Dodolev, *Mafiya vremen bezzakoniya* (Erevan, Izdatel'stvo AN Armenii, 1991).
7 *Moscow News*, no. 37 (1991), p. 6.
8 Stanislav Govorukhin, *Velikaya kriminal'naya revolyutsiya* (Moscow, 'Andreevskii flag', 1993).
9 Milovan Djilas, *The New Class* (New York, Praeger, 1957).
10 Zvi Gitelman, 'Working the Soviet System: Citizens and Urban Bureaucracies', in Henry W. Morton and Robert C. Stuart (eds), *The Contemporary Soviet City* (New York, M.E. Sharpe, 1984), p. 241.
11 J. F. Hough, *The Soviet Prefects: The Local Party Organs in Industrial Decision-making* (Cambridge, MA, Harvard University Press, 1969).
12 See Mary McAuley, 'Politics, Economics and Elite Realignment in Russia: a Regional Perspective', *Soviet Economy*, vol. 8, pp. 46–88.
13 Cf. Michael Voslensky, *Nomenklatura: Anatomy of the Soviet Ruling Class* (London, Bodley Head, 1980).
14 *Moscow News*, no. 37 (10 September 1993), p. 7.
15 Olga Kryshtanovskaya, 'Transformatsiya staroi nomenklatury v novuyu Rossiiskuyu elitu', *Obshchestvennye nauki i sovremennost'*, no. 1 (1995), p. 64.
16 Olga Kryshtanovskaya, *Izvestiya*, 10 January 1996; see also her 'The Transformation of the Old Nomenklatura Into a New Russian Elite', *Izvestiya*, 18 May 1994, p. 2; and 'Transformatsiya staroi nomenklatury v novuyu rossiiskuyu elitu', *ONS: Obshchestvennye nauki i sovremennost'*, no. 1 (1995), pp. 51–65.
17 The idea of a 'party of bosses' comes from Grigorii V. Golosov, 'Russian Political Parties and the "Party of Bosses": Evidence from the 1994 Provincial Elections in Western Siberia', mimeo, forthcoming in *Party Politics*, 1996; also *Vestnik moskovskogo universiteta: sotsial'no-politicheskie nauki*, forthcoming 1996.
18 Thomas Graham, 'The New Russian Regime', *Nezavisimaya gazeta*, 23 November 1995.
19 Guillermo O'Donnell, 'Delegative Democracy', *Journal of Democracy*, vol. 5, no. 1 (January 1994), pp. 55–69.
20 Guillermo O'Donnell, 'On the State, Democratization and some Conceptual Problems (A Latin American View with Glances at some Postcommunist Countries)', *World Development*, vol. 21, no. 8 (1993), pp. 1355–69, at p. 1367.
21 See Adam Przeworski, *Democracy and the Market: Political and Economic Reforms in Eastern Europe and Latin America* (Cambridge, Cambridge University Press, 1991); John F. Helliwell, 'Empirical Linkages Between Democracy and Economic Growth', *British Journal of Political Science*, vol. 24, no. 2 (1994), pp. 225–48.
22 E.g. Richard Lowenthal, 'Development Vs Utopia in Communist Policy', in Chalmers Johnson (ed.), *Change in Communist Systems* (Stanford, CA, Stanford University Press, 1970), pp. 33–116.

23 George W. Breslauer, 'On the Adaptability of Soviet Welfare-State Authoritarianism', in Karl Ryavec (ed.), *Soviet Society and the Communist Party* (Amherst, University of Massachusetts Press, 1978), pp. 3–25. See also Linda J. Cook, *The Social Contract and Why it Failed* (Cambridge, MA, Harvard University Press, 1993).

24 Solzhenitsyn, *Rebuilding Russia*, pp. 86–7.

25 *Rossiiskaya gazeta*, 29 October 1991, p. 2.

26 Cf. Paul Lewis, 'Civil Society and the Development of Political Parties in East-Central Europe', *The Journal of Communist Studies*, vol. 9, no. 4 (December 1993), pp. 5–20.

27 John Laughland, *The Death of Politics under Mitterand* (London, Michael Joseph, 1994).

28 W.M. Reissinger, A.H. Miller and V.L. Hesli, 'Political Norms in Rural Russia', *Europe-Asia Studies*, vol. 47, no. 6 (September 1995), p. 1030.

29 *Soviet Weekly*, 24 October 1991, p. 3.

30 *Literaturnaya gazeta*, 19 February 1992, p. 3.

31 *Guardian*, 30 December 1991.

32 Pavel Voshchanov, Yeltsin's former press secretary, interviewed by Jonathan Steele, *Guardian*, 21 December 1992.

33 Yu. G. Burtin and E. D. Molchanov (eds), *God posle Avgusta: gorech' i vybor* (Moscow, Literatura i politika, 1992), p. 247.

34 Burtin (ed.), *God posle Avgusta*, p. 129.

35 Yurii Afanas'ev, '"Narodovlastie" protiv demokratii', in Burtin (ed.), *God posle Avgusta*, pp. 111–16.

36 For a discussion of the problems of democratic consolidation in Russia, see Liliya Shevtsova, 'Vlast' v Rossii: problemy i tupiki konsolidatsii', in Burtin (ed.), *God posle Avgusta*, pp. 117–28.

37 *Argumenty i fakty*, no. 41 (1991), p. 2.

38 Burtin and Molchanov (eds), *God posle Avgusta*, in particular the article by Yu. Afanas'ev, pp. 1–12).

39 Urban, 'El'tsin, Democratic Russia and the Presidency', p. 202; their comments are reported by Valerii Vyzhutovich, 'My podderzhivaem El'tsina uslovno', *Izvestiya*, 7 October 1991.

40 *Moscow News*, no. 22 (31 May 1992), p. 2.

41 *Izvestiya*, 22 August 1992, p. 1.

42 In early 1992 Yeltsin was rated positively by 48 per cent of the electorate; by December 1992, when he was forced to sacrifice Gaidar, this had fallen to 32 per cent; and by December 1993, following the use of tanks against the Russian parliament, only 25 per cent admitted to confidence in him; while in 1994 a series of public relations disasters (the over-enthusiastic attempt to conduct an orchestra in Berlin on 31 August and the failure to come out of the plane to meet the Irish prime minister soon afterwards) saw his ratings fall below 12 per cent, and the Chechen war reduced this to 8 per cent, while 72 per cent lacked confidence in him, *Moskovskie novosti*, no. 13 (19–26 February 1995), p. 8.

43 *Moskovskie novosti*, no. 13 (19–26 February 1995), p. 9.

44 *Segodnya*, 23 February 1995.

45 *Moskovskie novosti*, no. 63 (11–18 December 1994), p. 2.

46 *Independent*, 4 November 1995.

47 Oleg Moroz, *Literaturnaya gazeta*, no. 46 (1995), p. 10.

48 Adam Michnik, 'My Vote Against Wałesa', *New York Review of Books*, 20 December 1990, pp. 47–50.

49 *Guardian*, 21 December 1992.

9 FEDERALISM AND THE STATE

1 *Rossiya*, 51 (109) (16 December 1992), p. 14. Professor Yasin led a research group under the Union of Industrialists and Entrepreneurs and later became economy minister.

2 Cited in Paul Dukes, *The Last Great Game: USA versus USSR* (London, Macmillan, 1989).

3 E. H. Carr, *The Bolshevik Revolution, 1917–1921*, vol. 1 (London, Penguin, 1966), p. 272.

4 On the creation of the USSR, see A. M. Salmin, *SNG: sostoyanie i perspektivy razvitiya* (Moscow, Gorbachev-Fond, 1992); Victor Swoboda, 'Was The Soviet Union Really Necessary?', *Soviet Studies*, vol. 44, no. 5 (1992), pp. 761–84.

5 Alan P. Pollard, (ed), *USSR: Facts and Figures Annual*, vol. 15, 1991 (Gulf Breeze, FL, Academic International Press, 1991), pp. 2, 504.

6 This certainly was the view of Khasbulatov, and in August 1990 he devised a constitution for a new federation of sovereign states, *The Struggle for Russia*, pp. 128–36.

7 *Moscow News*, no. 37 (1991), p. 5.

8 For Gorbachev's views, see his *Soyuz mozhno bylo sokhranit'* (Moscow, izd. 'aprel'-85', 1995).

9 Titular nationalities were an absolute majority in Dagestan (80.2 per cent), Chechen-Ingushetia (70.7 per cent, Chechens alone comprised 58 per cent of Chechen-Ingushetia), Chuvashia (67.8 per cent), Tyva (64.3 per cent), Komi-Permyak okrug (60.2 per cent), Kabardino-Balkaria (57.7 per cent), Buryats of the Aga-Buryat autonomous okrug (54.9 per cent), North Ossetia (53.0 per cent); and comparative majorities in Tatarstan (48.5 per cent), Kalmykia (45.4 per cent), and Mari-El (43.3 per cent), *All-Union Census of the Population of 1989* (Moscow, 1991), pp. 28–33.

10 Salmin, *SNG: sostoyanie i perspektivy razvitiya*, pp. 12, 19.

11 Calculations by A. I. Vdovin in A. S. Barsenkov *et al, Towards a Nationalities Policy in the Russian Federation*, Centre for Soviet and East European Studies, University of Aberdeen, 1993, p. 16.

12 Adygeya had been subordinate to Krasnodar krai; Gorno-Altai to Altai krai; Khakassia to Krasnoyarsk krai; and Karachai-Cherkessia to Stavropol krai.

13 *Politicheskii monitoring Rossii*, no. 3 (July–September 1992), pp. 44–5.

14 Ann Sheehy, 'Russia Republic's: A Threat to its Territorial Integrity?', *RFE/RL Research Report*, vol. 2, no. 20 (14 May 1993), p. 36.

15 The LDPR won 35.34 per cent of the party-list vote in Mordovia, 22 per cent in Tatarstan, 27.45 per cent in Khakassia and 22.53 per cent in Chuvashia (*Byulleten' TsIK*, no. 1 (12), 1994, pp. 52–4). Zhirinovskii's support was strongest where identities are the most strongly divided: for example, Russian soldiers in Tajikistan and the Russian population of Kaliningrad.

16 On 5 October 1990 Adygeya raised its status to an autonomous republic; on 8 October the Koryak autonomous okrug declared itself sovereign; on 10 October Buryatia; on 11 October Bashkiria; on 16 October Yamalo-Nenets autonomous okrug; on 18 October Kalmykiya; on 22 October Mari ASSR; on 24 October Chuvashia; on 25 October Gorno-Altai; and so on until Dagestan on 13 May 1991 and, last of all and not to be left out, Birobidjan (Jewish autonomous oblast) on 5 November 1991 declared itself sovereign.

17 Cited in Dunlop, *The Rise of Russia*, p. 62.

18 *Rossiiskaya gazeta*, 29 October 1991, p. 2.

19 Yelena Bonner, *Guardian*, 6 January 1992; *Nezavisimaya gazeta*, 5 January 1992.

20 *Gubernatorskie novosti*, no. 9 (March 1993), pp. 3–4.

21 Vladimir Lysenko, Deputy Chairman of the State Committee for Nationality Policy of the Russian Federation, *Rossiiskaya gazeta*, 1 December 1992, p. 4.

22 *Rossiiskaya gazeta*, 1 December 1992, p. 4.

23 *Rossiiskaya gazeta*, 5 November 1991, p. 1.

24 The plan is explained at some length by Rumyantsev, *Rossiiskaya gazeta*, 11 October 1991, p. 7.

25 *Rossiiskaya gazeta*, 11 October 1991, p. 7.

26 *Nezavisimaya gazeta*, 27 November 1991.

27 *Federativnyi dogovor: dokumenty, kommentarii* (Moscow, Supreme Soviet of the Russian Federation, 1992).

28 The three Federal Treaties are in *Konstitutsiya (osnovnoi zakon) Rossiiskoi Federatsii-Rossii* (Moscow, Izvestiya, 1992), pp. 81–108.

29 *Nezavisimaya gazeta*, 1 April 1992, p. 1.

30 *Federativnyi dogovor*, p. 4.

31 *Izvestiya*, 14 August 1992; *Nezavisimaya gazeta*, 15 August 1992.

32 *Konstitutsiya respubliki Tatarstan*, adopted on 6 November 1992 (Kazan, Tatarskoe knizhnoe izd., 1993), p. 14.

33 The Seventh Congress failed to adopt a constitutional amendment that would have allowed the Constitutional Court to rescind legislative acts of the republics if it found them unlawful, *Moscow News*, no. 6 (4 February 1993), p. 3.

34 Sergei Khrushchev, 'The Political Economy of Russia's Regional Fragmentation', in Douglas Blum (ed.), *Russia's Future: Consolidation or Disintegration?* (Boulder, CO, Westview Press), pp. 93–4.

35 *Moskovskie novosti*, no. 85 (10–17 December 1995), p. 9.

36 *Segodnya*, 13 November 1993, p. 2.

37 E.g. Sergei Shakhrai, *Kommersant-Daily*, 31 August 1995, pp. 1, 3.

38 Burbulis in *Nezavisimaya gazeta*, 28 November 1991, p. 1.

39 *Izvestiya*, 19 August 1992, p. 2.

10 NATIONALISM AND RUSSIA

1 Ivan Turgenev, 'On the Russian Language', in George Gibian (ed.), *The Portable Nineteenth-Century Russian Reader* (London, Penguin Books, 1993), p. 391.
2 Cf. Ronald Grigor Suny, 'States, Empires and Nations', *Post-Soviet Affairs*, vol. 11, no. 2 (1995), pp. 185–96, at p. 190.
3 Igor Klyamkin, *Ogonek*, no. 47 (1995), p. 19.
4 Len Karpinskii, cited by Tony Barber 'Democracy Tears Russia to Shreds', *Independent on Sunday*, 22 March 1992.
5 E.g. Mykhailo Hrushevs'kyi in S. Frederick Starr (ed.), *The Legacy of History on the Foreign Policies of the New States of the Former Soviet Union* (New York, M.E. Sharpe, 1994).
6 Alexander Zinoviev, *Katastroika* (London, Claridge Press, 1990).
7 This was the view of the 'patriots' associated with the newspaper *Den'* (*Day*) edited by Prokhanov, sponsored by the Union of Russian Writers.
8 Roman Szporluk, 'Dilemmas of Russian Nationalism', *Problems of Communism*, vol. 38, no. 4 (July–August 1989), pp. 15–35.
9 Mark R. Beissinger, 'The Persisting Ambiguity of Empire', *Post-Soviet Affairs*, vol. 11, no. 2 (1995), pp. 149–84, at p. 158.
10 *Argumenty i fakty*, no. 32 (August 1992), p. 2.
11 Vladimir Ilyushenko, *Literaturnaya gazeta*, 19 February 1992, p. 11.
12 For a good analysis of the rebirth of Russian nationalism, see Stephen K. Carter, *Russian Nationalism* (London, Pinter, 1990); and Dina Rome Spechler, 'Russian Nationalism and Soviet Politics', in Lubomyr Hajda and Mark Beissinger (eds), *The Nationalities Factor in Soviet Politics* (Boulder, CO, Westview Press, 1990), pp. 281–304.
13 Alexander Solzhenitsyn, *Letter to the Soviet Leaders* (New York, Harper and Row, 1974).
14 Igor Shafarevich, 'Separation or Reconciliation? – The Nationalities Question in the USSR' and 'Does Russia Have a Future', in Alexander Solzhenitsyn (ed.), *From Under the Rubble*, (London, Fontana, 1976), pp. 88–104, 279–94; and see also his 'Russofobiya', *Nash sovremennik*, no. 6, 1989; on allied questions see G. Popov and N. Adzhubei, 'Pamyat' i "Pamyat"': o problemakh istoricheskoi pamyati i sovremennykh natsional'nykh otnoshenii', *Znamya*, no. 1, 1988.
15 The roots of this thinking, the relationship between Nikolai Trubetskoi's anti-Western polemic *Europe and Humanity* (1921) and Nikolai Ustryalov's 'changing landmarks' (*smenovekhovtsy*) movement that endorsed the Bolshevik revolution since it appeared to augment Russian national power, are discussed by Jane Burbank, *Intelligentsia and Revolution* (Oxford, Oxford University Press, 1986), pp. 208–37.
16 E. A. Pozdnyakov, *Natsiya, natsionalizm, natsional'nye interesy* (Moscow, Progress-kultura, 1994), p. 61.
17 Pozdnyakov, *Natsiya, natsionalizm, natsional'nye interesy*, p. 74.
18 Solzhenitsyn, *Rebuilding Russia*, p. 15.
19 *Moscow News*, no. 37 (1991), p. 5.
20 An argument proposed by a leading Christian Democrat in Moscow, Victor Rott, 'The Truth will Make You Free', in *Khristianskaya Demokratiya*, no. 13, p. 2.
21 Cited in Hajda and Beissinger (eds), *The Nationalities Factor in Soviet Politics and Society*, p.13.
22 Hajda and Beissinger (eds), *The Nationalities Factor in Soviet Politics and Society*, p.17.
23 Henry A. Kissinger, 'The New Russian Question', *Newsweek*, 10 February 1991, pp. 12–13, at p. 13.
24 Likhachev described his experiences in the 1988 film about the prison, *Solovetskii Power*.
25 Dmitrii S. Likhachev, *Reflections on Russia* (Boulder, Westview Press, 1991), quotation from p. 80; his popular works in Russian include *Proshloe-budushchemu: stat'i i ocherki* (Leningrad, Nauka, 1985) and *Ya vospominayu* (Moscow, Progress, 1991).
26 *Rossiya*, no. 1 (9), (4–10 January 1991), p. 1.
27 See Reza Shah-Kazemi, 'Crisis in Chechnia', *Islamic World Report*, vol. 1, no. 1 (1995), p. 19.
28 The full story of Dudaev's coup and subsequent events is described in *Gosudarstvennaya Duma: parlamentarskaya kommissiya po issledovaniyu prichin i obstoyatel'stv vozniknoveniya kriznoi situatsii v Chechenskoi Respublike* (Moscow, 1995), chaired by Stanislav Govorukhin.
29 *Moscow News*, no. 37 (1991), p. 3.
30 *Moskovskie novosti*, no. 6 (19–26 February 1995), p. 6.
31 See Fiona Hill, *Russia's Tinderbox: Conflict in the North Caucasus and its Implications for the Future of the Russian Federation* (Cambridge, MA, Harvard University Kennedy School of Government, Strengthening Democratic Institutions Project, 1995).

32 For a more detailed analysis, see Richard Sakwa, 'The Chechen Crisis and Russian Political Development', Russian and CIS Programme, Royal Institute of International Affairs (RIIA), Chatham House, *Briefing Paper* no. 18 (March 1995).
33 *Independent*, 6 February 1995.
34 *Independent*, 22 February 1995, p. 13.
35 *Nezavisimaya gazeta*, 20 January 1995, p. 3.

11 REGIONAL AND LOCAL POLITICS

1 Robert W. Orttung, *From Leningrad to St. Petersburg: Democratization in a Russian City* (London, Macmillan, 1995), p. 4.
2 In Tomsk oblast, for example, the average urban district had 4,000 voters while rural districts had only 1,500, *Izvestiya*, 4 October 1991, cited by Darrell Slider; 'The CIS: Republican Leaders Confront Local opposition', *RFE/RL Research Report*, vol. 1, no. 10 (6 March 1992), pp. 7–11, at p. 7.
3 Gavin Helf and Jeffrey Hahn, 'Old Dogs and New Tricks: Party Elites in the Russian Regional Elections of 1990', *Slavic Review*, vol. 51, no. 3 (fall 1992), pp. 511–30. For an analysis of elite tactics in St Petersburg, Perm' and Arkhangel'sk, see Mary McAuley, 'Politics, Economics and Elite Realignment in Russia: A Case Study', *Soviet Economy*, vol. 8, no. 1 (1992), pp. 46–88, esp. pp. 59–66.
4 Jeffrey W. Hahn, 'Local Politics and Political Power in Russia: The Case of Yaroslavl'', *Soviet Economy*, vol. 7, no. 4 (1991), p. 328.
5 Joel C. Moses, 'Soviet Provincial Politics in an Era of Transition and Revolution, 1989–91', *Soviet Studies*, vol. 44, no. 3 (1992), pp. 479–509.
6 *Izvestiya*, 1 November 1991.
7 *Rossiiskaya gazeta*, 15 May 1991, pp. 1, 3.
8 Interviews with Makharadze in *Izvestiya*, 12 September 1991 and 1 November 1991.
9 The decree establishing 'representatives of the presidium of the Supreme Soviet of the RSFSR' had already been drafted in mid-June, but was shelved until a more opportune moment, provided by the coup, *Demokraticheskya gazeta*, no. 12 (15) (12 September 1991), p. 3. Following the coup the 'temporary instructions' made them envoys of the president rather than parliament, causing parliament yet more umbrage.
10 'Rasporyazhenie B. El'tsina o predstavitel'stve', *Izvestiya* and *Rossiiskaya gazeta*, 6 September 1991, p. 2.
11 *Rossiiskaya gazeta*, 6 September 1991, p. 2.
12 The regulations governing the work of the state inspector were adopted on 24 September and published in *Rossiiskie vesti*, no. 21 (October 1991), p. 3.
13 To three (Chuvashia, Kabardino-Balkiria and Ingushetia) out of the twenty-one republics for fear of exacerbating already tense relations; to all krais and oblasts (except Smolensk); to Birobidjan; to 7 out of 10 autonomous okrugs; and to Moscow and St Petersburg. Nearly half the envoys were radical deputies from the Russian CPD, and the other half came from local soviets, former USSR people's deputies, or were well-known public figures, *Nezavisimaya gazeta*, 6 November 1991, p. 2.
14 See, for example, James Hughes, 'Regionalism in Russia: The Rise and Fall of the Siberian Agreement', *Europe-Asia Studies*, vol. 46 (1994), pp. 1133–61.
15 Igor Mikhailov, 'V Rossii ne budet ispolkomov i koe-chego drugogo', *Kommersant*, no. 34 (19–26 August 1991), p. 14. See also Vladimir Kisilev, 'Yeltsin Appoints Administration Heads Across Russia', *Moscow News*, no. 36 (8 September 1991), p. 5.
16 *Zerkalo*, Vestnik Obshchestvennyi Komitet Rossiiskikh Reform, no. 2 (February 1992), p. 6.
17 *Vedomosti s"ezda narodnykh deputatov Rossiisskoi Federatsii i Verkhovnogo Soveta Rossiiskoi Federatsii*, no. 13 (26 March 1992), pp. 865–97.
18 *Vedomosti Mossoveta*, no. 3 (1992), p. 92.
19 A. N. Belyaev, chairman of the St Petersburg soviet, in *Vedemosti Mossoveta*, no. 4–5 (1992), pp. 131–5.
20 *Rossiiskaya gazeta*, 5 November 1991, p. 1.
21 In Rostov oblast, for example, the governor was a former Party secretary who went on to appoint former apparatchiki as heads of administration, see A. Nikolenko, 'Vivat, nomenklatura?', *Narodny deputat*, no. 5, 1992.
22 Ludmila Telen, *Moscow News*, no. 13 (29 March 1992), p. 7.
23 *Militsiya*, no. 1 (1992), p. 7.

24 For comment on this, see Michael Urban, 'The Politics of Identity in Russia's Postcommunist Transition: The Nation against Itself', *Slavic Review*, vol. 53, no. 3 (fall 1994), p. 760.

25 *Vedemosti Mossoveta*, no. 1 (1992), pp. 4–11. It had become increasingly difficult anyway to gain the necessary two-thirds quorum for meetings of the Mossoviet.

26 E.g. Keremovo, Jonathan Steele, *Guardian*, 27 November 1992.

27 *Rossiiskaya gazeta*, 22 December 1995.

28 *OMRI Daily Digest*, no. 248, Part I, 22 December 1995.

29 *Rossiya*, no. 51 (109) (16 December 1992), p. 14.

30 Alexander (*sic*) Salmin, *Nezavisimaya gazeta*, 10 December 1992, p. 5.

31 For their responsibilities, see 'Glaza i ushi prezidenta', *Trud*, 30 January 1992, p. 3; *Izvestiya*, 11 January 1992, p. 2.

32 Democratic Russia's objections are voiced in 'My podderzhivaem Eltsyna uslovno', *Izvestiya*, 7 October 1991, p. 2.

33 From west to east the economic regions are: Northern, North-Western, the Kaliningrad exclave (in effect part of the North-Western region but separated physically from Russia), Central, Central Black Earth, Volga, North Caucasian, Urals, Western Siberia, Eastern Siberia, and Far Eastern.

34 *Rossiiskaya gazeta*, 5 November 1991, p. 1.

35 *Politicheskii monitoring Rossii*, no. 3 (July–September 1992), p. 43; *Sotsial'no-politicheskii monitoring Rossii*, p. 28.

36 *Izvestiya*, 30 March 1992, p. 2.

37 Michael J. Bradshaw, 'Siberia Poses a Challenge to Russian Federalism', *RFE/RL Research Report*, vol. 1, no. 41 (16 October 1992), p. 6.

38 Bradshaw, 'Siberia Poses a Challenge to Russian Federalism', pp. 6–14.

39 For a discussion of regional associations, see Jean Radvanyi, 'And What if Russia Breaks Up? Towards New Regional Division', *Post-Soviet Geography*, vol. 33, no. 2 (1992), pp. 69–77.

40 *Izvestiya*, 26 May 1992.

41 K. Brown, 'Nizhnii Novgorod: A Regional Solution to National Problems?', *RFE/RL Research Report*, vol. 2, no. 5 (1993), pp. 17–23.

42 Aide to Nemtsov, cited by Adrian Campbell, 'Nizhnii Novgorod, St Petersburg and Moscow', in Coulson (ed.), *Local Government in Eastern Europe*, p. 240.

43 Kathryn Brown, 'Khabarovsk: Resurrecting the Nomenklatura', *RFE/RL Research Report*, vol. 1, no. 38 (25 September 1992), pp. 26–32, at pp. 26–7, citing articles by A. Druzenko and B. Reznik in *Izvestiya*, 14, 16, 17, and 20 July 1992. Their reports, however, should be taken with a pinch of salt, as in their rather simplistic characterisation of the krai soviet and the cadres policy of the local head of administration, *Izvestiya*, 16 July 1992, p. 2.

44 *Izvestiya*, 16 July 1992, p. 2.

45 Amongst the dozens of examples of local journals debating matters of historical and political development on the regional and national level, the one in Penza is among the best: *Zemstvo: arkhiv provintsial'noi istorii Rossii*.

46 See Stephen K. Wegren, 'Rural Migration and Agrarian Reform in Russia: A Research Note', *Europe-Asia Studies*, vol. 47, no. 5 (July 1995), pp. 877–88.

47 *Sotsial'no-politicheskii monitoring Rossii*, pp. 10–11.

48 *Sotsial'no-politicheskii monitoring Rossii*, p. 21.

49 Jeffrey W. Hahn, 'Local Politics and Political Power in Russia: The Case of Yaroslavl", *Soviet Economy*, vol. 7, no. 4 (1991), pp. 322–41, and quotation from p. 339.

50 Gaidar discussed regionalisation at a meeting of South Russian deputies on 23 November in Krasnodar, *Izvestiya*, 24 November 1992, p. 1.

51 *Rossiiskaya gazeta*, 19 June 1993, p. 9.

52 *Izvestiya*, 17 November 1992, p. 1.

53 The meeting took place on 24 November 1992 in Cheboksary, the capital of Chuvashia, *Izvestiya*, 24 November 1992, p. 1.

54 Cf. Elizabeth Teague, 'North-South Divide: Yeltsin and Russia's Provincial Leaders', *RFE/RL Research Report*, vol. 2, no. 47 (26 November 1993).

55 Abdulatipov insisted that the Federal Treaty gave the regions extensive economic and other powers that were not used by them, *Gubernatorskie novosti*, no. 9 (March 1993), p. 1.

56 *Kommersant-Daily*, 7 February 1995, p. 2.

57 *Rossiiskaya gazeta*, 12 October 1993.

58 Adrian Campbell, 'Regional Power in the Russian Federation', in Coulson (ed.), *Local Government in Eastern Europe*, p. 155.

59 *Review of the Russian Economy*, vol. 2, no. 4 (1993), p. 43.

60 *Pravda Rossii*, 30 November 1995, pp. 1, 2.
61 *Obshchaya gazeta*, no. 39 (1995), p. 8.
62 Sobchak's action led to an outcry on the grounds that only the CEC had the right to change electoral rules, *Segodnya*, 26 March 1994, p. 2.
63 *Segodnya*, 10 February 1994, p. 2.
64 *Rossiiskaya gazeta*, 12 March 1994.
65 *Izvestiya*, 2 February 1994, p. 1.
66 See Everett M. Jacobs (ed.), *Soviet Local Politics and Government* (London, George Allen and Unwin, 1983); Cameron Ross, *Local Government in the Soviet Union* (London, Croom Helm, 1987).
67 Jerry F. Hough, *The Soviet Prefects: The Local Party Organs in Industrial Decision-Making* (Cambridge, MA, Harvard University Press, 1969).
68 With the launching of radical economic reform the law was modified by the Fifth Congress on 1 November 1991 and later, 'Zakon RF o mestnom samoupravlenii v RF' (Moscow, Izvestiya, 1993).
69 E.g. in Ryazan, described by Jonathan Steele, *The Guardian*, 20 February 1993, p. 10.
70 McAuley, 'Politics, Economics and Elite Realignment in Russia', pp. 46–89.
71 *Vestnik Mossoveta*, no. 3 (1992), p. 85.
72 Popov's frustration is reflected in his speeches to the Moscow soviet on 25 May and 27 June 1990, *Materialy pervoi sessii Moskovskogo gorodskogo soveta narodnykh deputatov RSFSR dvadsat' pervogo sozyva* (Moscow, Moscow Soviet, 1991), pp. 38–9, 48–50.
73 Timothy J. Colton, 'The Politics of Democratisation: The Moscow Elections of 1990', *Soviet Economy*, vol. 6, no. 4 (1990), pp. 285–344.
74 Gavriil Popov, *What is to be Done?*, (Moscow, S.P. Lanit, 1990).
75 *Moskovskaya pravda*, 16 January 1991, p. 2.
76 *Rossiiskaya gazeta*, 29 October 1991, p. 1. Discussion of the administrative reorganisation of Moscow continued into 1992, see *Vestnik merii Moskvy*, no. 12 (June 1992), pp. 3–15.
77 Gavriil Popov, 'Moskvichi zasluzhivayut, chtoby nad nimi ne izdevalis', *Russkaya mysl'*, no. 3910 (27 December 1991), p. 6.
78 *Kuranty*, 6 June 1992, p. 1.
79 Cited by Campbell, 'Power and Structure', in Coulson (ed.), *Local Government in Eastern Europe*, p. 260.
80 The Moscow soviet provided a detailed case in its defence, citing acts of illegality by Popov and the vice-mayor Yurii Luzhkov, the fusion of executive and business structures, and much more, *Vedemosti Mossoveta*, no. 6 (1991), pp. 8–9.
81 Decree of 9 October, 'O reforme predstavitel'nykh organov vlasti i organov mestnogo samo-upravleniya v Rossiiskoi Federatsii', *Rossiiskaya Federatsiya*, 1 (13) (1993), p. 25.
82 The framework for local elections was established by presidential decree on 27 October 1993, *Byulleten' Tsentral'noi izbiratel'noi komissii Rossiiskoi Federatsii*, no. 1 (12) (1994), pp. 6–27.
83 *Rossiiskie vesti*, 26 October 1993.
84 Decree of 22 October 1993, 'Ob osnovnykh nachalakh organizatsii gosudarstvennoi vlasti v sub'ektakh Rossiiskoi Federatsii', *Byulleten' TsIK*, no. 1 (12) (1994), pp. 3–6.
85 Valerii Kirpichnikov, head of the Union of Russian Towns, *Rossiiskaya gazeta*, 24 December 1993, p. 2.
86 *Izvestiya*, 11 December 1993, p. 2.
87 *Rossiiskaya gazeta*, 29 December 1993, p. 4.
88 Solzhenitsyn gives details of his scheme in *Rebuilding Russia*, pp. 75–8.
89 For the earlier period, see Stephen Whitefield, *Industrial Power and the Soviet State* (Oxford, Clarendon Press, 1993).
90 Jadwiga Staniszkis, 'The Worrying Shift in the Kremlin', *European Brief*, vol.2, no. 4 (February 1995), p. 74.

12 TRANSFORMING THE ECONOMY

1 Boris Yeltsin, *Zapiski prezidenta* (Moscow, Ogonek, 1994), p. 300.
2 *Transition Report: Economic Transition in Eastern Europe and the Former Soviet Union* (London, EBRD, October 1994), p. 45.
3 *Soviet News*, 5 September 1990, p. 295.
4 Armenia, Belarus, Kazakhstan, Kyrgyzstan, Russia, Tajikistan, Turkmenistan and Uzbekistan.
5 *Soviet Weekly*, 31 October 1991, pp. 6–7.

6 Alistair McAuley, 'The Economic Consequences of Soviet Disintegration', *Soviet Economy*, vol. 7, no. 3 (1991), pp. 189–214, suggests a high degree of interdependence.

7 V. Samonis, 'Who Subsidized Whom? The Distorted World of Baltic-Soviet Economic Relations', *Current Politics and Economics of Russia*, vol. 2, no. 3 (1991), pp. 241–3.

8 *OECD Economic Surveys: The Russian Federation, 1995* (Paris, OECD, 1995), pp. 12–13.

9 *Soviet Weekly*, 5 December 1991, p. 10; John Tedstrom, 'Economic Crisis Deepens', *RFE/RL Research Report*, vol. 1, no. 1 (3 January 1992), pp. 22–6; Keith Bush, 'The Disastrous Last Year of the USSR', *RFE/RL Research Report*, vol. 1, no. 12 (20 March 1992), pp. 39–41.

10 Keith Bush, 'An Overview of the Russian Economy', *RFE/RL Research Report*, vol. 1, no. 25 (19 June 1992), p. 50.

11 *Soviet Weekly*, 10 October 1991, p. 11.

12 Anatolii B. Chubais and Sergei V. Vasil'ev, 'Privatisation as a Necessary Condition for Structural Change in the USSR', *Communist Economies and Economic Transformation*, vol. 3, no. 1 (1991), pp. 57–62, at p. 57.

13 *Soviet Weekly*, 5 December 1991, p. 2.

14 *Soviet Weekly*, 5 December 1991, p. 10.

15 *Guardian*, 2 March 1992, p. 21.

16 John Kenneth Galbraith, 'Revolt in Our Time: The Triumph of Simplistic Ideology', in Gwyn Prins (ed.), *Spring in Winter: The 1989 Revolutions* (Manchester, Manchester University Press, 1990), pp. 1–12.

17 *Moskovskie novosti*, no. 78 (12–19 November 1995), p. 5.

18 The outline of the government's policy is presented in a memorandum stressing the links with the IMF, *Ekonomika i zhizn'*, no. 10 (1992), pp. 4–5.

19 For their views, see Alec Nove, 'New Thinking on the Soviet Economy', in Archie Brown (ed.), *New Thinking in Soviet Politics* (London, Macmillan, 1992), pp. 29–38.

20 *Rossiiskaya gazeta*, 29 October 1991.

21 *Rossiiskaya gazeta*, 2 November 1991, p. 1.

22 *Russian Economic Trends*, vol. 1, no. 1 (1992), p. 5.

23 *Ekonomika i zhizn'*, no. 51 (1991), p. 1; Erik Whitlock, 'New Russian Government to Continue Economic Reform?', *RFE/RL Research Report*, vol. 2, no. 3 (15 January 1993), p. 23.

24 *Independent*, 23 September 1992.

25 Chubais and Vasil'ev, 'Privatisation', p. 59.

26 *OECD Economic Surveys*, p. 8.

27 *OECD Economic Surveys*, p. 10.

28 *Rossiiskaya gazeta*, 3 April 1992, pp. 1–2.

29 *Rossiiskaya gazeta*, 16 April 1992, p. 1.

30 *Izvestiya*, 14 January 1993.

31 Figures from the EBRD, *Independent*, 12 February 1993.

32 Erik Whitlock, 'Russia's Progress toward an Open Economy', *RFE/RL Research Report*, vol. 1, no. 47 (27 November 1992), pp. 35–40.

33 *Independent*, 29 April 1992.

34 *Independent*, 11 March 1995.

35 *OMRI Daily Digest*, no. 247, Part 1, 21 December 1995.

36 Dmitrii S. L'vov, 'The Social and Economic Problems of Perestroika', *Communist Economies and Economic Transformation*, vol. 4, no. 1 (1992), pp. 75–83, at pp. 78–9.

37 *OECD Economic Reviews*, p. 88. In Russia small firms (1–249 employees) made up 53 per cent of the total, in the USA 98 per cent.

38 *Rossiiskaya gazeta*, 10 January 1992, pp. 3–4, with an appendix on 15 January, p. 2.

39 See Alexander Bim *et al*, 'Privatization in the Former Soviet Union and the New Russia', in Saul Estrin (ed.), *Privatization in Central and Eastern Europe* (London, Longman, 1994), pp. 252–78.

40 *OECD Economic Surveys*, p. 72; Bim *et al*, pp. 262–7.

41 'Interview with Richard Layard', in Keith Bush, *From the Command Economy to the Market: A Collection of Interviews* (Aldershot, Dartmouth Publishing, 1991), pp. 142–7, at p. 143.

42 'Interview with Anders Aslund', in Bush, *From the Command Economy to the Market*, pp. 7–12, at p. 8.

43 'Interview with Milton Friedman', in Bush, *From the Command Economy to the Market*, pp. 49–57, at p. 51.

44 For a discussion of these issues, see Elizabeth Teague (ed.), 'Is Equity Compatible with Efficiency?', *RFE/RL Research Report*, vol. 1, no. 17 (1992), pp. 9–14.

45 *Literaturnaya gazeta*, 19 February 1992, p. 3.

46 *Russian Economic Trends*, December 1994, p. 7.
47 *OECD Economic Reviews*, p. 77.
48 John Tedstrom, 'Russia: Progress Report on Industrial Privatisation', *RFE/RL Research Report*, vol. 1, no. 17 (24 April 1992), p. 47.
49 Vladimir Capelik, 'The Development of Anti-monopoly Policy in Russia', *RFE/RL Research Report*, vol. 1, no. 34 (28 August 1992), pp. 66–70.
50 Anders Aslund, 'Reform Vs. "Rent-Seeking" in Russia's Economic Transformation', *Transition*, 26 January 1996, p. 13.
51 Boris Slavin and Valentin Davydov, 'Stanovlenie mnogopartiinosti', *Partiinaya zhizn'*, no. 18 (September 1991), pp. 6–16, at p. 15.
52 *Moscow News*, no. 37 (1991), p. 2.
53 'Sotsial'no-ekonomicheskoe polozhenie Rossiiskoi Federatsii v 1991 godu', *Ekonomika i zhizn'*, no. 4 (1992), pp. 4–5.
54 *Moscow News*, no. 37 (1991), pp. 8–9.
55 Tikhonov reported a steady rise in the number, stating that by the summer of 1991 there were about 300,000 production cooperatives employing some 7 million people permanently, *Russkaya mysl'*, 27 September 1991.
56 Vladimir Gimpelson, 'Russia's New Independent Entrepreneurs', *RFE/RL Research Report*, vol. 2, no. 36 (10 September 1993), pp. 44–8.
57 Tedstrom, 'Russia: Progress Report on Industrial Privatization', p. 49.
58 *Soviet Weekly*, 10 October 1991, p. 11.
59 Tedstrom, 'Russia: Progress Report on Industrial Privatization', p. 49.
60 The phrase comes from Roy D. Laird and Edward Crowley (eds), *Soviet Agriculture: The Permanent Crisis* (New York, Praeger, 1965). See also Stefan Hedlund, *Crisis in Soviet Agriculture* (New York, St Martin's Press, 1985). For a discussion of the historical context and Gorbachev's approach to agriculture, see the special issue of *Studies in Comparative Communism*, vol. 23, no. 2 (summer 1990).
61 *Pravitel'stvennyi vestnik*, no. 25 (51) (June 1990), p. 5.
62 Stephen K. Wegren, 'Private Farming and Agrarian Reform in Russia', *Problems of Communism*, vol. XLI, no. 3 (May–June 1992), pp. 107–21.
63 *Pravda*, 7 March 1990.
64 See Timothy N. Ash, Robert Lewis and Tanya Skaldina, 'Russia Sets the Pace of Agricultural Reform', *RFE/RL Research Report*, vol. 1, no. 25 (19 June 1992), pp. 55–63.
65 *Vedemosti S"ezda narodnykh deputatov RSFSR i Verkhovnogo Soveta RSFSR*, no. 1 (2 January 1992), pp. 48–51.
66 A. V. Rutskoi, *Agrarnaya reforma v Rossii* (Moscow, Prilozhenie k ezhenedel'niku 'Obozrevatel', 1992).
67 Decree 'On the Regulation of Land Relations and the Development of Agrarian Reform in Russia', *Rossiisskie vesti*, 29 October 1993, p. 2; see Don Van Atta, 'Yeltsin Decree Finally Ends "Second Serfdom" in Russia', *RFE/RL Research Report*, vol. 2, no. 46 (19 November 1993), pp. 33–9.
68 Stephen K. Wegren, 'Rural Reform in Russia', *RFE/RL Research Report*, vol. 2, no. 43 (29 October 1993), pp. 43–53.
69 Stephen K. Wegren and Frank A. Durgin, 'Why Agrarian Reform is Failing', *Transition*, 20 October 1995, p. 53.
70 Rutskoi stated that of the 128,000 individual farms registered in the first half of 1992, only 3,000 produced for the market, *Rossiiskaya gazeta*, 25 July 1992, p. 3.
71 Don Van Atta, 'Agrarian Reform in Post-Soviet Russia', *Post-Soviet Affairs*, vol. 10, no. 2 (April–June 1994), pp. 159–90.
72 Otto Latsis, *Izvestiya*, 23 January 1996, p. 2.
73 Michael Ellman, 'Shock Therapy in Russia: Failure or Partial Success?', *RFE/RL Research Report*, vol. 1, no. 34 (28 August 1992), p. 58.
74 Anders Aslund, *How Russia Became a Market Economy* (Washington, DC, The Brookings Institute, 1995).
75 *OECD Economic Surveys*, p. iii.
76 Marshall I. Goldman, *Lost Opportunity: Why Economic Reforms in Russia Have not Worked* (London, Norton, 1995).
77 Yeltin press conference, 21 August 1992.
78 *Izvestiya*, 19 August 1992, p. 3.
79 Outlined in the anti-crisis programme presented to parliament, *Rosiiskaya gazeta*, 27 November 1992, p. 1.

80 *Rossiiskaya gazeta*, 4 December 1992, pp. 3–4,
81 The IMF once again committed itself to Russian reforms, *Nezavisimaya gazeta*, 26 January 1993, p. 1.
82 Jude Wanniski, 'The Future of Russian Capitalism', *Foreign Affairs*, vol. 71, no. 2 (Spring 1992), pp. 17–25, at p. 17.
83 E.g. an industrialists conference in Moscow on 13–14 August 1992, Elizabeth Teague, 'Splits in the Ranks of Russia's "Red Directors"', *RFE/RL Research Report*, 1/35 (4 September 1992), pp. 6–10.
84 Gaidar, in *New York Review of Books*, 13 August 1992.
85 *Sed'moi s"ezd narodnykh deputatov Rossiiskoi Federatsii: byulleten'*, no. 24 (14 December 1992), pp. 3–4.
86 Centre for Economic and Political Research, directed by Grigorii Yavlinskii, 'Spring '92: Reforms in Russia', *Moscow News*, no. 21 (24 May 1992), pp. 6–7, and no. 22 (31 May 1992), pp. 6–11.
87 *Literaturnaya gazeta*, 19 February 1992, pp. 1, 3.
88 *Guardian*, 3 December 1992.
89 *Rossiisskaya gazeta*, 2 December 1992, pp. 1, 3–5.
90 *Rossiiskaya gazeta*, 4 December 1992, pp. 3–4.

13 SOCIAL TRANSFORMATION

1 Adam Smith, *The Wealth of Nations* (London, Penguin, 1970), I, 8.
2 Solzhenitsyn, *Rebuilding Russia*, p. 33.
3 *Soviet Weekly*, 24 October 1991, p. 5.
4 Solzhenitsyn, *Rebuilding Russia*, p. 33.
5 Barrington Moore, Jr, *Social Origins of Dictatorship and Democracy: Lord and Peasant in the Making of the Modern World* (Harmondsworth, Peregrine, 1967), p. 418.
6 A. Putko, *Soviet Weekly*, 5 December 1991, p. 4.
7 B. P. Pockney, *Soviet Statistics since 1950* (Aldershot, Dartmouth, 1991), pp. 63, 67.
8 John Tedstrom, 'Russia: Progress Report on Industrial Privatization', *RFE/RL Research Report*, vol. 1, no. 17 (24 April 1992), p. 48.
9 This issue is discussed by several contributors in Murray Yanovitch (ed.), *New Directions in Soviet Social Thought* (New York, M.E. Sharpe, 1989).
10 The Russian fertility rate is comparable to that in Estonia (1.44), Germany (1.39), Greece (1.35) and Italy (1.25), while in the former GDR it fell to 0.98 in 1991, Penny Morvant, 'Alarm over Falling Life Expectancy', *Transition*, 20 October 1995, p. 41.
11 In 1960 there were 23.2 births per 1000, 7.4 deaths per thousand, giving a natural growth of 15.8 per thousand, and the figure declined thereafter, Pockney, *Soviet Statistics since 1950*, p. 74.
12 *Nezavisimaya gazeta*, 26 January 1993, p. 1.
13 *Demograficheskii ezhegodnik RF, 1993* (Moscow, Goskomstat, 1994), p. 83; *Pravda*, 28 November 1995.
14 In 1970 the figure was 30 out of 100, and in 1980 40, *Naselenie Rossii* (Moscow, Goskomstat, 1993).
15 Viktor Perevedentsev, *Moskovskie novosti*, no. 49 (5 December 1993), p. 6.
16 *Independent*, 9 November 1992. In 1991 the birth rate fell from 12.1 to 11.1 per thousand population, while the death rate increased from 11.4 to 11.9 per thousand, *Nezavisimaya gazeta*, 26 January 1992, p. 1.
17 *Nezavisimaya gazeta*, 26 January 1993, p. 1, and the rate rose sharply in 1993 when Russia adopted international standards of measurement.
18 E.g. Vadim Pervyshin, 'Genotsid kak sistema', *Den'*, no. 36 (51), (6 September 1992), p. 3; see also Boris Khodov in *Pravda*, 30 March 1995. The theme is reflected in Stanislav Govorukhin's film of 1994, *The Russia that We Have Lost*.
19 Victoria Clark, the *Observer*, 26 November 1995, p. 26.
20 *Komsomolskaya pravda*, 25 July 1995. Hungary still has the highest suicide rate out of 84 developed countries, but Russia now comes in third.
21 *Soviet Weekly*, 3 October 1991, p. 10.
22 Figures from Dr. Alexander Nemtsov, in the *Observer*, 26 November 1995, p. 26.
23 On the anti-alcohol campaign, see Stephen White, *Russia Goes Dry: Alcohol, State and Society* (Cambridge, Cambridge University Press, 1995).
24 Stephen White, 'Hangover Cure for the Bear with a Sore Head', *Times Higher Educational Supplement*, 28 July 1995, pp. 17, 19.

25 *Rossiiskie vesti*, 7 July 1992, p. 3.

26 For the argument that social policies should reinforce the process of reform and avoid stimulating hyperinflation, see Michael Hay and Alan Peacock, *Social Policies in the Transition to the Market*, Report of a Mission to the Russian Federation Organised by the United Nations, January 1992 (London, The David Hume Institute, 1992).

27 S. A. Sidorenko, 'Moskovskie bezdomnye – pervye shagi v izuchenii problemy', *Ekonomicheskie i sotsial'nye peremeny: monitoring obshchestvennogo mneniya*, no. 4 (July–August 1995), p. 46.

28 *Observer*, 10 September 1995, p. 20.

29 Cf. Christopher M. Davies, 'Eastern Europe and the Former USSR: An Overview', *RFE/RL Research Report*, vol. 2, no. 40 (8 October 1993), pp. 31–43.

30 *Independent*, 30 August 1994.

31 *Izvestiya*, 23 January 1996.

32 Sheila Marnie, 'Economic Reform and the Social Safety Net', *RFE/RL Research Report*, vol. 2, no. 17 (23 April 1993), p. 2.

33 Sheila Marnie, 'The Social safety Net in Russia', *RFE/RL Research Report*, vol. 2, no. 17 (23 April 1993), pp. 17–23.

34 *Independent*, 26 February 1992.

35 *Soviet Weekly*, 31 October 1991, p. 4.

36 Khasbulatov, *The Struggle for Russia*, p. 96.

37 *Soviet Weekly*, 3 October 1991, p. 7.

38 Ivan Rybkin, *Rossiiskie vesti*, 21 November 1995, p. 1.

39 See Richard Rose, 'The Value of Fringe Benefits in Russia', *RFE/RL Research Report*, vol. 3, no. 15 (15 April 1994), pp. 16–21.

40 Details of presidential decrees, governmental acts and laws on social policy are in *Sotsial'naya politika v Rossii: sbornik dokumentov* (Moscow, Respublika, 1992).

41 *Ekonomika i zhizn'*, no. 22, 1991.

42 Alexander Shokhin, 'Labour Market Regulation in the USSR', *Communist Economies*, vol. 3, no. 4 (1991), pp. 499–509.

43 *OMRI Daily Digest*, no. 19, Part I, 26 January 1996.

44 *The Economist*, 20 November 1993, pp. 47-48.

45 *Rossiiskie vesti*, 5 May 1994, p. 4.

46 Shokhin, 'Labour Market Regulation in the USSR', p. 505.

47 For details, see Sheila Marnie, 'How Prepared is Russia for Mass Unemployment?', *RFE/RL Research Report*, vol. 1, no. 48 (4 December 1992), pp. 44–50; see also her 'Who and Where Are the Russian Unemployed?', *ibid*, vol. 2, no. 33 (20 August 1993), pp. 36–42.

48 See, for example, Russell Bova, 'Worker Activism: The Role of the State', Judith B. Sedaitis and Jim Butterfield (eds.), *Perestroika from Below: Social Movements in the Soviet Union* (Boulder, Westview Press, 1991), pp. 29-42.

49 For details on each union, see *Kto est' chto: politicheskaya Moskva 1993* (Moscow, Catallaxy, 1993), pp. 501–624; *Kyo est' chto*, vol. 2 *Profsoyuznye ob"edineniya i tsentry* (Moscow, 1994).

50 *Kto est' chto*, vol. 2, 1993, p. 219.

51 *Soviet Weekly*, 17 October 1991, p. 4.

52 Igor Klochkov, *Moskovskie novosti*, no. 30 (26 July 1992), p. 11.

53 For details, see Linda J. Cook, 'Russia's Labor Relations', in D.W. Blum (ed.), *Russia's Future* (Boulder, CO, Westview, 1994), pp. 69–89.

54 See John Thirkell, Richard Scase and Sarah Vickerstaff (eds), *Labour Relations and Political Change in Eastern Europe: a Comparative Perspective* (London, UCL Press, 1995).

55 *Tribune*, 22 October 1993.

56 See Elizabeth Teague, 'Organised Labour in Russia in 1992', *RFE/RL Research Report*, vol. 2, no. 5 (29 January 1993), pp. 38–41.

57 *Soviet Weekly*, 24 October 1991, p. 2.

58 Penny Morvant, 'The Beleagured Coal-Mining Industry Strikes Back', *Transition*, 30 June 1995, pp. 56–61, 70.

59 *Moskovskie novosti*, no. 11 (12–19 February 1995), p. 6.

60 See Boris Kagarlitskii, 'Profsoyuzy stoyat pered vyborom', *Nezavisimaya gazeta*, 25 August 1994, p. 4.

61 The most influential were the Independent Miners' Union, Sotsprof, the Kuzbass Confederation of Labour, and the trade unions for dockers, sailors, pilots, air traffic controllers, and locomotive railway workers, Lyudmila Alekseeva, 'Nesvobodnye profsoyuzy', *Moskovskie novosti*, no. 3 (22 January 1995), p. 14.

62 VTsIOM poll in 1993, cited in G. Rogova, 'Stanovlenie podlinnogo profsoyuznogo dvizeniya v Rossii', *MEMO*, no. 2 (1994), p. 47.

63 For a recent analysis of the question, see E. B. Gruzdeva and E. S. Chertikhina, 'Polozhenie zhenshchiny v obshchestve: konflikt rolei', in *Obshchestvo v raznykh izmereniyakh: sotsiologi otvechayut na voprosy*, compiled by V. E. Gimpel'son and A. K. Nazimova (Moscow, Moskovskii rabochii, 1990), pp. 147–67.

64 Pockney, *Soviet Statistics since 1950*, pp. 48–9.

65 Pockney, *Soviet Statistics since 1950*, p. 47.

66 Grigorii Gendler and Marina Gildingersh, 'A Socioeconomic Portrait of the Unemployed in Russia', *RFE/RL Research Report*, vol. 3, no. 3 (21 January 1994), p. 35.

67 *Rossiiskaya gazeta*, 18 February 1994.

68 Mikhail Gorbachev, *Perestroika: New Thinking for Our Country and the World* (London, Collins, 1987), p. 117.

69 See Penny Morvant, 'Bearing the "Double Burden" in Russia', *Transition*, 8 September 1995, pp. 4–9.

70 Valentina Bodrova, 'The Russian Family in Flux', *Transition*, 8 September 1995, pp. 10–11.

71 *Izvestiya*, 2 December 1993, p. 4.

72 Peter Lentini, 'Women and the 1989 Elections to the USSR Congress of People's Deputies', *Coexistence*, vol. 31 (1994), pp. 1–28.

73 *Rossiiskaya gazeta*, 3 December 1992, p. 1; women comprised 8.9 per cent of the Supreme Soviet.

74 Wendy Slater, 'Female Representation in Russian Politics', *RFE/RL Research Report*, vol. 3, no. 22 (3 June 1994), pp. 27–33.

75 S. V. Polenina, 'Zhenshchiny, vlast', demokratiya', *Byulleten' TsIK*, no. 1 (27) (1995), p. 15.

76 See Svetlana Aivazova, 'Zhenskoe dvizhenie v Rossii: traditsii i sovremennost'', *ONS*, no. 2 (1995), pp. 121–30.

77 *Nezavisimaya gazeta*, 12 January 1996, p. 2.

78 Cited in *Itogovyi otchet o rabote I nezavisimogo zhenskogo foruma* (Moscow, 1991), p. 7.

79 Elzbieta Matynia, 'Women After Communism: A Bitter Freedom', *Social Research*, vol. 62, no. 2 (summer 1994), pp. 351–77.

80 Cf. Mira Marody, 'Why I am not a Feminist', *Social Research*, vol. 60, no. 4 (winter 1993), pp. 853–64.

81 David Holloway, 'The Politics of Catastrophe', *The New York Review of Books* (10 June 1993), p. 36.

82 Mark Popovskii, *Delo akademika Vavilova* (Moscow, Kniga, 1991).

83 Douglas Weiner, *Models of Nature: Ecology, Conservation, and Cultural Revolution in Soviet Russia* (Bloomington, Indiana University Press, 1988).

84 See Charles E. Ziegler, 'Environmental Politics and Policy under Perestroika', in Sedaitis and Butterfield (eds), *Perestroika from Below*, pp. 113–32.

85 *Soviet Weekly*, 31 October 1991, p. 4.

86 For more details see Georgii S. Golitsyn, 'Ecological Problems in the CIS During the Transitional Period', *RFE/RL Research Report*, vol. 2, no. 2 (8 January 1993), pp. 33–46; on the Caspian Sea, *Izvestiya*, 11 December 1993, p. 15; on sunken nuclear reactors, *Independent*, 10 November 1993; and on whaling, *The Guardian*, 12 February 1994, p. 12.

87 *Soviet Weekly*, 31 October 1991, p. 4.

88 William Millinship, *Observer*, 31 May 1992, p. 49. For details of the crisis, see Murray Feshbach and Alfred Friendly, *Ecocide in the USSR: Health and Nature under Siege* (New York, Basic Books, 1992).

89 Divish Petrof, 'Siberian Forests under Threat', *The Ecologist*, vol. 22, no. 6 (1992), pp. 267–70.

90 *Moscow News*, no. 6 (4 February 1993), p. 3.

91 See Zhores Medvedev, *The Legacy of Chernobyl* (Oxford, Blackwell, 1991); see also Piers Paul Reed, *Ablaze: The Story of the Heroes and Victims of Chernobyl* (New York, Random House, 1992).

92 See David R. Marples, 'Nuclear Power in the CIS: A Reappraisal', *RFE/RL Research Report*, vol. 3, no. 22 (3 June 1994), pp. 21–26.

93 *Independent*, 25 January 1992.

94 Cf. Jeremy Russell, *Energy and Environmental Conflicts in East-Central Europe: The Case of Power Generation* (London, RIIA/World Conservation Union, 1991).

95 *Observer*, 26 March 1995, p. 1.

96 Cf. Duncan Fisher, *Paradise Deferred: Environmental Policy-making in Central and Eastern Europe* (London, RIIA/Ecological Studies Institute, 1992).

97 *Vedemosti S"ezda narodnykh deputatov Rossiiskoi Federatsii i Verkhovhogo Soveta Rossiiskoi federatsii*, no. 10 (5 March 1992), pp. 592–630.
98 D. J. Peterson, 'The Environment in the Post-Soviet Era', *RFE/RL Research Report*, vol. 2, no. 2 (8 January 1993), pp. 43–6.
99 *Russian Conservation News*, no. 3 (May 1995), p. 4. As of 30 March 1995 Russia had 89 Zapovedniki covering a total area of 29.1 million hectares (1.42 per cent of Russia's territory), and 29 National Parks, covering 6.6 million hectares, or 0.38 per cent of the Federation, with the final total expected to settle at about 100, *ibid.*, p. 11.
100 *Russian Conservation News*, no. 4 (August 1995), pp. 15–17.
101 *Russian Conservation News*, no. 3 (May 1995), p. 3.
102 Cf. M. Waller and F. Millard, 'Environmental Politics in Eastern Europe', *Environmental Politics*, vol. 2 (1992), p. 171.

14 FOREIGN POLICY

1 G. P. Fedotov, *Russia, Europe and Us: Collected Essays*, vol. 2 (Paris, YMCA Press, 1973), p. 232.
2 A. V. Kozyrev, 'Vneshnyaya politika preobrazhayushcheisya Rossii', *Voprosy istorii*, no. 1 (1994), p. 4.
3 Boris Pankin, *The Last Hundred Days of the Soviet Union* (London, I. B. Tauris, 1996), p. 104.
4 Suzanne Crow, 'The Twilight of All-Union Diplomacy', *RFE/RL Research Report*, vol. no. 1 (1992), pp. 27–8; *Moscow News*, no. 48 (1991), p. 4.
5 Suzanne Crow, 'Personnel Changes in the Russian Foreign Ministry', *RFE/RL Research Report*, vol. 1, no. 16 (17 April 1992), pp. 18–22, at p. 18.
6 Cited in A. V. Kozyrev, 'Vneshnyaya politika preobrazhayushcheisya Rossii', *Voprosy istorii*, no. 1 (1994), p. 6.
7 Andrei Kozyrev, 'Russia: A Chance of Survival', *Foreign Affairs* (spring 1992), pp. 1–16, at p. 4.
8 E.g. *Izvestiya*, 30 June 1992.
9 Pavel Baev, *The Russian Army in a Time of Trouble* (London, Sage, 1996).
10 *Nezavisimaya gazeta*, 28 March 1992. Andranik Migranyan later claimed to have rediscovered the notion of the Monroe Doctrine for Russia, 'Russia and the Near Abroad', *Nezavisimaya gazeta*, 12 January 1994.
11 'A Strategy for Russia', *Nezavisimaya gazeta*, 19 August 1992, p. 4.
12 Suzanne Crow, 'Russia Seeks Leadership in Regional Peace-keeping', *RFE/RL Research Report*, vol. 2, no. 15 (9 April 1993).
13 Kozyrev, 'Vneshnyaya politika', p. 3.
14 *Izvestiya*, 8 October 1993.
15 See Andrei Kozyrev, 'Partnership or Cold Peace?', *Foreign Policy*, no. 99 (Summer 1995), pp. 3–14.
16 E.g. Andranik Migranyan, *Nezavisimaya gazeta*, 10 December 1994.
17 *Moskovskie novosti*, no. 63 (11–18 December 1994), pp. 4, 6.
18 *Independent*, 13 January 1996, p. 9.
19 *Soviet Weekly*, 26 September 1991, p. 6.
20 Gennadi Charodeev, 'A New Priority Area for Russian Diplomacy: Relations with "Nearby Foreign Countries"', *Izvestiya*, 1 April 1992, p. 4; Suzanne Crow, 'Personnel Changes in the Russian Foreign Ministry', *RFE/RL Research Report*, vol. 1, no. 16 (17 April 1992), pp. 18–22, at p. 19.
21 A powerful critique of the performance of the new-style MFA is made by Aleksei Arbatov, 'Russia: National Security in the 1990s', *Mirovaya ekonomika i mezhdunarodnye otnosheniya* (*MEMO*), no. 7 (July 1994), pp. 5–15; Nos 8–9 (August–September 1994), pp. 5–18.
22 *Diplomaticheskii vestnik*, no. 16 (31 March 1992).
23 Suzanne Crow, 'Personnel Changes in the Russian Foreign Ministry', *RFE/RL Research Report*, vol. 1, no. 16 (17 April 1992), pp. 18–22, at p. 22.
24 *Izvestiya*, 7 August 1992, p. 6; Ambartsumov later claimed that the views of a discussion paper had been mistakenly attributed as his own, *Izvestiya*, 25 August 1992, p. 6.
25 *Rossiiskaya gazeta*, 31 March 1995, p. 5.
26 Konstantin Eggert, *Izvestiya*, 16 December 1995, p. 3.
27 *Moscow News*, no. 7 (11 February 1993), p. 9.
28 *Moskovski novosti*, no. 23 (5–12 June 1994), p. 11.
29 Yuri E. Fyodoroff, 'Foreign Policy-Making in the Russian Federation and Local Conflicts in the CIS', in Hans-Georg Ehrhart *et al* (eds), *Crisis Management in the CIS: Whither Russia?* (Baden-Baden, Nomos Verlagsgesellschaft, 1995), pp. 120–21.

30 *Izvestiya*, 30 June 1992.
31 *Nezavisimaya gazeta*, 27 May 1994, p. 5.
32 Cited in Suzanne Crow, 'Russia Prepares to Take a Hard Line on "Near Abroad"', *RFE/RL Research Report*, vol. 1, no. 32 (1992), pp. 21–4.
33 *Nezavisimaya gazeta*, 19 August 1992, p. 4.
34 *Nezavisimaya gazeta*, 27 May 1994, pp. 4–5.
35 *Nezavisimaya gazeta*, 27 May 1994, p. 4.
36 Cf. the testimony of the former deputy foreign minister from October 1991 to October 1992, Fedor Shelov-Kovedyaev, *Segodnya*, 31 August 1993.
37 Cf. V. P. Lukin, 'Rossiya i ee interesy', *Diplomaticheskii vestnik*, no. 21–2 (15–30 November 1992), pp. 48–53.
38 Sergei Stankevich, *Nezavisimaya gazeta*, 28 March 1992, p. 4.
39 Cf. Elgiz Pozdnyakov, 'National, State, and Class Interests in International Relations', in *MEMO: New Soviet Voices on Foreign and Economic Policy*, edited by Steve Hirsch (Washington, D.C., Bureau of National Affairs, 1989), pp. 471–90; originally in *MEMO*, no. 5 (May 1988).
40 E.g. Sergei Goncharov, head of the Sino-Russian relations department at the Institute of the Far East, RAN, *Izvestiya*, 25 February 1992, p. 6.
41 Pozdnyakov, *Natsiya, natsionalizm, natsional'nye interesy*, p. 78.
42 Sergei Stankevich, 'A Power in Search of Itself', *Nezavisimaya gazeta*, 28 March 1992, p. 4; see also Alexander Rahr, 'Atlanticists versus Eurasians in Russian Foreign Policy', *RFE/RL Research Report*, vol. 1, no. 22 (1992), pp. 17–22.
43 Tibor Szamuely, *The Russian Tradition*, (London, Fontana, 1988), p. 10.
44 Szamuely, *The Russian Tradition*, p. 10.
45 Dmitrii Likhachev, *Reflections on Russia* (Boulder, CO, Westview Press, 1991), p. 80.
46 See Elgiz Pozdnyakov, 'The Problem of Returning the Soviet Union to European Civilisation', *Paradigms: The Kent Journal of International Relations*, vol. 5, nos 1/2, 1991, pp. 45–57. See also Milan Hauner, *What is Asia for Us? Russia's Asian Heartland Yesterday and Today* (London, Unwin Hyman, 1990); and Mark Bassin, 'Russia Between Europe and Asia: The Ideological Construction of Geographical Space', *Slavic Review*, vol. 50, no. 1 (Spring 1991), pp. 1–17.
47 Assen Ignatow, *Der 'Eurasismus' und die Suche nach einer neuen russischen Kulturidentitat. Die Neubelebung des 'Jewrasijstwo'-Mythos* (Cologne, Berichte des BIOst 15, 1992).
48 Halford J. Mackinder, 'The Geographical Pivot of History', in his *Democratic Ideals and Reality* (New York, W. W. Norton and Co., 1962).
49 Cited in John M. Letiche and Basil Dmytryshyn, *Russian Statecraft: The Politika of Iurii Krizhanich* (Oxford, Basil Blackwell, 1985), p. 128.
50 Sergei N. Goncharov, 'Russia's Special Interests: What are They?', *Izvestiya*, 25 February 1992, p. 6.
51 P. Ya. Chaadaev, *Polnoe sobranie sochinenii i izbrannye pis'ma* (Moscow, Nauka, 1991), pp. 320–39.
52 Elgiz Pozdnyakov, 'Russia is a Great Power', *International Affairs* (Moscow), no. 1, 1993, pp. 3, 5.
53 Andrei Zagorsky, 'Russia and Europe', *International Affairs* (Moscow), no. 1 (1993), pp. 43–51.
54 *Observer*, 10 September 1995, p. 23.
55 Andrei Kozyrev, *Izvestiya*, 31 March 1992, p. 6; *Nezavisimaya gazeta*, 1 April 1992, pp. 1, 3.
56 *RFE/RL Research Report*, vol. 1, no. 29 (17 July 1992), p. 80.
57 *Izvestiya*, 30 June 1992.
58 *Diplomaticheskii vestnik*, no. 21–2 (15–30 November 1992), pp. 23–4.
59 Suzanne Crow, 'Competing Blueprints for Russian Foreign Policy', *RFE/RL Research Report*, vol. 1, no. 50 (18 December 1992), pp. 45–50.
60 *Nezavisimaya gazeta*, 19 August 1992.
61 'Kontseptsiya vneshnei politiki Rossiiskoi Federatsii', *Diplomaticheskii vestnik*, January 1993 (special edition).
62 Vladimir Lukin, *Foreign Affairs*, cited by Jonathan Steele, *Guardian*, 4 January 1993.
63 *Nezavisimaya gazeta*, 'Derzhava v poiskakh sebya', 28 March 1992, p. 4; *Literaturnaya gazeta*, no. 11 (1992); his views on the continuity with Russian imperial traditions and Great Power politics were developed in *Rossiiskaya gazeta*, 'Yavlenie derzhavy', 23 June 1992, p. 1.
64 Sergei Stankevich, *Izvestiya*, 7 July 1992, p. 3.
65 Milan Kundera, 'The Tragedy of Central Europe', *New York Review of Books*, 26 April 1984.
66 Marina Pavlova-Sil'vanskaya, 'Novyi panslavism?', *Nezavisimaya gazeta*, 25 June 1992, p. 5.
67 Solzhenitsyn, *Rebuilding Russia*, pp. 13, 17–21.
68 Cited by Alexander Rahr, '"Atlanticists" versus "Eurasians" in Russian Foreign Policy', *REF/RL Research Report*, vol. 1, no. 22 (29 May 1992), pp. 17–22, at p. 18.

69   *Argumenty i fakty*, no. 1, 1995.
70   *Izvestiya*, 14 February 1992.
71   *Literaturnaya Rossiya*, no. 34 (1992); *RFE/RL Research Report*, vol. 1, no. 35 (4 September 1992), p. 73.
72   Brzezinski's article 'The Cold War and Its Aftermath', *Foreign Affairs*, vol. 71, no. 4 (fall 1992), pp. 31–49, especially pp. 48–9, on the West's geopolitical policy towards Russia, was reproduced in *Den'*, no. 50 (78) (13 December 1992), p. 2.
73   Andrei Kozyrev, *Preobrazhenie* (Moscow, Mezhdunarodnye otnosheniya, 1995), p. 5.
74   *Izvestiya*, 22 February 1992, pp. 1, 3.
75   Kozyrev, 'Russia: A Chance of Survival', p. 10.
76   Andrei Kozyrev, 'Russia and Human Rights', *Slavic Review*, vol. 51, no. 2 (summer 1992), p. 289.
77   Kozyrev, 'Russia: A Chance for Survival', p. 10; *Trud*, 30 November 1991, p. 3; 'Rossiya obrechena byt' velikoi derzhavoi' ('Russia is Destined to be a Great Power'), *Novoe vremya*, no. 3 (1992), pp. 20–24; *Nezavisimaya gazeta*, 1 April 1992, pp. 1, 3. For the view that Russia has all that it takes to be a Great Power, in terms of population, resources and skills, see Yevgenii Bazhanov, 'Ne speshite otpevat' derzhavu', *Novoe vremya*, no. 2 (1992), pp. 16–18.
78   *Literaturnaya gazeta*, 13 September 1995, cited in *Transition*, 3 November 1995, p. 68.
79   See Chris Brown, *International Relations Theory: New Normative Approaches* (Hemel Hempstead, Harvester, 1992).
80   *Rossiiskaya gazeta*, 26 June 1992, p. 7.
81   Andrei Kozyrev, 'Peace with a Sword', *Moscow News*, no. 36 (9–15 September 1994).
82   Emil Pain, 'Russia and the Post-Soviet Space', *Moscow News*, no. 8 (25 February–3 March 1994).
83   Robert Seely, *Independent*, 8 March 1994.
84   *Independent*, 18 June 1992.
85   *Russkaya mysl'*, 19 April 1991.
86   *Independent*, 18 March 1995.
87   *Independent*, 16 February 1995.
88   *Independent*, 10 March 1995, p. 14.
89   *Nezavisimaya gazeta*, 20 August 1992, p. 4.
90   *Moskovskie novosti*, no. 59 (3–10 September 1995), p. 5.
91   *Russkaya mysl'*, 19 April 1991.
92   *Nezavisimaya gazeta*, 30 July 1992.
93   See E. Valkenier, *The Soviet Union and the Third World: The Economic Bind* (New York, Praeger, 1983); J. F. Hough, *The Struggle for the Third World: Soviet Debates and American Options* (Washington, DC, Brookings, 1986).
94   Solzhenitsyn, *Rebuilding Russia*, p. 27.
95   *Soviet Weekly*, 19 September 1991, p. 3.
96   *Nezavisimaya gazeta*, 1 April 1992, p. 3.
97   Vladimir Zubok, 'Tyranny of the Weak: Russia's New Foreign Policy', *World Policy Journal*, vol. IX, no. 2 (spring 1992), pp. 191–218.
98   *Moscow News*, no. 52 (31 December 1993), p. 1.
99   *Segodnya*, 14 July 1995, p. 5.
100 *Moscow News*, no. 37 (10 September 1993), p. 7.
101 Konstantin Eggert, *Izvestiya*, 16 December 1995, p. 3.

15 DEFENCE AND SECURITY POLICY

1   Osip Mandelstam, cited by Vasily Grossman, *Life and Fate* (London, The Harvill Press, 1995), p. 267.
2   Stephen Foye, 'Armed Forces Confront Legacy of Soviet Past', *RFE/RL Research Report*, vol. 1, no. 8 (21 February 1992, pp. 9–10.
3   Paul Hirst, 'The State, Civil Society and the Collapse of Soviet Communism', *Economy and Society*, vol. 20, no. 2, pp. 217–42. For a discussion of the size of the defence sector, see *Kommunist*, no. 1 (1991), pp. 54–64.
4   For a discussion of the army's ambiguous legal status at this time, see *Nezavisimaya gazeta*, 2 February 1992, p. 1.
5   *Soviet Weekly*, 19 September 1991, p. 2.
6   Shaposhnikov observed 'I am a citizen of Russia . . . whom do I serve if not Russia? But it is

Russia whose vital interests are conjugated with the interests of the other CIS nations', *Moscow News*, no. 6 (4 February 1993), p. 4.

7 *Izvestiya*, 3 July 1992, pp. 1–2.

8 *RFE/RL Research Report*, 1, 42 (23 October 1992), p. 41.

9 The defence minister, Konstantin Morozov, argued that the decision was prompted by Moscow's refusal to release around 20,000 officers of Ukrainian origin serving outside the republic who had asked to return to serve in Ukraine's armed forces, *Independent*, 8 June 1992.

10 *The Military Balance 1994–1995* (London, Brasseys for The International Institute for Strategic Studies, 1994), p. 104.

11 Cf. Adrian Karatnycky, 'The Ukrainian Factor', *Foreign Affairs*, vol. 71, no. 3 (summer 1992), p. 94.

12 *Krasnaya zvezda*, 9 May 1992.

13 *Moscow News*, no. 7 (11 February 1993), p. 3.

14 The lack of resources was used by Grachev against those who advocated such measures as the conversion of the Defence Ministry into a civilian organisation, e.g. Vladimir Lobov, 'How to Reform the Russian Army', *Rossiiskaya gazeta*, 25 January 1995.

15 Stephen Foye, 'Post-Soviet Russia: Politics and the New Russian Army', *RFE/RL Research Report*, vol. 1, no. 33 (21 August 1992), pp. 5–12.

16 Stephen Foye, 'Russian Troops Abroad: Vestiges of Empire', *RFE/RL Research Report*, vol. 1, no. 34 (28 August 1992), pp. 15–17, at p. 17.

17 *Krasnaya zvezda*, 17 February 1993, p. 1.

18 Dzintra Bungs, 'Soviet Troops in Latvia' *RFE/RL Research Report*, vol.1, no. 34 (28 August 1992), pp. 18–28, at p. 19.

19 Dzintra Bungs, 'Soviet Troops in Latvia' *RFE/RL Research Report*, vol. 1, no. 34 (28 August 1992), pp. 18–28.

20 *Independent*, 23 January 1993.

21 Stephen Foye, 'Russia's Defense Establishment in Disarray', *RFE/RL Research Report*, vol. 2, no. 36 (10 September 1993), pp. 49–54.

22 *RFE/RL Research Report*, vol. 1, no. 31 (31 July 1992), p. 61.

23 *Moscow News*, no. 7 (11 February 1993), p. 1.

24 Stephen Foye, 'Confusion in Moscow Over Military Base Directive', *RFE/RL News Briefs*, 8 April 1994.

25 The first 'Strategy for Russia' report in August 1992 had, indeed, singled Georgia out as Russia's key strategic ally in Transcaucasia.

26 *The Military Balance 1994–1995*, p. 109.

27 *Pravda*, 8 December 1988.

28 Estimates range as high as 15 million, Keith Bush, 'Conversion and Employment in Russia', *RFE/RL Research Report*, vol. 2, no. 2 (8 January 1993), p. 30; Brenda Hoorigan, 'How Many People Worked in the Soviet Defence Industry?', *RFE/RL Research Report*, vol. 1, no. 33 (21 August 1992), pp. 33–9.

29 *Rossiiskie vesti*, 22 May 1992.

30 Julian Cooper, *The Soviet Defence Industry: Conversion and Reform* (London, RIIA/Pinter, 1991), pp. 10–11, 14.

31 *RFE/RL Research Report*, vol. 1, no. 42 (23 October 1992), p. 40; for detailed analysis, see Christopher K. Hummel, 'Russian Conversion Policy Encounters Opposition', *RFE/RL Research Report*, vol. 1, no. 32 (14 August 1992), pp. 25–32; Keith Bush, 'Russia's Latest Program for Military Conversion', *RFE/RL Research Report*, vol. 1, no. 35 (4 September 1992), p. 32.

32 *Independent*, 26 September 1992.

33 Keith Bush, 'Russia's Latest Program for Military Conversion', *RFE/RL Research Report*, vol. 1, no. 35 (4 September 1992), pp. 32–5, at p. 33.

34 *Independent*, 12 October 1992.

35 See V. N. Tsygichko, 'Geopolitical Aspects of Shaping Russia's Nuclear Policy', *Military Thought/Voennaya Mysl'*, no. 3 (March 1994), pp. 2–9.

36 According to one report the Soviet nuclear arsenal included 45,000 warheads at its peak in 1986, 12,000 more than had been thought, *Independent*, 27 September 1993.

37 Stephen Van Evera, 'Managing the Eastern Crisis: Preventing War in the Former Soviet Empire', *Security Studies*, vol. 1, no. 3 (spring 1992).

38 Bohdan Nahaylo, 'The Shaping of Ukrainian Attitudes towards Nuclear Arms', *RFE/RL Research Report*, vol. 2, no. 8 (19 February 1993), pp. 21–33.

39 *Independent*, 4 June 1993.

40 *Nezavisimaya gazeta*, 7 December 1991, p. 1.
41 See John W. R. Lepingwell, 'Ukraine, Russia, and the Control of Nuclear Weapons', *RFE/RL Research Report*, vol. 2, no. 8 (19 February 1993), pp. 4–20.
42 E.g. the head of the Fifth Duma's foreign policy committee, Lukin, *Segodnya*, 28 March 1995.
43 Douglas L. Clarke, 'Rusting Fleet Renews Debate on Navy's Mission', *RFE/RL Research Report*, vol. 2, no. 25 (18 June 1993), p. 30.
44 Sergei Parkhomenko, *Segodnya*, 19 November 1994.
45 *Moscow News*, no. 30 (1990), p. 11.
46 *Independent*, 12 May 1992.
47 For a debate over the issue, see *Trud*, 27 March 1991.
48 Cf. Stephen Foye, 'Manning the Russian Army: Is Contract Service a Success?', *RFE/RL Research Report*, vol. 3, no. 13 (1 April 1994), pp. 36–45.
49 *The Military Balance 1994–1995*, p. 109.
50 Valerii Borisenko, *Moskovskie novosti*, no. 6 (1996), p. 9.
51 The *Independent*, 30 December 1993. Grachev gave a figure of 2.6 million in May 1992 (*Moskovsky komsomolets*, 20 May 1992), while the figure of 2.3 million he mentioned in April 1994 probably refers to total authorised strength. At that time he argued in favour of maintaining a force of 2.1 million, of whom some 780,000 were in Land Forces, *The Military Balance 1994–1995*, p. 109.
52 *Independent*, 1 March 1995, p. 12; 18 May 1996, p.11.
53 For details, see Douglas L. Clarke, 'Implementing the CFE Treaty', *RFE/RL Research Report*, vol. 1, no. 23 (5 June 1992), pp. 50–55.
54 *The Military Balance 1994–1995*, p. 108.
55 Cf. Douglas L. Clarke, 'The Russian Military and the CFE Treaty', *RFE/RL Research Report*, vol. 2, no. 42 (22 October 1993), pp. 38–43.
56 *Moscow News*, no. 5 (28 January 1993), p. 4.
57 Scott McMichael, 'Russia's New Military Doctrine', *RFE/RL Research Report*, vol. 1, no. 40 (9 October 1992), p. 45.
58 The draft was published in a special issue of *Voennaya mysl'*, May 1992.
59 The document was discussed by the Security Council on 3 March and 6 October 1993, and accepted at its session of 2 November, on which date the president decreed its adoption, 'Osnovnye polozheniya voennoi doktriny Rossiiskoi. Federatsii', special issue of *Voennaya mysl'*, November 1993, also in *Izvestiya*, 18 November 1993.
60 *Ibid*, p. 4.
61 E.g. V. K. Demedyuk and Yu. S. Kortunenko, 'On Organizational Structure of the Armed Forces', *Military Thought/Voennaya mysl'*, no. 5 (May 1994), pp. 2–6.
62 *Izvestiya*, 20 July 1992, p. 2.
63 *Vek*, no. 8 (1996), p. 3.
64 Christopher Bellamy, *Independent*, 19 February 1996, p. 11.
65 In his book, *Poslednii brosok na yug* (Moscow, Svetoton, 1994), Zhirinovskii argued that Russia's arrival on the shores of the Indian Ocean and the Mediterranean would signal the salvation of the Russian nation, removing the threat to Russia from the south forever.
66 *Segodnya*, 18 July 1995, p. 3.
67 *Independent*, 12 January 1995. This would have had the effect of removing operational control of forces from the defence minister, reducing him to the management of budgets and equipment.
68 Alex Pravda, 'Russia and European Security: The Delicate Balance', *NATO Review*, no. 3 (May 1995), p. 20.
69 For analyses of the CSCE process in the post-Cold War world, see articles by Dan Hiester (pp. 58–66), Yuri Deryabin (pp. 67–74), Andrei Zagorskii (pp. 76–88), Elaine Holoboff (pp. 91–110), and Pavel Baev (pp. 111–121), in *Paradigms: The Kent Journal of International Relations*, vol. 5, Nos 1/2 (1991).
70 Andrei Zagorskii, 'Khel'sinki: budushchee v tumane', *Moskovskie novosti*, no. 13 (29 March 1991), p. 5.
71 A. V. Kozyrev, 'Vneshnyaya politika', p. 9.
72 See Donald D. Asmus *et al*, 'NATO Expansion: The Next Steps', *Survival*, vol. 37, no. 1 (spring 1995).
73 For a discussion of the issues, see *Transition*, 15 December 1995, pp. 5–43.
74 Kozyrev, 'Partnership or Cold Peace?, p. 13.
75 *Soviet Weekly*, 31 October 1991, p. 4.
76 *Izvestiya*, 6 September 1994.

77 *Moskovskie novosti*, no. 15 (26 February–5 March 1995), p. 11.
78 *NATO Review*, no. 3 (May 1995), p. 5.
79 *OMRI Daily Digest*, no. 94, Part I, 16 May 1995.
80 E.g. Vladimir Lepekhin, editor of *Novaya ezhednevnaya gazeta*, 22 September 1994.
81 Kozyrev, 'Partnership or Cold Peace?', p. 13.
82 *Nezavisimaya gazeta*, 3 February 1995; see also the CFDP's theses on how Russia should respond to Nato expansion, *Nezavisimaya gazeta*, 21 June 1995, reproduced in *Transition*, 15 December 1995, pp. 27–32.
83 *Observer*, 29 October 1995, p. 21.
84 'Evolutionary Problems in the Former Soviet Armed Forces', *Survival*, autumn 1992, p. 37.
85 *Moscow News*, no. 5 (28 January 1993), p. 4.
86 For Yeltsin's vivid depiction of these events, see his *Zapiski prezidenta*, pp. 382–7.
87 *Independent*, 28 October 1995, p. 11.
88 *Independent*, 28 October 1995, p. 11.
89 Otto Latsis, *Izvestiya*, 13 October 1993.
90 *RFE/RL Research Report*, vol. 1, no. 36 (11 September 1992), p. 72. According to unofficial figures, some 25,000 officers had been dismissed by the end of 1992 for disagreeing with the government, *Guardian*, 13 January 1993.
91 Stephen Foye, 'The Defense Ministry and the New Military "Opposition"', *RFE/RL Research Report*, vol. 2, no. 20 (14 May 1993), pp. 68–73.
92 *Moscow News*, no. 7 (11 February 1992), p. 1.
93 *Moskovskie novosti*, no. 59 (3–10 September 1995), p. 7.
94 Televised broadcast of 22 December 1993.
95 *Independent*, 30 December 1993.
96 Pavel Felgengauer, *Segodnya*, 15 December 1993; and see *Sovetskaya Rossiya*, 21 December 1993, p. 1.
97 Zhirinovskii's support consistently reached 15 per cent, but this was balanced by growing support for Yavlinskii (rising from eighth to second place between March (6.6 per cent) and August 1995 (14.5 per cent)) because of his harsh criticisms of the government and president, while Zyuganov remained in third place with 14 per cent, *Moskovskie novosti*, no. 59 (3–10 September 1995), p. 6. A separate incomplete study in the Leningrad military district revealed solid support for the CPRF (21.9 per cent among senior oficers) and a sharp rise in the ratings of KRO (16 per cent, the same as the LDPR) once Lebed had joined them, *Moskovskie novosti*, no. 59 (3–10 September 1995), p. 7.
98 *Komsomolskaya pravda*, 30 March 1993, p. 1.
99 *Segodnya*, 5 August 1994; *Rossiiskaya gazeta*, 6 August 1994.
100 *Novaya ezhenedel'naya gazeta*, 17 August 1994.
101 *RFE/RL News Briefs*, 8–12 August 1994.
102 *Russkaya mysl'*, no. 4062 (26 January–1 February 1995), p. 20.
103 Pavel Baev, letter to the author, 23 March 1993.
104 *Nezavisimaya gazeta*, 19 August 1992.
105 Benjamin S. Lambeth, 'Russia's Wounded Military', *Foreign Affairs*, vol. 74, no. 2 (March/ April 1995), pp. 86–7.

16 COMMONWEALTH AND COMMUNITY

1 Niccolo Machiavelli, *Discourses on the First Decade of Titus Livius* (London, 1883), p. 175.
2 R. H. Jackson, *Quasi-States and Sovereignty: International Relations and the Third World* (Cambridge, Cambridge University Press, 1992).
3 Andrei Nuikin interviewed in *Vechernyaya Moskva*, 9 September 1991, p. 2. The Russian Christian Democratic Movement under Viktor Aksyuchits consistently held to this view.
4 A useful discussion of some of these questions is in A. V. Kortunov, 'Konfliktnyi potentsial "blizhnego" zarubezh'ya i adekvatnaya strategiya Rossii', *Diplomaticheskii vestnik*, no. 21–2 (15–30 November 1992), pp. 41–3.
5 *Pravda*, 27 November 1991.
6 The Almaty agreements of 21 December are in *Rossiiskaya gazeta*, 24 December 1991, p. 1.
7 Mikhail Gorbachev, 'Mir na perelome', *Svobodnaya mysl'*, no. 16 (1992), pp. 3–18, at p. 9.
8 M. A. Khrustalev, 'Evolyutsiya SNG i vneshnepoliticheskaya strategiya Rossii', *Diplomaticheskii vestnik*, no. 21–2 (15–30 November 1992), pp. 31–3.

9 Kozyrev, 'Vneshnyaya politika', p. 7.
10 Andrei Zagorskii *et al*, *The Commonwealth of Independent States: Developments and Prospects* (Moscow, Centre for International Studies, MGIMO, 1992), p. 6.
11 See Andrei Zagorskii, *SNG: ot dezintegratsii k reintegratsii?* (Moscow, MGIMO, 1994).
12 Zagorskii, *The Commonwealth of Independent States*, pp. 6–7.
13 *Literaturnaya gazeta*, 19 August 1992, p. 11.
14 *Nezavisimaya gazeta*, 18 August 1992, p. 2. Gorbachev remained consistent in this view, developed at length in his *Dekabr'-91: moya pozitsiya* (Moscow, Novosti, 1992).
15 Alexei Malashenko, 'Rossiya i islam', *Nezavisimaya gazeta*, 22 February 1992, p. 3.
16 *RFE/RL Research Report*, vol. 1, no. 42 (23 October 1992), p. 63.
17 *Nezavisimaya gazeta*, 9 October 1992, p. 3.
18 Suzanne Crow, 'The Theory and Practice of Peace-keeping in the Former USSR', *RFE/RL Research Report*, vol. 1, no. 37 (18 September 1992).
19 The text is in Stephen Foye, 'The Soviet Legacy', *RFE/RL Research Report*, vol. 2, no. 25 (18 June 1993), pp. 4–5.
20 Suzanne Crow, 'Russia Seeks Leadership in Regional Peace-keeping', *RFE/RL Research Report*, vol. 2, no. 15 (9 April 1993).
21 Pavel Baev, 'Russia's Experiments and Experience in Conflict Management and Peacemaking', *International Peace-keeping*, vol. 1, no. 3 (autumn 1994).
22 *Segodnya*, 25 December 1993, p. 1.
23 A development examined by Dmitrii Trenin, 'Collective Seurity and Collective Defence', *Nezavisimaya gazeta*, 4 November 1994.
24 See, e.g. General V. M. Barynkin, 'Local Wars at the Present Stage', *Voennaya mysl'*, no. 6 (June 1994), pp. 7–11.
25 Kozyrev, 'Vneshnyaya politika', p. 8.
26 Yurii Afanas'ev and Len Karpinskii, *Moskovskie novosti*, no. 32 (7–14 May 1995).
27 *Moskovskie novosti*, no. 15 (26 February–5 March 1995), p. 11.
28 *Nezavisimaya gazeta*, 10 October 1992.
29 *RFE/RL Research Report*, vol. 1, no. 3 (31 July 1992), p. 74.
30 Andrei Zagorskii, 'Reintegration in the Former USSR?', *Aussenpolitik*, no. 3 (1994), pp. 263–72.
31 Ruslan Khasbulatov, 'O vneshnei politike i diplomatii Rossii', *Rossiiskaya gazeta*, 6 March 1992, p. 7.
32 *Nezavisimaya gazeta*, 17 September 1992.
33 Zagorskii, *SNG*, p. 19.
34 *Nezavisimaya gazeta*, 1 September 1992.
35 Andrei Kozyrev, 'A Transformed Russia in a New World', *Izvestiya*, 2 January 1992, p. 3.
36 Andrei Kozyrev, 'Russia: A Chance of Survival', *Foreign Affairs* (spring 1992), pp. 10–12.
37 See *RFE/RL Research Report*, vol. 1, no. 29 (17 July 1992), p. 80. Apparently the Security Council on 1 July agreed to the creation of a separate CIS ministry, *RFE/RL Research Report*, vol. 1, no. 33, p. 4. Comparisons were drawn with Britain, where the Commonwealth Office handled relations with the former colonies before being merged in 1968 with the Foreign Office.
38 Suzanne Crow, 'Russia Prepares to take a Hard Line on "Near Abroad"', *REF/RL Research Report*, vol. 1, no. 32 (1992), pp. 21–4.
39 *Nezavisimaya gazeta*, 30 July 1992, pp. 1, 5.
40 Suzanne Crow, 'Russia's Relations with Members of the Commonwealth', *RFE/RL Research Report*, vol. 1, no. 19 (8 May 1992), pp. 8–12, at p. 11.
41 *Nezavisimaya gazeta*, 24 March 1992, p. 2.
42 *Nezavisimaya gazeta*, 21 June 1995, p. 2.
43 *Rossiiskaya gazeta*, 23 September 1995, p. 4.
44 *Nezavisimaya gazeta*, 19 August 1992; Suzanne Crow, 'Competing Blueprints for Russian Foreign Policy', *RFE/RL Research Report*, vol. 1, no. 50 (18 December 1992), pp. 48–9.
45 Andrei Zagorskii *et al*, *After the Disintegration of the Soviet Union: Russia in a New World* (Moscow, MGIMO, February 1992).
46 *Rossiiskaya gazeta*, 2 December 1992, p. 3.
47 Neil Melvin, *Forging the New Russian Nation* (London, RIIA Discussion Paper 50, 1994), p. 3.
48 Vittorio Strada, 'Old and New Borders: Soviet and Russian Borders as a Phenomenon', *Nezavisimaya gazeta*, 6 November 1991.
49 Ken Jowitt, *New World Disorder: The Leninist Extinction* (Berkeley, University of California Press, 1992), pp. 319–26 analyses the 'civic/ethnic identity issue'.

50 *Politicheskii monitoring Rossiii*, no. 3 (July-September 1992), p. 7.
51 *OMRI Daily Digest*, no. 11, Part I, 16 January 1996.
52 *Pravda*, 30 January 1992.
53 *Moscow News*, no. 37 (1991), p. 6.
54 Leonid Velekhov, *Segodnya*, 18 November 1995, p. 2.
55 *Soviet Weekly*, 10 October 1991, p. 5.
56 For details, see *Documents on British Foreign Policy, 1919–1939*, First Series, vol. XI, *Upper Silesia, Poland, and the Baltic States, January 1920–March 1921* (London, HMSO, 1961), pp. 1–197.
57 Alexander Golts, *Krasnaya zvezda*, 18 July 1992, p. 2.
58 Kozyrev, 'Vneshnyaya politika', p. 8.
59 Solzhenitsyn, *Rebuilding Russia*, p. 14.
60 *Loc. cit.*
61 *Ibid.*, p. 24.
62 *Nezavisimaya gazeta*, 3 July 1992, p. 3; *CDSP*, vol. XLIV, no. 27 (1992), pp. 11–12.
63 *Izvestiya*, 28 November 1991, p. 2.
64 *Rossiiskaya gazeta*, 6 February 1992.
65 *Rossiiskaya gazeta*, 14 July 1993.
66 Lowell Barrington, 'The Domestic and International Consequences of Citizenship in the Soviet Successor States', *Europe-Asia Studies*, vol. 47, no. 5 (July 1995), pp. 731–63.
67 C. Macartney, *National States and National Minorities* (London, Oxford University Press, 1934), p. 275 and *passim*. See also Hugh Miall (ed.), *Minority Rights in Europe* (London, Pinter, 1994).
68 Ann Sheehy, 'The CIS: A Shaky Edifice', *RFE/RL Research Report*, vol. 2, no. 1 (1 January 1993), p. 39.
69 See Chauncy D. Harris, 'The New Russian Minorities: A Statistical Overview', *Post-Soviet Geography*, vol. 34, no. 1 (1993), pp. 1–27.
70 Melvin, *Forging the New Russian Nation*, p. 3.
71 *Rossiiskaya gazeta*, 29 October 1991, p. 2.
72 For a good analysis of the 'Russians abroad' issue, see the Gorbachev Foundation's report, *Nezavisimaya gazeta*, 7 September 1993.
73 Speech of 29 April 1995, *OMRI Daily Digest*, no. 85, Part I, 2 May 1995.
74 *Independent*, 19 April 1995, p. 8.
75 Stephen Castles and Mark J. Miller, *The Age of Migration: International Population Movements in the Modern World* (London, Macmillan, 1993).
76 *Rossiya*, no. 19 (18–24 May 1994), p. 4.
77 See Benedict Anderson, *Imagined Communities: Reflections on the Origin and Spread of Nationalism* (London, Verso, 1983).
78 *Independent*, 19 April 1995, p. 8.
79 *Rossiiskie vesti*, 5 May 1994, p. 4.
80 *OECD Economic Surveys*, p. 130.
81 *Izvestiya*, 9 July 1992, p. 3.
82 Gaidar's report to parliament, 22 September 1992.
83 *Rossiiskaya gazeta*, 5 May 1994, p. 4.
84 *Argumenty i fakty*, no. 5 (February 1992), p. 4.
85 *Independent*, 8 May 1992.
86 *Rezultaty sotsiologicheskogo issledovaniya 'Sotsial'no-aktivnye sily Rossii: usloviya i puti ikh konsolidatsii* (Moscow, Institut sotsial'nykh i politicheskikh tekhnologii, 1991), pp. 10–11.
87 Sarah Helmstadter, 'The Export of Russian Labor: A Remedy for Unemployment?', *RFE/RL Research Report*, vol. 1, no. 37 (18 September 1992), pp. 50–54.
88 *Independent*, 12 October 1992.
89 UN International Organisation for Migration report, *Independent*, 17 February 1992.

17 PROBLEMS OF TRANSITION

1 Alexander Solzhenitsyn, *Rebuilding Russia* (London, Harvill, 1991), p. 9.
2 Robert O. Crummey, 'Introduction', in Crummey (ed.), *Reform in Russia and the USSR: Past and Prospects* (Urbana, University of Illinois Press, 1989), p. 9.
3 See, for example, Tim Mason, *Social Policy in the Third Reich: The Working Class and the National Community* (Providence, RI, Berg, 1993); and his *Nazism, Fascism and the Working Class* (Cambridge, Cambridge University Press, 1994).

4 Ralf Dahrendorf, *Society and Democracy in Germany* (London, Weidenfeld and Nicolson, 1968), p.342.

5 The problem of Russia's 'asococial subjectivity' and allied issues are discussed in my 'Subjectivity, Politics and Order in Russian Political Evolution', *Slavic Review*, vol. 54, no.4 (winter 1995), pp.943–64.

6 For a recent discussion of history and time, see Robert C. Tucker, 'Kakoe vremya pokazyvayut seichas chasy Rossiiskoi istorii' ('What Time is it in Russia's History'), *Problemy vostochnoi evropy*, nos. 31–32 (1991), pp. 58–78.

7 John Miller, *Mikhail Gorbachev and the End of Soviet Power* (London, Macmillan, 1993), p. 8.

8 *Political Archives of the Soviet Union*, vol. 2, no. 2 (1991), p. 119.

9 Nicolai N. Petro, *The Rebirth of Russian Democracy: An Interpretation of Political Culture* (Cambridge, MA, Harvard University Press, 1995).

10 N. Berdyaev *et al*, *Vekhi: sbornik statei o Russkoi intelligentsii* (Moscow, 1909; reprinted Frankfurt, Posev, 1967).

11 Geoffrey Hosking, *The Russian Constitutional Experiment: Government and Duma, 1907–1914* (Cambridge, Cambridge University Press, 1973).

12 Richard Pipes, *Russian under the Old Regime* (London, Weidenfeld and Nicolson, 1974).

13 See, for example, Sergei Pushkarev, *Self-Government and Freedom in Russia* (Boulder, CO, Westview Press, 1988); Nicolai N. Petro (ed.), *Christianity and Russian Culture in Soviet Society* (Boulder, CO, Westview Press, 1990).

14 A. V. Obolenskii, 'Mekhanizm tormozheniya: chelovecheskoe izmerenie', *Sovetskoe gosudarstvo i pravo*, no. 1 (1990), pp. 80–87; see also his 'Russian Politics in the Time of Troubles', in Amin Saikal and William Maley (eds), *Russia in Search of its Future* (Cambridge, Cambridge University Press, 1995), pp. 12–27.

15 Nicolai N. Petro, *The Rebirth of Russian Democracy: An Interpretation of Political Culture* (Cambridge, MA, Harvard University Press, 1995), pp. 2–3 and *passim*.

16 E.g. at the State Conference on 12–15 August 1917 in speeches by Georgi Plekhanov ('There can be no bourgeois revolution in which the bourgeoisie do not take part. There can be no capitalism in which there are no capitalists'), and Alexander Guchkov, a leader of the Octobrist Party, who urged the establishment of a strong government, *Moscow News*, no. 24 (16 June 1991), p. 9.

17 *Izvestiya*, 16 November 1993.

18 Alexander Yakovlev, 'Wake up Brother Russia', *Guardian*, 6 May 1992.

19 For recent assessments of 1917 in Russia, see Edward Acton, *Rethinking the Russian Revolution* (London, Edward Arnold, 1990); Edith Rogovin Frankel, Jonathen Frankel and Baruch Knei-Paz (eds), *Revolution in Russia: Reassessments of 1917* (Cambridge, Cambridge University Press, 1992). The best of recent analyses of the intelligentsia in revolution includes Jane Burbank, *Intelligentsia and Revolution: Russian Views of Bolshevism, 1917–1922* (Oxford, Oxford University Press, 1986); Christopher Read, *Culture and Power in Revolutionary Russia: The Intelligentsia and the Transition from Tsarism to Communism* (London, Macmillan, 1990).

20 Zdenek Mlynar, *Can Gorbachev Change the Soviet Union? The International Dimension of Political Reform* (Boulder, CO, Westview Press, 1990).

21 Lucian W. Pye, 'Political Science and the Crisis of Authoritarianism', *American Political Science Review*, vol. 84, no. 1 (March 1990), pp. 3–19.

22 Francis Fukuyama, 'The End of History', *The National Interest* (summer 1989), pp. 3–17; *The End of History and the Last Man* (New York, Free Press, 1992).

23 Dankwart Rustow, 'Democracy: A Global Revolution', *Foreign Affairs*, vol. 69, no. 4 (fall 1990), p. 75.

24 For a sophisticated attempt to analyse the relationship between modernisation and political development, see Andrew C. Janos, 'Social Science, Communism, and the Dynamics of Political Change', *World Politics*, vol. 44, no. 1 (October 1991), pp. 81–112.

25 For a discussion of these issues and the role of foreign aid, see Yavlinskii, *Nezavisimaya gazeta*, 8 July 1992, pp. 2, 5.

26 For a stimulating comparison of the governmental technologies of the Bolsheviks and the early modern police, see Agnes Horvath and Arpad Szakolczai, *The Dissolution of Communist Power: The Case of Hungary* (London, Routledge, 1992), esp. chapter 8.

27 For a challenging analysis of 'populist' and 'pluralist' definitions of democracy and the emergence of parliamentarianism in Russia, see Biryukov and Sergeev, *Russia's Road to Democracy*.

28 Chris Brown, '"Really Existing Liberalism" and International Order', *Millenium*, vol. 21, no. 3 (1992), pp. 313–28; see also his *International Relations Theory: New Normative Approaches* (Hemel Hempstead, Harvester Wheatsheaf, 1992).

29 Barrington Moore, Jr, *Social Origins of Dictatorship and Democracy* (Harmondsworth, Penguin, 1967), p. 418.
30 For example, Seymour Martin Lipset, *Political Man* (Garden City, NY, Doubleday, 1960), pp. 27–63; Charles Lindblom, *Politics and Markets* (New York, Basic Books, 1977); John Freeman, *Democracy and Markets* (Ithaca, NY, Cornell University Press, 1989).
31 Guillermo O'Donnell and Philippe Schmitter, *Transitions from Authoritarian Rule: Tentative Conclusions about Uncertain Democracies* (Baltimore, Johns Hopkins University Press, 1986).
32 For a classic example of the maturation argument, see Moshe Lewin, *The Gorbachev Phenomenon: A Historical Interpretation* (London, Hutchinson Radius, 1988).
33 Rustow, 'Democracy: A Global Revolution', p. 79.
34 Samuel P. Huntington, *The Third Wave: Democratization in the Late Twentieth Century* (Norman: University of Oklahoma Press, 1991); see also his 'How Countries Democratize', *Political Science Quarterly*, vol. 106, no. 4 (1991–92), pp. 579–616.
35 Laurence Whitehead, 'International Aspects of Democratisation', in Guillermo O'Donnell, Philippe Schmitter and Laurence Whitehead (eds), *Transitions from Authoritarian Rule: Comparative Perspectives* (Baltimore, Johns Hopkins University Press, 1986), pp. 3–46.
36 O'Donnell and Schmitter, *Tentative Conclusions*, pp. 15–36.
37 Alfred Stepan, 'Paths Toward Redemocratisation: Theoretical and Comparative Considerations', in O'Donnell *et al* (eds), *Comparative Perspectives*, pp. 64–84.
38 Samuel Huntington, *Political Order in Changing Societies* (New Haven, Yale University Press, 1968).
39 Dankwart Rustow, 'Transitions to Democracy: Toward a Dynamic Model', *Comparative Politics*, vol. 2, no. 3 (1970), pp. 337–63, at pp. 352–61.
40 Rustow, 'Transitions to Democracy', p. 352, Adam Przeworski, 'Some Problems in the Study of the Transition to Democracy'; Guillermo O'Donnell *et al* (eds), *Comparative Perspectives*, pp. 47–63, at p. 58; and Giuseppe Di Palma, *To Craft Democracies: An Essay in Democratic Transitions* (Berkeley, University of California Press, 1990), pp. 54ff.
41 Cf. Joseph Schumpeter, *Capitalism, Socialism and Democracy* (London, 1942/76); for a discussion of Schumpeter's relevance to the post-communist transitions, see Richard Bellamy, 'Schumpeter and the Transformation of Capitalism, Liberalism and Democracy', *Government and Opposition*, vol. 26, no. 4 (1991), pp. 500–19.
42 Rustow, 'Transitions to Democracy', p. 337.
43 For a defence of the concept of totalitarianism, see William E. Odom, 'Soviet Politics and After: Old and New Concepts', *World Politics*, vol. 45, no. 1 (1992), pp. 66–98; and for the view that the so-called 'totalitarianism' versus 'pluralism' debate obscured as much as it revealed, George Breslauer, 'In Defense of Sovietology', *Post-Soviet Affairs*, vol. 8, no. 3 (1992), pp. 197–238, esp. pp. 216–22.
44 Jadwiga Staniszkis, *The Dynamics of Breakthrough in Eastern Europe* (Berkeley, CA:, California University Press, 1991).
45 Joel Migdal, *Strong Societies and Weak States: State-Society Relations and State Capacities in the Third World* (Princeton, Princeton University Press, 1988).
46 Melvin Croan *et al*, 'Is Latin America the Future of Eastern Europe?', *Problems of Communism*, vol. XLI, no. 3 (May–June 1992), pp. 44–57.

18 DEMOCRACY IN RUSSIA

1 Max Weber, 'Bourgeois Democracy in Russia', in *The Russian Revolutions*, edited and translated by Gordon C. Wells and Peter Baehr (Oxford, Polity Press, 1995), p. 109.
2 Moore, *Social Origins of Dictatorship and Democracy*, p. 414.
3 *Peace Watch*, United States Institute of Peace, vol. 1, no. 2 (February 1995), p. 3.
4 A view repeated in his famous 1918 essay 'Politics as a Vocation': 'The state is considered the sole source of the "right" to use violence', in H. H. Gerth and C. Wright Mills (eds), *From Max Weber: Essays in Sociology* (New York, Oxford University Press, 1956), p. 78.
5 Jadwiga Staniszkis, 'The Worrying Power Shift in the Kremlin', *European Brief*, vol. 2, no. 4 (1993), pp. 73–4.
6 Frank Field review of Ronald H. Preston, *Religion and the Ambiguities of Capitalism* (London, SCM, 1992), *Independent*, 4 June 1992.
7 These ideas are discussed by Thomas Graham, *Moskovskie novosti*, no. 78 (12–19 November 1995), p. 23.

8 Samuel P. Huntington, 'The Clash of Civilizations?', *Foreign Affairs*, vol. 72, no. 3 (summer 1993), pp. 22–49; Zyuganov's views are in 'Rossiya i mir', in *Sovremennaya Russkaya ideya i gosudarstvo* (Moscow, Obozrevatel', 1995), pp. 10–26; see also his *Za gorizontom* (Moscow, 1995), p.8 and *passim.*

9 Jeffrey Sachs, *Moscow News*, no. 51 (28 December 1995), p. 3.

10 *Izvestiya*, 26 December 1995, p. 5.

11 *Observer*, 19 February 1995, p. 21.

12 Gordon A. Craig, 'Demonic Democracy', *New York Review of Books*, 13 February 1992, pp. 39–43, at p. 43; see also Wolfgang J. Mommsen, *Max Weber and German Politics, 1890–1920*, translated by Michael S. Steinberg (Chicago, University of Chicago Press, 1984).

13 *Delo*, no. 42 (1995), in *OMRI Russian Election Survey*, no. 2, 31 October 1995.

14 *Nezavisimaya gazeta*, 23 June 1994, p. 2.

15 Huntington, *Political Order and Changing Societies*.

16 As Schmitter demonstrated, presidential systems in Latin America were conducive to dictatorships, O'Donnell *et al*, vol. 2, *Southern Europe*, p. 9.

17 Leonid Nikitinskii, *Izvestiya*, 23 September 1993.

18 *Izvestiya*, 16 November 1993.

19 *Moskovskie novosti*, no. 85 (1995), p. 3.

20 *Moskovskie novosti*, no. 73 (22–9 October 1995), p. 6.

21 *Soviet Weekly*, 10 October 1991, p. 6.

22 Ken Jowitt, *New World Disorder: The Leninist Extinction* (Berkeley, University of California Press, 1992), p. 293.

23 Kozyrev, 'Russia: A Chance for Survival', p. 6.

24 *Izvestiya*, 4 May 1994, p. 5; *Observer*, 29 May 1994.

Select bibliography

CONTEMPORARY RUSSIAN POLITICS

Adelman, Jonathan A., *Torrents of Spring: Soviet and Post-Soviet Politics* (New York, McGraw-Hill, 1995).

Barner-Barry, Carol and Hody, Cynthia, *The Politics of Change: The Transformation of the Former Soviet Union* (London, Macmillan, 1995)

Billington, James H., *Russia Transformed: Breakthrough to Hope* (New York, Free Press, 1993).

Blum, Douglas W., *Russia's Future: Consolidation or Disintegration?* (Oxford, Boulder Press, 1994).

Buckley, Mary, *Redefining Russian Society and Polity* (Oxford, Westview Press, 1993).

Devlin, Judith, *The Rise of the Russian Democrats: The Causes and Consequences of the Elite Revolution* (Aldershot, Edward Elgar, 1995).

Dunlop, John B., *The Rise of Russia and the Fall of the Soviet Empire* (Princeton, NJ, Princeton University Press, 1993).

Isham, Heyward (ed.), *Remaking Russia: Voices from Within* (New York, M.E. Sharpe, 1995).

Kagarlitsky, Boris, *Restoration in Russia: Why Capitalism Failed*, translated by Renfrey Clarke (London, Verso, 1995).

Kagarlitsky, Boris, *Mirage of Modernisation* translated by Renfrey Clarke (London, Verso, 1995).

Kampfner, John, *Inside Yeltsin's Russia* (London, Cassell, 1994).

Lane, David (ed.), *Russia in Transition: Politics, Privatisation and Inequality* (Harlow, Longman, 1995).

Lapidus, Gail W. (ed.), *The New Russia: Troubled Transformation* (Boulder, CO, Westview Press, 1994).

Löwenhardt, John, *The Reincarnation of Russia: Struggling with the Legacy of Communism,1990–94* (Harlow, Longman, 1995).

McFaul, Michael, *Post-Communist Politics: Democratic Prospects in Russia and East Europe* (Washington, DC, Centre for Strategic and International Studies, 1993).

McFaul, Michael, *The Troubled Birth of Russian Democracy* (Stanford, Hoover Press, 1993).

Morrison, John, *Boris Yeltsin: From Bolshevik to Democrat* (London, Penguin Books, 1991).

Murray, Donald, *A Democracy of Despots* (Boulder, CO, Westview Press, 1996).

Nelson, Lynn D. and Kuzes, Irina, *Radical Reform in Yeltsin's Russia* (Armonk, NY, M. E. Sharpe, 1995).

Petro, Nicolai N., *The Rebirth of Russian Democracy: An Interpretation of Political Culture* (Cambridge, MA, Harvard University Press, 1995).

Ragsdale, Hugh, *The Russian Tragedy: The Burden of History* (New York, M.E. Sharpe, 1996).

Saikal, Amin and Maley, William, (eds), *Russian in Search of its Future* (Cambridge, Cambridge University Press, 1994).

Saivetz, Carol R. and Jones, Anthony, (eds), *In Search of Pluralism: Soviet and Post-Soviet Politics* (Boulder, CO, Westview, 1994).

Shaw, D. J. B., *The Post-Soviet Republics: A Systematic Geography* (London, Longman, 1995).

Solzhenitsyn, Alexander, *Rebuilding Russia: Reflections and Tentative Proposals* (London, Harvill Press, 1991).

Solzhenitsyn, Alexander, *The Russian Question at the End of the Twentieth Century* (London, Harvill Press, 1995).

Starr, S. Frederick (ed.), *The Legacy of History in Russia and the New States of Eurasia* (New York, M.E. Sharpe, 1994).

Tismaneanu, Vladimir (ed.), *Political Culture in Russia and the New States of Eurasia* (New York, M.E. Sharpe, 1995).

White, Stephen., Pravda, Alex, and Gitelman, Zvi, (eds), 3rd edn, *Developments in Russian and Post-Soviet Politics* (London, Macmillan, 1994).

White, Stephen, Gill, Graeme, and Slider, Darrell, *The Politics of Transition: Shaping a Post-Soviet Future* (Cambridge, Cambridge University Press, 1993).

SOVIET AND RUSSIAN HISTORY

Acton, Edward, *Russia: The Tsarist and Soviet Legacy*, 2nd edn (Harlow, Longman, 1995).

Amalrik, Andrei, *Will the Soviet Union Survive until 1984?* (London, Penguin Books, 1970).

Andrle, Vladimir, *A Social History of Twentieth Century Russia* (London, Edward Arnold, 1994).

Baradat, Leon P., *Soviet Political Society* 3rd edn (Prentice Hall, 1992).

Black, Cyril E. (ed.), *The Transformation of Russian Society: Aspects of Social Change since 1861* (Cambridge, MA, Harvard University Press, 1960).

Brown, Archie (ed.), *Political Leadership in the Soviet Union* (London, Macmillan, 1989).

Colton, Timothy J. and Levgold, Robert, (eds), *After the Soviet Union: From Empire to Nation* (New York, Norton, 1992).

Crummey, Robert O. (ed.), *Reform in Russia and the USSR: Past and Prospects* (Urbana, IL, University of Illinois Press, 1989).

Custine, Marquis de, *Letters from Russia*, translated and edited by Robin Buss (London, Penguin Classics, 1991).

Heller, M. and Nekrich, A. *Utopia in Power: A History of the USSR from 1917 to the Present* (London, Hutchinson, 1986).

Holloway, David and Nalmark, Norman, (eds), *Re-examining the Soviet Experience: Essays in Honor of Alexander Dallin* (Boulder, CO, Westview, 1996).

Hosking, Geoffrey, *The Russian Constitutional Experiment: Government and Duma, 1907–1914* (Cambridge, Cambridge University Press, 1973).

Hosking, Geoffrey, *A History of the Soviet Union* (London, Fontana, 1985/1990).

Hosking, Geoffrey, *The Awakening of the Soviet Union* (London, Heinemann, 1990).

Kagarlitsky, Boris, *The Thinking Reed: Intellectuals and the Soviet State from 1917 to the Present*, translated by Brian Pearce (London, Verso, 1988).

Kagarlitsky, Boris, *Farewell Perestroika: A Soviet Chronicle* (London, Verso, 1990).

Katkov, G. *et al*, *Russia Enters the Twentieth Century* (London, Methuen, 1973).

Keep, John L. H., *Last of the Empires: A History of the Soviet Union, 1945–1991* (Oxford, Oxford University Press, 1996).

Kennan, George, 'Communism in Russian History', *Foreign Affairs*, vol. 71 (winter 1990–1991), pp. 168–86.

Kort, Michael, *The Soviet Colossus: The Rise and Fall of the USSR*, 3rd edn (London, M. E. Sharpe, 1992).

Lieberman, Sanford R. *et al* (eds), *The Soviet Empire Reconsidered: Essays in Honor of Adam B. Ulam* (Boulder, CO, Westview Press, 1994).

Little, Richard D., *Governing the Soviet Union* (New York, Longman, 1989).

McAuley, Mary, *Soviet Politics, 1917–1991* (Oxford, Oxford University Press, 1992).

McCauley, Martin, *The Soviet Union, 1917–1991*, 2nd edn (Harlow, Longman, 1993).

Medish, Vadim, *The Soviet Union*, 4th edn (Prentice Hall, 1991).

Pearson, Raymond, *The Russian Moderates and the Crisis of Tsarism, 1914–1917* (London, Macmillan, 1977).

Riasanovsky, Nicholas V., *A History of Russia*, 5th edn (Oxford, Oxford University Press, 1993).

Rigby, T. H., *The Changing Soviet System: Mono-Organisational Socialism from its Origins to Gorbachev's Restructuring* (Aldershot, Edward Elgar, 1990).

Rogger, H., *Russia in the Age of Modernisation and Revolution, 1881–1917* (London, Longman, 1983).

Sakwa, Richard, *Soviet Politics: An Introduction* (London and New York, Routledge, 1989).

Shipler, D. K., *Russia: Broken Idols, Solemn Dreams* (London, MacDonald, 1983).

Smith, Gordon, *Soviet Politics*, 2nd edn, *Struggling with Change* (London, Macmillan, 1991).

Soros, George, *Opening the Soviet System* (London, Weidenfeld and Nicolson, 1990).

Steele, Jonathan, *Eternal Russia* (London, Faber, 1994).

Taranovski, Theodore, *Reform in Modern Russian History: Progress or Cycle?* (Cambridge, Cambridge University Press, 1995).

Thompson, John M., *Russia and the Soviet Union: An Historical Introduction from the Kievan State to the Present*, 3rd edn (Oxford, Westview Press, 1994).

Tolz, Vera and Elliot, Iain (eds), *The Demise of the USSR: From Communism to Independence* (London, Macmillan, 1994).

Treadgold, Donald W., *Twentieth Century Russia*, eighth edn (Oxford, Westview Press, 1994).

Von Laue, Theodore H., *Why Lenin? Why Stalin? Why Gorbachev? The Rise and Fall of the Soviet System* 3rd edn (New York, Harper Collins College Publishers, 1993).

Westwood, John, *Endurance and Endeavour: Russian History, 1812–1992*, 4th edn (Oxford, Oxford University Press, 1993).

THE FALL OF COMMUNISM

Arnason, Johann P., *The Future that Failed: Origins and Destinies of the Soviet Model* (London, Routledge, 1993).

Bialer, Seweryn, 'The Death of Soviet Communism', *Foreign Affairs*, vol. 70, no. 5 (winter-spring 1991).

Brzezinski, Zbigniew, *The Grand Failure: The Birth and Death of Communism in the Twentieth Century* (London, Macdonald, 1989).

Callinicos, Alex, *The Revenge of History: Marxism and the East European Revolutions* (Oxford, Polity Press, 1991)

Charlton, Michael, *Footsteps from the Finland Station: Five Landmarks in the Collapse of Communism* (St Albans, Claridge Press, 1992).

Cullen, Robert, *Twilight of Empire: Inside the Crumbling Soviet Bloc* (London, Bodley Head, 1991).

Daniels, Robert V., *The End of the Communist Revolution* (London, Routledge, 1993).

Goldman, Marshall I., *What Went Wrong with Perestroika* (New York, W. W. Norton, 1991).

Hill, Ronald J., *Communist Politics Under the Knife: Surgery or Autopsy* (London, Pinter, 1990).

Holmes, Leslie, *The End of Communist Power: Anti-Corruption Campaigns and Legitimation Crisis* (Oxford, Polity Press, 1993).

Hudelson, Richard H., *The Rise and Fall of Communism* (Boulder, CO, Westview Press, 1993).

Gill, Graeme, *The Collapse of the Single-Party System: The Disintegration of the Communist Party of the Soviet Union* (Cambridge, Cambridge University Press, 1994).

Jowitt, Ken, *New World Disorder: The Leninist Extinction* (Berkeley, University of California Press, 1992).

Kagarlitsky, Boris, *The Disintegration of the Monolith* (London, Verso, 1992).

Kiernan, Brendan, *The End of Soviet Politics: Elections, Legislatures, and the Demise of the Communist Party* (Boulder, CO, Westview, 1993)

Laqueur, Walter, *The Dream that Failed* (Oxford, Oxford University Press, 1994).

Malia, Martin ('Z'), 'To the Stalin Mausoleum', *Daedalus*, vol. 169, no. 1 (winter 1990), pp. 295–344.

Malia, Martin, 'Leninist Endgame', *Daedalus*, vol. 121, no. 2 (spring 1992), pp. 57–75.

Malia, Martin, *The Soviet Tragedy: A History of Socialism in Russia* (New York, The Free Press, 1994).

Mandelbaum, Michael, 'The End of the Soviet Union', *Foreign Affairs*, vol. 71, no. 1 (1992).

Remnick, David, *Lenin's Tomb: The Last Days of the Soviet Empire* (New York, Random House, 1993).

Robinson, Neil, *Ideology and the Collapse of the Soviet System: A Critical History of the Soviet Ideological Discourse* (Aldershot, Edward Elgar, 1995).

Sakwa, Richard, 'Commune Democracy and Gorbachev's Reforms', *Political Studies*, vol. 37, no. 2 (June 1989), pp. 224–43.

The National Interest, special issue devoted to the fall, spring 1993.

Ticktin, Hillel, *Origins of the Crisis in the USSR: Essays on the Political Economy of a Disintegrating System* (Armonk, NY, M. E. Sharpe, 1992).

Ulam, Adam, *The Communists: The Story of Power and Lost Illusions, 1948–1991* (New York, Macmillan, 1993).

White, Stephen., Gill, Graeme, and Slider, Darrell, *The Politics of Transition: Shaping a Post-Soviet Future* (Cambridge, Cambridge University Press, 1993)

The Gorbachev era

Balzer, Harley D. (ed.), *Five Years that Shook the World: Gorbachev's Unfinished Revolution* (Boulder/Oxford, Westview Press, 1991).

Bialer, Seweryn (ed.), *Politics, Society and Nationality inside Gorbachev's Russia* (Boulder, CO, Westview Press, 1989).

Boettke, Peter J., *Why Perestroika Failed: The Politics and Economics of Socialist Transformation* (London and New York, Routledge, 1993).

Boldin, Valery, *Ten Years that Shook the World* (London, Basic Books, 1994).

Breslauer, George, 'Evaluating Gorbachev as Leader', *Soviet Economy*, vol. 5, no. 4, (1989), pp. 299–340.

Brown, Archie, 'Gorbachev and the Reform of the Soviet System', *Political Quarterly*, 58, 2 (April–June 1987), pp. 139–51.

Brown, Archie (ed.), *New Thinking in Soviet Politics* (London, Macmillan, 1992).

Cerf, Christopher and Marina Albee, *Voices of Glasnost: Letters from the Soviet People to Ogonyok Magazine, 1987–1990* London, Kyle Cathie, 1990).

Chiesa, Giulietto, with Douglas Taylor Northrop, *Transition to Democracy: Political Change in the Soviet Union, 1987–1991* (Hanover, University Press of New England, 1993).

Cooper, Leo, *Soviet Reforms and Beyond* (London, Macmillan, 1991).

Dallin, Alexander and Gail W. Lapidus (eds), *The Soviet System: From Crisis to Collapse*, revised edn (Oxford, Westview Press, 1994).

Doder, Dusko and Branson, Louise, *Gorbachev: Heretic in the Kremlin* (London, Viking, 1990).

Gooding, John, 'Gorbachev and Democracy', *Soviet Studies*, vol. 42, no. 2, (1990), pp. 195–231.

Gooding, John, 'Perestroika and the Russian Revolution of 1991', *Slavonic and East European Review*, vol. 71, no. 2 (April 1993), pp. 234–56.

Gorbachev, M. S., *Perestroika: New Thinking for Our Country and the World* (London, Collins, 1987).

Hart, Gary, *The Second Russian Revolution* (London, Hodder & Stoughton, 1991).

Hewett, Ed A. and Victor H. Winston (eds), *Milestones in Glasnost and Perestroika: Politics and People* (Washington, DC, The Brookings Institution, 1991).

Hewett, Ed A. and Winston, Victor H., (eds), *Milestones in Glasnost and Perestroika: The Economy* (Washington, DC, The Brookings Institution, 1991).

Huber, Robert T. and Kelley, Donald R. (eds), *Perestroika-era Politics: The New Soviet Legislature and Gorbachev's Political Reforms* (Armonk, NY/London, M. E. Sharpe, 1991).

Kaiser, Robert G., 'Gorbachev: Triumph and Failure', *Foreign Affairs*, vol. 70, no. 2 (spring 1991), pp. 160–74.

Kaiser, Robert G., *Why Gorbachev Happened: His Triumphs and His Failure* (Hemel Hemstead, Simon and Schuster, 1992).

Lane, David, *Soviet Society under Perestroika* (London, Routledge, 1992).

Lane, David (ed.), *Russia in Flux: The Political and Social Consequences of Reform* (Aldershot, Edward Elgar, 1992).

Melville, Andrei and Lapidus, Gail W. (eds), *The Glasnost Papers: Voices on Reform from Moscow* (Boulder, CO, Westview Press, 1990).

Merridale, Catherine, and Ward, Chris (eds), *Perestroika: The Historical Perspective* (London, Edward Arnold, 1991).

Miller, John, *Mikhail Gorbachev and the End of Soviet Power* (Basingstoke, Macmillan, 1993).

Ruge, Gerd, *Gorbachev* (London, Chatto and Windus, 1991).

Sakwa, Richard, *Gorbachev and His Reforms, 1985–90* (Hemel Hempstead, Philip Allan, 1990).

Spring, D. W. (ed.), *The Impact of Gorbachev: The First Phase, 1985–90* (London, Pinter Publishers, 1991).

Urban, Michael E. (ed.), *Ideology and System Change in the USSR and Eastern Europe* (London, Macmillan, 1992).

Walker, Rachel, *Six Years that Changed the World: Perestroika the Impossible Project* (Manchester, Manchester University Press, 1993).

White, Stephen, *After Gorbachev*, 4th edn (Cambridge, Cambridge University Press, 1992).

The August 1991 coup and the disintegration of the USSR

Bonnell, Victoria E., Cooper, Ann and Friedin, Gregory (eds), *Russia at the Barricades* (Armonk, NY, M. E. Sharpe, 1994).

Crawshaw, Steve, *Goodbye to the USSR: the Collapse of Soviet Power* (London, Bloomsbury, 1992).

Gorbachev, Mikhail, *The August Coup: The Truth and the Lessons* (London, HarperCollins, 1991).

Grachev, Andrei, *Final Days: The Inside Story of the Collapse of the Soviet Union* (Oxford, Westview Press, 1995).

McDonnell, Lawrence, *October Revolution* (Staplehurst, Spellmount Limited, 1994).

Pankin, Boris, *The Last Hundred Days of the Soviet Union* (London, I. B. Tauris, 1995).

Roxburgh, Angus, *The Second Russian Revolution: The Struggle for Power in the Kremlin* (London, BBC Books, 1991).

Ruge, Gerd, *Der Putsch: Vier Tage, die die Welt veränderten* (Frankfurt, Fischer Taschenbuch Verlag, 1991).

Russian Information Agency, *Putsch. The Diary: Three Days that Collapsed the Empire* (Stevenage, SPA, 1993).

Sakwa, Richard, 'The Revolution of 1991 in Russia: Interpretations of the Moscow Coup', *Coexistence*, vol. 29, no. 4 (December 1992), pp. 27–67.

Sakwa, Richard, 'A Cleansing Storm: The August Coup and the Triumph of Perestroika', *Journal of Communist Studies*, vol. 9, no. 1 (spring 1993), pp. 131–49.

Sixsmith, Martin, *Moscow Coup: The Death of the Soviet System* (London, Simon and Schuster, 1991).

CONSTITUTIONALISM AND THE LAW

Barry, Donald D. (ed.), *Towards the 'Rule of Law' in Russia?: Political and Legal Reform in the Transition Period* (Armonk, NY, M. E. Sharpe, 1992).

Feofanov, Yuri and Barry, Donald P. *Politics and Justice in Russia: Major Trials of the Post-Stalin Era* (London, M.E. Sharpe, 1996).

Sharlet, Robert, *Soviet Constitutional Crisis: From De-Stalinisation to Disintegration* (Armonk, NY, M. E. Sharpe, 1992).

Crime, militia and the mafia

Gdlyan, Telman and Dodolev, E. *Mafiya vremen bezzakoniya* (Yerevan, Academy of Sciences, 1991).

Handelman, Stephen, *Comrade Criminal: The Theft of the Second Russian Revolution* (London, Michael Joseph, 1994).

Vaksberg, Arkady, *The Soviet Mafia* (London, Weidenfeld and Nicolson, 1991).

Security apparatus

Albats, Yevgenia, *KGB: State Within a State: the Secret Police and its Hold on Russia's Past, Present and Future* (London, I. B. Tauris, 1995).

Waller, J. Michael, *Secret Empire: the KGB in Russia Today* (Oxford, Westview, 1994).

PARTY DEVELOPMENT

CPSU and its fall

Gill, Graeme, *The Collapse of the Single-Party System: The Disintegration of the Communist Party of the Soviet Union* (Cambridge, Cambridge University Press, 1994).

Hill, Ronald J., 'The CPSU: Decline and Collapse', *Irish Slavonic Studies*, no. 12 (1991), pp. 97–119.

Hill, Ronald J., 'The CPSU: From Monolith to Pluralist', *Soviet Studies*, vol. 43, no. 2 (1991), pp. 217–35.

Millar, James R. (ed.), *Cracks in the Monolith: Party Power in the Brezhnev Era* (London, M. E. Sharpe, 1992).

White, Stephen, 'Rethinking the CPSU', *Soviet Studies*, vol. 43, no. 3 (1991), pp. 405–28.

From social movements to parties

Babkina, M. A. (ed.), *New Political Parties and Movements in the Soviet Union* (Commack, NY, Nova Science Publishers, 1991).

Berezovskii, V.N. *et al.*, *Rossiya: partii, assotsiatsii, soyuzy, kluby: ·sbornik dokumentov i materialov*, 10 vols (Moscow, RAU-Press, 1992).

Dallin, Alexander (ed.), *Political Parties in Russia* (Berkeley, University of California Press, 1993).

Fish, M. Stephen, *Democracy from Scratch: Opposition and Regime in the New Russian Revolution* (Princeton, NJ, Princeton University Press, 1995).

Golosov, Grigorii V., 'New Russian Political Parties and the Transition to Democracy: The Case of Western Siberia', *Government and Opposition*, vol. 30, no. 1 (winter 1995), pp. 110–19.

Hosking, Geoffrey A., Aves, Jonathan and Duncan, Peter J. S. *The Road to Post-Communism: Independent Political Movements in the Soviet Union* (London, Pinter Publishers, 1992).

Lohr, Eric, 'Arkadii Volsky's Political Base', *Europe-Asia Studies*, vol. 45, no. 5 (1993), pp. 811–29.

Mandel, David, *Perestroika and the Soviet People: Rebirth of the Labour Movement* (Montreal, Black Rose Books, 1991).

Orttung, Robert W., 'The Russian Right and the Dilemmas of Party Organisation', *Soviet Studies*, vol. 44, no. 3 (1992), pp. 445–78.

Petrenko, Viktor, Mitina, Ol'ga and Brown, Ruth 'The Semantic Space of Russian Political Parties on a Federal and Regional Level', *Europe-Asia Studies*, vol. 47, no. 5 (July 1995), pp. 835–57.

Sakwa, Richard, 'The Development of the Russian Party System', in Peter Lentini (ed.), *Elections and Political Order in Russia* (Budapest, Central European University Press, 1995), pp. 169–201.

Sedaitis, Judith B. and Butterfield, Jim (eds), *Perestroika From Below: Social Movements in the Soviet Union* (London, Westview, 1991).

Szajkowski, Bogdan (ed.), *New Political Parties of Eastern Europe and the Soviet Union* (Harlow, Longman, 1991).

Temkina, Anna, 'The Workers' Movement in Leningrad, 1986–91', *Soviet Studies*, vol. 44, no. 2 (1992), pp. 209–36.

Tolz, Vera, *The USSR's Emerging Multiparty System* (New York, Praeger, 1990).

Urban, Joan Barth and Solovei, Valerii D. *Hammer, Book and Sickle: Communism in Post-Soviet Russia* (Boulder, CO, Westview, 1996).

ELECTORAL POLITICS

Baglione, Lisa. and Clarke, Carol L. 'Participation and the Success of Economic and Political Reforms: A Lesson from the 1993 Russian Parliamentary Elections', *The Journal of Communist Studies and Transition Politics*, vol. 11, no. 3 (September 1995), pp. 215–48.

Berezkin, A. V. *et al.*, *Vesna 89: geografiya i anatomiya parlamentskikh vyborov* (Moscow, Progress, 1990); 'The Geography of the 1989 Elections of People's Deputies of the USSR', *Soviet Geography*, vol. 30, no. 8 (October 1989), pp. 607–34.

Colton, Timothy J., 'The Politics of Democratisation: The Moscow Election of 1990', *Soviet Economy*, vol. 6, no. 4 (October–December 1990), pp. 285–344.

Embree, Gregory J., 'RSFSR Election Results and Roll Call Votes', *Soviet Studies*, vol. 43, no. 6 (1991), pp. 1065–84.

Furtak, Robert K. (ed.), *Elections in Socialist States* (London, Harvester Wheatsheaf, 1990).

Hahn, Jeffrey W., 'An Experiment in Competition: The 1987 Elections to the Local Soviets', *Slavic Review*, vol. 47, no. 3 (fall 1988), pp. 434–47.

Hahn, W. G., 'Electoral "Choice" in the Soviet Bloc', *Problems of Communism*, vol. 36, no. 2 (March–April 1987), pp. 29–39.

Help, Gavin and Hahn, Jeffrey W. 'Old Dogs and New Tricks: Party Elites in the Russian Regional Elections of 1990', *Slavic Review*, vol. 51, no. 3 (fall 1992), pp. 511–30.

Kiernan, Brendan and Aistrup, Joseph 'The 1989 Elections to the Congress of People's Deputies in Moscow', *Soviet Studies*, vol. 43, no. 6 (1991), pp. 1049–64.

Lentini, Peter (ed.), *Elections and Political Order in Russia: The Implications of the 1993 Elections to the Federal Assembly* (Budapest, Central European University Press, 1995).

Remington, Thomas, 'The March 1990 RSFSR Elections', in Slider, Darrell (ed.), *Elections and Political Change in the Soviet Republics* (Durham, NC, Duke University Press, 1991).

Sakwa, Richard, 'The Russian Elections of December 1993', *Europe-Asia Studies*, vol. 47, no. 2 (March 1995), pp. 195–227.

Shlapentokh, Vladimir, 'The 1993 Russian Election Polls', *Public Opinion Quarterly*, vol. 58 (1994), pp. 579–602.

Slider, Darrell (ed.), *Soviet Politics and the 1990 Elections* (Durham, NC, Duke University Press, forthcoming).

Urban, Michael, 'December 1993 as a Replication of Late-Soviet Electoral Practices', *Post-Soviet Affairs*, vol. 10, no. 2 (1994), pp. 127–58.

White, Stephen, 'Reforming the Electoral System', *Journal of Communist Studies*, vol. 5, no. 4 (1988), pp. 1–17.
White, Stephen, 'From Acclamation to Limited Choice: The Soviet Elections of 1989', *Coexistence*, vol. 28, no. 4 (December 1991), pp. 77–103.
Whitefield, Stephen and Geoffrey Evans, 'The Russian Election of 1993: Public Opinion and the Transition Experience', *Post-Soviet Affairs*, vol. 10, no. 1 (1994), pp. 38–60.

REMAKING THE STATE: THE LEGISLATURE

Biryukov, Nikolai, and Sergeev, V.M. *Russia's Road to Democracy: Parliament, Communism and Traditional Culture* (Aldershot, Edward Elgar, 1993).
Hahn, Jeffrey W. (ed.), *Democratization in Russia: The Development of Legislative Institutions* (Armonk, NY, M.E. Sharpe, 1995).
Huber, Robert T. (ed.), *Perestroika-Era Politics: The New Soviet Legislature and Gorbachev's Political Reforms* (Armonk, NY, M. E. Sharpe, 1992).
Khasbulatov, Ruslan, *The Struggle for Russia: Power and Change in the Democratic Revolution*, edited by Richard Sakwa (London and New York, Routledge, 1993).
Myagkov, Mikhail G. and Kiewiet, D. Roderick 'Czar Rule in the Russian Congress of People's Deputies?', *Legislative Studies Quarterly*, vol. XXI, no. 1 (February 1996), pp. 5–40.
Remington, Thomas F. (ed.), *Parliaments in Transition: The New Legislative Politics in the Former USSR and Eastern Europe* (Boulder, CO, Westview Press, 1994).
Urban, Michael E., *More Power to the Soviets: The Democratic Revolution in the USSR* (Aldershot, Edward Elgar, 1990).

REMAKING THE STATE: THE EXECUTIVE

Colton, Timothy J. and Tucker, Robert C. (eds), *Patterns in Post-Soviet Leadership* (Boulder, CO, Westview Press, 1995).
Huskey, Eugene (ed.), *Executive Power and Soviet Politics: The Rise and Decline of the Soviet State* (Armonk, NY, M. E. Sharpe, 1992).
Lijphart, Arend (ed.), *Parliamentary versus Presidential Government* (Oxford, Oxford University Press, 1992).
Linz, Juan J., 'The Perils of Presidentialism', *Journal of Democracy*, vol. 1, no. 1 (1990), pp. 51–70.
Linz, Juan J. and Valenzuela, Arturo (eds), *The Failure of Presidential Democracy*, (Baltimore, MD, Johns Hopkins University Press, 1994).
Stepan, Alfred and Skach, Cindy 'Constitutional Frameworks and Democratic Consolidation: Parliamentarianism versus Presidentialism', *World Politics*, vol. 46, no. 1 (1993), pp. 1–22.
Urban, Michael E., 'Boris El'tsin, Democratic Russia and the Campaign for the Russian Presidency', *Soviet Studies*, vol. 44, no. 2 (1992), pp. 187–207.

THE POLITICS OF PLURALISM

Evans, Alfred B. 'Problems of Conflict Management in Russian Politics', *The Journal of Communist Studies*, vol. 9, no. 2 (June 1993), pp. 1–19.
Ra'anan, Uri *et al* (eds), *Russian Pluralism: Now Irreversible* (New York, St Martin's, 1992).
Saivetz, Carol R., and Jones, Anthony (eds), *In Search of Pluralism: Soviet and Post-Soviet Politics* (Boulder, CO, Westview, 1994).

Class, elite and leadership

Colton, Tim and Tucker, Robert C. (eds), *Patterns in Post Soviet Leadership* (Oxford, Westview, 1995).
Lane, David (1995), 'Political Elites under Gorbachev and Yeltsin in the Early Period of Transition: A Reputational and Analytical Study', in Colton, Tim and Tucker, Robert C. (eds), *Patterns in Post-Soviet Leadership* (Oxford, Westview, 1995).
Lane, David, 'The Gorbachev Revolution: The Role of the Political Elite in Regime Disintegration', *Political Studies*, vol. 42, no. 1 (March 1996), pp. 4–23.

FEDERALISM AND THE STATE

Smith, Graham (ed.), *Federalism: The Multi-Ethnic Challenge* (Harlow, Longman, 1995).

NATIONALISM AND RUSSIA

Nationalism in general

Alter, Peter, *Nationalism* 2nd edn (London, Edward Arnold, 1994).
Brzezinski, Z., 'Post-Communist Nationalism', *Foreign Affairs* (winter 1990–91), pp. 1–25.
Gellner, Ernest, *Nations and Nationalism: New Perspectives on the Past* (Oxford, Basil Blackwell, 1983).
Eriksen, T. H., *Ethnicity and Nationalism* (London, Pluto, 1993).
Hobsbawm, E. J., *Nations and Nationalism after 1870: Programme, Myth, Reality*, 2nd edn (Cambridge, Cambridge University Press, 1992).
Hutchinson, John and Smith, Anthony D. (eds), *Nationalism* (Oxford, Oxford University Press, 1994).
Kedourie, Elie, *Nationalism*, 4th edn (Oxford, Blackwell, 1993).
Ra'anan, Uri., Mesner, Maria., Armes, Keith and Martin, Kate (eds), *State and Nation in Multi-Ethnic Societies* (Manchester, Manchester University Press, 1991).
Smith, Anthony D., *Theories of Nationalism* (London, Duckworth, 1983).
Smith, Anthony D., *National Identity* (London, Penguin, 1991).

Soviet and post-communist nationality problems

Agursky, Mikhail, *The Third Rome: National Bolshevism in the USSR* (Boulder and London, Westview Press, 1987).
Azrael, Jeremy (ed.), *Soviet Nationality Policies and Practices* (New York, Praeger, 1978).
Bahry, Donna, *Outside Moscow: Power, Politics and Budgetary Policy in the Soviet Republics* (New York, Columbia University Press, 1987).
Bialer, Seweryn (ed.), *Politics, Society and Nationality in Gorbachev's Russia*, (Boulder, CO, Westview Press, 1989).
Bremmer, Ian and Taras, Ray (eds), *Nations and Politics in the Soviet Successor States* (Cambridge, Cambridge University Press, 1993).
Buttino, Marco (ed.), *In a Collapsing Empire: Underdevelopment, Ethnic Conflicts and Nationalisms in the Soviet Union* (Milan, Feltrinelli, 1993).
Carrére d'Encausse, Héléne, *Decline of an Empire: The Soviet Socialist Republics in Revolt* (New York, Newsweek Books, 1979).
Carrére d'Encausse, Héléne, *The Great Challenge: Nationalities and the Bolshevik State, 1917–1930* (New York, Holmes and Meier, 1992).
Carrére d'Encausse, Héléne, *The End of the Soviet Empire: The Triumph of the Nations* (London, Basic Books, 1994).
Connor, Walter, *The National Question in Marxist–Leninist Theory and Strategy* (Princeton, Princeton University Press, 1984).
Conquest, Robert (ed.), *The Last Empire: Nationality and the Soviet Future* (Stanford, CA, Hoover Institution Press, 1986).
Denber, Rachel (ed.), *The Soviet Nationality Reader: The Disintegration in Context* (Boulder, CO, Westview Press, 1992).
Diuk, Nadia and Karatnycky, Adrian *The Hidden Nations: The People Challenge the Soviet Union* (New York, William Morrow, 1990).
Drobizheva, Leokadia *et al* (eds), *Ethnic Conflict in the Post-Soviet World: Case Studies and Analysis* (New York, M.E. Sharpe, 1996).
Gleason, Gregory, *Federalism and Nationalism: The Struggle for Republican Rights in the USSR* (Boulder, CO, Westview Press, 1990).
Goble, Paul, 'Ethnic Politics in the USSR', *Problems of Communism*, vol. 38, (1989), pp. 1–14.
Hajda, Lubomyr and Beissinger, Mark (eds), *The Nationalities Factor in Soviet Politics and Society* (Boulder, CO, Westview Press, 1990).
Karklins, Rasma, *Ethnic Relations in the USSR: The Perspective from Below* (London, Allen and Unwin, 1986).
Katz, Z. (ed.), *Handbook of Major Soviet Nationalities* (New York, Free Press, 1975).

Kozlov, Victor, *The Peoples of the Soviet Union* (London, Hutchinson, 1988).

Kux, Stephan, *Soviet Federalism: A Comparative Perspective* (New York, Westview Press, 1991).

Lapidus, Gail W., 'Ethnonationalism and Political Stability: The Soviet Case', *World Politics*, vol. 4 (July 1984).

Lapidus, Gail W., Zaslavsky, Victor and Goldman, Philip (eds), *From Union to Commonwealth: Nationalism and Separatism in the Soviet Republics* (Cambridge, Cambridge University Press, 1992).

Lieberman, S. R. *et al* (eds), *The Soviet Empire Reconsidered: Essays in Honor of Adam B. Ulam* (Boulder, CO, Westview, 1994).

Mandel, William, *Soviet but Not Russia: The 'Other' Peoples of the Soviet Union* (Palo Alto, CA, Ramparts Press, 1985).

McLean, Fitroy, *All the Russias: The End of an Empire* (London, Viking, 1992).

Motyl, Alexander J., *Will the Non-Russians Rebel? State, Ethnicity and Stability in the USSR* (Ithaca, NY, Cornell University Press, 1987).

Motyl, Alexander J. (ed.), *Thinking Theoretically about Soviet Nationalities* (Oxford, Oxford University Press, 1992).

Motyl, Alexander J., *The Post-Soviet Nations: Perspectives on the Demise of the USSR* (New York, Columbia University Press, 1995).

Nahaylo, Bohdan and Swoboda, Victor *Soviet Disunion: A History of the Nationalities Problem in the USSR* (London, Hamish Hamilton, 1990).

McAuley, Alistair (ed.), *Soviet Federalism: Nationalism and Economic Decentralisation* (Leicester/ London, Leicester University Press, 1991).

Olcott, Martha Brill (ed.), *The Soviet Multinational State: Readings and Documents* (Armonk, NY, M. E. Sharpe, 1990).

Pavkovic, Aleksandar *et al* (eds), *Nationalism and Post-Communism: A Collection of Essays* (Aldershot, Dartmouth, 1995).

Rywkin, Michael, *Moscow's Lost Empire* (New York, M. E. Sharpe, 1994).

Simon, Gerhard, *Nationalism and Policy Toward the Nationalities in the Soviet Union: From Totalitarian Dictatorship to Post-Stalinist Society* (Boulder, CO, Westview Press, 1991).

Smith, Graham (ed.), *The Nationalities Question in the Post-Soviet States*, 2nd edn (Harlow, Longman, 1995).

Suny, Ronald Grigor, *The Revenge of the Past: Nationalism, Revolution and the Collapse of the Soviet Union* (Stanford, Stanford University Press, 1994).

Swoboda, Victor, 'Was the Soviet Union Really Necessary?', *Soviet Studies*, vol. 44, no. 5 (1992), pp. 761–84.

Szporluk, Roman, *Communism and Nationalism: Karl Marx Versus Friedrich List* (Oxford, Oxford University Press, 1988).

Zaslavsky, Victor, *The Neo-Stalinist State: Class, Ethnicity, and Consensus in Soviet Society* (Armonk, NY, M. E. Sharpe, 1982).

Zwick, Peter, *National Communism* (Boulder, CO, Westview Press, 1983).

Russian nation and nationalism

Agursky, Mikhail, *The Third Rome: National Bolshevism in the USSR* (Boulder, CO, Westview, 1987).

Allworth, Edward (ed.), *Ethnic Russia in the USSR: The Dilemma of Dominance* (New York, Pergamon Press, 1980).

Barghoorn, Frederick C., *Soviet Russian Nationalism* (Westport, CT, Greenwood, 1976).

Berdyaev, Nikolai, *The Russian Idea* (London, Geoffrey Bles, 1947).

Carter, Stephen K., *The Politics of Solzhenitsyn* (London, Macmillan, 1977).

Carter, Stephen K., *Russian Nationalism: Yesterday, Today, Tomorrow* (London, Pinter Publishers, 1990).

Duncan, W. Raymond and Paul Holman (eds), *Ethnic Nationalism and Regional Conflict: The Former Soviet Union and Yugoslavia* (Boulder, CO, Westview Press, 1994).

Dunlop, John B., *The New Russian Revolutionaries* (Mass., Nordland, 1976).

Dunlop, John B., *The Faces of Contemporary Russian Nationalism* (Princeton, NJ, Princeton University Press, 1983).

Dunlop, John B., *The New Russian Nationalism* (New York, Praeger, 1985).

Hammer, D. P., 'Vladimir Osipov and the Veche Group, 1971–74', *The Russian Review*, vol. 43, (1984).

Hammer, D. P., *Russian Nationalism and Soviet Politics* (Boulder/London, Westview Press, 1989).

Hosking, Geoffrey A. (ed.), *Church, Nation and State in Russia and the Ukraine* (London, Macmillan, 1991).

Hughes, Michael, 'The Never-Ending Story: Russian Nationalism, National Communism and Opposition to Reform in the USSR and Russia', *The Journal of Communist Studies*, vol. 9, no. 2 (June 1993), pp. 41–61.

Krasnov, Vladislav, *Russia Beyond Communism: A Chronicle of National Rebirth* (Boulder, CO, Westview Press, 1991).

Labedz, Leopold (ed.), *Solzhenitsyn: A Documentary Record* (London, Pelican, 1974).

Laqueur, Walter, *Black Hundred: The Rise of the Extreme Right in Russia* (New York, HarperCollins, 1993).

Likhachev, Dmitri S., *Reflections on Russia*, edited by Nicolai N. Petro, translated by Christina Sever (Boulder, CO, Westview Press, 1991).

Parland, Thomas, *The Rejection in Russia of Totalitarian Socialism and Liberal Democracy: A Study of the Russian New Right* (Helsinki, The Finnish Society of Sciences and Letters, 1993).

Petro, Nicolai N. (ed.), *Christianity and Russian Culture in Soviet Society* (Boulder, CO, Westview Press, 1990).

Petro, Nicolai N., '"The Project of the Century": A Case Study of Russian Nationalist Opposition', *Studies in Comparative Communism*, winter/fall 1987, pp. 235–52.

Petro, Nicolai N., 'Rediscovering Russia', *Orbis*, (winter 1990), pp. 33–50.

Petro, Nicolai N., 'New Political Thinking and Russian Patriotism: The Dichotomy of Perestroika', *Comparative Strategy*, vol. 9, no. 4, 1990, pp. 351–70.

Pushkarev, Sergei, *Self-Government and Freedom in Russia* (Boulder, CO, Westview Press, 1988).

Russian Nationalism Today, special edition of *Radio Liberty Research Bulletin*, 19 December 1988.

Scammell, Michael, *Solzhenitsyn: A Biography* (London, Hutchinson, 1985).

Smith, Hedrick, *The New Russians* (New York, Random House, 1991).

Szporluk, Roman, 'Dilemmas of Russian Nationalism', *Problems of Communism*, vol. 38, no. 4 (July–August 1989), pp. 15–35.

Szporluk, Roman (ed.), *National Identity and Ethnicity in Russia and the New States of Eurasia* (New York, M.E. Sharpe, 1994).

Walicki, A., *The Slavophile Controversy* (Oxford, Oxford University Press, 1975).

Yakunin, Gleb *et al*, *Christianity and Government in Russia and the Soviet Union* (Boulder, CO, Westview Press, 1989).

Yanov, A., *The Russian New Right: Right-Wing Ideologies in the Contemporary USSR* (Berkeley, CA, Institute of International Studies, 1978).

Yanov, A., *The Russian Challenge and the Year 2000* (Oxford, Basil Blackwell, 1987).

Urban, Michael, 'The Politics of Identity in Russia's Postcommunist Transition: The Nation against Itself', *Slavic Review*, vol. 53, no. 3 (fall 1994), pp. 733–65.

REPUBLICS AND NATIONS OF RUSSIA

The republics of Russia

Alatalu, Toomas, 'Tuva – a State Reawakens', *Soviet Studies*, vol. 44, no. 5 (1992), pp. 881–96.

Goldenberg, Suzanne, *Pride of Small Nations: The Caucasus and Post-Soviet Disorder* (London, Zed Books, 1994).

Rorlich, Azade-Ayze, *The Volga Tatars: A Profile in National Resilience* (Stanford, Hoover Institution Press, 1986).

The nations of Russia

Armstrong, T., *Russian Settlement in the North* (Cambridge, Cambridge University Press, 1965).

Bawden, C., *Shamans, Lamas and Evangelicals* (London, Routledge and Kegan Paul, 1985).

Forsyth, James, *A History of the Peoples of Siberia: Russia's North Asian Colony 1581–1990* (Cambridge, Cambridge University Press, 1992).

Freedman, I. (ed.), *Soviet Jewry in the 1980s* (Durham, NC, Duke University Press, 1989).

Gitelman, Zvi, *A Century of Ambivalence: The Jews of Russia and the Soviet Union, 1881 to the Present* (New York, Schocken Books, 1988).

Humphrey, Caroline, *Karl Marx Collective: Economy, Society and Religion in a Siberian Collective Farm* (Cambridge, Cambridge University Press, 1983).
Kochan, Lionel (ed.), *The Jews in Soviet Russia since 1917*, 3rd edn (Oxford, Oxford University Press, 1978).
Lallukka, Seppo, *The East Finnic Minorities in the Soviet Union: An Appraisal of the Erosive Trends* (Helsinki, Suomalainmen tiedeakatemia, 1990).
Pinkus, Benjamin, *The Jews of the Soviet Union: A History of a National Minority* (Cambridge, Cambridge University Press, 1988).
Ro'i, Yaacov, *The Struggle for Soviet Jewish Emigration, 1948–1967* (Cambridge, Cambridge University Press, 1990).
Rorlich, Azade-Ayse, *The Volga Tatars: A Profile in National Resilience* (Stanford, CA, Hoover Press, 1986).

The deported peoples

Allworth, Edward (ed.), *Tatars of the Crimea: Their Struggle for Survival* (Durham, NC, Duke University Press, 1988).
Conquest, Robert, *The Nation Killers: The Soviet Deportation of Nationalities* (London, Macmillan, 1970).
Fisher, Alan W., *The Crimean Tatars* (Stanford, CA, Hoover Press, 1978).
Koch, F. C., *The Volga Germans in Russia and the Americas from 1763 to the Present* (Pennsylvania, Pennsylvania University Press, 1977).
Kreindler, I., 'The Soviet Deported Nationalities: A Summary and an Update', *Soviet Studies*, vol. 38, no. 3, 1986, pp. 387–405.
Nekrich, Alexander, *The Punished Peoples: The Deportation and the Fate of Soviet Minorities at the End of the Second World War* (New York, Norton, 1978).

REGIONAL AND LOCAL POLITICS

Bobrick, Benson, *East of the Sun* (London, Heinemann, 1993).
Bradshaw, Michael J. (ed.), *The Soviet Union: A New Regional Geography?* (London, Belhaven Press, 1991).
Buroway, Michael and Pavel Krotov, 'The Economic Basis of Russia's Political Crisis', *New Left Review*, no. 198 (March–April 1993), pp. 49–69.
Coulson, Andrew (ed.), *Local Government in Eastern Europe* (Aldershot, Edward Elgar, 1995).
Dienes, Leslie, 'Siberia: Perestroika and Economic Development', *Soviet Geography*, vol. 32, no. 7 (1991), pp. 445–57.
Friedgut, Theodore H. and Hahn, Jeffrey W. (eds), *Local Power and Post-Soviet Politics* (New York, M.E. Sharpe, 1994).
Hahn, Jeffrey W., *Soviet Grassroots: Citizen Participation in Local Soviet Government* (Princeton, NJ, Princeton University Press, 1988).
Hahn, Jeffrey W., 'Local Politics and Political Power in Russia: The Case of Yaroslavl'', *Soviet Economy*, vol. 7, no. 4 (1991), pp. 322–41.
Hahn, Jeffrey W., 'Developments in Soviet Local Politics', in Rieber, Alfred J. and Rubinstein, Alvin Z. (eds), *Perestroika at the Crossroads* (Armonk, NY, M. E. Sharpe, 1991).
Hughes, James, 'Regionalism in Russia: The Rise and Fall of the Siberian Agreement', *Europe-Asia Studies*, vol. 46 (1994), pp. 1133–61.
Kirkow, Peter, 'Regional Warlordism in Russia: The case of Primorskii Krai', *Europe-Asia Studies*, vol. 47, no. 6 (September 1995), pp. 923–47.
Kotkin, Stephen and Wolff, David (eds), *Rediscovering Russia in Asia: Siberia and the Russian Far East* (New York, M. E. Sharpe, 1995).
McAuley, Mary, 'Politics, Economics and Elite Realignment in Russia: A Case Study', *Soviet Economy*, vol. 8, no. 1, 1992, pp. 46–88.
Moses, Joel C., 'Soviet Provincial Politics in an Era of Transition and Revolution, 1989–91', *Soviet Studies*, vol. 44, no. 3 (1992), pp. 479–509.
Orttung, Robert, *From Leningrad to St Petersburg: Democratization in a Russian City* (London, Macmillan, 1995).

Popov, Gavriil, *What's To Be Done?* (London, Centre for Research into Communist Economies, 1992).
Schiffer, Jonathan R., *Soviet Regional Economic Policy: The East-West Debate over Pacific Siberian Development* (London, Macmillan, 1989).
Shaw, Denis, *The Post-Soviet Republics: A Systematic Geography* (Harlow, Longman, 1995).
Slider, Darrell *et al*, 'Political Tendencies in Russia's Regions: Evidence from the 1993 Parliamentary Elections', *Slavic Review*, vol. 53, no. 3 (fall 1994), pp. 711–32.
Stephan, John J., *The Russian Far East: A History* (Stanford, CA, Stanford University Press, 1994).
Valencia, Mark J., *The Russian Far East in Transition: Opportunities for Regional Economic Cooperation* (Boulder, CO, Westview Press, 1995).
Wood, Alan and R. Anthony French (eds), *The Development of Siberia: People and Resources* (London, Macmillan, 1989).

REBUILDING THE ECONOMY

Aganbegyan, Abel, *The Challenge: Economics of Perestroika* (London, Hutchinson, 1988).
Aslund, Anders, *Gorbachev's Struggle for Economic Reform*, 2nd edn (London, Pinter Publishers, 1991).
Aslund, Anders (ed.), *The Post-Soviet Economy: Soviet and Western Perspectives* (London, Pinter Publishers, 1992).
Aslund, Anders and Richard Layard (eds), *Changing the Economic System in Russia* (London, Pinter Publishers, 1993).
Aslund, Anders (ed.), *Economic Transformation in Russia* (London, Pinter Publishers, 1994).
Aslund, Anders (ed.), *Russian Economic Reform in Jeopardy* (London, Pinter, 1995).
Aslund, Anders, *How Russia Became a Market Economy* (Washington, DC, The Brookings Institute, 1995).
Bush, Keith, *From the Command Economy to the Market: A Collection of Interviews* (Aldershot, Dartmouth Publishers, 1991).
Clarke, Simon, 'Privatization and the Development of Capitalism in Russia', *New Left Review*, no. 196 (November/December 1992), pp. 3–27.
Cooper, Julian, *The Soviet Defence Industry: Conversion and Reform* (London, RIIA/Pinter Publishers, 1991).
Dyker, David, *Restructuring the Soviet Economy* (London and New York, Routledge, 1992).
Ellman, Michael and Kontorovich, Vladimir (eds), *The Disintegration of the Soviet Economic System* (London and New York, Routledge, 1992).
Goldman, Marshall I., *Lost Opportunity: Why Economic Reforms in Russia Have not Worked* (London, Norton, 1995).
Gregory, Paul R. and Stuart, Robert C. *Soviet and Post-Soviet Economic Structure and Performance*, 5th edn (London, HarperCollins, 1993).
Jones, Anthony and Moskoff, William *Ko-ops: The Rebirth of Entrepreneurship in the Soviet Union* (Bloomington, Indiana University Press, 1991).
Kaminski, Bartlomiej, *Economic Transition in Russia and the New States of Eurasia* (New York, M.E. Sharpe, 1996).
Kornai, Janos, *The Road to a Free Economy: Shifting from a Socialist System. The Example of Hungary* (New York, Norton, 1990).
Lavigne, Marie, *The Economics of Transition: From Socialist Economy to Market Economy* (London, Macmillan, 1995).
Lazeur, Edward P. (ed.), *Economic Transition in Eastern Europe and Russia* (Stanford, CA, Hoover Press, 1995).
Leitzel, Jim, *Russian Economic Reform* (London, Routledge, 1995).
Mau, Vladimir, '*Perestroika*: Theoretical and Political Problems of Economic Reforms in the USSR', *Europe-Asia Studies*, vol. 47, no. 3, (1995), pp. 387–411.
Mau, Vladimir, 'The Road to *Perestroika*: Economics in the USSR and the Problems of Reforming the Soviet Economic Order', *Europe-Asia Studies*, vol. 48, no. 2, (1996), pp. 207–24.
McAuley, Alistair, 'The Economic Consequences of Soviet Disintegration', *Soviet Economy*, vol. 7, no. 3, (1991), pp. 189–214.
Nelson, Lynn D., *Property to the People: The Struggle for Radical Economic Reform in Russia* (Armonk, NY, M. E. Sharpe, 1994).
Puffer, Sheila M. (ed.), *The Russian Management Revolution: Preparing Managers for a Market Economy* (London, M. E. Sharpe, 1992).

Rutland, Peter, *The Politics of Economic Stagnation in the Soviet Union: The Role of Local Party Organs in Economic Management* (Cambridge, Cambridge University Press, 1992).

Smith, Alan, *Russia and the World Economy: Problems of Integration* (London, Routledge, 1993).

Sutela, Pekka, *Economic Thought and Economic Reform in the Soviet Union* (Cambridge, Cambridge University Press, 1991).

Wanniski, Jude, 'The Future of Russian Capitalism', *Foreign Affairs*, vol. 71, no. 2 (spring 1992), pp. 17–25.

Wigley, John, *The Rebirth of Russia* (London, Macmillan, 1995).

Privatisation

Clarke, Simon, 'Privatization and the Development of Capitalism in Russia', *New Left Review*, no. 196 (November/December 1992), pp. 3–27.

Cox, Terry, *From Perestroika to Privatisation: Property Relations and Social Change in Soviet Society, 1985–1991* (Aldershot, Avebury, 1996).

Estrin, Saul, (ed.), *Privatization in Central and Eastern Europe* (London, Longman, 1994).

Filatotchev, Igor, Buck, Trevor and Wright, Mike 'Privatisation and Buy-outs in the USSR', *Soviet Studies*, vol. 44, no. 2 (1992), pp. 265–82.

Frydman, Roman, Rapaczynski, Andrzej, Earle, John S. *et al.*, *The Privatisation Process in Central Europe* (Budapest, Central European University Press, 1993).

McFaul, Michael and Tova Perlmutter (eds), *Privatization, Conversion, and Enterprise Reform in Russia* (Boulder, CO, Westview Press, 1994).

Agriculture

Channon, John, *Agrarian Reforms in Russia, 1992–5* (London, RIIA, 1995).

Reissinger, William M., Miller, Arthur H. and Hesli, Vivki L. 'Political Norms in Rural Russia: Evidence From Public Attitudes', *European-Asia Studies*, vol. 47, no. 6, 1995, pp. 1025–42.

Rutskoi, A. V., *Agrarnaya reforma v Rossii* (Moscow, Prilozhenie k ezhenedel'niku 'Obozrevatel'', 1992).

Van Atta, Don, 'Agrarian Reform in Post-Soviet Russia', *Post-Soviet Affairs*, vol. 10, no. 2 (April–June 1994), pp. 159–90.

Wegren, Stephen K., 'Rural Migration and Agrarian Reform in Russia: A Research Note', *Europe-Asia Studies*, vol. 47, no. 5 (July 1995), pp. 877–88.

Wegren, Stephen K., 'Understanding Rural Reform in Russia: A Response to Reissinger', *Europe-Asia Studies*, vol. 48, no. 2, (1996), pp. 317–29.

For comparative purposes

Bird, Graham (ed.), *Economic Reform in Eastern Europe* (Aldershot, Edward Elgar, 1992).

Crawford, Beverly (ed.), *Markets, States and Democracy: The Political Economy of Post-Communist Transformation* (Oxford, Westview Press, 1995).

Islam, Shafiqul, and Michael Mandelbaum (eds), *Making Markets: Economic Transformation in Eastern Europe and the Post-Soviet States* (New York, Council on Foreign Relations Press, 1993).

Milanovic, Branko, 'Poland's Quest for Economic Stabilisation, 1988–91: Interaction of Political Economy and Economics', *Soviet Studies*, vol. 44, no. 3 (1992), pp. 511–32.

Poznanski, Kazimierz (ed.), *The Evolutionary Transition to Capitalism* (Boulder, CO, Westview Press, 1995).

SOCIAL TRANSFORMATION

Society and social Policy

Adam, Jan (ed.), *Economic Reforms and Welfare Systems in the USSR, Poland and Hungary: Social Contract in Transformation* (London, Macmillan, 1991).

Deacon, Bob *et al.* (eds), *The New Eastern Europe: Social Policy Past, Present and Future* (London, Sage Publications, 1992).

Deacon, Bob (ed.), *Social Policy, Social Justice and Citizenship in Eastern Europe* (Aldershot, Avebury, 1992).

Millar, James R. and Wolchik, Sharon L. (eds), *Social Legacies of Communism* (Cambridge, Cambridge University Press, 1994).

Yanowitch, Murray, *Controversies in Soviet Social Thought: Democratisation, Social Justice and the Erosion of Official Ideology* (Armonk, NY, M. E. Sharpe, 1991).

Gender Politics

Attwood, Lynne, *The New Soviet Man and Woman: Sex-Role Socialisation in the USSR* (Bloomington, IN, Indiana University Press, 1991).

Bridger, Sue *et al.*, *No More Heroines? Russia, Women and the Market* (London, Routledge, 1995).

Buckley, Mary (ed.), *Perestroika and Soviet Women* (Cambridge, Cambridge University Press, 1992).

Clements, B. E., Engel, B. A. and Worobec, Christine D. (eds), *Russia's Women: Accommodation, Resistance, Transformation* (Berkeley, University of California Press, 1991).

Edmondson, Linda (ed.), *Women and Society in Russia and the Soviet Union* (Cambridge, Cambridge University Press, 1992).

Einhorn, Barbara and Molyneux, Maxine (eds), *Feminist Review*, Special Issue, no. 39 (1991) on Soviet Union and Eastern Europe.

Funk, N. and Mueller, M. (eds), *Gender, Politics and Post-Communism* (London, Routledge, 1993).

Goscilo, Helena (ed.), *Fruits of Her Plume: Essays on Contemporary Russian Women's Culture* (London, M. E. Sharpe, 1993).

Gray, Francine du Plessix, *Soviet Women: Walking the Tightrope* (London, Virago Press, 1991).

Kagal, Ayesha and Perova, Natasha *Present Imperfect: Stories by Russian Women* (Boulder, CO, Westview, 1996).

Pilkington, Hilary (ed.), *Gender, Generation and Identity in Contemporary Russia* (London, Routledge, 1996).

Posadskaya, Anastasiya, *Women in Russia* (Oxford, Blackwell, 1994).

Rai, Shirin, Pilkington, Hilary and Phizacklea, Annie (eds), *Women in the Face of Change: The Soviet Union, Eastern Europe and China* (London, Routledge, 1992).

Youth

Adelman, Deborah, *The 'Children of Perestroika': Moscow Teenagers Talk about their Lives and the Future* (London, M. E. Sharpe, 1991).

Bushnell, J., *Moscow Graffiti: Language and Subculture* (London, Unwin Hyman, 1990).

Pilkington, Hilary, *Russia's Youth and its Culture: A Nation's Constructors and Constructed* (London, Routledge, 1994).

Riordan, James (ed.), *Soviet Youth Culture* (London, Macmillan, 1989).

Riordan, James *et al.* (eds), *Young People in Post-Communist Russia and Eastern Europe* (Aldershot, Dartmouth, 1995).

Environmental politics

Bridges, Olga and Bridges, J.W. *Losing Hope: The Environment and Health in Russia* (Aldershot, Avebury, 1996).

DeBardeleben, Joan and Hannigan, John (eds), *Environmental Security and Quality after Communism* (Boulder, CO, Westview Press, 1994).

Feshbach, Murray and Friendly, Jnr, Alfred *Ecocide in the USSR: Health and Nature under Siege* (New York, Basic Books, 1992).

Pryde, Philip R., *Environmental Management in the Soviet Union* (Cambridge, Cambridge University Press, 1991).

Pryde, Philip R. (ed.), *Environmental Resources and Constraints in the Former Soviet Republics* (Boulder, CO, Westview Press, 1995).

Stewart, John Massey (ed.), *The Soviet Environment: Problems, Policies and Politics* (Cambridge, Cambridge University Press, 1992).

Wages, labour and trade unions

Connor, Walter D., *Tattered Banners: Labor, Conflict and Corporatism in Post-communist Russia* (Boulder, CO, Westview, 1996).
Waller, Michael, Courtois, Stephanie and Lazar, Marc (eds), *Comrades and Brothers: Communism and Trade Unions in Europe* (London, Frank Cass, 1991).

CULTURAL CHANGE

Culture and society

Balzar, Marjorie (ed.), *Russian Traditional Culture: Religion, Gender and Customary Law* (London, M. E. Sharpe, 1992).
Condee, Nancy and Padunov, Vladimir 'Perestroika Suicide: Not by *Bred* Alone', *New Left Review*, no. 189 (September–October 1991), pp. 67–89.
Graffy, J. and Hosking, G. (eds), *Culture and the Media in the USSR Today* (Basingstoke, Macmillan, 1989).
Hosking, Geoffrey, *Beyond Socialist Realism: Soviet Fiction since Ivan Denisovich* (London, Granada, 1980).
Jones, Anthony (ed.), *Education and Society in the New Russia* (London, Sharpe, 1994).
Marsh, Rosalind, 'The Death of Soviet Literature: Can Russian Literature Survive?', *Europe-Asia Studies*, vol. 45, no. 1, (1993), pp. 115–39.
Marsh, Rosalind, *History and Literature in Contemporary Russia* (London, Macmillan, 1995).
Piitman, Riita H., 'Writers and Politics in the Gorbachev Era', *Soviet Studies*, vol. 44, no. 4 (1992), pp. 665–85.
Siefert, Marsha (ed.), *Mass Culture and Perestroika in the Soviet Union* (New York/Oxford, Oxford University Press, 1991).
Shalin, Dmitri N. (ed.), *Russian Culture at the Crossroads: Paradoxes of Postcommunist Consciousness* (Boulder, CO, Westview, 1996).

The media

Androunas, Elena, *Soviet Media in Transition: Structural and Economic Alternatives* (Westport, Praeger, 1993).
Benn, David Wedgwood, *From Glasnost to Freedom of Speech: Russian Openness and International Relations* (London, Pinter Publishers/RIIA, 1992).
Mickiewicz, Ellen, *Split Signals* (Oxford, Oxford University Press, 1988).
Murray, John, *The Russian Press from Brezhnev to Yeltsin: Behind the Paper Curtain* (Aldershot, Edward Elgar, 1994).
Nove, Alec, *Glasnost' in Action: Cultural Renaissance in Russia* (London, Unwin Hyman, 1989).
Urban, Michael E., 'The Russian Free Press in the Transition to a Post-Communist Society', *The Journal of Communist Studies*, vol. 9, no. 2 (June 1993), pp. 20–40.

Church and religion

Anderson, John, *Religion, State and Politics in the Soviet Union and Successor States* (Cambridge University Press, 1994).
Bourdeaux, Michael, *Gorbachev, Glasnost and the Gospel* (London, Hodder and Stoughton, 1991).
Bourdeaux, Michael (ed.), *The Politics of Religion in Russia and the New States of Eurasia* (New York, M.E. Sharpe, 1995).
Davis, Nathaniel, *A Long Walk to the Church: A Contemporary History of Russian Orthodoxy* (Oxford, Westview Press, 1994).
Ellis, Jane, *The Russian Orthodox Church: A Contemporary History* (London, New York, 1986).

Hill, Ken R., *The Puzzle of the Soviet Church: An Inside Look at Christianity and Glasnost* (Portland, Multnomah Press, 1989).

Michel, Patrick, *Politics and Religion in Eastern Europe* (Oxford, Polity Press, 1991).

Moizes, Paul, *Religious Liberty in Eastern Europe and the USSR: Before and After the Great Transformation* (Boulder, CO, Westview, 1992).

Moss, Vladimir, *The Sacred Struggle of the True Orthodox Christians of Russia, 1917–92* (Woking, 1992).

Nielsen, Niels C. (ed.), *Christianity after Communism: Social, Political and Cultural Struggle in Russia* (Boulder, CO, Westview, 1994).

Ramet, Sabrina Petra (ed.), *Religious Policy in the Soviet Union* (Cambridge, Cambridge University Press, 1992).

Shirley, Eugene B. and Rowe, Michael (eds), *Candle in the Wind: Religion in the Soviet Union* (Washington, DC, University Press of America, 1989).

Weigel, George, *The Final Revolution: The Resistance Church and the Collapse of Communism* (Oxford, Oxford University Press, 1993).

Political culture and public opinion

Almond, Gabriel A., 'Communism and Political Culture Theory', *Comparative Politics*, no. 15, (1983), pp. 127–38.

Brown, Archie and Jack Gray (eds), *Political Culture and Political Change in Communist States* (London, Macmillan, 1977).

Fleron, Frederic J., 'Post-Soviet Political Culture in Russia: An Assessment of Recent Empirical Investigations', *Europe-Asia Studies*, vol. 48, no. 2, (1996), pp. 225–60.

Gozman, Leonid and Etkind, Alexander *The Psychology of Post-Totalitarianism in Russia* (London, Centre for Research into Communist Economies, 1992).

Hahn, Jeffrey W., 'Continuity and Change in Russian Political Culture', *British Journal of Political Science*, vol. 21, pp. 393–412.

Mason, David S., 'Attitudes towards the Market and Political Participation in the Postcommunist States', *Slavic Review*, vol. 54, no. 2 (summer 1995), pp. 385–406.

Pye, Lucian W., and Verba, Sidney (eds), *Political Culture and Political Development* (Princeton, NJ, Princeton University Press, 1965).

Reissinger, William M., Miller, Arthur H. and Hesli, Vicki L. 'Political Norms in Rural Russia: Evidence from Public Attitudes', *Europe-Asia Studies*, vol. 47, no. 6 (september 1995), pp. 1025–42.

White, Stephen, *Political Culture and Soviet Politics* (London, Macmillan, 1979).

Wyman, Matthew, *Public Opinion in Postcommunist Russia* (London, Macmillan, 1996).

FOREIGN POLICY

Aron, Leon and Kenneth M. Jensen (eds), *The Emergence of Russian Foreign Policy* (Washington, DC, US Institute of Peace, 1994).

Bassin, Mark, 'Russia Between Europe and Asia: The Ideological Construction of Geographical Space', *Slavic Review*, vol. 50, no. 1 (spring 1991), pp. 1–17.

Brzezinski, Zbigniew, 'The Cold War and its Aftermath', *Foreign Affairs*, vol. 71, no. 4 (fall 1992), pp. 31–49.

Checkel, Jeff, 'Russian Foreign Policy: Back to the Future?', *RFE/RL Research Report*, vol. 1, no. 41 (16 October 1991), pp. 15–29.

Crow, Suzanne, 'Competing Blueprints for Russian Foreign Policy', *RFE/RL Research Report*, vol. 1, no. 50 (18 December 1992), pp. 45–50.

Dawisha, Adeed and Dawisha, Karen (eds), *The Making of Foreign Policy in Russia and the New States of Eurasia* (New York, M.E. Sharpe, 1995).

Dukes, Paul, *Russia, The West and the World: Problems of Historical Interpretation* (London, Routledge, 1996).

Ehrhart, Hans-Georg, Kreikemeyer, Anna and Zagorski, Andre (eds), *Crisis Management in the CIS: Whither Russia?* (Baden-Baden, Nomos Verlagsgesellschaft, 1995).

Fleron, Frederic J. Jr., Hoffmann, Erik P. and Laird, Robbin F. (eds), *Soviet Foreign Policy: Classic and Contemporary Issues* (New York, Aldine de Gruyter, 1991).

Golan, Galia, *Moscow and the Middle East: New Thinking on Regional Conflict* (London, Pinter/RIIA, 1992).

Hauner, Milan, *What is Asia for Us? Russia's Asian Heartland Yesterday and Today* (London, Unwin Hyman, 1990).

Karaganov, Sergei A., *Russia: The New Foreign Policy and Security Agenda. A View from Moscow* (London, Brassey's for the Centre of Defence Studies, 1992). [UKC DK 289]

Kerr, David, 'The New Eurasianism: The Rise of Geopolitics in Russia's Foreign Policy', *Europe-Asia Studies*, vol. 47, no. 6 (September 1995), pp. 977–88.

Kozyrev, Andrei, 'Russia: A Chance for Survival', *Foreign Affairs*, vol. 71, no. 2 (spring 1992), pp. 1–16.

Kozyrev, Andrei, 'Russia and Human Rights', *Slavic Review*, vol. 51, no. 2 (summer 1992), pp. 287–93.

Kubalkova, Vendulka, 'The Post-Cold War Geopolitics of Knowledge: International Studies in the Former Soviet Bloc', *Studies in Comparative Communism*, vol. XXV, no. 4 (December 1992), pp. 405–17.

Kull, Steven, *Burying Lenin: The Soviet Revolution in Ideology and Foreign Policy* (Boulder, CO, Westview Press, 1992).

Lynch, Allen, *The Cold War is Over – Again* (Boulder, CO, Westview Press, 1992).

Malcolm, Neil, Pravda, Alex, Allison, Roy and Light, Margot *Internal Factors in Russian Foreign Policy: Domestic Influences in the Post-Soviet Setting* (London, RIIA/Oxford University Press, 1996).

Pravda, Alex, *Russian Foreign Policy in the Making* (London, Pinter, 1995).

Ragsdale, Hugh (ed.), *Imperial Russian Foreign Policy* (Cambridge, Cambridge University Press, 1993).

Roucek, Libor, *After the Bloc: The New International Relations in Eastern Europe* (London, RIIA Discussion Papers no. 40, 1992).

Sestanovich, Stephen (ed.), *Rethinking Russia's National Interests* (Washington, DC, Centre for Strategic and International Studies, 1994).

Shearman, Peter, 'New Thinking Reassessed', *Review of International Studies*, vol. 19, no. 2 (1993).

Shearman, Peter, 'Russia's Three Circles of Interests', in Thakur Ramesh and Thayer, Carlyle (eds), *Reshaping Regional Relations: Asia Pacific and the Former Soviet Union* (Boulder, CO, Westview, 1993).

Shearman, Peter, *New Directions in Russian Foreign Policy* (Boulder, CO, Westview, 1993).

Shearman, Peter (ed.), *Russian Foreign Policy Since 1990* (Boulder, CO, Westview Press, 1995).

Simes, Dimitri, 'America and the Post-Soviet Republics', *Foreign Affairs*, vol. 71, no. 3 (summer 1992), pp. 73–89.

Taylor, Trevor (ed.), *The Collapse of the Soviet Empire: Managing the Regional Fall-Out* (London, RIIA and International Institute for Global Peace, Tokyo, 1992).

Timmermann, Heinz, 'Russian Foreign Policy under Yeltsin: Priority for Integration into the "Community of Civilised States"', *The Journal of Communist Studies*, vol. 8, no. 4 (December 1992), pp. 163–85.

Russia and Europe

Baranovsky, Vladimir (ed.), *Russia and Europe: The Emerging Security Agenda* (Oxford, OUP/SIPRI, 1996).

Duke, Paul, *World Order in History: Russia and the West* (London, Routledge, 1995).

Lucas, Michael R. and Zagorskii, Andrei *The European Challenge for Russia* (forthcoming).

Malcolm, Neil (ed.), *Russia and Europe: An End to Confrontation?* (London, Pinter Publishers, 1994). [UKC ordered]

Naarden, Bruno, *Socialist Europe and Revolutionary Russia: Perception and Prejudice* (Cambridge, Cambridge University Press, 1992).

Neumann, Iver B., *Russia and the Idea of Europe* (London, Routledge, 1995).

Russia and America

Midlarsky, Manus, John Vasquez and Peter Gladkov (eds), *From Rivalry to Cooperation: Russian and American Perspectives on the Post-Cold War Era* (New York, HarperCollins, 1994).

DEFENCE AND SECURITY POLICY

Baev, Pavel, *The Russian Army in a Time of Troubles* (London, Sage, 1996, 1996).

Bluth, Christoph, *The Collapse of Soviet Military Power* (Aldershot, Dartmouth, 1995).

Colton, Timothy J. and Gustafson, Thane (eds), *Soldiers and the Soviet State: Civil-Military Relations from Brezhnev to Gorbachev* (Princeton, NJ, Princeton University Press, 1990).

Cox, David, *Retreating from the Cold War: Germany, Russia and the Withdrawal of the Western Group of Forces* (London, Macmillan, 1995).

Currie, Kenneth M., *Soviet Military Politics: Contemporary Issues* (New York, Paragon House, 1992).

Danopoulos, Constantine and Zirker, Daniel (eds), *Civil-Military Relations in Soviet and Yugoslav Successor States* (Oxford, Westview Press, 1995).

Donnely, Christopher, 'Evolutionary Problems of the Former Soviet Armed Forces', *Survival*, vol. 34, no. 3 (autumn 1992), pp. 28–42.

Dunay, Pal, Kardos, Gabor and Williams, Andrew *New Forms of Security: Views from Central, Eastern and Western Europe* (Aldershot, Dartmouth, 1995).

Galeotti, Mark, *The Age of Anxiety: Security and Politics in Soviet and Post-Soviet Russia* (London, Longman, 1994).

Galeotti, Mark, *The Kremlin's Agenda* (London, Jane's Intelligence Review, 1995).

Holden, Gerard, *Russia after the Cold War: History and the Nation in Post-Soviet Security Politics* (Boulder, CO, Westview Press, 1994).

Lambeth, Benjamin S., 'Russia's Wounded Military', *Foreign Affairs*, vol. 74, no. 2 (March/April 1995).

Lepingwell, John, 'Soviet Civil-Military Relations and the August Coup', *World Politics*, vol. 44, no. 4 (July 1992), pp. 539–72.

Marples, David R., *Ukraine, Byelorus and the Nuclear Dilemma* (London, Macmillan, 1995).

Mearsheimer, John, 'Back to the Future: Instability in Europe After the Cold War', in Sean Lynn-Jones (ed.), *The Cold War and After: Prospects for Peace* (Cambridge, MA, MIT Press, 1991), pp. 141–92.

Parrott, Bruce (ed.), *State Building and Military Power in Russia and the New States of Eurasia* (New York, M.E. Sharpe, 1995).

Quester, George H., *The Nuclear Challenge in Russia and the New States of Eurasia* (New York, M.E. Sharpe, 1995).

THE BIRTH OF NATIONS

Russia and the successor states

Bremmer, Ian and Taras, Ray (eds), *Nations and Politics in the Soviet Successor States* (Cambridge, Cambridge University Press, 1993).

Dawisha, Karen and Parrott, Bruce *Russia and the New States of Eurasia: The Politics of Upheaval* (Cambridge, Cambridge University Press, 1994).

Szporluk, Roman (ed.), *National Identity and Ethnicity in Russia and the New States of Eurasia* (Armonk, NY, M.E. Sharpe, 1994).

The Baltic republics

Allworth, Edward (ed.), *Nationality Group Survival in Multi-Ethnic States: Shifting Support Patterns in the Soviet Baltic Region* (New York, Praeger, 1977).

Clemens, Walter C. Jr., *Baltic Independence and Russian Empire* (Basingstoke, Macmillan, 1991).

Hiden, John and Salmon, Patrick *The Baltic Nations and Europe: Estonia, Latvia and Lithuania in the Twentieth Century*, revised edition (Harlow, Longman, 1994).

Lieven, Anatol, *The Baltic Revolution* (New Haven, Yale University Press, 1993).

Misiunas, Romuald and Taagepera, Rein *The Baltic States: Years of Dependence, 1940–1980* (Berkeley, CA, University of California Press, 1983).

Smith, Graham (ed.), *The Baltic States: The National Self-Determination of Estonia, Latvia and Lithuania* (London, Macmillan, 1994).

Trapans, Jan Arvads (ed.), *Towards Independence: The Baltic Popular Movements* (Boulder, CO, Westview Press, 1991).

Vardys, V. Stanley and Misiunas, Romuald J. *The Baltic States in Peace and War* (University Park, PA, Penn State University Press, 1978).

Von Rauch, Georg, *The Baltic States: Years of Independence, 1917–1940* (Berkeley, CA, University of California Press, 1974).

Estonia

Arter, David, 'Estonia after the March 1995 Riigikou Election: Still an Anti-Party System?', *The Journal of Communist Studies and Transition Politics*, vol. 11, no. 3 (September 1995), pp. 249–71.

Parming, Tonu and Jarvesoo, Elmar *A Case Study of a Soviet Republic: The Estonian SSR* (Boulder, CO, Westview Press, 1978).

Raun, Toivo, *Estonia and the Estonians*, 2nd edn (Stanford, CA, Hoover Press, 1991).

Raun, Toivo, 'Post-Soviet Estonia', *Journal of Baltic Studies*, spring 1994.

Taagepera, Rein, *Estonia: Return to Independence* (Boulder, CO, Westview, 1993).

Latvia

Dreifelds, Juris, 'Latvian National Rebirth', *Problems of Communism*, vol. 38, 1989, pp. 77–94.

Dreifelds, Juris, *Latvia in Transition* (Cambridge, Cambridge University Press, 1996).

Plakans, Andrejs, *The Latvians: A Short History* (Stanford, CA, Hoover Press, 1995).

Plakans, Andrejs, 'The Tribulations of Independence: Latvia 1991–1993', *Journal of Baltic Studies*, spring 1994.

Rudenshiold, Eric, 'Ethnic Dimensions in Contemporary Latvian Politics: Focusing Forces for Change', *Soviet Studies*, vol. 44, no. 4 (1992), pp. 609–39.

Lithuania

Krickus, Richard, *Bloody Sunday: The Lithuanian Rebellion and the Collapse of the Soviet Empire* (London, Brassey's, 1996).

Remeikis, T., *Opposition to Soviet Rule in Lithuania, 1945–1980* (Chicago, Institute of Lithuanian Studies Press, 1980).

Senn, Alfred Erich, *Lithuania Awakening* (Berkeley, University of California Press, 1990).

Senn, Alfred Erich, *Gorbachev's Failure in Lithuania* (London, Macmillan, 1995).

Vardys, V. Stanley, *The Catholic Church: Dissent and Nationality in Soviet Lithuania* (Boulder, CO, Westview Press, 1978).

Vardys, V. Stanley and Sedaitis, Judith *Lithuania: Rebel Nation* (Boulder, CO, Westview, 1996).

Moldova

Bruchis, Michael, *Nations – Nationalities – People: A Study of the Nationalities Policy of the Communist Party in Soviet Moldavia* (Boulder, CO, East European Monographs, 1984).

Crowther, William, 'Moldova after Independence', *Current History*, October 1994.

King, Charles, *Post-Soviet Moldova: A Borderland in Transition* (London, Royal Institute of International Affairs, 1995).

Manoliu-Manea, Maria (ed.), *The Tragic Plight of a Border Area: Bessarabia and Bucovina* (Arcata, CA, Humboldt State University Press, 1983).

Nicholas, Dima, *From Moldavia to Moldova: The Soviet–Romanian Territorial Dispute* (New York, 1991).

Belarus

Guthier, S., 'The Belorussians: National Identification and Assimilation, 1897–1970', *Soviet Studies*, vol. 29, no. 1 (January 1977), pp. 37–61, and vol. 29, no. 2 (April 1977), pp. 270–83.

Lubachko, Ivan S., *Belorussia under Soviet Rule, 1917–1957* (Lexington, KY, University Press of Kentucky, 1972).

Marples, David R., 'Post-Soviet Belarus' and the Impact of Chernobyl", *Post-Soviet Geography*, vol. 33, no. 7 (September 1992), pp. 419–31.

Marples, David R., 'Belarus: The Illusion of Stability', *Post- Soviet Affairs*, vol. 9, no. 3, 1993, pp. 253–77.

Marples, David R., *Belarus: From Soviet Rule to Nuclear Catastrophe* (London, Macmillan, 1996).

Urban, Michael, *An Algebra of Soviet Power: Elite Circulation in the Belorussian Republic 1966–1986* (Cambridge, Cambridge University Press, 1989).

Urban, Michael and Zaprudnik, Jan 'Belarus: A Long Road to Nationhood', in Ian Bremmer and Raymond Taras (eds), *Nations and Politics in the Soviet Successor States* (Cambridge, Cambridge University Press, 1993).

Vakar, Nicholas P., *Belorussia: The Making of a Nation* (Cambridge, MA, Harvard University Press, 1956).

Zaprudnik, Jan, *Belarus: At a Crossroads in History* (Boulder, CO, Westview, 1993).

Ukraine

Armstrong, John, *Ukrainian Nationalism* (Ukrainian Academic Press, 1990).

Dzyuba, Ivan, *Internationalism or Russification? A Study in the Soviet Nationalities Problem* (New York, Monad, 1974).

Karatnycky, Adrian, 'The Ukrainian Factor', *Foreign Affairs*, vol. 71, no. 3 (Summer 1992), pp. 90–107.

Kohut, Zenon E., *Russian Centralism and Ukrainian Autonomy: Imperial Absorption of the Hetmanate, 1760s–1830s* (Boston, MA Harvard University Press, 1988).

Krawchenko, Bohdan (ed.), *Ukraine after Shelest* (Edmonton, University of Alberta, Canadian Institute of Ukrainian Studies, 1983).

Krawchenko, Bohdan, *Social Change and National Consciousness in Twentieth-century Ukraine* (London, Macmillan, 1985).

Kuzio, Taras, *Ukraine: The Unfinished Revolution* (London, Institute for European Defence and Strategic Studies, 1992).

Kuzio, Taras and Wilson, Andrew *Ukraine: From Perestroika to Independence* (London, Macmillan, 1994).

Lewytzkyj, Borys, *Politics and Society in Soviet Ukraine, 1953–1980* (Edmonton, University of Alberta, Canadian Institute of Ukrainian Studies, 1984).

Liber, George O., *Soviet Nationality Policy, Urban Growth, and Identity Change in the Ukrainian SSR 1923–1934* (Cambridge, Cambridge University Press, 1992).

Little, David, *Ukraine: The Legacy of Intolerance* (Washington, DC, United States Institute of Peace Press, 1991).

Marples, David, *Ukraine Under Perestroika: Ecology, Economics and Workers' Revolt* (London, Macmillan, 1991).

Motyl, Alexander J., *Dilemmas of Independence: Ukraine After Totalitarianism* (New York, Council on Foreign Relations, 1993).

Nahaylo, Bohdan, *The New Ukraine* (London, Royal Institute of International Affairs, 1992).

Solchanyk, Roman, 'Ukraine, the (Former) Center, Russia and "Russia"', *Studies in Comparative Communism*, vol. 25, no. 1 (March 1992), pp. 31–45.

Solchanyk, Roman, 'Back to the USSR?', *The Harriman Institute Forum*, vol. 6, no. 3 (November 1992).

Solchanyk, Roman, *Ukraine; From Chernobyl' to Sovereignty: A Collection of Interviews* (Basingstoke, Macmillan, 1992).

Subtelny, Orest, *Ukraine: A History* (Toronto, University of Toronto Press, 1988).

Wolchik, Sharon L. and Zviglyanich, V. A. (eds), *Building a State: Ukraine in a Post-Soviet World* (Budapest, Central European University Press/OUP, 1996).

Transcaucasia

Aves, Jonathan, *Post-Soviet Transcaucasia* (London, RIIA/Post-Soviet Business Forum, 1993).

Suny, Ronald Grigor (ed.), *Transcaucasia: Nationalism and Social Change* (Ann Arbor, MI, University of Michigan Press, 1983).

Armenia

Hovannisian, Richard G., *The Armenian People from Ancient to Modern Times*, vol. 2, *Foreign Dominion to Statehood* (Cambridge, Cambridge University Press, 1994).

Lang, David M., *The Armenians: A People in Exile* (London, Unwin Hyman, 1988).

Libaridian, Gerard J. (ed.), *Armenia at the Crossroads: Democracy and Nationhood in the Post-Soviet Era* (Watertown, MA, Blue Crane Books, 1991).

Matossian, Mary K., *The Impact of Soviet Policies in Armenia* (Leiden, Holland, E. J. Brill, 1962).
Walker, Christopher J., *Armenia: The Survival of a Nation* (London, Croom Helm, 1980).

Azerbaijan

Altstadt, Audrey L., *The Azerbaijani Turks: Power and Identity under Russian Rule* (Stanford, CA, Hoover Press, 1992).
Martin, Robert, *The Economy and Foreign Relations of Azerbaijan* (London, RIIA, 1996).
Swietochowski, Tadeusz, *Russian Azerbaijan 1905–1920: The Shaping of National Identity in a Muslim Community* (Cambridge, Cambridge University Press, 1985).

Nagorno-Karabakh

Chorbajian, Levon *et al.*, *The Caucasian Knot: The History and Politics of Nagorno-Karabagh* (London, Zed Books, 1994).
Dragadze, Tamara, 'The Armenian-Azerbaijani Conflict: Structure and Sentiment', *Third World Quarterly*, vol. 11, no. 1, (1989).

Georgia

Allen, W., *A History of the Georgian People* (New York, Barnes and Noble, 1971).
Aves, Jonathan, *Path to National Independence in Georgia, 1987–90* (London, School of Slavonic and East European Studies, 1991).
Aves, Jonathan *Georgia: From Chaos to Stability?* (London, RIIA, 1996).
Gachechiladze, Revaz, *The New Georgia: Space, Society, Politics* (London, UCL Press, 1995).
Jones, Stephen, 'The Establishment of Soviet Power in Transcaucasia: The Case of Georgia 1921–1928', *Soviet Studies*, vol. 40, no. 4 (October 1982).
Lang, David M., *A Modern History of Georgia* (New York, Grove Press, 1962).
Nelson, Lynn D. and Amonashvili, Paata 'Voting and Political Attitudes in Soviet Georgia', *Soviet Studies*, vol. 44, no. 4 (1992), pp. 687–98.
Parsons, Robert, 'National Integration in Soviet Georgia', *Soviet Studies*, vol. 34, no. 4 (October 1982).
Suny, Ronald Grigor, *The Making of the Modern Georgian Nation*, 2nd edn (Bloomington, IN, Indiana University Press, 1994).

Central Asia

Akiner, Shirin, *Islamic Peoples of the Soviet Union* (London, Kegan Paul, 1983).
Akiner, Shirin (ed.), *Cultural Change and Continuity in Central Asia* (London, Kegan Paul, 1991).
Akiner, Shirin (ed.), *Political and Economic Trends in Central Asia* (London, I. B. Tauris, 1993).
Allworth, Edward (ed.), *The Nationality Question in Soviet Central Asia* (New York, Praeger, 1973).
Allworth, Edward, *Central Asia: 130 Years of Russian Dominance, A Historical Overview* 3rd edn (London, Duke University Press, 1994).
Banuazizi, Ali and Weiner, Myron *The New Geopolitics of Central Asia* (London, I. B. Tauris, 1993).
Bennigsen, A. and Broxup, M. *The Islamic Threat to the Soviet State* (London, Croom Helm, 1983).
Bennigsen, A. and Enders Wimbush, S. *Muslim National Communism in the Soviet Union* (Chicago, University of Chicago Press, 1979).
Bennigsen, A. and Enders Wimbush, S. *Muslims of the Soviet Empire: A Guide* (London, Hurst, 1986).
Eickelman, Dale F. (ed.), *Russia's Muslim Frontier: New Directions in Cross-Cultural Analysis* (Indiana, Indiana University Press, 1993).
Fierman, William (ed.), *Soviet Central Asia: The Failed Transformation* (Boulder, CO, Westview Press, 1991).
Gleason, Gregory, *The Central Asian States: Discovering Independence* (Boulder, CO, Westview Press, 1996).
Haghayeghi, Mehrdad, *Islam and Politics in Central Asia* (London, Macmillan, 1995)
Hambly, G., *et al.*, *Central Asia* (London, Weidenfeld and Nicolson, 1969).

Hiro, Dilip, *Between Marx and Muhammed: The Changing Face of Central Asia* (London, HarperCollins, 1994).

Hyman, Anthony, 'Moving out of Moscow's Orbit: The Outlook for Central Asia', *International Affairs*, vol. 69, no. 2 (April 1993), pp. 289–304.

Kulchik, Y.G., Fadin, A.V. and Sergeev, V.M. *Central Asia After the Empire* (London, Pluto Press, 1996).

Lubin, Nancy, *Labor and Nationality in Soviet Central Asia* (Princeton, NJ, Princeton University Press, 1984).

Manz, Beatrice (ed.), *Soviet Central Asia in Historical Perspective* (Boulder, CO, Westview, 1994).

Olcott, Martha Brill, 'Central Asia's Catapult to Independence', *Foreign Affairs*, vol. 71, no. 3 (summer 1992), pp. 108–30.

Olcott, Martha Brill, 'Central Asia on its Own', *Journal of Democracy*, January 1993.

Paksoy, H. B. (ed.), *Central Asia Reader: The Rediscovery of History* (London, M. E. Sharpe, 1994).

Poliakov, Sergei P., *Everyday Islam: Religion and Tradition in Rural Central Asia* (London, M. E. Sharpe, 1992).

Rashid, Ahmed, *The Resurgence of Central Asia* (London, Zed Books, 1994).

Rumer, Boris Z., *Soviet Central Asia: 'A Tragic Experiment'* (London, Unwin Hyman, 1989).

Rywkin, Michael, *Moscow's Muslim Challenge: Soviet Central Asia*, revised edn (Armonk, NY, M. E. Sharpe, 1990).

Starr, S. Frederick, 'Making Eurasia Stable', *Foreign Affairs*, vol. 75, no. 1 (1996), pp. 80–92.

Wheeler, G., *The Modern History of Soviet Central Asia* (New York, Praeger, 1964).

Kazakhstan

Akiner, Shirin, *The Formation of Kazakh Identity* (London, RIIA/Plymbridge, 1995).

Olcott, Marth Brill, *The Kazakhs*, 2nd edn (Stanford, CA, Hoover Press, 1995).

Kyrgyzstan

Huskey, Eugene, 'The Rise of Contested Politics in Central Asia: Elections in Kyrgyzstan, 1989–90', *Europe-Asia Studies*, vol. 47, no. 5 (July 1995), pp. 813–33.

Tajikistan

Rakowska-Harmstone, Teresa, *Russia and Nationalism in Central Asia: The Case of Tadzhikistan* (Baltimore, MD, Johns Hopkins University Press, 1970).

Uzbekistan

Allworth, Edward, *The Modern Uzbeks: From the Fourteenth Century to the Present* (Stanford, CA, Hoover Press, 1990).

Critchlow, James, *Nationalism in Uzbekistan: A Soviet Republic's Road to Sovereignty* (Boulder, CO, Westview Press, 1992).

Kangas, Roger, *Uzbekistan in the Twentieth Century* (New York, St Martin's Press, 1995).

Regional internationalism

Herzig, Edmund, *Iran and the Former Soviet South* (London, RIIA/Plymbridge, 1995).

Mastny, Vojtech (ed.), *Turkey and Europe: Perspectives on a Rising Regional Power* (Boulder, CO, Westview Press, 1995).

Mastny, Vojtech (ed.), *Italy and East-Central Europe: Dimensions of the Regional Relationship* (Boulder, CO, Westview Press, 1995).

Rubinstein, Alvin Z. and Oles M. Spolansky (eds), *Regional Power Rivalries in the New Eurasia* (New York, M.E. Sharpe, 1995).

Starr, S. Frederick (ed.), *The Legacy of History on the Foreign Policies of the New States of the Former Soviet Union* (New York, M.E. Sharpe, 1994).
Szporluk, Roman (ed.), *The Influence of National Identity* (New York, M. E. Sharpe, 1994).
Webber, Mark, *The International Politics of Russia and the Successor States* (Manchester University Press, 1995).
Winrow, Gareth, *Turkey in Post-Soviet Central Asia* (London, RIIA/Plymbridge, 1995).
Zviagelskaia, Irina, *The Russian Policy Debate on Central Asia* (London, RIIA/Plymbridge, 1995).

COMMONWEALTH AND COMMUNITY

The Commonwealth of Independent States

Zagorski, Andrei *et al.*, *The Commonwealth of Independent States: Developments and Prospects* (Moscow, Centre of International Studies, MGIMO, 1992).

Borders and citizenship

Bondarevsky, Grigory and Englefield, Greg, *Boundary Issues in Central Asia* (London, RIIA, 1996).
Barrington, Lowell, 'The Domestic and International Consequences of Citizenship in the Soviet Successor States', *Europe-Asia Studies*, vol. 47, no. 5 (July 1995), pp. 731–63.
Pogany, Istvan (ed.), *Human Rights in Eastern Europe* (Aldershot, Edward Elgar, 1995).

Minorities and Russians abroad

Chinn, Jeff and Robert Kaiser, *Russians as the New Minority: Ethnicity and Nationalism in the Soviet Successor States* (Boulder, CO, Westview, 1996).
Kolstoe, Paul, *Russian Minorities in the Former Soviet Republics* (forthcoming).
Melvin, Neil, *Forging the New Russian Nation: Russian Foreign Policy and the Russian-Speaking Communities of the Former USSR* (London, Discussion Paper no. 50, RIIA, 1994).
Melvin, Neil, *Russians Beyond Russia: The Politics of National Identity* (London, RIIA/Pinter, 1995).
Shlapentokh, Vladimir *et al.* (eds), *The New Russian Diaspora: Russian Minorities in the Former Soviet Republics* (New York, M.E. Sharpe, 1994).

Migration and refugees

Ardittis, Solon (ed.), *The Politics of East-West Migration* (London, Macmillan, 1994).
Waever, Ole, Barry Buzan, Morten Kelstrup and Pierre Lemaitre, *Identity, Migration and the New Security Agenda in Europe* (London, Pinter, 1993).

PROBLEMS OF TRANSITION

Bermeo, Nancy (ed.), *Liberalization and Democratization: Change in the Soviet Union and Eastern Europe* (Baltimore, MD, Johns Hopkins University Press, 1992).
Brabant, Joseph M. van, *Remaking Eastern Europe: On the Political Economy of Transition* (Dordrecht, Kluwer, 1990).
Breslauer, George W. (ed.), *Dilemmas of Transition in the Soviet Union and Eastern Europe* (Berkeley, CA, Berkeley- Stanford Program in Soviet studies, Center for Slavic and East European Studies, 1991).
Breslauer, George, 'In Defense of Sovietology', *Post-Soviet Affairs*, vol. 8, no. 3, (1992), pp. 197–238.
Csaba, Laszlo (ed.), *Sytemic Change and Stabilisation in Eastern Europe* (Aldershot, Dartmouth Publishing, 1991).
Di Palma, Giuseppe, *To Craft Democracies: An Essay in Democratic Transition* (Berkeley, University of California Press, 1990).
Evans, Peter, Rueschmeyer, Dietrich and Skocpol, Theda (eds), *Bringing the State Back In* (Oxford, Oxford University Press, 1985).

Fleron, F. and Hoffman, E. *Post-Communist Studies and Political Science: Methodology and Empirical Theory in Sovietology* (Boulder, CO, Westview, 1993).

Gellner, Ernest, *Conditions for Liberty* (London, Hamish Hamilton, 1994).

Gill, Graeme, 'Liberalization and Democratization in the Soviet Union and Russia', *Democratization*, vol. 2, no. 3 (Autumn 1995), pp. 313–36.

Hankiss, Elemer, *East European Alternatives* (Oxford, Clarendon Press, 1990).

Huntington, Samuel, *Political Order in Changing Societies* (New Haven, Yale University Press, 1968).

Kukathas, Chandran, Lovell, David W. and Maley, William (eds), *The Transition from Socialism: State and Civil Society in the USSR* (Melbourne, Longman Cheshire, 1991).

Lemke, Christiane and Marks, Gary (eds), *The Crisis of Socialism in Europe* (Durham/London, Duke University Press, 1992).

Migdal, Joel, *Strong Societies and Weak States: State-Society Relations and State Capacities in the Third World* (Princeton, NJ, Princeton University Press, 1988).

Miliband, Ralph and Leo Panitch (eds), *Communist Regimes: The Aftermath, Socialist Register*, (London, Merlin Press, 1991).

Odom, William E., 'Soviet Politics and After: Old and New Concepts', *World Politics*, vol. 45, no. 1, (1992), pp. 66–98.

O'Donnell, Guillermo and Schmitter, Philippe C. *Transitions from Authoritarian Rule: Tentative Conclusions about Uncertain Democracies* (Baltimore, MD, Johns Hopkins University Press, 1986).

O'Donnell, Guillermo, Schmitter, Philippe C. and Whitehead, Laurence (eds), *Transitions from Authoritarian Rule: Comparative Perspectives* (Baltimore, MD, Johns Hopkins University Press, 1986).

O'Donnell, Guillermo, 'On the State, Democratization and Some Conceptual Problems: A Latin American View with Glances at Some Postcommunist Countries', *World Development*, vol. 21, no. 8 (1993), pp. 1355–69.

Pei, Minxin, *From Reform to Revolution: The Demise of Communism in China and the Soviet Union* (Cambridge, MA, Harvard University Press, 1994).

Pridham, Geoffrey (ed.), *Securing Democracy: Political Parties and Democratic Consolidation in Southern Europe* (London, Routledge, 1990).

Pridham, Geoffrey (ed.), *Encouraging Democracy: The External Context of Regime Transition in Southern Europe* (London, Pinter Publishers, 1991).

Pridham, Geoffrey, George Sanford and Eric Herring (eds), *Building Democracy? The International Dimension of Democratisation in Eastern Europe* (London, Pinter, 1994).

Przeworski, Adam, *Democracy and the Market: Political and Economic Reforms in Eastern Europe and Latin America* (Cambridge, Cambridge University Press, 1991).

Pye, Lucian W., 'Political Science and the Crisis of Authoritarianism', *American Political Science Review*, no. 84, (1990), pp. 3–19.

Ramet, Sabrina P., *Social Currents in Eastern Europe: The Sources and Meaning of the Great Transformation* (Durham, NC, Duke University Press, 1991).

Remington, Thomas F., 'Regime Transition in Communist Systems', *Soviet Economy*, vol. 6, no. 2, 1990, pp. 160–90.

Remington, Thomas F., 'Sovietology and System Stability', *Post-Soviet Affairs*, vol. 8, no. 3, (1992), pp. 239–69.

Rustow, Dankwart, 'Transitions to Democracy: Toward a Dynamic Model', *Comparative Politics*, vol. 2, no. 3 (1970), pp. 337–63.

Rustow, Dankwart, 'Democracy: A Global Revolution', *Foreign Affairs*, vol. 69, no. 4 (fall 1990), pp. 75–91.

Saunders, Christopher T. (ed.), *Economics and Politics of Transition* (London, Macmillan, 1992).

Staniszkis, Jadwiga, *The Dynamics of Breakthrough in Eastern Europe* (Berkeley, University of California Press, 1991).

Staniszkis, Jadwiga, *The Ontology of Socialism* (Oxford, Clarendon Press, 1992).

MEMOIRS AND THOUGHTS

Boldin, Valery, *Ten Years that Shook the World: The Gorbachev Era as Witnessed by his Chief of Staff* (Glasgow, HarperCollins, 1994).

Gorbachev, Mikhail, *The August Coup: The Truth and the Lessons* (London, HarperCollins, 1991).

Gorbachev, Mikhail, *Dekabr'-91: moya pozitsiya* (Moscow, Novosti, 1992).

Gorbachev, Mikhail, *Soyuz mozhno bylo sokhranit': belaya kniga*, Mezhdunarodnyi Fond sotsial'no-ekonomicheskikh i politologicheskikh issledovanii (Gorbachev-Fond) (Moscow, izd. 'aprel'-85', 1995).

Gorbachev, Mikhail, *Zhizn' i reformy* (*Life and Reforms*), 2 vols (Moscow, Novosti, 1995).

Gorbachev, Raisa, *I Hope* (London, HarperCollins, 1991).

Grachev, Andrei, *Final Days: The Inside Story of the Collapse of the Soviet Union*, foreword by Archie Brown (Boulder, CO, Westview Press, 1995).

Khasbulatov, Ruslan, *The Struggle for Russia: Power and Change in the Democratic Revolution*, edited by Richard Sakwa (London and New York, Routledge, 1993).

Ligachev, Yegor, *Inside Gorbachev's Kremlin: The Memoirs of Yegor Ligachev* (Boulder, CO, Westview, 1996).

Nazarbaev, Nursultan, *Bez pravykh i levykh: stranitsy avtobiografii, razmyshleniya, pozitsiya* (Moscow, Molodaya gvardiya, 1991).

Ryzhkov, Nikolai, *Perestroika: istoriya predatel'stv* (Moscow, Novosti, 1992).

Shevardnadze, Eduard, *The Future Belongs to Freedom* (London, Sinclair-Stevenson, 1991).

Sobchak, Anatoly, *For a New Russia* (London, HarperCollins, 1992).

Tsipko, Alexander, *Is Stalinism Really Dead?* (New York, HarperCollins, 1990).

Yakovlev, Alexander, *Muki prochteniya bytiya; perestroika: nadezhdy i real'nosti* (Moscow, Novosti, 1991).

Yakovlev, Alexander, *Predislovie, obval, posleslovie* (Moscow, Novosti, 1992).

Yakovlev, Alexander, *The Fate of Marxism in Russia*, introduced by Thomas F. Remington, foreword by Alexander Tsipko (New Haven, Yale University Press, 1993).

Yakovlev, Alexander, M., *Striving for Law in a Lawless Land: Memoirs of a Russian Reformer* (New York, M.E. Sharpe, 1995).

Yeltsin, Boris, *Against the Grain: An Autobiography* (London, Pan Books, 1990).

Yeltsin, Boris, *The View from the Kremlin*, (London, HarperCollins, 1994); *The Struggle for Russia* (New York, Times Books/Belka Publishing Company, 1994).

Index